BRITISH POLICY TOWARDS WEST AFRICA

WEST AFRICA

Select Documents, 1786–1874

BRITISH POLICY
TOWARDS
WEST AFRICA

Select Documents
1786–1874

C. W. NEWBURY

CLARENDON PRESS · OXFORD
1965

327.42066
N 535 b
107318

Printed in Great Britain by
The Camelot Press Ltd., London and Southampton

PREFACE

The purpose of this first volume is to provide materials for the history of European relations with West Africa from the suppression of the slave trade till the decade before international partition. It is essentially a book of sources from state papers, most of which are published here for the first time and are not easily accessible to students. But for a fuller understanding of their context, value, and limitations they require to be supplemented in a number of ways.

First, the edition has its place in the wider documentation illustrating British expansion and the growth of responsible government overseas already available in collections by K. N. Bell and W. P. Morrell, Vincent Harlow and Frederick Madden, W. P. M. Kennedy, Arthur Berriedale Keith, C. H. Philips, G. Bennett, and in the *Records* of Cape Colony, Australia, and New Zealand. With few exceptions, however, very little in these general or regional works relates to West Africa. Conversely, the more readily accessible parliamentary speeches and statutes laying down the broad trends of imperial policy have been omitted here, even where they touch on West African affairs.

Secondly, there are for West Africa itself a few editions of basic sources, limited to particular areas or themes. Among these are C. Howard and J. H. Plumb, *West African Explorers* (London, 1951), J. J. Crooks, *Records relating to the Gold Coast Settlements from 1750 to 1874* (Dublin, 1923), and the monumental work by Christian Schefer, *Instructions générales données de 1763 à 1870 aux gouverneurs et ordonnateurs des Établissements français en Afrique occidentale* (Paris, 1927). For diplomatic agreements between European powers and with African states the reader is referred to Sir E. Hertslet's three volumes, *The Map of Africa by Treaty* (London, 1894 and 1909), and the thirty-one volumes of his father's *Treaties between Great Britain and Foreign Powers* (London, 1835–1926). Also useful for their publication of materials are Freda Wolfson, *Pageant of Ghana* (London, 1958), Thomas Hodgkin, *Nigerian Perspectives. An Historical Anthology* (London, 1960), and C. Fyfe, *Sierra Leone Inheritance*, (London, 1964). For the major supplement to this edition, however, one must await selections of documents from West African archives, collections of local traditions and the publication of source materials in Arabic which now claim the attention of European and African scholars.

The treatment of the growth and protection of British interests in West Africa from the last decades of the eighteenth century is largely from the point of view of government departments and their agents. For reasons of space, materials collected to illustrate the work of missionary societies and the beginnings of education on the coast had to be omitted. Similarly, it was originally intended to supplement the documentation on commercial developments and financial administration with statistical appendices. But a survey of the Customs and Board of Trade records revealed such large discrepancies between manuscript and published data that compilation of tables demanded more editorial commentary than could be contained in a mere appendix. On the whole, it was felt better to leave the analysis of materials for West African economic history for another occasion.

The usual editorial conventions have been followed in the presentation of the text. Selections from Parliamentary Papers, where reproduced, have been checked against the original manuscripts and changes noted by the use of the symbol 'A' (Additional), or 'D' (Deleted). The same procedure has been followed in the case of amended drafts of despatches. Capitals and punctuation have been retained as in the originals, unless the meaning of a sentence is notably obscured or ambiguous.

The maps presented with the text have been treated as documents, though they have had to be re-drawn and reduced for convenience of publication. Nos. 2, 3, and 7 are Crown copyright and are reproduced by permission of the Controller of H.M. Stationery Office.

Finally, it is a pleasure to acknowledge the initial guidance given by the late Professor Vincent Harlow and by Dr. John Fage, Dr. Margery Perham and Mrs. E. M. Chilver, when the plan for collection was in its early stages. As the edition has neared completion, my personal debt to the Committee for Commonwealth Studies, Oxford, has grown, and with it an equal sense of gratitude to the staffs of Rhodes House Library, the Bodleian Library and the Public Record Office, London. For advice on the text and the draft Introduction, I would also wish to thank Professor J. Gallagher, Dr. Frederick Madden, Mr. D. K. Fieldhouse, Mr. Christopher Fyfe and Mr. Robin Hallett; and for invaluable assistance in transcription and the preparation of the Index I have to thank my wife.

C. W. N.

INSTITUTE OF COMMONWEALTH STUDIES, OXFORD,
May 1964.

LIST OF CONTENTS

LIST OF MAPS

LIST OF SELECT DOCUMENTS, 1786–1874

I. EXPLORATION AND SURVEY

II. LEGITIMATE TRADE
A. Navigation Acts and Tariffs

III. SLAVE TRADE
A. METHODS OF SUPPRESSION

B. African Resettlement

IV. RELATIONS WITH AFRICAN SOCIETIES

A. Senegal, Gambia

C. Gold Coast

V. COMPANY AND CROWN ADMINISTRATION
A. THE WEST AFRICAN SETTLEMENTS

2. Constitution and Government

B. Courts and Extra–Territorial Jurisdiction

C. Defence

D. Land, Finance and Customs

GENERAL INTRODUCTION

FOR much of the nineteenth century the European and African trading frontier followed the line of the coast. Settlements declined at some points; at others they increased in size and number; a few posts were opened up on the navigable rivers. But on the whole, before the 1870's, the business of European agents kept them to the seaward markets, even as knowledge of the interior increased. The reasons for this are understood: the climate was feared; penetration of the interior was opposed by African coastal societies; communications and the high cost of settlement in the hinterland were beyond the means of the small-scale enterprises that operated well enough on the coast. In short, the weight of circumstances lay heavily in favour of preserving the traditional location of European contact and in maintaining the customary relations of buyer and seller established first by the Portuguese.

Yet it was not to last. A complete account of the interplay of opinions and events which modified European relations with West Africa and led to territorial dominion is beyond the scope of this essay. Its purpose, rather, is to define the policy of one European power during the period before 1874, when British experience of trade and administration on the coast was casual and limited. What elements of the international 'scramble' of later decades are traceable to this period? Do all the factors behind that forceful and sudden conquest lie in Europe and in the African continent at the time of the Berlin Conference; or were some of the attitudes of imperialism already present well before 1885? Moreover, annexation, protection, and partition were exercises of state sovereignty through unilateral and international agreements on behalf of private and public interests in the metropolis. This extension of British government overseas was not, of course, new outside of Africa. But intervention on a continental scale in the Western Sudan and the interior of the Guinea coast in the 1880's was at first sight a novel and dramatic event in that sector of the tropical world. How far was it prepared by government actions there in the past?

These questions presume that in the last analysis the criterion of imperial interests in Western Africa was territorial acquisition. To some extent this is true, though there were areas of Africa—the Congo, for example—where British official and private intervention stopped short of annexation in a situation which contained many factors encouraging political control. The fact remains that the establishment of protectorates and colonies was more usually the

last act of a long series, often debated and postponed, but providing
at length metropolitan responsibility for law, order, and human
welfare on the traders' unstable frontier. This was not the only method
by which British interests in West Africa had been safeguarded. In
some ways the 'scramble' was an alternative to other forms of
imperial pressure and international agreement which had been tried
out in previous decades.

However one looks at the outcome of European contact, there were
certain constants in British policy towards West Africa. These were
summed up once and for all by Lord John Russell, writing to the
Governor of Sierra Leone in 1840: 'The general object . . . is to
provide for the establishment of Peace, and innocent Commerce,
and for the abolition of the Slave Trade'.[1] Undoubtedly this proposition would have found favour with secretaries of state from the
Napoleonic Wars till the 1870's. But beneath these simple phrases
lay chasms of disagreement about how they were to be put into
practice and who was to pay the cost. Above all, up till the date
of Russell's dispatch, it was by no means clear what place there
was for British settlements on the coast to further these aims, or
what the rôle of the British Government in their administration was
to be.

The uncertainties and shifts in British policy, then, were not so
much a result of any failure to appreciate the nature of British
interests in Africa (it was always assumed that some national advantage could be derived from trade and from prohibiting the export of
slaves by other powers). The long exchanges between the Colonial
Office, Foreign Office, Treasury, Admiralty, War Office, Board of
Trade, commercial and philanthropic societies and, not least, between
colonial governments and their agents, revolved around methods. In
discussion and action on the coast three phases can be distinguished.
The first which lasted till about 1840 reveals a series of policies
which relied heavily on eighteenth-century precedents; the second
which it is convenient to terminate by the Select Committee Report
of 1865 was remarkable for a change in British relations with African
coastal societies and was mildly expansionist till the early 1860's;
the third featured a concentration on the reform of settlement
administration and a certain complacency about the consequences
of European contact which was shattered by the Ashanti war of
1872–3.

I

The two principal lessons learned by the British from their early
experience on the West African coast were that separate traders were

[1] C.O. 268/35, Russell to Doherty, 30 September 1840, ff. 380–401.

more efficient than monopoly companies and that administration by agents of the Crown was expensive in money and lives and possibly unnecessary for the protection of national interests. In the past these interests were trade in slaves, gum, ivory, and gold dust. To ensure their continued supply and the upkeep of shore stations without the use of privilege a compromise solution was arrived at in the Act of 23 Geo. II, c. 31 of 1750 which wound up the affairs of the Royal African Company. A committee of the regulated 'Company of Merchants trading to Africa' was allowed to administer the Gambia and Gold Coast forts with the help of a parliamentary grant, while joint-stock trading by the Company was forbidden and the facilities of its posts were opened to British subjects rent-free.[1] As a second compromise with the commercial spirit of the age, the African possessions were denied the status of plantations or colonies and their position under the Navigation Acts was for long left in doubt.

Another answer to the problem of protection had been to set up the full apparatus of Crown colony government in the captured 'Province' of Senegambia in 1764.[2] Governor, council, chief justice, and a colonial corps were luxuries in West African conditions of service. Relations between officials in Senegal and their subordinates at James' Island in the Gambia were disrupted by dismissals, incarceration, and suits at law; and what was made unworkable by intrigue was also left defenceless and lost again to the French in 1779. On the whole the experiment confirmed the wisdom of leaving West Africa to the merchants; and in 1783 when Senegal and Gorée were returned to France the British Government was content to safeguard rights to a share of the gum trade and hand over the Gambia fort to the care of the African Committee.[3] Official withdrawal from responsibility for African plantations or posts was almost complete for twenty-five years; and active interest was reawakened only when new values were attached by the Government in time of war to African trade and exploration.

British participation in West African trade by the last decades of the eighteenth century was largely the business of Liverpool, Bristol, and London trading houses. Regardless of the abolition of the slave trade on which much of this business had been built, the total value of imports and exports remained steady during the war in Europe. Between 1781 and the 1830's, tropical imports from the

---

[1] For the organization of the African Committee and its work, see E. C. Martin, *The British West African Settlements* (London, 1927), pp. 9–14, 29–42.

[2] Martin, pp. 57–102.

[3] Vincent T. Harlow, *The Founding of the Second British Empire 1763–1793* (London, 1952) I, pp. 402–3; J. M. Gray, *A History of the Gambia* (Cambridge, 1940), pp. 234–75.

region of 'Western Africa' amounted to about £250,000 a year, while exports from Great Britain, including materials for public works, averaged about £500,000 in the same period, after a temporary rise during the foundation of a new settlement in Sierra Leone. So far as merchants were concerned, protection meant the removal of foreign competition. In time of war this was possible. But in time of peace the conditions of West African trade made it particularly difficult to apply to the settlements rules and regulations designed to preserve a national monopoly of exchanges and shipping. In so far as they prohibited inter-colonial traffic and the foreign carrying trade the Navigation Acts were held to apply to West Africa by a ruling of the Crown Law Officers made in 1787.[1] But in practice only Sierra Leone and captured French posts were constricted by late eighteenth-century mercantilism: the Gold Coast forts escaped regulation till 1821.[2] It was not the kind of commercial protection British traders desired; and as the full rigour of the Acts began to be felt in West Africa, they looked to the principles of freer trade which were already being evolved for imperial possessions elsewhere. These principles were, in turn, extended to Sierra Leone and its dependencies in 1829 and consolidated by a local enactment of 1834 which ended discriminatory tariffs and opened the British ports to foreign goods.

The results of freer trade and the export of new staples—timber, groundnuts, and palm products—which became significant in the 1830's are not easy to assess. Reciprocity in commerce did nothing to reconcile British separate traders to foreign competition in the Gambia or in the Bight of Benin, particularly as the French took longer to dismantle the barriers of mercantilism in their West African posts.[3] But this rivalry apart, available statistics are defective in their range of information and inequable in their basis for the calculation of values. For some years they do not exist; for others, the general rubric 'West Africa' may mean a region from Morocco to the Cape or from the Gambia to the Cameroons. Customs records kept at the forts and settlements themselves do not cover more than a fraction of British and African trade.

So far as rough estimates can be made two general developments can be discerned: one is the expansion of imports of tropical produce from areas outside British control; the second is the absolute growth in quantity and value of a narrow range of staples to meet the demands of the market in Europe. For example, in 1829 nearly

---

[1] B.T. 6/7, Jules to Fawkner, 8 August 1787.

[2] B.T. 6/250, Minutes, 18 October 1819, 1 March 1823; and below, Introductory Note, p. 97.

[3] B. Schnapper, 'La fin du régime de l'exclusif: le commerce étranger dans les possessions françaises d'Afrique tropicale (1817–1870)', *Annales africaines* (1959), pp. 149–99. Gorée, however, was an entrepôt and duty-free port from 1822.

two-thirds of the total value of British imports from West Africa (£258,570) came from the Bight of Benin or Portendic; only half of the total of British manufactures sent to the coast went to the forts and settlements of the merchants and the Crown.[1] It is not surprising that the Committee of Privy Council for Trade and Plantations raised no objections to a Colonial Office suggestion to abandon the Gold Coast at the end of the 1820's;[2] and in 1841 the Delta palm oil trade was contrasted favourably with the small amounts exported from ports under British rule.[3] The lesson was obvious enough: African possessions offered little commercial advantage in return for their upkeep, in relation to coastal trade as a whole. The merchants' case for the retention of African posts which was still based on the eighteenth-century premise that a fort offered protection of the principal national interest in the African market was, by the 1830's, an extremely weak one.

The second sphere for government support of British enterprise was African exploration which by the end of the eighteenth century had become a field for scientific and commercial investment and part of the strategy of the war with France. A private institution of aristocrats, amateurs, and parliamentarians backed by the massive and comprehensive authority of Sir Joseph Banks showed the way. The practical object of the 'Association for promoting the Discovery of the Interior Parts of Africa', founded in 1788, was to 'open to Britain a commercial passage to rich and populous nations' by investigating the course and region of the Niger.[4] Mungo Park by 1797 had verified the river's direction and published a book which further stimulated interests in the human geography and possible wealth of the Western Sudan. An expensive plan to profit by this knowledge and set up a permanent consulate in the Senegambia to open diplomatic relations with the Tokolor and Fulbe states never materialized, though it indicated, as did the routes chosen for the first explorers, a preference for tackling the Niger problem and reaching the distant Hausa states from the western rivers of Africa. Strategic motives and the partial extension of the struggle in Europe to the African continent helped to finance Park's second—and fatal —expedition of 1805. Government interest revived again in 1815, when Sir John Barrow at the Admiralty and Lord Bathurst's Colonial Office backed the costly and unsuccessful expeditions of Captain

[1] Trade and commerce are still among the more neglected aspects of West African history. Their investigation is basic to a number of assumptions about European and African relations and the history of African societies on the Atlantic coast and in the interior. Statistics here have been taken from Parliamentary Papers and checked, where possible, against Board of Trade Customs returns. The total value of British exports to West Africa in 1829 was £511,799: Customs 8 (1829); *Parl. Papers*, 1831, xix (260).

[2] Document 4, p. 106.   [3] Document 7, p. 111.
[4] Document 1, p. 47; Introductory Note, p. 42.

Tuckey and Major Peddie to the Congo and the Niger. Thereafter, important missions were sponsored by traders and officials in Sierra Leone and on the Gold Coast for commercial information and diplomatic contact with the forest and savanna states. Simultaneously to the north, after a series of false starts, the Sahara route to the Niger was opened to European travellers when the Treasury agreed in 1821 to pay £5,000 towards the cost of sending Denham, Clapperton, and Oudney from Tripoli to Bornu. On the coast in the early 1820's detailed hydrographic surveys reduced the ignorance which was the principal danger to navigation in eighteenth-century charts. Meanwhile, Clapperton's death on his second expedition and the return of Richard Lander in 1828 still left the course of the Niger undetermined—though there had been some shrewd guesswork about its probable outlet based on information picked up from Hausa traders in the Bight of Benin.[1] In the end, it was Lander himself, encouraged by Sir John Barrow, who offered to solve cheaply and competently the mystery which had haunted the early years of the African Association and cost over a score of lives; and in 1831 the journey of the Lander brothers down-river to the Delta rounded off the period of West African exploration begun in the last decades of the eighteenth century.

Immediately the interest of government departments lapsed. It was laid down that no missions were to be sent from Sierra Leone or the Gambia at the administration's expense.[2] Requests by the Royal Geographical Society for funds to explore the Gambia and the Casamance were refused.[3] The 'African Inland Commercial Company' formed for the exploitation of Lander's discoveries was denied a charter and Treasury backing.[4] In spite of this, Laird Oldfield, and Lander took steam navigation to the African coast and as far inland as the Benue. Fittingly, the historians of the first British commercial expedition to the Niger dedicated their narrative to the Merchants and Philanthropists of Great Britain;[5] and in 1834, Lieutenant William Allen who had commanded one of the Niger vessels offered to turn his experience and knowledge into 'judicious colonization on a small scale' by settling emancipated slaves along the river and changing the pattern of interior trade.[6] This offer, too,—in some ways the logical conclusion of investment

<hr />

[1] Royal Geographical Society, Banks Papers. Admiral Sir James Yeo to the Admiralty, 12 May 1817; see, too, James MacQueen, *A Geographical and Commercial View of Northern Central Africa.* Edinburgh, 1821.

[2] C.O. 401/1, Hay to Rendall, 2 October 1832.

[3] C.O. 87/22, C.O. to F.O., 8 February 1839.

[4] C.O. 2/19, Forsyth to Hay, 7 April 1832.

[5] M. Laird and R. A. K. Oldfield, *Narrative of an Expedition into the Interior of Africa, by the River Niger in 1832–4,* 2 vols. London, 1837.

[6] C.O. 2/19, Allen to Barrow, 6 October 1834, encl. in Admiralty to C.O., 14 October 1834; Hay, Minute, 28 October 1834.

in exploration—was rejected by the Colonial Office. Nevertheless, British interest in the Western Sudan had at length swung away from the Gambia and the Senegal to the 'Houssa' of the African Association's early informant, Shabeni, whose account of the Niger and its markets had excited wealthy eighteenth-century gentlemen and nobles to action. It was in that direction, from the Sahara and the coast, that exploration was resumed at a later date.[1]

Thus, both African trade and African exploration had ceased to attract the support of the British Government by the 1830's. A third enterprise requiring even more official aid was the anti-slavery campaign and the resettlement of Africans in Sierra Leone. Philanthropy on this scale, too, was begun in the eighteenth century; and of all the West African activities inherited from that century the freeing of Africans was the most difficult for government either to withdraw from or to prosecute effectively. In the end the campaign proved the most permanent feature of British policy till the 1860's and one which influenced every other activity sponsored by official or private agents on the coast.

Once again, as in the case of trade and exploration, the work of a few dedicated enthusiasts helped to create commitments for government departments which had been glad to renounce the West African coast as profitless and unhealthy in 1783. Promoters of 'legitimate' trade and African resettlement worked to interest Pitt's administration in the distress of England's Black Poor and in the foundation of a colony in Sierra Leone.[2] To the Department of Home affairs and colonies, philanthropy in this direction meant ridding England of undesirables. To Granville Sharp and his friends it meant the foundation of a 'Province of Freedom' as a centre of enlightened government on the African coast and an example of a colony of free men to compare with the slavery of the West Indies. Persuaded by reports of a bountiful location[3] and by the insistence of the Black Poor themselves, the philanthropists and the Treasury founded the new settlement in 1787 with a handful of artisans, 340 blacks and some seventy London prostitutes on territory annexed by the Crown.

As the difficulties encountered by the colonists grew, the promoters turned to more traditional methods of eighteenth-century settlement. The St. George's Bay (Sierra Leone) Company, launched by Sharp,

---

[1] Introductory Note, p. 45.

[2] Christopher Fyfe, *A History of Sierra Leone* (Oxford, 1962), pp. 13–27.

[3] Henry Smeathman, traveller and botanist, had spent some time at the Banana Islands off Sierra Leone and was instrumental in persuading Quakers and the Committee for the Black Poor to consider the area as suitable for a colony. B.T. 6/7, Smeathman to Knowles, 21 July 1783; see too his *Plan of a Settlement to be made near Sierra Leone on the Grain Coast of Africa*, London, 1786.

Thomas Clarkson, and the banker, Henry Thornton, in 1790, combined some of the idealism of the visionaries with a solid expectation to cover costs. Incorporated in 1791 by the Act of 31 Geo. III c. 55, the Company came more under the direction of Thornton and his Board, and less under the impractical fringe of the abolitionists. But it was still severely inhibited by the circumstances of its formation: commercial monopoly was forbidden; experience of its directors in the African market was slight; and the colony itself was ruined by a succession of disasters—a French raid in 1794, settlers' revolts in 1796 and 1800, and Temne wars in 1801. The principal lesson learned before transfer to the Crown in 1807 was that philanthropy could not be run at a profit, or indeed survive at all without parliamentary grants; and secondly that the representative institutions outlined by Sharp demanded a sense of justice on the part of governors and councillors and a community discipline among the settlers which neither group was fitted by their experience of tropical colonization to display.

Nevertheless, these efforts by a struggling company made their mark on British policy in West Africa and the interests of the settlement continued to be safeguarded by the African Institution which was supported by most of the original directors and subscribers. The influence of the Institution itself has, perhaps, been exaggerated by historians, though it continued to advise and intrigue in West African affairs till 1827. Much of this advice about commerce was ill-informed and further evidence of the kind of ignorance that had helped to defeat the purposes of the Sierra Leone Company; the intrigues for appointments did not help the government of the settlement either. On the whole Sierra Leone policy lay now in the hands of the Department of War and Colonies, and behind it, in the Treasury, while the Foreign Office and the Admiralty sought to enforce in the Atlantic and Caribbean the anti-slavery principles that had helped to found the settlement and remained its justification.

Heir to the liabilities of the Company in 1807, Lord Grenville's administration and its successors were bound to end the slave trade. Limited means on the coast and at sea and the impossibility of seizing foreign vessels in time of peace left only the resources of diplomacy to secure reciprocal abolition by other maritime powers. Until 1839, the anti-slavery campaign centred around the legal problems of examination on the high seas and the collection of sufficient evidence for prosecution. Partial co-operation was obtained by treaties with Portugal, Spain, Holland, Brazil, and France, and by the establishment of a Court of Mixed Commission at Freetown to adjudicate captures.[1] But as the slave trade increased, the colony became a centre for liberated Africans far beyond the calculations of Clarkson

[1] Introductory Note, p. 133.

or Sharp; and as the cost of resettlement through the Liberated African Department mounted,[1] the administration of the settlement and the suitability of its location came under critical review.

At the same time, by the 1830's, the type of government inherited from the Sierra Leone Company and the African Merchants had been modified, but not entirely replaced. A general tendency towards autocratic administration of the Crown colony variety, unity under Sierra Leone, and a desire to separate the functions of traders and officials can be discerned in the correspondence of the early decades of the nineteenth century, where West Africa is concerned. Freetown had been established 'to afford the Asylum of an equal and good government' to liberated slaves;[2] the forts were run by merchants who made what profit they could from their position as 'governors' and commandants. Sierra Leone administration under the Company had been far from equal, as it was far from good; and the Merchants' Committee was subjected to complaint and scrutiny during the period of debate on the slave trade.[3] Yet both Freetown and the forts retained much of their eighteenth-century rule and precedent: Freetown was still an 'Asylum', after 1807, and the forts were trading-houses. Like the African Institution (though more effectively), the Merchants' Committee survived the legislation that ended one of the main sources of profit for its Bristol and Liverpool members, by accepting the fact that its African possessions were unreservedly under the ultimate control of Parliament.[4] The powers of the Governor of Cape Coast over his council were increased in 1804, and salaries of officials in the service of the Merchants were raised to compensate for loss of trade in 1808. On the whole, the African Company made the transition to legitimate trade without difficulty and defended itself successfully against the criticisms of the commissioners sent to report on British West African possessions in 1810.[5] An annual parliamentary grant defrayed the cost of the forts and their garrisons. Only the presence of Dutch competitors and the return of the French to the coast with permission to export slaves for five years under the peace treaty of 1814 left the Merchants angry and dismayed.[6]

At Sierra Leone a Charter of Justice issued to the Company in 1799 remained the basis of Crown administration. The governor and council of three were assisted in municipal administration by a mayor

[1] Amounting to £194,273, 1826–1842, compared with £116,850 expended on the civil establishment in Sierra Leone for the same period. *Parl. Papers*, 1843, xxxiii (622), p. 4.
[2] Document 3, p. 464, n. 2.
[3] See, for example, the charges by the Chief Justice of Senegambia, Edward Morse in 1784: C.O. 267/8.
[4] Martin, pp. 146–7.   [5] *Parl. Papers*, 1812, x (101); C.O. 267/29.
[6] C.O. 267/39, African Committee to Bathurst, 22 June 1814.

and aldermen, and in district administration by nominated superintendents. Trial by jury for civil and criminal cases was retained,
and in 1811 a chief justice was appointed. For the rest, the governor's
instructions of the same year added a few clauses similar to those
issued to West India governors concerning the powers and duties of
the council:[1] the Company system of 1799 was largely left intact.

On the Gold Coast, however, further surveys by commissioners,
charges of extravagance, and a plan for unified settlements by Governor MacCarthy, brought about the abolition of the African Company
in 1821, when the forts were placed under Sierra Leone. Very few
of the implications of establishing a united government were thought
out. MacCarthy's recommendations for a supreme court with power
to appoint magistrates in the dependencies were ignored; the legislative powers of the governor's council of nine at Freetown were
couched in the vaguest terms in the new Charter of 1821,[2] and the
executive powers of the governor outside of Sierra Leone were not
mentioned at all. James Stephen, as Permanent Under-Secretary
to the Colonial Office, was sufficiently mystified by this constitution
to suggest an Act of Parliament and changes to the governor's
commission to remedy its defects. But nothing was done, except to
hand back the administration of the forts to a new committee of
merchants in 1828. In the Gambia settlement which was tied to the
Sierra Leone Council, a lieutenant-governor was appointed for the
first time in 1829—unable to pass his own legislation and subjected
to the multiple delays of a system of administration which was in
need of abolition or reform.

Reforms had indeed been planned by Lord Bathurst in 1826 to
give to the Gold Coast and the Gambia their own governors and to
institute a unified colonial service on the model of Ceylon.[3] But in
the same year the Colonial Office began to consider the transfer of
the Mixed Commission Court and liberated African establishment
from Freetown to Fernando Po. Orders for the move were issued
in 1827.[4] The scheme was delayed, however, by the need to survey
the island and set up a rudimentary settlement there—made more
urgent by land shortage in Sierra Leone and the resolutions of a
Parliamentary Select Committee in 1830.[5] The new settlement
proved no healthier than the old one; no money could be voted to
pay the Spanish Government £100,000 for freehold rights—a sum
equal to the amount already wasted on the scheme; and in 1832, the
decision was made to break up the establishment at Fernando Po.

---

[1] Document 8, p. 482.
[2] Document 15, p. 494.
[3] C.O. 268/20, Bathurst to Turner, 30 April 1826, ff. 260–3.
[4] C.O. 268/26, Bathurst to Campbell, 20 March 1827, ff. 209–11.
[5] C.O. 267/98, Ricketts to Murray, 27 May 1829; Parl. Papers, 1830, x (661),
pp. 3–5.

Official interest in West Africa sank to its lowest point in the nineteenth century.[1]

The final legacy of the eighteenth century in West Africa includes the political, religious, and economic changes in the interior, partly appreciated by early explorers, increasingly important for European relations with African societies of the forest and savanna regions. These relations between European agents and coastal societies near the forts and settlements were complex and subject to a variety of motives and pressures on both sides. For merchants, administrators, missionaries, consuls, and naval officers, the dominant considerations were trade, good government, the progress of the missions, and the suppression of the slave trade. For African societies none of these developments proceeded in isolation from the total political and economic environment of the region south of the Sahara, any more than European activities on the coast were completely distinct from wars in Europe, or changes in metropolitan attitudes to tropical trade. Neither Africa nor Europe contained completely 'static' communities; and on the coast where European and African relations were closest, events in the interior had time, over the period of a century, to influence the course of settlement and government.

The most consequential of the changes in West Africa were the Islamic revolutions that began with the foundation of the Fulbe theocracy in the Futa Jallon in the eighteenth century and continued with the rise of a Tokolor Muslim confederation in the Futa Toro.[2] East of the Niger, the Fulani revolt and conquest of the Hausa states and Nupe in the early nineteenth century helped to complete the disintegration of the Yoruba empire under Oyo, between the 1820's and the 1860's. And again, to the west the creation of a Muslim state in Massina where the Fulbe overthrew their Bambarra rulers, and were themselves overthrown by Al Haj 'Umar in 1852, affected the partially islamized or pagan societies of the Senegambia and Guinea region. The huge area from Senegal to Lake Chad was the scene of a religious and political transformation which at points directly touched the areas south of the Western Sudan in the Futa Jallon hills, or in Ilorin, Nupe, and Adamawa. Political instability leading to partition, revolt, and reconquest continued throughout the period of Islamic consolidation, when time was needed for the development of the legal and administrative structure of the emirates. Not the least

---

[1] C.O. 82/5, Admiralty to C.O., 16 October 1832. For a general discussion of plans for withdrawal, see *The Cambridge History of the British Empire*, vol. ii, *The Growth of the New Empire 1783–1870* (Cambridge, 1940), pp. 650–2.

[2] Much is still obscure about the economic and religious background to the *jihad* of the Western Sudan. See the suggestive article by H. F. C. Smith, 'The Islamic Revolutions of the 19th Century', *Journal of the Historical Society of Nigeria* (1961), vol. ii, no. 1, pp. 169–85; and J. Spencer Trimingham, *A History of Islam in West Africa* (Oxford, 1962), pp. 155–81; Thomas Hodgkin, *Nigerian Perspectives* (London, 1960), pp. 38–47.

important result of these changes was to influence the reorientation of trade in the sahel and savanna—in the direction of the coast, rather than across the Sahara—a development which preceded the Islamic revolutions, as well as being assisted by them. All the principal river routes to the sea grew in importance as the slave trade drew on fresh supplies from the interior. The gradual decline of the desert routes to North Africa, with the exception of the Tripoli-Bornu and Kano axis, made the new states look south for their arms, powder, salt, and cloth and took Fulbe and Hausa traders to settle in communities at the coastal ports and markets from the beginning of the nineteenth century.

These political and economic changes were very marked in the Senegambia area and in Yorubaland. The Wolof states and Bondu were subjected to military intervention from Fulbe and Tokolor in the early nineteenth century, just as the successor states to Oyo later came under pressure from the Fulani. Both movements were checked in the lower Senegal, 1805–6, and at Oshogbo in 1843. But the spread of Islamic clerics and traders continued and eventually threatened the position of Wolof and Mandinka overlords in the Senegambia (though there is no evidence of similar revolts following infiltration among the Yoruba). Economically, the Senegal and the Gambia basins became tributary to the Futa Toro, Kaarta, and the Futa Jallon, while the Nunez and Casamance were closely connected with upper Senegal and upper Niger trade through Timbo.[1] In Yorubaland no one of the Yoruba states was strong enough to dominate trade routes to southern Dahomey, Badagri, Lagos, or Benin, though the Egba and Ijebu were slightly better placed as middlemen dealing with Yoruba and Hausa to the north.

South and west of the Futa Jallon the militant element in the spread of Islam was not so evident as it was between the Senegal and Gambia rivers or to the east of the Niger. But one result of the consolidation of the Fulbe theocracy at Timbo was the spread of pagan and islamized Susu through Limba territory to the Temne and Bulom area bordering Sierra Leone in the eighteenth and early nineteenth centuries, and, secondly, the migration of Yolunka (Solima) to Falaba, a new trading capital near the Niger watershed. Sierra Leone trade was greatly influenced by the internal tension arising from these movements in neighbouring Temne, Loko, Susu, and Bulom societies.[2] Two areas were of prime importance: Port Loko and the Rokel river, reaching inland from the head of the Sierra Leone estuary through Koya and Masimera country to Falaba; and, again, on the coast north of Freetown, as far as the Isles de Los and inland to the Futa Jallon highlands. Interest in a third area to the south-east in the Sherbro developed in the 1850's, as a result of activity against

[1] See Map 1, facing p. 1.   [2] See Map 2, p. 69.

the slave trade and increased exports of rice, palm oil, ivory, and timber. There, too, as among the Temne, Loko, and Bulom, there were Mandinka, Susu, and Fulbe immigrants competing for trade and leadership among the Mende and the Vai.

The pagan kingdoms of Ashanti and Dahomey largely escaped the direct consequences of the spread of Islam in the interior, though Ashanti relations with Muslim centres to the north were old and close,[1] and it is possible that Dahomey's capacity for trade in slaves was increased by Bariba resistance to the Fulani in Borgu. But so far as Europeans were concerned, these two states constituted by far the greatest threat to settlement throughout the first half of the nineteenth century, after their irruption into the politics and trade of the coastal chiefdoms between 1730 and 1807. Thereafter, the problem of European contact with the Fanti of the Gold Coast and the Gun of southern Dahomey was how to keep the peace between these coastal middlemen and their overbearing clients to the north when the former aspired to freedom from Ashanti or Dahomey controls, while the latter possessed military superiority.

The delta states in the Oil Rivers were sheltered from Islamic expansion. In the nineteenth century, after the abolition and decline of the slave trade, they offered examples, however, of a different kind of internal tension—between traditional rulers and former slaves, at a time when the rising value of the palm oil trade and the trust system by which it was carried on made Ibo, Ijo, and Ibibio society particularly vulnerable to European pressure from without and political competition for economic controls from within.[2]

Europeans, then, in the nineteenth century were faced with the consequences of their own activities and with the results of changes in the interior and on the coast outside their short range of influence. Their knowledge of the interior increased remarkably during the forty years after Park's first mission to the Niger: by the 1820's officials in London could distinguish nicely between Bornu and the Fulani-Hausa emirates; there was detailed information on the politics and trade of the Senegambia region; and from Park himself had come a picture of the free African, new to Europeans who began to see possibilities of increased productivity in a society needing only 'example to enlighten the minds of the natives'.[3] It was still a very partial and incomplete picture; but it was better than Cadamosto or Leo Africanus, and more comprehensive than most of the early coastal authors. On the whole, the missions to the Niger and the Sierra Leone explorations left the impression in England that there

[1] Ivor Wilks, *The Northern Factor in Ashanti History*, Ghana, 1961.

[2] G. I. Jones, *The Trading States of the Oil Rivers*. International African Institute (Oxford, 1963), pp. 63–87, 107–30.

[3] *Report of the Committee of the African Institution, 15 July 1807* (London, 1807), p. 40.

existed paramount authorities—'sultans' and *almamys*—with whom business could be arranged in the manner of the North African states or the Ottoman Turks. For West Africa the age of the paper convention had arrived.

The transition in European and African relations on the coast from the years of the company concessions to the years of colonial government may be described as a progression from diplomacy to clientage. The diplomacy continued, particularly during periods of exploration or forays into the interior to mediate in African disputes; and the status of equal partners was formally acknowledged by the correspondence passing between the Foreign Office and Sokoto, or by the periodic communications between Freetown and Timbo up till the 1870's. Clientage on the coast had occasionally meant protection by African chiefs and the surrender of freedom of movement by Europeans in return for the right to trade. But broadly speaking, by the end of the 1830's, experiments were in progress to secure African clientage to colonial government, particularly near Sierra Leone, at the Gold Coast forts, and in the next decade at Lagos and in the Delta.

The methods by which the Merchants' Committee had kept open communications on the Gold Coast by the regular payment of presents and rents amounting to £500 or £600 a year[1] were not continued by the colonial administration after 1821. The system of making annual gifts in kind was, however, still basic to the Senegambia gum trade and helped to keep the British market open at Portendic, when Senegal was returned to France. Thereafter, presents from government stores to the Trarza Moors were made till the decline of the trade itself by the early 1840's. The presents were then sent to the Gambia where a similar policy of making regular payments to secure favourable conditions of trade had been followed since the 1820's. An attempt to extend this system to the chiefs of the upper Gambia in return for a monopoly of gum exports was discouraged by the Colonial Office in 1829, when it was suspected that commercial enterprise of this kind implied a new settlement above MacCarthy Island. By then, the Secretary of State for Colonies was sceptical of largesse in Africa, 'as experience has shown the fallacy of expecting any national benefit from arrangements which rest upon a system of tributary presents . . . . Some sacrifices must of course be made occasionally to obtain the goodwill of the influential tribes; but no expense should be incurred for that purpose exceeding what the rules of courtesy may prescribe as sufficient'.[2]

This rejection of tribute was in keeping with Crown policy on the Gold Coast in the 1820's. But it was out of touch with the develop-

---

[1] *Parl. Papers*, 1821, xxi (724), pp. 8–10.
[2] C.O. 401/1, Glenelg to Rendall, 25 June 1830, ff. 112–14.

ment of the clientage system between the Sierra Leone Government and Bulom, Temne, Susu, and Mandinka chiefs for the preservation of peace and trade. Promises of military assistance such as those made by Governor Thompson in an 'Offensive and Defensive' alliance of 1808, it is true, were premature and not sanctioned.[1] But the provision of arms to African allies certainly continued on a small scale, and they feature in a 'Return of Articles required for the Payment of Customs and Presents' drawn up by Governor Mac-Carthy in 1823 to cover the purchase of goodwill from chiefs in Sierra Leone, the Gold Coast, and the Isles de Los.[2] The idea of a formal contract with African rulers, begun abortively by Thompson, was attempted also on the Gold Coast in the treaties of 1817 and 1820 which were concluded with the Ashanti by representatives of the Merchants and the British Government.[3] In both documents, however, the issues at stake between the Ashanti, Fanti, and the British were stated, but not solved. Their terms provided no inducement for a lasting settlement, and they were rejected by the Merchants for over-generous recognition of Ashanti claims to Fanti states. Refusal to allow the payment of rents to Kumasi resulted in a clash in 1824 and the defeat of the Ashanti at Dodowa in 1826. After the return of the forts to a Committee of Merchants two years later, there was no formal peace till 1831, when George Maclean as President of the Cape Coast Council succeeded in delimiting the Ashanti confederation north of the buffer states of Denkyera and Assin, and secured a bond, hostages, and rules to leep open paths for trade and guarantee the independence of the Fanti. The idea of paying rents for the forts was never revived. So long as Ashanti accepted this state of affairs, the truce of 1831 was kept.

In Sierra Leone, by contrast, the administration evolved very detailed agreements between 1831 and 1835 to put an end to Loko, Temne, and Susu hostilities, to arrange for reciprocal surrender of liberated Africans and domestic slaves, and to fix regular annual stipends to chiefs in place of traders' rents for timber concessions and trade.[4] More chiefs were brought into this system in 1837, when it was extended to include the Limba and was proposed to the Fulbe of the Futa Jallon. The Colonial Office approved—except for clauses concerning slaves. Stipends were suspended, until this important revision could be made. By the end of 1839, however, the Governor of Sierra Leone reported the refusal of chiefs to surrender their claims to fugitives;[5] and this report reached the Colonial Office in time to be weighed in the balance of British policy towards African

---

[1] Document 1, p. 243.
[2] C.O. 267/58, MacCarthy to Bathhurst, 30 June 1823.
[3] Documents 2, 4, pp. 284, 288.   [4] Documents 6–8, pp. 250–3.
[5] C.O. 267/148, Doherty to Glenelg, 7 September 1838; and 267/154, Doherty to Normanby, 7 October 1839. Stipends had been suspended since June 1837.

societies, when Lord John Russell began to give treaties a greater content and wider application to deal with the problems of legitimate and slave trade as a whole.

In a number of ways, therefore, the inheritance from the eighteenth century in West African policy contained attitudes which were as out of date as most of the fortified emplacements that looked seaward from the settlements. The predilection was still for islands off the coast—St. Mary's, Bulama, the Isles de Los, Fernando Po—or a peninsula, if no island was available. Monopoly companies were not revived for over a century after 1750, as a means of encouraging national trade, but the regulated companies that were used proved inadequate for either philanthropy or managing the forts. Finally, government aid to exploration came to an end for a time, once the Niger problem was solved. Possible abandonment of the settlements was then considered. But the new responsibility of the campaign against the slave trade made such a step undesirable: the Crown continued to hang on to its scattered posts, leaving the forts to a caretaker administration of merchants. This, too, was an eighteenth-century solution for officials who were still unwilling in the 1830's to pay for the cost of administrative reform. Parallel to the responsibility of the anti-slavery campaign there developed in Sierra Leone and in the Gambia the beginnings of a formal series of treaty relations with African rulers—a policy rejected or made unworkable on the Gold Coast. The consequences of this policy were not, as yet, foreseen.

II

The year 1840 marked the date in British West African policy when nineteenth-century ministers and officials ran out of eighteenth-century ideas. Evidence of an increase in the slave trade and the suspicion that the Gold Coast forts were being used to supply slavers shook the Colonial and Foreign Offices out of the attitude of makeshift and compromise that had prevailed since about 1828. The immediate results of the investigations carried out by Captain Tucker in 1839 and by Commissioner R. R. Madden in 1841[1] made it clear that the old system of using merchants as caretaker administrators could not continue; and at the end of 1842, Lord Stanley's Colonial Office accepted most of the recommendations of a Select Committee of the House of Commons for the return of the forts to the Crown and the separation of the Gambia from Sierra Leone.[2] The decision was made after a sharp inter-departmental debate on

[1] Introductory Note, p. 133.

[2] Documents 22–26, pp. 509–15. The importance of this decision was not lost on the ministries for marine and colonies, agriculture and commerce, in France, where it was interpreted as evidence of expansion and French posts were pressed for as compensation. Bernard Schnapper, *La politique et le commerce français dans le Golfe de Guinée de 1838 à 1871* (Paris, 1961), pp. 28–29.

the implications of British jurisdiction at the forts and, indeed, the necessity for any forts or settlements at all. In this debate Under-Secretary James Stephen played a less constructive part than is sometimes assumed.[1] His meticulous attack on the administration of the Gold Coast by the Merchants weakened by 1843, when he came to understand the domestic slavery question better; and, on the whole, the reorganization of the British settlements was carried out along lines suggested by the Parliamentary Under-Secretary, G. W. Hope, and accepted by Stanley against Stephen's judgement. But for the world at large it was not constitutional change, but the anti-slavery campaign and the Niger expedition of 1841 which aroused optimism or ridicule about West Africa. For a time the Government was deeply involved in the support of both ventures in ways which showed some originality of thought.

The foundation of a 'Society for the Extinction of the Slave Trade and the Civilization of Africa' in 1840 resumed in its title an old theme already propounded by Wilberforce and Sharp—that if the soil of Africa were made to produce more goods for export the sale of Africans would cease. Nevertheless, T. F. Buxton, Dr. Lushington, and the group which framed the Society's policy were inclined to see themselves as innovators in the humanitarian field. When they paused to look at the work of eighteenth-century abolitionists and at the African Institution, they were careful to dissociate themselves from the ineffectiveness of their predecessors by pointing to a number of new factors which they felt gave them a better chance of achieving their ends.[2] The advance from sail to steam (they argued) would revolutionize the African trade; the Niger discoveries opened a way to the interior and a site for experimental agriculture in the heart of the slave trade; the practice of making treaties with chiefs—not merely with the nations of Europe, as the African Institution had urged—would stop the market for slaves at source.

These developments in legitimate commerce and in relations with African rulers did, indeed, have an important bearing on the anti-slavery campaign and on the role of the British Government in West Africa, though not in ways that immediately justified the enthusiasm of the Civilization Society in 1840 and 1841. It was in some ways a curiously old-fashioned idea to set up a plantation in a region of the world where all previous British and French efforts to found one had failed, and on a river where Liverpool and Bristol traders had demonstrated the type of investment that succeeded best.[3] Eventually,

---

[1] *The Cambridge History of the British Empire*, vol. ii, pp. 661, 665–6.
[2] *The Friend of Africa* (1841) i, pp. 26–27.
[3] The Buxtonites were not alone in this dream: at least one company promoter in 1843 tried to form an 'African Agricultural Association' to cultivate Fernando Po and the Amboises Islands, 'as if they were West Indian Estates'. Rhodes House MS., R. Dillon Tennent, 'Prospectus. African Agricultural Association', 10 January 1843.

the losses sustained by the Niger expedition killed the hope that somehow freed labour would dramatically redeem Africa from 'idleness and servitude'.

A second and more successful contribution to British policy was the action of Captain Denman in the Gallinas in 1841, when a naval blockade and the destruction of slavers' property offered the first effective example of suppression since 1807. The possible illegality of the action, however, bred a new caution on the part of the Government for a time. Opposition to the use of the Preventive Squadron was not defeated till the early 1850's—by Parliamentary manœuvre, by favourable decision in Denman's case, and by further examples of naval tactics inshore at the Gallinas and at Lagos. Another decade and changes in the Brazilian and Cuban markets were needed, before the export of slaves from West Africa was finally overcome. But it was made extremely difficult to continue the old illegal traffic in the Bights after 1851, and the bulk of the trade was confined to the Congo or to well-known areas north of Sierra Leone. Throughout the campaign after 1840 it was the Navy and the treaty system outlined in Buxton's plan (and not his agricultural experiment) which played the more significant part.

Already in 1839 James Bandinel in the Foreign Office had drawn up a draft treaty for West Africa, consisting of twenty-two articles copied from agreements with the Sultan of Muscat and the Hova of Madagascar.[1] Most of these articles dealt with liberation of slaves and sought safeguards for British property and lives in far greater detail than the early Sierra Leone, Gold Coast, or Delta treaties. But, unlike its models, the draft did not allow West African chiefs jurisdiction over British subjects. The inducements to sign were much the same: revenue might be collected on imports and handed over to the chiefs; or payments were promised annually or in a lump sum. Among the additional terms appended to this draft was a promise of British protection, if the African signatory was attacked by rivals. Two other clauses dealt with the cession of territory and with the abolition of human sacrifice. The whole draft treaty of 1839 became the basis for the treaty forms taken to Africa by the Niger Commissioners; and towards the end of 1840 it was circulated among Government departments and members of the Cabinet.[2] The Cabinet approved, though the Chancellor of the Exchequer, Sir Francis Baring, raised objections to the proposed payment of chiefs. Russell had already written to the Treasury to explain the purpose of the expedition and had secured agreement to go ahead with the purchase of three steam vessels.[3] The Niger Commissioners received their final

---

[1] F.O. Confidential Print (1839). Africa. Expedition and Mission proposed. Some points for consideration. Draft of Treaty. Annex. B.

[2] C.O. 325/37, Stephen, Minute, 8 December [1840]; Vernon Smith, Minute, n.d.

[3] Parl. Papers, 1843, xlviii (472), Russell to Treasury, 26 December 1839.

instructions in January 1841.[1] By then, the much amended draft Niger treaty, on the suggestion of Under-Secretary Robert Vernon Smith, served in turn as a model for relations with African chiefs in the Gambia and Sierra Leone.[2]

Russell forwarded the treaty to West Africa in July 1840 with orders to use it in the rivers near Sierra Leone and in the Futa Jallon. More detailed explanations followed, emphasizing the need to encourage the cultivation of produce in much the same terms as those sent to guide the Niger Commissioners.[3] Of the four additional articles appended to the treaty 'for special cases', Russell explained, the one concerned with the payment of compensation for ending the slave trade was intended as a temporary measure, until the benefits of legitimate trade were appreciated. Great store was set by the abolition of human sacrifice, where it existed, in order to render Africans 'more ready and open to communicate amicably with civilized nations; to adopt their habits, their arts, their religion'. No land was to be purchased without Government permission; and, cautioned Russell, terms for the protection of African allies were to be entered into with care and only with chiefs near to the sea or on navigable rivers. Finally, Russell laid down that Customs duties levied on British goods were not to exceed 5 per cent. of their value; in special cases some other duty or anchorage charge might be made over to chiefs; but the 5 per cent. limit to the general *ad valorem* duty already levied at Freetown was not to be exceeded by any additional charges to meet the cost of payments.

Russell's anti-slavery treaty which married the aims of the Buxtonites to past policy in Sierra Leone towards neighbouring rulers represented the most serious attempt in the nineteenth century to arrive at a contract with African states. In its final form the draft treaty was nothing less than an agreement to social and economic revolution in return for doubtful promises of financial aid and eventual well-being. The principal objection to it (as Stephen did not fail to point out) was that it could not be enforced, if the terms were broken, unless an expensive and vigorous policy was adopted in West Africa.

There were other objections, too, which came to light, when the first of the new treaties from Sierra Leone were forwarded to the Colonial Office in 1841; and the threat of involvement in a military expedition on behalf of an African signatory in the Gambia in the same year brought Russell's system under closer scrutiny from his

[1] Document 16, p. 154.
[2] C.O. 267/159, Doherty to Russell, 22 April 1840; Vernon Smith, Minute, 17 June 1840.
[3] C.O. 268/35, Russell to Doherty, 30 September 1840, ff. 380–401; Document 12, p. 260. A copy of these instructions and a draft treaty were also sent to Governor Huntley at Bathurst.

successor, Lord Stanley.[1] Promises of military assistance were disallowed, and in 1843 the Foreign Office requested the omission of all complex commercial clauses from anti-slavery treaties.[2] A new model was supplied, based on a treaty for the chiefs of Bimbia in the Cameroons concluded that year.

In the Delta and on the Slave Coast, the principle of compensation by annual subsidies was retained, though it was not really applied till two treaties were obtained from Bonny in 1848. Such inducements were not enough for chiefs in Dahomey and at Lagos—the least successful test for Russell's policy. By the 1840's the area was still one of the strongholds of resident slavers on the coast; and in addition to this reason for intervention a small number of traders began to export palm oil from Badagri, while T. B. Freeman of the Cape Coast Methodist Mission pioneered relations with the Yoruba. Like the Methodists, the Church Missionary Society followed the lead of African immigrants returning from Sierra Leone. By 1846, a mission had been established at Abeokuta, using Badagri as a port of supply. Inevitably, missionaries and traders were involved in the struggle between the Yoruba and the Fon of Dahomey and in a civil war at Badagri arising out of the expulsion of King Akitoye of Lagos by his nephew, Kosoko. To secure their communications with the sea, British residents petitioned for protection in 1843 and obtained a small garrison from the Gold Coast to guard the British flag at Badagri for a few months in 1844. Neither of these steps was approved; and the Foreign Office fell back on the anti-slavery treaty as a means of securing peace.

Like King Pepple of Bonny, Ghezo of Dahomey was hard to convince that an offer of $2,000 for a few years was adequate compensation for the loss of profits on trade in slaves, which was still open to his neighbours on the coast; and as the reasons for the King of Dahomey's reluctance were better understood, after an official mission to Abomey in 1848, Lord Palmerston appointed a vice-consul to Whydah to expound the benefits of legitimate trade.

The use of consuls in the Bights and at the Sherbro from the end of the 1840's was less a return to diplomacy in dealings with African chiefs than a Foreign Office measure to enforce clientage relations with the British Government, once they had been established by treaty. Instructions to explorers, compared with Palmerston's orders to Consul Beecroft, present a different conception of the two roles of European agents—as ambassadors and as a constabulary.[3] Beecroft the explorer, appointed to lead the Niger expedition of

---

[1] C.O. 267/163, Jeremie to Russell, 20 January 1841; 4 March 1841; and 267/164, Stephen, Minute, 22 September 1841; Documents 6-8, pp. 224-7; Introductory Note, pp. 215-16.
[2] C.O. 267/167, Leveson to Stephen, 3 August 1841.
[3] Documents 13 and 9, pp. 73 and 384.

1854, was to go as a dispenser of 'suitable presents and samples of goods'; as consul at Fernando Po, he was selected for his experience 'and because of the influence which you appear to have acquired over the Native Chiefs'. Once involved in contractual relations and accessible to naval action, African signatories to treaties after 1840 no longer enjoyed the same status with European officials. Indeed, as Stephen reminded Lord Stanley at the outset of the new campaign started by Russell, Lord Palmerston had forbidden the use of the word 'treaty' in the African context 'to mark the distinction between Agreements with barbarous Chiefs and the international Compacts of Civilized States'.[1] The duty of the consuls was to see that the terms of these second-class agreements were kept.

The consequence of consular appointments to the Bights was increased reliance on the Navy to secure the aims of British policy. Beecroft's overtures at Abomey and Abeokuta in 1850 failed to win over King Ghezo to the anti-slavery cause and brought the British into temporary alliance with the Yoruba. The Navy was ordered to blockade the Slave Coast and to make a show of force if necessary at Lagos. The bombardment which followed in 1851 on Beecroft's initiative and the installation of King Akitoye at Lagos as signatory to an anti-slavery treaty produced a crop of agreements along the coast. At Abeokuta, after the repulse of Dahomey forces in March 1851, British prestige was at its highest: Commander Forbes supplied ammunition and advice at the end of the year; and in 1852 Commodore Bruce renewed the alliance. The kind of commitment which the Colonial Office had tried to avoid in the Gambia and in Sierra Leone had now been entered into by the Foreign Office and the Admiralty in the Lagos interior.

The establishment of a new consulate at Lagos in 1852 and the abolition of the post at Whydah completed a process begun by the missionaries to secure protection of trade and evangelism in Yorubaland. Dahomey was not forgotten in future considerations of policy in the area; but Lagos had been accessible to the Navy and Abomey was not. The use of the Navy in the style developed by Denman at the Gallinas to secure treaties took Government interference in West Africa a step further than the stipend system of Sierra Leone or the 'protection' begun on a narrow juridical basis among the Fanti on the Gold Coast. The policy adopted by the consuls towards King Akitoye and his successors in the 1850's made Lagos Island a British Protectorate in all but name. Lagos was not a fort, circumscribed by rules about the limits of a governor's authority; it was an expanding trading community where, by the end of the decade, the need for adequate jurisdiction over foreigners and British subjects and the political influence gained by the consuls over the Yoruba chief of

[1] Document 7, p. 226.

DBP

the island counted for much alongside other factors of trade and French competition, when, in 1861, the decision to annex was made.

Elsewhere in the Bights, too, consular policy went beyond supervising the treaty system at Bonny, New Calabar, Old Calabar, and Bimbia. Elections of chiefs were managed and approved in the Cameroons' ports; Beecroft imposed fines on traders to settle disputes; and in 1854 the political influence of the consulate at Fernando Po was extended to Bonny, where the consul assisted an alliance of traders and chiefs in deposing and sending into exile King Dappa Pepple.[1] Consul Lynslager went further and destroyed by bombardment a town at Old Calabar.

During the last years of the 1850's, these and other actions raised the question of consular jurisdiction in the palm oil markets. The Foreign Office, without consulting other departments, proposed to extend magisterial powers of consuls by an Order-in-Council, if suitable treaties could be arranged to cede jurisdiction to officers of the Crown.[2] Only two treaties were obtained—an insufficient basis for consular courts.[3] Deposing chiefs, however, was forbidden in 1861. At most, the consuls were permitted to frame rules for courts of equity in which they could not sit and to protect British subjects whose status, in the case of liberated Africans, was still doubtful even after the Liberated African Act of 1853.[4] Meanwhile, the problems which had encouraged their illegal intervention in the past and had led to the annexation of Lagos grew more acute, particularly at Bonny, where new leaders sought to control the palm oil market as the authority of traditional chiefs declined.

Elsewhere on the coast, Sierra Leone, the Gambia, and to some extent the Gold Coast forts had similar difficulties arising from the increased volume of trade and the ambiguous attitude of colonial governments to domestic slavery and to the control of British subjects beyond the limits of colonial rule. Different remedies were proposed. In general, the Freetown administration continued to develop the stipend system as the basis of native policy in and near Sierra Leone, defraying the cost from the colonial chest.[5] A list of annual sums paid out between 1835 and 1847 suggests they were far from regular, varying from as little as £5 in one year to £246 in another.[6] More stipendiary chiefs were added to the budget in 1849, at the end of a

---

[1] Document 13, p. 391.

[2] F.O. 84/1087, 1088, F.O. to Hutchinson and Campbell, 23 May 1859 (and draft treaty encl.); Brand to Russell, 31 December 1859.

[3] F.O. 84/1117, Hutchinson to Russell, 12 February 1860; and 84/1176, F.O. to Burton, 23 August 1862.

[4] Document 18, p. 564.

[5] C.O. 267/205, Treasury to C.O., 11 July 1848.

[6] C.O. 267/204, Pine to Grey, 18 October 1848.

civil war in the Sherbro where treaties and a naval force brought an uneasy peace. Four years later the whole policy was questioned by Governor Kennedy who advised a change from paying goods measured in devaluated 'bars' to payments of money and suggested terminating stipends on the death of signatories to past treaties.[1] The Colonial Office accepted this advice, but Kennedy's local successors did not, and 'bars' continued to be used.

None of this experience in Sierra Leone appears to have influenced policy on the Gold Coast. Any pretence of cementing Anglo-Fanti relations by payments had long been given up with the African Company in 1821 and was overshadowed by problems of administration near the forts, and threats from Ashanti. The resumption of Crown control in 1843 brought a series of muddled attempts to define more closely the notion of 'protection' over African society on the coast, while restricting nominal sovereignty to the forts. Under the Foreign Jurisdiction Act of 1843 and the declarations obtained from Fanti chiefs in 1844,[2] judgement of criminal cases by a Judicial Assessor and a doubtful military security against Ashanti were the principal contributions of the Crown in return for Fanti 'allegiance'. After the separation of the Gold Coast from Sierra Leone in 1850, the premise of co-operation on which joint jurisdiction had been assented to by the Fanti chiefs was gradually replaced by the assumption of unique authority in civil and criminal matters by the Supreme Court. Chiefs, moreover, could be punished and deposed, as Lieut.- Governor Winniett demonstrated in 1848 by his expedition against Appollonia, and as his successors showed during the Krobo 'rebellion' a decade later.[3] But the notion of 'protection' underwent a change during these ten years. The meagre benefits resulting from the poll tax introduced in 1852 and failure to make use of an assembly of chiefs and district councils weakened confidence in the intentions of the protecting power. Moreover, the state of local defences against Ashanti incursions in 1853 and 1863 did nothing to reassure the Fanti that British assistance would be effective. For the colonial government 'protection' came to mean not merely military readiness, but internal security in relations with the Fanti against real and imaginary threats to colonial authority.

In Sierra Leone, on the other hand, the need for asserting the authority of the administration outside the colonial boundaries was neither so pressing as on the Gold Coast, nor was it tolerated by the Colonial Office. When Governor Pine tried to make extra-territorial offences by British subjects cognizable at Freetown courts in 1849, the matter was thought to depend on the content of treaties ceding

[1] Document 20, p. 271.
[2] Documents 7 and 12, pp. 549 and 298. See also, David Kimble, *A Political History of Ghana* (Oxford, 1963), pp. 192–217.
[3] Document 21, p. 309.

such jurisdiction to the Crown and on the status of Liberated Africans.[1] While these points were being settled, the paradox existed whereby jurisdiction over the Fanti slowly increased in an area where no sovereignty had been acquired outside the forts, while the protection of British laws was found not to exist for the bulk of the inhabitants of Sierra Leone. Although it was pointed out that the Foreign Jurisdiction Act did not apply solely to British subjects, the idea that former slaves carried with them the rights and duties of Britons abroad was accepted with great reluctance, even after the Liberated African Act of 1853. Indeed, unless some additional treaty with a native chief was obtained, the status of Africans returning from Sierra Leone to their own territory in the Delta could hardly be equated with that of a British subject at all. Nearer to Sierra Leone, however, further agreements with Temne and Loko chiefs in 1860 and the Offences Act of 1861 (24 and 25 Vict., c. 31) provided for the surrender of British offenders to colonial justice at Freetown.

In the Gambia, the situation was different again. There, by the 1850's, the old treaty policy was breaking down because of external factors arising from trade rivalries and political instability in African societies adjacent to British posts. The whole of British policy towards the Gambia Wolof and Mandinka chiefdoms which had reposed on occasional agreements and stipends was destroyed between 1852 and the mid-1860's by a series of political and religious revolts. The pan-Islamic elements in the 'Marabout' confederation which emerged among the scattered trading settlements of Mandinka and Fula clerics were appreciated by the Gambia administration and the Colonial Office. But policy was not determined so much by this consideration (indeed, Palmerston preferred Muslims to 'fetish Negroes'),[2] as by the limited garrison available to defend British territory against attack. There was little Governor D'Arcy or his successors could do to influence the course and outcome of the Mandinka-Wolof-'Marabout' wars, unless African contestants agreed to submit to arbitration—a policy which the Colonial Office was unwilling to encourage and which held little appeal for the Gambia chiefs.

At Lagos, too, the administration after 1861 was vulnerable to disruption of interior trade and local market supplies. The reaction of officials was to undo the careful diplomacy of the missionary and consular period in an effort to assert preponderant influence over the nearest of the Yoruba states. Administrator Glover's defeat of the Egba at Ikorodu opposite Lagos Island in 1865 achieved his immediate aim of opening trade routes to Lagos. But the action marked the decline of the early British alliance with Abeokuta which had begun

[1] Documents 11-13, pp. 557-60.   [2] Document 14, p. 233.

to weaken in 1861 or 1862, as the new colony sought to manage conditions outside the colonial boundary.

By the mid-1860's, then, the method of combining anti-slavery treaties with clauses from traditional conventions for 'amity and commerce' had produced about 107 signed documents in all.[1] Some 82 of these had been contracted by the Navy and the Sierra Leone administration (though very few of the 23 treaties for territorial cessions had been approved). The remainder mostly concerned the Gambia and Lagos areas. For the Gold Coast there was little in addition to the 1831 treaty with Ashanti and the 'Bonds' of 1844. The results of this method are not easy to assess. Wars in the Gambia exposed the weakness of the system where it was incomplete and unsupported by military or naval resources. The stipend system, on the other hand, in Sierra Leone and to a limited extent in the Lagos Protectorate, restricted disaffection. On the Gold Coast the cession of Fanti chiefs' judicial powers, without compensation, opened the way to further encroachments, while the treaty with Ashanti was more in the nature of a truce than an agreement of the clientage type.

The fact that so many of the treaties were made with chiefs outside the British settlements reflected the pattern of trade on the coast and the spread of British interests since the 1830's. By the 1850's, total trade between the United Kingdom and British West Africa was valued at only half a million pounds; and by 1874 this value had tripled.[2] Yet, for the 1850's and the 1860's respectively, this share represented only 18 per cent. and 28 per cent. of total British trade with West Africa during these two decades; and the slight increase of the contribution of the British forts and settlements may be attributed almost entirely to the annexation of Lagos. The trading frontier, on the whole, lay outside British possessions. Timber, groundnuts, and palm products accounted for over three-quarters of the value of African exports from Sierra Leone and its hinterland, the Gambia, and the Bights.

The latter area from Lagos to the Cameroons was undoubtedly the most important market of the three. Against this background in which traders were content to see Africa produce cash crops without special schemes for the introduction of West India plantation and labour models, the protection offered by Government for operations on the Niger in the 1850's appears exceptional. Much of the reason for the enthusiasm for penetration of the lower Niger, however, can be traced to false hopes raised by speculation in cotton, to a renewal of officially supported exploration by the Foreign Office, and

---

[1] *Parl. Papers*, 1865, v (412), Qq. 114–18.
[2] W. Page, *Commerce and Industry. Tables of Statistics for the British Empire from 1815.* London, 1919; *Parl. Papers*, 1874, xlvi [C. 941].

finally to the enterprise of Macgregor Laird who provided the ships, and to W. B. Baikie who was a source of information on the Niger interior second only to Barth.[1]

After the ascent of 1854 which left Baikie in Nupe, the insistence of Laird and the promptings of the British Association for the Advancement of Science moved the Foreign Office and the Treasury to accept a new contract for annual expeditions in 1857.[2] The first relief vessel sent by Laird was wrecked at the beginning of 1858 and was followed by two others. This initiative caused difficulties over the contract, when Laird demanded £6,000 for the extra vessel. The Admiralty proposed half this sum and a foreclosure of the contract at the end of 1859, instead of in 1861. In the end, Laird got only £22,500 (and not the £35,000 originally stipulated) for the whole operation between 1857 and the end of 1859.[3] This niggardliness left Baikie in a precarious position. Laird pressed for further expeditions in 1860 and received support for the plan from John Wodehouse at the Foreign Office and Lord Palmerston who agreed with the implication that force should be used to keep open the river, if necessary.[4] A new scheme was produced for three voyages up the Niger for £6,000 per season. The Articles of Agreement, furthermore, accepted these terms for three years, and the Foreign Office promised naval protection during the passage through the Delta. This the Admiralty failed to provide and the expedition had to be abandoned in 1860. Laird died the following year; the Treasury paid £4,000 to his executor; and the contract once more lapsed, though a vessel with supplies reached Baikie at the end of 1861.[5] The opposition encountered in the lower river again raised the question of naval protection and reprisals. Baikie's answer was to propose annexation of territory in 1862, but Lord John Russell ordered him to send more information on the value of Niger trade before coming to a decision. By August 1862, Russell had decided against a colony.[6] The initiative then passed to the Company of African Merchants who requested a subsidy for annual expeditions in 1863, and though

---

[1] For efforts to increase cotton growing: *Colonial Report*, 1852, pp. 200-1; F.O. 84/1031, Clarendon to Campbell, 9 March 1857; Campbell to Clarendon, 16 May 1857; F.O. 2/24 and 25, F.O. to Hutchinson, 6 May 1858; F.O. 2/32, Baikie to Russell, 8 August 1859; Manchester Cotton Growing Association to Russell, 3 November 1859; C.O. 267/272, Murdoch to Rogers, 22 February 1861 (British West African Cotton Company application for 10,000 acres in Sierra Leone). Documents 8, 10 and 12, pp. 113, 115 and 118.
[2] F.O. 2/18 and 2/23 for the organization of the expedition; Admiralty to F.O., 15 April 1857 (for the Articles of Agreement).
[3] F.O. 2/27 A and 2/31.
[4] Document 14, p. 120; F.O. 2/34.
[5] F.O. 97/433, Admiralty to F.O., 6 March 1861; F.O. to Treasury, 20 June 1861; Treasury to F.O., 25 June 1861.
[6] F.O. 97/434, Baikie to Russell, 20 February 1862; Russell, Minute, August 1862.

the Foreign Office went so far as to recommend the proposal to the Treasury the hostility of Liverpool and other traders killed the scheme.[1] At the same time, the Admiralty and the Colonial Office sought to reverse Palmerston's policy of supplying naval protection. Further visits to the river by naval vessels were approved in 1865, but the African Merchants were informed in 1866 that the Government had done enough.[2]

The Niger expeditions of the 1850's and early 1860's demonstrated the difficulty of depending on Government aid beyond the coast. The muddle and discord between departments were as great a danger to Laird's finances or Baikie's life as hostility from African middlemen. Furthermore, the bulk of the Delta traders saw to it that privileged companies were not allowed, as yet, to undertake the commercial exploitation of markets above the Niger-Benue confluence on terms which gave them a monopoly of transport and endangered the position of traditional suppliers on the coast. Macgregor Laird's greatest single contribution in the West African market was not up-river, but in supplying a monthly mail service for a Government subsidy from 1853. This did much to encourage small commission agents and merchants between Gorée and Fernando Po and linked the settlements and the free ports with Europe in an undramatic but regular manner. It was not as spectacular as an expedition to the Benue, but it was sound business.

The general administration of British possessions was equally unspectacular, but contained the seeds of important developments. Seen against the background of the anti-slavery campaign, the growth of trade, and the experiment in contractual relations with African rulers, the government of the forts and settlements in the 1840's and 1850's appeared as a restricted attempt to preserve imperial control. The effort was a disjointed one: even in 1843 when the Government accepted the abolitionist and merchant thesis that posts were necessary, although they could not be maintained in private hands, there was no return to the amalgamation of dependencies under a single administration as in 1821. The separate governments were allowed to take root independently of each other in 1843 and in 1850, before constitutional reform in 1866 brought a period of unity through the establishment of a government-in-chief in Sierra Leone. Moreover, by the West African and Falkland Islands Act of 1843, the Colonial Office Parliamentary Under-Secretary, G. W. Hope, denied the settlements the title of 'colonies' with its contemporary connotations about the rights of Britons abroad, and treated them as conquered territories, where the Crown could rule by Order-in-Council as its

[1] Documents 17 and 18, pp. 124–5.
[2] C.O. 267/285, Hammond to Cardwell, 9 October 1865; Romaine to Layard, 20 September 1865; F.O. 97/436, F.O. to African Merchants, 10 January 1866.

advisers thought fit.[1] The Gambia was immediately given a constitution of the crown colony type with executive and legislative
councils, a full range of colonial officials and a separate military
command;[2] the Gold Coast was organized under a similar charter of
government in 1850; and Lagos was constituted a settlement with
protected dependencies and a provisional legislative council in 1862.
Sierra Leone had to wait till 1863 for a new constitution to replace
the curious machinery that governors and chief justices had fashioned
according to their interpretation of the charter of 1799. The frag-
mentation begun by the Select Committee of 1842 was for a short
time complete.

Each of the settlements, then, after 1843, had its own budget,
garrison, officials, and methods of elementary representation for a
community which was prohibited from organizing assemblies. If
Britons and British subjects in West Africa were not to be allowed
institutions for which they could not pay, at least some unofficial
spokesmen were nominated to seats on the legislative councils—
though not in the Gambia, where traders' petitions for a say in the
administration were quashed by James Stephen in 1842.[3] Three
unofficial members appear in the Sierra Leone Council from 1843
(there had been spasmodic representation since 1815); and two
merchants were appointed to the Gold Coast Council from 1850.[4]
Governor Blackall used a method of selection adopted from Cape
Colony to obtain approval by Sierra Leone merchants for first one,
then two nominations to the reconstructed legislative council of
1863. At Lagos, on the other hand, Governor Freeman's appointment
of three traders to his provisional council was not approved, and
Glover preferred to dispense with representation altogether.

As the settlements remained isolated they duplicated departments
and personnel. By the early 1860's, the administration at each capital
was run by thirty or more officials—colonial secretaries, customs
collectors, chief justices, magistrates, surveyors, military commandants, landing waiters, and clerks. But outside the seat of government
administration was sketchy and improvident. Civil commandants
were appointed on the Gold Coast and in Lagos Protectorate after
1863. Sierra Leone which for long had relied on village 'superintendents', supplied for a period by the Church Missionary Society,
changed their title in 1827 to Managers whose duties were laid down

---

[1] Documents 26 and 27, pp. 513-14. But in 1844 Cape Coast and Sierra Leone
were 'appointed' as British colonies for the trial and sentence of British subjects.
See below, p. 555.
[2] Reasons for this speedy donation of a charter to the Gambia were the need
for better courts at Bathurst and the provision of local enactments to regulate
changing conditions of trade: C.O. 268/38, Stanley to Macdonald, 30 July 1842;
Document 28, p. 515.
[3] Document 23, p. 509.
[4] Parl. Papers, 1845, xxxi (589); C.O. 96/15, Winniett to Grey, 10 December 1849.

by Governor Kennedy in 1854.[1] In the Gambia there were no district officials at all.

The principal aim of Crown administration was to keep the traders' peace and make colonial government pay for itself. Economy had been one motive behind the return of the forts to the merchants in 1828; it was no less a consideration from the 1840's on, when Customs duties were looked to increasingly as a means of paying for local expenditure, while parliamentary estimates and grants met the cost of defence, the West Africa Squadron, and the resettlement of captured slaves. Experiments with direct taxes on persons, property and produce were tried at various times, since the days of the Sierra Leone Company's quit rents. Contributions from such sources were very small, because of the opposition of Africans, or because the basis for assessing property and land was untrustworthy where title registration and survey were incomplete. Only in the Gambia at Kombo was an effort made to allocate Crown land by methods tried out in colonies elsewhere. A heavy land and produce tax was levied from 1864—higher than anywhere else in the British Empire—and yet failed to account for more than a fifth of Gambia revenues.[2] By the 1860's it was clear that only increased indirect taxes or imperial grants and loans could save most of the settlements from insolvency. Average total revenues for the British possessions on the coast in the 1840's were not much more than £30,000 a year. In the 1860's the annual average total rose to just over £100,000 of which Lagos Colony accounted for more than a quarter. Customs revenue rose proportionately, as new departments were added to each administration and each settlement was asked to support more of the cost of local defence. Financial difficulties on the coast were reflected, too, in Colonial Office exchanges with the Treasury which would not accept the cost of the Ashanti war, 1863–4, and would not ask Parliament for a special vote.[3] By that date Parliament was in a mood for fresh scrutiny of the West African possessions.

Need for revenue, too, was a factor which combined with humanitarian motives to persuade the Colonial Office to approve between 1850 and 1863 a number of territorial acquisitions. The period of restraint from about 1827 till 1848 ended when Earl Grey agreed to the purchase of the Danish forts as Customs posts in 1850 and to the annexation of land at Kombo to support Bathurst settlers.[4] In the Bight of Benin, as a result of the growth of consular authority and the promise of a new field for trade, the Foreign Office persuaded

---

[1] Document 6, p. 619. [2] Document 13, p. 628.
[3] C.O. 96/64, Elliott, Minute, 13 February 1864. Statistics for revenue and expenditure are taken from the Blue Books and *Colonial Reports* for the 1860's. They should be used with caution: returns for any year were often altered subsequently as arrears of accounts were completed.
[4] Documents 15 and 16, pp. 424 and 425.

the Colonial Office to agree to the annexation of Lagos in 1861. Annexations of Bendu and of Sherbro Island in the name of the anti-slavery campaign and the timber trade followed soon after. Bulama Island which had been formally annexed in 1849 and Koya were declared part of the colony of Sierra Leone and occupied in 1861.[1] On the Gold Coast the administration of the eastern districts was expanded towards the Volta mouth as far as Keta; and Badagri, Palma and Lekki were added to Lagos to ensure control of the lagoon markets for customs in 1863.

For the moment this represented the limit of Colonial Office patience under the Duke of Newcastle and Edward Cardwell with imperial arguments based on humanitarian principles, finance, or trade. Permission to settle more liberated Africans in the Gambia was not given in 1861 to avoid offering a pretext for further local expansion.[2] Suggestions for exchange or purchase of the Dutch forts, made between 1860 and 1862, were not considered seriously at this date. Further acquisitions were forbidden in the vicinity of Lagos, outside the forts, north of Sierra Leone, or in the Gambia. On the other hand, there was no support for the idea of giving up British possessions. This assumption of restricted, but continuing, British control of areas already annexed helps to explain the attitude of traders who testified before the Select Committee of 1865, when only two—Swanzy of the Gold Coast and McCrosky of Lagos—out of the six witnesses with business on the coast favoured West African possessions.[3] The others wanted protection, but preferred no government interference for which they might be asked to pay. What existed to date was sufficient as a base for this protection. This view was reflected in the Committee's ambiguous recommendations for retrenchment and partial retreat which are often cited as influential in the formation of British policy towards West Africa.[4] Restraint had, of course, already begun in 1863, and retrenchment in administration was nothing new where the settlements were concerned. Too much should not be made of the 1865 Committee's Report: though

---

[1] The Portuguese flag had been removed from the island and replaced by the British flag in 1849. Governor Kennedy was ordered to send a resident there in 1853. C.O. 267/273, Newcastle to Hill, 2 November 1861; Hill to Newcastle, 7 January 1861. It was placed under the Gambia administration in 1864. The Anglo-Portuguese dispute was submitted to international arbitration in 1868 which found for Portugal. C.O. 267/296 and 300.

[2] C.O. 87/71, Newcastle to D'Arcy, 23 September 1861; Introductory Note p. 408

[3] *Parl. Papers*, 1865, v (412). Of the others, the Sherbro merchant, J. Harris agreed that protection should be paid for by traders: Qq. 4987-9; J. A. Tobin, the Liverpool merchant, wanted government subsidies for Niger trade: Qq. 5218-5372; Capt. J. Croft and D. Chinery, director of the London and African Trading Co., were outspoken in their dislike of regulations and controls at the settlements. See, too, John D. Hargreaves, *Prelude to the Partition of West Africa* (London, 1963), pp. 73-90.

[4] Document 35, p. 529.

its resolutions were considered and occasionally quoted during the next decade, the constitutional proposals for amalgamation of the settlements were the more important feature of its work; and these were not new either, having already been made by Governor Blackall and Commissioner Ord in 1864.[1] Strictures about non-expansion were not accepted without reservation even in the Colonial Office where the revenue factor and possible rivalry with other nations on the coast had been seriously observed since 1850 and emphasized again by Assistant Under-Secretary T. F. Elliot in 1863 and by Governor Blackall in 1864.[2] The need to control areas of the coast for customs had been well established and was not really contested in 1865. Even such a cautious Secretary of State as Edward Cardwell, in 1866, while detesting additions to Lagos Protectorate, was still prepared to 'keep sovereignty over the sea-board and the waters of the Lagoon' for revenue purposes;[3] and it was also Cardwell who favoured reopening negotiations on the Dutch exchange scheme as a financially sound proposal in 1866, though the details were not completed in his term of office. Some concern about the French remained, too. In the longer term Elliot's anxiety about 'elbow room' near foreign neighbours and Blackall's conception of 'judicious expansion' were by no means forgotten under the immediate impact of the Select Committee's resolutions, as administration grew more, not less, expensive and the problems of protection more acute.

III

Two years after the provision of separate Crown colony constitutions for all the settlements, they were united again under Freetown by the Charter of 1866. The four sets of legislatures and councils were, however, preserved, as the lieutenant-governors wished; and no provision was made, as Colonel Ord had suggested, for a council of general government at the centre. Regular visits of inspection by the governor-in-chief to co-ordinate policy were planned, but depended on improved communications. Correspondence was directed through Sierra Leone, as were the annual estimates for each settlement, before being passed on to the Colonial Office with the recommendations of the head of the administration. A supreme court with appellate jurisdiction completed this reorganization in 1867.

One feature of the 1865 Committee Report was not observed—the economy for which most of the recommendations had been made. With the best intentions in the Colonial Office, steps were taken to bring the administration on the coast into line with practice elsewhere, and invariably the result was greater expenditure. The average of thirty officials per settlement in 1860 had, by 1874, risen

[1] Documents 33 and 34, pp. 525–528. [2] Documents 32 and 33, pp. 437 and 524.
[3] Document 20, p. 365.

to 110.[1] Departments which numbered five or six expanded to as many as sixteen in Sierra Leone and fifteen on the Gold Coast. As befitted posts eager to pay their way, the Gold Coast Treasury and Audit alone employed in the early 1870's nearly one-third of all official personnel in the Colony. The next largest departments in all settlements were judiciary and police, the smallest education and medical services. Compared with this expansion, events such as the retrocession of part of Koya in Sierra Leone and the withdrawal from MacCarthy's Island in the Gambia were of minimal importance to the local budget.

Unification, such as it was, cost the Treasury immediately £61,000 in 1866 to pay off the settlements' accumulated debts and purchase two steamers, in return for a saving of only £9,500 on troops sent back to the West Indies. Stricter methods of accounting and a complete overhaul of the West African Customs departments in 1869 did much to reduce sources of confusion and waste. Africans who cost less than Europeans were encouraged by Governor Kennedy and other administrators to enter local administrative services by examination:[2] and by 1871 there were twenty-two African officials at Sierra Leone and a dozen or so at Lagos and the Gambia. But despite these measures, the settlements at the beginning of the 1870's were forced to rely on the Imperial Government to an extent unforeseen by the earlier advocates of retrenchment. The Colonial Office disliked, but tolerated, Governor Pope Hennessy's casual abolition of the Sierra Leone House and Land Tax; loans for Sierra Leone and Lagos were raised on the London market in 1871 and 1873; the Office fought successfully to retain the Treasury subsidy for steamers carrying West African mails. Finally, in 1874 it was discovered that the Ashanti expedition had cost £815,000—about six times as much as total parliamentary grants to the Sierra Leone Company at the beginning of the century, and the equivalent of five or six years' revenue for the settlements at the time of the campaign. To this burden was added in the same year an advance of £35,000 to pay for additional salaries and public works on the Gold Coast, when that colony and Lagos were separated from Sierra Leone and the Gambia.

While more was spent on public works and personnel, less was available on local and imperial budgets for military and naval forces, before the crisis of 1873. Defence policy for the settlements was the least explicit aspect of British responsibilities on the coast, and the easiest item to prune, after the decline of the slave trade in the 1860's.[3] Basically, West African defence was a copy of the

---

[1] *Colonial Office Lists*, 1874 and 1875: Sierra Leone, 92 (16 departments); Gambia, 35 (9 departments); Gold Coast 153 (15 departments); Lagos, 52 (10 departments).
[2] C.O. 267/293, Kennedy to Buckingham, 15 May 1868.
[3] Introductory Note, p. 584.

eighteenth-century coastal fort—limited to the seaboard and likely to prove unready when tested. In the 1850's and early 1860's, the settlements were practically undefended, except for the Navy, until the Ashanti invasion of 1863 brought in a total of two regiments from the West Indies to back up small local detachments already on the coast. Immediately after the invasion, most of the West India force was withdrawn and numbered no more than 375 men in West Africa by 1871, while the settlements bore the cost of their individual miscellanies of Hausa police, militia, and unarmed 'volunteers', in the hope that the Navy would provide vessels and men for emergencies. But the Navy was no longer in a position to do this. The total failure of this policy to meet the defence of the Gold Coast, without recourse to the use of European troops in 1873, merely underlined the flaw in the reasoning which expected West African traders to pay for protection by taxes levied at the colonial ports.

There was a corresponding decline during the 1860's of official willingness to provide protection for traders at all in areas outside colonial jurisdiction. No subsidies were available for navigation on the Niger; a consular post at Lokoja was withdrawn in 1869; and in 1871 Lord Granville decided to end the annual naval expeditions up the river and to warn a deputation from the African Association that the Government would not interfere in the Delta, so long as British traders took sides in local wars.[1] The active policy pursued by Palmerston and contemplated by Russell and Clarendon in the 1850's gave way to a Foreign Office deference to Colonial Office views from 1870 till 1874. This change of attitude towards the use of force was keenly felt by William Wylde, formerly head of the Foreign Office Slave Trade Department, to whom correspondence on the Bonny-Opobo dispute in the Delta was sent in 1870. Sensing hesitation in the Office, he wrote:

I have from the beginning of this quarrel been of one opinion that the only way to put a stop to it and to bring about a satisfactory settlement would be by stating ourselves the terms that should be agreed upon, and insisting on their acceptance, and I would put a stop to *all* trade until an understanding had been come to.

When the Chiefs know that we are in earnest, it will take very little pressure to compel them to agree to our terms. One Gun Boat will be sufficient. This was the plan adopted during the ten years I was head of the S[lave] T[rade] Dept., and I never knew it to fail.[2]

In this wistful backward look to the days of blockade and bombardment, Wylde was supported by John Glover, then on leave in England, to whom the Bonny case was also referred.[3]

---

[1] C.O. 147/22, Granville to Hopkins, 25 December 1871.
[2] F.O. 84/1326, Wylde, Minute, 29 December 1870; Introductory Note, p. 99.
[3] Ibid; Vivian, Minute, 29 December 1870.

Their views were rejected. In the precarious state of West African defences the colonial steamers at Lagos were unfit for service in the Delta. Consul Livingstone did call in a warship, but obtained no permanent settlement. None of this was approved by Lord Granville who noted: 'I confess I am not in favour of our dictating terms of peace to these rival Chiefs, for if we [do] we make ourselves responsible for their being observed. The utmost I think we should do is to tell them that if they do not make peace, their interests will suffer as Merchants will not resort to a country where there is no security for commerce'; and an invitation to the consul to fall back on force if necessary was removed from Granville's dispatch.[1]

The same reluctance to 'meddle' in the African interior adjacent to the settlements had, of course, been part of Colonial Office policy since 1863. It was reinforced by the recommendations of 1865, but was subjected to scrutiny and some revision after 1870. In Sierra Leone, the old stipend system still remained the basis of dealings with neighbouring Temne, Susu, Mende, and Fula chiefs. The system had been extended to the Scarcies in 1861 and to the chiefs of the Sherbro in 1869. Any suggestion, however, that these areas were 'protected' in the formal Gold Coast sense of the word was firmly rejected by the Colonial Office.[2] Governor Kennedy who had backed exploratory journeys into the interior by Winwood Reade in 1869 sent two more ambassadors inland in 1871 and 1872. The next year Edward Blyden secured a trade treaty from the paramount chief of Timbo in the Futa Jallon, in return for an annual stipend of £100 from a colonial government nearly 200 miles away at Freetown. This marked the radius of Sierra Leone influence on interior conditions of trade. Within this area, by the early 1870's, a total of £959 was paid out annually to sixty-three chiefs on the registers of the colony in amounts varying from £2 to an average of £20.[3] There was talk in the Colonial Office of applying this method to the Gold Coast, where in 1871 there appeared to be only two courses open to keep the peace, according to Sir Robert Herbert:

It is a question of moderate (continual) bribery or greater expenditure in military force, & loss to the colony, or some (periodical) breaking out of these Native Chiefs. I think the bribery is preferable & cheaper.[4]

It is hard to see how stipends could have helped Anglo-Fanti relations which had seriously deteriorated in the 1860's, or how judicious 'bribery' could have halted the drive of the Ashanti for direct access to the coast and control of the lower Volta. The tendency of officials to look on the Fanti as colonial subjects was challenged by

[1] Document 22, p. 402.
[2] C.O. 267/293, Buckingham to Kennedy, 15 April 1868.
[3] C.O. 267/320, Keate to Kennedy, 28 February 1873.
[4] C.O. 96/89, Minute, 1 December 1871.

the King of Cape Coast, John Aggery, and his advisers, 1865–6, when he disputed the right of the Judicial Assessor to reverse decisions made in his court. Furthermore, with the aid of educated Africans he chose to interpret literally the resolutions of the 1865 Committee concerning the withdrawal of British administration from the coast. When there was no sign of withdrawal, the Governor's authority over Fanti chiefs was questioned, and Aggery was deposed for sedition. A second challenge of a more serious kind came after 1868 from the Fanti confederation, formed initially to oppose the Elmina, and endowed by a constitution of 1871 with an executive council and two assemblies of Fanti representatives and chiefs. Suspected for starting separate negotiations with Ashanti, this proto-nationalist movement was condemned as a 'dangerous conspiracy' and was sufficiently discredited for the Colonial Office to reject the advice of the Governor-in-Chief in 1872 to heed Fanti proposals for judicial and financial reforms. Protectorate jurisdiction had brought colonial autocracy in its train.

Yoruba relations with Lagos were largely conditioned by fears of a similar situation arising, if colonial government were allowed to exercise economic and judicial controls in Egba and Ijebu territory. The official interpretation of affairs in Yorubaland, based on information sent to the Foreign and Colonial Offices by Glover, was strictly in terms of Lagos trade, with an occasional thought for the export of slaves through southern Dahomey. The aim of Glover's policy, therefore, was to exert economic pressure on the Yoruba trading states nearest to the coast and to open routes inland through Ibadan, as far as the Niger. His methods were open coercion in the case of Porto-Novo, blockade, the extension of police posts beyond the colonial frontier, and unauthorized missions to the interior. None of this really improved relations with the Yoruba or guaranteed open roads. Given his way, Glover would have turned most of the Lagos interior into a series of clientage states; but he was sufficiently restrained and was refused the military forces needed for this to happen. Lagos remained an economic dependency of the region Glover failed to control.

A third method of building up the 'informal empire'—other than by stipends or threats of force—was through the consuls. The legal basis for extra-territorial jurisdiction, restricted for want of necessary treaties in the 1850's, steadily grew after the Sierra Leone Offences Act of 1861. A decade later, the need was felt not merely for the surrender of British offenders by independent chiefs, but for redress in crimes and offences committed against British subjects by Africans outside British territory. The Law Officers advised that such an extension of jurisdiction could be made;[1] and the Foreign Jurisdiction Act of 1871 made the subjects of 'uncivilized Powers' liable for

[1] Document 27, p. 574.

acts committed within twenty miles of Sierra Leone boundaries.[1] Further afield in the Delta, the jurisdiction of consuls over British subjects was confirmed by the West African Order-in-Council of 1872; and a series of regulations were framed to reorganize the Courts of Equity for the settlement of minor disputes between traders and Delta chiefs.

None of these new developments in European and African relations after 1870 required the prior sanction of formal treaties with African chiefs. Jurisdiction over British subjects in African territories was exercised under Acts of the Imperial Parliament and by a certain amount of 'usage, treaty and sufferance' accumulated from the past in the Delta and near Sierra Leone. After 1870 this kind of 'usurpation', once criticized by James Stephen on the appointment of a Judicial Assessor to the Gold Coast in 1843, had become accepted as a practical method of keeping order on the borders of the Freetown settlement and in the Oil Rivers. The criterion for deciding such an extension of jurisdiction was no longer a prior agreement with African society, but classification of that society as an 'uncivilized state'.

The final aspect of relations with African society—direct military confrontation—had been consistently avoided after 1866. Even as a theoretical consequence of breaking treaty obligations, the use of force was discouraged after the decline of the slave trade, when the Navy was no longer willing to provide such a force. On the Gold Coast, however, by the end of the 1860's, defence, not diplomacy or courts, was the paramount consideration. After a truce in 1863 and the accession of a new *Asantehene* in 1867, Ashanti policy towards the British hardened. In the west the Fanti attack on Elmina in 1869, occasioned by the Anglo-Dutch exchange of forts, threatened an Ashanti ally and source of supply; in the east, an over-zealous administrator faced an Ashanti army with an assertion of British claims to protect states along the lower Volta. The cession of Elmina to the British by the Dutch in 1871 sparked off a series of Ashanti demands to Elmina fort and to the Assin, Akim, and Denkyera states; and a full-scale invasion of the Fanti coast had to be resisted in 1873. The use of European troops, the decision to annex the area of the Fanti protectorate, to invest in the administration of the Gold Coast, to legislate against domestic slavery, and to separate the Colony and Lagos from Sierra Leone—all this marked a departure from the line of policy begun in 1863 and confirmed by the Select Committee of 1865. The Government still showed a preference for keeping peace on the West African frontier by other means; but the question of the rôle of Government in time of crisis, when these means proved inadequate had now been answered in a more positive way than at any time since the Ashanti War of 1826.

[1] Document 28, p. 575.

Behind the hesitations of British policy on the West African coast in the nineteenth century lay not simply indifference, but the difficulty of interpreting the course and outcome of European contact with African society. On this interpretation the rôle of government depended. In the previous century and for most of the 1820's traders and officials were concerned as much about the Dutch or the French as about conditions in the coastal states. As anxieties about foreign competition decreased, the anti-slavery campaign intensified and African and European commission agents and separate traders moved farther afield in search of groundnuts and palm products. The conditions of trade no longer depended so completely on the ability of African chiefs to maintain peaceful contact. The major item of European traffic had been forbidden; other items were encouraged, and their market value increased the importance of previously unimportant areas of cash-crop production and the wealth of the middlemen and political rulers controlling them. By the 1840's, a common interpretation of economic and political changes, as seen by European agents, was summed up by Captain William Allen—twice explorer of the Niger and planner of colonies—in a dispatch to Lord Stanley written from the Cameroons:

It is, my Lord, much to be deplored, that the long intercourse which the Europeans have had with the Africans has but tended to increase their innate avidity for gain, while the white merchants who have succeeded to the Slave-dealers, in order to protect themselves from fraud and extortion, frequently have recourse to arbitrary measures, which are as repugnant to all principles of justice as they must be to those of good policy. A mutual reaction of evil is thus induced, and on it has been based a system which must be not only an effectual bar to the introduction of civilization, but must bring the parties into continual collision. I would therefore take the liberty of respectfully suggesting to your Lordship that the natives having arrived at that point where lawful trade has become a necessity, the interference of Government would be very salutary, on the one hand, in establishing such simple regulations as, without throwing any impediment in the way of trade, may afford protection to the merchants against the extortion of the natives, and enable them to recover their just debts, and on the other hand, may protect the natives against arbitrary proceedings on the part of the whites, by preventing the necessity of having recourse to them.[1]

For the moment this advice was ignored, at least until the establishment of consular posts in the early 1850's, though the analysis of conditions on the African frontier was accepted in the Colonial Office and the Foreign Office which had ample evidence of similar situations all along the coast. Increasingly, there was a tendency from this date to look to the British Government to cut the Gordian knots that

---

[1] *Parl. Papers*, 1843, xlviii (472), p. 61; Allen to Stanley, 9 May 1842.

bound small communities of European traders and officials to the leaders of local African society and impose a solution to the problems of contact on European terms. The Government, however, was limited in its choice of methods, inhibited by the need for economy and by a general desire to avoid acquiring an empire in Africa. The forts and settlements had been retained and administered largely for humanitarian reasons in the case of Sierra Leone and the Gold Coast, for the gum trade in the case of the Gambia, and as a base for legitimate trade on the Slave Coast in the case of Lagos. After 1865, the humanitarian argument for the posts weakened. But by then they had developed into Crown colonies and the pressure of the apostles of Buxton was redirected against domestic slavery and for the reform of native law and custom. The rôle to be played by Government, therefore, was still not uninfluenced by what was loosely termed 'public opinion'. In the case of West Africa this meant the small parliamentary group from the Aborigines Protection Society,[1] traders from Liverpool, Manchester, Bristol, and London, and occasionally missionary societies. The first two groups made themselves felt twice after 1850—in the matter of subsidies for Niger navigation and over the question of the Anglo-French Gambia exchange scheme. In both examples successful agitation was negative in aim—against the possibility of commercial monopoly and against the rational demarcation of French and British spheres of interest on the coast. The missions were less important, making their voices heard effectively only when stations were opened in the Gambia and in Yorubaland. But whatever influences from private quarters were exercised, only three courses of action were open to Government where the settlements were concerned: to abandon, to maintain, or to expand.

Abandonment of all posts was never really considered seriously in the 1860's; and the case of the Gambia between 1866 and 1870[2] demonstrated not that the Colonial Office was prepared to follow unthinkingly extremists like Sir Charles Adderley in self-denial, but that the major problem was what to ask for in exchange. The rationalization of the West African settlements, moreover, could not be attempted without considering foreign pressure groups in addition to British traders and humanitarians. Gradually, international considerations outside the suppression of the slave trade made themselves felt again in British West African policy, after a period of relative unimportance between the 1820's and the 1850's. After earlier suggestions, the first official overture from France for an exchange of territory including the Gambia was made in 1865. The Colonial Office accepted the idea, but was not attracted by the Ivory Coast or the Gaboon posts as compensation. Nor could the scheme be

---

[1] Charles Buxton, E. Eastwick, A. Kinnaird, W. McArthur.
[2] For an analysis of Anglo-French negotiations, see Hargreaves, pp. 136–95.

linked satisfactorily with the exchange of forts arranged with the Dutch in 1867. Governor Kennedy pressed for continued negotiations, aiming at the withdrawal of French trade and political influence from the Melakori and Scarcies; and this conception of partition around Sierra Leone was favoured by Lord Granville at the Colonial Office in 1869. The plan was very nearly carried through. But the final steps were delayed by the need for parliamentary approval, mounting opposition from French and British firms with interests at Bathurst and, not least, by opposition from the Anglo-African population who feared the loss of rights and property. The delay in submitting legislation to Parliament was accepted by Lord Kimberley; and the Franco-Prussian War cut off discussion of a proposal he was beginning to refuse in 1870[1] and definitely abandoned in 1871.

A second field for international co-operation lay in joint military operations or in agreements over trade on the coast. The French had assisted in the Gambia in 1831, but the British Governor was not allowed to reciprocate during the campaign against Maba in the 1860's. During the Ashanti invasion of 1873, a suggestion was made by the French for a joint prohibition by Britain, France, and Portugal of imports of arms and powder on the coast to prevent other uprisings. Lord Kimberley considered this important proposal carefully, before pointing out obvious objections:

I would answer that an arrangement by which the importation of arms &c. could be checked seems desirable in the interest of these Powers, and that any measure by which the destructive wars which desolate the interior of the country could be mitigated must be favourable to the progress of peaceful commerce so that any loss sustained by European merchants by the stoppage of the trade in arms would be probably more than compensated by the increase of other trade, but it would be necessary that there should be liberty to import arms for the use of the tribes under the protection or control of the colonial Governments and I should be glad to know how the French Govt. would propose to regulate such importations. It is also observed that there are points on the coast not under European control through which supplies of arms and ammunition would no doubt be largely sent into the interior when other means of access were closed. For example Whydah and Porto Novo since the retirement of the French and the rivers known as the oil rivers are under native rule, and the proposed measure would therefore not apply to them. It would also be desirable to obtain the co-operation of the Govt. of Liberia.[2]

The question was also referred to West African governors; and on their evidence Carnarvon at the Colonial Office and Lord Derby at

---

[1] Document 44, p. 445.
[2] C.O. 96/106, F.O. to C.O., 19 September 1873, encl. French ambassador to Granville, 13 August 1873; Kimberley, Minute, 24 September 1873.

the Foreign Office decided that international co-operation on the matter was impracticable.

Thus, two efforts at agreement with France broke down. Both illustrated that by the early 1870's the British Government was neither prepared to withdraw from the coast nor willing to undertake expensive (and possibly useless) prohibitions to influence the kind of trade done in the West African interior.

A second course of action—reform of the existing administration—was pursued with vigour throughout the 1860's, when expenditure tripled between the beginning and end of the decade.[1] The question whether the settlements provided facilities of the kind useful to West African traders was still reopened from time to time by commercial firms which used them as a base. In response to complaints in 1872 and 1873 the Colonial Office claimed that to abolish the system of a single government-in-chief would run counter to the recommendations of the 1865 Committee, but agreed to examine proposals for improving appeals to Privy Council, defining boundaries, enlarging the legislative councils and recruiting Hausa police.[2] Little of this was accomplished, however, while the Ashanti War was in progress. But petitions aimed at better government in each settlement continued to arrive. It was left to Carnarvon to carry out the work prepared by Kimberley and Holland, after 1873. The separation of the eastern settlements from Sierra Leone in 1874 was to some extent a recognition of traders' agitation for smaller units of colonial administration. It was also made because of the size and importance of the newly annexed colony south of Ashanti and because of the need for a jurisdiction separate from Freetown courts.

Reform of the West African judiciary went to the heart of the accumulation of complaints at the settlements since 1865. The problem to be faced was not the provision of legal redress for British subjects (though there was argument enough on the matter of appeals), but the extension of some form of jurisdiction for civil cases in areas adjacent to British territory. The use of the Foreign Jurisdiction Act in Sierra Leone had offered one solution; the Judicial Assessor's court outside the forts on the Gold Coast had been another. A clash of jurisdictions in the early 1860's and the rejection of the Fanti confederation for political reasons brought a lot of this work of the Assessor in civil cases to an end, until his functions were revived by D. P. Chalmers as Gold Coast magistrate and queen's advocate, 1869–74.[3] But he was not in favour of reviving the jury

---

[1] From £55,968 for Gambia, Sierra Leone, Gold Coast, in 1860, to £167,958 for these settlements and Lagos in 1870: Blue Books, 1860–1, 1870–1.

[2] C.O. 147/29, Clare to Kimberley, 13 October 1872; 267/324, memorials from the Manchester Chamber of Commerce and Banner Bros. to Kimberley, 3 June 1873; 147/29, Holland to Blood, 10 September 1873.

[3] C.O. 96/94, Chalmers to Ussher, 4 April 1872.

system for civil cases, preferring to retain 'summary trial' as 'more suited to the habits and ideas of the complainants and witnesses' in the towns, and the Assessor's court for 'bush-natives'. After the Ashanti War, this division was abolished and only the magistrates' courts and English laws were left in operation, before the Supreme Court Ordinance of 1875. Lord Carnarvon's view of the implications of extended jurisdiction by annexation left no place for Fanti tribunals:

> The employment of Native magistrates must for the present at all events be considered impracticable. The gradual but early extinction of the [Fanti] Kings' courts—where the Kings have any substantial authority in the decision of cases—and of their virtually uncontrolled jurisdiction in prisons should be aimed at. . . .[1]

But elsewhere on the coast this kind of judicial assimilation was either impossible or undesirable, although the same basis for the powers of the Crown through the Foreign Jurisdiction Acts was claimed. After 1872 Lagos became a place of imprisonment for offenders tried in Delta consular courts. Offenders near Sierra Leone could be tried at Freetown courts. In both areas the nature of African trade with its use of extended credit precluded refined forms of debt recovery. The Chief Magistrate of Lagos, R. D. Mayne, summed up the peculiar relationship between a colony and its interior in West Africa, where commercial litigation exceeded the bounds of colonial authority:

> From the position of Lagos, a greater part of what is called trade really partakes much more of the nature of diplomacy. The court would be compelled to act in a great degree [if applying rules of bankruptcy] on information received from up the Country which could be only very imperfectly verified, and which might be manufactured & manipulated by unscrupulous men in a way which might lead to serious difficulties. This is certainly a political rather than a legal view of the question, but it is a view which ought to be considered.[2]

Glover had certainly had this matter in mind, but his methods of meeting the problem of jurisdiction by using political missions and constabulary to keep the traders' peace were in advance of his time.

'It may be true', continued Mayne, 'that the system of credit has in Lagos been stretched too far but such as that system is, under it Lagos has risen in ten years from the position of an obscure native town to that of a not unimportant English settlement.'

Much the same could have been said of Freetown, Bathurst, and the Delta ports, with the difference that the latter markets had not been annexed and were only under a form of consular protection. But the lesson of the 1860's was becoming clear: the administrative and

[1] C.O. 96/112, Carnarvon, Minute, 1 January 1875.
[2] C.O. 147/30, Mayne to C.O., 16 May 1874.

commercial stake in the settlements had greatly increased by financial investment and the improvement of market facilities. There was still no Bank of West Africa—as planned in 1871—for want of a suitable ordinance of incorporation; the proportion of British trade with the settlements still remained low compared with West African trade as a whole. Nevertheless, William Allen's request for Government-regulated trade in 1842 was no less pertinent in the early 1870's, when it was recognized by the Colonial Office that West African possessions with 'powerful and savage neighbours' were a special case.[1] Such neighbours could be dealt with by conquest, but such a course was a failure rather than a success in terms of the type of economic and legal relationship sought by British policy in West Africa after 1841. Other conquests, apart from Ashanti, had been formally considered and discouraged—in southern Dahomey, where invasion was planned by Governor Freeman in 1862, in the upper Gambia, or on the coast north of Freetown. Again, for financial and judicial reasons the expansion of the settlements continued to receive close attention after 1873. In general, the verdict was against expansion,[2] though there were signs from Under-Secretary Knatchbull-Hughessen and the junior official, A. W. L. Hemming, in the Colonial Office that opposition was not a matter of principle, but to be considered according to the merits of each case. In this they were closer to Blackall and Glover than to the Committee of 1865. The compromise policy which the Office was working towards in 1874, as a result of French expansion and the need for increased Customs revenue, aimed at the extension of posts into independent areas of coast near Sierra Leone, without the formal establishment of a protectorate. At the same time, a confidential dispatch was sent to the Administrator of Lagos after complaints had been received from traders concerning the market at Porto Novo. E. D. Fairfield, the Colonial Office Clerk, urged annexation (as Glover had often done); Carnarvon was doubtful whether such a step would improve trade; finally, it was Herbert's suggestion for a transfer of Customs collection from the King's officials to the Lagos administration which was recommended as a solution to be investigated.[3] The pragmatism which had led to the purchase of the Danish and Dutch forts was again at work, and for much the same purpose of financial control.

By 1874, the British West African settlements amounted to only about 15,500 square miles of coast—an area twice as big as Natal or the Fiji group. The population of half a million British subjects, about four-fifths of whom were in the Gold Coast Colony, equalled that of Jamaica. The revenue of the settlements—just over £200,000

---

[1] Document 37, p. 533.   [2] *Hansard*, Vol. ccxix, 12 April 1874.
[3] C.O. 147/30, Banner Bros. to Herbert, 20 August 1874; Carnarvon to Strahan, 4 September 1874; and Document 56, p. 458.

—was small, comparable to that of Trinidad and only one-third of the revenue of Mauritius. Total trade with the United Kingdom was less than trade with Newfoundland or the Channel Islands. Over a century of European contact lay behind their location and administration. Yet it was not till the early 1840's that the rôle of Government in their administration became certain. Other responsibilities of Government (including the supervision of emigrant labour to the West Indies) were extended about the same time. The years from 1839 to 1844 were a watershed for British policy towards West Africa as a whole. Decisions taken then ended the indifference of the previous decade to the inheritance of the eighteenth century on the coast; and from these decisions about the conduct of the anti-slavery campaign and the organization of the forts and settlements derived most of the consequences which involved Government, officials, and traders more closely in African affairs during the rest of the century. The development of clientage relations with African rulers, extra-territorial jurisdiction, and financial investment in administration were the most important of these consequences. There were still hesitations and minor withdrawals, particularly in the mid-1860's. But a decade later the feeling that Britain had acquired obligations to be met by well-tried imperial methods and a few experiments in informal empire amounted to a certainty. If there had ever been a time to retire quietly from West African possessions (as the Danes and the Dutch did), it was in the 1830's. After 1842, disengagement became more difficult; and by 1874 the accumulative results of remaining and expanding made it unlikely.

I

EXPLORATION AND SURVEY

Introductory Note

THE impetus for European exploration in Western Africa came mainly from the scientific enthusiasm of the African Association which sought a solution to the problem of the course and outlet of the Niger. Commercial and strategic advantages, derived from improved knowledge of the interior, brought support from the British Government after 1804; and when the Lander brothers proved in 1830 what was already guessed—that the Niger flowed south from the Hausa states to the sea—the prospect of increased trade and a touch of philanthropy were sufficient to stimulate further expeditions from North Africa and from the coast.

Of the seven missions financed by the African Association between 1788 and 1815, the first three were a failure, in terms of their object, till Mungo Park verified the course of the Niger, 1795–7. New evidence about the interior combined with an interest in markets to widen the scope of British policy in the Senegambia-Niger region, as the Association and the Government digested information from the Sierra Leone Company, the North African consulates, the Bulama Association, and from explorers' reports. A political and commercial consulate was planned for the Senegambia, and elaborate instructions were drawn up for James Willis to fill the post in 1795. But the African Association concentrated on sending out Park; and after an adverse report on the estimates needed for Willis, the plan for a consulate was dropped at the beginning of 1796. Similar grandiose elements entered into the project drawn up by the War Department for Park's second mission in 1805. By the time the Niger had been reached, commercial and strategic pretensions had been left far behind, and the death of Park near Bussa curtailed official interest (but not geographical speculation) for nearly ten years.

When it was revived again by the publication of Park's works, Captain Tuckey was sent to the Congo and Major Peddie, Captain Campbell, and Lieutenant Stokoe to the Senegambia in 1815 to make a double strike for the Niger by different routes and set at rest the question of its ultimate course. Neither expedition was successful: Tuckey did not get far beyond the Congo mouth; Peddie and Campbell died in 1817; their successors, Major W. Gray and Staff Surgeon Dochard, got no farther than Kaarta in 1820. In the interests of Sierra Leone's trade Brian O'Beirne was sent to the Futa Jallon in 1821 and Major Laing to the Scarcies and Falaba in 1822.

The northern route proved more promising, despite an early failure of Hornemann to return from the Niger and the short expeditions of Ritchie and Lyon to the Fezzan in 1818. With assistance from the Pasha of Tripoli and instructions from Lord Bathurst, Major Denham, Captain Clapperton, and Dr. Walter Oudney left Tripoli for Chad in 1822. Clapperton visited Kano and Sokoto, Denham Bornu. Together they met at Kuka and returned to Tripoli at the beginning of 1825. A second expedition led by Clapperton from the coast, 1825-6, reopened the subject of the slave trade discussed with Sultan Bello in 1824; but it was left to Richard Lander and his brother to complete the exploration of the Niger from Bussa to the Delta in 1830. Government sponsorship—which had continued in other ways by the dispatch of Consul Dupuis to Kumasi in 1820 and Consul Tyrwhit to Kuka (where he died in 1825)—now lapsed.

After the failure of the Niger expeditions of 1832 and 1841-2 James Richardson persuaded Lord Palmerston to finance a mission across the Sahara in which the scientific work was to be left to Dr. Heinrich Barth and Dr. Adolph Overweg, while Richardson established treaty relations with the Sudan states. Both objectives were carried out by Barth during his five years in the interior. A complementary expedition up the Niger was organized by the Foreign Office and the Admiralty, and was led by Dr. W. B. Baikie in 1854. Macgregor Laird and the British Association for the Advancement of Science urged further Niger ascents to be undertaken under contract over a period of five years. Baikie returned to Nupe; but the loss of Laird's *Dayspring* in 1858, and difficulties with the Admiralty over payments for extra vessels, resulted in the foreclosure of the contract in 1859. When the Niger voyages were resumed after 1860 their purpose was less for exploration than for the protection of trade.[1]

I

THE AFRICAN ASSOCIATION: EXPEDITION OF MAJOR HOUGHTON, 1790-1[2]

SINCE the publication of the Proceedings of the Society for promoting the Discovery of the Interior Regions of Africa, two years have elapsed; and in that period their Committee has received, through the medium of distinct and unconnected channels, new and interesting intelligence.

An account which an Arab, of the name of Shabeni,[3] had given them of an empire on the banks of the Niger, excited their early attention; for he said that the population of Houssa, its capital, where he resided two years, was equalled only (so far as his knowledge

[1] See below, II B, p. 99.
[2] *Proceedings of the Association for Promoting the Discovery of the Interior Parts of Africa.* 2 vols. (London, 1810), pp. 239-41; 254-6. Sections of Major Houghton's journal for 1791 are in the Banks Papers, Royal Geographical Society, ff. 129-31. He proceeded as far as Kaarta, between the Gambia and the Niger, where he was murdered.
[3] A Moroccan who visited Europe in 1790. J. G. Jackson (ed.), *An Account of Timbuctoo and Housa in the Interior of Africa, by El Hadje Abd Salam Shabeeny.* London, 1820.

extended) by that of London and Cairo: and, in his rude unlettered way, he described the government as monarchical, yet not unlimited; its justice as severe, but directed by written laws; and the rights of landed property as guarded by the institution of certain hereditary officers, whose functions appear to be similar to those of the Canongoes of Hindostan, and whose important and complicated duties imply an unusual degree of civilization and refinement.

For the probity of their merchants, he expressed the highest respect; but remarked, with indignation, that the women were admitted to society, and that the honour of the husband was often insecure.

Of their written alphabet he knew no more than it was perfectly different from the Arabic and Hebrew characters; but he described the art of writing as common in Houssa. And when he acted the manner in which their pottery is made, he gave, unknowingly to himself, a representation of the ancient Grecian wheel.

In passing to Houssa from Tombuctoo, in which last city he resided seven years, he found the banks of the Niger more numerously peopled than those of the Nile from Alexandria to Cairo; and his mind was obviously impressed with higher ideals of the wealth and grandeur of the empire of Houssa, than of those of any kingdom he had seen, England alone excepted.

The existence of the city of Houssa, and of the empire thus described by Shabeni, was strongly confirmed by the letters which the Committee received from his Majesty's Consuls at Tunis and Morocco, and with this additional circumstance of information from them, that both at Tunis and Morocco the eunuchs of the seraglio were brought from the city of Houssa.

Anxious to investigate the truth of these accounts; and impatient to explore the origin and course of a river that might possibly open to Britain a commercial passage to rich and populous nations, the Committee embraced the proposals which the ardour of a new emissary offered to their acceptance. For Major Houghton, who was formerly a captain in the 69th regiment, and in the year 1779 had acted under General Rooke as Fort-Major, in the island of Goree, expressed his willingness to undertake the execution of a plan which he heard they had formed, of penetrating to the Niger by the way of the Gambia.

His instructions, accordingly, were to ascertain the course, and, if possible, the rise and termination of that mysterious river; and after visiting the cities of Tombuctoo and Houssa, to return by the way of the Desert, or by any other route which the circumstances of his situation at the time should recommend to his choice. . . .

[Houghton left England in 1790 and proceeded up the Gambia as far as the kingdoms of Wuli and Bambuk on the Faleme river; he is continuing his exploration in the direction of Timbuktu.]

. . . His journey from the Gambia to the kingdom of Bambouk has enlarged the limits of European discovery; for the intermediate kingdom of Bondou was undescribed by geographers: and the information he has obtained from the king of Bambouk, as well as from the native merchants with whom he conversed, has not only determined the course, and shewn, in a great degree, the origin of the Niger, but has furnished the names of the principal cities erected on its banks; fortunately, too, the accounts which he has thus transmitted, are strongly confirmed by the intelligence which his Majesty's Consul at Tunis[1] has collected from the Barbary merchants, who trade to the cities of Tombuctoo and of Houssa, and whose commercial connexions extend to the highest navigable part of the Niger. Nor is this the only advantage for which the Committee are indebted to the public spirit and indefatigable zeal of Consul Magra; for the specimens of the vegetable productions of the countries on the south of the Desert, which the acquaintance he has cultivated with the conductors of the caravans, has enabled him to send to the Committee afford a satisfactory proof that the account which their printed narrative, on the authority of the Shereef Imhammed, has given of several of those productions, is faithful to the objects it describes. And the relation he has transmitted of the routes from Tunis to Ghedesmes, and from thence to Cashna and Tombuctoo,[2] have furnished important materials for elucidating the geography of the desert.

But though we have now an assurance that the Niger has its rise in a chain of mountains which bound the eastern side of the kingdom of Bambouk, and that it takes its couse in a contrary direction from that of the Senegal and the Gambia which flow on the opposite side of the same ridge, yet the place of its final destination is still unknown; for whether it reaches the ocean; or is lost, as several of the rivers of Mount Atlas are, in the immensity of the Desert; or whether, like the streams of the Caspian, it terminates in a vast inland sea, are questions on which there still hangs an unpenetrated cloud. . . .

[1] Possibly based on a report by Acting Consul Robert Traill, 1789, on the caravan traffic from Tunis to the Niger: F.O. 77/3.

[2] I.e. Tunis–Ghadames–Katsina–Timbuktu, one of the three main trans-Saharan routes. The information furnished by Imhammed at Tripoli is discussed in the *Proceedings of the Association*, pp. 73–74. See too Robin Hallett (ed.), *Records of the African Association, 1788–1831* (London, 1964), pp. 25–28; 120–140.

2

HENRY BEAUFOY: REMARKS ON THE EXPEDIENCY OF APPOINTING A CONSUL TO SENEGAMBIA [26 JUNE 1793[1]]

A LUCRATIVE commerce, the extent of which is unknown, but which, from the best Information, appears to be much under-rated at a Million Sterling p. Annum, is carried on from the different states of Barbary to the Nations on the banks of the Niger: And tho' the Intercourse is burthened with the expence & the Hazards of a Land Carriage of 1200 miles across the Desart of Zahara; & has also to contend with the frequent & varying exactions of the Barbary Governments, yet the large compensation which the Profit affords has constantly yielded an ample Encouragement, & has uniformly upheld the Trade.

It was in a similar Mode, & under Disadvantages nearly correspondent, that the Trade from Europe to the East Indies was anciently conducted. In that Trade, the discovery of the Cape of Good Hope produced an entire Revolution; & another Geographical Discovery, less important indeed, but not less unexpected, now offers the means of effecting as complete a revolution in the Mercantile Intercourse with the inland Countries of Africa.

On the first institution of the Society for promoting the Discovery of the interior Nations of Africa, the course of the Niger was unexamined & unknown; nor were the Ideas entertained of it such as to suggest a belief that it would prove of importance to the inland Navigation of the Country.

Fortunately, however, it now appears,—

That the Niger is navigable at the distance of three hundred or three hundred & fifty miles from the highest navigable reach of the Gambia:

That its Course is from the South and South West to the North, the North & East:

That it flows thro' the several Countries to which the Trade from the Coast of the Mediterranean is carried on:

That a Land carriage of 300 or 350 Miles will therefore enable the Merchants of Britain to reach the same Markets to which the Traders of the States of Barbary travel by a route of 1200 Miles.

That the country between the Gambia & the Niger is possessed by

[1] C.O. 267/10. *Henry Beaufoy*, Whig politician and liberal dissenter, was a foundation member of the African Association and Secretary to the Board of Control, 1791–3. This memorandum was delivered personally to Evan Nepean, Under-Secretary to the Home (and Colonial) Department, and Beaufoy was interviewed by Henry Dundas (President of the Board of Control) and William Pitt. Date marked in pencil on the MS.

a Sovereign who has expressed the strongest desire of establishing a Commercial Intercourse with the English; and whose obvious Interests affords a probable pledge of his Sincerity.

That the Gold Mines of Bambouk by which name his country is known to Europeans, apparently furnish the means of payment for the Muskets & Military Stores of which he acknowledges the want, & which are requisite for his defence against the hostile attacks of a neighbouring state:

That this King, having no Interest in the Slave Trade, & no particular connection with the Slave Traders, has no inducement for discouraging an exchange of Military Stores for Gold, the native produce of his Country:

That the Jealousy of the Slave Traders on the Gambia (whose Intrigues endangered the safety of Major Houghton in his passage up the River, & whose attempts were repeated with more effectual success on his approach to Tombuctoo) can only be resisted by Persons who carry with them the sanction of a public character, & the Respect that is paid to the Representative of the British Government:

That if assurances of protection on the River Gambia (unquestionably a part of the British Possessions) could be given to the British Merchants, a commercial Intercourse from the Gambia to the Niger would be opened by Mercantile Houses of great character in London:

That the appointment of a Consul to Senegambia would ensure that protection; & should Instructions be given him to proceed to Bambouk would, in all probability, establish a commerce that would soon transfer to Great Britain the Trade which is now carried on by the Barbary States to the inland Nations of their Continent, & consequently superadd to her commerce a profitable Export of much greater extent than the whole of her present Traffic with the Coast & Western Rivers of Africa.

3

JOHN SULLIVAN: MEMORANDUM OF INSTRUCTIONS TO MUNGO PARK, 1804[1]

MR. PARK should be dispatched early in the month of Octr. in a Troop Ship with an armed Brig and a Gunboat. He should be accompanied by a detachment of 130 of the African Corps, 20 of the Corps of

[1] C.O. 2/1, ff. 72–91 and v. For the final instructions, signed by Earl Camden, Secretary of State for War and Colonies, 2 January 1805, see C. Howard and J. H. Plumb (eds.), *West African Explorers* (London, 1951), pp. 142–3. *John Sullivan* was Under-Secretary to the War Department, 1801–3. Park's last letters and accounts are in C.O. 2/2; and see *Travels in the Interior Parts of Africa, with an Account of a Subsequent Mission to that Country in 1805.* 2 vols. London, 1816.

Artificers, the Goree Pilot and two or three Intelligent Naval Officers, who should be encourage[d] by allowances in addition to their Pay.

He should be directed to stop at the Cape de Verd Islands and to purchase there Wine and as many Draft Mules & Horses as the Ship may be able to convey to Goree and to enter into a Contract for fifty more.

At Goree the party should be reinforced by a Detachment of 100 Men from that Garrison and immediately proceed to the Gambia for the purpose of dislodging the French from their Factory at Albreida. This effected the officer in command should be instructed to concert with the Naval Officer and Mr. Park the Measures which it might be adviseable to take with a view to the conveyance of the Troops and Stores up the Gambia to Pisania and Barraconda. And upon this Subject their attention should be particularly directed to the account of the Expedition up that River in Moore's book.[1] —authority should be given them to engage as many canoes and native boatmen as they might judge to be necessary for that Service and for the further Navigation of the Gambia about the falls of Barraconda.

It should be left to the discretion of Mr. Park whether to precede the Troops to Barraconda or to proceed with them and in what mode he should announce to the King of Wooli his arrival for the purpose of reestablishing the British Factories on the River Gambia,[2] and of extending the relations of Commerce with that and the neighbouring countries. Mr. Park should be furnished with the means of concilating this Chief by giving him presents, and he should be directed after having fixed a Tariff of duties to take the measures which may appear to him most proper for obtaining his concurrence & assistance towards the establishment of a Post at Koogar,[3] or at some other convenient place near the N.E. Frontier of Wooli.

In negotiating these points, favorable opportunities may offer for buying Horses & other animals to assist in the conveyance of Troops and Stores, and it may be politick, if there should be any Slaves for Sale, to purchase some of them and thereby to guard against the counteraction of the Slatees or Slave Dealers who might otherwise throw such obstacles in our way, as might materially retard our progress. The Slaves might be employed to open the road to assist in the conveyance of Stores.

When Mr. Park shall have concluded this Negotiation and concerted with the officer in command of the detachment, the nature of the Post it may be proper to establish upon the Gambia & the modes of keeping open a communication to the Sea and with the parties as

[1] Francis Moore, *Travels into the Inland Parts of Africa.* London, 1738.
[2] Factories had been established by two British traders at Karantaba (Pisania) in the 1780's.
[3] Or Koojar, visited by Park in 1795.

they may advance, he should move forward as expeditiously as possible for the frontier of Wooli, taking with him such a proportion of the Military force and Stores as from information may appear to be necessary, and such guides and Messengers, bearing the authority of the Chief, as may engage the people of Koogar or of whatever place he may fix upon near the Frontier to assist in forming a Station of security there.

From that Station Mr. Park should open a communication with the Chief of the adjoining District of Bondou, for the purpose of obtaining his consent to the passage of our party and to the establishment of a Post at Ganado, distant from Koogar about 54 Miles, and another Station at Naye,[1] distant from Ganado about 63 Miles, or at some other convenient Situation upon the Eastern Frontier of Bondou. The same course should be observed with the King of Bondou and all the Chiefs thro' whose Countries we should have occasion to pass, as has been proposed with regard to Wooli, avowing everywhere, that, being at War with France, it became necessary that we should take possession of Fort St. Joseph and any other establishment which might belong to that Nation upon the Senegal and the Falimé, and that our Merchants would furnish every Article of Trade that might be wished for in Africa.

While Mr. Park shall be employed in opening the route in an eastern direction for the division under Col. Stevenson,[2] it would be advisable that the Naval Officers appropriated to this Service should be employed in proceeding up the Gambia with such craft as can navigate at that favorable Season above the falls of Barraconda taking with them at least Ten of the most seasoned Soldiers, a sufficient number of Goree blacks to navigate the craft & two or more Interpreters, with arms ammunition and provisions including Wine and Spirits, and a Surgeon with Medicines.

The Naval Officer in the command of this Party should be directed to trace the course of the River & to take Soundings with as much accuracy as possible—to communicate with the Natives; to pay for everything they may furnish him with, & to make small presents to those who may assist his progress or from whom he may be able to collect information.

When he shall approach the Nerico[3] which falls into the Gambia about 60 Miles S.E. of Barraconda, he should make particular enquiries as to the distance, by the course of the River, from Ganado, & whether it be navigable and by what sized canoes. Similar enquiries

[1] Ganado and Nae were small villages near the Faleme river where Park had passed on his first mission.
[2] The plan for a military expedition originated with Colonel Charles Stevenson in a memorandum, 10 March 1804: C.O. 2/1. The reasons for its modification (shortage of troops and shipping) are discussed in W. O. 6/22.
[3] The Nieri Ko.

should be made relative to every considerable Stream that may fall into the Gambia on either side. When the navigation of the Gambia shall cease to be practicable the Officer should be instructed to collect the best information he can, as to the distance he may be at from the Falimé in the N.E. and if he should judge it practicable, he should advance to that River and descend to Naye. If that course should not be found adviseable, he should endeavour to open a communication with the Town of Laby[1] on the S.E. leaving, in either case, the canoes and such Articles as he may not be able to take away with him, under the protection of the Chief of the nearest Town on the River.

In the event of his taking the Route to the Falimé, he should be instructed to embark at the nearest place where he may meet with canoes or be able to make a raft, and if upon his arrival at Nayé, he should not find a Post already established there, or in the Vicinity, he should immediately dispatch a Messenger to Barraconda and endeavour to conciliate the Chief of Bondou, by purchasing Horses and taking such further measures as circumstances may enable him, for facilitating the progress of the Troops when they should arrive. He should inform himself of the further course of the Falimé until it falls into the Sengal, at the Village of Tafaliga[2] and be governed in his future conduct by such instructions as he may receive from the Officer Commanding the party with Mr. Park.

If on the other hand, he should find it necessary to take the route towards Laby, the abstract of the Journey of Messrs. Watts & Winterbottom[3] will furnish him with much useful information and as those Gentlemen represent the people of that Town to be well disposed, he may be able to open a communication from thence thro' the Capital of Teemboo with Sierra Leone and also find means of discovering whether the River Danso forms a branch of the Rio Grande, at what distance from Laby and Teemboo it becomes navigable, and where it falls into the Rio Grande. . . .

Colonel Stevenson with the Troops & Stores ought to Sail from England before the end of October. He should touch at Cape de Verd Islands to take in further Supplies of Wine, Horses and Mules, and at Goree for information and such aid in canoes and native Boatmen as may have been collected.

He should use all possible diligence in getting up the Gambia to the place of disembarkation, & in proceeding by the tract Mr. Park may have opened leaving one hundred Men on board the Ships to be conveyed to Sierra Leone. One of the armed Brigs and one Gunboat

---

[1] Labé, capital of the Fulani *diwal* of Labé in the Futa Jallon, Guinea.
[2] Or Tafalisga on James Rennell's map (1798).
[3] For a summary of this exploration from the Nunez to Timbo in 1794, see Hugh Murray (ed.), *Historical Account of Discoveries and Travels in Africa*, 2 vols. (Edinburgh, 1818), vol. i, pp. 330–6.

with the Store & Hospital Ships should remain in the Gambia, and the naval officer in command be directed to have an accurate survey of the River taken, and if necessary to reinforce the Party that may have advanced by water above the Falls of Barraconda.

When Colonel Stevenson shall have taken possession of the French Fort of St. Joseph on the Senegal River and of its Dependencies whether on that River or on the Falimé and in Bambouk—He should be directed to concert with Mr. Park, the course which it may be most adviseable to pursue with a view of advancing a detachment to the Niger and of conveying the frame of the Gunboat with such Stores and other articles as might be necessary for the establishment of a Post on the bank of that River & of enabling Mr. Park to proceed in the Gunboat and such craft as could be armed, on his Mission to Sego, Tombuctoo and such other places as the Navigation of the River may admit of his approaching.

Mr. Park should be instructed to dispatch a Canoe with as little delay as possible after his arrival upon the bank of the Niger, with a Letter in Arabic to the King of Sego, informing him that he had been sent by his Government with Letters and Presents for him, and that as soon as the necessary conveyance for himself and his Attendants could be got ready He should proceed by the River to Sego.

The Naval Officer in command of the Gunboat should be directed to concert upon all occasions with Mr. Park and to be governed in every thing, but the management of the boat and Craft by him—great care should be taken not to excite an alarm, but on the contrary to conciliate the Natives and the Chiefs of the principal Towns, by paying for everything they may furnish and abstaining from all kind of traffic beyond the purchase of necessaries, referring Traders to the Factories upon the Gambia and the Senegal and assuming the Character of an Envoy from the British Government to the Kings of Sego, Tombuctoo and Houssa.

If upon his arrival off Sego, measures should not have taken for his public reception, he should signify that the orders of his Government would not admit of his landing, and that he should proceed on the further objects of his Mission to Tombuctoo and Houssa by such an hour; unless the King of Sego should previously send proper persons to invite Him on shore.

He should act upon this intimation and not be induced to relax but by preparing solicitation—with a view to the security of himself and the party that may land with him he should represent them as Attendants necessary to his dignity and upon that ground not suffer them to be separated from him. He should endeavour to obtain permission for the establishment of a Factory, and when he shall have dispatched an account to Colonel Stevenson of the occurences of his voyage, and of the information he may have collected, he should

FBP

proceed down the River, observing the same Conduct at Tombuctoo and other principal places that have been pointed out for his guidance with regard to Sego; endeavouring every where to give the most favorable impression of the British Character and power and sending Dispatches regularly if possible but otherwise employing Messengers whenever he may have any thing important to communicate.

It must be left to the discretion and judgment of Colonel Stevenson to employ the force that may remain with him, either in the establishment of various posts in the Country of Bambouk, or to strengthen the lines of communication E. & W. always keeping in his mind that a free & secure intercourse of trade with the Natives is the great object to be attained, that their prejudices and caprices must be studied, and that the force under his command is only to be employed to repel Force and ensure protection. . . .

[Communications will be kept open from Sierra Leone and along the Rio Grande; a new settlement may be established at Bulama Island with hired labour.]

4

EARL BATHURST TO MAJOR PEDDIE: EXPEDITION TO THE NIGER, 23 AUGUST 1815[1]

SIR,

It being extremely desirable with a view to the Improvement of the Geographical Knowledge of the Interior of Southern Africa and eventually to the extension of British Commerce in that Quarter to prosecute those discoveries which have at different times been made by His Majesty's Subjects and more recently by Mr. Park; His Royal Highness the Prince Regent has signified His Commands that an Expedition should be undertaken for that purpose and having received the most satisfactory Testimony of your Zeal Perseverance and Activity in the various Services in which you have heretofore been engaged His Royal Highness has been pleased to select you for its Command. Captain Campbell of the Royal Staff Corps an Officer equally recommended, and Staff Surgeon Cowdry, who to great professional skill unites a competent Knowledge of Astronomy and Minerology and has before been a Traveller in Southern Africa, where he has acquired a Knowledge of Arabic, will be associated with you in the Expedition and placed under your Command, and you will be authorized to select either from the Royal African Corps, or

---

[1] C.O. 268/19. A good deal of valuable information on interior trade was collected by Campbell: C.O. 2/5; Gray's letters and Campbell's journals are in C.O. 2/7.

from the Captured Negroes in the British Settlements in Africa, such numbers of persons not exceeding altogether 100 as may volunteer for the Service and you may consider it expedient to employ; From this source you will by means of a careful selection be amply provided with Guides Artificers and Interpreters necessary to the Conduct and successful Issue of the Expedition. To these persons you will consider yourself authorized to promise the following Advantages upon their return provided they shall have conducted themselves faithfully to the termination of the Journey. Each Serjeant may be assured of receiving the value of One Thousand Dollars, each Corporal of 500 Dollars, and each Private of 300 Dollars besides his accruing Pay during the period of Absence. It is only necessary to direct you in making choice of Native Africans to select excepting under very particular circumstances such only as were originally free in those Countries in which you may intend to pass. Supplies of all Articles required as presents for the Inhabitants or for the purposes of Trade with them will be placed at your disposal previous to your departure from England and the Officer Commanding in Africa will be instructed to afford you such further assistance as to Stores provisions and means of Transport as you may upon your arrival in Africa find it necessary to require.

The main Object of the Expedition (and that to which your Attention will be so far exclusively directed as to consider every other as of secondary Importance) is the discovery of the Mouths of the Niger, and the Course of that River from the point at which it was visited by Mr. Park to that at which it may be found to terminate. Having once ascertained this point you will adopt the safest mode of communicating the Result of your discoveries to this Country and of effecting the Return of your party either collectively or separately as circumstances may render the one or the other most safe and practicable.

The Success of the Expedition materially depends upon it being undertaken at the Season of the Year least obnoxious to an European constitution. As that Season commences in December and as some time will be required for preparation in Africa, it is proposed that you should leave this Country on the first of September at latest proceed to Senegal which has been selected [as the] point of your ultimate departure both on account of the facility which it affords for procuring a supply of the requisite articles and for conveying them either by Land or Water to a very considerable distance into the Interior; Should you however after your arrival in Senegal have reason to believe that the route from thence is less practicable than that which Mr. Park followed or that there are any circumstances which render it more advisable to proceed by any other, directions will be given for your being conveyed to that point on the Coast of

Africa from whence you may finally deem it most expedient to commence your Journey.

The Object of the Expedition itself points out how desirable it must be that no time should be unnecessarily lost in reaching the Niger. But I must urge as a paramount consideration the Importance of not hazarding by any premature exertion the Safety or Health of those under your Command. Should you therefore on attaining the Niger or even in the earlier Stages of your Journey forsee any obstruction to your future progress arising either from the State of the Season, the disposition of the Inhabitants, a defficiency of your means or the Sickness of your party, you will consider yourself as fully authorized to arrest your Advance and to select some eligible post in which your party may establish themselves in security until you may receive from some of His Majesty's Possessions in Africa such assistance as you may deem requisite to the successful prosecution of your enterprize. In establishing such a post however you will carefully avoid exciting the jealousy of the Inhabitants. The ground necessary for your purpose must be fairly and openly purchased of the Chief or Proprietor to whom it may belong and you may as far as is practicable explain the necessity which induces you to require it.

From the moment at which you commence your Expedition down the Niger the mode of conducting it must be left entirely to your own judgement and discretion. Whether your object will be best effected by navigation down the River, or by travelling along its Shores; whether it may or may not be expedient in the later, as has been already recommended in the earlier Stages of the Journey, temporarily to establish yourself in a post of security for the purpose of recruiting your means, you alone will be able to determine. I feel that I should only contribute to your embarrassment by attempting to give you any precise Instructions upon these points which could only be drawn from the Memoranda of Mr. Park and other Travellers with which you are already acquainted and of the value which you are perfectly qualified to judge. I content myself with enclosing for information the last Memoire[1] by Mr. Park to Earl Camden which contains upon these subjects much useful detail.

It is equally out of my power to offer any observations as to the best mode of effecting your Return after the Objects of the Expedition shall have been accomplished. Should the Niger terminate as has been supposed by some in a Morass or Lake in the interior of Africa, your Return must depend entirely upon your own exertions. Should it flow into the Nile as has been supposed by some or into the Zair or Congo as has been with a great appearance of probability asserted by others, opportunities may offer of affording you assistance. In contemplation of the latter hypothesis proving true His Royal

1 See E. Smith, *The Life of Sir Joseph Banks* (London, 1911), p. 150.

Highness The Prince Regent has been pleased to order an Expedition to proceed simultaneously up the Zair[1] for the purpose of aiding in your progress in the latter Stages of your Enterprize, and directions will also be transmitted to His Majesty's Resident in Egypt to adopt any measures which he may consider effectual for diminishing the difficulty of descending the Upper Nile in the Event of your arriving in that Quarter. . . .

[He is to survey the Niger, keep an accurate Journal of events, and correspond with the Secretary of State for Colonies.]

5

DRAFT OF INSTRUCTIONS TO MAJOR DENHAM: EXPEDITION TO BORNU, 20 SEPTEMBER 1821[2]

The Bashaw of Tripoli having made an offer to His Majesty of convoy to Bornou and of bringing back from thence after a certain Interval any Travellers whom His Majesty might entrust to his Protection His Majesty has thought this a favourable opportunity of renewing the attempts which have latterly been made for exploring yet further the Interior of Africa and having received the strongest assurances of Your Zeal & Ability has been pleased to select You as the Person to be so employed. You will be accompanied by Lieutenant Clapperton of the Royal Navy whose Character for enterprise perseverance and professional talents cannot but render him a most valuable Assistant. This Gentleman will not be the less entitled to Your Consideration from the Circumstances of his having volunteered to join an Expedition placed under Your Command without any reference to his relative Rank in His Majesty's Service.

As the Season of the Year is approaching which has been pronounced the fittest for undertaking a Journey from Tripoli to Bornou you will lose no time in proceeding to Malta and from thence to Tripoli in any manner which the Commander of His Majesty's Naval Forces at Malta may consider most advisable to secure your early

---

[1] At the same time Captain J. K. Tuckey was to explore the Congo: *Narrative of an Expedition to explore the River Zaire, usually called the Congo, in South Africa, in 1816, under the Direction of Captain J. K. Tuckey, R.N.* London, 1818.

[2] C.O. 2/13. Two drafts were prepared and corrected by *Henry Goulburn*, Under-Secretary in the Colonial Office, 1812–21, and by Lord Bathurst. The second version is printed here. See D. Denham, H. Clapperton, W. Oudney, *Narrative of Travels and Discoveries in Northern and Central Africa in 1822–24.* London, 1826; and for letters and Denham's dispute with Clapperton over leadership, C.O. 2/13. Also included here are letters and translations from Sultan Muhammad Bello, son of Dan Fodio and intellectual leader of the Fulani *Jihad*, and from Muhammad al-Amin al-Kanemi, Sultan of Bornu.

arrival. You will either at Malta or Tripoli join Lt. Clapperton who proceeded a short time since to the former place and who will have secured the Services of some Naval Carpenter from the Yard at Malta to accompany You and will have made some other necessary preliminary arrangements for Your Journey. You will also find there Dr. Oudeney who has been nominated Her Majesty's Vice Consul to the Sultan of Bornou and who will proceed to His destination at the same time with Yourself under the Bashaw of Tripoli's protection. To Him has been confided the Presents necessary to ensure his own reception at Bornou. He will obtain permission from the Sultan for your proceeding from thence on Your Journey of Discovery; and will both during your stay at Bornou & after Your Departure afford you every Assistance & support which His Situation admits.

As you will be conveyed to Bornou by the Bashaw of Tripoli the Instructions which I shall have to convey to You will principally relate to Your Conduct after Your arrival in that place. You will of course however on Your Journey thither omit no opportunity of observing and recording whatever may be either Interesting to future Travellers or may give an insight into the nature of the Country through which You Travel or the Manners & habits of the People taking care however on this as on all other occasions so to conduct Your observations as to give no cause of Jealousy to the Inhabitants & rather to forego enquiry than risk any proceeding which might interfere with the ultimate objects of Your Expedition.

The main object of Your Journey is to explore the Country to the Southward and Eastward of Bornou, principally with a view to tracing the course of the Niger and ascertaining its Embouchure. You must judge on the spot whether this may be best effected by navigating the River itself or by traversing the Country through which it flows. It appears requisite to Your Success that You should after Your arrival at Bournou remain there some time in order to collect information as to the Countries thro' which You propose to Travel & to make Yourself to a certain degree master of the language which may be most generally useful to You. It might even be desirable that You should make short Excursions from Bornou to neighbouring Towns in order to accustom Yourself to the manner of Travelling and the habits of the People; but you will at all events be careful not to precipitate your final departure until you have adequately qualified Yourself in these particulars.

Should the Country beyond Bornou be in a state of tranquillity, the Caravans which are understood to proceed from thence to the South East would in all probability afford You the safest and most advantageous mode of prosecuting Your Journey so long as their direction corresponded with that which is prescribed to you. Should the Sultan of Bornou be at War with the neighbouring Powers and undertake any Military Expedition, in the direction which You may wish to take, You might find it adviseable to solicit His permission to accompany him, without however engaging in the War, and avail Yourself of this means of exploring the Country but in suggesting these modes of proceeding I am far from wishing to prescribe to You the course which it may be most advisable to pursue in a Country of which nothing is known. Your own discretion and the information You may obtain on the Spot must direct Your course. I would only impress upon You that the objects of Your attention will be principally the Characters of the People, Geography of the Country, its Rivers, Lakes Mountains and relative Situation & distances of the Towns through which you may pass. Not that I would undervalue the importance of obtaining Information & specimens of its Animal, Vegetable or Mineral productions if consistent with the other objects, but I would guard against Your making those which ought to be incidental, the leading objects of Your Enquiry. You will not fail at all times immediately to record any discovery which You may make or any information which You may consider deserving of Credit respecting the Interior of the Country and to transmit a Minute or Copy of it to me through Dr. Oudeney at Bornou or any other channel which you consider equally safe. Much of our present ignorance with respect to the Country arises from the omission of former Travellers in this Respect & the loss of Information which had only been by them committed to Memory and I am anxious that in Your Case this evil should be avoided.

For some time after Your departure from Bornou the more easy mode of Communication with this Country or of supplying any Wants which may occur will be through Mr. Oudeney & Consul Warrington but as in the event of Your reaching the Niger & successfully pursuing the course You may be brought nearer to Upper Egypt or the Countries bordering upon it, His Majesty's Consul in that quarter has been instructed to take such measures as may ensure You a favourable reception and to furnish You with all that may be necessary to supply Your wants in the Country or to secure Your return Home from that Quarter.

I have only to add that during the time of Your Employment You will be entitled to receive a personal Allowance of Three Hundred Pounds a Year to commence from the 12th. June last the day on which Your Engagement took place. The Expenses of Your Journey to Bornou will be defrayed by the Bashaw of Tripoli and with respect to Your Expences after arriving at Bornou, Mr. Oudeney has been instructed from time to time to provide on Your Application to Him such Means as may be required for the prosecution of the ulterior objects of Your Expedition.

6

JOHN BARROW TO CAPTAIN W. F. W. OWEN: SURVEY OF THE AFRICAN COAST, 30 JUNE 1824[1]

SIR,

It being the intention of my Lords Commissioners of the Admiralty, that on your return to England from the surveys in which you have been engaged on the eastern side of Africa, you should employ yourself with the vessels under your orders in making a complete survey of the western coast of Africa, from Cape Mesurado to the River Gambia, and the Bight of Benin; I am commanded by their Lordships to signify their directions to you, to return with the Leven and Barracouta to the Cape of Good Hope, to report their labours in time to enable you afterwards to reach the coast between Cape Mesurado and the Gambia about the middle of November 1825, when you are accordingly to employ yourself in making accurate surveys of the coasts and dangers above mentioned, and having completed the same, you are then to make the best of your way with the said vessels to Spithead, and report your arrival and proceedings for their Lordships' information.

I am further to acquaint you, that a packet containing some charts and a memorandum from the Hydrographical Department of this office for your information, in regard to the surveys above directed on the western coast of Africa, is forwarded for you to the naval store-keeper at the Cape of Good Hope, to whom you are to apply for the same.

7

P. WALKER: MEMORANDUM, SURVEY OF THE AFRICAN COAST, 30 JUNE 1824[2]

THEIR Lordships being desirous of having the Coast of Africa, between Sierra Leone, and the River Gambia, with its dangers, completely surveyed, have directed me to give you a detailed account,

[1] H. Robinson (ed.), *Narrative of Voyages to explore the Shores of Africa, and Madagascar; performed in H.M. Ships 'Leven' and 'Barracouta', under the Direction of Captain W. F. W. Owen, R.N.* 2 vols. (London, 1833), vol. i, pp. xii–xv. *Captain Owen* was appointed to command the *Leven* in 1821 and surveyed the Cape of Good Hope, Delagoa Bay, the coast of Madagascar and Arabia, before completing this mission in the Bight of Benin and the Gambia in 1826. For the *Leven* Log, Admiralty 52/3254; and for charts and views, Capt. W. F. W. Owen, *Hydrographical Survey of the Coast of Africa*, London, 822–6. (*Sir*) *John Barrow* who had travelled extensively in China and the interior of Cape Colony was appointed Secretary to the Admiralty in 1804 and occupied the post for forty years.
[2] Ibid., p. xv.

not only of what we possess, but also of our wants, that you may be the better enabled to fulfil them. I shall also give you a short statement of the whole coast, that you may know what is wanted to complete it.

I should recommend you to begin at Cape Mesurado, a little to the southward of the shoals of St. Ann, where Mr. De Mayne left off. A survey of these shoals lately made by Lieutenant Hagen, will accompany this, which may be of use for you, either to verify or amend if necessary. We know nothing whatever of the River Sierra Leone, as far as is necessary for navigation: it will, therefore, be desirable to obtain the requisite information. The Isles de Loss are frequently resorted to by His Majesty's Ships; you have a copy of the only plan we possess, in the first volume of plans you were furnished with, but it is reported to be very erroneous; a survey, therefore of them, on a good-sized scale, is very desirable. The whole coast line from Sierra Leone to Cape Roxa, we know little or nothing about, though it contains the entrances of four large rivers, besides a number of smaller ones, but the most dangerous part is the Bissagos Archipelago, or as they are generally called in the charts, the shoals of Rio Grande. The French have lately made a survey of the two channels which nearly surround these shoals, the one leading into the Rio Jaba, the other into the Rio Grande, a copy of which accompanies this: you will see they only just touch upon the Islands and Shoals; a more detailed one would be desirable, as far as prudence will allow you to risk your ships.

From Cape Roxo to the River Gambia, being a straight coast and no dangers, you will have little to do, as it was surveyed in a former voyage in the Leven, by Lieutenants Vidal and Mudge, except the entrances of three or four rivers which were thought too insignificant to lose their time about; but the Gambia it will be necessary to survey very minutely, so far up as may be necessary for navigation, it being a place of great trade; and there are said to be many dangers, but which we are totally unacquainted with.

The Coast from the Cape of Good Hope to Benguela, has been fully examined and surveyed by Captain Chapman, of His Majesty's Ship Espiegle, and as we have a former survey of that part taken in one of His Majesty's ships, these combined with Mr. De Mayne's survey from Benguela to the Congo, will be fully sufficient for every purpose of navigation. But from the Congo to the Bight of Benin, we are very defective; it is represented as a straight coast, and I believe no dangers exist on it. Yet it is desirable to have its situation exactly ascertained, and to know what rivers may empty themselves into the sea within that space. Should you therefore arrive on that part of the coast before the fair weather commences, (about the middle of November), or be driven away from it before you have completed the survey of that part between Sierra Leone and the Gambia, you might take that opportunity to inspect that between the Congo and the Bight of Benin. When these two objects are accomplished, I conceive the whole western coast of Africa will be sufficiently known for every purpose of navigation. . . .

8

EARL BATHURST TO HUGH CLAPPERTON: EXPEDITION TO SOKOTO, 30 JULY 1825[1]

SIR,

His Highness Mahomet Bello, Sultan of the Fellatas, having expressed a strong desire to establish friendly intercourse with Great Britain, & His Majesty having been pleased to direct that a Mission should proceed forthwith to Sockatoo, the Residence of His Highness, in order to accomplish so desirable a purpose, I have the King's commands to nominate and appoint you to conduct the said Mission, & to furnish you with the following Instructions for your guidance therein; not doubting that, from the zeal and ability you have already displayed in exploring the hitherto unknown regions of Central Africa, & from the friendly manner in which you were received by all classes of Nations, you will be able to accomplish the important objects which His Majesty's Government have in view.

As soon as the preparations necessary for the voyage shall be completed, you are to proceed to Portsmouth where the Commander of His Majesty's Ship Brazen has been ordered to receive you on board, & to convey you to the Bight of Benin near to Whydah, or such other place as you may find, on your arrival on the Coast, to be the most safe & convenient for communicating with Soccatoo or Raca, the latter of which (from the information you obtained at Soccatoo) appears to be the nearest town in the Sultan's dominions to the Sea-Coast, & the place fixed upon by himself for the ultimate residence of a British Agent or Consul.

From our present imperfect knowledge of this part of Africa beyond the line of the Coast, much must necessarily be left to your discretion, and your proceedings therefore will in a great degree be regulated according to the information you may be able to collect on your arrival at the Coast. You will, in the first place however, make every possible enquiry at Whydah whether any of the Sultan's people are, or have been there, conformably with an engagement

[1] C.O. 2/16. For the mission to Sokoto (where no treaty was obtained) and to Kano, *Journal of a Second Expedition into the Interior of Africa . . . by the Late Commander Clapperton, of the Royal Navy. To which is added the Journal of Richard Lander from Kano to the Sea-coast.* London, 1829; R. Lander, *Records of Captain Clapperton's last expedition.* 2 vols. London, 1829; and for letters and journals, C.O. 2/15 and 2/16.

entered into by you to that effect; & if still there, you will first dispatch them to their Master with an account of your arrival and that you are ready to proceed either to his Capital, or to Raca, as he may judge most expedient, to deliver to him a letter from your Sovereign & several valuable Articles for his acceptance, on his sending down a proper escort to conduct you & them to his presence. Or, if the Sultan's Messengers shall be able to satisfy you of the road being perfectly open & safe, you are at liberty to proceed with them yourself, leaving the presents in the Brazen in charge of one of the Gentlemen, hereafter named, who will accompany you on the present Mission.

Failing in your endeavour to obtain any tidings of the Sultan's servants having been at Whydah, you are to enquire and consider well whether, from the information you obtain, it will be most advisable to proceed yourself with a few presents to bestow on the intermediate Chiefs thro' whose territories you would have to pass in your way to Raca; Or, whether it might not be more prudent to engage some respectable Native, under promise of reward on his return, to conduct Columbus (who will accompany you in the capacity of Interpreter & Servant) to that place, or to Soccatoo, if necessary, with a letter from you to the Sultan advising him of your arrival, & requesting that persons may be sent down for the conveyance of the presents and baggage & an escort for yourself and companions.

If however after your arrival on the Coast, & after due enquiries, you should entertain doubts as to the success of either of these plans of proceeding from Whydah, it may be advisable to take the Brazen to the mouth of the River of Benin, where it is understood that you will find no difficulty in communicating with Mr. Houston, an English Merchant residing at Gatto, a town about sixty miles up the river. This Gentleman is said to speak the language of the Natives, & to have collected much valuable information from the Moorish Traders, who come down thither from Houssa & other provinces of Soudan; he had intended it seems to accompany the late Mr. Belzoni[1] a considerable way on his journey towards Timbuctoo. As the distance from Benin to Racca is little more than that from Whydah, the great advantage of procuring the assistance & information of a resident English Merchant will perhaps be considered to outweigh any plan of proceeding from Whydah, with the exception of meeting with, or hearing of, the Sultan's Messengers at the latter place. But these are considerations which must necessarily be left entirely to your discretion when on the spot.

It is understood that Mr. Houston has also an Establishment at Lagos, close to Whydah, & it may be important to communicate with him, at any rate, whether or not he may be at Lagos or Gatto, as he may be of eventual service to the Mission.

[1] An Italian traveller who died at Benin in 1823.

On your arrival at the residence of Bello, & after delivering His Majesty's letter & presents, you are to assure him of the satisfaction which His Majesty feels in thus being able to open an amicable intercourse between the two Nations, & the opportunity it affords for cultivating that mutual friendship, which cannot fail, in due time, to produce mutual benefit. You will endeavour by every means in your power to impress on his mind the very great advantages he will derive by putting a total stop to the sale of Slaves to Christian Merchants, thro' Native Slave-dealers on or near the Coast, & by preventing other powers of Africa from marching Koffilas or Slaves thro' his dominions. You will inform him of the anxious desire which the King your Master feels for the total abolition of this inhuman & unnatural traffic, & the measures he has adopted to that effect; and you will assure him that the happy result of his cordial cooperation will cause him to be ranked among the benefactors of mankind; that the benefits arising from the suppression of the Trade to foreigners will speedily be felt by all the surrounding states; for that all the Articles of Merchandize, which are now brought into Africa, & given in return for human beings, will, when that traffic has ceased, be brought by English Merchants, in exchange for such Articles as Soudan may produce, & which may be sought for in the Markets of Europe; & that when once the road is open between Raca & the Sea-Coast, he will receive whatever articles of Merchandize he may require at a much cheaper rate than he now pays for those which are brought accross the long desert.

You will endeavour to ascertain, & to note down, such products of Soudan as may appear most suitable for the European Markets, & to what extent they might be procured by the increased industry of the Natives, the certain result of a cessation in the trade of Slaves.

You will also endeavour to ascertain in what manner & from what parts of the Country, both within the Sultan's dominions, & in those to the Southward of them, & also in what numbers from the several States such Slaves are procured which are brought down to, & shipped by Slave-dealers at, the mouths of those great Rivers which fall into the Bights of Biafra & Benin; & you will consider and report to me what measures may appear most advisable for putting a stop to, or at least materially checking, this inhumane traffic, not only in those districts under the controul of the Sultan Bello, but also in those parts from which the trade is chiefly supplied with victims.

You will consider it an important part of your duty to use your best endeavours in ascertaining the leading features in the Geography of Central Africa, which yet appear to be left undetermined, more particularly the direction of the Mountain ranges, & the courses of the Rivers. It will be highly desirable to trace the course of that river which is known with certainty to flow past the Kabra, or the port of

Timbuctoo, & which has been known in modern times by the name of Niger. If this river, contrary to ancient & modern testimonies, should, according to the information which you received at Sockatoo, be found to bend its course to the Southward & to fall into the Bight of Benin, instead of continuing to flow to the Eastward, as has hitherto been supposed; and if it should be found to be navigable thro' the Sultan's territories, or any part thereof, such a discovery may prove of the utmost importance in facilitating the objects of the present Mission & our future intercourse with that Sovereign.

You will make every enquiry within your power, & ascertain personally, if practicable, the sources of those numerous large rivers which empty their waters into the Bights of Biafra & Benin, to what extent they are navigable, & by what description of Vessels. You will also, during your stay in Coastal Africa, endeavour to visit the city of Timbuctoo, provided you shall not have heard that Major Laing[1] had already accomplished that object; & in the former event, you will enquire into the nature and extent of the commerce carried on there with the various natives of Africa.

You will employ your liezure time in collecting and preserving specimens of such materials, manufactures, & other products of Soudan, as you may deem to be valuable, in a commercial point of view; & also such objects of Natural History as may appear to you to be rare and curious.

To assist you in the performance of your various duties I have appointed Captain Pearce, a Commander in the Navy, who is to act in your stead, in the event of your death or absence; & you will also be accompanied by Mr. Dickson[2] & Mr. Morrison both of whom you will present to the Sultan as Gentlemen well skilled in the practice of Medicine. By both of these Gentlemen you will be aided in making collections of Natural History & in settling the geography of the Country.

As soon as convenient after your arrival at Soccatoo you are to dispatch Captain Pearce with a letter from me, & a suitable present from the King, to the Sheik of Bornou, with whom he is to be instructed by you to remain for some time, to cultivate the friendship of that Chief. In the course of his residence there, he is to be directed to take every opportunity that may offer, of endeavouring to explore that portion of the Eastern Shore of the great Lake Tsed, which was left unexamined by Major Denham, & to proceed as far beyond the Lake towards Fittré,[3] or to the Eastward, as circumstances may allow

---

[1] For Laing's journal and last letters on his mission from Tripoli to Ghadames and Timbuktu, 1825–6, C.O. 2/15.

[2] Thomas Dickson attempted an alternative route through Abomey where he spent some months in 1825 and 1826. Morrison and Pearce died shortly after arrival on the Slave Coast.

[3] Lake Fitri some 200 miles east of Chad.

him to do with safety to himself; but he is, on no account to attempt to undertake journeys of this kind, without having previously obtained the concurrence of the Sheik of Bornou. And as the direct route between Sockatoo & Bornou has twice been travelled over by yourself; & as, according to your information, the province of Addmouah is within the dominions of the Sultan, it will be highly desirable that Captain Pearce either in his journey to Bornou, or on his return, should take his route through Addmouah, more especially as it is probable that the great navigable river Shary runs thro' that province. And as you have His Majesty's permission to return to England whenever you conceive that the object of your Mission shall have been accomplished or brought into a train of being so, either by the Bight of Benin or accross the Northern Desert to Tripoli. You are in such an event to recal[l] Captain Pearce from Bornou, & instruct him to remain at Sockatoo or Raca, as the Sultan may determine, in the capacity of Consul or Agent to concert such measures with the Agent which he has promised to appoint on his part, as may be most effectual to put a stop to the passage of Slaves from Houssa & the other provinces of the Fellatah Nation to the Sea Coast; & for his further guidance you are to leave with him a Copy of these Instructions.

With regard to Mr. Dickson he may either remain at Soccatoo or Raca as it may be agreed upon with the Sultan, or return with you to England, according as he may feel disposed to do. And Mr. Morrison is to consider himself as attached to Captain Pearce, & to accompany him to Bornou. . . .

[Conditions of pay and allowances. Regular correspondence and copies of journals are to be sent home.]

9

JOHN BARROW TO R. W. HAY: MISSION TO THE NIGER, 19 SEPTEMBER 1829[1]

MY DEAR HAY,

. . . The thing most to be desired is, to follow up the Benin River to ascertain whether or not it is a continuation of the Niger—the distance is very triffling, and with a few trinkets of a hundred pounds value the thing would easily be done. Then to follow the valley of Adamowa to the Lake Tsad, and ascertain whether it be watered by the Strang [sic] or any other river. To proceed from Bornou easterly towards the Nile. This I think is feasible. But, would not Lander, who

---

[1] C.O. 2/18. *R. W. Hay* was Permanent Under-Secretary in the Colonial Department, 1825–36.

has been pressing to go again,[1] be the fittest person to send? None in my opinion would make their way so well, and with a bundle of beads & bafts and other trinkets, we could land him somewhere about Bonny, and let him find his way.

The two letters of Bello to Clapperton which Salamé kept back,[2] place the conduct of the former in a better point of view than he appears from Clapperton's narrative; it appears from them that, circumstanced as he then was, he could not well have acted otherwise than he did. If therefore Mr. Coulthurst[3] is bent upon Soccatoo, there can be no objection to let him have a letter to Bello, though it would be prudent not to furnish him, in that case, with credentials to his Enemy, the Sheik of Bornou.

10

R. W. HAY TO RICHARD LANDER: MISSION TO THE NIGER, 31 DECEMBER 1829[4]

SIR,

I am directed by Secretary Sir George Murray to acquaint you, that he has deemed it expedient to accept the offer which you have made, to proceed to Africa, accompanied by your brother, for the purpose of ascertaining the course of the Great River which was crossed by the late Captain Clapperton, on his journey to Soccatoo; and a passage having been accordingly engaged for you and your brother on board of the Alert, merchant vessel, which is proceeding to Cape-Coast Castle, on the western coast of Africa, I am to desire that you will embark directly on board of that vessel.

In the event of your falling in with any of his Majesty's ships of war on the coast of Africa, previously to your arrival at Cape-Coast Castle, you will prevail on the master to use every endeavour to speak with such ship of war, and to deliver to the officer commanding her, the letter of which you are the bearer, and which is to require him to convey yourself and your brother to Badagry, to present you to the king, and to give you such assistance as may be required to enable you to set out on your journey.

[1] C.O. 2/17, Lander to Hay, 13 November 1829. Richard and John Lander proceeded in 1830 from Badagri to Bussa and down the Niger to Brass. *Journal of an Expedition to explore the Course and Termination of the Niger*. 3 vols. London, 1832.

[2] A. V. Salamé was a translator of Arabic documents for the Foreign Office. These two letters may refer to those forwarded from Bello, in C.O. 2/13; see *Narrative of Travels and Discoveries in Northern and Central Africa in 1822–24*, Appendix, pp. 139–45.

[3] C. D. Coulthurst was an amateur adventurer seeking Government support—which was not granted.

[4] Richard and John Lander, *Journal of an Expedition to explore the Course and Termination of the Niger*, i, pp. lii–lvii.

You should incur as little delay as possible at Badagry, in order that, by reaching the hilly country, you may be more secure from those fevers which are known to be prevalent on the low lands of the sea-coast. You are to proceed by the same road as on a previous occasion, as far as Katunga, unless you shall be able to find, on the northern side of the mountains, a road which will lead you to Funda, on the Quorra or Niger, in which case you are to proceed direct to Funda. If, however, it should be necessary to go as far as Katunga, you are to use your endeavours to prevail on the chief of that country to assist you on your way to the Quorra, and with the means of tracing down, either by land or water, the course of that river as far as Funda.

On your arrival at this place, you are to be very particular in your observations, so as to enable you to give a correct statement—

1st. Whether any, and what rivers fall into the Quorra at or near that place, or whether the whole or any part of the Quorra turns to the eastward.

2nd. Whether there is at Funda, or in the neighbourhood, any lake or collection of waters, or large swamp; in which case you are to go round such lake or swamp, and be very particular in examining whether any river flows *into* or *out* of it, and in what direction it takes its course.

3rd. If you should find that at Funda the Quorra continues to flow to the southward, you are to follow it to the sea, where, in this case, it may be presumed to empty its waters; but if it should be found to turn off to the eastward, in which case it will most probably fall into the Lake Tshad, you are to follow its course in that direction, as far as you conceive you can venture to do, with due regard to your personal safety, even to Bornou, in which case it will be for you to determine whether it may not be advisable to return home by the way of Fezzan and Tripoli: if, however, after proceeding in an easterly course for some distance, the river should be found to turn off towards the south, you are to follow it, as before, down to the sea. In short, after having once gained the banks of the Quorra, either from Katunga, or lower down, you are to follow its course, if possible, to its termination, wherever that may be.

Should you be of opinion that the Sultan of Youri can safely be communicated with, you are at liberty to send your brother with a present to that chief, to ask, in the king's name, for certain books or papers which he is supposed to have, that belonged to the late Mr. Park; but you are not necessarily yourself to wait for your brother's return, but to proceed in the execution of the main object of your mission, to ascertain the course and termination of the Niger.

You are to take every opportunity of sending down by the coast a brief abstract of your proceedings and observations, furnishing the bearer with a note, setting forth the reward he is to have for his trouble, and requesting any English person, to whom it is presented,

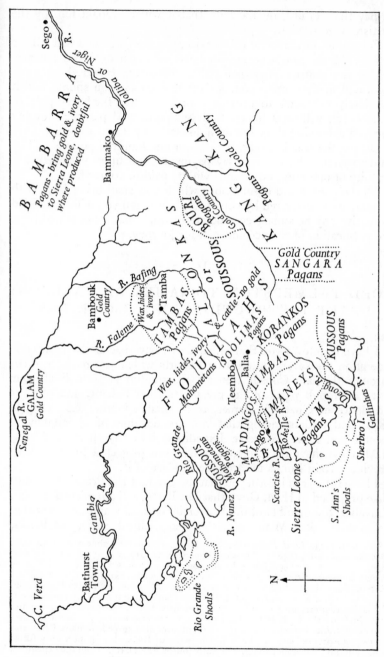

Map 2: Robert Pearce. The Sierra Leone and Senegal–Niger Interior, 1825. No scale.

to pay that reward, on the faith that it will be repaid him by the British Government.

For the performance of this service, you are furnished with all the articles which you have required for your personal convenience, during your journey, together with a sum of two hundred dollars in coin, and in case, upon your arrival at Badagry, you should find it absolutely necessary to provide yourself with a further supply of dollars, you will be at liberty to draw upon this department for any sum not exceeding three hundred dollars.

During the ensuing year, the sum of one hundred pounds will be paid to your wife, in quarterly payments, and upon your return a gratuity of one hundred pounds will be paid to yourself.

All the papers and observations which you shall bring back with you, are to be delivered by you at this office, and you will be entitled to receive any pecuniary consideration which may be obtained from the publication of the account of your journey.

11

LORD PALMERSTON TO JAMES RICHARDSON: DRAFT INSTRUCTIONS, NOVEMBER 1849[1]

SIR,

I have to inform you that H.M. Govt. have had under their consideration the several interesting Reports which you made to them through the late Consul General Warrington at Tripoli of your travels through parts of the great Desert of Sahara; and of your Residence at Ghat, Ghadames, & Moorzook in the years 1845 & 1846; and understanding that you are desirous of undertaking a second and more extensive Expedition into that part of Africa, H.M. Govt. have decided to sanction your projected Journey, & to provide certain Funds towards the expense of it.

I have further to inform you that the Govt. of His Prussian Majesty have proposed to H.M. Govt. that Dr. Barth, a distinguished African Traveller, & a member of the University of Berlin, and Dr. Overweg, a Geologist, & a Member of the Geographical Society at Berlin,

[1] F.O. 101/23. *Lord Palmerston* was Foreign Secretary almost continuously, 1830–41, and again, 1846–51. He was Home Secretary, 1852–3, and Prime Minister, 1856, 1857–8 and 1859. *James Richardson* was a member of the Anti-Slavery Society and had written three books of travels from materials collected in the Sahara, 1845–6. The mission to Lake Chad was proposed by Richardson to Palmerston, 5 October 1848, as a 'Journey of Exploration and Philanthropy'. A second draft of his instructions in November 1849 commissioned him to enter into treaties with chiefs on the basis of the 1844 revised treaty (see below, p. 164) with extra articles on trade. Palmerston, in the same month, also agreed to allow Barth and Overweg to proceed beyond Lake Chad—without Richardson if necessary (draft memorandum, November 1849). The early journals and letters from the expedition are in F.O. 101/26 and 34.

should accompany you in your journey; and H.M. Govt. have gladly accepted this handsome offer deeming it an important advantage to have thus secured the assistance of these eminent & distinguished persons in the prosecution of those investigations with a view to which your Expedition is to be undertaken.

The Experience which you have acquired in your former travels in the Interior of Africa, and your knowledge of the habits & manners of the African Arabs, will tend to afford you facilities for your intended Journey, and will be useful in directing and in assisting your inquiries.

The Countries you are about to visit are as yet so little known to the Nations of Europe that every information of every kind respecting them which you may be able to collect will be interesting & useful; but besides those Political & Scientific Subjects of investigation to which your attention will of course be directed, it is the wish of H.M. Govt. that you should specially endeavour to ascertain by what means the Commercial intercourse between Great Britain and Africa might be extended and developed; what are the Districts and what the Lines of communication in that Country which offer the greatest facilities for Commerce; what are the European Commodities which are most sought after by the Natives; and what are the main articles of African produce which could best be obtained in payment for the productions of Europe.

You will not fail to take advantage of every suitable opportunity to impress upon the minds of the African Chiefs with whom you may come in contact, the great advantages which they and their country would derive from the extension of Legitimate Commerce with the Natives of other parts of the World; and you will assure them that H.M. Govt. in seeking to put an end to the trade in Slaves are endeavouring most effectually to promote the welfare & prosperity of the Nations of Africa.

Though the general conduct of the Expedition will be entrusted to your guidance [D. and discretion] yet it will be your duty, as I am convinced it will be your desire, to act with entire unreserve and in the most cordial union with the Prussian Gentlemen with whom you are to be associated; and you will of course give all due attention to their wishes & suggestions with respect to the course of your common Proceedings.

You will as far as circumstances may admit keep yourself in communication with H.M. Consular Agents in Africa; and those Officers have been instructed to afford you every assistance in their power to aid you and your companions in the performance of the Duties which you have undertaken.

12

H. U. ADDINGTON TO THE SECRETARY TO THE ADMIRALTY: EXPEDITION TO THE NIGER AND BENUE, 15 APRIL 1853[1]

SIR,

By accounts received either directly at this Office or indirectly through the Prussian Minister at this Court, from Drs. Barth and Overweg, who accompanied Mr. Richardson in his expedition, by Tripoli and Mourzuk, into the Interior of Africa, and who, since Mr. Richardson's death, have been engaged in pushing their researches far to the Southward of Lake Tchad, the great fact seems to be already established that a vast navigable river, in connexion with the Quorra or Niger, exists in the very heart of Central Africa, having its source towards the 9th. degree of N. Latitude and the 14th. or 15th. degree of East Longitude, & flowing in a broad & deep stream from East to West until under the names of the Tchadda & the Benue, it joins the Quorra, or Niger, about the 8th degree of N. Latitude.

The Reports respecting this great & important watercourse, which have been received at this office direct from Drs. Barth and Overweg are somewhat disjointed, having been written at various times in the course of their adventurous travels; but a map of the countries explored by those enterprizing travellers, wh. has been transmitted by Dr. Barth to this office, is now in the hands of Mr. Petermann, the Hydrographer, who is also thoroughly acquainted with the whole course of Drs. Barth's & Overweg's proceedings & who, on being called on, will be able to point out to the Admiralty in detail, the Districts, hitherto unknown, which have been laid open by those intrepid & persevering Pioneers of Science.

The maps when ready will be communicated to the Admiralty. In the meantime I enclose herewith Extracts from a Letter which the Chevalier Bunsen has addressed to this office, and which give the most connected account in the possession of the office of the great fact above recorded.

It appears to the Earl of Clarendon that considering the importance of so vast a Channel in Central Africa to the Commerce of this Country, & the increase in power which may also be acquired by means of such access to the interior of Africa for the repression of the Slave Trade, no time whould be lost in thoroughly exploring the River so stated to exist.

I am therefore directed by His Lordship to request that you will call the attention of the first Lord of the Admiralty to this matter, and

[1] F.O. 101/34. *Henry Addington* was Under-Secretary at the Foreign Office, 1842–54. Richardson had died in March 1851, a few days' march from Lake Chad. Barth was requested to take charge of the expedition, with the same instructions. H. Barth, *Travels and Discoveries in North and Central Africa*. 5 vols. London, 1857. For Petermann's maps see particularly vol. 2, nos. vii, viii, and vol. 5, no. xiv.

that you will state to him, that in Ld. Clarendon's opinion, it wld. be desirable to make preparations for sending out a Steam Vessel of fitting dimensions and Steam power, & otherwise properly equipped, with instructions to the officer, who may be appointed to command her, to ascend the Qworra, or Niger, to the point of confluence of the Tchadda, and up the large navigable branches of that River, which are credibly stated, if not actually shown to exist at least as high as 400 miles from the point of confluence of the Tchadda and Niger.

It is believed that in the season of the rains when the rivers are full, that is between the end of June and the end of Septr., the navigation of the Qworra and the Tchadda may be effected rapidly & without difficulty.

13

DRAFT INSTRUCTIONS TO CONSUL JOHN BEECROFT: EXPEDITION TO THE NIGER AND BENUE, MAY 1854[1]

SIR,

Her Majesty's Government having determined to send an expedition to the river Chadda in Central Africa, and understanding that you have expressed your willingness to be the leader of such an expedition, and H.M. Secretary of State for Foreign Affairs having granted permission to you to be absent from your Consulate, I am commanded by my Lords Commissioners of the Admiralty to acquaint you that they have accepted your offer, and you are hereby directed to take charge of the expedition for exploring the river Chadda, and all those forming a part of the said expedition are required to obey your orders.

You will be accompanied by Dr. Baikie,[2] M.D. a medical officer of the Royal Navy who is a naturalist, and has been preparing himself during the past year with this object. Possibly also Dr. Beach, Ph.D. of Bonn, an Ethnologist, will be of the party. It is further understood that the Revd. Mr. Crowther,[3] from Sierra Leone, will avail himself of this opportunity of ascending the river.

[1] F.O. 2/18, ff. 91–93A and v. In Admiralty to F.O., 14 May 1854. The plan for a new scientific expedition to the Niger was accepted by the Admiralty, 30 April 1853. *John Beecroft* had been explorer, trader, and Governor of Fernando Po for Spain, 1843–9, and was British Consul to the Bights of Benin and Biafra, 1849–54. He accepted this appointment in Feburary 1854, requesting instructions giving 'free scope to my own judgment'. The instructions were approved by the Foreign Office, 23 May 1854.

[2] In July 1854 the Foreign Office was informed of Beecroft's ill-health and later of his death. *Dr. William Balfour Baikie* who took command of the expedition after its arrival at Fernando Po had served in the Mediterranean and at Haslar Hospital. He successfully penetrated as far as the Hausa states and returned without loss of life. See his *Narrative of an Exploring Voyage up the Niger*. London, 1856; and Foreign Office, Confidential Print, 1855 [132].

[3] *Samuel Adjai Crowther*, C.M.S. missionary teacher and later Bishop of Western Equatorial Africa, 1864–92.

The vessel prepared for this expedition is the 'Pleiad', an iron screw-steamer of 260 tons burthen, rigged as a schooner. She is 100 feet in length, 24 feet beam, engines of 60 horse power, and having 7 feet draught of water, with three months provisions and stores on board, and 20 days coal of 12 hours each. She is officially reported on her trial of speed at Liverpool to have made 10 knots an hour in smooth water. There will be, in addition to this vessel, two 50 feet sectional iron trade boats and the Consular boat, all three of which will be towed from Fernando Po as far as the entrance of the Chadda, or farther if necessary.

The expedition has two main objects. One is to explore the river Chadda or Benueh, the Eastern branch of the Kawára, from Dagbó, the highest point reached by Oldfield and Allen in 1833[1], to the country of Adamauá, a distance of about 400 miles, where the river was crossed at the junction of the Benueh and Faro by Dr. Barth in June 1851; and thence again, if the season permits and the waters are still rising, to the limit of navigation.

The other is to endeavour to meet and afford assistance to that excellent traveller Dr. Barth, who left England for Africa towards the start of the year 1849, and who from the latest accounts received from him, would after reaching Tumbuktu, make his way to the banks of the Benueh. On all occasions every possible enquiry is to be made for Dr. Barth, and no presents spared in endeavouring to obtain information respecting him. The same instructions hold good respecting Dr. Vogel, who left England in 1853, and who may have succeeded in penetrating to the banks of the Chadda.

In carrying out these two objects it is the desire of Her Majesty's Government, for the benefit of commerce and civilization, to take advantage of every opportunity for opening trade with the Natives at each large town on the banks of the river, and within a moderate distance on either side. One hundred pounds worth of suitable presents and samples of goods have been supplied by Government for this purpose, to be delivered to you by the Sailing Master of the 'Pleiad', and a list of which is enclosed. These are to be freely given on all occasions, it is left to your judgment to limit the amount, but the practice is always to be observed in conformity with the custom of the Country. It is further desirable to make careful enquiries as to the political power of the several chiefs, as to the state of civilization among them, as to the existence of foreign slave trade, and, if so, whether they would consent to put an end to it, if lawful trade could be insured to them, and a market opened for the ivory, and other products of their country. Mr. Crowther will naturally enquire into the apparent disposition, willingness, or aptitude of the Natives to receive religious or secular instruction.

From your experience as a traveller in Central Africa, it is almost

[1] See below, p. 107 and n.

unnecessary to give you any detailed instructions, yet it is right to call your attention to the most recent and best Map of Central Africa accompanied by a Memorandum compiled by Mr. Petermann from the papers of Messrs. Richardson, Barth, Overweg, and Vogel, placed at his disposal by the Earl of Clarendon, H.M. Secretary of State for Foreign Affairs. A copy of this work is supplied for your use. In it you will see that the town of Doma on the north of the Chadda, Wukári the capital of Korrórofa on the South, Juggum a settlement of the Koána, Hamárrua, and Yola the capital of Adamaua are places of importance. Wukári is described as a very large town lying 8 miles South of the river, and the capital of the populous country of Korrorofa, with the chief of which it is hoped an extensive trade may be established. Within 30 miles of Yola, Mount Alantika is said to reach an altitude of 10,000 feet; if the highest point could be attained it would be an admirable position for a round of angles or bearings, as on a clear day in that climate, the radius of vision from it would be fully 100 miles.

It is essential as you ascend the Chadda to make a rapid survey of the windings of the river noting the depths of water, and width of stream, with the character and height of its banks, laying the work down at once on prepared sheets of paper by careful compass bearings, and measured on estimated distances, checking the whole by astronomical observations at every halt for the night.

For this latter purpose you will be provided with three Chronometers and the necessary instruments. In using the Compass it must not be forgotten that the observations are made on board an iron ship; and all bearings should therefore be taken from the standard compass, and carefully corrected for local deviation, which should be ascertained by swinging the vessel at Fernando Po before starting, and testing it every evening by bearings of the Pole Star, which in those latitudes will be always within 7° or 8° of the horizon. On all occasions you will endeavour to ascertain the height of any hill or mountain which may be in sight, if no means are afforded of measuring it by angles or by barometer, never omit to estimate its altitude, and mark down its position and height while on the spot. Trust nothing to memory.

In the Admiralty Manual of Scientific Enquiry, a copy of which is supplied, you will find useful suggestions in geography, hydrography, and in all other departments of science.

Dr. Baikie is to act as Medical Adviser to your party. He has been supplied with all the necessary medicines, and a sufficient stock also to enable him to prescribe for the Natives whose goodwill is readily obtained by medical advice and medicine, more so perhaps than by any other means. It will therefore be politic to offer his services on many occasions.

Dr. Baikie will also act as Naturalist to the Expedition; he is so well acquainted with the branches of Zoology and Botany that no special instructions are required, but a few suggestions are offered by Professor Edward Forbes,[1] as well as some Hints on Geology by Sir Roderick Murchison,[2] on Ethnology by Dr. Latham,[3] and on Terrestrial Magnetism by Colonel Sabine,[4] with instruments, instructions, and blank forms for Meteorological Observations. You will see that Dr. Baikie is provided with boats or the necessary means for facilitating his researches, and that every care be taken of any collections he may make.

The Commander of the 'Pleiad' is engaged to comply with all your requisitions as you will observe by a copy of the Contract, and if his Instructions from his Owners which are are annexed.

The 'Pleiad' being armed with a 12 pounder pivot gun, four swivels, Minié rifles and double barrelled guns for the Officers, muskets for the crew and with boarding nettings of wire, it is not probable that she will meet with any opposition in the lower parts of the river, where there may be danger. But you will remember that the best security from attack consists in the Natives knowing you are well prepared to meet it. At the same time you are strictly enjoined to use the greatest forbearance towards the people, and while returning proper formness in the event of any misunderstanding, to endeavour to conciliate, as far as can possibly be admitted with safety to your party. You will on all occasions enforce the strictest justice, and never on any account permit one of your party to illtreat, insult, or cheat the Natives.

You will comply with the First Article of War in Her Majesty's Naval Service, in causing Divine worship to be celebrated on board on Sundays, and allow no unnecessary work to be done, or trading operations to be carried on on that day. At the same time you will be careful to observe the spirit rather than the letter of the law, and never allow the vessel or your party to remain in any dangerous or unhealthy position or risk being caught on a falling river, or defer any work of positive necessity on that day.

You should not delay your departure from Fernando Po beyond the 1st. July at latest, if the vessel can be ready it would be better to leave earlier, as this late period will only leave you two months for your ascent of the river, since you must commence your return voyage as soon as the river ceases to rise, probably about the beginning of September.

[1] Naturalist, Professor of Botany, King's College, London.
[2] President of the Royal Geographical Society.
[3] R. G. Latham, philologist and director of the ethnological department of the Crystal Palace.
[4] Sir Edmund Sabine, general secretary of the British Association and later president of the Royal Society.

In the possible, but it is trusted most improbable case of the loss of the 'Pleiad' on any of the numerous rocks and banks which may be expected in an unexplored river, the Consular boat and two trade boats will ensure you the means of a safe return to the sea, and their Lordships will direct the Mail packets to call off the mouth of the river each voyage from the middle of September to the end of the year, to make enquiries as to your safety, and to afford you assistance in case of need.

During the whole of the expedition you will keep a full journal of your proceedings, and if an opportunity offers of sending home despatches from time to time you will not fail to avail yourself of it transmitting at the same time a tracing, however rough, of the chart of the river as far as you may have advanced, so that in case of accident to your own papers, the results of the expedition so far, will be recorded...

[Beecroft is to resume his consular duties after the expedition.]

Finally you are strictly enjoined to be careful of the health of the party entrusted to your charge, and to afford them the benefit of your experience as to the best mode of maintaining health in African rivers; and should, unfortunately, fever break out and assume a threatening appearance, you are to remember that you are not called upon to persevere in the ascent of the river, but that your first care is the safety of your people.

14

DRAFT INSTRUCTIONS TO DR. W. B. BAIKIE: EXPEDITION TO THE NIGER, 1 MAY 1857[1]

SIR,
Her Majesty's Government having decided to send an expedition to Central Africa [D: with a view to the extinction of the Foreign Slave Trade] and having understood that you have expressed your willingness to be the leader of such an expedition, and the Lords Commissioners of the Admiralty having given their sanction thereto, I have [D: directed by Her Majesty's Principal Secretary of State for Foreign Affairs] to acquaint you that your offer has been accepted, and you are hereby directed to take charge of the expedition for exploring the rivers of Central Africa, and all the officers and men forming part thereof are required to obey your orders. . . .

[1] F.O. 2/23, ff. 190–205. *Macgregor Laird* (see below, p. 114, n.), explorer and shipbuilder, was the principal source of inspiration for the new series of Niger expeditions. By Articles of Agreement with the Admiralty, 1 January 1857, he contracted to send one steamer out annually for five years for a government subsidy of £35,000. The *Dayspring* was wrecked in January 1858, and subsequent failures to assure regular contact left Baikie isolated at Bida and Lokoja. Baikie's voluminous reports on the interior before his death in 1864 are in F.O. 2/23, 32, 34 and 97/433, and have yet to be fully studied to assess his contribution to the history of Nigeria.

[He is to be accompanied by Lieutenant Glover, R.N., Mr. Daniel May, Second Master, R.N., Assistant Surgeon Davis, R.N., a geologist, a botanist, and the Revd. Samuel Crowther, on the *Dayspring*, a steamer of 170 tons.]

4. The main objects of the expedition are, to explore the river Niger and its tributaries, to ascertain the natural productions and capabilities of the countries through which they flow; to enter into friendly relations with the native chiefs; to facilitate the return of liberated Africans to their homes; and practically to show the advantage of legitimate trade over the debasing and demoralizing traffic in slaves.

With these ends in view the steps to be taken would appear to be:

1st. To lay a firm foundation of friendly intercourse and establish a good understanding not only with the tribes that inhabit the more immediate banks of the rivers Kawára and Bénueh, and their tributaries, but with the people and chiefs of that portion of Africa generally of which those rivers form the principal outlets.

2nd. By frequently putting up and down the river in the steamer to convince the Natives who dwell near the lower portion of the Kawára that their habit of attacking the canoes of other tribes, and levying heavy tolls upon all goods that pass up and down the stream can on longer be tolerated [D: and so to establish a system of river police that will keep] that the highway of the river shall be kept open [D: and permit] for all persons to trade without let or hindrance to all parts of the [D: river] country that may wish, and especially that the liberated Africans from Sierra Leone may be enabled to return unmolested and with a feeling of security to their relative homes.

3rd. To navigate as far as practicable the upper waters of the Kawára and Bénueh and their affluents, as well as the lagoons and network or rivers that form the Delta, in order to ascertain the full advantage that may be derived from water communication either by canoes or steamers of light draught. Also by means of journeys by land to open out the principal routes by which the liberated Africans resident at Abbeokúta and in the Yaribah country to the west, may freely trade with Rabbah and Busah, and the Housah country on the east; and to explore the hitherto unvisited, and it is believed the fertile and wealthy, district of Adamáwa lying to the southward of the headwaters of the Bénueh.

Lastly, to embrace every opportunity of friendly intercourse with the natives, to point out the suicidal effects of the foreign slave trade to impress upon them the advantages of lawful trade, the benefit they would derive from an exchange of the natural productions of Africa for the manufactures of Europe, the probable advantage that would arise to them from the culture of cotton, and generally to hold out every encouragement in order to induce them to give up their warlike and predatory habits and substitute instead the more peaceable pursuits of agriculture and commerce.

5. All accounts concur in representing the Fellatah Chief, whose principal residence is at Sákatú, as the most influential and powerful in Central Africa. It is of importance therefore in the outset of your proceeding that friendly relations and direct communication should be opened and established with him; you will therefore be accredited by H.M. Government to Alibu[1] the Sultan of Sákatú, and you will lose no time in proceeding to that place well provided with suitable presents, and you will remain there as long as may be necessary to accomplish your object. . . .

[The route to Sokoto is through Rabba and Bussa; list of equipment needed.]

9. During your absence on this journey a good opportunity will be afforded to the party left on board the Steamer for opening a trade with the very populous town of Rabbah, said to contain 40,000 inhabitants. It is most desirable, both on the present and on all occasions to impress upon the chiefs and people that you are there as traders, not as colonists, not as acquirers of land, but simply as traders and as protectors of trade. This title is fully understood and recognized by all natives in Central Africa, and in all your language, and by every act you and all your people should be careful to make it appear that such is the *bona fide* intention and desire of Great Britain. The two or three months that the steamer will spend at Rabbah, could not be more usefully or more profitably employed than in impressing upon the people this fact . . .

[He may visit Yoruba country from Rabba. The steamer is to go to the Benue where Laird intends to establish a trading station.]

13. It will now be necessary to despatch the steamer on her biennial trip down the river to Fernando Po, and probably to Lagos. The Captain of the vessel, or the officer who goes in command, should be charged to call at all the trading stations on his way, to make enquiries whether any acts of aggression have been committed, to express the disapproval of H.M.'s Govt. of all the acts of aggression and its determination to uphold the aggrieved party however small or weak. At the same time he will not fail to make a present to each of the chiefs who may have acted a friendly part, as an encouragement to persevere in similar conduct. Such is to be the practice in cases of passing up and down the river, and Her Majesty's Government attach much importance to this instruction being strictly complied with, in order that the steamer by her visits and her presence may impart a feeling of security to the lawful trader, and protect any establishment that may be found . . .

[If possible the Lagos lagoons and the Calabar river are to be explored. Specifications of the *Dayspring*; personnel; equipment.]

[1] Aliyu Babba, Sultan of Sokoto, 1842–59.

II

LEGITIMATE TRADE

A. NAVIGATION ACTS AND TARIFFS

Introductory Note

THE two fundamentals of colonial mercantilism—the exclusion of foreign manufactures and the use of British vessels in the carrying trade—were not strictly enforced at the Company forts in the eighteenth century; and although the Law Officers of the Crown were prepared to classify these factories as British Plantations in 1787 and prohibit importation of American rum, this definition of the West African settlements found no favour among the merchants and was allowed to lapse. In Sierra Leone, however, both before and after transfer to the Crown, foreign vessels were excluded from trade; and, by a Colonial Act of 22 August 1812 (C.O.269/1), a differential tariff of 4 per cent. applied to goods of foreign origin landed at Freetown. The same regulations were extended to Bathurst in 1822 and to the Gold Coast forts as dependencies of Sierra Leone, 1821–8. Thereafter, the forts escaped the restrictions which hampered the trade of the northern ports till the resumption of Crown control in 1843.

From 1815 till 1834, Bathurst and Freetown traders were slow to benefit from the relaxation of the Navigation Acts, though United Kingdom duties on imports of African produce were progressively reduced. Most of the local African markets lay outside the colonies themselves; and after 1817 there was strong competition from the French, increased by the reoccupation of the factory at Albreda in 1819 and by the creation of an entrepôt at Gorée in 1822. Gorée furnished the whole of the Guinea Coast with goods of many origins, while British traders were still required to import directly from the United Kingdom and were forbidden to make transhipments between the two northern settlements and the Gold Coast forts after 1821.

The early governors of Sierra Leone did their best to mitigate the worst effects of the system. Governor MacCarthy, after assimilating the Gold Coast forts to the tariff policy of Sierra Leone and applying duties of 2 per cent. on British and 6 per cent. on foreign goods landed at Cape Coast and Accra, tried, in vain, to obtain permission to admit foreign vessels. It was not till 1825 that French vessels could safely enter the Gambia and run past Bathurst to Albreda, contrary to the wishes of British merchants who were still prohibited from the Senegal and the Casamance. When Bathurst itself was opened to foreign vessels for the export of timber and hides, the provisions of freer trade, as consolidated in Acts of 1825 (6 Geo. IV, c. 73 and 114) were considered in relation to West African conditions as a whole and a complicated exchange of correspondence in 1828 between the Commissioners of Customs, the Board of Trade, and the Treasury determined which statutes were to be extended to the West African settlements. Although this was done by an Order in Council of 12 October 1829, many of the older regulations were left in force for want of local enactments, until Acting Governor Cole swept them away in 1834 and consolidated in one Colonial Act for Sierra Leone the main features of the British Possessions Acts for North America and Mauritius. This Act of 1834 went beyond the principles of reciprocity which had set limits to British free trade. But it was not repealed; and its provisions were extended to Bathurst in February 1835. The few restrictions that remained on the importation of certain articles by French vessels were waived for the Gambia in 1837 where the only alternative to complete freedom of trade was widespread smuggling and loss of revenue. In 1846, by the Act of 9 & 10 Vict., c. 94, British colonies were permitted to repeal these restrictions.

By 1849, the fiscal rather than the mercantilist aspect of West African trade was more important at the settlements. Two Orders in Council of that year drew up a complex set of rules covering port entry, collection of fees, and warehousing for Sierra Leone and the Gambia. In 1852 the general supervision of the Board of Customs was ended and a new Order in Council made the government of each settlement responsible for controlling conditions of trade and raising revenue on goods and shipping according to financial needs.

I

R. P. ARDEN, A. McDONALD (LAW OFFICERS) TO THE COMMISSIONERS OF CUSTOMS: FOREIGN IMPORTS INTO THE SETTLEMENTS, 22 JULY 1787[1]

MESSRS. ATTORNEY AND SOLICITOR GENERAL are requested to give their opinion:

Whether there is any Law which prohibits the Importation of American or other Foreign Rum in British or Foreign Ships either into the British Settlements or Factories on the Coast of Africa or into the Countries on the said Coast in Alliance with the British Nation?

Opinion.

No goods whatever can be imported into a British Plantation but in British built Ships manned and navigated according to Law—with respect to Foreign Rum, by which we suppose is meant Rum the produce of the American States or of some Foreign Plantation in

[1] B.T. 6/7. Encl. in Custom House to Board of Trade, 8 August 1787, in reply to a request for instructions from the Committee of African Merchants by the Governor and Council of Cape Coast.

America, We find no Law whereby the Importation of the same is prohibited if made in British built Ships. The Act of the 4th Geo. 3 Ch. 15. S 10[1] prohibits the Importation of Foreign Rum into any of His Majesty's Colonies or Plantations in *America*, and the 15 Ch. 2 C. 7. S 6.[2] prohibits the importation into any British Plantation of goods the produce of Manufacture of Europe, except immediately from England (now extended to Scotland and Ireland). But the importation of American commodities though of Foreign growth or manufacture into a plantation on the Coast of Africa does not appear to us, upon the best search we have been able to make, to be prohibited by any Law, supposing the Regulations with Respect to Ships and packages be complied with, and therefore we are of opinion that it would be proper that a prohibitory Law[3] should be proposed to Parliament at their next meeting for the purpose of preventing a commerce which must be extremely injurious to the British Planter or British Distiller.

2

MERCHANTS OF LIVERPOOL TO THE COM-MITTEE OF THE COMPANY OF MERCHANTS: TRADE REGULATIONS, 5 JUNE 1815[4]

GENTLEMEN,

We beg leave to state to you, in the hope that you will represent the same to His Majesty's Government, that the trade to the Coast of Africa is exposed to the most serious interruption, and that many merchants and ship-owners engaged in it, have been subjected to very heavy losses by the proceedings of the persons exercising authority at Sierra Leone, who have lately made numerous seizures of vessels and goods, upon the pretence that the owners or masters have been guilty of some infraction of the revenue and navigation laws of Great Britain.

As the particular cases will be made the subject of individual remonstrance or procedure on the part of the persons aggrieved, we do not think it necessary to go into the details of them on the present occasion, but we beg to submit to your consideration the necessity of obtaining, as soon as possible, some public declaration from Government, in what light merchants and ship-owners are to consider the British Settlements on the Coast of Africa.

Until the last 12 or 18 months, we believe the trade to the British

---

[1] Lord Grenville's 'Sugar' Act of 1764.   [2] The Staple Act of 1663.
[3] This prohibition against American imports of rum into the African settlements was not, however, contained in the Act of 1788, 28 Geo. III, c. 6, which regulated exports from British possessions in the West Indies and North America.
[4] *Parl. Papers*, 1816, vii (506), p. 84.

Settlements in Africa had, from the periods of their original establishment, been subject to no restrictions but such as arise out of war; but now, under some local regulations, the persons holding office at Sierra Leone have thought fit to make, of which no publication that we can learn has ever been made in England, those persons exercise the power of demanding the papers of every vessel that touches at that place, and, without regard to what the intention of the parties may be, if any thing appears to them to be contrary to the strict regulations of the Revenue Laws, as applicable to the British plantations, an immediate seizure, condemnation and sale, is the inevitable consequence.

Being satisfied that the Government, in conferring upon the officers at Sierra Leone the necessary power to put a stop to the Slave Trade, and to introduce and encourage a different species of commerce in its stead, could never intend to give them the destructive authority which they now exercise without restraint, to the ruin of a valuable trade that would otherwise be established with that country; we entreat that you will, as soon as possible, take the requisite measures for making Government acquainted with this most serious evil, being perfectly assured, that nothing more is necessary to the attainment of a speedy remedy.

In the cases of seizures and condemnations which have occurred, the claimants in general find the greatest difficulty in prosecuting an appeal, from the almost impossibility of finding persons competent and willing to undertake the task of serving the officers in question with the Admiralty Process, for compelling the transmission of the accounts and proceeds; and we therefore beg particularly to call your attention to the necessity of some general peremptory order being given, for the immediate transmission of the accounts and proceeds to this country.

We are, &c.

J. & N. Bold & Co, John Caton, W. McIver, Hughes & Tobins, Philip Quirk & Co, Geo. Robertson, James Penny & Co, J. & R. Fisher, Thos. Brancker, Robert Kitchen, Mercer & Antrobus.

3

JOHN REEVES TO THE COMMITTEE FOR TRADE: TRADE REGULATIONS, 6 JULY 1816[1]

... In obedience to Their Lordships' Commands, I have considered the case of Seizure, made by the Custom House officer at Sierra Leone, of British Goods there imported from Senegal, under Stat. 15 Car: 2 c. 7.

[1] C.O. 267/44. *John Reeves* was Law Clerk to the Committee of the Council for Trade and Foreign Plantations. This opinion was forwarded to the Colonial Office, 8 July 1816.

The design of that Statute was, to confine to the Mother Country the whole supply of European articles to the Colonies: no European Goods are to be imported into the Colonies from any other place; they must go direct from this Kingdom.

Whatever might heretofore be argued in favour of such importation from one Colony to another, as if it might be allowed in respect of goods that had once been imported conformably with the act, such construction seems more to be quite taken away by Stat. 45 Geo. 3 c. 57[1] and Stat. 50 Geo. 3 c. 100. These acts permit such an importation of European goods from one colony to another in America and the West Indies. They are, therefore, a testimony of the practice, which needed such a parliamentary interposition; and they are a legislative declaration, what ought to be the construction in the present case; namely that an importation of European goods cannot be made at Sierra Leone from Senegal, till it shall be permitted in like manner, by these two Acts, between Colonies in the West Indies & America. . . .

4

COMMITTEE FOR TRADE: STATEMENT OF PROPOSED DUTIES ON AFRICAN IMPORTS, 1 DECEMBER 1818[2]

Articles of African Produce	Present Duty £. s. d.			Proposed Duty £. s. d.		
Elephants' Teeth viz						
weighing about 21 lbs. each, the Cwt.	3	19	2	4	–	–
weighing 21 lbs. each, or under the Cwt.	3	19	2	2	–	–
Gold Dust Duty free						
Grains, viz						
Guinea Grains, the lb.	–	–	$9^{10/20}$	–	2	–
Grains of Paradise the lb.	–	1	$11^{15/20}$	–	2	–
Gum Senegal the Cwt.	–	11	$10^{10/20}$	–	12	–
Arabic the Cwt.	–	11	$10^{10/20}$	–	12	–
Copal the lb.	–	1	7	–	1	8
Hides viz						
Buffalo, Bull, Cow, or Ox Hides, in the Hair, not being tanned, tawed, curried, nor in any way dress'd, imported from the West Coast of Africa—The Hide	–	–	$4^{15/20}$	–	–	6

[1] The Free Port Act for the West Indies (which still excluded American vessels).
[2] C.O. 267/48. Duties on important staples were further reduced. By May 1840, palm oil paid 1s. 3d. per cwt., and in 1843 this was lowered to 6d.

Articles of African Produce	Present Duty £. s. d.			Proposed Duty £. s. d.		
Palm oil, the Cwt.	–	6	4	–	2	6
Guinea Pepper the lb.	–	1	7	–	2	6
Rice						
The Produce of, and imported directly from any British Colony, Plantation, or Territory, the Cwt.	–	7	6 5/20	–	2	6
Bees Wax, unmanufactured, the Cwt.	3	6	6	3	6	6
Wood viz Bar Woods, for every £100 of the Value	20	–	–	–	15	–
Red or Guinea Wood, the Ton	1	18	–	–	15	–
Cam Woods. The Ton	1	18	–	–	15	–
Ebony the Ton	1	–	7	–	15	–
Cotton Wool. The 100 lbs.	–	8	7	–	8	7
Teak Wood, the Growth & Production of the West Coast of Africa & imported directly from thence 8 Inches Square or upwards, the Load containing 50 Cubic Feet	–	–	–	1	10	–

5

THOMAS LACK TO WILMOT HORTON: ADMISSION OF FOREIGN VESSELS, 30 AUGUST 1823[1]

SIR,

Having laid before the Lords of the Committee of Privy Council for Trade your Letter of the 9th. Inst. inclosing Copy of a Letter from Governor Sir Charles Macarthy[2] requesting permission to admit Foreign Vessels to carry on Trade with the British Forts on the Gold Coast, as was the case previous to the abolition of the late African Company; I am directed to acquaint you, for the information of Earl Bathurst, that the Lords of the Committee do not conceive that there exists any Authority under which such a permission can be granted; and that they consequently are of opinion, that if the Ports are to be opened to Foreign Vessels in the manner proposed by Governor Macarthy, he must do it either upon his own Responsibility, acting from the Necessity of the Case, or under special

[1] C.O. 267/59. *Thomas Lack* was Clerk to the Committee for Trade. *Robert Wilmot Horton* was Under-Secretary for War and Colonies, 1821–7.

[2] *Governor Sir Charles MacCarthy* administered Sierra Leone and the Forts, 1814–24, before his death on the Gold Coast.

Instructions from the Secretary of State for the Colonies, in either of which cases a Bill of Indemnity may be necessary.[1]

6

RESOLUTIONS OF THE GAMBIA BOARD OF COMMERCE, 1 AUGUST 1827[2]

[France dominates the trade of the Gambia, using Albreda and the free port of Gorée; American tobacco is thereby admitted at a lower price than tobacco transhipped from England.]

. . . THE Board is of opinion that the Settlement at Bathurst, bears no relation whatever with our West India Colonies, and whatever the difference may be between Great Britain and America with respect to the trade of these Colonies, it is unfair that they should extend it to the interest of this Infant Settlement, with the French Factory at Albreda, in the vicinity, and where it is impossible to prevent Tobacco being imported direct from America through Goree.

7

THOMAS LACK TO R. W. HAY: FOREIGN TRADE WITH THE GAMBIA, 14 NOVEMBER 1827[3]

SIR,

The Lords of the Committee of Privy Council for Trade having received a Petition from Messrs Forster & Smith,[4] stating, that the Collector of Duties at St. Mary's, on the River Gambia, has refused, until he has instructions from Home, to allow the Merchants there, to sell and ship to Foreigners any of the Red Teake Wood, of which the Petitioners have, after great Exertions and Expence, made a Trade in the River; I am directed to transmit to you, a Copy of the said Petition and also a copy of a Report from the Commissioners of His Majesty's Customs, wherein it is stated that St Mary's being a British Possession in Africa, within the meaning of the Colonial and Navigation Law, there is nothing to prevent Foreign Ships generally [A. provided they be the Vessels of States which reciprocate] from taking in Cargoes at that place for the purpose of being carried to Foreign Countries; and as it appears from a recent Enquiry which

[1] By Statute 34 Geo. III, c. 35, for example, governors might be indemnified for permitting trade in foreign vessels in cases of necessity.
[2] C.O. 267/83. Signed Edward Lloyd, Thomas Chosen, William Forster, Charles Johnston, C. Grant; encl. in Lumley to Goderich, 30 August 1827.
[3] C.O. 267/84. This ruling was reported in Huskisson to Lumley, 20 November 1827: C.O. 268/28, ff. 35–36.
[4] Forster and Smith to the Committee for Trade, 16 October 1826: C.O. 267/84.

has been made by their Lordships' Directions, that the Collector of Duties still persists in his refusal to permit such Shipments, I am to request that you will move Mr. Secretary Huskisson to give the necessary directions for acquainting the Collector that such practice is contrary to the true intent and meaning of the Act of 6. Geo: 4. C: 114.[1] the provisions of which Act, apply both to the Import and Export Trade of that Settlement. . . .

[A copy of the Order in Council of 16 July 1827 setting out the privileges of foreign countries trading with British possessions is to be sent to the Gambia.]

8

THE COMMISSIONERS OF CUSTOMS TO THE TREASURY: REGULATION OF WEST AFRICAN TRADE, 27 SEPTEMBER 1828[2]

. . . WE have received a Report from the Collector at Sierra Leone[3] . . . representing that the existing Colonial Laws are inadequate to the due Protection of the Revenue, and suggesting that some of the Provisions of the Act 6th Geo: 4th. Cap. 114 regulating the Trade of the British Possessions Abroad may be extended to that Colony; also stating that a doubt exists whether under His Majesty's Order in Council, dated the 16th. July 1827, all articles subject to an ad valorem Duty, may be imported into the British Possessions on the Western Coast of Africa, in French Ships, or such Goods only as are enumerated in the Table annexed to the Order in Council of the 1st. of June 1826.

That in our Memorial of the 6th May last, No. 34, founded upon a Letter from the Collector of the Customs at St Mary's Gambia, we submitted whether it might not be your Lordships' pleasure, that so much of the Table of Prohibitions contained in the Act 6th. Geo: 4th. Cap: 114. Sec. 7 as was then in force, should be extended to the British Possessions on the Western Coast of Africa, and with reference to the present Representation from the Collector at Sierra Leone, We take leave further to submit for your Lordships' Consideration, the expediency of an Order in Council being issued, under the Power vested in His Majesty, by the 3rd. Sect. of the said Act, extending to the Colony of Sierra Leone, and to other British Possessions on the Western Coast of Africa, the Provisions of the

---

[1] The British Possessions Act, 5 July 1825, which laid down the conditions of freer trade and reciprocity with foreign countries. West Africa was mentioned in Art. LXXIII which stated that trade there was to be regulated by Order in Council.
[2] C.O. 267/96. Signed G. Stewart, H. Richmond, W. T. Roi, C. C. Smith.
[3] Logan Hook to Commissioners of Customs, 18 April 1828, ibid.

following Acts, so far as the same relate to the Entry of Vessels and Goods Inwards and Outwards, and to the Prevention of Smuggling, vizt

6th Geo. 4th. C. 114

7th Geo. 4th. C. 48

7th & 8th Geo. 4th. C. 56

9th Geo. 4th. C. 76

and with respect to the Articles which are admissable in French Ships, We will with your Lordships' sanction, issue the same Instructions to the Collector at Sierra Leone as we proposed in our Memorial above mentioned, to transmit to the Collector at St Mary's Gambia, vizt. that the Order in Council of 16th July 1827 which permitted French Vessels to import into the British Possessions on the Western Coast of Africa, the Articles enumerated or described in the Table subjoined to the Order in Council of 1 July 1826 (except Wine, which by the Order in Council of 16th Decr. 1826, is excluded) refers to the Goods therein specified, and to such articles as are subject under the 6th. Geo. 4th. Cap. 114. Sec. 9th. to a duty ad valorem, not exceeding $7\frac{1}{2}$ Per Cent, upon Importation into the Possessions in America, and the West Indies, and does not refer to goods which are liable under Colonial Authority to a rate of Duty not exceeding $7\frac{1}{2}$ Per Cent upon Importation into the British Possessions on the Western Coast of Africa.

9

J. D. HUME TO R. W. HAY: GAMBIA DUTIES, 19 JANUARY 1830[1]

SIR,

The Lords of the Committee of Privy Council for Trade have had under their consideration your Letter of the 23d. November last, relating to the state of Trade of the Port of Bathurst in the River Gambia.

The Lords of this Committee assume from the observations contained in your Letter, that the Duties payable at the Port of Bathurst are not deemed by Sir George Murray, to be necessary for the local expenses of the Settlement, and as it appears that the Goods, to which the Duties attach, are wanted for the purposes of a Barter Trade with the neighbouring Tribes of Africans, their Lordships can see no objection to the removal of those Duties. But if the Merchants of Bathurst, when desiring that the privileges of a 'Free Port' may be extended to that Place, contemplate the general admission of

---

[1] C.O. 87/4. *J. D. Hume* who was largely responsible for consolidating British Customs laws in 1825 was joint-secretary to the Board of Trade, 1828–40.

all foreign vessels, the Lords of this Committee are of opinion that such admission cannot be granted to those vessels which are excluded by the Laws and by the Orders in Council made for regulating the Intercourse of foreign Vessels with British Possessions abroad.

10

ACTING GOVERNOR T. COLE TO T. SPRING-RICE: SIERRA LEONE DUTIES ACT, 25 NOVEMBER 1834[1]

SIR,

As great confusion and difficulty was likely to prevail in the Collection of the Revenue of the Colony in consequence of the accumulation of no less than thirteen Acts, and which must eventually have become a great embarrassment to commerce from the Merchant not being able to ascertain the amount of Duties for which he was liable, I have with the advice and consent of the Council deemed it proper to simplify the Laws as much as possible by consolidating those which have been passed from time to time into one Act, and which will show at one View the Resources from which the Revenue is derived.

The adoption of this measure is rendered the more desirable at the present time, it having been found expedient by His Majesty's Government to order the repeal of every Colonial Statute under which higher Tonnage Duties are imposed upon the Shipping of Foreign Countries (with which Conventions of Commerce extending to the Colonies subsist) than upon British Shipping or the Shipping of Sierra Leone.

In framing this Statute the Council have endeavoured to act strictly in accordance with the wishes of His Majesty's Government in order that the Duties which are established may not effect Navigation or Commerce, nor tend in any way to injure those interests which [it] is the object of the Government to protect.

The Duties previously to the passing of the present Act were levied under the following heads:—

1st. An import duty of 2 pr. cent upon British and 6 pr. cent upon Foreign Produce or Manufactures.

2nd. A Tonnage duty of 1s. per Ton Register measurement on all British Vessels and 1s. 6d. per Ton on all Foreign Vessels, at each entrance into the Port; Vessels built in any of the British Possessions on the Western Coast of Africa or owned by any person or persons

[1] C.O. 267/124. *Thomas Cole* was Colonial Secretary at Sierra Leone, 1834–40, and Acting Governor, 1834–35 and 1837. *Thomas Spring-Rice* was Secretary of State for War and Colonies, June–November 1834.

there resident and employed in Coasting and Dragueing [*sic*] subject to the said Duty once in every year.

3rd. Wharfage at the rate of 5s. pr. Ton, and for any quantity under a Ton landed, and for bulky articles such as lumber 7s./8d. for every 2,000 feet, and the same sum upon every 40 Cubic feet of Casks, Crates, hampers, boxes, containing Tin ware, Glass, etc.

4th. An Extra Duty of 1s. pr Gallon upon Rum and 1s./6d. upon Brandy, Gin, Geneva and Hollands.

5th. An additional duty of 1s. pr. Cwt. on Tobacco.

6th. A Duty of $2\frac{1}{2}$ pr. Cent upon the Gross amount of sales of all Prize Goods and Vessels.

The Collection of the first impost having been found open to much abuse, in consequence of its being left in a great measure to the Importer to make the Entry of his Goods, either as 'British' or 'Foreign', it has been thought advisable to equalise the Import Duty by fixing it at 3 pr. Centum and thus prevent the possibility of fraud, while at the same time it encourages a free interchange of Commodities with Foreign Countries (with which Conventions of Commerce have been made) and will tend rather to increase than diminish the Revenue.

The Act for levying the Second Impost having been disallowed by His Most Gracious Majesty in consequence of its exacting a discriminating Tonnage duty, the present rate is established at 9d. pr ton upon all British and Foreign Vessels.

The Third Impost has been altered in regard to the rate of wharfage to be charged for any quantity of goods landed under a Ton. Formerly it was fixed at five Shillings, and if a package of the size of a Hat Box, valued only at 4s. was landed, it became subject to the amount due upon a Ton. This has been much complained of, and the objection is removed by making the wharfage duty in the Present Act 2s./6d. for any Quantity under a Ton landed. The charge of 7s./6d. for every 40 Cubic feet of Bulky articles such as Casks, Crates, Hampers, Boxes, etc. has never been exacted, owing to the great difficulty and expense which must necessarily be incurred in employing extra landing waiters to ascertain the cubic contents; but the wharfage Duty having hitherto been collected upon all Packages, of this description as well as upon all others according to a comparative Table; the distinction is omitted in the present Act.

From 1816 up to the present time the Duty on Rum has varied from one Shilling to one Shilling and sixpence pr. Gallon and upon Brandy, Gin, Geneva and Hollands from one Shilling to two Shillings pr. Gallon. An Act was passed by the Governor and Council on the 8th day of November 1831, authorising the levying of an additional duty of 6d. pr. Gallon on Brandy, Gin, Geneva and Hollands and one Shilling pr. Cwt. on Tobacco 'to defray the expenses then and thereafter to be incurred in consequence of the Treaty entered into with the Timmanee Natives on the 23 September 1831'.[1] That Statute expired on the 9th. Inst. and the Council have thought it expedient to fix by the present Act an additional Duty on all Spirituous Liquors at the rate of one Shilling and sixpence pr. Gallon and additional one farthing pr. pound on Tobacco.

The sixth Impost on the amount of Sales of all Prize Goods and Vessels has been altered to 3 per centum, in order to bring the Duty equal with that upon 'Imports', and the Council humbly conceive that this triffling increase cannot possibly effect any of the arrangements subsisting between Great Britain and Foreign Powers in regard to the abolition of the Slave Trade.

With the exception of the 12th Clause the entire Act has been framed strictly in conformity with the Provisions of the Act of Parliament for 'Regulating the Trade of the British Possessions abroad',[2] as far as the same are applicable; but the Council being of opinion that the punishment consequent upon 'Felony' for obstructing Officers in the exercise of their Duty, as prescribed by the 6th Section of that Act, is of so severe a nature as to be calculated under the peculiar circumstances of the Colony and Condition of the People, to defeat the ends of Justice; it was considered more consonant with reason and Policy to fix the offence as a 'Misdemeanor'. It is however necessary to observe that the Chief Justice, altho' he concurred in the propriety of lessening the punishment in a Colony situated as this is, yet he dissented from the opinion of the Council on technical Grounds considering himself bound to do so by the 3 & 4 of William the 4 Cap 59 Sect 62.

The Lieutenant Governor of the Gambia having on former occasions repeatedly represented the difficulty he laboured under in consequence of having no Fiscal Regulations for the Port of 'Bathurst', it has been deemed expedient to extend the Provisions of the Act now submitted to that Settlement in so far as the same related to the amount of Duties and payment thereof and the Regulations therein made for securing and enforcing payments of the said Duties, and all Fines and Penalties thereby imposed for breach of any such Regulations.

On reference to the Custom House Returns of the Imports into the Colony for the three last years, it is found that the Revenue will be increased to a small amount by the present rate of Duties, and I trust

---

[1] For the Temne Treaty see below, p. 251.
[2] The British Possessions Act of 1833 (3 & 4 Will. IV, c. 59). Encl., 'An Act for Regulating the Customs House Duties within the Colony of Sierra Leone, and Certain Dependencies thereon', 8 November 1834. A new Colonial Act of 18 February 1835 raised the import duty at Bathurst to 3 per cent. *ad valorem*; and a further Act of 25 March 1835 allowed a special drawback of 6*d*. per gallon on spirits imported into Sierra Leone for British factories in Koya.

that the fixed Expenditure upon the Colonial Fund as detailed in the enclosed Statement, and the expense to be incurred in the execution of the Works now in progress; as well as the repairs to Buildings which will be hereafter necessary will justify their adoption.

11

THE EARL OF ABERDEEN TO LIEUT.-GOVERNOR H. D. CAMPBELL; SIERRA LEONE DUTIES ACT, 12 MARCH 1835[1]

SIR,

I have had under my consideration Acting-Governor Cole's Despatch, No. 35, of the 25th of November last, transmitting an Act, passed by the Governor and Council of Sierra Leone on the 8th of the same month entitled:

'An Act for regulating the Custom House Duties within the Colony of Sierra Leone and certain Dependencies thereon.'

The object of this Act is to consolidate the Laws respecting the duties of Customs payable in the Colony, with some amendments: and in signifying to you the King's Pleasure upon it, it is necessary that I should trouble you with some observations with regard to certain of its provisions.

First. The local Legislature, on a former occasion imposed discriminating duties in favor of British, and to the prejudice of all Foreign Shipping. The Act imposing such duties was disallowed; because the Treaties of Commercial reciprocity with some Foreign States (Sweden and the South American Republics for example) pledge this Kingdom to admit the Vessels of those Countries in all British Colonies, on the same terms as British Vessels. By the present Act, to avoid that error, the Legislature of Sierra Leone, have rendered Foreign Shipping of every description exempt from all duties of Tonnage, or duties upon their Cargoes by which British Vessels are not equally affected. By thus passing over from one extreme to the other, the Colonial Legislature appear to have rather varied the form than escaped the substance of the error into which they formerly fell. They are still in opposition to the principles of Parliament, and of the King's Government upon this subject. That principle is to raise the level of British Shipping in respect of Commercial advantages in the direct Trade between Foreign Countries, and the British Colonies, the Vessels of those States, and of those only, which having Colonies of their own, concede in the Colonies

---

[1] C.O. 268/33, ff. 17–26. *Lord Aberdeen* was Secretary of State for War and Colonies, November 1834–April 1835. *H. D. Campbell* was administrator of Sierra Leone, 1835–7.

the corresponding advantages to the Shipping of this Country; or which, being without such Colonies, have placed the Trade of this Country on the footing of the most favored nation. To States which have performed either the one, or the other of those conditions as the case may be, Parliament has secured a direct access to the British Colonies, for their commercial marine. To such of those States as have gone further, and entered into Treaties of reciprocity extending to the Colonies it has been promised, that, in availing themselves of that right of access, they shall not be impeded by any fiscal Regulations affecting their Trade, unless such Regulations shall also reach, and apply to British Ships engaged in the same Trade. The former Act of Sierra Leone, which was disallowed would have been a direct breach of this promise. The present Act renders the engagement comparatively valueless. It confounds the distinctions between those Nations which do, and those which do not perform the required conditions in our favor; and gives to all the benefit which Great Britain is specially pledged to impart to a comparatively small number. Moreover the distinction is lost sight of by which, in another form, Parliament have thought it right to secure some peculiar advantage for British Shipping in the British Colonies. The importation of Goods in Foreign Vessels is allowed only when such goods are the product of the Foreign Country to which the Ship herself belongs, and are brought directly from the Ports of that Country. Under this Act, on the contrary, it seems to be designed, that the cargo of any Foreign Vessel, from whatever quarter brought, and of whatever Articles composed, shall be received on the same terms as if the importing ship were British.

Secondly. A duty of 3 per cent ad valorem is proposed on the amount of all sales of prize Vessels, and Goods by Public Auction, after deducting the charges of the same. If this impost were now for the first time to be established, I should think it a matter of very grave doubt, how far it would be proper to sanction it. The Colony of Sierra Leone derives great advantages from being the seat of the various Mixed Commissions for the suppression of the Slave Trade. Without subjecting the settled Inhabitants to any cost whatever, it opens to them many sources of Emolument, of which they would otherwise be destitute. The sale of the condemned Slave Trading Ships at that place gives to the Merchants there the constant opportunity of making most beneficial bargains, from the contractedness and consequent want of competition of that market. The hardly earned remuneration of the Captors is thus reduced in favor of persons who have certainly in this respect no special claim to the consideration of the Public at large. The deduction made from the Proceeds of such sales for the support of the Public expenditure of the Colony is entirely at the expense of the Captors; and, by abridging the amount of direct taxation, is in another sense also a benefit to the resident Merchants and others by whom that burthen would be properly sustained. At present all captures are, and probably ever will be, effected by British Cruizers. But there is nothing in the terms of the Treaties to prevent the fitting out and employment of Foreign Ships of War for the same purpose. If a Slave Trader should be brought into Sierra Leone for condemnation by a Portuguese or Netherlands Vessel, the Captor would complain, and, as I think, with reason, of an infringement of the Treaty, when informed, that part of his Prize was to be employed for the support of the Civil Government of Sierra Leone. The impost, however, has been so long levied without objection, that it may seem unreasonable to agitate the question now, although, for the reasons which I have stated, this appears to me a very objectionable source of Revenue.

Thirdly. By the English Act of Parliament from which the provisions of this Act are chiefly borrowed, the resistance to a Customs House Officer in the discharge of his duty is felony. By the 12th Section of this Act, the offence is reduced to a misdemeanor in consequence of circumstances which, in such a place, and amongst such a Population would have rendered the exaction of the higher penalty either impracticable or inexpedient. The Chief Justice is stated to have acquiesced in the propriety of this measure, but to have thought it unlawful for certain technical reasons. What these reasons may be, is not explained, and I can only state my inability to discover any legal objection technical, or substantial to this part of the enactment.

On the whole I do not consider the objections which I have pointed out to certain provisions of this Act to be of such weight as to require its disallowance, and I am therefore to convey to you His Majesty's confirmation and allowance of it. It will, however, be requisite, that you should bring under the consideration of your Council the necessity of passing a supplementary Enactment which shall declare that on the admission of Foreign Vessels and their Cargoes at Sierra Leone, the same Rules should be observed as are established by the Statute 3 and 4 Will. IV Cap. 59. S. 5 and by any Orders made by His Majesty in Council in pursuance of that Statute, or by any Commercial Treaties in force in any Foreign State, for the regulation of the Trade of His Majesty's Possessions in America and the West Indies.

12

THE COLLECTORS OF CUSTOMS TO THE TREASURY: SUSPENSION OF REGULATIONS AT THE GAMBIA, 8 OCTOBER 1845[1]

... WE Report

That in our Report of the 18th October 1844 No. 1528 upon an application from Messrs. Forster & Smith complaining of the injury sustained by those interested in British Shipping in consequence of the Provisions of the Navigation Act of the 3 & 4 Will. 4 Cap. 54 not having been strictly enforced at Bathurst (St Mary's) in the River Gambia, we took occasion to request your Lordship's attention to our former Report of the 30th Nov. 1837 No. 1651 upon a letter which you had been pleased to refer to us from Mr. Hay transmitting by desire of Her Majesty's Principal Secretary of State for Colonies Copy of a Despatch from the Lieut-Governor of Bathurst setting forth the reasons which had induced him to allow, until the pleasure of Her Majesty's Government should be signified to him, the Importation into that Settlement of certain Goods in French Vessels —such Importations being at variance with the Law of Navigation— in which Report after adverting to the Provisions of the Navigation Act of the 3 & 4 Will. 4 Cap. 54, We stated that so long as the French retained possession of the Factory called Albreda, situated in the River Gambia, 30 miles above the Town of Bathurst, the Vessels of that Country would at all times be enabled to proceed to Albreda with Cargoes which are prohibited by the Laws of Navigation and Her Majesty's Order in Council to be imported into Bathurst, and that under those circumstances it had been found necessary to permit all goods brought by French Vessels from the neighbouring Settlements of Senegal and Goree, to be landed on payment of the same duties to which Goods of a similar description imported in due course of Trade would be liable; and we expressed our concurrence in the opinion of the Lieut-Governor of the Gambia, that it would not be expedient to enforce the Provisions of the Navigation Law with respect to the French Vessels arriving in that Settlement; and Your Lordships were pleased by Mr. Spearman's Letter of the 17th May 1838 to acquaint us that you had informed the Secretary of State for the Colonies that under the very peculiar circumstances of the case, it would not be expedient to direct the revocation of the authority which had been given for the non enforcement of the Provisions of the Navigation Law at the Gambia. And in reply to the complaint of

[1] C.O. 87/36. Encl. in Treasury to C.O., 31 October 1845, and signed E. Stewart, H. Spring-Rice, H. Lushington, G. Dawson. This relaxation of the British Possessions Acts and the Order in Council of 1829 was continued till 1849.

Messrs. Forster & Smith, the subject of our Report of the 18th October 1844 before referred to, Your Lordships were pleased by Mr. Trevelyan's Letter of the 16th December following to transmit to us Copy of your Minute of the 25th October acquainting us that those Parties had been informed that the whole subject having been very fully considered, by the late Government in the year 1837 when the relaxation of the Navigation Laws to which they adverted in favour of French Vessels trading to the Gambia was assented to— Your Lordships on a review of the correspondence which then took place, were not of opinion that any advantage would result from giving directions on the subject as suggested by the Applicants.

With respect to the question put in Mr. Hope's Letter vizt. whether the same relaxation of the Navigation Law in regard to Importations into St. Mary's in French Ships, has been extended to Goods brought in American Vessels, we have to state that American Ships can only legally import from that Country Goods the produce of the United States direct from thence into Bathurst on the Gambia, and not from any other place—and the law in this respect, has not so far as we are aware been violated. . . .

13

ORDER IN COUNCIL: GAMBIA AND SIERRA LEONE CUSTOMS REGULATIONS, 5 MARCH 1852[1]

WHEREAS by a certain Act of Parliament made in the Session of Parliament holden in the eighth and ninth years of the reign of Her present Majesty, intituled, 'An Act to regulate the Trade of the British Possessions abroad',[2] it is amongst other things enacted, that it shall be lawful for Her Majesty, by and with the advice of Her Privy Council, by any Order or Orders in Council to be issued from time to time, to give such directions and make such regulations touching the trade and commerce to and from any British possessions in or near the continent of Europe, or within the Mediterranean Sea, or in Africa, or within the limits of the East India Company's Charter (excepting the possessions of the said Company), as to Her Majesty in Council shall appear most expedient and salutary: And whereas by certain orders made by Her Majesty in Council on the 31st day of January 1849, and on the 13th day of February 1849,[3] in pursuance of the said Act Her Majesty made certain regulations

[1] *Parl. Papers*, 1855, xxxvii (383), pp. 35–36.   [2] Statute 8 & 9 Vict., c. 93.
[3] Further local ordinances were passed to regulate Gambia trade and customs in 1853 and 1862. A general consolidation ordinance was passed by the Legislative Council of Sierra Leone in 1866.

touching the trade and commerce of Her settlements on the River Gambia, and touching the trade and commerce of the colony of Sierra Leone respectively: And whereas it is expedient to enable the legislatures of the said Settlements and colony respectively to alter or repeal all such regulations as are made in and by the said Orders respectively:

Her Majesty doth therefore, with the advice of Her Privy Council, and in pursuance and exercise of the powers so vested in Her by the said Act of Parliament, and of all other powers enabling her in that behalf, order, and it is hereby ordered,—

That if and whenever the legislatures of the said Settlements on the River Gambia and their dependencies, and of the colony of Sierra Leone respectively, shall make or pass any Act or Ordinance in the manner and subject to the conditions which are or may be by law required in respect of Acts or Ordinances of such legislatures respectively, altering or repealing all or any of the regulations made in and by the said Orders in Council respectively; and if Her Majesty shall confirm such Act or Ordinance, in such manner as Acts or Ordinances passed by such Legislatures respectively are or shall be by law subject to Her confirmation, such regulations shall, upon the proclamation of such confirmation in the said Settlements or Colony, or at any time thereafter which may be fixed by such Act or Ordinance, be so altered and repealed as if such alteration or repeal had been effected by Order of Her Majesty, with the advice of Her Privy Council. . . .

B. STAPLES AND TRADERS

Introductory Note

THE outstanding feature of West African trade in the nineteenth century, during and after the gradual abolition of the export of slaves, was the change in the type and quantity of products sent to Europe. By the 1850's, gum, gold, spices, and ivory had given way to timber, palm oil, and groundnuts. The development of these staples in the British and French spheres of action and the encouragement of cotton formed the basis of European economic enterprise in West Africa. To protect this enterprise, the British Government was expected to assist traders against the real or imagined threats of foreign competition, against the establishment of trading monopolies under official patronage, and against the consequences of European lawlessness on the African frontier.

From the 1780's till well after 1815, the bulk of traders' correspondence reaching the Committee of Trade and Plantations and the Colonial Office was concerned with French rivalry for the Senegambia gum trade and possible French settlements on the Gold Coast and in the Bight of Benin.

Strategy and commercial competition were inseparable, as an official memorandum of 1802 pointed out; and when strategy was no longer an issue, there were loud voices in the Committee of the Company of Merchants which linked foreign competition with the African slave trade and condemned the peace treaty of 1814 for allowing the French to return to their former possessions. The development of freer trade tended, if anything, to increase this rivalry in the Gambia and on the Guinea Coast where British firms complained of unfair methods and were outraged when France established a few posts in the 1840's. By then, neither the Foreign Office nor the Colonial Office took such petitions very seriously. The main weight of British West African policy was still directed against the slave trade and not against commercial competition. It took some twenty years of spasmodic diplomacy to settle the question of the French factory at Albreda, ceded to Britain in 1857; but this did not improve the British position in the centre of a French market. With the possible exceptions of Lagos, the Sherbro, and the purchase of the Danish and Dutch forts, international rivalry arising from commercial competition counted for little in British policy till the early 1870's.

Similarly, purchase of territory to increase legitimate trade, inherent in the arguments of the Buxton group in the early 1840's, was considered but not accepted by Lord Russell and Lord Stanley. This attitude owed much to the discovery that the bulk of British trade with West Africa was done with areas where no colonies existed: the gum trade and the palm oil market, on the whole, incurred no imperial expense. A decade later, it was equally certain that the two other staples, groundnuts and cotton could safely be left to the independent African peasant to produce. By 1852, the Gambia alone exported about £150,000 of groundnuts, grown outside the colony and marketed to Bathurst traders. Gold, ivory, teak, and gum had been completely replaced. Again, in 1857, after unsuccesful attempts to encourage cotton growing in Sierra Leone, the Foreign Office and British consuls looked outside the settlements for new supplies. Careful reports were prepared by government and missionary agents on cotton varieties and methods of ginning; W. B. Baikie put forward grandiose schemes of his own for plantations of cotton in the Hausa states; and the Gambia administration distributed seeds and machinery in the interior. In the end little came of these experiments, except in the vicinity of Lagos where exports of baled cotton were valued at £60,000 a year by the end of the 1860's, after which prices fell and production quickly declined. By then, the trading economy of the settlements was clearly defined: each depended on markets and producers beyond its frontiers and played the part of an entrepôt rather than a plantation, in a region of many alternative markets to the colonial ports.

Rejection of annexation to foster national trade in Africa derived in part from the British attitude to company monopolies. If the separate traders could make their own way in return for a modest subsidy to help pay for the forts, so much the better. The Committee of Merchants, in its turn, took umbrage at the formation of the St. George's Bay (Sierra Leone) Company in 1790, though their anxiety was set at rest by the charter of 1791. The bankruptcy of the Company and the dissolution of the

Merchants' Committee in 1821 ended these last vestiges of exclusive corporations on the coast.

The idea of some form of government aid to commercial enterprise however, did not disappear. The short-lived African Inland Commercial Company, formed in 1832, applied in vain for a charter and reduction of duties on its produce; and from then, till the 1870's, the Niger remained the central point for appeals for official protection and support. The beginning of regular steamer lines to the Bights after 1852 and government encouragement of exploration from the Western Sudan and the Delta in 1854 committed the Foreign Office and the Treasury to paying subsidies to Macgregor Laird to keep open communications with the Hausa and Nupe states. Contracts made in 1857 and 1860 broke down when Niger steamers were attacked, or when the Navy failed to provide an escort in time for the annual ascent. Subsidized exploration ended in 1861, the year of Laird's death; but Lord Palmerston's contention that commerce could only be protected by keeping the river open by force was given practical effect by sending a government steamer annually up the Niger, 1862–71.

Force, not finance or settlements, was the Government's gift to the traders for the decade. W. B. Baikie, who was allowed to remain in Nupe, had his proposal for a Niger colony rejected by Russell as a method of protecting trade in 1862. Applications for Treasury subsidies by the Company of African Merchants and the West Africa Company, though favourably considered, were refused as a result of pressure from independent trading firms in 1863 and 1864. But force was not unlimited either: the Admiralty opposed intervention in traders' disputes on African rivers and was strongly supported by the Colonial Office in 1865; the Foreign Office warned merchants in 1866 that they were responsible for their conduct on the Niger and in the Delta; finally, the consulate at Lokoja, opened in 1866, was abandoned three years later after hostilities and a siege. The five firms with steamers on the Niger were required to look after themselves, with only a promise of a gunboat at the Delta, after the last official survey up-river by a government agent in 1871.

I

/ o 7 3 ι 8

REPORT OF THE COURT OF DIRECTORS; SIERRA LEONE TRADE, 19 OCTOBER 1791[1]

(a)

THE information received by the Company, from their own agents, and from various other quarters, exceedingly confirms the above account of Lieutenant Matthews;[2] and Mr. Falconbridge[3] has

[1] *Substance of the Report of the Court of Directors of the Sierra Leone Company . . . 19th October 1791* (London, 1792), pp. 12–13, 18–20. The directors were Henry Thornton, Philip Sanson, Sir C. Middleton, Sir G. Young, W. Wilberforce, Rev. T. Clarkson, J. Hardcastle, J. Kingston, S. Parker, Granville Sharp, W. Sandford, Vickeris Taylor, G. Wolff.

[2] John Mathews, *A Voyage to the River Sierra Leone, on the Coast of Africa.* London, 1788.

[3] *Alexander Falconbridge* was surgeon and commercial agent to the Company till 1794.

collected several specimens of native produce, particularly of woods, iron ore, gum copal, pepper, rice, cotton, and sugar-cane, which afford the most favourable hopes to the Company.

The Directors do not however enter into any further detail of particulars, but they have to observe in general, that all the most valuable productions of the tropical climates seem to grow spontaneously at Sierra Leone; and that nothing but attention and cultivation appear wanting, in order to produce them of every kind, and in sufficient quantities to become articles of trade, and even of great national concern. Besides the prospect of trading to Sierra Leone for the immediate productions of that country, it appears also, that a coast and river trade, and, through the rivers, an important inland trade, may easily be established by means of small vessels calculated for that purpose: These might deposit at Sierra Leone productions of Africa, brought from other parts. The coast of Africa, neighbouring to Sierra Leone, is more intersected with rivers navigable for small craft, than any other portion of it whatsoever: by which circumstance an extensive commerce might be greatly facilitated.

(b)

The Directors having now stated the very great and uncommon natural advantages of Sierra Leone on the one hand, and its present forlorn and miserable situation on the other, are led to observe, that it is evidently not merely a commercial factory that they have to establish, but that in order to introduce either a safe trade, or any considerable degree of civilization and cultivation, it must be an especial object of the Company to provide effectually for the protection of property, and for the personal security of the settlers on their district.

The Directors have therefore felt themselves bound to take care, that together with their first adventure, a sufficient strength shall be sent out for security against external violence, and maintaining domestic tranquillity.

They have resolved, that three or four vessels shall sail at once with a considerable number of persons who will thus be an effectual protection and accommodation to each other, and the ships will carry a sufficient quantity of articles, both for opening a store in the way of commerce, and for the use of the colony itself.

It seems obvious both from general reasoning on the subject, and from past experience, that a small and feeble attempt to set up a colony, or to begin a new trade at Sierra Leone, under all the circumstances of that place, is in no respect so likely to prosper, as an attempt made upon a larger scale, carrying out a stronger body of persons from hence, and supported by the weight of so large a capital as may imply a determination to persist.

Besides the advantages of general security to the settlement, and personal convenience to the settlers, from the formation of a respectable establishment at once, the Directors are of opinion also, that a much more profitable trade is eventually to be expected by conducting it on a large scale, than by confining it to a narrow mercantile speculation.

The expense of protection to a factory, and of demurrage to the ships waiting or trading about for the scattered produce of Africa, has hitherto been so great, that the usual advantage in the barter, which is extremely great, has perhaps been no more than what was necessary to indemnify the trader for his high charges, and leave over and above these the ordinary profit of trade. The advantage therefore of introducing a great degree of cultivation on one spot, of collecting a great body of consumers of British articles on the side of one river, of storing a large quantity of goods in their factory rather than a small one (for the factory and superintendence must in either case be nearly an equal standing expense); the advantage also of thus providing the means of a more prompt sale, and quicker returns in the African trade than have yet been effected, must be very obvious.

To the attainment of these objects in any degree worth mentioning, a considerable capital appears indispensably necessary, and upon the whole, the Directors have thought proper to name the sum of not less than One Hundred Thousand Pounds. . . .

2

[JOHN SULLIVAN]: 'MEMORANDA, ON CERTAIN PARAGRAPHS CONTAINED IN THE *MONITEUR*, RELATIVE TO THE FRENCH ESTABLISHMENTS IN AFRICA', AUGUST 1802[1]

A PUBLICATION has lately appeared in France, under the Title of 'Fragmens d'un Voyage en Afrique',[2] the object of which appears evidently to be, to set up a pretension, on the part of the French Nation, to a priority of Right, from the first discovery of the Territory from Cape Blanco to Cape Palmas on the Coast of Africa, comprehending near 25 degrees of Latitude, & including the most Valuable parts of that Coast, whether with Relation to the Trade which has been heretofore carried on there by Europeans, or to the more enlarged plans of Commerce which late discoveries, & the Establishment of the Sierra Leone Company may give rise to.

[1] C.O. 2/1, ff. 1–4 and v.
[2] Xavier de Golberry, *Fragmens d'un voyage en Afrique fait pendant les années 1785, 1786, 1787, dans les contrées occidentales de ce continent comprises entre le Cap Blanco et le Cap des Palmes*. Paris, 1802.

IBP

This Work having fallen under the Consideration of Sir Joseph Banks,[1] he immediately saw the important Consequences which might result from it, if time were given for its full operation on the enterprising Spirit of the French People, who allured by the representations which the author makes of the Climate and Soil, & encouraged by their Government, might be tempted to proceed to the Several parts of the Coast which have been pointed out as favourable to Establishments, and by the act of possession shut us out from many Sources of Advantageous Commerce.

Sir Joseph Banks was the more awake to this danger, & the better qualified to judge of its extent, from having, in the year 1799, been led to turn his attention particularly to the Subject.

In the month of June of that year he communicated the accompanying Resolutions of the African Association to Government,[2] and strongly expressed his Sentiments on the importance of our opening a Commercial Intercourse with the Interior of Africa from the Same Line of Coast to which the Views of the French are now diverted; and as the War with France gave us, at that time, the opportunity, he recommended that we should dislodge them from the Senegal, lest they Should, upon the Return of Peace, push their Establishments up that River, so as to be enabled to interrupt the Communication which we might open from the Gambia.

The Return of Peace has left the French Government in possession of the advantages which the Navigation of the River Senegal and its tributary Streams offer to their activity; & from the Work already alluded to it is not improbable that they will avail themselves of these advantages, and endeavour to exclude us from competition by the route which has hither-to been thought by us to be the most favourable, namely, that from the Gambia.

This Consideration would seem to render it necessary that measures Should be taken, without delay, for the resuming the possession of James's Island[3] at the entrance of the Gambia, & re-establishing the Works there; for securing to ourselves, by Treaties with the Natives, the Priviledges of a Free-Trade, and their permission to Establish factories on the Gambia as high up as it is Navigable for boats; & from thence, by extending ourselves to the Falime, which empties itself into the Senegal, to anticipate the French in that direction.

Another, and a Shorter, Channel of Intercourse with the Interior of Africa, towards that most interesting part of it through which the Niger flows in an Easterly Course, offers itself to us in the navigation of the Rio Grande. This River discharges itself into the Atlantic

[1] C.O. 2/1. Banks to Sullivan, 1 August 1802, ff. 7–8 and v.
[2] Ibid., Banks to Liverpool, 9 June 1799, ff. 9–19; Resolution, 25 May 1799, ff. 11–13; *Proceedings of the Association*, ii, pp. 5–6.
[3] James Island in the Gambia was not reoccupied till 1816.

nearly midway between the mouth of the Gambia and that of the River of Sierra Leone. It was navigated in the year 1793, for the extent of 72 miles, by Captain Beaver of the Navy, who, after a Residence of two years on its banks, makes the most favorable Report of the fertility of the Soil, and the disposition of the Natives, from whom he had obtained, in the name of His Majesty, a Cession (which it would now be advisable to get renewed) of the Islands of Bulama and Areas, and of a Very extensive Tract of Country on the Continent.[1]

The Report that was made by Captain Beaver to the Bulama Association, in whose service he was employed, and the Reports that have been made to the Sierra Leone Company by their agents[2] coincide in their general Result, & leave no room to doubt but that a most important Commercial Intercourse with the Various Natives who Inhabit the Vast Extent of the Interior of Africa, might be established thro' the agency of these Two Societies, or by their union, under the protection and direction of Government, and in cooperation with the Factories that may be formed on the Gambia.

3

REPORT OF THE COMMITTEE OF THE AFRICAN INSTITUTION: WEST AFRICAN PRODUCE, 25 MARCH 1808[3]

[The Institution will encourage cotton-growing in Africa by distributing seed in Sierra Leone.]

... THE Committee are aware, that it may be objected to this attempt to extend the cultivation of cotton, that the supply of that article is already equal to the demand; and that therefore the measures pursued by the Committee are impolitic. But they would observe in reply to this objection, that cotton is an article the growth of which in Africa will occasion less of competition with our own Colonies than almost any other article of tropical produce which could be named; and that it is important to be preparing sources from which a supply of cotton may be drawn, should circumstances arise to interrupt our commercial relations with America, or with the other places which now

[1] C.O. 2/1. Beaver to the Bulama Association, 24 June 1794, ff. 20-28. For the details of this fruitless experiment, see Captain Philip Beaver, *African Memoranda: relative to an Attempt to establish a British Settlement on the Island of Bulama, on the Western Coast of Africa, in the Year 1792.* London, 1805.

[2] Ibid., Zachary Macaulay to Sullivan, 4 September 1802, 'On the Means of Establishing a Commercial Intercourse between the Western Coast of Africa and the River Niger', ff. 32-45.

[3] *Second Report of the Committee of the African Institution* (London, 1808), pp. 6-13. See also, Vincent Harlow and Frederick Madden (eds.), *British Colonial Developments 1774-1834* (Oxford, 1953), pp. 388-9 and n.

furnish it. But independently of these considerations it may be presumed, that in proportion as the natives of Africa supply us with the raw material, they will be capable of paying for a larger quantity of the manufactured article.

The Committee think that it may be of use to enumerate in this place, for the information of the Subscribers, what other articles there are which Africa may be expected to furnish as a return to the British merchant for the goods he may send thither.

The first they will specify is Gold. This precious metal is found in many parts of Africa, sometimes in small lumps, in a pure state; but for the most part it is procured by merely washing, with care, the sand taken from the bed of the river. The quantity obtained in this way, indeed, will barely pay the labour required to free it from the sand. It nevertheless proves the existence of gold mines in the country, which, it is presumed, may be found and opened, should the advancing civilization of Africa admit of that free intercourse, which would give an opportunity to European mineralogists of exploring this source of wealth.

Ivory has hitherto formed, next to slaves, the largest branch of African commerce, and its quantity will of course not be lessened by the new circumstances in which Africa is placed.

Bees Wax may be obtained in every part of Africa; and in some places, particularly the Rivers Gambia and Gaboon, it forms a considerable part of the present exports. It might of course be greatly increased by encouraging the rearing of Bees.

Dye-Woods, of various kinds, including Camwood, Barwood, and Fustick, are now exported, the two first in considerable quantities from Africa. Requiring no previous cultivation, but only to be cut down in order to be brought to market, and thus affording a present temptation to exertion, the commerce in articles of this description, has not been equally affected by the Slave Trade, as the commerce in those articles which require previous culture, and the profits of which are remotely prospective. Without doubt, however, when the intercourse with the interior of Africa shall become more open and secure not only may the trade in the Dye-Woods already specified be increased, but other valuable Dye-Woods will probably be discovered.

Many kinds of Timber are likewise produced in Africa, which are supposed to be well adapted for the use of *Cabinet Makers*, *Inlayers*, and even of *Shipwrights*. The importation of these is discouraged by the high duties payable on *unrated woods*, amounting at present to about £27 per Cent. ad valorem.

Potash might also be procured from Africa: the clearing of the forests would be course supply materials for the manufacture of this useful article.

Gum Senegal and Gum Copal are now imported into this country from Africa, in a quantity nearly equal to the demand. Besides these, there are many other gums in Africa, which, if properly examined, might prove useful both to our manufacturers and chemists. Gums, as was observed in the case of Dye-Woods, require no cultivation, and hardly any labour to prepare them for market.

Palm Oil, which is useful in the manufacture of soap, may be obtained in considerable quantities.

Indigo grows wild in almost every part of the African Coast, and might therefore easily be brought into cultivation. Almost all the Indigo which is now consumed in Europe, is imported from the East Indies, under the disadvantage of a voyage more than thrice as long as that from Africa. Besides the Indigo, there is another plant which the natives use as a blue dye, which appears to impart a more indelible colour, and which, should it stand the test of experiment, might also be cultivated.

Rice forms the principal food of the Africans, and might doubtless become an article of export, for the supply of the West Indies and Europe.

Several varieties of the Coffee, one of a kind not inferior, it is supposed, to the Mocha, are found growing wild in the mountains of Sierra Leone. The cultivation of this article has been begun at that Colony, and promises to succeed. It may thence be extended to every part of the continent.

Sugar Cane of an excellent quality grows, with hardly any culture, in many parts of Africa. The Committee do not recommend this, at the present moment, as an article to be cultivated with a view to exportation. Still its existence, and luxuriant growth, serve to show what are the capabilities of that country.

Malaguetta Pepper, an article in considerable demand, grows wild in great abundance on the windward coast.

A variety of other Spiceries, including the Cayenne, Ginger, Cubebs, Cardamums, species of Nutmeg, and Cinnamon, are found in Africa, and might be cultivated with advantage, Castor Oil, Musk, and various other drugs might also be brought thence, together with the Indian Arrow Root, Tapioca and Sago.

Tobacco is cultivated on a small scale, in various parts of Africa, and might, if it were desirable, be cultivated still more extensively.

A few Hides are now imported from the River Gambia: the number will doubtless increase, as cattle can be more securely reared.

Sponge may also be procured thence.

But besides the articles above enumerated, as already existing in Africa, there are others of a very valuable kind, such as Opium, which might be transported thither. The Cochineal and the Silk Worm might also be reared there. In short, it may be said that there are no articles, produced between the tropics, which may not be naturalized in that part of Western Africa, which has hitherto been the theatre of the Slave Trade. . . .

4

THOMAS LACK TO R. W. HAY: GOLD COAST TRADE, 3 MARCH 1828[1]

SIR,

The Lords of the Committee of Privy Council for Trade, having had under Consideration, your Letter of the 21st. January last, wherein you request to receive their Lordships' Opinion as to the Importance to this Country of the Traffic carried on along the Coast of Guinea; I am directed to acquaint you, for the Information of Mr. Secretary Huskisson, that as the Statement of the value of Imports and Exports from Great Britain to the Western Coast of Africa, which accompanied your Letter did not enable their Lordships to judge to what degree the Apprehensions expressed by the Merchants trading to the Gold Coast as to the probable loss of that Branch of Commerce, if the British Settlements there should be given up, were well founded, their Lordships thought fit to call for an account of the Value of the Exports from Great Britain to Cape Coast, and British Accra in the Year 1827 (a Copy of which is herewith transmitted). From this account it appears that the total value of those Exports was £47,265, that the Articles of greatest Export, were

East India Cottons—£11,340.
Rum—£9,410.

That the largest Export of Articles of British manufacture consisted of

Cotton Goods—£11,905.
Gunpowder & Arms—£5,608.

The Lords of this Committee, however, are inclined to think that if the Supply of the above mentioned Articles, through the Channels which are now open, should be interrupted in consequence of the abandonment of the British Forts on the Gold Coast, it may fairly be presumed that a very considerable Portion will continue to find its way into the Countries where they are consumed, through other Routes; and under these Circumstances their Lordships are of opinion that if, for reasons which it does not belong to this Department to decide upon, it should be thought desirable to withdraw our Establishments on the Gold Coast, there is no reason to apprehend any such Injury to the Trade and Manufactures of this Country as should interfere with, or embarrass that decision.

[1] C.O. 267/96.

5

THOMAS FORSYTH TO R. W. HAY: AFRICAN INLAND COMMERCIAL COMPANY, 7 APRIL 1832[1]

SIR,

Several highly respectable merchants of Liverpool, desirous of ascertaining whether the late discoveries made by Mr. Richard Lander might be rendered beneficial to the Commerce of Great Britain have associated themselves together under the designation of 'The African Inland Commercial Company'. They are preparing two Steam Boats, with every convenience for ascending the River Niger under the direction of Mr. Lander. A sailing vessel will accompany them, with such goods as Mr. Lander may suggest, as suitable for trading with the Natives on the Banks of the River. This vessel is to remain on the Coast, until Mr. Lander returns down with the Steam Boats. Such is the outline of the projected expedition. The Lords of the Admiralty have expressed a wish to send out a Naval Officer[2] for the purpose of obtaining the accurate positions of the various places on the Banks of the Niger, and of taking astronomical observations.

As this is an extremely hazardous enterprise, and if successful, may lead to very important results to the Country at large, I am directed by the Company to request the favor of your laying our case before Lord Goderich, and to beg His Lordship's influence to obtain for them a Charter for a few years, permitting the produce which they may collect, to be imported on a reduced scale of Duties. The articles collected may in the first instance be scarcely worth the Duty now imposed, but if released from this, the Company would order home every species of Commodity. It thus could be ascertained, how far the quality of each may be improved, and rendered beneficial to the future commerce of Great Britain. I am also desired to request the favor of Lord Goderich granting leave to Mr. Richard Lander to accompany the expedition.

[Lord Goderich[3]]: Minute, 9 April [1832].

[1] C.O. 2/19. *Thomas Forsyth* was secretary to the 'African Inland Commercial Company'. Richard Lander was at this date employed by the Treasury. He was subsequently killed during the course of the expedition in the Lower Niger. His correspondence and that of his brother is in C.O. 2/19. See M. Laird and R. A. K. Oldfield, *Narrative of an Expedition into the Interior of Africa, by the River Niger* 2 vols. London, 1837.
[2] Captain William Allen who commanded the expedition in 1832 and took part in the later ascent, 1841–2.
[3] *Lord Goderich* was Secretary of State for War and Colonies, April–August 1827 and November 1830–April 1833.

L[ord] G[oderich] is glad to hear of yr. proposal but cannot undertake to recommend to the Bd. of Trade that any reduction of duties or Charter shd. be granted.

Treasury shall be written to respecting Lander's leave.

6

DR. S. LUSHINGTON AND SIR T. F. BUXTON TO LORD JOHN RUSSELL: NIGER PLANTATIONS, 7 AUGUST 1840[1]

. . . YOUR LORDSHIP is probably aware that it is in contemplation, by some persons interested in the welfare of Africa, to make at this time an attempt to cultivate a district of that country. As a mere mercantile venture, few would be disposed to embark in it; with a view to profit, it would be obviously expedient to wait till more was known, both of the advantages which the soil of Africa offers, and of the dangers to which the adventurers would be exposed. But gentlemen of the most acknowledged sagacity in the mercantile world, urged by a desire of rendering benefit to Africa, and convinced that there is no way of doing this so effectual, as by demonstrating her agricultural resources, are willing to embark their capital, provided only that such facilities and securities are afforded them as the Government have the power of bestowing.

For this purpose they require and trust that there will be no difficulty on the part of the Government in giving them a charter, limiting responsibility; they then will be prepared to make the experiment of cultivating a tract of country bordering on the Niger, and of raising, in the first instance, 50,000 *l.*, with the intention, if this trial be successful, of hereafter inviting the public to unite with them in finding the funds for more extended tillage.

We now proceed to inquire what are the necessary conditions, in order that this attempt may be made under the most favourable circumstances, and may lead to the most complete and striking exhibition of the effects which cultivation will produce, and the blessings it will bring with it.

In these settlements, persons, property, and lawful occupations

[1] *Parl. Papers.*, 1843, xlviii (472), pp. 16–17, 18. *Dr. Stephen Lushington* was a distinguished lawyer and Member of Parliament. As Wilberforce's successor to leadership of the anti-slavery movement, *T. F. Buxton* had already fought a successful campaign for abolition by 1836. His attention then turned to the slave trade in Africa itself—to be countered by the promotion of legitimate trade and plantation settlements, as outlined in *The African Slave Trade and its Remedy*, London, 1839. *Lord John Russell* was Colonial Secretary from August 1839 till June 1841. He led his own ministry, 1846–51, was Foreign Secretary, 1852–3, and returned to the Colonial Office briefly from February till July 1855, before serving again as Palmerston's Foreign Secretary and as Prime Minister.

must be protected; the produce of free labour must receive encouragement in the European market. Finally, a fitting example must be presented to surrounding nations of the benefits of Christianity, and of the advantages to be derived from civilized institutions. The simple enumeration of these particulars may suffice to show the impossibility of combining or securing them under any known form of native Government. All that is known of Africa, whether from British officers or missionaries, or scientific travellers, seem to concur in proving the settlements of this description must be kept apart from the contamination of prevailing native practices, and that their internal prosperity, not less than their external security, can be maintained in no other way than by placing them under the protection of the British Crown.

It is clear that in the districts where the experiment is made, the sovereign power must be held by the British Government, and the natives obey our laws, or we must be subject to their authority, and submit to such laws as they may impose. Our rule and institutions would be a pure gain to the Africans. We might then insure security of person and property within the precincts of our settlement, and we might take care that there, at least, none of the native superstitions and bloody rites were practised.

It is not too much to say, that wherever British sovereignty shall be firmly established, there religious and civil liberty would instantly prevail, intestine wars and anarchy would cease, the aborigines would be protected, equal rights be enjoyed by all, and every motive, aid, and opportunity which public or private benevolence or enterprise might contribute towards the civilization of Africa would be most succesfully brought into operation.

But supposing the natives to be rulers, we must submit to all their abominations, and consent to see human sacrifices made, and to be thwarted by the evil influence which such sights exercise on all attempts at civilization. We believe that no Company could be induced to endure this; and if that difficulty could be got over, we do not believe that our presence, under such circumstances, could effect any great advance in civilization.

If the districts cultivated by the persons to whom we have alluded are under the dominion of Great Britain, slavery must be abolished. This was done in Bulama, and is done at Liberia, and all persons resorting to those tracts of territory have been declared to be free; and it is remarkable that we have from Captain Beaver, on the one part, and Governor Buchanan, on the other, the strongest acknowledgments of the benefits which they severally derived from refusing to tolerate slavery under any form. But advantages of this kind are not the strongest arguments for our insisting upon free labour. The extended cultivation of the soil of Africa, if unaccompanied with precautions against slavery, may even aggravate and perpetuate this lamentable system; and every step towards extending and improving the resources of these countries may, with them, as with Egypt, prove a step towards promoting and encouraging predial bondage, In short, our paramount object is to establish free-labour cultivation, and to prove its superiority, thus providing wholesome and profitable occupation, and undermining the Slave Trade. If the district cultivated be British territory, there can be no slavery, and it is hardly too much to say that, under native rule, there will be no such thing at present as free labour . . .

[The land must belong to the Crown to encourage investment in a plantation.]

Unless the territory which it is intended to till be subject to Great Britain, we shall be deprived of a large portion of the money which is to form the capital of our agricultural establishment. We look to members of the Society of Friends, or Quakers, for a considerable portion of this capital. Some of them are ready to undertake agriculture in Africa, provided that, in that country, they are circumstanced as they are already in England. The Government here finds them protection; they have no act or part in the matter; their scruples are not offended by having to ask for the aid of an armed police; they do not carry arms themselves, neither do they ask others to carry them. But unless we are sovereigns in the district we cultivate, our people must protect themselves, and must be ready, on every occasion, to turn out against the enemy.

Lastly. The British Government proposes to engage for 'the admission for consumption in this country, on favourable terms, of goods, the produce or manufacture of the territories subject to them'.[1] And we readily admit that no inducement could be devised more efficacious for the purpose of leading the native powers to unite with us in the suppression of the Slave Trade; it would provide for them the two things which they most require—a market for their own products, and a liberal supply of European goods; but we are at a loss to conceive how this boon can be conceded, unless the territory on which these products are grown be British. In the latter case, the duties we impose may be as light as we please, and there will be no restraint as to the measure of encouragement which we may chose to give to the infant cultivation of Africa. But if the district belong to a native power, we shall be controlled by all our treaties with other nations, engaging to receive their commodities upon the same terms as those of the most favoured nations. We propose, for example, to grow sugar in Africa by free labour, to come into competition with

[1] Ibid., Russell to the Treasury, 26 December 1839, p. 3. For the Niger expedition, 1841–2, see below, p. 154.

the sugar of Brazil; we shall naturally be disposed to favour that which is intended as a blow against the Slave Trade, in preference to that which is produced by means of the Slave Trade.

In short, if the territory on which our capital is to be expended be British, we have it in our power to offer the most effectual encouragement for its growth; but the contracts we have formed with other nations forbid us to give this natural and powerful stimulus to the industry of tribes who are under native dominion. . . .

7

DR. ROBERT MADDEN: THE PALM OIL TRADE, 31 JULY 1841[1]

Is chiefly carried on in the River Bonny, but it is beginning to become of some importance on the Gold Coast, and especially at Accra, where at the Danish settlement about five or six ship-loads of it were exported in the course of the preceding year, as I was informed by the principal Danish merchant in that settlement.

The average import of palm oil into Liverpool for some years past has been about 12,000 tons a year, value about 400,000 *l.* sterling. Three-fourths of this quantity are exported from the Bonny, and the other outlets of the Niger, and gives employment to 12,000 or 15,000 tons of shipping in the year. In the year 1840, 13,170 tons of shipping were employed in this trade in the River Bonny and its immediate vicinity. There were 36 vessels employed in it, and the crews of these vessels amounted to 736 men. In the Appendix will be found the details as communicated to me during my voyage to the coast, by a commander of one of these vessels, Captain Brown, of the 'May,' who had made 11 voyages to the coast, and has a thorough knowledge of the trade and of the people of the Bonny. He states that the oil is brought down from the interior, a distance of about 150 miles, and sold to the Bonny traders in small quantities. It is purchased from them by the English trader, and paid for in gunpowder, guns, cutlasses, lead and iron bars, and boilers, tobacco, rum, and Manchester goods. The imports into Great Britain,
in the year 1808 did not exceed 200 tons a year.

ditto 1827 ditto 4,700 ditto
ditto 1834 ditto 13,945 ditto

In 1816 the official value of all the palm-oil imported from the coast of Africa did not exceed 23,831 *l.* sterling; in 1828, 126,572 *l.*

[1] *Parl. Papers*, 1842, xi (551), Pt. ii, 33–34. *Dr. Robert Madden*, formerly a special magistrate appointed to supervise the abolition of slavery in Jamaica, and judge of the Havana Court of Mixed Commission, was selected as a West Africa Commissioner by Lord Russell to investigate charges of domestic slavery and trading with slave vessels at the Gold Coast Forts.

and in 1834 the official value of the palm oil imported from the coast of Africa amounted to 458,810 *l.* sterling. The quantity of shipping employed in this trade since 1820 has largely increased; in 1840, in the Bonny alone, it amounted to 13,170 tons. These data are sufficient to show the extraordinary growth of this trade.

From the British settlements on the Gold Coast the amount of palm oil exported is still extremely small; from the Gambia, in 1839, the whole quantity exported was 15,093 gallons, the value of which was 2,396 *l.* sterling; and from Sierra Leone, in 1839, it amounted to 7,993 *l.*; only about one-half of which was the value of the quantity sent to Great Britain. In 1838, of the whole amount of palm-oil exported from Africa, the value of the quantity exported from the Gold Coast amounted to only 7,350 *l.* sterling; and in 1829 it fell off to 7,000 *l.* sterling; while in the Bonny, and in the Bights of Benin and Biafra, it increased that year upwards of 50,000 *l.* sterling. It is a very singular circumstance, and one deserving of serious consideration, that nearly the whole of this trade has sprung up within the last 30 years, in a place where we have no government agents, forts or settlement. That without any protection or a single British merchant or mercantile agent residing at the place where this great trade is carried on, namely, the River Bonny, that trade has originated, grown up, and steadily augmented up to the year 1834, when it reached the amount of 269,907 cwts. exported from Africa, and chiefly from this river and its vicinity. . . .

[Palm oil trade in the Bight of Biafra varies according to the demand for slaves.]

The price of palm oil, duty paid, varies from 33 *l.* to 34 *l.* a ton. If we compare the trade of the Bonny with that of any one of our settlements on the coast of Africa, where we have large and costly establishments, we find the trade of the latter, with all the protection afforded them, fall far short of that of the Bonny, that has no aid or support of any kind from Government. These are facts which I feel called upon to state, but from which I do not desire to draw any inference unfavourable to our settlements on the coast of Africa. These settlements are there ill chosen and ill governed no doubt; but the first great expense of their establishment is gone to, and it seems to me the best policy now is, to render them efficient and beneficial to commerce and advantageous to the inhabitants; and where these establishments have become cumbrous and expensive, and where public money has been lavished to a very great extent, to reduce these establishments to the level of the trade and resources of the colony; and in other settlements where the mode of government is injurious to the national character, calculated only to retain the monopoly of the whole trade of the Gold Coast in the hands of a few individuals, where its jurisdiction is injuriously oppressive to the natives, and unsatisfactory to all who are employed under it, from the narrowness of the means placed at the disposal of the local administration, that another system of government should be adopted, having in view the general extension of British commerce, and not the particular interests of any individual merchants; and the promotion of African civilization, instead of the enlargement of our settlement at the expense of the natives' territorial rights. . . .

8

EARL GREY TO GOVERNOR N. W. MACDONALD: SIERRA LEONE COTTON, 5 OCTOBER 1850[1]

SIR,

I transmit to you a copy of a letter addressed to the Board of Trade by Mr Abraham Bauer[2] who is about to proceed to Sierra Leone & who proposes during his stay there, to institute enquiries as to the practicability of obtaining in the Colony & its vicinity regular supplies of Cotton suitable for the English Market.

You [A. are already fully aware of the earnest desire of H.M.'s Govt. to afford the utmost encouragement in their power to] the growth of Cotton at S. Leone [judging from the] specimens [A. you have sent home] of the indigenous Cotton which is to be obtained there. [A. It seems highly probable the colony is capable of yielding a large supply of this valuable material. Nothing is more likely to contribute to the] attainment of this object [which I regard as one] of the greatest [A. national] importance [A. than that a gentleman of intelligence well acquainted with the trade of our manufacturing district shd. visit the Coast of Africa for the purpose of ascertaining by personal observatn. what means can be adopted for obtaining a supply of Cotton from the Continent]. I have accordingly to request that you will render all the assistance which may be in your power to Mr. Bauer in the prosecution of his enquiries on that subject.

[1] C.O. 267/218. Draft by Sir George Barrow with additions by Grey. *Earl Grey* was Under-Secretary in the Colonial Department, 1830–3, and Secretary of State for War and Colonies, 1846–52. *N. W. Macdonald* had been a writer and Colonial Secretary at Sierra Leone which he governed from 1846 till 1852.

[2] C.O. 267/218, Bauer to Porter, 23 September 1850. Bauer was a Director of the Exchange Bank, London, and intended to investigate Sierra Leone at his own expense.

9

MACGREGOR LAIRD TO EARL GREY: STEAM COMMUNICATION WITH AFRICA, 25 MARCH 1851[1]

My Lord,

I beg respectfully to submit, for your Lordship's consideration, a Memorandum on the advantages of a direct steam communication, by screw vessels, with the coast of Africa, between Cape Verde and the Equator, with a table of the distances between the principal ports, and the time required for the performance of the proposed service.

The portion of the trade that would be more immediately benefited by the proposed communication, is that carried on in the rivers flowing into the Bights of Benin and Biafra; on the average there are 20,000 tons of British shipping constantly lying in them, bartering English goods for palm oil and other productions of the country. The unhealthiness of these rivers is unfortunately too well known; they have all formidable bars at their entrances, which frequently, for a length of time, prevent the egress of loaded vessels; and when clear of the river a merchant ship has great difficulty from currents and baffling winds in getting off the coast. A common passage from Bonny or Calabar being from three to four months, there are no means of sending bills of lading or letters, except by the casual departures of laden ships; the consequence is, that merchants have not the usual facilities common to other trades, and though, since the slave trade has been put down on those rivers, legitimate trade has increased rapidly, yet it has never been fully and fairly developed, and cannot be, until a regular communication is established with this country. To the great increase that will take place in the trade of these rivers, down which the produce of central Africa must ultimately come, I look for the principal means of supporting a steam communication; it will convert a most uncertain and precarious trade into a regular and steady one, diminish the risk of life, and free a large portion of the capital at present engaged in it, for its extension or other pursuits.

By making the French port of Goree the first port of call, and Fernando Po the terminus of the line of postal communication, every European community on the coast will be brought into direct communication with England in from 12 to 26 days.

[1] *Parl. Papers*, 1852, xliv (284), pp. 423–4. Brother of John Laird the shipbuilder, *Macgregor Laird* had survived the Niger expedition of 1832. He promoted the British and North American Steam Navigation Company in 1837 and backed private enterprise on the Niger from 1854 till his death in 1861, through the African Steamship Company.

Looking forward to the development of trade, and the increased personal intercourse that a monthly line of steamers would create along the coast and with this country, not only of the European residents, but amongst the higher classes of natives, I am ready to enter into a contract with Her Majesty's Government for a term of years, for the performance of the monthly service described in the memorandum, in vessels specially constructed for the purpose and capable of entering all the principal rivers, at the rate of 4s. 3d. per mile of the distance run per annum, subject to the usual conditions attached to such contracts.[1]

The vessels to be ready to commence the service in six months from this date.

10

CONSUL BENJAMIN CAMPBELL TO LORD CLARENDON: YORUBA COTTON, 16 MAY 1857[2]

... THE Reverend Samuel Crowther, the highly intelligent native Clergyman attached to the Church Missionary Society's Establisment at this station, through whose instrumentality the Chiefs and others at Abeokuta have extended their cultivation of the cotton plant as a commercial export, having returned from a visit to that Town I lost no time in making him acquainted with the wishes and intentions of Her Majesty's Government in regard to promoting the cultivation of the Cotton plant.

Mr. Crowther is of the opinion that in the present stage it would not be advisable to distribute the seeds of a foreign and more valuable description of Cotton to the Chiefs and others at Abeokuta; the native cotton now grown by them is of that description of which the greatest quantity is used, and is known at Manchester, 'good ordinary', and fetches to the cultivators a remunerating price; but, Mr. Crowther is of the opinion that seed of a higher priced description of Cotton would be advantageously placed in the hands of the Native Converts to Christianity many of whom are planters, because they would readily submit to any Instructions and directions as to the mode and manner of cultivating the new seed, in fact that under the advice

---

[1] The final Articles of Agreement, signed by Laird and the Admiralty, 29 January 1852, arranged for monthly conveyance of mails for ten years in return for an annual government subsidy, decreasing from £23,250 to £18,750 over that period.

[2] F.O. 84/1031. *Benjamin Campbell* was consul at Lagos, 1853–9. A copy of this report was forward to Macgregor Laird and to the Manchester Cotton Supply Association. *Lord Clarendon* was Foreign Secretary, 1853–8, 1865–6, 1868–70, and requested this information in March 1857.

and instruction of the Missionary Agents these converts would readily cultivate a model plantation, to which, after a time, the attention of the Chiefs and other cultivators might be invited. I think highly of this suggestion of Mr. Crowther's and beg respectfully to submit to your Lordship that seed of the higher priced description of cotton be sent out to me to be placed in the hands of the Native Christian Converts.

The great drawback hitherto experienced has been the want of good machines for separating the Cotton from the seed. Those hitherto used are the description called the saw Gin, but as they deteriorate the Cotton a halfpenny and more the lb., in consequence of the tearing of the fibre, another description called the roller Gin was sent out, but this machine being unadapted for the cotton cultivated in this part of Africa, not cleaning five lbs of Cotton per day while the saw Gin cleaned upwards of 30 lbs., the natives refused them even as a gift; another great drawback also has been the want of a press, but this will be soon remedied as two presses have arrived out and will be seen set up in Abeokuta; and Signor Scala the Sardinian Consul a man of energy and enterprise who is forming a Commercial establishment at Abeokuta expects a press from England by the next Packet. Unhappily a large quantity of Cotton in the raw state of the crop of last season, stored in various depots at Abeokuta waiting the arrival of more cleaning Gins and the presses was destroyed by a fire some months since which burnt down a large portion of the town of Abeokuta.

As it is a great desideratum with a people who have no other capital than their labor that they should possess machines for cleaning the Cotton, simple, cheap, and inexpensive, I beg to submit to Your Lordship that Her Majesty's Consuls in those Southern States of America, and in other countries where Cotton is extensively grown, be directed to forward to Your Lordship drawings and diagrams of the description of cleaning machines most used in those Countries, with such descriptions as would render them quite intelligible to a Manchester Merchant; and, as an increased cultivation of the Cotton plant in other parts of the Yourbah Country is confidently expected and there are neither rail roads nor canals by which to transport cheaply so bulky a material and only very narrow foot paths at best, I beg further to submit to Your Lordship that Her Majesty's Consuls at Pernambuco and Para be directed to send plans and descriptions of the rude but powerful wooden presses which I am informed are used in the interior of those provinces in Brazil, to compress the Cotton into small bales which are then carried on the backs of mules to the Ports on the Coast.

I beg again respectfully to suggest to Your Lordship that the Conductors of the trading expedition up the Niger should be earnestly requested to direct their attention to cotton as an article of Export, and, that the Expedition should be provided with all the means necessary for purchasing it from the Natives, cleaning it, and pressing it in the state fit for shipment.

11

GOVERNOR L. S. O'CONNOR TO HENRY LABOUCHERE: GAMBIA TRADE, 27 JULY 1857[1]

[Forwarding the Blue Book for 1856.]

. . . 13. In Mungo Park's time, that famous epoch in the annals of Western Africa, and from which so many of its events date, the trade of the River Gambia was carried on by two or three vessels, and the annual exports were under 20,000 *l.*

14. The colony steadily progressed until 1840, when the imports and exports advanced with rapid strides. . . .

15. In 1840, 255 merchant vessels entered Gambia; their tonnage amounting to 14,009 tons; the imports, 105,441 *l.*; and the exports, 124,587 *l.*

16. In 1845, 241 merchant vessels entered Gambia; their tonnage, 21,132 tons; the imports, 119,187 *l.*; and the exports, 154,801 *l.*

17. In 1851, 239 merchant vessels entered Gambia; their tonnage, 25,491 tons; the imports, 107,011 *l.*; and the exports, 186,404 *l.*

18. In 1855, 211 merchant vessels entered Gambia; their tonnage 32,619 tons; the imports, 126,454 *l.* 3*s.* 10*d.*; and the exports, 215,803 *l.*

19. In comparing the exports and imports of Sierra Leone for 1855, it appears from the Blue Book the former amounts to 114,910 *l.* and the latter to 170,547 *l.*; there is, therefore, an excess in favour of Gambia of 11,544 *l.* on imports, and of 45,256 *l.* on exports in 1855.

20. This great increase in the exports may be fairly attributed to the ground nuts, an article in Gambia commerce of comparatively recent date.

21. In 1836 the value of ground nuts exported was only 838 *l.*, and in one year it sprung up to 8,053 *l.*; in four years, that is in 1840, the exportation of ground nuts was 15,209 *l.*; and in twelve years, 1852, ground nuts were exported to the value of 153,008 *l.*

22. In 1855 the exportation of ground nuts was 149,713 *l.* 13*s.*, while the same exported from Sierra Leone amounted only 27,617 *l.*,

---

[1] *Colonial Reports*, 1856 (London, 1858), pp. 183–5. *Lieut.-Colonel O'Connor* was Governor of the Gambia, 1852–9. *Henry Labouchere* had been briefly Under-Secretary for War and Colonies in February 1839 between periods as Vice-President and President of the Board of Trade, before becoming Secretary of State for Colonies, November 1855–February 1858.

leaving an excess on ground nuts in favour of Gambia of 122,096 *l.*
The trifling decline from 1852 is attributable to the war in Barra, the
disturbances up the river, and the insurrection in Combo during
some years to 1852, all harassing the natives, destroying large farms,
and checking the trade.

23. The subsequent restoration of tranquillity in the river, Barra
and Combo, the increased cultivation, and favourable season, raised
the exportation of ground nuts during the half year ending 30 June
1857 to 9,424 tons, or 133,093 *l.* 9*s.* for six months. . . .

24. It is a singular fact, and well worthy of observation, that four
principal articles of exportation from Gambia have sunk into
insignificance in a brief space of time. . . .

In five years, the exportation of gold dwindled from 5,010 *l.* to
1,289 *l.*; gum, from 20,809 *l.* to 1,636 *l.*; ivory from 7,055 *l.* to
4,759 *l.*; teak wood, from 12,355 *l.* to 5,176 *l.*

25. Pass we over ten years, and in 1851 the gold exported from
Gambia was nil, gum 1,361 *l.*, ivory 846 *l.*, and teak wood nil.

26. In five years more, 1856, the gold exported was 202 *l.*, gum
212 *l.* 2*s.* 6*d.*, ivory 218 *l.* 4*s.*, teak wood nil.

27. Thus four articles of exportation, yielding in 1836 45,229 *l.*,
in 1856 returned 632 *l.* 6*s.* 6*d.*

28. In truth it demanded some singularly productive and profitable
article of commerce to pull up the lee-way of such an unprecedented
falling off, and this proved the 'ground-nut' trade;—a trade that, as
cultivation spreads, the circulation of articles for general consumption
increases, commercial reciprocity is encouraged, and good faith
preserved with the various tribes;—the monopoly, hitherto enjoyed
by a few large houses, terminates, and the profits of the trade no
longer engrossed by them, but subdivided amongst a greater number
of humble, industrious, persevering natives;—a trade, I say, that
will render Her Majesty's Settlements in the River Gambia progressive, prosperous, and profitable, and raise them to their legitimate
position among the first colonies of the western coast of Africa. . . .

12

G. R. HAYWOOD TO LORD JOHN RUSSELL;
WEST AFRICAN COTTON,
3 NOVEMBER 1859[1]

MY LORD,

I am desired to convey to Your Lordship the thanks of the
Executive Committee of the Cotton Supply Association for Your
Lordship's courtesy in forwarding to them Dr. Baikie's despatch

[1] F.O. 2/32.

No. 58 on the subject of the Cultivation of Cotton on the West Coast of Africa.[1]

Your Lordship is perhaps not aware that this Association has already, with a view to encourage the Cultivation of Cotton in Africa, taken active measures by giving seeds, and more particularly machines for separating the seeds from the cotton fibre to various persons at Lagos, Abbeokuta, Sierra Leone, to the Gold Coast Agricl. Society,[2] and to the President of Liberia.

They have every wish to avail themselves of Dr. Baikie's kind offer of cooperation and trust Your Lordship will permit them to accept his offer. They beg to enclose a Letter addressed to Dr. Baikie on the subject which they hope Your Lordship will sanction and forward to him.

It will be of great assistance to this Association if Your Lordship will permit the Gins referred to in the letter to Dr. Baikie to be conveyed to him with other Government stores.

This Association is prevented by its constitution from taking a pecuniary interest in the cultivation or purchase of Cotton on its own account but will take immediate steps to bring Dr. Baikie's recommendations before parties now trading to Africa.

13

W. G. ROMAINE TO HERMAN MERIVALE: THE TIMBER TRADE, 2 MARCH 1860[3]

SIR,

With reference to your letter of the 31st. Decr. last, respecting the difficulties experienced in procuring Timber in the neighbourhood of Sierra Leone in consequence of the constant wars between the native chiefs; I am commanded by my Lords Commissioners of the Admiralty to state, for the information of His Grace the Duke of Newcastle, that orders have been given to the Senior Officer of Her Majesty's Ships on the West Coast of Africa to instruct the commanding officers of Cruizers in the neighbourhood of Sierra Leone to place themselves in communication with the Governors of that Colony, and to afford such protection as may appear to be proper and practicable to the British Timber Trade in the Rivers and Creeks

---

[1] Baikie to Russell, 8 August 1859: ibid.

[2] Promoted by the missionary, T. B. Freeman; see *Colonial Report*, 1852 (London, 1854), pp. 200–1.

[3] C.O. 267/269. *W. G. Romaine* was second secretary to the Admiralty, 1857–69. *H. Merivale* had been Permanent Under-Secretary since 1848 in the Colonial Office, but had already transferred to the India Office in 1859. The Admiralty (without informing the Sierra Leone Government) had entered into a timber contract with the Sierra Leone trader Charles Heddle for supplies from along the Bagru river in the Sherbro Estuary.

of the Coast, observing due precaution not needlessly to incur risk
to the health of the crews of the Vessels.

14

LORD PALMERSTON: MINUTE, PROTECTION OF TRADE, 22 APRIL 1860[1]

... THE extension of our trade on the West Coast of Africa generally
and up the Niger in particular is an object which ought to be actively
& increasingly pursued, but it cannot be accomplished without
physical efforts for the Protection of that Trade. It may be true in one
sense that Trade ought not to be enforced by Cannon Balls, but on
the other hand Trade cannot flourish without security, and that
security may often be unattainable without the Protection of physical
force.

It might be said of an European Country that Trade ought not to
be enforced by the Cudgels of a Police or the Sabres & Carbines of a
Gendarmerie, but those Cudgels & Sabres & Carbines are necessary
to keep quiet the ill disposed People whose violence would render
Trade insecure and thus prevent its operations.

So it is in Africa; the Slave Traders African & European endeavour
by violence to put a stop to, and to drive away Legitimate Commerce
in order that it may not interfere with Slave Trade, and if we wish
Commerce to prosper we must employ Force or the threat of Force
to keep these Enemies of Legitimate Commerce quiet.

For this purpose some armed vessel ought to go up the Niger at the
proper season, for the purpose of dissuading or forcing those villages
whose People have fired on our trading vessels to desist from Inter-
rupting our Commercial Enterprizes and I believe the occupation of
Lagos would be a very useful and important step for the suppression
of Slave Trade & for the promotion of Legitimate Commerce.

It is said that Commerce will put an end to Slave Trade, but it is
equally true that Slave Trade puts an end to Commerce; and
experience tends to shew that it is necessary to begin by rooting out
the overshadowing weed Slave Trade, before the nourishing Crop of
Legitimate Commerce, can rear its head and flourish to useful
Purpose.

It is not easy to put a limit upon the Resources which Africa affords
for advantageous Commerce with England. Cotton, Palm oil,
Ground nuts, Coffee, Ivory may be obtained in immense Quantities,
and of course in exchange for the Productions of British Industry.
The advantages to be derived from a great Increase of our Trade with

[1] F.O. 2/34. On a report from the Admiralty Hydrographer, Captain Washing-
ton, concerning the navigation of the Niger, in Admiralty to C.O., 14 April 1860.

Africa, would infinitely counterbalance the small expenditure necessary for protecting that Trade in its Infancy.

15

WILLIAM WYLDE: MINUTE, NIGER TRADE, 8 JANUARY 1862[1]

I WOULD venture to submit the following statement with reference to Sir Baldwin Walker's[2] inquiry whether any further steps should be taken to chastise the villages which shewed themselves hostile to the late expedition up the Niger.

It has been shewn by the reports received from Dr. Baikie and from the Commanders of the several Expeditions that have at various times ascended the Niger that the Chiefs and People in the Upper part of that River are peaceably disposed and very anxious to trade with Europeans. The produce of the Country is valuable and can be increased to any extent that there may be a demand for it, in fact the supply is only limited by the quantity of suitable European goods that can be brought into their markets. The River moreover is navigable for vessels of 300 Tons burthen for a distance of upwards of 500 miles thus opening a highway into the very heart of Africa. It has been shewn also that from the Regions visited by Dr. Baikie in the neighbourhood of the River, large Caravans depart and arrive annually, carrying European goods that find their way up from the Coast into the Centre of Africa. In fact the Trade that used to pass from the Northern Shores of the Mediterranean to Central Africa is now being diverted to the Western Coast, sensibly diminishing the supply of Slaves that used formerly to be taken to the Mediterranean Coast. If therefore, it is found more profitable for the Caravans to procure their supplies of European Goods from the Western Coast, when these supplies have to be filtered through the hands of several Chiefs and are enhanced in value by a long and dangerous land carriage how much more profitable would it be if the supplies they required were to be found in Markets established on the Upper banks of the Niger. But it is impossible that these markets should be established and the trade of the River developed as long as the navigation in the Delta is practically stopped by the hostility of some of the Native Chiefs. Render the Navigation safe and the Merchants will soon push their way up the River and establish Trading Posts.

[1] F.O. 97/434. *William Wylde* was Superintendent of the Slave Trade Department and of the Commercial and Consular Department in the Foreign Office. Minute on Admiralty to F.O., 3 January 1862. The Delta middlemen had attacked Laird's Niger steamers in 1857, 1859, and 1860.
[2] Rear-Admiral Sir Baldwin Walker, Commander-in-Chief at the Cape, 1861–4.

It should moreover be borne in mind that Dr. Baikie is still in the interior and will have to be withdrawn or some decision come to respecting him next summer when the River is again navigable.

It would appear to be a pity when so much money has been spent, that the scheme for opening the Navigation of the Niger should be given up, when it has been proved to be practicable, as far as the navigation of the River is concerned, and is only prevented by the hostility of a few insignificant Native Chiefs.

I would therefore venture to suggest, that Adml. Walker should be authorized to use the means at his disposal for punishing the hostile Chiefs, particularly the Chief of Aboh regarding whom Ld. Palmerston, on reading the Command. of the 'Espoirs' proceedings at that place says, 'It is much to be regretted that this barbarous Chief was not properly punished for his misdeeds and Breach of Engagements.'

Unless events should render it necessary to weaken the Afr. Squadron, Adml. Walker will have vessels at his disposal next summer fitted for the Navigation of the Niger, and if it should be decided that an Expedition is to be undertaken for the punishment of the hostile Chiefs, it would I think be useful to make known some little time beforehand that an Expedition is going to ascend the River in order that Merchants might take advantage of the escort for purposes of Trade. Perhaps the most practicable way of opening the Navigation of the Niger would be to send a Ship of War, or two if necessary, up the River for two or three years in succession and to give notice to the Traders that this will be done, and that they may take advantage of the Escort. The Native Chiefs, who are sharp enough, seeing that the Traders are protected will find it more to their advantage to trade than to fight. If our Merchants do not choose to take advantage of the opportunities that would be thus afforded them of opening out a Trade into the interior of Africa, the Govt. will have done its duty and the Merchants will only have themselves to blame. Such a scheme would, I submit, be preferable to entering into any new Contract for the Navigation of the River.

16

THE COMPANY OF AFRICAN MERCHANTS TO LORD JOHN RUSSELL, PETITION FOR A SUBSIDY, 22 JULY 1863[1]

MY LORD,

We have the honour to inclose for your Lordship's information a Copy of the Prospectus of the Company of African Merchants which is now finally constituted with the whole of its Capital £400,000, subscribed.

The Capital thus subscribed will be ample for the present purposes of the Company; but they have power, should it be necessary, to raise additional Capital. The objects of the Company are partly sketched out in the Prospectus;[2] but the Directors are more particularly desirous of coming to a decision as to immediate operations in the River Niger. They are prepared to negociate with Her Majesty's Government for continuing and extending the operations of the late Macgregor Laird, and otherwise to give effect to the valuable labours of Dr. Baikie.

For the purpose of maintaining Steam Communication with the Interior, the Directors are convinced that Government support is necessary for a few years until the Trade is established; after which they are equally persuaded it will be sufficiently developed to be selfsupporting; and eventually be the means of securing to this Country the Trade of the interior of Africa by the Rivers Niger and Chadda, and opening up a promising and boundless field for the supply of Cotton; while at the same time the operations of legitimate Commerce will prove as they have already done on the various Coast Rulers, the most effectual means of destroying the Slave Trade from the interior by which the foreign Slave Trade is supplied.

We beg leave therefore respectfully to express a hope that in view of the great national importance of these objects, Her Majesty's Government will accord to the Company of African Merchants such assistance and support as may be found necessary for the fully carrying out of the plans contemplated by the Directors of this Company.

[1] F.O. 97/434. Signed, W. Dent and A. Hamilton, Directors, V. Fitzgerald, Secretary. The Company was formed by representatives of the Liverpool and Manchester firms, Fred. Huth & Co., and Thomas Tobin & Son. The subsidy requested was refused: F.O. 97/434, Layard to African Merchants, 13 August 1863.

[2] Ibid., encl. Prospectus, describing African exports—palm oil, cotton, copper ore—and attacking the slave trade.

17

MERCHANTS OF LIVERPOOL TO LORD JOHN RUSSELL: NIGER SUBSIDY, 3 MAY 1864[1]

MY LORD,

We the undersigned merchants, including every house in Liverpool trading to the West Coast of Africa (with the exception of the 'Company of African Merchants Limited', and one gentleman connected with it), employing 66 ships, of 30,228 tons register, entirely in the African trade, view with surprise and alarm the application of the 'Company of African Merchants, Limited', for a subsidy from Government, on the ground of developing the trade of the Niger, with the further professed objects of extending civilization in Central Africa, and of assisting to suppress the slave-trade.

Our surprise is occasioned by the fact of an application for Government aid being made by a purely trading company, in the face of the enlightened policy of the present day, and the very proper opposition offered to any system of legislation resulting in the advantage of the few to the injury of the many.

The merchants engaged in the African trade have hitherto competed with the entire world without any assistance from Government, beyond the protection to life and property afforded to Her Majesty's subjects in all parts of the globe, and we cannot but view with alarm the possibility of a subsidy being granted to a powerful company which is in active competition with us in most parts of the West Coast of Africa. A Government grant, however moderate, and even if paid exclusively for work done on the Niger, would give a company so subsidised an undue importance in the eyes of the natives, and an unfair advantage over private firms in other parts of the coast.

Whilst Government aid was given, as in the case of the late Macgregor Laird, to a private individual not engaged in trade in other parts of Africa, but solely for the purpose of opening up the Niger, and with the view of extending civilization, so far from offering any protest, we have viewed with deep interest the efforts made, and have wished them complete success; but as the Niger has been effectually explored to the furthest navigable point, namely, the rapids at Rabbah both by private philanthropists and the Government, at a great outlay of public money as also of private money, and unfortunately at the sacrifice of many valuable lives, we consider the time has passed for any further grants from Government solely for the purpose of exploration.

[1] *Parl. Papers*, 1864, x (424), p. 16. Merchants of Bristol and London sent in similar petitions dated 6 and 30 May 1864.

If so successful a trade is to be prosecuted up the Niger (as the Company represents in its prospectus herewith), we think it should be left to private enterprise, which will be amply rewarded, and it would be manifestly unjust to tax the community at large for the benefit of private interests.

That there is no slave-trade to be lessened or entirely suppressed by the proposed enterprise for furthering which a grant from the public purse is now sought, is evident from the incontrovertible fact that not a single slave has been exported from the Niger or any of it mouths for at least 10 years.

We therefore respectfully submit to your Lordship our objections to the grant to the 'Company of African Merchants, Limited', not on the ground of its being excessive, but solely because of the principle involved, and in the fervent hope that Government will not entertain with favour the proposed subsidy, but decide, on the contrary, that it would be both an impolitic precedent and an improper expenditure of the public money.

Thomas Harrison & Co.; Hatton & Cookson; Tyron, Richmond & Jones; David Clark; Alfred Aspinall; Charles Horsfall & Sons; Stuart & Douglas; George J. Cornish.

18

W. G. ROMAINE TO A. H. LAYARD: PROTECTION OF TRADERS, 20 SEPTEMBER 1865[1]

[The crew of H.M.S. *Zebra*, summoned by the Governor of Sierra Leone to patrol the Melakori rivers, have suffered severely from tropical sickness.]

... My Lords [Commissioners of the Admiralty] are of opinion that the Instructions to H.M.'s Naval Officers to assist the Governors of Colonies in protecting British Life and Property should not be held to extend to those British & other European traders who establish themselves beyond the limits of British territory in the midst of barbarous and savage tribes.

My Lords therefore propose to request Mr. Secr[etary] Cardwell to inform the Govrs. on the West Coast of Africa that they are not at liberty to call on the Comm[anders] of H.M.'s Ships of War to send their boats up the Rivers to protect traders who have settled themselves in such places as the Mellacourie River;—that the Govrs. should be directed to acquaint merchants & their agents trading among the tribes of Western Africa that if they choose to risk their lives & property without the limits of British territory, they must so

[1] C.O. 267/285. *A. H. Layard* was Under-Secretary at the Foreign Office, 1852, 1861–6.

conduct their affairs as to be at peace with their savage neighbours.

My Lords propose to give instructions to Comm[odore] Wilmot to the above effect for his future guidance in similar cases. My Lords would remark that this Expedition up the Mellacourie river was requested by the Govr. & carried out by the 'Zebra', in the unhealthy season of the year, contrary to the standing orders of the Station, and that the result was such as has usually attended any stay beyond a few hours in the Rivers of this part of the world. The 'Zebra' has been compelled to return to England in consequence of the prostration of the men employed on the Expedition through fever and other disease.

My Lords consider that assistance tendered to traders under such circumstances is purchased too dearly by the loss of the service of a cruiser engaged in the suppression of the Slave Trade, and at the expense of the health, if not the lives of officers and men of H.M.'s Naval Service.

19

T. F. ELLIOT TO W. G. ROMAINE: PROTECTION OF TRADERS, 30 SEPTEMBER 1865[1]

... MR. CARDWELL agrees in the general principle laid down by the Lords of the Admiralty in regard to the amount of protection to be granted to British and other European Traders who may establish themselves beyond the limits of British Territory, but he presumes that its application must be a matter requiring the exercise of much discretion. Mr. Cardwell makes no claim on the part of Colonial Governors for authority to interfere officially in cases occurring at a distance from their Governments. ...

20

E. HAMMOND TO T. F. ELLIOT: PROTECTION OF TRADERS, 9 OCTOBER 1865[2]

... LORD RUSSELL desires me to state that he would view with very greatest regret the issue of any such orders as those contemplated in the Admiralty letter, because the effect would be to withdraw British protection from the Merchants and Traders established in the Oil Rivers on the West Coast of Africa, where a very valuable and increasing trade is carried on, and where a vast amount of British

[1] C.O. 267/285. *T. F. Elliot* had been head of the Colonial Land and Emigration Commission, 1837–47, and was Assistant Under-Secretary at the Colonial Office, 1849–68.

[2] Ibid., *E. Hammond* was head of the Oriental Department at the Foreign Office and Permanent Under-Secretary, 1854–73.

property, as well as many British Lives, are dependent for their safety on the knowledge possessed by the Native Chiefs and People that they will be severely punished by a British Naval Force in the event of their causing any injury to the Lives or Properties of British Subjects established in their Territories.

At the present moment, when there is every reason to believe that a Cargo of Slaves has not been shipped from the West Coast of Africa for the last eighteen months, and when it may be hoped that the Export trade of Slaves from that Coast is approaching its total Suppression, Lord Russell is of opinion that it is the policy of this Country to assist by all legitimate means the development of lawful trade on the African Coast and Rivers, and that instead of protection being withdrawn from British traders, they should be encouraged to pursue, and if possible increase their trading transactions with the Natives; for it is only by the establishment of legitimate trade that we may hope totally to eradicate the Slave Trade.

I am to transmit for Mr. Cardwell's information, copies of a Correspondence which has passed between this Department and the Admiralty, relative to an application made to the latter Department by Lord Russell's directions that facilities should be afforded to Her Majesty's Consuls on the West Coast of Africa to visit periodically the Oil Rivers within their Consular Jurisdiction, with a view to enable them to attend to British interests, and to settle disputes that are constantly arising between British and Native Traders, and which, if not attended to in time, are apt to lead to serious consequences.

I am to state that if the Lords Commissioners of the Admiralty cannot find the means of placing a Steam-Vessel occasionally at the disposal of Her Majesty's Consuls in order to enable them to carry out their duties, Lord Russell proposes to request the Lords Commissioners of Her Majesty's Treasury to sanction the expense necessary for the purpose of equipping a Steam-Vessel to be employed on this Service, but before making any communication either to the Treasury or to the Admiralty on this subject His Lordship would wish to be favoured with Mr. Cardwell's views in the matter.

I am to add that the reason assigned by the Admiralty for their instruction to the Commanders on the West Coast of Africa, namely the vicinity of barbarous and savage Tribes might be extended to other parts of the Globe, and might lead to the refusal of protection to all British Subjects who do not reside in civilized countries.

21

THE SECRETARY TO THE TREASURY TO A. H. LAYARD: NIGER SUBSIDY, 15 MAY 1866[1]

... THEIR LORDSHIPS desire me to state, for the information of the Earl of Clarendon, that, having again considered this proposal, they are not at present prepared to submit to Parliament a Vote for such a Subsidy [for Niger expeditions] as is sought by the African Merchants and recommended by the African Aid Society.

Lord Clarendon: Minute, 18 May 1866.

We can do no more in this matter as Mr Gladstone told me he was sure that the vote wd. be successfully opposed in the H. of C.

22

GOVERNOR SIR ARTHUR KENNEDY TO THE DUKE OF BUCKINGHAM AND CHANDOS: FRENCH COMPETITION IN THE MELAKORI, 3 JULY 1868[2]

[France has occupied part of the Melakori.]

... THE French Governments have taken possession of the mouths of these Rivers,[3] and levy a duty of Four per cent on all produce leaving the River, and will doubtless soon impose other duties at a place called 'Benti' commanding the mouth of the Mellicourie River, where a formidable Block House is in the course of erection, though this place has, with the full sanction and under protection of Native Chiefs, long been occupied by British Traders who have established Factories there.

6. Similar proceedings have been adopted by the French Government in the Rivers Nunez and Pongas.

7. I have, when referred to, or visited by Native Chiefs laying their complaints before me, confined myself to counselling Peace, and the avoidance of Collision with French Forces.

[1] F.O. 97/436. The Company of African Merchants had renewed their request for a subsidy, 30 June 1865. F.O. 97/435.

[2] C.O. 267/294. *Sir Arthur Kennedy* had retired from the Army in 1848. He acted as Governor of the Gambia and of Sierra Leone, 1851–4, and after governorships in Western Australia and Vancouver Island, he was appointed Governor-in-Chief of the West African Settlements, 1867–72.

[3] A French fort was built at the mouth of the Nunez in 1865; a protectorate agreement was made in the Melakori in 1867 and a military post was set up at Gbinti at the mouth of the river.

8. These proceedings will, without doubt, seriously affect the Trade of this Colony, as the distrust created among the Native population has already driven many away, and is drying up the productive power of the Country.

9. There can be no doubt that the policy of the French Government is directed to the occupation of all the Rivers lying between Sierra Leone and 'Gorée'; and I think it not improbable that in furtherance of this policy, the 'Great' and 'Little Scarcies' Rivers, on the Northern boundary of the Colony may ere long be similarly occupied. I would therefore beg for Your Grace's instructions to guide me in such an event. The Chiefs in these Rivers have expressed their apprehension of such an occurrence.

10. Your Grace will observe on reference to Treaties at pages 390 and 393 of Volume 2 Local Ordinances, that we are guaranteed *the free Navigation* of these Rivers, and any interruption to it would prove a fatal blow to the Commerce and progress of this Colony.

11. Already the Natives of the Interior at the head of the Fouricariah and Mellicoorie Rivers, alarmed at the French occupation, begin to bring their produce (which has hitherto found an outlet by those Rivers) to Sierra Leone via Scarcies Rivers. . . .

23

SIR F. R. SANDFORD TO THE FOREIGN OFFICE: FRENCH COMPETITION IN THE MELAKORI, 9 MARCH 1869[1]

[France is willing to place British and French coastal trading vessels on an equal footing in their respective areas of West Africa.]

. . . LORD GRANVILLE desires me to request that you will call the attention of the Earl of Clarendon to the observations contained in the letters from this Department of the 21st. May and 27th. November last, with reference to which Lord Granville would remark that the French Government appear still to ignore the main question at issue viz. the rights enjoyed by British Subjects under Treaties entered into with the Native Chiefs of these Countries on the West Coast of Africa in which the French have assumed authority.

Meanwhile the following general considerations on the whole subject have suggested themselves to Lord Granville. It appears to His Lordship that the British Government ought to have no such

---

[1] C.O. 267/299. Drafted by Sir Frederic Rogers Sandford. *F. R. Sandford* was Assistant Under-Secretary at the Colonial Office 1868–70. *Lord Granville* had been Under-Secretary in the Foreign Office, 1840–1 and Secretary of State there in 1851 and 1852. He was Secretary of State for Colonies, December 1868–July 1870, before transferring to the Foreign Office again.

desire for the extension of their own political influence in the neighbourhood of Sierra Leone, as would lead them to oppose the establishment of a French Protectorate, provided it do not extend to Tribes (if any) who are already practically dependencies of S. Leone; and further that if in a French territory, or territory under French Protectorate, English Merchants have the same freedom of trade that French Merchants have, the British Government have no cause to be dissatisfied, even though they may lose their right to absolute exemption from duties.

Lord Granville is however of opinion that if such freedom of trade is not granted by the French Government, Great Britain may properly insist on the rights guaranteed to her by the Treaties abovementioned.

[D. Nor would his Lordship be disposed to concede the right of the French Govt.] [A. And a question may be whether & to what extent the right of the French] to impose Customs Duties on British Merchants contrary to those treaties [A. shd. be recognized] except in territories where the French accept the correlative duty of maintaining order.

With these views it seems to Lord Granville that it would be desirable [D. 1st. to draw a line round S. Leone, embracing all that Great Britain wishes to retain or acquire.][1]

1st. to come to an arrangement with the French that they should not attempt to acquire political influence [D. beyond that line] [A. in Territory within a certain distance from S. Leone—to be defined–] and that Great Britain on her part would not interfere with their acquiring political influence [A. beyond that territory to the North].

2nd. to establish reciprocally perfect equality of trade French and English being in all respects on the same footing throughout French & English territories, and to make some special arrangements, if it be considered advisable, regarding the acquisition of land in either territory.

[D. At the same time, Lord Granville is alive to the consideration that to insist, wherever Customs Duties are levied, that the recipient power should be responsible for protecting Commerce might involve the British Govt. in difficult obligations].

I am to add that if Lord Clarendon should concur in this general view of the case, Lord Granville would propose to refer it to Sir A. Kennedy for his report, prior to its being communicated to the French Govt.

---

[1] Deleted because Sierra Leone had no dependencies to the north and no claims to territory, except Bulama.

24

FOREIGN OFFICE TO THE COLONIAL OFFICE: LIBERIAN INDEMNITY, 10 AUGUST 1869[1]

. . . WITH reference to my letter of the 4th instant, upon the subject of the measures to be adopted with the view to procure & redress from the Liberian Government for outrages committed by Liberian Authorities upon British Subjects in the Manna River District, I am directed by the Earl of Clarendon to transmit to you, to be laid before Earl Granville, the accompanying copy of a letter from the Admiralty, stating that Her Majesty's Ship 'Sirius', a Captain's command, will be ready to sail from Sierra Leone early this week and could embark the Governor-in-Chief of the West African Settlements, and convey him to Monrovia with the view to his communicating with the Liberian authorities.

I am also to transmit a copy of the reply which by Lord Clarendon's directions has been returned to the inquiry of the Admiralty as to the nature of the coercive measures to be adopted in the event of a non-compliance on the part of the Liberians with the Governor-General's demands and I am to suggest that, if Lord Granville concurs, Instructions in a similar sense should be addressed to Sir Arthur Kennedy.

25

FOREIGN OFFICE TO THE SECRETARY TO THE ADMIRALTY: PROTECTION OF NIGER TRADE, 11 OCTOBER 1869[2]

SIR,

I have laid before the Earl of Clarendon your letter of 29th. ult. inquiring, with refce. to a report from Commor. Dowell upon his proposed distribution of the naval force on the W. Coast of Africa, what are Ld. Clarendon's present views as to the necessity of continuing the annual exp[edition] up the Niger & the S[lave] T[rade] Blockade of the Coast.

In reply, to the 1st. question I am to request that you will inform the Lds. of the Admy. that, upon the conclusion in April last of the

---

[1] C.O. 267/303. Signed by Arthur Otway. The issue was the right of Liberia to assert a claim to the Gallinas and to enforce payment of Customs by Sierra Leone traders. At Monrovia, Kennedy secured the return of a trading schooner and the payment of an indemnity of £3,370, in instalments.

[2] Ibid. For the agreement over the distribution of naval forces, see below, p. 596.

arrangement of the naval forces on the Coast, which included as provision for the employment of a vessel in the annual Niger Exp-[edition] the Merchants interested in the Niger Trade were informed that, altho' the Consulate at Lukoja[1] had been abolished, the moral support of the annual visit of a Ship of War to the Niger would probably be extended to them so long as it was warranted by the necessities of their trade & the success of their operations, & Ld. Clarendon thinks it would be a breach of faith with the merchants if the Exp[edition] were to be immediately abandoned. His L[ordshi]p also considers that it would be impolitic to withdraw all protection and support from this trade at a time when it appears to be satisfactorily increasing and developing itself into a valuable commerce. . . .

[The slave trade blockade of the Western Coast is to be continued.]

26

FOREIGN OFFICE TO THE COLONIAL OFFICE: PROTECTION OF NIGER TRADE, 5 FEBRUARY 1872[2]

[Forwarding a copy of W. H. Simpson's *Report of the Niger Expedition*, November 1871.]

. . . I AM to state that Lord Granville, while adhering to his decision to discontinue the annual Government Expedition up the River, has suggested to the Admiralty the expediency of sending a vessel of light draught of water as far as the Delta about the time when the Trading Steamers annually start up the River, to protect them from attack, and to prevent the chances and lamentable consequences of a collision between the Natives and armed Merchant Vessels. . . .

[1] There had been a temporary consulate at the Niger-Benue Confluence, 1866–9, under J. L. McLeod.
[2] C.O. 147/25. *W. H. Simpson* was Collector of Customs and Acting Administrator of Lagos Colony.

III

SLAVE TRADE

A. METHODS OF SUPPRESSION

Introductory Note

THE humanitarian campaign against slavery and the slave trade profoundly influenced the course of British policy in West Africa. Of the three effective achievements of this campaign—Lord Mansfield's judgement of 1772 and the two Acts of 1807 and 1833—the first and the last guaranteed emancipation in England and in British possessions abroad, while the second attacked British traffic in slaves. On this basis, an Order in Council of 1808 authorized the seizure and condemnation of slave vessels under prize commission in time of war and began the long and costly naval campaign in the Atlantic and on the coast.

The implications of the use of a Preventive Squadron were foreseen as early as 1811: a limited number of men and ships could be concentrated in special areas, or employed extensively to make occasional captures from Senegal to the Congo. Disagreement over the most effective naval strategy persisted throughout the campaign, not least when the number of warships had risen from a mere half-dozen to twenty or more in the 1840's.

Another serious drawback after 1815 was the legal inability of the Squadron to examine vessels under foreign flags, unless permitted by treaty with the country concerned. Until 1839, suppression off the coast of West Africa centred around this problem which was only partially solved by early agreements made with Portugal, Spain, and Holland, 1815–18, and by the establishment of a Court of Mixed Commission at Sierra Leone. Vessels could not be taken unless slaves were found on board; and vessels under the Portuguese flag were prohibited from slave-trading north of the Equator only. Reports of the Senior Officer of the West Africa Squadron pointed to the general inadequacy of the campaign at sea and the difficulties of presenting evidence before the Mixed Commission Court whose members were either unsure of their jurisdiction or unwilling to see their own nationals punished. Other methods were considered: Governor Turner's plan for a 'floating force' of colonial gunboats was approved by Lord Bathurst in 1825, but systematic blockade of slave ports was prohibited and the force was never provided. Similarly, the Admiralty refused to place vessels under the orders of colonial governors or to station them for long periods inshore at river mouths. More sweeping proposals for annexation of parts of the coast were rejected.

By the end of the 1830's, diplomatic action had secured the concession of the right of search from Brazil and France and the addition of equipment clauses to a treaty with Spain. Failing to obtain a new treaty from

Portugal, Lord Palmerston declared the slave trade under the Portuguese flag a piracy, north and south of the Equator (as urged by Admiral Collier in 1820), whether vessels were carrying slaves or merely equipped for the task. This Act of 1839, it was claimed, marked the 'epoch when the right of search system first became complete'.[1]

In 1839, too, the anti-slavery movement in England planned to supplement diplomacy and naval action by ending the slave trade at its source. The main points in the programme of economic and social regeneration proposed by Thomas Fowell Buxton at the formation of the African Civilization Society were expanded in the Society's *Prospectus* of 1840; and the two most important of them were adopted by Lord John Russell. A widespread system of treaties with African chiefs was to ensure the prohibition of slave-dealing on the coast; legitimate trade in African produce was to be encouraged by an expedition to the Niger and by the establishment of model plantations.

A draft treaty containing the main requirements for African co-operation was sent to the Governor of Sierra Leone in 1840; and a similar treaty was appended to the instructions of the Niger Expedition Commissioners at the beginning of 1841. By the end of that year, difficulties of navigation and loss of life had forced the withdrawal of the three Niger steamers to Fernando Po, leaving only a tender at the Niger-Benue confluence where land had been purchased for a 'Model Farm'. Two treaties with the chiefs of Abo and Ida, above and below Lokoja, were little enough to show for the expenditure in money and men; and when it was clear that the farm had failed, the expedition was officially abandoned by Lord Stanley in March 1842.

A second blow to the active opponents of the slave trade, and one which crippled the naval tactics used with success by Captain Denman at the Gallinas in 1841, was a decision by the Law Officers and Lord Aberdeen that blockade and the destruction of foreigners' stores were illegal.

As a result of this setback to the policies initiated by Buxton and Russell, new instructions for naval officers were drawn up by a committee appointed in 1842, and included a short draft treaty of six articles which promised neither British protection nor any form of payment to African chiefs. Meanwhile, opposition to the use of the Preventive Squadron as an instrument of humanitarian policy mounted and reached a climax in the unfavourable conclusions of a Select Committee of the House of Commons in 1848. But a change of legal opinion and the failure of an action for damages brought by slave-dealers against Captain Denman, allowed the destruction of slave stations on the coast to continue, where treaties had been broken.

This acceptance of the use of force inshore, begun by Denman and continued at the Gallinas, Cape Mount, New Cestos, Sherbro, and Lagos, and the favourable recommendations of the Lords' Committee of 1850, did not by themselves constitute a policy which ended the slave trade. There could be no final solution, unless all the coast were annexed (which was not seriously considered), or until the markets of the Americas were closed. On the coast as a whole the most significant results of the

---

[1] Captain the Hon. Joseph Denman: below, p. 168, n.1.

campaign were the extension of the treaty system and the appointment of consuls. Between 1841 and 1853, some sixty-five agreements to end the slave trade were made with chiefs from the Gambia to the Delta. Only a few of the early treaties for the Gambia and Sierra Leone contained the terms of the draft of 1840, and these had later to be changed. The bulk, obtained in 1847 and 1848, were based on the draft of 1844, and with the exception of some of the Delta and Slave Coast chiefs, their signatories were promised no compensation. Consuls and consular agents were appointed between 1849 and 1853 to the Delta, the Gallinas, Porto-Novo, Lagos, and the Sherbro to see the terms of the treaties were observed. Inevitably, in the Bights where consular activity was longest their activities involved Great Britain more closely in the affairs of legitimate traders on the coast.

I

ORDER IN COUNCIL: RECAPTURE OF SLAVES, 16 MARCH 1808[1]

. . . AND whereas it is expedient and necessary to provide for the due execution of the said Act of Parliament,[2] by such orders, appointments and regulations, as His Majesty in Council is thereby empowered to make, His Majesty is pleased, by and with the advice of His Privy Council, to order and appoint, and doth hereby order and appoint, that the Collector, or Chief Officer of the Customs for the time being, resident in any of His Majesty's Islands, Settlements, or Colonies, being Seats of Courts of Vice-Admiralty, for the time being, and also the Governor or Person having and exercising the Chief Civil Command, for the time being, at the Colony of Sierra Leone, on the Coast of Africa, do receive, protect, and provide for all such Natives of Africa, as have been, or shall be condemned, either as Prize of War or for forfeitures to His Majesty's Use, pursuant to the said recited Acts, in the said several Islands, Settlements, or Colonies respectively; and the said persons shall have full power and authority to receive, protect and provide for all such Natives of Africa as shall be condemned as aforesaid, and to enter and enlist the same into His Majesty's Land or Sea Service, as Soldiers, Seamen, or Mariners; and to bind the same Apprentices, pursuant to the powers given by the said recited Act, upon such terms and conditions, and subject to such regulations as His Majesty shall, from time to time, think fit to prescribe by His Order, or Orders in Council, in that behalf; and to make and execute Indentures of Apprenticeship for that purpose; and also to grant certificates for entitling the captors or seizors and prosecutors of any such Negroes, to receive the Bounties, by the said receited Act and herein-after appointed . . .[3]

[1] C.O. 267/24. Forwarded to the Governor of Sierra Leone, 11 April 1808.
[2] The Slave Trade Abolition Act, 25 March 1807 (46 Geo. III, c. 36).
[3] £40, £30 and £10 for every man, woman and child adjudicated.

2

REPORT OF THE COMMISSIONERS OF AFRICAN INQUIRY: USE OF THE NAVY, 1811[1]

THE interruptions and annoyance which the Slave Trade has lately met with between Goree and Sierra Leone, has given it a considerable blow. As long as it is carried on by vessels liable to seizure (such as the Spanish Americans), the coast from the latter place to the River Nunez, would be nearly free from this evil, were it not for the Portuguese settlement of Bissao, which, instead of furnishing, as formerly, a small number of slaves annually to Brazil, is now becoming the emporium of the Slave Trade in this part of Africa. There the ships lay secure from seizure, and thither the slaves are safely conveyed, along the shore in canoes and small craft, from the Scarcies, Pongas, Nunez, and other rivers in the neighbourhood. No good remedy seems applicable to this evil, but the direct interference of the Portuguese Government.

But the great scene of the Slave Trade is on the coast of Whydah, the Bight of Benin, Gaboon, and the Portuguese settlements in Congo and Angola. We have no means here of ascertaining the extent to which it is carried on: but according to the general opinion of the best informed Spaniards and Portuguese who have been brought into this port, the annual importation was (in the beginning of 1810) considered, at a moderate computation, to be 40,000 for Brazil, 40,000 for the Havannah and Cuba. The Portuguese part of this trade is carried on almost entirely in ships and vessels actually Portuguese. Some British merchants are supposed to be the real owners of a few; and the Americans, of a few more. Very few real Spanish ships are employed; the great mass of vessels under the Spanish flag on the coast of Africa, are actually Americans; several are supposed to belong to British merchants.

The slave vessels which are by far the most numerous, and of course most obvious to the examination of our cruizers, are Americans, commonly under Spanish, but in some few instances under other false colours. The decision of the Privy Council, on a case of appeal, has determined that vessels so circumstanced are liable to confiscation. But the difficulty of producing the necessary proofs, renders their detention generally hazardous; and the increasing experience of

[1] *Parl. Papers*, 1812, x (101), pp. 1–2. *Thomas Ludlam* and *William Dawes*, both former Governors of Sierra Leone, were appointed with *Governor E. H. Columbine* to report on the settlements and the slave trade. They completed their first report early in 1810 and submitted the rest in April 1811. C.O. 267/29; and *Sixth Report of the Directors of the African Institution, 25 March 1812* (London, 1812), pp. 69–72.

those traders rendering detection more and more difficult every day, nothing is to be expected from our cruizers in any degree commensurate to the extent of the evil.

But allowing that no vessel be permitted to pass which is liable to good ground of suspicion, still, it is to be feared, that without some great restriction by Spain and her colonies, and some further limitation on the part of Portugal, no effectual means are in the power of Great Britain to stop such an extensive and lucrative trade. It is also extremely difficult even to catch the vessels which are supposed contraband: most of them sail extremely well, are perfectly on their guard, and have the advantage of directing their voyage to too many distant ports across the Atlantic, to allow of any important molestation from our cruizers.

The cruizers at present on this station have lately made four distinct sweeps along the coast down to Prince's Island. Out of many slave ships which were boarded, only one has been caught under circumstances which would admit her being brought up for adjudication.

Upon a careful review of the whole case, it would seem that the following conclusions may fairly be drawn:—

That we have not sufficient means to prevent the Slave Trade in general from being carried on; but if instead of opposing it generally, we confine ourselves for the present to some one branch of it, there is a great probability of our success there, and of a constant gradual extension of that success at a more remote period.

No difficulty can occur in choosing the particular part to which we should confine our exertions. The leeward coast, all that part which is generally called the Bight of Benin, is too unhealthy to admit much cruizing, or the formation of a new establishment on some of the islands, if Portugal would cede one of them for that purpose. As to the Gold Coast, we have already as many forts as can be desired there; but little benefit is to be expected from their co-operation in the extinction of the Slave Trade, as they do not possess authority or influence enough to prevent its being carried on, even under their guns.

We must therefore turn our views to Sierra Leone, from whence will probably emanate any degree of civilization which may be attained by the adjacent parts of Africa in the south-east quarter. But no progress worth speaking of can be made until the Slave Trade shall be so completely prevented, that the trading chiefs and other natives no longer entertaining any hopes of its restoration, shall feel the necessity of raising produce sufficient to purchase those European commodities, which the sale of their slaves at present furnishes to them. For this purpose our cruizers in Africa should be generally limited to the coast between Goree and the Kroo country; paying a more decided attention to the coast from the river Nunez to the Sherbro. This unceasing interruption would compel the traders to withdraw from this part of the coast; but finding little or no mole-station to the eastward of the Gold Coast, they would naturally direct their voyages thither, and leave western Africa at rest, and with a fair opportunity of bettering its condition.

3

W. DAWES: ADDITIONAL REPORT, USE OF THE NAVY, 1811[1]

... I FEEL myself called upon for these reasons to dissent entirely from that part of the report, which would restrain the naval efforts of Great Britain to suppress this trade, within narrower limits than are fully adequate to meet all the exigencies of the case on every part of the African coast; and I cannot doubt that Captain Columbine would have concurred in my views, had he known of the circumstances to which I have alluded as affecting the capture of slave ships, or could he have believed that a naval force sufficient to scour the whole coast would be afforded by Government.

I feel it incumbent on me to express my decided opinion, that a powerful and concurrent effort made by an adequate number of cruizers along the whole line of the African coast, continued during the succeeding twelve months, would do more effectually to suppress this traffic, than the continuance of a smaller force on the coast for a much greater length of time. The trade might receive a blow during that time from which it would hardly recover. Should His Majesty's Government determine on making such an effort, the island of Princes would afford a most convenient rendezvous for a small squadron, such as Captain Columbine proposes should be stationed to windward, from whence it would give most effectual annoyance to illicit slave ships throughout the Bight of Benin, and even occasion-ally as far as Cape Three Points, westward, and Angola, southward.

I concur also in the general statements of the report with respect to this colony. Its situation is extremely well chosen, and it possesses other advantages which give it a decided superiority over every other possession of the Crown in Western Africa. I also anticipate many benefits to Africa and to Great Britain from its maintenance.

[1] *Parl. Papers*, 1812, x (180).

4

C. ROBINSON (KING'S ADVOCATE) TO EARL BATHURST: SEIZURE OF FOREIGN VESSELS, 28 JUNE 1816[1]

... IN obedience to Your Lordship's directions I am of the opinion that there is not any Jurisdiction in the Courts of Vice Admiralty, under the original Commission of the Judges, or under any Acts of Parliament, which have extended that Jurisdiction, that will empower them in time of peace to take Cognizance of the Act of trading in Slaves, as an offence committed by foreign vessels, in parts not connected with His Majesty's Dominions, although that trade may be prohibited by their own Governments.

The Jurisdiction which has been exercised in such Cases during the late War has been under the Prize Commission and following the Authority of a Decision of the Court of Appeal, which rejected the claim of the Proprietor, exceptione turpis causa, or on account of illegality of the transaction, in which the Parties were engaged.

The seizure in the first Case had originated in a Case connected with War—and though Condemnation passed on the collateral ground as above stated, it was conformable to Principles, that had been applied to other Cases of illegal Trade.

That mode of reaching Cases of this description must cease with the Prize Commission of the Courts of Vice Admiralty, and I am of opinion that those Courts as at present constituted have not in their Civil or Criminal Jurisdiction, any authority to take Cognizance of such Cases.

5

THE LORDS COMMISSIONERS OF THE ADMIRALTY TO COMMODORE SIR G. R. COLLIER: INSTRUCTIONS, 3 NOVEMBER 1819[2]

... WE have issued to the commanders of vessels[3] employed on the coast of Africa, the following documents, viz.—

Two Acts of Parliament, passed to carry into effect the treaties concluded with Portugal and Spain,[4] for the prevention of an illicit

[1] C.O. 267/43. [2] Parl. Papers, xxiii (366), p. 84.
[3] The warships Pheasant, Morgiana, Snapper, Thistle.
[4] The treaty of 22 January 1815 and additional convention, 28 July 1817, between Great Britain and Portugal; the treaty of 23 September 1817 with Spain. Both these treaties authorized mutual right of search and capture of vessels carrying slaves.

traffic in slaves, (copies of which treaties were transmitted with our said instructions to you;)

The necessary orders, signed by us, to authorize the commanders of His Majesty's ships to search vessels bearing the flags of the said two nations;

And, a treaty concluded, for the same object, with the King of the Netherlands;[1] with the Act of Parliament, and signed instructions relating thereto.

We now send you documents of the descriptions here mentioned, and strictly enjoin you to be governed by them, in your conduct towards all ships bearing the flags of the nations alluded to; observing, that any of these ships, which may be captured for illicit trafficking in slaves, are to be sent for adjudication to the following places, as may be most convenient, according to the situation in which the capture may be made, viz—

Ships of *any of the three nations* to Sierra Leone, or *Portuguese* ships to Rio de Janeiro, *Spanish* ships to the Havannah, and *Dutch* ships to Surinam; courts having been established at these places for the trial of offences of the above description, committed by vessels of those nations respectively, as above detailed.

Vessels under English colours may be sent to, and tried at either of the places enumerated. . . .

6

COMMODORE SIR G. R. COLLIER: SECOND ANNUAL REPORT, 16 SEPTEMBER 1820[2]

. . . My public letters, reciting a variety of atrocious facts, will, I trust, have satisfied their Lordships, that this more than ever cruelly conducted Slave Company's trade is, contrary to their anxious expectations, far from being on the decline. I therefore feel it my duty, before I conclude this report, to give some general understanding of what the Slave Trade really is at present; and I humbly hope, I shall the more readily be excused this, as the naval force of His Majesty, which their Lordships have been pleased to place under my command, is fitted expressly for the object of suppressing this abominable traffic. England certainly, the whole world must acknowledge, has most faithfully abandoned the trade. America may be considered next in good intention. She has passed laws, forbidding the trade by her subjects, and has decreed heavy punishments on those who shall engage in it. She has also sent an armed force to the

---

[1] Treaty of 4 May 1818 on mutual right of search and capture.
[2] *Parl. Papers*, xxiii (366), pp. 76–77. *Sir George Collier* was Commodore of the West African Squadron.

coast of Africa, and this force has captured vessels, the property of American subjects. Still, her measures are not yet complete, and American vessels, American subjects, and American capital, are unquestionably engaged in the trade, though under other colours and in disguise; but it may be hoped, time will effect in America, as it has in England, a total discontinuance of this traffic, as the Government of America appears to have engaged in its suppression with great sincerity.

Spain, by her decrees, in consequence of her engagements with Great Britain, has relinquished the trade; but her colonies still carry it on in defiance of those engagements; and as a Spanish vessel is not subject to capture, unless she shall have slaves on board, although as I have frequently observed, landing those embarked on the appearance of a British man of war. She will, by her colonies, continue the traffic, though not with the same security she formerly had, yet certainly to a great extent. If Spain be sincere, she can shew it only by *compelling* her colonies to observe her engagements.

Holland, it is true, has entered into engagements similar to those of Spain; but in her colonies also the trade is encouraged, and vessels under the flag of the King of the Netherlands are frequently met on the slaving coast, and some have been sent into Sierra Leone, which, after much opposition by those whose duty it was to have acted otherwise, have been condemned.

Portugal, though restricted by her treaties, to the continuance of the trade south of the line, permits her subjects of St. Thomas's and Prince's Island to carry on the traffic to a very considerable extent; and in the month of February last, no fewer than six vessels arrived at Prince's Island with cargoes, ultimately for the West Indies.

But France, it is with deepest regret that I mention it, has countenanced and encouraged the Slave Trade, almost beyond estimation or belief. Under pretence of supplying her own colonies, and furnishing only the means required for their cultivation, she has her flag protected, and British cruizers can only retire when they shall see her ensign; for search being forbidden, power and force become unavailing. Under this security, France is engrossing nearly the whole of the Slave Trade, and she has extended this traffic beyond what can be supposed, but by one only who has witnessed it. In truth, France now supplies the foreign colonies, north of the line, with Africans. I exaggerate nothing in saying, that thirty vessels, bearing the colours of France, have nearly at the same time, and within two or three degrees of distance, been employed slaving, without my daring to offer interruption, but at considerable risk; yet I was induced, under some circumstances, to detain vessels bearing the French flag, in the hope of checking the bold and frequent outrages committed by the French on our own coast. I will add, that in the last twelve months, not less than 60,000 Africans have been forced from their country, principally under the colours of France, most of whom have been distributed between the Islands of Martinique, Guadeloupe, and Cuba. The confidence under which vessels navigate, bearing the French flag, has become so great, that I saw at the Havannah, in July last, no fewer than forty vessels fitting avowedly for the Slave Trade, protected equally by the flags and papers of France and Spain. France has certainly issued her decrees against this traffic, but she has done nothing to enforce them. On the contrary, she gives to the trade all countenance short of public avowal.

Piracy upon the coast of Africa is increasing, for a vessel so engaged has only to show the flag of France, and search by a British officer, incurs a penalty; and unless His Majesty's ships, employed on that coast in suppression of slavery, shall, against slaving vessels, have the full powers of a belligerent, all prohibitory laws against this trade will become a mockery. . . .

7

EARL BATHURST TO GOVERNOR CHARLES TURNER: PLAN FOR GUNBOATS, 19 DECEMBER 1825[1]

[No military posts can be established along the coast to prevent the slave trade.]

. . . No similar objection, however, exists to the foundation of a floating force on a very limited scale, to be stationed with the consent of the Tribes to which the Territory may belong, either up the Rivers, or at the mouth of such as are known to be the most frequent resort of the Slave Dealers.

I leave you to the selection of the Spots on this Coast where the experiment may be made with the greatest advantage. A Gun boat or vessel of a similar description capable of containing 40 or 50 men, who should be chosen from those most inured to the Climate, would I should imagine, fully answer the purpose intended, & would serve as a rallying point for such of the Neighbouring Tribes as may be disposed to cooperate heartily in repressing the Slave Trade; and would materially relieve the Cruizers employed on this Coast. And you will not fail to have inserted in the Treaties which you will have to negotiate with the Native Powers, such stipulations as will enable His

---

[1] C.O. 268/20, ff. 295-8. For Turner's expansionist policy, see below, p. 417. The use of small armed vessels on the coast had been urged by Governor Maxwell in 1813, but was postponed by Bathurst during the war with France: C.O. 268/19 f. 8. The first colonial steamer, the *African*, sent out in 1827, lasted less than a year and was not replaced at Sierra Leone till 1866 by the *Corra Linn*.

Majesty to station a floating force in the manner above described, & will receive every facility of landing on either side of the Rivers respectively, as the urgency of the case may require.

8

EARL BATHURST TO GOVERNOR SIR NEIL CAMPBELL: BLOCKADE, 25 OCTOBER 1826[1]

SIR,

By the letters which I have received from the Acting Governor Mr. Macaulay, since the date of my letter addressed to you on the 1st. Inst., I find that the Proclamation of Blockade had been enforced, & that Mr. Macaulay had purchased an additional Vessel for that purpose.

Although this measure of force obviates in some degree the objections to such a blockade, I trust that it will have been removed & that the measures taken by the Acting Governor Mr. Smart will have put an end to the hostilities with the Gallinas.

You are in possession of instructions in the event of these hostilities continuing, or being renewed, so as to render a blockade in your judgment necessary; & the Colonial force which appears to be now at your disposal will give facilities to its due establishment. But I must remind you on no account to place under blockade any part of the Coast which does not belong to a Country with which His Majesty may not be in a state of actual hostility. A blockade is strictly a belligerent measure, and authorized only by a state of War. It is not one to which you can have recourse solely for the purpose of putting down the Slave Trade to whatever extent, there may be too much reason to believe that, this odious traffic exists on that part of the Coast.

I have in my former instructions to General Turner (19 Dec. 1825)[2] explained the utmost extent to which you can be authorized to go for putting down this odious traffic, & you must always bear in mind that these measures must not be adopted without the consent formally given by the Tribes to whom the Territory belongs, wherever you may deem it necessary that they should be applied; & that they must not be so exercised as to interrupt the free navigation of the River, where it may be rightfully claimed by those Tribes who shall not have given their consent.

[1] C.O. 268/26, ff. 111–14. *Major-General Sir Neil Campbell*, like Turner, had served in the Napoleonic Wars. He governed Sierra Leone from August 1826 till his death a year later.

[2] See above, no. 7, p. 142.

9

EXTRACTS FROM THE REGULATIONS FOR THE GUIDANCE OF THE SLAVE TRADE COMMISSIONS, 1830[1]

THESE Commissions are framed in pursuance of the following Treaties between His Britannick Majesty, and His Most Faithful Majesty the King of Portugal, His Catholick Majesty the King of Spain, and His Majesty the King of the Netherlands.

The Treaty with Portugal was made on the 28th July 1817, and Ratifications were exchanged at Rio Janeiro on the 27th November 1817.

The Treaty with Spain was made on the 23d September 1817, and Ratifications exchanged at Madrid on the 22d November 1817.

The Treaty with the King of the Netherlands was made the 4th May 1818, and Ratifications exchanged at the Hague on the 25th May 1818.

It may not, in the first place, be improper to take a short review of these Treaties, as they regard the illicit traffick in slaves.

The Treaties between this Country and Portugal, and Spain, and the Acts of Parliament for carrying these Treaties into effect, declare illicit, all traffick in slaves by British ships;—all traffick in slaves by Portuguese or Spanish ships in parts therein specified, and all such traffick in other parts, by Portuguese or Spanish ships, for account of the subjects of any other Government, or bound for any port, not in the dominions of the Sovereign to which the ship may belong.

By the Treaty with the King of the Netherlands, that Sovereign engages within 8 months, or sooner if possible, from the exchange of the Ratifications, to prohibit all his subjects, in the most effectual manner, and especially by penal law the most formal, to take any part whatever in the trade of slaves; and in the event of the measures already taken by the British Government, and to be taken by that of the Netherlands, being found ineffectual or insufficient, the High Contracting Parties mutually engage to adopt such further measures, by legal provision or otherwise, as may, from time to time, appear best calculated to prevent all their respective subjects from taking any share whatever in this nefarious traffick.

It is expressly stipulated by all the High Contracting Powers, that no vessels shall be detained, but those having slaves actually on board: that they are to be carried as soon as possible for judgement to the nearest place, where one of the Mixed Commissions is sitting, or

[1] *Parl. Papers*, 1831, *Slave Trade* (A). *Correspondence with British Commissioners*, pp. 15–16.

which the captor thinks he can soonest reach from the spot where the slave-ship shall have been detained; and no cruizer is legally authorized to detain any vessel, unless such cruizer forms part of the British, Portuguese, Spanish, or Netherland Royal Navies, and is furnished with the special instructions, pointed out in the Treaties, for visiting merchant vessels suspected of having slaves on board; the visitation and search are directed to be done in the most mild manner; and in no case is the search to be made by an Officer holding rank inferior to that of Lieutenant in the British, Portuguese, or Netherland Royal Navies; or of Ensign of a ship of the line in the Spanish Navy.

By the Treaty with Spain, it is declared to be illegal at present, for any Spanish subject to carry on the slave-trade, on any part of the coast of Africa, North of the Equator, upon any pretext, or in any manner whatever; and His Catholick Majesty engages that the slave-trade shall be abolished, throughout the entire dominions of Spain, on the 30th May 1820, and after that period it shall not be lawful for any Spanish subject to purchase slaves, or carry on the slave-trade; but the same is then to cease entirely. A term, however, of 5 months, from the said 30th May 1820, is allowed for completing the voyages of those vessels, which shall have cleared out lawfully previous to the said 30th May 1820.

By the Separate Article to the Additional Convention with Portugal, dated London, 11th September, 1817, it is stipulated, that as soon as the total abolition of the slave-trade, for the subjects of the Crown of Portugal, shall have taken place, the two High Contracting Parties agree to adapt, to the state of circumstances, the stipulations of the said Convention, dated 28th July 1817; but in default of such alterations, the Additional Convention of that date shall remain in force, until the expiration of 15 years, from the day on which the general abolition of the slave-trade shall so take place, on the part of the Portuguese Government.

All traffick in slaves by the Portuguese, to the northward of the Equator, is prohibited, and the only trading in slaves to south of the Equator, which is at present allowed to the Portuguese, by the Treaty or Convention of 28th July, 1817, is limited to the territories, possessed by the Crown of Portugal, upon the coast of Africa; viz. the territory lying between Cape Delgado Bay, and the Bay of Laurenco Marques, upon the eastern coast of Africa; and, upon the western coast, all the territory which is situated from the 8th to the 18th degree of south latitude.

By the 2d article of the Treaty it is declared, that the territories over which the King of Portugal has retained the rights of sovereignty, on the coast of Africa, south of the Equator, are those of Molembo and Cabinda, upon the eastern coast, from the 5th degree 12: to the

8th degree south. This must be an error, as those places are on the western coast of Africa.

Every Portuguese or Spanish vessel engaged in this trade, must be provided with a Royal Passport permitting such traffick.

The Mixed Commissions are to consist of two Commissary Judges, and two Commissioners of Arbitration; one of each to be named by His Britannick Majesty, and the others by the Kings of Portugal and Spain, as they shall be established in their respective dominions. To each Commission is to be attached a Secretary or Registrar, whose appointment is vested in the Sovereign of the country in which the Commission may reside, and the proceedings under the Commissions are to be written down in the language of the country where the same may be respectively established.

The British Government has undertaken to indemnify the proprietors of all Portuguese vessels improperly detained after the 1st of July 1814; but no claim for compensation can be admitted, for a larger number of slaves than was permitted according to the rate of tonnage of the vessel captured; and the individuals having a just claim, are to be paid the same within the space of a year, at farthest, from the decision of each case.

It has been before observed, that no vessels are legally liable to be captured, but those having slaves actually on board for the express purpose of the traffick; so that a vessel having negro servants or sailors on board, is not for that reason to be detained: and no merchantman or slave-ship is to be visited or detained, whilst in the port or roadstead belonging to either of the High Contracting Powers, or within cannon-shot of the batteries on shore, excepting on the continent of Africa, north of the Equator; but no slave-ship, either Portuguese or Spanish, is to be detained near the land, or even on the high seas, south of the Equator, unless after a chase, which shall have commenced north of the Equator; and if any vessel be detained south of the Equator, the proof as the illegality of the voyage is to be exhibited *by the Captor*; and in all cases of slave-ships detained to the north of the Equator, the proof of the legality of the voyage is to be furnished *by the vessel so detained*.

It is stipulated, that notwithstanding the number of slaves found on board any vessel may not agree with the number contained in the passport, yet that shall not be a sufficient reason to justify the detention of the ship.

When a slave-ship shall be detained, the Master thereof, and a part at least of the crew are to be left on board, and the Captor is directed to draw up in writing, an authentick declaration, which shall exhibit the state in which he found the detained ship, and the changes which may have taken place in it; and to deliver to the Master of the slave-ship, a signed certificate of the papers seized on board such detained vessel, as well as the number of slaves found on board. None of the slaves are to be disembarked, till after the vessel shall have arrived at the place where the legality of the capture is to be tried, unless urgent motives, deduced from the length of the voyage, the state of health of the negroes, or other causes, should make a disembarkation (entirely or in part) necessary before the vessel's arrival: the Commander of the capturing ship, however, takes upon himself the responsibility of such disembarkation, and the necessity thereof must be stated in a certificate, in proper form. . . .

[Forms of declarations and certificates to be used.]

10

LORD PALMERSTON TO HIS MAJESTY'S COMMISSIONERS, SIERRA LEONE: USE OF THE NAVY, 31 DECEMBER 1830[1]

GENTLEMEN,

Your despatches up to those of the 30th of October, 1830, have been received.

I have communicated to the Board of Admiralty, your despatches of September 21st, and October 18th, reporting the increase of slave-trade in the neighbourhod of Sierra Leone, and suggesting, that a vessel of war, furnished with instructions under the Treaties, should be stationed at that place, and made subject to the orders of the Governor of that Settlement.

The Board of Admiralty have answered, that they cannot comply with this suggestion, as it is contrary to the custom of the service to place any of His Majesty's ships under a Colonial Government; but that strict orders are given to the senior Officer on the African station, for the prevention of the slave-trade, and the protection of the British settlements and commerce.

11

SIR THOMAS FOWELL BUXTON: MEMORANDUM FOR THE AFRICAN CIVILIZATION SOCIETY, APRIL 1839[2]

THE principle has been sufficiently explained:—It is the deliverance of Africa, by calling forth her own resources.

[1] Ibid., p. 19. The Slave Trade Commissioners at this date were *Lieut.-Colonel A. Findlay*, Governor of Sierra Leone, 1830–3, and *Commissary Judge William Smith*.
[2] Charles Buxton (ed.), *Memoirs of Sir Thomas Fowell Buxton, Baronet. With Selections from His Correspondence* (London, 1848), p. 448.

In order to do this, we must:—1. Impede the traffic; 2. Establish commerce; 3. Teach cultivation; 4. Impart education.

To accomplish the first object we must increase and concentrate our squadron, and make treaties with coast and inland chiefs.

To accomplish the second, we must settle factories and send out trading ships.

To accomplish the third, we must obtain by treaty lands for cultivation, and set on foot a company.

To accomplish the fourth, we must revive African institutions: look out for Black agents, &c.

What then is actually to be done now by Government? Increase the squadron; obtain Fernando Po; prepare and instruct embassies (or authorize governors) to form treaties, including, prevention of traffic; arrangements for trade; grants of land. By us; form a trading company; revive the African Institution.

12

LORD JOHN RUSSELL: MEMORANDUM ON THE AFRICAN SLAVE TRADE, 23 SEPTEMBER 1839[1]

THERE are three kinds of measures proposed to be taken for the prevention of the dreadful trade in Slaves, carried on by African Chiefs, & European merchants—the sellers & buyers in this Traffic.

1. The first is a more vigilant and systematic course of naval operations. The Admiralty are giving directions in conjunction with the Govt. upon this subject.

2. The next is a combination of treaties made with the Princes & Chiefs both of the Coast, & the Interior, for the substitution of innocent commerce for the Trade in Men. The expedition [is] about to sail, & the Governors on the Coast will be furnished with instructions for this purpose.

3. The remaining point, and the one on which the greatest difficulty exists, relates to the acquisition of territory in Africa by the Crown. Mr. Buxton, who is the most earnest in favour of this measure, does not seem to have thoroughly considered it. In speaking of the necessary conditions he states 'first, the territory shall be freely offered to us without any kind of constraint—and an *annual rent should be paid for it*'. I must remark upon these conditions that besides the vagueness of the first, the proposal to pay an annual rent for Sovereignty is I believe new, & I am sure is advisable. Sovereignty must be absolute; the Crown paying a rent to an African Chief would appear in the humiliating & precarious situation of a tenant of such barbarous Chief. I agree however with Mr. Buxton that the Commissioners should not be instructed peremptorily to refuse in all cases 'the

[1] C.O. 325/37.

sovereignty over any Province or Place'. What I should propose is this. That the Commissioners should be instructed to enquire & report on the practicability, advantages, & dangers of acquiring sovereignty for the Crown of any place or situation in the interior of Africa. They should not be satisfied with ascertaining that a single Chief is willing to barter his dominions for manufactured goods. They should weigh the hazard of jealousy, & hostility being excited among neighbouring Chiefs by the appearance of the British flag in the midst of their possessions as a token of sovereign power. They should calculate the force that would be necessary to maintain & defend the territory that might be acquired—the facility or difficulty of relief—the extent of territory necessary to protect those who might seek shelter & security within its borders—the danger of invasion from any European power, which might have settlements on the Coast. If upon examination of these & many other points they should be of opinion that the acquisition of territory by the Crown is essential to the success of the great objects of the Expedition, they will yet conclude no Treaty for that purpose, but make an ample report of all the facts for the information of Government. In my opinion so large a scheme could not be adopted, even to a limited extent, without consulting the House of Commons, & perhaps submitting the facts to a committee in both Houses.

13

LORD PALMERSTON TO HER MAJESTY'S COMMISSIONERS, SIERRA LEONE: PORTUGUESE SLAVE VESSELS, 2 NOVEMBER 1839[1]

GENTLEMEN,

With reference to my Despatches, marked Slave Trade, of the 25th of August and of the 3rd of September last; the first enclosing copies of an Address upon Slave Trade from the House of Peers to Her Majesty, and Her Majesty's most gracious answer thereto; and the second enclosing a copy of an Act of Parliament[2] recently passed for the suppression of the Slave Trade,—I have to acquaint you, that the Queen has been pleased to command, that orders should be given to the commanders of Her Majesty's cruizers to detain vessels engaged in Slave Trade, and sailing under the flag of Portugal, wherever met with; and also to detain vessels engaged in Slave Trade,

[1] *Parl. Papers*, 1839, *Slave Trade* (A), *Correspondence with British Commissioners*, p. 7.
[2] Act 2 & 3 Vict., c. 73 (24 August 1839). The Act was repealed in 1843, after a new treaty with Portugal on illegal equipment of vessels for the slave trade. A similar Act of 8 August 1845 (8 & 9 Vict, c. 122) subjected vessels sailing under the Brazilian flag to Admiralty jurisdiction if similarly equipped.

MBP

but hoisting no flag, and destitute of any papers proving their nationality.

Orders have also been given to establish British Courts of Vice Admiralty at any places within Her Majesty's Dominions and Colonies abroad, where such Courts may be requisite for the adjudication of vessels detained as before mentioned.

Thirdly, orders have been given, that the crews of Portuguese slave-vessels so detained shall be sent to that port of the Portuguese dominions, to which it may be most convenient to convey them, in order that they may there be delivered up to the Portuguese authorities.

Fourthly, orders have been given that negroes found on board such detained vessels shall be landed at the nearest British port or settlement, and shall there be placed under the care of the Governor or other officer in command.

And fifthly, orders have been given to the Governors of Her Majesty's forts and settlements abroad, to make the necessary arrangements for the care and support of the negroes who may be landed and set free under these orders.

The officers commanding Her Majesty's cruizers employed for the suppression of the Slave Trade, have, at the same time, been acquainted, that nothing contained in the before-mentioned Act of Parliament is intended to confer upon British cruizers any new right of search as to any vessel sailing under the flag of a State, with which Great Britain has no Treaty granting a mutual right of search, and that with respect to vessels sailing under the flag of a State, with which Great Britain has a Treaty granting a mutual right of search, that Act of Parliament is not intended to authorize Her Majesty's naval officers to visit and search such vessels, in any other way than that which is prescribed by such Treaties and by the instructions annexed thereto.

14

DRAFT AGREEMENT WITH AFRICAN CHIEFS, JULY 1840[1]

Object

THERE shall be peace and friendship between the people of England and the people of——and the slave trade shall be put down for ever in ——, and the people of England and the people of——shall trade together innocently, justly, kindly and usefully. And A and B do make the following agreement for these purposes:—

---

[1] *Parl. Papers*, 1865, v (412), pp. 424–5.

Terms.

1. No white Christian persons shall be made slaves in the —— country in any case; and if any white Christians are now slaves in the ——country, or shall be brought into it as slaves, they shall instantly be set free by the Chief of ——, and he shall assist them to return to their own country.

2. No persons of any colour, or wherever born, shall be taken out of the——country as slaves; and no person in the——country shall be in any way concerned in seizing, keeping, carrying, or sending away any persons for the purpose of their being taken out of the —— country as slaves. And the Chief of —— shall punish severely all those who break this law.

3. The officers of the Queen of England may seize every vessel or boat of —— found anywhere carrying on the trade in slaves, and may also seize every vessel or boat of other nations found carrying on the trade in slaves in the waters belonging to the Chief of ——, and the vessels and boats so seized shall be taken into an England possession to be tried by English law; and, when condemned, shall be sold, and the produce of the sale shall be divided equally between the Queen of England and the Chief of ——, and the slaves who were found on board shall be made free.

4. English people may come freely into the —— country, and may stay in it or pass through it; and they shall be treated as friends while in it, and shall receive every supply they need there; they may freely practice the Christian religion there, and shall not be harmed nor troubled on that account; and they may leave the country when they please.

5. English people may always trade freely with the people of —— in every article which they may wish to buy or sell; and neither the English people nor the people of —— shall ever be forced to buy or to sell any article, nor shall they be prevented from buying or selling any article; and the customs and dues taken by the Chief of —— on English goods shall in no case be more altogether than 1/ th part of the price of the goods sold.

6. The paths shall be kept open through the —— country to other countries, so that English traders may carry goods of all kinds through the —— country to sell them elsewhere; and the traders of other countries may bring their goods through the —— country to trade with the English people.

7. English people may buy and sell or hire lands and houses in the —— country, and their houses shall not be entered without their consent, nor shall their goods be seized, nor their persons touched; and if English people are wronged or illtreated by the people of ——, and Chief of —— shall punish those who wrong or illtreat the English people.

8. But the English people must not break the laws of the —— country; and when they are accused of breaking the laws, the chiefs shall send a true account of the matter to the nearest place where there is an English force; and the commander of such English force shall send for the English person, who shall be tried according to English law, and shall be punished if found guilty.

9. If the —— people should take away the property of an English person, or should not pay their just debts to an English person, the Chief of —— shall do all he can to make the —— people restore the property and pay the debt; and if English persons should take away the property of the —— people, or should not pay their just debts to the —— people, the Chief of —— shall make known the fact to the Commander of the English force, nearest to the —— country, or to the resident agent, if there is one; and the English Commander, or the agent, whichever it may be, shall do all he can to make the English persons restore the property and pay the debt.

10. The Queen of England may appoint an agent to visit —— or to reside there, in order to watch over the interests of the English people, and to see that this agreement is fulfilled; and such agent shall always receive honour and protection in the —— country, and the —— Chiefs shall pay attention to what the agent says; and the person and property of the agent shall be sacred.

11. The Chief of —— shall, within 48 hours of the date of this agreement, make a law for carrying the whole of it into effect; and shall proclaim that law, and the Chief of —— shall put that law in force from that time for ever. . . .

[Form of signatures.]

Additional Terms for special cases.

Article 1. Moreover, the Queen of England, for —— years to come, will have ready every year, at ——, the following articles, viz: —— and an English officer shall inquire in each year whether the Chief of —— and his people have faithfully kept the foregoing agreement, and if, after enquiry, he shall be satisfied that they have kept the agreement, he shall then deliver the articles to the chief, or to the chief's agent for him; but when the English officer is not so satisfied, he shall not deliver the articles.

Article 2. The practice of making human sacrifices, on account of religious or political ceremonies or customs, shall cease for ever in ——.

Article 3. The Chief of —— sells and makes over to the English people for the Queen of England, the land from —— to —— and everything in it, entirely and for ever, for the sum of ——, of which

—— is now paid to him. And the English people shall have possession of the said land, and of whatever may be upon it, when they shall have paid to the Chief of —— the remainder of the price above stated; and when the land shall be delivered over to the English people, they may do with it what they please.

Article 4. The Queen of England will assist in protecting the Chief and people of —— against any attack which other chiefs and people may make on them on account of anything they may do for the purpose of giving up the slave trade according to the present agreement.

15

JAMES STEPHEN: MINUTE ON THE PROPOSED INSTRUCTIONS FOR THE NIGER EXPEDITION, 8 DECEMBER [1840][1]

MR. TREVELYAN[2] called here yesterday and told me that they had received at the Treasury (I think from Captain Trotter[3]) copies of the proposed Instructions and Treaties, and that the Chancellor of the Exchequer[4] had a very strong objection to so much of them as related to the present expenditure for obtaining those Treaties by gifts to the African Chiefs—that he also regarded those Treaties as the certain and fertile source of great expences in future—that he objected to any such Treaties being made—and that Mr. Macauley was of the same opinion. Mr. Trevelyan observed that these Instructions must go to the Treasury for their formal sanction in reference to the proposed Expenditure. I told him that it was only just now that Captain Trotter's report on them had been received, and that it was impossible for Lord John Russell to consult the Treasury on a project on which he had not been able as yet to determine exactly what to recommend for their sanction—that determination being impossible until after Captain Trotter had been heard on the subject.

I am very much afraid that the main principle of all this arrangement is not, even yet, clearly understood and agreed upon by the Members of the Govt. among themselves, supposing Mr. Trevelyan

---

[1] C.O. 325/37. *James Stephen* had been appointed part-time counsel to the Colonial Department in 1813 and permanent counsel in 1825, Assistant Under-Secretary in 1834, and remained as Permanent Under-Secretary from 1836 till 1847.

[2] *C. E. Trevelyan*, Assistant Secretary to the Treasury, 1840–59.

[3] *Captain Henry Dundas Trotter*, Senior Officer of the West Africa Squadron, 1830–5, and commander of the *Albert* during the Niger Expedition.

[4] *F. T. Baring*, Chancellor, 1839–41.

to be accurately informed, and supposing me to have accurately understood him respecting the opinion of Messrs Baring and Macaulay.

For my own part I think it right to say (whatever may be the value of my judgement on such a matter) that I never could see a clear path on this business, beyond the *preliminary step of an exploration, with a view to a Report* as to what it would be right to do hereafter. I may very possibly be wrong, for I am certainly very ignorant about the internal State of Africa, but it seems to me (with the most sincere deference to the very high judgements which are ranged on the opposite side) that few schemes could be more unpromising or hazardous than that of sending Ships many hundred miles into the heart of that Continent, there to make compacts which apparently at least we should not have the slightest power of enforcing, and the breach of which by the Native Chiefs may be regarded as almost a certainty. They will take our presents, and sign what we like, and then do just what they like; and who is to prevent them? We shall establish relations which may be very embarrassing, and if we begin by showing that engagements with us may be violated with impunity, we shall certainly labour under great disadvantages in any future attempt to compas [*sic*] the same ends. . . .

16

LORD JOHN RUSSELL: INSTRUCTIONS TO HER MAJESTY'S NIGER COMMISSIONERS, 30 JANUARY 1841[1]

(*a*)

. . . 10. ON your arrival at each native settlement, you will ascertain the proper mode for opening a communication with the Chief; and in all your intercourse with him, you will take care that you are treated by him with proper respect; and you will not neglect, also, to treat him with the respect which is due to the rank which belongs to him.

11. You will tell the Chief that you are sent by the Queen of Great Britain and Ireland to express Her Majesty's wish to establish friendly relations with him; and to settle and agree with him for the extinction of the Foreign Traffic in Slaves in his dominions; and for the substitution instead thereof of a full and free intercourse and

[1] *Parl. Papers*, 1843, xlviii (472), pp. 6–10, 15. The Niger Commissioners were Captain H. D. Trotter, Commander W. Allen, Commander Bird Allen and William Cook.

barter of all articles of innocent trade between the subjects of Her Majesty and those of such Chief, for his profit and advantage, and for the mutual use, comfort, and benefit of the subjects of both countries. You will ask him what articles he and his subjects are in want of, and you will express generally the readiness of this country to supply them; you will ask him what articles of trade he and his subjects wish to dispose of; and you will express generally the readiness of this country to purchase them. You will inquire what further articles of native growth, or produce, or manufacture his country can supply as articles of useful export with Great Britain; and you will encourage him to the cultivation or production thereof, by expressing generally the readiness of this country to take off his hands, on fair and reasonable terms of barter, all such articles of useful trade for this country as he can supply, in return for all such articles of use, and comfort, and advantage to himself as he requires.

12. You will show to him the advantages of putting down the Foreign Slave Trade, and of building upon the abolition a lawful and innocent trade. You will say to him, that his subjects will thereby be induced to cultivate the soil, to value their habitations, to increase their produce, and to behave well, in order to keep the advantage which that produce will give to them; that they will thus become better subjects, and better men, and that his possessions will thus become more full of what is valuable. You will impress upon him, that he himself will no longer need to make, or to keep up, quarrels with his neighbours, or to undertake distant and dangerous wars, or to seek out causes of punishment to his own subjects, for the sake of producing from the odious Trade in Slaves an income for himself. You will explain to him, that the people of his country will, out of the produce of labour in cultivating, gathering, and preparing articles for trade, bring to him more revenues, and be consequently more valuable to him.

13. You will tell him, that Her Majesty, desirous to make that innocent commerce which is a benefit to all nations, a peculiar benefit to himself, proposes that, upon his abolishing the Slave Trade, not only he and his subjects shall have this free and advantageous commerce; but that he himself shall have, for his own share, and without any payment on his part, a sum not exceeding one-twentieth part value of every article of British merchandize brought by British ships and sold in his dominions; such proportion to be taken by himself without any reference to the amount of articles for which the remaining nineteen-twentieths shall be bartered with him or with his subjects; and you will make agreements with him on this subject conformable, as far as possible, with the draft agreement.[1] You will, where possible, stipulate in return for a free right of barter for his

1 Ibid., pp. 13–14; and above, no. 14.

subjects, and the abolition of any monopoly in his own favour, should such exist.

14. While explaining to the Chief the profit to be derived from the cultivation of the soil, you will not fail on all proper occasions, as far as you may deem it expedient and compatible with the main objects of your mission, to draw his attention to the superior advantages of free over slave labour: to impress upon him the impolicy as well as the injustice of slavery: and to acquaint him with the abhorrence in which it is held by Her Majesty and the people of England. You may remind him of the large tracts of waste land in his possession; state how unprofitable they are to him at present; and inform him that if he could procure such land to be cultivated by his subjects on a system of free labour, he would be justly entitled to receive a considerable share of the increased profits: far more than enough to counterbalance all the profits which could possibly arise from the continuance of the Slave Trade. You may further remind him that every man naturally works harder for himself than for another, and is more economical and more careful of his own property; consequently, that the produce of his country would be much greater by free labour than by any other system, and that he would derive a double advantage, first, from his share of the produce as a landlord, and afterwards from the duties he would get as Chief on the sale of the remainder. You may further intimate to him, that a compliance with the wish of Her Majesty's Government and her people, in this respect, would certainly increase Her Majesty's interest in his welfare, and enable Her Majesty and her people to render much greater assistance and encouragement in improving the condition of himself and his people, than could be afforded them during the continuance of a system of slave labour. But you must always bear in mind that the main object of your commission is the extinction of the Foreign Slave Trade, and all other points must for the present be considered subordinate.

15. You will, at the proper time, exhibit the presents with which you are furnished from Her Majesty, as proofs of the desire of friendship which the Queen entertains towards the Chief, and as samples of the articles, with which, among others, this country will be glad to supply himself and his subjects in as great a quantity as they shall want and wish, on fair and reasonable terms of barter. You should not distribute these presents to any of the Chiefs, except in those cases where you are satisfied that the interests of the commission in which you are employed imperatively require it; and further, you will also bear in mind the necessity of giving no more than is absolutely requisite; and especially with a view to avoid all possibility of in future impeding ordinary traffic with British or other merchants. In case any of the Chiefs or Head-men of the country

should be willing to make presents, you are authorized to exercise your discretion in receiving or rejecting the same; all presents received being for the use of Her Majesty.

16. You will finally propose to him an Agreement upon the basis of the draft with which you are herewith furnished.

17. If, after earnestly discussing this matter with the Chief, you shall find that your arguments have not so far prevailed with him, as to induce him to enter into this Agreement for the Extinction of the Foreign Slave Trade in his dominions; and if he shall resolutely resist your suggestions and the wishes of Her Majesty to that effect; you will entreat and urge him to reconsider this matter, you will ask him to assemble his elders or head-men, and consult with them, before he finally rejects the proposals made by you.

18. You will, if permitted to be present at such conference, declare that the Queen your Sovereign, however powerful, is anxious only to promote peace and prosperity among them; that she offers them, through you, every advantage that they can want and that she can give, towards increasing, in a harmless and sure way, the wealth and power of the country; that you come but to ask them to give up the custom of exporting human beings as slaves, and in return to offer them a more profitable substitute in innocent trade; that if they wish moreover any help towards the production of any article, or introduction of any commodity or art for the benefit of their country, your Sovereign is disposed to assist them, and her subjects will be willing to supply at a moderate rate what they desire; and that you will express to Her Majesty their wishes, and forward their views to that effect.

19. While you describe the power and wealth of your country, you will, in all your interviews with the African Chiefs, and with other African natives, on the subject of the suppression of the Slave Trade, abstain carefully from any threat or intimation, that hostilities upon their territory will be the result of their refusal to treat. You will state that the Queen and people of England profess the Christian Religion; that by this religion they are commanded to assist in promoting good will, peace, and brotherly love, among all nations and men; and that in endeavouring to commence a further intercourse with the African nations Her Majesty's Government are actuated and guided by these principles. You will make allowance for the motives of fear, of distrust, of jealousy, of suspicion, by which native Africans, unaccustomed to treat with Europeans in this formal way, may, at first, naturally view the overtures made to them; you will make allowance also for misunderstanding, either of language, of manner, or of conduct, or of your object in seeking intercourse with them; you will also allow for any hardness of feeling you may witness in them on the subject of Slave Trade, a hardness naturally engendered by the

exercise of that traffic, and, perhaps, in some cases, increased by intercourse with the lowest and basest of Europeans. You will endeavour to convince them by courtesy, by kindness, by patience and forbearance, of your most persevering desire to be on good terms with them; and you will be most careful to exhibit no signs of needless mistrust. You will on all occasions keep a strict watch, so that no mischief may, from open force or secret wile of the natives, ensure to the lives, liberties, and properties of yourselves, and of others committed to your care; and with this view you will be careful to be provided with adequate means of defence as far as possible; but you will on no account have recourse to arms, excepting for the purpose of defence; and you will bear in mind, that the language and conduct prescribed to you in this paragraph is that which you are to observe on all occasions in the course of your commission.

20. If, after all your attempts to attain the immediate object of your commission, you shall fail in it, you will conclude by telling the Chief and his head-men, that Her Majesty is bound to use all her naval means in conformity with the treaties already entered into with other Great Powers to endeavour entirely to put a stop to the exportation of Slaves from the dominions of every African Chief; and that the Chief and his subjects will, when perhaps too late, see cause to regret their conduct.

21. In those cases in which, all your arguments and representations failing, you will have been obliged to leave the Chief and his country, without accomplishing the immediate objects of your mission, you will be careful still even at parting to leave that Chief and his country in a friendly manner, in order to give room for future overtures, and for a reconsideration of the kindly meant efforts of Her Majesty; and you will, if time and circumstances allow it, take an opportunity of visiting again those Chiefs, who in your first visit declined your overtures; and strengthened by the weight which your success elsewhere may have given to your negotiations, you will again urge the Chiefs to conclude an agreement, on the before-mentioned basis of the abolition of the Slave Trade. . . .

. . . It is considered desirable by Her Majesty's Government to have power to erect one or more small forts on the Niger, from whence, and by means of which, to watch over the due execution of the Agreements, to assist in the abolition of the Slave Trade, and to protect and further the innocent trade of Her Majesty's subjects.

Bearing these views in mind, you will, in your course up that river, select some one or more appropriate spots for the erection of forts for the above-mentioned purposes; and you will make with the Chief of the country a conditional bargain for the land, stating the purpose for which it is intended: you will pay down a small portion of the price, as security for the purchase and permission; and you will send or bring home, for the consideration and ultimate decision of Her Majesty's Government, reports and drawings explanatory of the spot and its capabilities.

The spots should be chosen with reference both to defence and salubrity; to soil and to climate, not only of the spots themselves, but also of the immediate neighbourhood on both sides of the river; because the miasma from one side of a river will frequently, if carried by winds, produce diseases on the other side. They should be places where vessels may securely anchor and ride in safety. They should be in situations to which natives are likely to resort for trade; and if possible, in situations where natives have been accustomed to resort for the purpose. Means of a ready communication with the interior are also desirable for the positions; so that persons wishing to visit the interior from thence, for purposes of commerce or otherwise, may there find facilities for those objects. They should be in a neighbourhood where supplies for vessels may be got; and in a country where the inhabitants are well disposed towards friendly communication with British subjects; and they will be preferably situated if not far from some considerable mass of habitations. The establishment of a position near to the confluence of the rivers Niger and Tchadda, would, with its other advantages, have the additional and important one, that it would assist the British trade with both rivers. . . .

. . . 33. If at any place, in an independent State within the range of your commission, it shall appear to you to be desirable, that a resident agent on the part of Her Majesty, shall be immediately appointed, and enter on his duties, you are empowered to leave at such a place provisionally, as British resident agent, any one of the gentlemen of your commission, or of the officers or others of the expedition, whom you may think competent and fitted to the duties of that situation. You may assure to such gentleman an allowance proportioned to the circumstances of his situation, for one year only.

LORD JOHN RUSSELL: INSTRUCTIONS TO HER MAJESTY'S NIGER COMMISSIONERS, 30 JANUARY 1841[1]

(b)

GENTLEMEN,

In my general Instructions of this day's date, I have authorized you to make a conditional bargain of a site of land on the Niger, for the erection of a fort. But I have also instructed you that you are not authorized to accept, on behalf of Her Majesty, the sovereignty over any province or place which might be offered through you to the Crown.

[1] Based on a minute by Robert Vernon Smith, 12 August 1840, C.O. 325/37.

The question of establishing British sovereignty in Africa must be reserved for future consideration and decision. But you will perceive, from the accompanying copy of a letter which has been addressed to me by Dr. Lushington and by Sir Fowell Buxton,[1] that they have urged the establishment of such sovereignty as indispensable, in their judgement, for the success of the views of an Agricultural Society, who contemplate the prosecution of the special objects explained in that letter.

Dr. Lushington and Sir Fowell Buxton are desirous for the purchase of the sovereignty over a territory not exceeding 100 miles square, in which the Agent of the Agricultural Society adverted to would, on behalf of that body, purchase, in fee simple, the most eligible spot for the purposes of the Society.

I can only, however, at present instruct to make this proposition the subject of your most careful inquiry, with a view to your reporting:—

1st. Whether a tract of land of the nature of that required could easily be obtained, and upon what terms.

2ndly. Whether such territory might be acquired in a district deemed tolerably healthy for Europeans.

3rdly. Whether the neighbouring tribes would be likely to be friendly or hostile to the proposed agricultural establishment; and

4thly. What force would be required for the protection of such territory.

You will have carefully to weigh, therefore, the practicability, advantages, and dangers of acquiring sovereignty for the crown over a considerable territory. You are not to satisfy yourselves that a single Chief is willing to sell his dominions, or a portion of them, but are to consider the hazard of jealousy and of hostility being excited among neighbouring Chiefs by the appearance of the British flag as a token of sovereign power in the midst of their possessions. You will have to calculate the force that would be necessary to maintain and defend the territory that might be acquired,—the facility or difficulty of relief,—the extent of territory necessary to protect those who might seek shelter and security within its borders, as well as the danger of invasion from any European Power, which might have settlements on the coast.

[1] *Parl. Papers*, 1843, xlviii (472), pp. 15–18, Lushington and Buxton to Russell, 7 August 1840; and above, p. 108.

17

LORD JOHN RUSSELL TO GOVERNOR SIR JOHN JEREMIE: DESTRUCTION OF SLAVE FACTORIES AT GALLINAS, 15 APRIL 1841[1]

SIR,

I have to ack: the receipt of your predecessor's despatch No. 67 of the 7th of Decr. last together with your own No. 2, of the 4th Jany, the former reporting the proceedings of Commander Honble. Joseph Denman in the Gallinas, by which that Officer has effected the recovery of two of HM's Subjects, the destruction of eight Slave factories, and the liberation of 841 Slaves; and your own despatch reporting the circumstances under which the Slave dealer Canot[2] has surrendered himself with 104 Slaves to Lieut: Seagram.

I entirely approve of the proceeding of your predecessor in urging the interposition of Comr. Denman on behalf of the two individuals in question; and I have requested the L.C. of the Admy. to express to the Commr. the high sense which HM's Govt. entertain of his very spirited and able conduct & of his important results to the interests of humanity.

Upon this Subject generally you will understand that HM. Govt. are of the opinion that operations similar to those undertaken by Comr. Denman at the Gallinas, should be executed against all piratical Slave Trade Estabts. which may be met with on all parts of the Coast not belonging to any civilized power. . . .

With regard however to the Slave dealer Canot, it is very desirable to encourage a breach of the confidence of Slave dealers in each other: but particular cases such as that of the individual above named must be left to your descretion, guided as you will be by such information as you can obtain from the most respectable persons at Sierra Leone.

18

THE NIGER EXPEDITION: HOUSE OF COMMONS, 4 MARCH 1842[3]

LORD STANLEY said that the Niger expedition had been undertaken with the most humane and philanthropic intentions—with a desire

[1] C.O. 268/38, ff. 45–46. *Sir John Jeremie* was the first civilian governor of Sierra Leone, 1840–1. He had championed the cause of slave emancipation as Chief Justice in the West Indies.

[2] *Theodore Canot*, a Florentine slaver-trader in the Rio Pongas and at Cape Mount.

[3] *The Friend of Africa*, ii, 18 (1842), p. 59. For the results of the expeditino, see *Parl. Papers*, 1843, xlviii (472); Captain W. Allen, T. R. H. Thomson, *A Narrative of the Expedition to the Niger River in 1841*, 2 vols. London, 1848.

to improve, if possible, the interior of Africa, by introducing and promoting commerce, and by putting a stop, as far as it could be done, to the practice or encouragement of the slave trade on the part of the chiefs who occupy territories on the banks of the Niger. Now, it was impossible to deny, that to a certain, and indeed to a lamentable extent, the expedition had proved a failure. He would not say it had been altogether a failure, for there was on the part of the inhabitants of that country a desire to enter into trade, and to encourage commercial intercourse with this country; and if, in addition to that desire, it could be proved that there was any law recognized amongst those chiefs under which such commerce could be carried on successfully, there was nothing but the dangers of the climate that could prevent its being carried on by whites. But it was clear that the climate—upon the banks of the river at all events, nor did it appear to improve in the interior, but was rather worse, perhaps— was so deadly in its nature to white men, and likely therefore to produce such disastrous effects amongst expeditions composed of white men, that Her Majesty's Government did not feel themselves justified, even for the important objects for which it was thought right to despatch the last expedition, to run the risk of sacrificing the health and lives of more of Her Majesty's Subjects by renewing the attempt; so far, then as white men were concerned, it was not the intention of Her Majesty's Government to renew the expedition to the Niger. . . .

19

LORD ABERDEEN TO THE LORDS COMMISSIONERS OF THE ADMIRALTY: BLOCKADE AND THE DESTRUCTION OF SLAVE FACTORIES, 20 MAY 1842[1]

MY LORDS,

I beg to call your Lordship's attention to the subject of the instructions given to Her Majesty's naval officers employed in suppressing the slave trade on the coast of Africa, and to the proceedings which have taken place with reference thereto as detailed in the papers named in the margin of this letter.

Her Majesty's Advocate-general, to whom these papers have been submitted, has reported that he cannot take upon himself to advise that all the proceedings described as having taken place as Gallinas, New Cestos, and Sea Bar, are strictly justifiable, or that the instruc-

---

[1] *Parl. Papers*, 1842, xi (551), p. 516. The *Earl of Aberdeen* was Secretary of State for War and Colonies, November 1834–April 1835.

tions to Her Majesty's naval officers, as referred to in these papers, are such as can with perfect legality be carried into execution.

The Queen's Advocate is of opinion that blockading the rivers, landing and destroying buildings, and carrying off persons held in slavery in countries with which Great Britain is not at war, cannot be considered as sanctioned by the law of nations, or by the provisions of any existing treaties; and that however desirable it may be to put an end to the slave trade, a good, however eminent, should not be attained otherwise than by lawful means.

Accordingly, and with reference to the proceedings of Captain Nurse at Rio Pongas, on the 28th April 1841, as well as to the letters addressed from this department to the Admiralty on the 6th of April, the 1st and 17th of June, and the 28th of July last year, I would submit to the consideration of your Lordships, that it is desirable that Her Majesty's naval officers employed in suppressing the slave trade should be instructed to abstain from destroying slave factories and carrying off persons held in slavery, unless the power upon whose territory or within whose jurisdiction the factories or the slaves are found, should by treaty with Great Britain, or by formal written agreement with British officers, have empowered Her Majesty's naval forces to take these steps for the suppression of the slave trade; and that if, in proceeding to destroy any factory, it should be found to contain merchandise or other property which there may be reason to suppose to belong to foreign traders, care should be taken not to include such property in the destruction of the factory.

With respect to the blockading [of] rivers, it appears to the papers referred to, that the terms blockade and blockading have been used by British naval officers, when adverting to the laudable practice of stationing cruisers off the slave-trading stations, with a view the better to intercept vessels carrying on slave trade, contrary to treaties between Great Britain and the powers to which such vessels belong.

But as the term blockade properly used extends to an interdiction of all trade, and indeed all communication with the place blockaded, I beg leave to submit for your Lordship's consideration, whether it will not be proper to caution Her Majesty's naval officers upon this head, lest by the inadvertent and repeated use of the term blockade, the exercise of the duty confided to British officers in suppressing slave trade might, by any one, be confounded with the very different one of actual blockade.

20

ENGAGEMENT WITH THE CHIEFS OF BIMBIA, CAMEROONS, 17 FEBRUARY 1844[1]

LIEUTENANT EDWARD CHARLES EARLE, Commander of Her Britannic Majesty's brig 'Rapid', on the part of Her Majesty the Queen of England, and the Chiefs of Bimbia and of the neighbourhood, on the part of themselves and of their country, have agreed upon the following Articles and Conditions:—

Article I.

The Export of Slaves to foreign countries is for ever abolished in the territories of the Chiefs of Bimbia, and the Chiefs of Bimbia engage to make and proclaim a law prohibiting any of their subjects, or any person within their jurisdiction, from selling or assisting in the sale of any Slave for transportation to a foreign country; and the Chiefs of Bimbia promise to inflict a severe punishment on any person who shall break this law.

Article II.

No European or other person whatever shall be permitted to reside within the territories of the Chiefs of Bimbia, for the purpose of carrying on in any way the Traffic in Slaves; and no houses, or stores, or buildings of any kind whatever, shall be erected for the purpose of Slave Trade within the territory of the Chiefs of Bimbia.

Article III.

The Queen of Great Britain, to show her friendship for the Chiefs of Bimbia, and because they have made this Agreement, engages to give them goods to the value of twelve hundred dollars.

Article IV.

If at any time it shall appear that the Slave Trade has been carried on through or from the territory of the Chiefs of Bimbia, the Slave Trade may be put down by Great Britain by force upon that territory, the British officers may seize the boats of Bimbia found anywhere carrying on the Slave Trade, and the Chiefs of Bimbia will subject themselves to a severe act of displeasure on the part of the Queen of England.

---

[1] *F.O. Confidential Print*, 1845. Signed: Commander E. C. Earle, H.M.S. *Rapid*, William King of Bimbia, Prince John, Dick Merchant Duke Merchant, John Bimbia, Old Ambic, chiefs of Bimbia.

Article V.

The subjects of the Queen of England may always trade freely with the people of Bimbia, in every article they may wish to buy and sell, in all the places and ports within the territories of the Chiefs of Bimbia, and throughout the whole of their dominions; and the Chiefs of Bimbia pledge themselves to show no favour and give no privilege to the ships and traders of other countries, which they do not show to those of England.

Done at King William's Town, Bimbia, this 17th day of February, 1844.

21

ADMIRALTY INSTRUCTIONS TO SENIOR OFFICERS FOR NEGOTIATING WITH CHIEFS OF AFRICA, 12 JUNE 1844[1]

By the Commissioners for executing the Office of Lord High Admiral of the United Kingdom of Great Britain and Ireland, &c.

1. The suppression of the Slave Trade may be materially assisted by obtaining the co-operation of the Native Chiefs of Africa in the object; you are therefore authorized to conclude Engagements for this purpose with the African Chiefs; but you must strictly adhere to the regulations herein laid down on the subject.

2. You will procure the fullest and most correct information as to the state of those parts of the coast in which Slave Trade is carried on, so as to enable you to determine, with what Chiefs it may be expedient to enter into negotiations for the conclusion of Engagements.

With this in view, you will endeavour to ascertain the power and influence of the several Chiefs; their personal character, and the habits of the people; the extent and force of the country; the sources, amount, and description of the legitimate trade carried on.

You will endeavour to obtain the most accurate information as to the Slave Trade; its present extent, and whether it has recently increased or diminished: you will inquire by whose agency, whether native or foreign, it is principally prosecuted; in what mode it is conducted; in what form the price of Slaves is received, whether in money or goods, and if in goods, the description of the same; how

---

[1] *Parl. Papers*, 1844, *Instructions for the Guidance of Her Majesty's Naval Officers employed in the Suppression of the Slave Trade*, pp. 15–17. Additional instructions of the same date covered the seizure of British and foreign vessels engaged in the slave trade. All drafts were originally prepared in 1843 by a committee consisting of Captain Denman, Dr. Lushington, James Bandinel, and a lawyer. Denman later complained that some of the drafting had been needlessly complicated by alterations in the published instructions.

they are obtained; from whom and into what places imported; from what parts of the country the Slaves are brought, and how procured; from what parts of the coast they are usually embarked, and whether with the assistance of any, and what Chiefs.

You will investigate the means whereby the Slave Trade may most effectually and speedily be extinguished, and you will enquire into the inclination and the power of the Chief to carry into effect an Engagement for that purpose, and the means which Great Britain may have for enforcing it.

3. You are not to attempt to enter into any negotiation until you have obtained the fullest information that the circumstances admit of with respect to all the matters of enquiry before specified. And you must not enter into any Engagements excepting with independent Chiefs of considerable power and influence upon the coast.

4. When you shall desire to open negotiations with any African Chief, you will, after taking every proper precaution for the safety of yourself and your people, at the same time avoiding giving offence to the Natives, obtain a personal interview with the Chiefs, and endeavour to induce them to conclude an Engagement according to the Draft of Engagement forming the Appendix to this Instruction.

5. If at the time of the negotiation the foreign Slave Trade actually exists in the territory of the Native Chief, you will propose the two Articles marked 'Additional', annexed to the Draft, and will consider them an indispensable part of the Engagement.

6. Every opportunity is to be taken of impressing the minds of the Native Chiefs and their people with a conviction of the efforts Great Britain has made for their benefit, and of her earnest desire to raise them in the scale of nations. It is most desirable to excite in them an emulation of the habits of the Christian world, and to enable them to make the first practical step towards civilization by the abandonment of the Slave Trade.

7. Special care must be taken not to offend the prejudices of the Natives; and every proper respect must be paid to their peculiar usages, so far as the same are not of an inhuman character; and allowance must be made for any jealousy or distrust that may be shewn by them.

8. You will not conclude the Engagement without reference home, except it be completed in the exact terms of the Draft of Engagement forming the Appendix to this Section; and if any further stipulation should appear to you to be necessary or desirable, whether on commercial or on other grounds, it will be your duty to make a report on the subject to your Government.

9. Threats or intimidation are never to be used, to induce the Native Chiefs to conclude the Engagement: on the contrary, forbearance and conciliation must be in all cases the rule of conduct; and if the Native Chiefs refuse the Engagement, every means must be taken

to encourage in them feelings of confidence, and to leave a favourable impression that may facilitate the renewal of negotiations at a future period.

10. On the conclusion of an Engagement, according to the Draft, you will consider yourself authorized to declare Her Majesty's approval of the same.

The Engagement must always be signed in duplicate.

11. Immediately after the conclusion of the Engagement, you will require the Chiefs to proclaim a law to their people, by which its stipulations shall be publicly made known.

12. In case the Slave Trade is actually carried on within the jurisdiction of the Chief at the time the Engagement is concluded, and that, consequently, the two Additional Articles form part of the Engagement, you will then require, that all the Slaves held for exportation shall be delivered up to you to be made free at a British colony. You will also demand, that all implements of Slave Trade, such as shackles, bolts, and handcuffs, chains, whips, branding-irons, &c., or articles of Slave equipment for fitting up vessels to carry Slaves, shall be given up to you, or destroyed in your presence. You will also insist on the immediate destruction of the barracoons, or buildings exclusively devoted to the reception of Slaves, and, if necessary, you will enforce all these demands.

13. Upon the fulfilment of the Engagement thus far, you will use every effort to induce the Chiefs to carry into effect the other provisions of the Engagement, especially as regards the white Slave-dealers; and you are for this purpose to afford any assistance that the Native Chiefs may require, but you are not to use force, unless at their signed request in writing.

14. You are not, without the signed consent in writing of a Native Chief, to take any step upon his territory for putting down the Slave Trade by force, excepting when, by Engagement, Great Britain is entitled to adopt coercive measures on shore for that purpose.

15. After the conclusion of an Engagement, and the carrying of the same into effect so far as above directed, you will send home one of the originals of the Engagement, and a report of your proceedings thereupon, for further instructions. You will cause a vigilant watch to be kept over the proceedings of the Chiefs, until you are satisfied of their fidelity to their Engagements. After which, you will visit the Chiefs in person, or send a Commander of one of Her Majesty's Ships, at least once in six months, to see to the due execution of the Engagements on the part of the Chiefs.

16. In the event, however, of ultimate failure of the negotiation, you will finally state to the Chief, that every civilized Naval Power in the world has declared that it has abandoned the Slave Trade; that most nations have united with Great Britain in endeavours to put it down;

that Great Britain will not allow the subjects of the Chief so far as to frustrate those endeavours, as to carry Slaves for sale, to or from any places beyond the limits of his own territory, and that Her Majesty's Officers have orders to liberate Slaves when found embarked in boats of his subjects for that purpose.

17. All the proceedings adopted in conformity with these Instructions, whether with regard to the Negotiation or the carrying into effect of Engagements, are to be conducted by you; but if circumstances prevent you from doing so in person, you may specially authorize for the purpose another Officer; but you will take great care, in such case, to select one on whose judgement and discretion you can rely with confidence.

18. You will forward to the Admiralty a detailed report of all proceedings which may have taken place on the occasion of visiting any port or place for the purposes mentioned in this Instruction. And in those cases in which you shall have deputed to another Officer the duty of visiting the place, the Officer so deputed will forward direct to the Admiralty a duplicate of his report to you.

19. You will make to the Admiralty an annual detailed Report on the state of legal commerce, and the extent of Slave Trade, throughout your station, recapitulating therein the principal points of your occasional reports during the year, and adding thereto such other information, as may serve to give Her Majesty's Government a correct view of the course of your proceedings and of their result in the service of suppressing the Slave Trade.

Given under our hands, this 12th day of June, 1844.

G. Cockburn.
W. H. Gage.

By the Command of their Lordships,
Sidney Herbert.

22

SELECT COMMITTEE ON THE SLAVE TRADE: EVIDENCE OF CAPTAIN THE HON. JOSEPH DENMAN, 1 APRIL 1845[1]

... Q. CONFINING ourselves to the West Coast, of what extent is the coast upon which the trade is carried on?

[1] F.O. *Confidential Print* (1845). *Minutes of Evidence taken before the Duke de Broglie and the Rt. Hon. Stephen Lushington, D.C.L., March 31, April 1, 2, 3, and 4, 1845*, pp. 21–25, 28–29.

Captain Denman, after his destruction of the Gallinas slave factories in 1841 and the publication of Aberdeen's letter to the Admiralty, 20 May, 1842, faced legal actions amounting to some £300,000 begun by slave-dealers. In 1848 he was found not to be personally liable for damages. See C. Lloyd, *The Navy and the Slave Trade* (London, 1949), pp. 95–99.

A. It is carried on at intervals almost along the whole coast from Cape Verd down to beyond Loando.

Q. Down to where it becomes impossible, from the nature of the coast?

A. Yes; about 20 degrees south latitude.

Q. What is about the extent of it in distance?

A. I should think it was something more than 3000 miles.

Q. Do you think it would be possible to blockade that extent of coast so as to stop the Slave Trade?

A. Yes; I think it is possible to blockade all the places where the Slave Trade is carried on within those limits.

Q. So that assuming that a sufficient force could be obtained, you could effectually prevent the Slave Trade?

A. I have not the slightest doubt about it. The suppression would be greatly accelerated by breaking up the slave factories.

Q. Are you of opinion that operations on land would materially assist in the attainment of that object?

A. Certainly.

Q. What species of operations?

A. The destruction of the slave factories, the encouragement of commerce, and the establishment of commercial posts at convenient intervals.

Q. And treaties with the native chiefs?

A. Yes; I would destroy the slave factories under treaty with the native chiefs.

Q. Do you think there would be any difficulty in obtaining permission from the native chiefs, for a reasonable consideration, to destroy all the existing factories?

A. I think you might do so, after by blocking up their factories for a long period, you had made them despair of further prosecution of the Slave Trade, but not till then.

Q. In fact when you had reduced the value of the factory by blockade for a certain time, and the maintenance of the factory had become of less importance, they would then part with it for a consideration?

A. Yes; according to the system of blockade which I have before recommended, I believe you may prevent the embarkation of one single slave. Under the pressure of that system the natives will soon consider the Slave Trade a thing of past days and of no further value, and they will be ready to enter into treaties for its total abolition.

Q. Supposing it be practicable to obtain treaties with all the native Powers engaged in the Slave Trade, to allow you by force to destroy the factories, that would be one of the most useful auxiliary measures?

A. It would certainly be one of the most useful auxiliary measures;

but I would recommend that we should at once begin to form treaties to this effect with natives upon whose territory the Slave Trade does not at present exist; because directly you have put it down in one place, they will endeavour to get it up in another, and if you are already armed with powers of that description, which the chiefs of parts where there is at present no Slave Trade will be ready enough to give you; then you would render the establishment of the Slave Trade in those countries impossible.

Q. Then you would advise forming treaties with the whole of the native Powers, whether they at present carry on the Slave Trade or not; giving you the right and authority to put it down by force, in case of need?

A. Certainly.

Q. You have considered the question of suppressing the Slave Trade very maturely?

A. I have given my mind to the subject a great deal for some years.

Q. Have the goodness to state what measures you would propose to adopt, with the view to extinguishing that trade?

A. I consider in the first place a universal right of search upon the parts of the ships of war, of whatever nation, employed upon that service, to be indispensable, whether under particular treaties or whether under some substitute for the existing system; but that right I take to be quite essential. The next thing in importance, I think, would be to affix a personal penalty or punishment upon the persons who may be found engaged in the traffic. Thirdly, the breaking up of the slave depôts.

Fourthly, the entering into treaties with the native Powers, providing for the destruction of the slave factories. Fifthly, the establishment of commercial posts in the neighbourhood of all present slave trading districts, the encouragement of legitimate commerce, the instruction and improvement of the natives by means of missionary labours and otherwise. And lastly, the liberated African population of Sierra Leone may be made use of, with the greatest advantage, in disseminating improvement and a horror of the Slave Trade amongst the natives from whence they originally came. . . .

23

EXTRACTS FROM THE GENERAL STANDING ORDER BOOK: WEST AFRICA SQUADRON, 3 NOVEMBER 1846[1]

(a) 3 November 1846

THE boats are never to be employed in the rivers during the sickly season, nor at any period, unless some extraordinary emergency

[1] *Parl. Papers*, 1850, ix (53), p. 422.

should occur, and the fulfilment of the public service render it imperatively necessary.

(b) 21 January 1848

The boats are never to be detached from ships stationed on the line of coast between Cape Palmas and the River Gambia, except in pursuit of a suspected vessel actually in sight.

24

COMMODORE SIR CHARLES HOTHAM TO THE SECRETARY TO THE ADMIRALTY: USE OF THE NAVY, 1 NOVEMBER 1848[1]

Penelope,
St. Helena,
1 November 1848.

Sir,

1. The anxiety which the House of Commons has shown, during the last Session, to arrive, [*sic*] as well as the nature of the service on the West Coast of Africa, as of the results obtained in suppressing the Slave Trade, induce me to depart from the rule which has hitherto been considered applicable to all agents of the public service; and request their Lordships to permit me to reply to an assertion made by Commander Matson, in a pamphlet styled 'Remarks on the Slave Trade and African Squadron', and which, I see, has already run through two editions.[2]

2. I am in no way desirous that my remarks should have publicity, or go beyond the walls of the Admiralty; but I think their Lordships are entitled to require from me the fullest and most complete explanation on every point connected with the peculiar service on which the squadron under my command are employed; and that I, on my part, coveting the largest share of their Lordships' approbation, am not deviating from the rules of propriety and discretion in bringing such subjects to their notice.

3. Commander Matson says, page 31, 'I believe he has removed the vessels to a greater distance from the coast, and has forbidden the employment of boats on detached service; this latter restriction must certainly have crippled the exertions of the squadron.'

4. I request you inform their Lordships that this statement is, generally speaking, inaccurate, as the two enclosed General Orders[3]

---

[1] Ibid., p. 422.
[2] Commander H. J. Matson, *Remarks on the Slave Trade.* London, 1848.
[3] See above, no. 23.

issued to the commanders of the cruisers, the first of the 3d November 1846, the second on the 21st January 1848, will show.

5. I interdicted boat-service in rivers, because humanity required it. Their Lordships will not have forgotten the result of the 'Wanderer's' boat excursion up the River Pongos, or the number of lives which it cost.

6. I also interdicted boat-service on the line of coast between Cape Palmas and the River Gambia, because the service they could perform was in no degree adequate to the risk; but this is only on one-third of the station, and there is no prohibition as to the employment of boats on any other part of the coast; on the contrary, consistently with discipline and health, it has rather been encouraged.

7. I am quite aware that officers of more experience in this service might have managed matters better; but it should be borne in mind that I had difficulties to encounter unusually great, and that there were obstacles which required both time and patience to remove.

8. And I trust that the return of vessels captured, empty and with slaves, during the last 12 months—100 vessels and 7,000 slaves—will show that with whatever faults we may be charged, inactivity, at all events, cannot reasonably be included in the number.

25

COMMODORE SIR CHARLES HOTHAM TO THE SECRETARY TO THE ADMIRALTY: DESTRUCTION OF SLAVE FACTORIES AT GALLINAS, 13 FEBRUARY 1849[1]

Penelope,
Sierra Leone,
13 February 1849[1]

SIR,

1. In my despatch, No. 32 of 1848, dated 20th January, I requested you to inform my Lords Commissioners of the Admiralty, that Commander Dixon, of Her Majesty's Sloop 'Rapid', had, in compliance with their Lordships' instructions, notified to the chiefs of Gallinas, 'that if they did not entirely discontinue and put an end to the Slave Trade, the British Government would be compelled to use the means at its disposal to force them to do so'.

2. Their Lordships replied by enclosing a copy of the Advocate-General's opinion, pronouncing, 'That Her Majesty's Government will be justified in directing hostilities to be commenced against Gallinas, in consequence of the chiefs having refused to abide by the

[1] *Parl. Papers*, 1850, ix (53), pp. 460–1.

treaty or agreement concluded by them with Captain Denman.'[1] The Advocate-General further continues: 'I think that the white slave-dealers, whose exclusion from the Gallinas was the principal object of Captain Denman's Treaty, will not, under the circumstances, be able successfully to maintain an action in the courts of this country, for the loss of their property.'

3. Armed with the opinion of Her Majesty's principal legal adviser, I determined to enforce the terms of the Treaty, as soon as the season of the year and the state of the surf on the beach would enable me with prudence to land a force sufficiently overwhelming to prevent opposition.

4. On the 3d instant I assembled the ships named in the margin,[2] off Gallinas, and with their boats, under the charge of their Commanders, containing a force of 300 men, passed the bar at 7.30 a.m., and landed at Dombocorro, took possession of it, and the neighbouring factories and barracoons, and planted sentinels to guard the property. In the meantime, Captain Jones, with the boats of the 'Penelope', pushed on to the Solyman factories, established within the limits of the Gallinas boundary; these, three in number, were, with the goods they contained, as well as the village of Dreesing, known for its intimate connexion with the Slave Trade, totally destroyed. He returned to Dombocorro at 7 p.m. on the same evening having met with no resistance beyond an occasional straggling fire from the bushes on the side of the river, by which a native prisoner was wounded. Commander Murray also conducted a party to Mineh, and destroyed the factories and barracoons which it contained.

5. On the following morning, the 4th instant, the three large factories in the vicinity of Dombocorro were, with the goods which they contained, entirely destroyed; and at 1 p.m. on the same day, Dombocorro itself, with all its contents, was burnt to the ground.

6. By sunset on the 4th, the force returned to their respective ships, without a single casualty of any sort or kind, or appearance of fever.

It is impossible for me to speak too highly of the exertions of the officers, or good conduct of the seamen and marines. Captain Jones conducted the service entrusted to him entirely to my satisfaction. Commander Murray rendered me, in a variety of ways, essential service; and the behaviour of the men was beyond all praise. Surrounded by temptation of every kind, I did not hear of a case of inebriety or plunder. In short I met with the same support which has characterized the commanding officers of the African squadron since my arrival on the station.

7. The operations already described were complete as far as they went; still they only checked the Slave Trade; left there, in one year

[1] Treaty, 21 November 1840.
[2] *Penelope, Favorite, Sealark, Waterwitch, Bonnetta, Dart, Pluto.*

it would again break forth with increased vigour. It was evident that something more was required to extirpate the slave dealers, and destroy their profits, and this I hope to effect through the medium of a blockade in its legal sense.

The Advocate-General says, 'It will be competent to Her Majesty's Government to direct that all the means allowed by the law of nations may be used in carrying on the war.' The first of these is clearly the right of blockade. I have therefore notified, according to the form already transmitted, the existence of the blockade between Solyman Point on the south, and Cazee on the north, lat. 6° 57' N., long. 11° 35' W., and lat. 7° 5' N., long. 11° 45' W.; and I have the pleasure of informing their Lordships that the Commanding Officers of the French and American forces have expressed their satisfaction at the adoption of an intelligible measure, likely, in their opinion, to fulfil the object in view.

8. The enclosed answers to a form of questions submitted to the several Commanding Officers immediately after their return to their ships, as well as the journal of the pilot (Mr. Parker),[1] many years a resident in this country, and intimately acquainted with the affairs of Gallinas, will, I hope, satisfy their Lordships that there was abundant proof of Slave Trade in each factory; and that the goods they contained were destined to be exchanged for slaves, and were landed for no other purpose.

26

REPORT BY THE LORDS' SELECT COMMITTEE ON THE SLAVE TRADE, 15 JULY 1850[2]

[The means used against the slave trade have been international treaties, treaties with African chiefs, the maintenance of the African forts, and the African Squadron.]

. . . THE general tenor of the Evidence establishes in our minds, beyond all doubt, (1.) That the English Cruisers have greatly checked and crippled the Slave Trade. (2.) That their removal would be the signal for its breaking out with unexampled vigour at every available port along the whole sea-board. (3.) That this would lead, amongst other results, to the whole coast swarming with piratical vessels, which would utterly destroy the legitimate trade, now daily increasing in value between Great Britain and Africa; whilst all the beginnings of civilization, and all attempts to Christianize Africa, would be wholly defeated and destroyed. All the Witnesses agree that the legitimate trade cannot co-exist with the Slave Trade; and that its

---

[1] Journal enclosed, ibid., pp. 462–3.
[2] *Parl. Papers*, 1850, ix (590), pp. 5–8.

slower returns cannot compete in immediate apparent profit to the Chiefs with the Slave Trade; but that if the Slave Trade be suppressed for any lengthened period, its revival would be prevented by the lawful trade.

Turning now to the suggestions which have been made to the Committee for rendering these more effectual, they would call the attention of the House to the following as most worthy of consideration:—

(1.) The habitual disregard of Treaties on this subject with this country, on the part of Brazil, and, to a great extent, also, on the part of Spain, appears to be the main hindrance to the suppression of the Trade; and to this, therefore, especially, the attention of Her Majesty's Ministers and of Parliament should, in our opinion, be directed.

The suppression of the Slave Trade can never be declared impossible to England, until she has at least attempted to oblige Brazil to fulfil her Treaties.

A plan for obtaining greater practical efficiency for these Treaties has been suggested, which will be found fully detailed in the Evidence, and which the Committee consider worthy of the best consideration. Its main feature is the giving, by Treaty, to Mixed Commission Courts at Rio and the Havannah, power to declare free all Slaves brought before them who shall have been imported after a day to be fixed. There appears to be in Cuba a large, and in Brazil an increasing, party, who might be expected to support this country in requiring and maintaining such a Treaty.

It is also, in our judgment, worthy of consideration, whether the three great Maritime Powers, France, the United States and Great Britain, could not at the present time be brought to combine in joint representations, and, if need be, active measures, for obtaining from Spain and Brazil an actual suppression of this traffic.

The admission of Slave-grown Sugar into the markets of Great Britain, which, in the judgment of all the Witnesses, is a great and direct stimulus to the Slave Trade, seems to require of Great Britain that she should use every effort in her power to prevent so great an evil accruing to Africa from her new commercial policy.

(2.) The Committee would recommend the consideration of the wisdom of extending further our Forts and Settlements on the Coast of Africa; of encouraging the free Settlement of Liberia, which secures 350 miles of coast. The Committee have learned with satisfaction that a Treaty has already been entered into with Denmark for the purpose of obtaining possession of the Danish Settlements on the Gold Coast.

(3.) Of countenancing the Settlement, on different parts of the Coast of Africa, of Free Blacks from our own possessions.

(4.) Of establishing Consular Agents on the points of the Coast where the Slave Trade has been extinguished, and which are best fitted to become emporiums of trade.

This last recommendation leads them to another. The Slave Trade cannot be permanently suppressed by any means which do not at the same time foster a lawful trade by which the desires of the native Chiefs for European goods can be supplied. To promote, therefore, this trade should be one chief object of our exertions; it appears to be capable of almost unlimited increase. The present great hindrance to its extension is the existence of the Slave Trade, which, wherever it continues, renders all security for life and property impossible in Africa; prevents the due cultivation of its most fertile soil, and the consequent increase of lawful commerce. Cotton and almost all tropical productions might, it appears, be largely produced in Africa if this one master impediment were removed; whilst the habits and inclinations of the Africans are such as would naturally incline them to become an eminently commercial people, and thus at once secure a supply of most important productions for our own markets, and open an unlimited demand for our manufactures. Direct trading establishments should be encouraged under the protection of every British Fort on the Coast of Africa. Various important suggestions bearing upon this point will be found in the Evidence we have reported.

(5.) As the maintenance of the cruising Squadron on the Coast of Africa is, in our judgment, an essential condition towards the success of every other effort, we have paid especial attention to any suggestions made to us for increasing its efficiency....

[The Committee recommends the use of smaller vessels, more detailed instructions to commanders, the punishment of all nationalities found on slave ships, and alterations in the system of paying prize-money. The sufferings of transported Africans are not a reason for withdrawing the Squadron.]

... Finally, we would report, from a full examination of all the Evidence brought before us, that in our opinion—

1. The past efficiency of the cruising Squadron has been greatly undervalued.

2. That its cost has been much exaggerated.

3. That, with proper precautions, it is not an unhealthy Service.

4. That to withdraw the Cruisers in part, and to administer a regulated Slave Trade, (as has been suggested), would be impossible of execution, no material saving of the cost of the present system, and utterly at variance with every past profession of Great Britain on this subject since she abolished the British Slave Trade.

5. That against the present cost of the Squadron should be set the

advantage of nourishing and maintaining a valuable and increasing lawful trade, which must be utterly extirpated if the Cruisers were withdrawn, and which might be developed to an unlimited extent if the Slave Trade were suppressed.

6. That to abandon the suppression of the Trade, to which, in the face of the whole civilized world, Great Britain is solemnly and repeatedly pledged, would be a fatal blow to her national honour.

7. That there is every reason to believe that the present system is susceptible of a large and immediate increase of efficiency by the adoption of such improvements as we have recommended; and that if these improvements be adopted, aided by other measures recommended, there is reason to believe that this great object may be speedily and certainly obtained. . . .

27

COMMODORE EDMONSTONE TO REAR-ADMIRAL SIR B. WALKER: STATE OF THE SLAVE TRADE, 7 NOVEMBER 1861

Arrogant, at Sea,
7 November 1861[1]

North Division

I FEAR this inhuman Traffic has increased; 4 vessels have been captured since my last Report, and I got off from the River Nunez. King Catty is supposed to have supplied the slaves in the latter case; but as reliable information of the movements of those known to be interested in the Trade is easily procured on this part of the coast, which is the most civilized, and where legal commerce is developed to a greater extent, there is no hope of its ever reviving very much.

19. At present it is conducted by a Spanish Company, who employ small vessels to suit the navigation of the rivers, as will be seen on referring to Inclosure 3, but I am thankful to say as yet they cannot have succeeded in their discreditable enterprise; this, in a great measure, is owing to the exertions of Commander Smith, who has during his service on the North Coast captured 5 vessels.

20. It appears that slaves are procured and shipped principally in the Nunez, Pongas, Debruka, Sherbro, and in the Gallinas; but the River Pongas is without doubt the head-quarters of slavery in this Division, and the Sherbro and its neighbourhood the market from whence supplies are chiefly procured.

---

[1] F.O. *Confidential Print* (1862), *Report by Commodore Edmonstone*, pp. 3–4.

21. With regard to the Pongas our cruizers obtain good information of any contemplated shipment through the Mission established at Falanghia, who take every opportunity of assisting us.

22. As King Catty is evidently engaged in connection with Mrs. Lightbourne in carrying on the Slave Trade in this river, I have issued directions in compliance with Admiralty letter of the 24th of June last, addressed to you or the Senior Officer at Sierra Leone, to punish the Chief for breaking his Treaty with Her Majesty's Government, should sufficient proof of his having done so be established, communicating on the subject with Governor Hill.

23. At the Gallinas, Prince Mannah keeps us in possession of all information on the subject; it is, however, reported that he takes care first to promise a cargo, and has been known to receive part payment beforehand; so by giving timely notice he avoids the necessity of parting with his property.

24. I look forward to the permanent establishment of a timber trade in the Bagroo with great interest, as it will certainly be the means of doing away with the Slave Trade from the Sherbro in a great measure, by the wholesome check it must afford to the movements of those engaged in that illegal Traffic, as also tending to introduce legitimate commerce to a greater extent in that river.

25. I may here mention that I am in receipt of an Admiralty communication directing me to furnish a ten-oared pinnace and a whaleboat, at a valuation, to Mr. Hanson,[1] who has entered into an engagement with Her Majesty's Government to supply our dockyards with timber from the Sherbro country. I will take the earliest opportunity of complying with their Lordship's instructions, and hope to be able to procure these boats at Ascension.

26. Slaves are occasionally taken from the Sierra Leone River in canoes, but I have not heard to what extent. The principal description of Slave Trade in the North Coast is, however, domestic, and I consider the absence of vessels mentioned on the Suspected List as a good proof of the very small limit to which the export of slaves can safely be assigned. The Spanish Company already alluded to has only been recently set on foot, and appears not to have answered as yet.

27. That portion of the Coast over which the Liberian Government have any influence is, I am happy to say, entirely free from the taint of slavery.

28. I have the honour to bring under your notice some information which has reached me regarding the legal trade in this Division.

29. At Cape Settlement there appears to be a very flourishing trade in palm oil, cane, and other description of dye-woods, ivory, and sometimes a little gold dust; but I hear that at present we are not represented: there is, however, a factory belonging to the house at

[1] Consul at the Sherbro.

Hatton and Cookson of Liverpool, about three miles from the entrance of the Cavalla River.

30. The palm-oil season commences here in December, when the nut is gathered, and the oil is ready for shipment during the months of May and June; the quantity exported, exclusive of the English factory, of which no statistics could be obtained, is about 300,000 gallons annually.

31. The 'Falcon' visited Cape Palmas by my order in July last, when Commander Heneage ascertained without a doubt that suspicious vessels do frequently call in there, and also at Monrovia, information of the movements of our cruizers, and to procure their letters, &c., that arrived by the mail.

32. The export of slaves from the Bights Division is chiefly carried on within that part of the Coast over which Dahomey's power and influence is felt, and as a rule it may be said from nowhere else in this Division to any serious extent. The usual shipping-places are Aghwey, Great and Little Popoe, and Whydah.

33. I have only positive knowledge of one shipment having taken place, and that is supposed to have been the 'African' from the Coast between Quittah and Addah, as shown in Inclosure 5.

34. I learn, however, with regret from Major de Ruvignes, lately the Commandant at Accra, that two known slave-vessels under the American flag have been seen at anchor in the Dutch roads; in all probability they have got off, as I have not heard further news of them, nor have they been met with by any of our cruizers.

35. That officer also informs me that slave factories are in existence in the Volla Islands. I have therefore ordered Commander Bedingfeld to cause this part of the Coast to be constantly watched for some time to come.

36. In the Brass River I am happy to say this illegal Traffic has entirely ceased to exist, no vessel of a suspicious nature having been seen in its vicinity since the one captured by the 'Archer', about two years ago; but there appears to be a little slaving in the Segama River, principally carried on during the dry season, and by small vessels. In this instance slaves are collected between the Segama and Nun, and taken outside the Bar, from whence they are shipped.

37. In the rivers in the Bight of Biafra the palm-oil trade has altogether superseded this nefarious Traffic, but domestic slavery still exists, and a great inclination to rise against their masters has lately manifested itself on the part of the former, but no disturbances have taken place, and the rivers are being constantly visited by our cruizers.

38. It is to be hoped that our new position at Lagos will have the wholesome effect in time of checking the Slave Trade in Dahomey's country, which I can confidently assert is the only part of the Coast in this Division where it prevails to any serious extent.

39. There is no doubt that the destruction of Porto-Novo is the greatest blow that has been for some time past inflicted on this illegal traffic, and I believe it has had a good moral effect on the neighbouring tribes, and now that our traders are permitted to enjoy the same privileges of residing there, which formerly was only accorded to the Brazilians and other known slave-dealers, a check will necessarily be placed on the movements of those interested in this barbarous traffic.

B. AFRICAN RESETTLEMENT

Introductory Note

THE transportation of Africans after capture and liberation was a minor chapter in the history of Atlantic migration. Those landed at Sierra Leone joined the descendants of the Black Poor, Nova Scotians, and Maroons settled there between 1787 and 1800. By 1840 some 70,000 slaves had passed into the colony since the abolition of the slave trade: and at least a third as many again were adjudicated there up till the early 1860's. Those who remained or drifted to other parts of the coast deeply influenced the structure of local trading society, not only at Freetown, but also at Bathurst, Lagos, and the Delta ports.

The conditions of resettlement and the apprenticeship of freed slave children were roundly condemned by Governor Thompson in 1808, though his legislation against the system did not end it. In 1824 an indenture fee of 10s. per head was introduced and raised to £1 in 1836. Abolished in the West Indies, indenture lingered on in Sierra Leone where there were still 2,680 apprentices in 1841, before the practice was stopped six years later. It had been a symptom of the condition of society in the recaptive and African community and evidence of the inability of the administration to turn all liberated slaves into peasant farmers with the limited means at its disposal; and as the population of the colony grew and well-meant schemes for land grants failed, other remedies were sought.

The Sierra Leone Government was requested by the Colonial Office in 1831 and 1832 to send as many liberated Africans as possible to the Gambia, after a preliminary shipment of 145 on the initiative of Lieut.-Governor Rendall. By June 1836 a further 2,000 had been transported north. A Liberated African Department on the Sierra Leone model was opened at MacCarthy Island and lasted till 1843, after receiving a further 914 Africans from Freetown. At the same time unofficial emigration eastwards to the Bights was organized by the liberated African community in Sierra Leone. A petition for official protection at Badagri was rejected by Lord John Russell; but the news of willingness to leave the colony, reported by Governor Doherty in March 1840, encouraged the Colonial Office to begin correspondence with West India governors on recruitment and transport.

In all, during the period of regulated emigration between 1841 and

1863, some 8,700 liberated slaves were taken from Sierra Leone to Jamaica, Trinidad, Grenada, St. Lucia, St. Vincent, Tobago, and St. Kitts.[1] An additional 13,355 Africans were sent to British Guiana between 1835 and 1865, though it is not clear from official returns how many of these were recruited outside Sierra Leone. Compared with the transportation of labourers from the East Indies, Madeira, or China, West Africa provided only about 8 per cent. of the total number of official migrants taken to the West Indies, 1835–72. But the encouragement of this African source of supply raised some difficult points of principle concerning the purpose of the Sierra Leone settlement.

In general, recruitment from Sierra Leone was voluntary, though Lord John Russell laid down in his preliminary instructions that the Sierra Leone Government was not obliged to provide subsistence for liberated Africans beyond a period of three months after landing. Those who could not maintain themselves were required to leave. In 1844 the period of free subsistence was abolished (in the face of protests from Buxton and the anti-slavery group); and the period of residence in Sierra Leone required of prospective migrants was reduced to no more than a week. Finally, in 1847, the West India Committee and the Land and Emigration Commissioners suggested that captured slaves might be shipped directly to the British West Indies without landing at Freetown at all. The Foreign Office saw no objection to this, nor did Earl Grey; and the idea of compulsory emigration was accepted, though it is difficult to say how far it was applied in actual cases of capture, until more work on slave trade records has been done.

As it operated, African transportation was financed partly by a bounty system paid for by each of the governments of the West Indies and partly by Treasury grant. From 1843 all arrangements were supervised by the Colonial Land and Emigration Commissioners, and the earlier practice of leaving selection to Emigration Agents from the West Indies was abandoned in favour of a greater measure of control through a single agent under the Governor of Sierra Leone. Vessels were chartered at first by the Imperial Government, and free return passages after five years were promised. The system was revised again in 1847, after a decline in the supply of migrants, and the regular dispatch of transport was stopped. Exhortation to migrate (and the policy of refusing subsistence) stimulated another wave of Sierra Leone Africans and Kru labourers between 1847 and 1853, transported by contract with the shipping firm of Hyde, Hodge & Co. The offer of return passages was dropped. In 1853 recruitment was suspended after critical reports had appeared in the *Liberian Herald*. Liberated African transportation dwindled to nothing. There was a brief revival again in 1858 when return passages were allowed; but reluctance to leave the colony and the decline of captures caused the whole scheme to be abandoned, after the last shipload left Freetown for St. Kitts in May 1863.

[1] F. H. Hitchens, *The Colonial Land and Emigration Commission* (Philadelphia, 1931), Appendix 12, pp. 324–5; C.O. 267/175, Fergusson to Stanley, 30 January 1842. The totals cited from Commission reports by Hitchins do not include figures for 1841–2 to some of the West India islands. They do include Kru labourers transhipped to Freetown.

OBP

I

LORD SYDNEY TO THE LORDS COMMISSIONERS OF THE ADMIRALTY: SIERRA LEONE SETTLERS, 7 DECEMBER 1786[1]

My Lords,

A Plan having been laid before the King, for sending out of this Country a Number of Black Poor (many of whom have been discharged from His Majesty's Naval Service at the Conclusion of the late War, and others after having been employed with the Army in North America) who have since their Arrival in England been reduced to the greatest Distress, in order that a Settlement may be formed in or near the River Sierra Leone, on the Coast of Africa; and His Majesty having been pleased to approve of the Plan, and in Consequence thereof to direct that Measures should immediately be taken for acquiring from the Native Chiefs a Territory of sufficient Extent for the settling of the said Black Poor, and also for furnishing them with Tools and Implements, &c. for the Cultivation of the Land, as well as with Provisions for their Subsistence, until it is supposed that they will be able to raise Food for their future Support, I have received His Royal Commands to signify to your Lordships His Majesty's Pleasure, that as soon as the said Black Poor shall be embarked on Board of the Vessels which are prepared for their Reception, together with the Stores and Provisions before mentioned, you do appoint a Ship of War to escort the said Vessels to the River Sierra Leone, directing her Commander, upon his Arrival there, to give every possible Assistance to the Superintendant or Overseer who will accompany the said Black Poor, in the Execution of the Plan, whilst the said Ship may remain in the said River. I shall transmit to your Lordships, as soon as may be, a Copy of the Plan, for your full Information upon this Business.

[1] *Parl. Papers*, 1789, xxiv (626), p. 3. *Lord Sydney* was Home Secretary, responsible for colonial and plantation affairs till 1786. For the handbill advertising conditions of settlement issued by the Committee for the Black Poor in 1786, see J. J. Crooks, *A History of the Colony of Sierra Leone Western Africa* (London, 1903), pp. 359–60. A little over 400 settlers were landed at Sierra Leone in May 1787. Desertion and death quickly reduced this number (and a score more who arrived in 1788) to about half. Their settlement was destroyed by the Temne at the end of 1789.

2

GOVERNOR T. P. THOMPSON TO LORD CASTLE-REAGH: APPRENTICED SLAVES, 27 JULY 1808[1]

... I AM afraid, my Lord, I shall discover that the natives of Africa have been introduced into the Colony of Sierra Leone, and have existed in a situation in no essential circumstance differing from that of slaves, not only without authority but in opposition to the Orders of His Majesty's Government. If this should be the fact, I should be unworthy of His Majesty's confidence if I did not immediately endeavour to remedy the evil.

If the information I have collected is exact, it will appear that a misapplication of the permission given by the Order in Council for apprenticing slaves natives of Africa who shall have been condemned for apprenticing or forfeiture, has been the source from which this evil has arisen.[2]

I cannot conceal from your Lordship my apprehensions that in the present circumstances of Africa it will not be practicable to introduce into His Majesty's Colony natives of Africa as apprentices without reducing their situation in all essential points to that of slaves, & that effects of such a competition of compelled labour will be exceedingly prejudicial to the welfare of His Majesty's Colony, the anxiety of some of the traders who have heretofore trafficked in slaves on the coast of Africa, to be permitted to have and possess natives of Africa under the name of apprentices in His Majesty's Colony, & to procure them from the natives, gives me strong reasons for suspecting that the terms *apprentice* & *slave* are by these men considered as synonemous. ...

3

JOSIAH PRATT TO HENRY GOULBURN: SLAVE CHILDREN, 1 NOVEMBER 1816[3]

[The Church Missionary Society cannot be responsible for the care of more than 200 liberated African children in Sierra Leone.]

[1] C.O. 267/24. *T. P. Thompson* was the first Governor of Sierra Leone appointed by the Crown, 1808–10, before being recalled home to explain his policy. *Viscount Castlereagh* was Secretary of State for War and Colonies, 1805–9.
[2] In February 1808 Governor Ludlam had disposed of 167 captured slaves by taking 40 of the men into government service and apprenticing the rest to settlers. Thompson published two ordinances to end all apprenticeship and to prevent slave-dealing in the Colony. *Sierra Leone Gazette*, No. 7, 1 August 1808; No. 9, 20 August 1808.
[3] C.O. 267/44. *Josiah Pratt* was Secretary to the C.M.S., 1802–24.

... I HAVE in consequence, in command from the Committee of the Society to beg the favour of you to state this matter to the Earl Bathurst, and to request that Instructions may be given to Governor MacCarthy to that effect. The Society will wholly exonerate Government from expence respecting the maintenance, clothing, and education of 200 of the recaptured children, in succession—Government allowing to its representatives in the Colony, as proposed, the sum of £5 for each child, beyond that number, that shall be committed to its care—and the whole of their management and education being subject to the inspection of the Governor. . . .

4

JOSIAH PRATT TO EARL BATHURST, VILLAGE SUPERINTENDENTS, AUGUST 1818[1]

... THE Committee [of the Church Missionary Society] propose therefore, to provide, for the approbation of the Governor, an English or Lutheran Clergyman, to be appointed to the office of Superintendent in each Town of Liberated Negroes, now formed or hereafter to be formed; and to grant to such Superintendent, in addition to the Stipend of £150 per anm. which he will receive as an officer of Government, the sum of £100 per annum in consideration of his charging himself with the moral and religious instruction of the Negroes under his care.

The Committee further propose to provide, for the approbation of the Governor, in such Towns as may require further assistance, a Schoolmaster to relieve the Superintendent & to take charge of the Children, at a salary not exceeding £150 per anm.

As a new town has probably by this time been added to those of Gloucester, Bathurst, Leopold, Charlotte, Regent, Wilberforce, & Kissey, mentioned in the last Returns, it is obvious, that, when all these Towns come to request both a Superintendent & a Schoolmaster, that this proposal will bring to the Society under an annual charge of £2000; beside that of £500 for the Colonial Schools, and the support of 200 children at Leicester Mountain; leaving on the funds an annual charge, on the whole, of little less than £4000, to be expended in behalf of the Liberated Negroes. This proposal I am authorized to lay before your Lordship, as that which the Committee are willing to act upon for the present, under all the circumstances before stated, and with the hope already expressed of future relief from this charge: it being understood, that provision is or will be made by Government, for the erection, in the respective Towns, of Churches, School Houses, & Dwellings for the Superintendents & Schoolmasters.

[1] C.O. 267/48.

5

GOVERNOR CHARLES TURNER TO EARL BATHURST: LIBERATED AFRICAN DEPARTMENT, SIERRA LEONE, 25 JANUARY 1826[1]

MY LORD,

Amongst the many objects which in this Colony lay claim to my attention, there are very few which require to be considered more than that which is called the 'Liberated African Department'.[2] However adequate the arrangements might have been to the early state of this establishment, it is very evident that they have not been so for some time past, and equally evident that, from the numbers of captured slaves brought into the Colony, they become every day less so. There have been more than 20,000 Slaves landed in this Colony, and during the last year upwards of 2,400 have been emancipated. Should the trade in Slaves continue to increase in the manner in which it has done for the last two years, there is no doubt, from the activity of our cruizers, but the number brought in here will increase also, and will very shortly become a very large and unwieldy mass of people; indeed, they are so already: and it becomes a matter of very serious consideration how they are to be disposed of, or how they are to maintain themselves. Under the arrangements hitherto prevailing, they have been distributed amongst the villages, where they have been for years supported in idleness by the Government; but the villages and the poor land of the mountains where they are situated, already begin to refuse to them a scanty subsistence, and they have begun to wander in search of better soil and easier sustenance:—and the evident tendency of this is, that they will retrograde in the woods, into a state of nature and barbarism, or become vagrants about Freetown and the more populous villages. I, in some degree, meet this evil at present, by employing them on the public works, carrying bricks and other materials, giving them food, lodging, and some clothing, at the public expense; and I have given them in small numbers and under registry, to respectable people to cultivate land and for domestic purposes. And it is found that under this system of putting them to easy and regular labour, such as they have been used to on their landing from the slave ships, that they become very orderly good labourers; but in the cases where they have been located in the villages, and have received gratuitous maintenance, they can with difficulty be induced to give a day's labour even for good

[1] *Parl. Papers*, 1826, xxii (389), pp. 4–5.
[2] This title was changed from the Captured Negro Department in 1822. The Department was not finally abolished (after years of inactivity) till 1891.

wages. The expense of this establishment has been very great; I believe that the regulations under which I have reduced it during the last year . . . may be safely persevered in, and a still greater reduction made; but as the whole system is defective, I cannot persuade myself that I can do more than to alleviate the evil. It would but lead to disappointment to imagine, that a large mass of poor ignorant people, without capital, skill or industry, could be brought to maintain themselves, and to raise articles of export, without the assistance of labour wages;—could such a system succeed even in England, the poor rates might soon be abolished.

There are twelve Villages established for the purpose of civilizing, instructing and keeping together these people, and with establishments apparently very suitable, although practically very inefficient: —a clergyman, a schoolmaster, and a superintendent to each village, has the appearance of meeting every possible purpose, but unfortunately the untowardness of the climate, the privations, fatigues, and uncongeniality of the situations with the former habits of the people who hold them, and the absence of personal interest or hope of progressive advancement, soon cause a decrease of numbers. At present there are in the Colony but *one* Church Missionary (Mr. Raban), and three Lutheran clergymen, five schoolmasters, and four superintendents. Amongst these there is not one person who has the slightest knowledge of Agriculture, nor can I learn that there ever has been any person employed in the colony, who had any acquaintance either with European or Tropical Agriculture. Under such disadvantages, it is not to be wondered that cultivation has not made much progress. Should it meet your Lordship's approbation that twelve superintendents from the West India Islands, where cotton and coffee cultivation is best understood, men of colour, with an assistant or overseer to each, should be brought to this colony for the purpose of instructing these Liberated Africans, and for superintending such plantations, as would not fail, under such facilities, to be formed here by capitalists. I am satisfied, that under such arrangement, more would be done for the permanent improvement of the colony and the condition of these people, in a few years, than is to be expected under the present system in half a century. Europeans cannot accomplish such objects here, and there are no native people capable of conducting such matters. . . .

6

REPORT OF THE COMMISSIONERS OF INQUIRY: LIBERATED AFRICANS, 29 JUNE 1827[1]

. . . HAVING considered it a part of our duty to represent to your Lordship the sufferings and privations to which the negroes are frequently subjected, in their passage from the usual place of capture to Sierra Leone, as well the sickness and loss of life consequent upon it; it will probably be expected that we should be prepared to suggest some remedy for the removal of an evil, the existence of which we feel assured your Lordship will greatly deplore. As long as the great majority of the slave captures shall be made in the Bights of Biafra and Benin, and the place of their location is so far to windward as Sierra Leone, we fear it will be exceedingly difficult to remove the evil altogether; yet we indulge the hope that even under these circumstances it may be considerably mitigated. With this view we venture to propose, that should His Majesty's government continue to direct the location of captured negroes at Sierra Leone, (or any part of the Coast farther to windward,) a leeward station should be selected for the establishment of the Courts of Mixed Commission, and a depôt formed there for the reception of liberated Africans, where they should remain under proper regulations and superintendence till their state of health, and other circumstances, admitted of their being forwarded by eligible conveyances to their ultimate destination.

We are aware that in forming such a depôt for the reception of the negroes, a considerable expense would be incurred, and should therefore feel greater hesitation in proposing it, were we not persuaded that, wherever the liberated Africans are to be received in charge, when first landed after capture, such an establishment is absolutely essential to any systematic plan for their due classification; and when it is considered that, independently of the benefit to the negroes, it would lay the foundation for an improved mode of treatment, and for introducing a regular gradation of responsibility and controul, the objection on the score of expense will lose much of its force, perhaps altogether disappear.

Supposing such an establishment as we have suggested, a difficulty may present itself as to the means of conveying the negroes thence to their ultimate destination. The appropriation of a vessel to that

---

[1] *Parl. Papers*, 1827, vii (312), pp. 45–47, 55–56. *Major James Rowan* and *Henry Wellington* were appointed as commissioners by Bathurst in 1825 and spent the next two years touring the settlements. Their MS. reports and returns are in C.O. 267/90 and 91.

specific object, would perhaps be the simplest and most eligible plan. If not, the slave vessels might still be employed in this service, under regulations such as would remove many of the evils now complained of. They might, after landing their cargo, and being properly cleansed, and supplied with fresh provisions and water, be required to carry to Sierra Leone, the Gambia, or elsewhere, a regulated number of negroes, selected from those who had been longest in charge of the superintendent, and otherwise in a proper state for embarkation. In this way the greater part of the negroes might be removed with little additional expense or inconvenience, particularly as the captured vessels would, in all probability, be necessarily sent to windward for sale; it being unlikely that purchasers would be found at any station to leeward, where such an establishment would be formed.

If, however, this measure should not be approved of, and it should be decided still to send the captured negroes direct to Sierra Leone for adjudication; we beg leave to recommend the establishment of a floating lazaretto or receiving ship, under proper regulations, for the reception of these negroes who arrive there under the influence of infectious disease; or, when no disease exists, for the purpose of removing a part of the over-crowded cargoes, and thereby meliorating the circumstances of the whole, while detained on board awaiting adjudication. We feel confident, that with proper management such an establishment might be maintained at a very moderate expense. Were a vessel well adapted to the object sent out from England, and moored in the Sierra Leone river (an eligible station for this purpose), little additional expenditure would be required. A naval assistant surgeon might be appointed to her, who should live on board, and, in addition to his pay, receive the salary as surgeon of the Mixed Court. A trifling expense would probably not be considered when the question was one of humanity; but, if it should, the objection might be obviated by a per-centage deducted from the head money now paid to the captors.

Their benevolence would doubtless incline them to this measure, even were it not, as it unquestionably is, their interest to promote a plan, having in view the preservation of the negroes for adjudication.

The delays which occasionally take place in this adjudication are greatly to be regretted, from the consequences thereby entailed upon the negroes. In one instance delay is known to have arisen from the simultaneous absence (for some weeks) of the governor and the acting chief justice, who held appointments in the Mixed Courts, and without whom a court could not be formed; an evil, the recurrence of which, it would seem right to guard against. . . .

7

SIR GEORGE MURRAY TO ACTING GOVERNOR H. J. RICKETTS: MISSIONARY CO-OPERATION, 3 JULY 1829[1]

SIR,

I transmit, herewith, for your information a copy of a communication which I have received from the Church Missionary Society, explanatory of the reasons which induce them to relinquish the arrangement, which they entered into with His Majesty's Government in the Year 1824.

Although it was to be lamented that the benevolent objects of the Society have been, in a great measure frustrated by the difficulty of securing the services of an adequate number of intelligent Missionaries, yet I am not without hopes that the Society will not, therefore, be discouraged from prosecuting their original views, so far as the comparatively limited means at their disposal, can serve. In accordance with this expectation, I have assured the Society that you would lend your cordial assistance and cooperation to their servants in the Colony, in furtherance of the ends of their Mission, and it will therefore be convenient that I should point out to you, the extent to which your cooperation should be carried.

Under the arrangement of 1824, the Society charged themselves with the task of providing religious instruction for the inhabitants of the Colony: and the Government undertook to provide dwelling houses for the Missionaries, Churches for the performance of Divine Worship, as well as School Education for the youth of the Colony.

Assuming, as I do, that the Society will continue, as well as they are able, to provide the means of affording religious instruction to the Colony, it will be only reasonable that we should continue to provide their Missionaries with dwelling houses. It would certainly be desirable too that there should be a Church in every Village: but as no special provision has been made for so large an expenditure as would be necessary for that purpose, I would have you consider whether it might not be possible to stimulate the inhabitants of the most populous Villages, where there may be no Churches, to contribute their Labours at least, the Government undertaking to furnish the expense of materials, towards erecting decent places of worship, which might serve at the same time as Schools in those Villages, where there may be none: and if you will have the goodness to transmit to me, at your earliest convenience, a statement of the number and situation of the

---

[1] C.O. 268/28, ff. 265–71. *Sir George Murray* was Secretary of State for Colonies, 1828–30.

Churches which are extant, together with an estimate of the expense which would be necessary upon the principle which I have suggested for building Churches in the Villages which have none, I shall lose no time in signifying to you the determination of His Majesty's Government on the subject.

With respect to the Schools which the Society revived, I see no reason for apprehending that any serious inconvenience could arise from these Establishments being placed under the exclusive controul of the Missionaries: but it will be necessary that you should come to some understanding with the Servants of the Society in regard to the description of children over which the Governor of the Colony is to abstain from exercising any controul.

I am of opinion that all children, who have been born in the Colony of Liberated African Parents, and are not at the charge of Government, may be admitted into those Schools, subject to the controul of their Parents only: and although I see no reason why the Society should be precluded from imparting the benefits of education to Children who, have been rescued from Slavery and brought into the Colony at an early age, yet such of those children who are deprived of their parents, must remain subject to the controul of Government, so long as they are subsisted at the Public expence.

I would not have you interfere, unnecessarily, with the course of education, which they may receive from the Missionaries, but it must be for you to prescribe the period when that education shall terminate, and their instruction, under Indentures of apprenticeship, in the arts of industry commence.

Upon reference to the Blue Book of your Government which I have consulted with the view of ascertaining the present state of efficiency of the Government Schools, I have been surprised to find that, with the exception of some teachers of the Missionary Society, who are included in the Education Return, there is not one Teacher reported to be in the service of the Colonial Government. . . .

8

GOVERNOR A. FINDLAY TO R. W. HAY: GAMBIA RESETTLEMENT, 7 MAY 1832[1]

. . . A VESSEL being here at present from the Gambia, and about to return with a cargo, I have, with a view of complying with His Lordship's wishes, engaged her to carry one hundred Libd. Africans to Saint Mary's for which I have agreed to pay 13/- per head for their passage. Being afraid to send an unarmed vessel to Sea, with those people, in case of a Pirate or Slaver falling in with her, who would no

[1] C.O. 267/114. Approved in Hay to Findlay, 11 July 1832, C.O. 268/30.

doubt take the Africans out and destroy the vessel, I made a requisition to Commodore Hayes to send one of his Tenders as a convoy, and
to carry some specie to the Gambia, which I did not wish to trust in a
merchant vessel. He readily agreed to convoy the vessel and specie
there himself, on his way to England. The 60 men and 40 women
whom I have slected for the Gambia have just been emancipated, and
I regret that I have not the means of sending some more of the same
cargo. I have given directions for the Assist. Superintendent to draw
the Six Months Allowance for them, out of which he is to put 3 weeks
provisions on board, and pay 13/- per head for their passage; the
balance will be sent to Lieut. Govr. Rendall and if he should require
any further subsistence for them I have recommended him to make a
requisition on the Commisariat instead of drawing Bills on the
Treasury. The usual clothing and utensils have been issued to the
people, the agricultural implements, with six months further supply
of clothing, and twelve months supply of medicine have been sent in
the vessel, to be placed at the Lieut. Governor's disposal. . . .

9

GOVERNOR A. FINDLAY TO R. W. HAY: RESTRIC-
TIONS ON LIBERATED AFRICANS,
2 MARCH 1833[1]

SIR,
    In consequence of the numerous instances of Liberated Africans
leaving their locations, and settling themselves in various parts of the
Colony, whereby it became impossible for the Managers of the
Villages to account for the Population placed under their immediate
care, it was deemed necessary to issue an order of the Governor and
Council to impose a fine on any person who should afterwards
harbour or entertain any runaway among Liberated Africans in his
or their Hamlet.
    It has been represented to many of the Liberated Africans by Mr.
Savage[2] that this order is illegal, and he has pointed it out to them as
a hardship and a great grievance by this means endeavouring to sow
the seeds of discontent and rebellion among a large population, a
great part of whom have been but a short time in the Colony, consequently, they are the more easily led away by what is represented to
them, by persons of their own Color, through the influence of Mr.
Savage. . . .

    [Citing his evidence before the Slave Trade Commissioners, 20 January
1831.]

[1] C.O. 267/119.
[2] *W. H. Savage*, coloured trader, lawyer, and business partner of W. Gabbidon.

. . . In consequence of the great influence which the Mahommadan Priests have over the Liberated Africans, I have by the advice of the Council issued a Proclamation prohibiting them from settling in any of the Liberated African Villages, and directing the Liberated Africans as far as their circumstances will admit to conform to the European mode of dress.

Many of the discharged soldiers settled in several of the Villages of the Colony have adopted their original native Superstitious Customs, by following the Faith and assuming the Garb of the Mahommedans, this I have forbid[den] on pain of the forfeiture of their pensions. . . .

10

R. W. HAY TO LIEUT.-GOVERNOR O. TEMPLE: FORCED RECRUITMENT, 28 MAY 1834[1]

My Dear Sir,

I have received a Communication from the Secretary to the General Commanding in Chief, enclosing a copy of a Letter addressed to him by a Captain Fraser, relative to an opinion which it is stated that you had formed, as to the practicability of effecting the forcible enrolment of Liberated Africans into the Military Service. Lord Hill has expressed a decided opinion as to the propriety of abstaining from such a course, and as Mr. Stanley[2] fully concurs with him in that view of the question, it will be advisable to avoid in future attempting any thing like constraint in procuring recruits from the Liberated Africans.

11

LIEUT.-GOVERNOR G. RENDALL TO LORD GLENELG: GAMBIA RESETTLEMENT, 14 JULY 1836[3]

[The difficulties of supervising the Liberated Africans; a recommendation for funds to erect sawmills and cornmills using African labour.]

. . . The views which have guided me in the location of the Liberated Africans upon [the Gambia] River have been powerfully controlled

[1] C.O. 268/30, ff. 469–70. *Major O. Temple* was Lieut.-Governor of Sierra Leone, 1833–4.

[2] *E. G. S. Stanley* (Lord Stanley and Earl of Derby), Under-Secretary to the Colonial Office, 1827–8, and Secretary of State for War and Colonies, April 1833–June 1844, September 1841–December 1845.

[3] C.O. 87/14. *George Rendall* was Chief Justice of the Gambia, 1820–30, and Lieut.-Governor, 1833–4. *Lord Glenelg* was Secretary of State for War and Colonies, 1835–9.

by the necessity which I considered existed for the Government to be relieved from the expense of their support as quickly as possible and for that purpose have devised the best means I could of employing them so as to obtain some profit from their labor which would relieve the Government from a part of the burthen. It was with this view I established the Brick Works, Lime Making, &c.

Another object I had was to give to this Settlement a permanent population of Mechanics, Artisans, Sailors and laborers and I therefore apprenticed as many as I could to the Merchants and Inhabitants of the Settlement in whose families I considered they would be well taken care of.

This Settlement was formed by the English Merchants in Goree and Senegal until possession of those Colonies was given up and then they brought down here a great Number of Artisans, Workmen, and laborers from those places besides which Several Hundred of the natives have been in the habit of coming from the mainland to this Settlement annually for about 8 months to look for work consisting of several tribes, Joloffs, Syrias, Salums, Toucolores[1] and Tilliboukoes, they could never be depended upon as they came only when it suited their convenience.

To obviate this uncertainty I allowed a number of the Libd. Africans to be located to Goderich (as I have called the district between Joalla Town and the end of the Island) a distance of about three miles where they make their farms during the rainy season and at other times obtain employment from the Merchants and Inhabitants.

The Liberated Africans at Berwick Town are those which I apprenticed and placed with the discharged Soldiers to learn to be Farmers, and to add to the strength of Fort Bullen in case of need.

At MacCarthy's Island as many have been apprenticed as could find good masters, and the others located, being placed for the first year with their Countrymen having each a small Town lot and making their farms on the best land they can find vacant . . .

[The Settlement needs a qualified land surveyor]

. . . The only supervision I have exercised was in having all the Apprentices before me in 1834, and which I propose doing again this year. This Town is so small that the Colonial Secretary, the Director, or myself must be made acquainted with any improper treatment should any persons be inclined to subject them to it. I make it a point whenever I visit the several stations to see every body.

My only reason for apprenticing considerable numbers to individuals has been owing to their having greater means of employing them as Sailors, Canoemen, Farmers and Squarers of Mahogany.

[1] *Sic*, Wolof, Sereres, Wolof of Salum, Tukolor.

12

LIEUT.-GOVERNOR H. D. CAMPBELL TO LORD GLENELG: SIERRA LEONE RESETTLEMENT AND APPRENTICESHIP, 5 SEPTEMBER 1836[1]

MY LORD,

Taking the Liberated Africans as a body they are a remarkably well conducted people nor have we as much crime as in England and certainly not of that enormity; the vice of drunkenness is principally confined to the Europeans and little known among the Africans with the exception of the Pensioners and those in Freetown who have been much associated with the Europeans; humiliating as it is to acknowledge the fact it is beyond contradiction that some of the most degraded and worthless characters here are from our own Country.

They are all well intentioned kind hearted people charitable to one another and will give a share to the Stranger of what they have; once gain their confidence and you may lead them by a thread; they have been much neglected, in fact as to civilizing them little has been done except by themselves in readily adopting what is European; the whole system that has been adopted is in my opinion (formed by actual observation and residence) extremely bad.

The Slave Vessel arrives in the harbour generally crammed with the unfortunate Slaves of all ages from fifty to two years old. They are first visited by the Marshall and Surgeon of the Mixed Commission Court who make their report; an order is then given and they are landed at the Liberated African Yard (the sick being sent to Kissy Hospital direct by water) where they remain a week until emancipated by the Court of Mixed Commission. They are then employed on the Public Works for three months after which located in the villages receiving at the rate of 2d. per day for three months more when they are left to themselves.

No regard has been paid to the time of the year whether it is the rainy or dry season; their time being up they must be located and the poor creature is given one square Chain of land in some village to build a Hut; no matter whether his lot is on rock there he is to live and to raise produce to support himself the best way he can and were it not for their kind feeling towards each other many would perish for want.

No regard has generally been had to the nature of the Soil or situation where Villages have been formed the most barren and inconvenient seem to have been selected. These causes and the want

[1] C.O. 267/133. Approved in Glenelg to Campbell, 1 December 1836, C.O. 268/33.

of good roads must account in a great degree for the number that leave the Colony.

The Apprenticeship System is most abominable it is nothing more than Slavery of the worst description any person who wanted an Apprentice had one by paying 10/- in many cases the parties receiving the unfortunate Children had been but a short time in the Colony themselves and [were] as uncivilized as the child they obtained which was then taken to their home in Freetown the Villages or into the bush where many live in a state of nature. After they are located it is their first object to procure an apprentice who is obliged to do all the hard work or druggery [sic] for his Master; the girls are brought up much in the same way those in Freetown too generally in prostitution their mistresses living by their infamy and when any girl is manageable and a man wishes to have her he makes the best bargain he can with the Mistress purchases the girl and marries her or not as suits his convenience; the women were in the habit of being given to any person who would take them or sent to the Villages where they were disposed of in the same way.

In the first instance the Colonial Surgeon who has virtually the care of them ought to be the person to see them on their arrival. This may be easily obtained by his being appointed by the Foreign Office instead of the Surgeon of the African Corps who takes no more trouble than he can avoid with the poor creatures knowing that they are only in his care for a few days in fact the Colonial Surgeon has the greater part of the duty to do from their first arrival as the sick are now sent to Kissy Hospital.

I have as far as possible checked the bad effects attending the giving away the women by sending them to the Villages placing each under the care of a resident married female of good character who is glad to support her for the work until she gets married to a man she likes.

With regard to the Apprentices I raised the fee from 10/- to one pound to obtain a better class of persons and now only give them to such persons as I know will bring them up properly.

I have altered the Indentures obliging the Master or Mistress to clothe and make them attend a place of worship and Sunday School as also after the first year to pay two dollars annually towards a School fund, this will have the effect of making the Managers see the Children & their Masters twice a year and prevent the probability of their making away with them with impunity.

13

LIBERATED AFRICANS TO GOVERNOR R. DOHERTY: PETITION FOR PROTECTION, 15 NOVEMBER 1839[1]

THE humble petition of the undersigned persons most respectfully sheweth. That your humble petitioners are Liberated Africans, and we feel with much thankful[ness] to Almighty God, and the Queen of England who has rescued us from being in a state of slavery, and has brought us to this Colony, and set us at Liberty, and thanks to be the God of all Mercy, who has sent his servant to declare unto us poor Creatures the way of Salvation, which illuminates our understanding, so we were brought to know that we have a soul to save, and when your humble petitioners look back upon their poor Country people, who now living in darkness, without the light of the Gospel, so we take upon ourselves to direct this our humble petition to your Excellency.

That the Queen will be graciously [pleased] to sympathize with her humble petitioners to establish a Colony at Badagry that the same may be under the Queen's Jurisdiction, and beg of Her Royal Majesty [that she] will be pleased to send us to the above mentioned place, and also beg and solicit of her Royal Majesty to send [a] Missionary with us, and by so doing the slave trade can be abolished, because the slave dealers can be afread [*sic*] to go up to the said place so that the Gospel of Christ can be preached throughout our Land. . .

Thomas Wills	John Macaulay	John Turner
John Ezzidio	John Thompson	John H. Atkins
Emanuel Cline	Edward Davis	John T. Nottidge
Thos. Pinches	George Randle	James Will
James Gording	Thomas Crook	John Lewis
John James	Peter Campbell	William Findlay
Christopher Taylor	William Sawyer	James Lewis

[1] C.O. 267/154. *Lieut.-Colonel Richard Doherty* was Governor of Sierra Leone, 1837–40. The first vessel with migrant Yoruba, Nupe, and others had sailed for Badagri in April 1839. This exodus was not approved: Russell to Doherty, 1 May 1840, C.O. 268/35, ff. 312–14.

14

GOVERNOR R. DOHERTY TO LORD JOHN RUSSELL: LIBERATED AFRICAN EMIGRATION, 20 MARCH 1840[1]

MY LORD,

I have the honour to acquaint your Lordship that a pretty extensive and growing disposition exists at present among the Liberated African population both of Freetown and the villages to emigrate from the Colony to their native countries to the northward and eastward. Some time ago two small parties of twenty and fourteen sailed from Badagry in the Bight of Benin; of which the first were, at their own request, landed and left at the British Settlement of Accra, while of the second no intelligence has yet been received. At this moment not fewer than two hundred persons, belonging chiefly to the Houssa Country and the Kingdom of Yarriba, lying east and west of the Niger, having subscribed the amount of four dollars each towards the formation of a fund, have purchased with it a condemned prize vessel, in which it was their intention to proceed to Badagry and from thence to seek their native homes at a distance of some hundred miles inland. But as with this party were about to embark one hundred children, I have deemed it imperative to prohibit for the present their departure and that of their parents. I have allowed passports for not more than forty-four men and seventeen women, and of an age so mature as renders them not likely to become the prey of the slave dealers: and I shall await until I am made acquainted with your Lordship's sentiments in the matter, before I permit the others to follow.

I have in vain cautioned them all against the dangers to which they may expose themselves, in returning without protection to those parts of the continent, of being again made captives and again sold into slavery. They reply that in their own countries they are free persons and therefore not liable to be sold there, unless taken in war; and that in travelling through other territories in large bodies they encounter no risk. They allege that in this colony they are retarded in the career of improvement, that no opportunity is afforded them of increasing their means and further ameliorating their condition; and certainly they receive little encouragement from the Maroons and settlers, or from Europeans themselves, who on all occasions prefer for employment the tribes of Kroomen and Timmanees. The villagers complain that they are without a market for their produce.

[1] C.O. 267/159.

And to these causes is no doubt to be added a restless spirit of change which appears to be natural to Africans.

At this moment it likewise happens that many of the Maroon and Settler population having been informed of the management given to immigration in Trinidad and others of the West Indies, express the wish and purpose of removing thither with their families; and in my opinion nothing ought to be done to discourage their departure, which if, as they conceive, it would be beneficial to themselves, would undoubtedly be not less so to the Colony. But I am desirous of knowing from your Lordship what course it would be adviseable for me to pursue in the event of any considerable number of Liberated Africans being induced by this example to decide upon removing likewise to the same part of the world.

15

LORD JOHN RUSSELL TO GOVERNOR R. DOHERTY: MUSLIMS AND LIBERATED AFRICANS, 3 APRIL 1840[1]

SIR,

I have to acknowledge the receipt of your Despatch No. 77 of the 4th of December last with its enclosures relating to the extension of the doctrines and practices of Mahometanism among the Liberated Africans.

I concur in the view which you have taken of the injurious consequences which must result from the introduction and spread of Mahometan habits and superstitions in the Colony; and I agree with you that the persons who openly profess Mahometanism should be removed to the verge of the Colony.

It appears that you will have no difficulty in breaking up their settlement at Fourah Town; and with regard to the other Settlement at Fourah bay, you will take such measures for dispossessing the individuals located there, as upon a view of all the facts of the case, the Official Legal Adviser of Your Govt. shall consider to be most in accordance with Law.

[1] C.O. 268/35, ff. 309–10.

16

LORD JOHN RUSSELL TO GOVERNOR SIR JOHN JEREMIE: LIBERATED AFRICAN EMIGRATION, 20 MARCH 1841[1]

. . . I CONSIDER the establishment of a regular intercourse between Africa and the West Indies will tend greatly not only to the prosperity of the British West Indian possessions, but likewise to the civilization of Africa.

A new epoch has arrived for the African race. We have in the West Indies 800,000 negroes, of whom perhaps three-fourths are Christians, in the enjoyment of practical freedom, of means of education, and of physical comfort, to a very high degree. There is no reason to suppose that their advances in wealth, knowledge, and religious improvement, may not be in proportion to the most hopeful anticipations. Nothing like this state of society exists among the African race elsewhere. In Hayti there is a very low standard of government and civilization; in Cuba, in Brazil, and in the United States, slavery; in Africa, slavery, human sacrifices, and the most degrading superstitions.

We have made in the last ten years a wonderful and successful experiment. But its consequences are yet to be developed, and may far exceed the present good which has been effected, great and surprising as that has been.

. . . Applying the preceding observations to the subject of emigration, I am entirely opposed to any plan for taking the liberated Africans to the West Indies against their will. But, on the other hand, I consider that we are not bound to maintain in the colony of Sierra Leone all the captured negroes who are sent thither; and that Africans landed there in future should, at the expiration of three months, be bound, 1st, to show that they are in a state to maintain themselves on the spot; or, 2dly, to signify their consent to emigrate to the West Indies; or, 3dly, to leave the colony.

In laying down the rule that liberated Africans should be able to maintain themselves after the expiration of three months from the time of their being landed in the colony, I do not include the expense of their superintendents and of other administrative officers.

I think it desirable that you should communicate fully and openly on all these points with the ministers of religion in the colony.

[1] *Parl. Papers*, 1842, xxxi (301), pp. 447–9. The Sierra Leone administration had been informed in January 1841 that an Agent-General (James Hackett) would arrive to supervise emigration to Jamaica in vessels contracted from Messrs. Stewart and Westmoreland, according to the provisions of the Passengers' Act of 1840 (5 & 6 Will. IV, c. 63).

I further consider that it is time to appoint an agent, whose duty it shall be to watch over the execution of the laws and regulations affecting emigration. I enclose a sketch of these instructions, which you will give to that agent.[1] I do not prescribe these instructions as an inflexible rule, but as ambodying my views of the principles by which I consider that it is at least desirable that emigration from the colony should be regulated in the first instance. You will perceive that I have omitted to lay down any rule as to the proportion of females who may accompany the male emigrants. Undoubtedly, it would be desirable that the number of the former should equal the number of the latter; but it is obvious that the adoption of such a rule would have the effect of restricting emigration within limits so narrow, as to amount to a total prohibition. I should feel satisfied, therefore, if you could apply in all cases the rule adopted by the Legislature of Jamaica, which requires that the females accompanying male emigrants should be in the proportion of one-third. But I do not expect that you should feel yourself enable to insist upon that rule generally. It would be wholly inapplicable, for instance, to the Kroomen, whose custom is not to bring their wives with them to the colony, but who may be very desirous of engaging themselves to the West Indian agents.

Upon the whole, therefore, I consider it most advisable that emigration from the colony should be chiefly regulated by the laws of those colonies to which the emigrants are to proceed. . . .

17

HEADS OF INSTRUCTIONS FOR THE GOVERNMENT EMIGRATION AGENT, SIERRA LEONE, 1841[2]

. . . 1. WITH respect to the mode of collecting emigrants, four conditions are indispensable.

1st. The emigrants should have been resident upwards of at least six weeks in the colony previously to their embarkation.

2d. The emigrants at the time of their embarkation should be in a good state of bodily health.

3d. They should embark with their free consent, and without the practice of any force, fraud, or imposition, to induce them to do so.

4th. They should be made to comprehend, by adequate explanations, the nature and probable consequences of their removal, so far as they themselves would be affected by it.

---

[1] See below, no. 17.   [2] *Parl. Papers*, 1842, xxxi (301), pp. 449–51.

The first condition is a necessary precaution to prevent slave-dealers from bringing slaves to Sierra Leone to be exported as emigrants.

Should this precaution prove insufficient, the Government emigration agent for Sierra Leone will apply to the Governor of that colony for further instructions on the subject.

To insure the fulfilment of the second condition, a medical practitioner should examine every emigrant before he is accepted for a passage. A medical certificate should then be given to the master of the ship, to be delivered by him to the agent for emigration in the colony to which the ship is bound. Every emigrant should also have been vaccinated before he embarks.

With respect to the third and fourth conditions, every emigrant before he embarks should have communicated in person with the emigration agent of the colony to which he may agree to proceed, and should have received from such agent full information on those points connected with his removal which have been before adverted to. . . .

18

LIEUT.-GOVERNOR W. FERGUSSON TO THE COLONIAL OFFICE: EMIGRATION TO THE WEST INDIES, 30 JANUARY 1842[1]

. . . TRANSATLANTIC Emigration commenced in April 1841 and was for some months carried on with a degree of energy and success that threatened to depopulate the Colony. The great advantages of the West Indies were represented in glowing language, plenty of work, wages ranging from 1/8 to 2/- per diem, liberal allowances of food, gratuitous medical attention and medicine, and no compulsory labour, all these were freely offered and produced an electrical effect among our population, the public mind was violently agitated, ordinary avocations were neglected, distant visits were paid by persons anxious to canvass with each other the whole merits of the new measure, and its probable results on their future welfare.

The first vessels obtained their Complement of Emigrants with astonishing rapidity, the Agents had in fact several hundred names enrolled of eager candidates for Emigration for whom no accomodation could be found in the vessels then about to proceed. The chagrin of the disappointed candidates was great, but they were consoled by the assurance that other and early opportunities would be afforded them.

[1] C.O. 267/175. *Dr. William Fergusson* was Staff Surgeon and Acting Governor and Governor of Sierra Leone, 1841–1845.

Meantime there arose in the minds of the more shrewd and calculating a certain measure of distance and caution which prompted them to wait the issue of the first experiment, before resolving on that more extended measure of expatriation to which by the eagerness of the Emigration Agents they were invited.

For this purpose they determined to delegate certain persons to proceed with the first Emigrant Ships to Jamaica, Trinidad and Demerara, under an express understanding that such delegates were to be taken away free of expense, maintained while absent, and returned to Sierra Leone also free of expense.

With the issue of this arrangement entered into with the best motives, and in entire good faith on the part of the West Indian Agents, commenced that check to the progress of Transatlantic Emigration which has since become final and complete.

The enthusiasm created in the public mind on the arrival of the first Emigrant vessels subsided rather rapidly; after they had sailed, a calm survey of the whole matter, induced a general idea that the comforts and advantages of Sierra Leone were not outweighed by the prospects held out by Emigration.

The delegates sent to Demerara returned to the Colony in the Superior, they landed in a uniform of fine blue cloth, with scarlet cuff and collar, elegant forage caps, a scarlet waistband and fine cloth trowsers, these adornments proved in the event to be a very great mistake intended as they no doubt were, to allure Emigrants, they had precisely an opposite effect. The Scheme partook too much of artifice and delusion.

It had been arranged by Mr. Barclay, the Commissioner General for Emigration for Jamaica, that the Jamaica delegates should be returned to this colony by a small brig in August. The Brig according to promise left Jamaica in June but soon thereafter was wrecked, the delegates in consequence did not arrive at Sierra Leone until [May][1] this though entirely the effect of accident, had on the already declining cause of Emigration all the adverse consequences of a deliberate breach of faith.

Matters were still worse with the delegates to Trinidad. Mr. Hamilton the Emigration Agent for that Island had formerly resided many years among the Liberated Africans of Sierra Leone, by whom he was highly esteemed—great confidence was reposed in him and he distinctly promised that the delegates chosen to accompany him to Trinidad, should also accompany him on his return to Sierra Leone within a few months—month after month however rolled on without bringing either Mr. Hamilton or his delegates. Mr. Hamilton at last arrived in December, but he came alone unaccompanied by the delegates; nor have they up to this day returned from Trinidad.

[1] *Sic*, May 1842—over a year since they had left the colony.

Accident as well as mismanagement have thus alike contributed and each in no slight degree to the overthrow of Transatlantic Emigration from this place.

This Government did not in any respect interfere with the increase of Emigration neither encouraging to it, nor dissuading from it, those whom it was meant to concern.

The body of Wesleyan Missionaries was supposed by the Emigration Agents to have interfered in dissuading the people from going to the West Indies. I have not been able however to ascertain that this charge against that body was well founded.

It may be proper notwithstanding to mention that the Wesleyans have uniformly expressed a decided preference for Emigration coastwise over Transatlantic Emigration, and that for reasons which appear to be entitled to some respect. The great aim and object of Missionary labour and enterprize in Western Africa is the civilization and Religious improvement of its people. Transatlantic Emigration from Sierra Leone if successful would necessarily withdraw from Africa and transfer to the West Indies a large portion of that people upon whose agency the missionaries had calculated in their endeavour to accomplish the great ends of Missionary labour whereas the voluntary removal of a considerable body of people from Sierra Leone to their own country, who had for several years been habituated to the customs of civilized men and had participated largely in the privileges of the Christian Church, was held to be the opening of a new, a welcome, and unexpected avenue, for the extension of that great cause to which they had devoted their lives.

The force and cogency of these views were enhanced by the fact that the first Emigrants to Badagry soon after their arrival there, addressed to the Wesleyan body a communication earnestly representing their spiritual wants and requesting the aid of a Christian Missionary.

The future proceedings of those Liberated Africans who by removing to Badagry had thus removed themselves beyond the precincts of British jurisdiction necessarily became a subject of much anxious concern to this Government; a request has accordingly been made to the Senior Officer of the Naval Squadron that such of Her Majesty's Cruizers as may be in the neighbourhood may be instructed to pay them an occasional visit, as well as to repress any attempt at irregularities that may arise among them, as to impress the surrounding natives with the idea that they are not wholly unprotected and uncared for. Although Emigration in the very limited influence which it has as yet exerted on the population of this Colony, has, it must be owned, taken away several valuable, industrious and rising members of the community, yet one of its remarkable effects, or perhaps concomitants, cannot be omitted in this Report; vizt. that contemporaneously with its progress, there occurred a sensible and very evident falling off in the number of cases brought for trial at the police court. Of this fact I am assured by Mr. McCormack the police magistrate.

The number of persons who have emigrated from this Colony to the West Indies, during the year ended 30 Sept. 1841 has been 1019 and of those who have emigrated to the Leeward Coast during the same period 150 making a total of 1169.

19

LIEUT.-GOVERNOR W. FERGUSSON TO LORD STANLEY: RESISTANCE TO EMIGRATION, 9 JULY 1844[1]

MY LORD,

Adverting to my despatch No 9 of the 13th ultimo, and more especially to that part of it which relates to your Lordship's directions concerning the future disposal of Liberated Africans, videlicet, that such of them as should refuse to emigrate by the first opportunity that may offer after their adjudication by the Courts of Mixed Commission are to be placed on their own resources for maintenance, clothing, and such other allowances as have heretofore been supplied them at the expense of the British Government, I have now the honour to acquaint your Lordship with the issue of the first practical trial of this measure.

When this determination on the part of Her Majesty's Government was announced in the Proclamation and Government notice, copies of which I had the honour to forward to your Lordship in my despatch No 10 under date the 15th ultimo, it excited considerable commotion in the public mind. Grave apprehensions were entertained by many persons as to the perfect safety—as a measure of Police—of turning loose on the public some hundreds of Africans, houseless, penniless, and in a condition of great barbarism. Scenes of violence and of bloodshed were anticipated as likely to ensue in the defence of private property.

There were at that time 180 persons—adult males—in the Liberated African Yard at Freetown. These had been frequently canvassed but always unsuccessfully, by the respective agents for Emigration. They steadily persisted in their refusal to emigrate notwithstanding the manifest evils of the position in which, by such refusal, they were about to be placed. The *Glen Huntley* Transport arrived from Jamaica on the 7th June; and shortly thereafter I took steps for their dispersion.

[1] C.O. 267/184.

An addition of twenty persons had recently been made to the Constabulary Force of Freetown; and in order that the dispersion of the Liberated Africans should partake as little as possible of the nature of a grievance inflicted on the public, I directed that parties of from 20 to 40 should be sent to the several rural districts of the Colony—having regard to the density of the population, the pecuniary means of the inhabitants, and other considerations by which their quiet settlement might probably be effected.

This measure was not however followed by any of the anticipated causes of alarm. The persons thus placed on their own resources were received with much gladness wheresoever they were sent, and, as a separate body they were almost instantly lost in the general mass of the people.

The great eagerness with which they were picked up, in the rural districts, by the Liberated Africans already settled there, has added another to the reasons under which I expressed to your Lordship, in a former despatch [No 12, 3 July 1844] my opinion, that the main obstacle to the success of Transatlantic Emigration from this place, has arisen from the unfounded representations of the Liberated Africans themselves.

These persons who have thus refused to emigrate, and have been so readily picked up by the already located Liberated Africans, are employed by them altogether as unpaid servants—they are fed—scantily, if at all clothed—and have no pecuniary allowance whatever.

It thus becomes a matter of individual interest with the Liberated Africans already settled in the Colony, to represent Emigration in a light, so unfavorable as effectually to prevent the new-comers from viewing it as a measure calculated for their advantage—and their zeal in this respect has met with a measure of success, which may be found difficult to counterbalance. . . .

20

INSTRUCTIONS TO THE CHIEF EMIGRATION AGENT FOR THE WEST INDIA COLONIES
[MARCH 1847[1]]

1. ONE of Her Majesty's steamers will repair almost immediately to the coast of Africa for the purpose of taking emigrants from Sierra Leone and the Kroo Coast to the colonies of British Guiana and Trinidad.

2. The Chief Agent for Emigration will select forthwith and

[1] *Parl. Papers*, 1847, xxxix (191), pp. 8–9. Drawn up by the Land and Emigration Commissioners, T. F. Elliot, C. Wood, F. Rogers, and forwarded to Governor Macdonald at Sierra Leone, 13 March 1847. C.O. 268/41.

despatch to the places which he judges best on the Kroo Coast, a few trustworthy subordinate agents to endeavour to collect free emigrants from Her Majesty's steamer [Growler.][1]

3. The subordinate agents may explain that the steamer is one of Her Majesty's vessels of war.

4. The Chief Agent will also be at liberty to furnish the subordinate agents for their use with any printed papers which may from time to time be officially communicated to him for the purpose, containing information relative to the respective West India colonies. The intelligence thus conveyed will consist of any general statements which it may be practical to supply from authentic sources, of the average rates of money-wages for different kinds of labour, the other advantages afforded by employers, and the sort of labour which is most in demand.

5. The different agents will inform all emigrants from the coast of Africa, whether from Sierra Leone or elsewhere, that they will be entitled to demand a free passage back after five years from their arrival, provided they shall, during that time, have been engaged under written agreements to labour for owners of land in the colony.

6. The Chief Agent will assign to the subordinate agents, with the approval of the Governor, moderate salaries in addition to an allowance of half a dollar a head to each of them for all the emigrants despatched from his station. The Chief Agent's report of such salaries with any remarks which they may require in explanation, being transmitted by the Governor at the earliest opportunity to the Secretary of State for confirmation.

7. The subordinate agents are to be placed no where except within the proper limits of the Kroo Coast, nor on any pretence to go or be sent to any place where slave trading has prevailed—a rule which is enjoined on pain of the immediate dismissal of any officer concerned in its violation.

8. In case it should be necessary to establish any depôts on the Kroo Coast for the reception of emigrants waiting for the steamers, the Chief Agent will make the requisite arrangements, and report them through the Governor of Sierra Leone for approval; but he will avoid every unnecessary measure of this description.

9. On the first, and if possible each succeeding voyage of the steamer, it would be desirable that the Chief Agent should proceed in her to visit the other agents, and attend to the embarcation of the people on the Kroo Coast. With regard to the mode of returning to Sierra Leone, he should make an early report on the means of communication coastwise; and in the meantime may incur, with the

---

[1] The *Growler* was sent to the Kru Coast (Liberia) and to Sierra Leone which she left in July 1847 with 477 emigrants, only 164 of whom were adults: Macdonald to Grey, 22 July 1847, C.O. 267/200.

Governor's approval, any expenditure indispensable for that purpose, and may hire a coaster expressly for it if no better arrangement can be made.

10. While these arrangements are made on the Kroo Coast, the steamer is also to be available for the conveyance of any emigrants who may be procurable at Sierra Leone.

11. The Chief Agent should spare no endeavour to secure, if possible, the presence of an interpreter in the steamer for each voyage.

12. He will inspect personally every emigrant to ascertain that he goes out with his free consent, and has not been deceived, but really understands the nature of the countries to which he is going, and the contract he is about to enter into.

13. He will see that each emigrant has such clothing or blankets as may be requisite for decency and for health during the voyage.

14. He will render all the assistance in his power to facilitate the embarcation of the emigrants, and will furnish the officer in command with a nominal list, in Form (A.), of all the passengers embarked. He will sign this list himself, and see that there be appended to it a certificate from the surgeon on board that he has examined all the emigrants previous to embarkation, and found them to be in good bodily health, and with no infirmity or defect incapacitating them from labour.

15. He will transmit through the Governor, for the information of Her Majesty's Government, a quarterly return of emigration, according to the Form (B.); and he will make a general report at the close of every year, upon the mode in which the plan has worked, and upon the alterations, if any, which may have occurred to him as desirable for its improvement.

16. The Chief Agent will continue to receive a salary of 300 *l.* per annum, but divided for the present between British Guiana and Trinidad; and will also receive an allowance of a dollar a head for each emigrant despatched respectively to those two colonies.

17. For his salary and head-money he will draw bills quarterly upon the Colonial Land and Emigration Commissioners; being careful duly to advise their Secretary of each bill, and also to transmit a certificate from the Governor of Sierra Leone, that he has been in the performance of his duties for the period referred to, as well as a statement signed by the officer in command of the steamer, showing the number of free emigrants despatched by him during the quarter to British Guiana and Trinidad respectively.

18. For the pay and head-money of the sub-agents, and for all miscellaneous and petty disbursements, the Chief Agent will also draw bills duly advised on the same Board, carefully forwarding at the same time any accounts which may be necessary, together with

proper receipts for all sums paid by him. As regards the amount of head-money paid by him to the sub-agents, he should transmit a certificate signed by himself, of the accuracy of the numbers in respect of whom payment is thus made. All bills to be drawn at sixty days' sight.

21

COLONIAL OFFICE TO H. U. ADDINGTON: COMPULSORY EMIGRATION, 11 NOVEMBER 1847[1]

SIR,

I am directed by Earl Grey to request that you will state to Viscount Palmerston that he has had under his consideration the propriety of not allowing in future any newly liberated Africans to settle [A. at Sierra Leone] but of removing them at once to the West Indies a measure which he thinks would be both of essential benefit to the Africans themselves, & of no small importance to the West Indian Colonies.

The mode in which the Africans, who were liberated at Sierra Leone, were formerly disposed of, was, by placing them in villages, where, from the poverty of the soil, and their innate love of ease, no improvement took place in their condition, & no advantage accrued to the Colony.

Dr. Madden who was at S. Leone in 1841 as Commissioner, states in his report, that the allotments of land to the Liberated Africans, had not tended much to increase cultivation, or to the advantage of the settlers, & that if they were not a patient race, it would have been impossible to have kept them in the villages—that vast numbers of them had thrown up their farms & gone to Free Town, where they became Hucksters, Hawkers, Pedlars &c. But even then safety was not secured by this mode of locating them, for their number in 1841 was computed to be 37,000, being very little more than half the number of those who had been emancipated in the Colony. None of them at that period had been sent to the West Indies, & no one knew what had become of them.

Of the 37,000 only 2680 were apprenticed, & these were distributed amongst the poorest of the colonial people, who usually seek for apprentices. The common rate of wages is stated by Dr. Madden to be from 3d. to 5d. a day, at any kind of practical labour—the average 4d. a day in the country villages, & in the Towns about 7d. a day for Porters' work, or employment on the wharf, or in boats.

In this state of things at S. Leone, & there being little or no demand

[1] C.O. 267/200. Based on a draft by Sir George Barrow and Earl Grey, Minute, 21 October 1847. The question had been raised by the West India Committee with the Land and Emigration Commissioners who referred it to the Colonial Office.

for labour or employment there, H.M. Govt. have of late years, done all in their power to encourage emigration from that Colony to the West Indies, where the liberated African would not lead the unprofitable life, which he must pass at S. Leone, but would on the contrary, find at once, full employment & instead of earning 2d. or 3d. a day, would get [D. as many Shillings] [A. wages more than equal to those for similar labour in this country] & would be placed in a far higher state of civilization.

But notwithstanding the superior advantages to be gained by the Liberated African in the West Indies, great difficulty has been experienced in inducing them to go there [A. altho' every facility has been given them for that purpose] & H.M. Govt. have been for some time compelled, on their refusal to emigrate, to make them provide for themselves, with the exception of the children, & of the sick [A. and of such as may enlist in the W. Indian Regiment stationed at S. Leone].

It has been found that the settled Colonists, are not only reluctant to emigrate themselves, but that they do all they can to dissuade the newly emancipated African, from consenting to be removed from the Colony. To defeat in some measure these attempts, it has been the practice of late, to confine the newly emancipated Africans in, what is called the African Yard, in order to keep them as much as possible from communication with the Colonists until an opportunity might offer of embarking them with their consent, for the West Indies. With the uncertainty however whether any captured Africans would be found to go to the West Indies, it was often found impossible to engage ships for the purpose. Under such circumstances it was not thought right to detain the liberated Africans in the Yard for an indefinite period, independently, of the great expense, which was incurred; the result was that when they were set free & had communicated with the Colonists, they declined generally to emigrate, tho' they had previously given their consent.

Under the circumstances above stated Lord Grey is of opinion that it would be perfectly consistent with justice & on every account advisable that the British Govt. should take upon itself to decide where these people should be settled, acting as their guardian on the ground that they are incapable of judging for themselves what is best for them. His Lordship therefore proposes that in future liberated Africans should not be permitted to settle in S. Leone, but should be removed to the W. Indies.

Before however, His Lordship proceeds to give any directions to this effect, he would be glad to be informed whether Lord Palmerston is of opinion that any objection to this course can be urged by Foreign Powers, in consequence of the terms of our Treaties for the suppression of the Slave Trade. . . .

22

LORD STANLEY TO HERMAN MERIVALE: COMPULSORY EMIGRATION, 18 NOVEMBER 1847[1]

[Lord Palmerston has considered the Colonial Office communication of 11 November and can find no objection to the plan to ship Liberated Africans directly to the West Indies.]

. . . It follows therefore that all negroes found in vessels captured under the Flags of Spain, the Argentine Confederation, Bolivia, Chile, Mexico, the Netherlands, & Sweden and Norway, and all negroes found in vessels which in pursuance of the Powers of the Acts of the 8th and 9th Victoria Cap: 122, and 2nd and 3rd Victoria, Cap: 73,[2] may be captured under the Brazilian Flag, or without any national character, may be sent to the West Indies instead of being settled at Sierra Leone.

23

EARL GREY TO GOVERNOR N. W. MACDONALD: CONDITIONS OF EMIGRATION, 20 JUNE 1850[3]

[Acknowledgement of Macdonald's dispatch, No. 53, 22 April 1850: approval of his organization of emigration.]

. . . 4. I AM surprised at the amount of discouragement of unmarried Emigrants which you state to result from the high price of cooking and washing in some of the West India Colonies, but I shall communicate these parts of your despatch to the Governors of these Colonies, and doubt not that if any practical hardship exist on this point, they will consider of the means of providing a remedy.

5. In the proposal that free grants of land should be made to the African Emigrants I cannot concur. It would be inconsistent with the established policy of H.M.'s Govemt. on the disposal of waste lands.

6. I quite agree in your remarks on the inability of Captured Africans, under the circ[umstances] in which they are first delivered from the Slavers, to exercise a judgment of their own upon the comparative advantage of different Colonies: and the condition in which they so often fall in Sierra Leone is the best proof of the propriety of removing them to the West Indies. The suggestions

[1] C.O. 267/201. *E. J. Stanley* (*Baron Stanley*) was Under-Secretary at the Foreign Office, 1846–52.
[2] The Acts of 24 August 1839 and 8 August 1845 which outlawed Portuguese and Brazilian slave vessels. Sir George Barrow, however, in a minute, 19 November 1847, considered that a treaty with Portugal, 2 July 1842, required Africans landed in Sierra Leone from Portuguese vessels to be left there. But there was no Portuguese commissioner at Freetown after 1842 to argue this point.
[3] C.O. 268/43, ff. 160–61.

however which you throw out of the employment of the Receiving Ship cannot be adopted. Independently of other objections which it is unnecessary for me to specify, the heavy cost of such vessels must alone be a conclusive bar to the proposal. The remedy of attempts to tamper with the Captured Africans must be found in strictly excluding improper persons, and in efficient superintendence.

7. On the employment of John Macaulay, the Akoo Chief[1] who was named to the African Yard by Mr. Pine whilst Acting Governor, the reasons which you have assigned for wishing to reverse Mr. Pine's act appear to me insufficient, and I must entirely dissent from your proposal. In this as in other matters, I am of opinion that it is proper and advisable to make a legitimate use of the influence of the Chiefs, and that they should be conciliated, instead of making attempts, which your own reasoning proves would be vain to overrule them by the authority of Europeans incapable of knowing what is said either to or by their people. Nor could it have any other than the worst effect to overrule in this matter, without any ostensible reason whatever, the act of your predecessor in the Administration of the Govemt. approved by the Secretary of State. . . .

24

THE DUKE OF NEWCASTLE TO GOVERNOR SIR ARTHUR KENNEDY: KRU COAST EMIGRATION, 13 JANUARY 1854[2]

SIR,

I have had under my consideration your Despatch No. 184, of the 10th of October last, accompanied by copies of various correspondence which had passed on the subject of the circumstances to which the President of Monrovia had drawn attention connected with Emigration from the Kroo Coast.[3]

With reference to this Despatch and to the previous correspondence noted in the Margin, as well as to information which has reached me through the Foreign Department I have to instruct you that it is no longer considered proper to admit of Emigration from any parts of Africa lying beyond British jurisdiction, and that no resort for Emigrants to the Kroo Coast can any longer be sanctioned. The Emigration must until further directions be confined exclusively to the Port

[1] The Sierra Leone Yoruba recaptives and their descendants were headed by John (Atapa) Macaulay, 1840–67. His official post was then abolished by Governor Kennedy, though he remained their leader till his death.
[2] C.O. 268/45. ff. 234–6. *The Duke of Newcastle* was Secretary of State for Colonies, 1854, 1859–64.
[3] And Kennedy to Newcastle, 28 April 1853, encl. *Liberian Herald*, 6 April 1853, C.O. 267/232.

of Sierra Leone, and can only be conducted from thence under the same precautions which have always hitherto been taken for ensuring the free agency of the parties who Emigrate, and for guarding them against the influence of misrepresentations.

In conveying these instructions to you, I think it right to explain that they are only elicited by a consideration of the risk of abuse to which it would appear from the facts communicated by you that all Emigration from African places not under the immediate control of British authority must be exposed, and that I hold the respectable firm of Messrs. Hyde Hodge & Co.[1] entirely free from any imputation of having wished to promote, directly or indirectly, by improper means, the Emigration upon which they were employed on behalf of the Colony of British Guiana.

25

HENRY LABOUCHERE TO GOVERNOR S. J. HILL: CONDITIONS OF EMIGRATION, 25 FEBRUARY 1858[2]

SIR,

I collect from the monthly returns which reach me from S. Leone that during the last six months upwards of 800 Liberated Africans have been brought into the Colony, and as H.M. Govt. have always considered it a matter of great importance that these persons should be induced if possible to emigrate to the W.I. Colonies both for the relief of these Colonies & for their own benefit, I have authorised the emigration C[ommissioners] to conclude such an arrangement as may seem to them an opportunity of doing this at the expense of the Imperial Govt.

I enclose copies of a Report from the Commissioners and of an agreement which they have concluded with Messrs. Hyde, Hodge & Co.[3] by which that firm is bound to supply a succession of ships for the conveyance of the Africans and to contribute largely towards their maintenance in the Govt. Yard until they are taken off in these vessels.

By reference to the documents cited by the C[ommissioners] you will perceive that the agreement is in all material aspects identical

[1] The Liberian Proclamation, 6 February 1853, against emigration was also specifically directed against Hyde Hodge & Co.'s offer, as shipping contractors, of $10 to Kru chiefs for every person persuaded to emigrate.

[2] C.O. 268/47, ff. 226–30. *Colonel Stephen Hill* had commanded expeditions in the Gambia in 1849; he was Governor of the Gold Coast, 1851–4, and of Sierra Leone, 1854–62.

[3] Land and Emigration Commissioners to Colonial Office, 2 February 1858: C.O. 267/262. The Colonial Office approved the Articles of Agreement, 4 February 1858.

with one under which a previous Emigration of the same kind was carried on, and you will easily collect the duties which devolve on yourself and under your superintendence, on an Emigration Agent whom it will be necessary for you to appoint for the practical management of this Service at Sierra Leone. [A. These duties will affect first: the emigration of Liberated Africans brought into the Colony and next any members of the resident population who may be inclined to seek profitable employment in the W.I.]

With regard to the first class of persons I wish you to maintain in the Govt. Yard and at the Govt. expense all Liberated Africans who may be brought thither till they have refused at least one opportunity of emigrating and even after such a refusal in case there should be any likelihood of their changing their minds you will be at liberty to defer their discharge till the contractors' liability for maintenance money shall have ceased under the 12th Article of the enclosed agreement. Meanwhile you will take care that they are made to understand the advantages of Emigration and are not exposed to the solicitations of those who are interested in oppositing it. The rate of wages in B. Guiana, Trinidad. St. Lucia & Grenada (to which the first ships will be sent) appear in one of the enclosures to this despatch.

The duration of the contract into which Africans above 15 years of age will probably be required to enter on their arrival in the W.I. is 8 years. If below that age they will probably be indentured till the age of 18. You will of course not embark Liberated Africans in any ship but those employed in pursuance of the enclosed contract.

It is also very desirable that you should encourage to the utmost of your power any tendency to emigrate which may show itself among the resident and especially the recently located populations. The 16th Article of the agreement provides for the payment of a bounty on all such persons shipped under your authority for the W.I. For the present however you will authorise such shipments only for B. Guiana, St. Lucia or Trinidad those being the only Colonies for which I am now at liberty to offer such a bounty. This emigration must be confined to able bodied labourers under the age of 40 and their families. They must also be prepared to enter into contracts for three years on their arrival in the Colony.

You will of course (if this is not already done) issue the Proclamation which is necessary under the Act 16 & 17 Vict. cap. 84[1] (of which I enclose a copy) in order to enable these ships to carry passengers in the proportion of one adult to every 12 superficial feet of the Passengers' Deck.

The Duties of the Emigration Agent (besides those which may devolve upon him under the Imperial Passengers Act) are prescribed

[1] An Imperial Passengers' Act of 1853.

by the Instructions referred to by the E[migration] C[ommissioners]. You will be at liberty to offer him, without any fixed salary, a fee of a dollar per adult on every Liberated[African]emigrating up to the no. of 2000 and one quarter of a dollar per adult for all embarked above that no. This fee will be payable by you on behalf of the Imperial Govt. For Emigrants not embarked from the Govt. yards he will receive a dollar per adult from the colonies to which the Emigration proceeds.

26

ACTING GOVERNOR W. HILL TO THE DUKE OF NEWCASTLE: GAMBIA RESETTLEMENT, 31 JULY 1861[1]

My Lord Duke,

I have the honour to receive your Grace's despatch No 188 of the 11th June last on the subject of the Liberated Africans sent to the Gambia, and favouring me with your Grace's opinion with respect to the destination of any of those people that may in future be landed in the Colony.

With respect to the 200 sent to the Gambia, they were selected by Governor D'Arcy who visted the African yard, and had his choice, after the whole of the Liberated Africans had expressed their willingness to proceed with him.

Your Grace may be assured that every precaution is taken to permit the Liberated Africans being tampered with; Overseers are placed in charge of them, the premises in which they reside are isolated, and no person is allowed to visit them, excepting the Colonial Surgeon and the clerk in charge, every pains are [sic] also taken to explain to them, the nature of the Emigration to the West Indies and the better prospects there open to them, and my own opinion is, their repugnance is not so much on account of the change to the West Indies as a disinclination to again embark on board ship after experiencing the miseries of a crowded Slaver. However, I have no doubt I shall be able to give effect to your Grace's wishes whenever a vessel may be sent to convey Liberated Africans to the West Indies.

[1] C.O. 267/271. *Major William Hill* (son of Stephen Hill) was Acting Governor of Sierra Leone in 1861.

IV

RELATIONS WITH AFRICAN SOCIETIES

A. SENEGAL, GAMBIA

Introductory Note

RELATIONS with the Moors, Wolof, and Mandinka of the Senegal and Gambia till the early 1840's centred around the organization of the gum trade. Competition with the French gave rise to a system of annual presents from British Government stores and the protection of a naval vessel at Portendic from 1829. A treaty was arranged with the Trarza Moors in 1836, but was never ratified. After an investigation by the Board of Trade, the Foreign Office insisted on the continued payment of annual presents to the Moors; but when the export of gum declined, these goods were diverted to the Gambia in 1843 where a similar policy of purchasing favourable conditions of trade had been followed irregularly since 1826. An attempt to create a monopoly of trade on the upper river with Wuli and Bondu was disapproved in 1829. The chiefdoms along the Gambia, however, were well known and their commercial relations with the Futa Jallon and the upper Senegal and Niger understood. Little was done to profit from this knowledge, and British intervention in the affairs of the Wolof and Mandinka states was limited to a punitive expedition against the King of Barra at the Gambia mouth in 1831 and to expeditions to Wuli and to Upper Niani in 1834 and 1835.

In 1841 the Colonial Office was made to see the full implications of Russell's new treaty policy when an agreement was signed with the chief of Kataba (in Niani). Because of the terms of international reciprocity treaties and a reluctance to extend British protection to an African chief, the treaty was disallowed and troops were withdrawn from Kataba in 1842. Disapproval had already been anticipated by Acting Governor Ingram who suspended negotiations along the river till less demanding terms had been prescribed. Six new agreements to end the slave trade were concluded in 1843 and were approved by the Foreign Office and Lord Stanley, after the exclusion of detailed commercial clauses. No arrangement for the payment of Customs on trade to chiefs was made; and Gambia administrators fell back on stipends and occasional presents to buy good will, supplemented by a punitive expedition to Kunnong (in Kiang) in 1849.

This limitation of official relations with the Gambia states was questioned at the outset of a long series of 'Marabout' (*Murabit*) revolts which destroyed most of the Mandinka states in the nineteenth century. Help from the French at Senegal enabled the Bathurst administration to check the uprising in 1855 and arrange for a truce. But an expedition against Baddibu touched off another Marabout revolt and disrupted a system of stipends and customs arranged by treaty in 1861. With limited means at their disposal and restrained by Colonial Office sanctions against the use of unnecessary force, Governor D'Arcy and his successors could do little except report on the civil war and make minor expeditions in which they inclined towards upholding the Mandinka chiefs—in contradiction to the policy laid down by Cardwell in 1865 which prohibited intervention or alliance with either side.

I

EARL BATHURST TO LIEUT.-COLONEL CHARLES MACCARTHY: TRARZA MOORS, 6 SEPTEMBER 1813[1]

. . . H.M.'s. GOVERNMENT view with entire approbation the Efforts which you have made to reestablish the Gum Trade on its ancient footing in the neighbourhood of Senegal, & in a great degree attribute the Success which has attended them to the judicious Energy, with which you have uniformly acted. The Wars which unfortunately prevail between the Moors & the various Negro Tribes present serious obstacles no less to the improvement of the Trade than to the general Civilization & Prosperity of that part of Africa. But so long as the Negro Tribes continue from their Indolence and their Divisions to present so alluring a prey to the plundering spirit of the Moors, I fear that there is but little Ground to expect any Peace of long duration. Whatever influence you possess with either Party, you will continue to exert it, as you have hitherto done, for the purpose of promoting general, or even partial, Pacification & of mitigating the Cruelty of their mode of Warfare: But while you throw every obstacle in the way of the hostile aggression of either Party, you will not fail to be particularly cautious to avoid every act which by indicating Partiality to either, may engage this Country in Hostility or Dispute with their oponents.

[The policy of making presents to the King of the Trarzas is approved.]

. . . In making any such Present, however, you will be careful to explain clearly the Condition upon which it is granted, to be the previous success of the Gum Trade, & you will at the same time specially guard against any claim to such Present on the part of the family of the present King of the Trasars, whenever they may be

[1] C.O. 268/19, ff. 9–10. MacCarthy had been to Podor to arrange a new trade treaty with the Trarza *Almamy*. MacCarthy to Bathurst, 9 April 1813, C.O. 267/36.

deprived (by the Elevation of another family) of their present Influence on their Trade. . . .

2

W. HUTTON TO R. W. HAY: AGREEMENTS WITH WULI AND BONDU, 18 MAY 1829[1]

SIR,

I have the honor to state to you, for the information of the Right Honorable Sir George Murray, that since Major Findlay's departure from Bathurst, I have been induced, at the unanimous wish of the Merchants, to undertake a Mission to the Upper River, with the view of forming a Settlement above McCarthy's Island; which has long been deemed an object of great importance, not only with the Merchants here, but with the late Sir Neil Campbell and other Governors.

In complying therefore with the wish of the Merchants, upon this occasion, I knew I was carrying into effect the plans and intentions of men more experienced than myself, and particularly Major Findlay, who I know contemplated a similar Mission for some months before his departure; but was prevented from carrying it into effect, by long and severe indisposition.

I have now the satisfaction to acquaint you, that after a tedious passage of twelve days, I arrived at *Fattatenda*, in the King of Woolli's Dominions; where, after much discussion and with some triffling presents, I effected a Treaty with his sable Majesty who came down from his capital (Medina) to the river side, accompanied by a large body of his people, consisting of his Captains and Soldiers, his Son and Brothers, all mounted on Horses richly caparisoned.

A copy of this Treaty I have now the honor to enclose; from which you will perceive, that the conditions entered into by me, on the part of His Britannic Majesty, are entirely subject to the approval of the Right Honorable Sir George Murray. I shall therefore anxiously look for the arrival of a vessel with your answer to this letter, as much will depend upon Sir George Murray's decision. I mean not only as regards his approbation or disapprobation of the measures I have taken, but also as regards other measures, which it may still be prudent to adopt, to induce the King of Bondou to co-operate with the King of Woolli, in securing the Gum Trade to the British

[1] C.O. 87/2. *William Hutton* traded on almost every part of the coast from Bathurst to the Bights. He had been Acting Consul in Kumasi in 1820 and was to be a principal witness before the 1842 Select Committee. See his *Voyage to Africa*, London, 1821. His treaties of 11 and 13 April 1829 with Mansakoi, King of Wuli, and Kantalaba, Chief of Kantalakunda, were disallowed: Hay to Jackson, 7 November 1829, C.O. 401/1, ff. 74–75.

Merchants at Fattatenda. The French having exclusively possessed the advantage of this important and profitable article of commerce at *Galam,* on the Banks of the Senegal, which is only about two or three days walk from Fattatenda, it will be an object of the utmost importance if we can divert the Gum Trade from *Galam,* by prevailing on the King of Bondou to co-operate with the King of Woolli in directing the Traders in Gum to Fattatenda.

This I conceive may be accomplished with the King of Woolli's friendship and assistance (which is now secured) and the payment of a certain sum annually to the King of Bondou, in addition to what I have already agreed to pay the King of Woolli annually. The object indeed of three or four hundred Dollars, is trifling to the advantages that would result from such a powerful connexion with these Kings, whose influence extends not only through the whole of Bondou and Woolli, but also to the adjoining countries of *Tenda and Shroudou,*[1] which are celebrated for Gold, Gum, and other Articles of Commerce; as will be seen on reference to Mungo Park's Travels in this part of Africa.

But as the advantages (although ultimately beneficial to Great Britain) would more immediately be felt by the Merchants trading in this River, it would perhaps be only reasonable that they should pay a part, if not the whole, of the annual sum allowed both to the King of Bondou and to the King of Woolli. Such an arrangement, if Sir George Murray thought it proper, I have no doubt I could easily effect with the Merchants here, who I am sure would willingly bear a part, if not the whole, of the Annual Custom to these powerful Monarchs. Indeed I was authorised, on the part of the Merchants, to assure the King of Woolli (which I did) that he should receive 2000 Dollars as soon as the first British Vessel was loaded with Gum at Fattatenda; so that with this temptation held out to him, and the 200 dollars annually, there is every reason to believe he will (as he assured me he would) use his most strenuous exertions to direct the Trade to our new Settlement at Fattatenda.

With respect to the 200 Dollars to be paid to the King annually, I beg leave to remark that as this is to be paid *in British Merchandize,* the amount in Sterling is only £43. 6. 8, which, when paid by any of the Merchants in articles of traffick, *at the prices charged in the Upper River,* will be *little more than one half* the sum mentioned in the Treaty (say about £30); so that the amount is really *so trifling,* that I feel assured Sir George Murray will not disapprove of what I have done, when the great importance of extending our Commercial Intercourse with the Interior, is taken into consideration; Fattatenda being at least *500 Miles in the Interior* (Vide Park's Travels in Africa.)

[1] Tenda and Shrudu were small kingdoms between the Upper Gambia and the Falime river.

I have further to state to you, for Sir George Murray's Information, that in addition to the Treaty with the King of Woolli, at *Fattatenda*, I also effected an arrangement with the Chief of *Contacunda*[1], in the Carbo[2] Country, a place of considerable Trade, sixty miles above Fattenda, and on the opposite side of the River.

Contalacunda being deemed a place of importance by the Merchants, from its immediate connexion with *Mana*, *Cardi*, *Colli*, *Foota Jalloo*,[3] and other countries, celebrated for Commerce, I did not consider that 50 Dollars annually (or £10 Sterling) to secure the friendship of the Chief of Contalacunda would be ill bestowed. But a copy of my agreement, is herewith transmitted to you, from which you will see that this arrangement is also subject to the approbation of Sir George Murray.

It may not be unnecessary to observe that Vessels of *a hundred Tons Burthen*, can be navigated to both these Settlements with ease; and in addition to the advantages which are likely to result to the Mercantile Interest of Great Britain, we have now a British Settlement *nearly 600 Miles in the Interior of Africa*!

Fattatenda is situated on a high hill and is a place of commercial Importance, not only on account of its Connexion with *Bondu*, *Tenda*, *Sego*, and other Countries, on the North side of the Gambia, but also as the Traders in Gold and Ivory, *cross the River at this place*. . . .

3

LORD GODERICH TO LIEUT.-GOVERNOR G. RENDALL: KING OF BARRA, 28 NOVEMBER 1831[4]

SIR,

My Under-Secretary of State has laid before me the dispatch which you addressed to him under date of the 24th of July last, announcing the disposition of the King of Barra and of the Settonoko[5] people to become turbulent: and I have also received your dispatch No. 46, with its enclosures, from which it appears, that a large body of armed natives had compelled a small detachment of H.M. Troops and discharged soldiers of the Royal African Corps to evacuate the settlement at Barra Point, and retire across the River to Bathurst.

These hostile proceedings of the King of Barra, attended, as they

---

[1] *Sic*, Kantalakunda, at the junction of several important trade routes, was situated about thirty miles below Barakunda Falls at the head of the Gambia.

[2] Kabu, between the Upper Gambia and the Rio Grande in Guinea.

[3] *Sic*, Rio Mana, Kade, and Kalla on the trade route to the Futa Jallon.

[4] C.O. 401/1, ff. 185–8.

[5] Barra and Sittanunku on the bank opposite Bathurst at the mouth of the Gambia were part of a strip of territory annexed in 1826, but not effectively occupied.

have been, with the loss of a number of men, and calculated as they are, to interrupt for a time the commercial operations of our Traders, are deeply to be regretted, altho' I am happy, on the other hand, to find that no very serious apprehensions need be entertained for the safety of Bathurst, resolved, as you have shewn yourself to be, whether the King of Barra has the means of attempting further aggression.

At the same time H.M. Government have thought it right to dispatch the Gun Brig 'Brisk' to your assistance, with a detachment of Marines, who will be landed, if necessary, at Bathurst, or distributed in the vessels in the Harbour, should any aggression be meditated against the Settlement.

The great advantage, however, which I would wish you to draw from the presence of the Gun Brig will be, by shewing that you are fully prepared for aggression, the better to enable you thereby to make peace with the King of Barra; for it would be not less useless than I am sure it would be inexpedient for you to attempt undertaking any warlike operations in the field against the numerous tribes of barbarous people who would be arranged against you. I must desire, therefore, that you will renounce all projects of that nature, and content yourself in endeavouring to review an amicable understanding with the refractory Chiefs, upon such terms as may appear to you proper and calculated to ensure a durable peace.

4

LIEUT.-GOVERNOR G. RENDALL TO R. W. HAY: MANDINKA AND WOLOF STATES, 9 FEBRUARY 1835[1]

[There has been an increase in expenditure on presents for chiefs.]

. . . IT is my duty to state that some peculiar circumstances have caused an increase in this expenditure.

First—the Coronation of the King of Barra, on which occasion it is usual to give extraordinary presents. Next his visit to this Settlement when he came to give himself up (as he called it) which was merely to shew his confidence in this Government and his determination to be on friendly terms in future.

The King of Combo also paid a visit to this Settlement with a numerous retinue.

Another expense was caused by the bad conduct of the Chiefs of Seine, seizing the articles belonging to our Traders which rendered it necessary to send Messengers to obtain restitution.

A still further expense was incurred by my voyage to MacCarthy's

[1] C.O. 87/12.

Island in His Majesty's Sloop 'Britomart' to disperse a large body of natives that were assembled in the neighbourhood of that Island with a supposed intention of attacking it.

The outrageous conduct of Kementang obliged me to send Messengers to the Upper River with presents to the Chiefs, to obtain their good offices in facilitating the removal of Merchants' property to MacCarthy's Island, and generally to assist in establishing the blockade of Kementang's Territory.[1]

The King of Barra has also received larger presents than usual in consideration of his having stopped the trade of his own people in Salt, Cloths, Fish, and Corn with the Upper River.

The Officer commanding MacCarthy's Island also has been obliged to give small presents to some of the numerous Chiefs and Messengers who have visited him in consequence of the affair of Kementang.

Some changes will also be observed in the account for presents to the Kings of Salum, and of Baddiboo upon the restoration of some runaway Liberated Africans.

In addition to the presents purchased within the Settlement, I have upon occasions been in the habit of giving some of those Articles sent from England—namely Guns, Bafts, Cocked Hats, Coats, Swords, Pistols, Medals, and Canes. . . .

RIGHT BANK OF THE RIVER[2]

Kings and Chiefs	Remarks	Trade &c.
King of Barra	Has two tributary Kings, Vizt. Jocada, & Kolai, seven Samars, besides many Alcaides of Towns	Timber, Rice, Corn, Cattle, Poultry, Palm Wine and small quantities of Hides, and wax
King of Seine	Has one Lingard, a Giraffe, and several Geliwars	Corn, Hides, Wax, & Ivory
King of Baddi-boo	Has a number of Geliwars, and a Joloff prince residing in his Country who claims the throne of Salum with his Geliwars	Hides, Wax, Ivory, Corn, Rice & Pagnes
King of Sabba & Sanjally	Formerly tributary to Salum now independent having their Alcaides at their Towns near the River	Ditto
King of Salum	Has a Lingard, Boomeys of Provinces, Geliwars, and Giraffes	Ditto
Kings of Joynee, Gidore, & Jaffy Jaffy	Tributary to Salum	Corn, Rice, Ivory, and Hides

[1] An expedition against the Mandinka chief Kemintang of Upper Niani failed to obtain satisfaction for the plunder of a schooner.

[2] Encl. 'Return of Native Kings and Chiefs on the Banks of the River Gambia in Communication with the Settlement of Bathurst'. Among the variety of political titles the following are identifiable: *Sumar* (Chief, Mandinka and Soninke); *gelowar* (Mandinka warrior nobility); *Jaraf* or *Diaraf* (Wolof freeborn official or judge); *Linger* (Wolof: the king's mother or sister, as headwoman); *bumi* (Wolof tax official); *alkati* (Muslim clerics, chiefs of trade centres).

Kings and Chiefs	Remarks	Trade &c.
Chiefs of Barti- dae	Formerly tributary to Salum but now independent	Same as Salum with the addition of Timber
King of Nyani- bantang	Has under him the King of Cassan and and Chiefs of Tanimaroo	Trade same as Barti- dae. At these places it is expected Gum may be bought from the Joloff Country
King of Konyol &c.		Same as Nayniban- tang
King of Keeo and Coombijan		Same as Nyaniban- tang
King of Cartebar	Has several Slatees and Alcaides	Trade same as Salum without Timber
King of Upper Yani	Has Slatees and Alcaides	Hides, Wax & Ivory
King of Wooli	Has Princes Slatees & Alcaides	Gold, Hides, Wax & Ivory & pagnes, the great trade from the N.E. Interior comes through this Country

LEFT BANK OF THE RIVER

Kings and Chiefs	Remarks	Trade &c.
King of Combo	Has several Samars, Alcaides, & Joala, or Feeloop Chiefs tributary to him	Hides, Wax, Corn, Rice, Cattle, Poultry and Palm wine
King of Brekama	Has Alcaides and Joala[1] Chiefs tributary to him	Trade same a Combo with the addition of Timbers
Farang of Fara- bar	Has Alcaides	Trade same as Brek- ama
King of Berefet	Has Farang, and Alcaides, with Joala Chiefs tributary to him	Hides, Wax, Ivory, Rice, poultry, Cattle, and Timber
Alcaide of Vin- taia	Has Joala Chiefs tributary to him	Same as Berefet
King of Keong [Kiang]	Has Alcaides and Joala Chiefs tribu- taries and the King of the Binunkos is is in some degree subject to him, through his country is one great path to Cobo and Foota Jallon	Gold, Ivory, Wax and Hides—Timber is also cut
King of Mandoar	Has the Chiefs of Taakrowall, Tendu- bar, Queen Alla, and Jamaly, with their Alcaides tributary to him. Tende- bar has another great path to Cabo, and Foota Jallon	Same as Keong
King of Jara	Has under him the Chiefs of Joniatiba, Bye, Badamar, Jassan, Boareme, and Dumasensang	Hides, Wax, Ivory, Cattle, & Timber

[1] Diola or Dyula, Islamized Mandinka traders who settled throughout the area from Senegal to the Ivory Coast.

Kings and Chiefs	Remarks	Trade &c.
King of Yanima [Niamina]	Has Alcaides	Timber, Rice, Cattle, Hides, Wax & Ivory
Chief of Curopina [Eropina]	Has Alcaides	Same as Yanima
Chiefs of Beckama, Bursensang & Chaconda	Have Alcaides	Hides, Wax, Ivory and Cattle
King of Jemaroo [Kimara]	Has Geliwars and Alcaides	Ditto
King of Toomani	Has under him Chiefs of Sottoomai, Bassy and Bardai, with their Alcaides	Ditto
King of Cantor [Kantora]	Has under him the Chiefs of Perai, Sonkunda, Kantalicunda, and Farangtombo, with their Alcaides. This also has a great path for the Gold Traders, and others from Boari, Foota Jallon, and Tendah	

It is proper to remark that the Kings of Jamaroo, Toomani, and Cantor, and the Chief of Chaonda are normally tributary to the King of Cabo. Messengers are often received from the Kings of Baol and Cayor, to the Northwards—the Almamy of Bondou, the Kings of Cassau, and Kartar, Bambara in the East, and the Almamy of Foota Jallon to the South East.

5

G. J. PENNINGTON TO THE HON. FOX STRANGE-WAYS: TRARZA MOORS, 8 JUNE 1839[1]

Sir,

With reference to your Letter of 3d. Inst. requesting information as to the Presents which it has been customary to make annually to the Moorish Chiefs on the Coast of Africa connected with the Gum Trade, I have it in command from the Lords Commissioners of Her Majesty's Treasury to acquaint you for the information of Viscount Palmerston, that it would appear from the Documents in this Office, that Presents to the Moorish Chiefs concerned in the Gum Trade had been given by the British Authorities while the French Settlements on the Senegal were in the possession of Great Britain; and that after the restoration of those Settlements to France, the Presents were continued to the Chiefs at Portendick for the same object. It also appears that the Articles required for this purpose have been regularly supplied from this Country through the Ordinance department until the year 1831; but in that, and the following year no Trade

[1] F.O. 2/2. *G. J. Pennington* was adviser to the Treasury. *Fox Strangeways* was Under-Secretary to the Foreign Office.

was carried on at Portendick and the Presents were consequently not required.

Since the resumption of the Trade at that Port in 1833, the articles for Presents have been annually supplied by direction of this Board, in accordance with recommendations from the Board of Trade, or from the Foreign Office, and altho' it was uncertain whether any Trade would be attempted in the last year, the Articles were sent out to the Gambia, to be presented, or not, as the Lieutenant Governor of that Settlement, after consultation with the Merchants might see fit. . . .

6

THE KATABA TREATY, 23 APRIL 1841[1]

[The Slave Trade in Niani (Upper Gambia) is abolished.]

. . . THE Officer of England may seize every vessel or boat of Cartabar found anywhere carrying on the trade in Slaves, in the waters of Cartabar and the vessel and boats so seized shall be taken to an English possession to be tried by English law, and if condemned, shall with appurtenances and cargo be sold, the produce of the sale being equally divided between the Queen of England and the King of Cartabar.

Two Additional Articles.

1. The King of Cartabar seeing that he is unable of himself to prevent the incursion of neighbouring ill-disposed Chiefs delighting only in war and who have heretofore annually ravaged his Country, carrying off his people as Slaves; the cattle and produce; now and for ever places the Country of Cartabar under the sole protection of the Sovereign of England and he begs that Her Majesty Victoria the 1st. Queen of England may become in his own royal person and for Her Heirs and successors, the protecting Sovereign of the Cartabar Country; And the King of Cartabar freely cedes forever, to the Queen of England Her Heirs and successors one square mile of land in such part of his country as shall be pointed out by the Lieutenant Governor of the British Settlements of the Gambia or other officer authorized to do so.

2nd. The King of Cartabar agrees that he will not enter any alliances, negotiations or communication of any political nature whatever, with any power in the world without the knowledge and consent of the Queen of England; and the King of Cartabar declares the whole of the annexed Treaty, and these two additional articles

[1] C.O. 87/25. Encl. in Huntley to Russell, 24 April 1841. The Foreign Office approved.

to be binding equally to himself as to His Heirs and successors for ever. . . .

<h1 style="text-align:center">7</h1>

JAMES STEPHEN: MINUTE, IMPLICATIONS OF THE KATABA TREATY, 6 SEPTEMBER 1841[1]

. . . When the Niger Expedition was resolved on, it was also resolved to make war on the Slave Trade by Treaties with the Chiefs of the Interior. A model of such a Treaty was prepared, and was sent to each of the Governors. Capt. Huntley, the Governor of the Gambia, accordingly made a Treaty with a Chief called the King of Cartabar. He reported this in his Despatch No 1067. I would refer you to Lord John Russell's note of the 30th June on the back of that Despatch.[2] In pursuance of his Lordship's directions it was communicated to the late Cabinet. On the 23d. of July, Lord Palmerston's opinion was desired as to the Ratification of the Treaty. On the 31st. of July Lord Palmerston recommended that it should be approved. On the 16th. of August the concurrence of the Treasury was requested.

In the meantime the Officer commanding the Troops at the Gambia, Major Perry, reported to Lord Hill that he had been ordered to make an advance with certain fieldpieces, beyond the precincts of the Colony for the defence of our new ally the King of Cartabar.

On the 18th of August Lord Hill sent that Report to Lord John Russell with the remark that it appeared somewhat imprudent to employ fieldpieces with a Body so inadequate in point of number to their due protection.[3]

This Letter was on the 25th of August referred to the Lieut. Governor, who is now in England, for explanations.

On the 28th of August, the Lieut-Governor in No 1489, made his report accordingly. You will see on the back of that report Notes which led to a Minute in Lord John Russell's hand writing, which though undated, was I think written on the 2d or 3d Instant.[4] It was manifestly intended as a Minute for his Lordship's Successor, and, very fully states the principles by which Lord John Russell thought the Govt. of this Country should be guided in regard to these Treaties.

On the same day, namely the 20th. of Sept. a Treasury Letter was written in answer to the reference of the 16th of August in which Letter the Treasury proposed the question whether Lord John Russell had ascertained the compatibility of the Lieut. Governor's

---

[1] Ibid.   [2] Ibid. Russell, Minute, 30 June 1841.
[3] C.O. 87/26. War Office to Colonial Office, 18 August 1841.
[4] This minute does not appear to be extant; it probably repeated Russell's views on the slave trade, recorded elsewhere: see above, no. 12, p. 148.

Treaty with the Treaties of Reciprocity with Foreign Countries. To that question the answer must be in the negative.

The questions to be disposed of are therefore as follows:

1st. Is the Treaty with the King of Cartabar to be ratified? But preliminary to or involved in this question are the following—

2nd. Are the Expences consequent upon it to be undertaken—a point on which the Treasury have reserved their judgment?

3dly. Are the military operations undertaken by Major Perry to be approved and continued or disapproved and arrested?

4thly. Should the question about the Reciprocity Treaties be more distinctly proposed to the Foreign Office? It is possible that Lord Palmerston's general approbation of Capt. Huntley's Treaty may have been given without any distinct reference to that point. Until it is cleared up we shall hear nothing from the Treasury about the expense.

I have called this Agreement with the King of Cartabar a *Treaty*, but it should be observed that in devolving all these arrangements on this Office, Lord Palmerston expressly stipulated against the use of and such Diplomatic language. He desired that the compacts to be made with the African Chiefs should be described as '*Arrangements* or *Agreements*', or by some other word which should exclude them from the class of Diplomatic Conventions. The distinction is not verbal or trivial. It means to reserve to the Secretary of State for Foreign Affairs his own exclusive power of negociating Treaties, and it is also meant to mark the distinction between Agreements with barbarous Chiefs and the international Compacts of Civilized States. For example a Treaty must be ratified under the Great Seal, and with the advice of the Privy Council—form which would be totally misplaced in these cases.

I pass these Papers with this brief account of the state of the question, because the matters to which that question relates are of national and permanent importance, and will probably engage the personal attention of Lord Stanley and of his collegues in the first instance—and because Lord John Russell has already recorded an opinion which unless it should be over-ruled by his Lordship's successor must, by myself at least, be regarded as Conclusive.

8

ACTING GOVERNOR T. L. INGRAM TO LORD STANLEY: MANDINKA AND WOLOF TREATIES, 23 DECEMBER 1841[1]

MY LORD,

I have had the honour to receive your Lordship's Despatch, dated the 8th November last,[2] and numbered 2, on the subject of the treaty concluded at Cartabar on 23d April 1841 between Sir H. Huntley, on behalf of Her Majesty, and the Chief of Cartabar, in which your Lordship prohibits me from making any treaty or agreement which shall have the effect of binding Her Majesty's Government to afford military aid to African chiefs, or to assume any right of sovereignty or protection over any portion of the soil or waters of this continent.

Previously to the receipt of your Lordship's Despatch, I had made some arrangements for entering on agreements of a somewhat similar nature with several of the influential kings and chiefs of various countries bordering on the Gambia. I have not yet concluded any, as they can only be entered into in the countries under the direction of the chiefs who are disposed to agree to them. I consider my present position of Acting Governor does not leave me at liberty to absent myself from Bathurst or its immediate vicinity without your Lordship's permission; but to enable me to conclude such agreements, it would be necessary that I should visit the different chiefs, and my absence from Bathurst would necessarily be a protracted one; but while I only fill temporarily the office of Lieutenant Governor at the Gambia, I do not believe your Lordship would approve of my leaving the colony at all. I have, therefore, reluctantly deferred my negotiations with several native kings and chiefs, although the preliminary arrangements are made, informing them I should wait your Lordship's further directions before the signing of the agreements. I have strong reasons to feel assured that such agreements will be advantageous to British interests at the same time that they will confer considerable benefit on the natives.

A brief outline of the 'Agreement' forwarded to this colony by Her Majesty's Government has been given to several native chiefs, but I refrained from acquainting them of that part which specifies that protection, under certain circumstances, would be afforded them. I also omitted that portion of the 'Agreement' which allows a custom

[1] *Parl. Papers*, 1865, v (412), pp. 426–7. *T. L. Ingram* was Acting Governor of the Gambia in 1839 and 1841.

[2] Ibid., p. 426. The terms of this dispatch were exactly the same as Stanley to Carr, 8 November 1841 (rejecting annexation of territory along the River Nunez): see below, p. 419.

to be levied on all merchandise entering their territories. Leaving out these clauses, I consider the 'Agreement' still affords many advantages to the chiefs or kings, all of whom are happy to enter into it.

I have the honour to acquaint your Lordship that I have not at any time contemplated affording military protection or assistance to the Native Powers who have been desirous of entering into the proposed 'Agreement'; neither have I sought to obtain from them the sovereignty of any fresh portion of the soil or waters of this part of Africa, because experience has convinced me that this colony is not likely to be benefited by any accession to its extent, unless it also receives a proportionate increase of military force, defences, &c., which I am aware would entail a very heavy expenditure—one, in my opinion, exceeding the value of any territory which might be acquired on the banks of the Gambia.

I feel very happy to have anticipated your Lordship's instructions to refrain from promising to afford military aid to any African chief, and also from assuming or accepting the sovereignty of any country within the limits of my negotiations in respect of the form of 'Agreement' received from Her Majesty's Government.

9

ACTING GOVERNOR T. L. INGRAM TO LORD STANLEY: MANDINKA AND WOLOF TREATIES, 30 MARCH 1843[1]

MY LORD,

I have the honor to enclose for Your Lordship's approval the Copies of Six 'Agreements', or Treaties which I have entered into with the Kings and Chiefs therein specified in pursuance of Your Lordship's instructions conveyed to me in despatch No. 23 of 18th March 1842.

[Enclosed are accounts for the cost of an expedition up the Gambia amounting to £195. 16. 6.]

... Your Lordship will perceive that no payment has been made for the Bafts mentioned in the various agreements as having been given to the Chiefs who entered into them. I reported in my despatch No. 8 of 2nd. February last, that I had taken a supply of this article from the quantity sent from England for the Moors at Portendick, whereby some expenditure has been saved.

[1] C.O. 87/30. Encl. treaties with the chiefs of Lower Niani and Dobakunda, Koro, Wuli, Chakunda, and Kantalakunda on the Upper Gambia. Approved in F.O. to C.O., 11 September 1843: C.O. 87/32. For the final version of these treaties, see *Parl. Papers*, 1865, v (412), p. 405.

In proceeding up the River, I made it my duty to see every King and Chief between MacCarthy's Island and Cantalicunda. I did not think it necessary to enter into 'Agreements' with all of them, although I should have had no difficulty in doing so, because I believed that in selecting the most influential, as I have done, the views of Her Majesty's Government would be equally well carried out. I have, however, been obliged to conform to the Custom of the Country and to give a present to each of the Chiefs whom I visited. The expense thus incurred has not yet been defrayed, as I did not consider myself authorised to include in the cost of the Mission any other sums than those of the articles supplied to the contractory parties, and the hire of the Vessel to convey me to the Upper River. I shall, therefore, cause the extra expenditure, which is inconsiderable, to be charged in the quarterly accounts of Presents to Native Kings and Chiefs, and direct it to be paid from the Colonial Revenue.

I deeply regretted to find the Trade of the River above MacCarthy's Island in a most deplorable state. The competition between the traders appeared to me anything but profitable. The Jolas, or native brokers, complained grievously of the Merchants having raised the prices of their goods, or rather refusing to give more than what the Jolas considered half the value of the River produce. The Native Traders attributed the decrease of Trade entirely to the conduct of the Merchants. I concur to a certain extent, in the opinion they have expressed. In Africa it is difficult to effect changes in things even the most unimportant. In matters of consequence it is dangerous to attempt them. I consider that the Resident Merchants have acted unwisely in making the alteration in the price of African produce, as they have done. It is customary among the African Tribes to send for the Kings, Chiefs and headmen to announce the intention wished to be carried out, and to request their co-operation and assistance. A present must be sent to them with every Messenger, for nothing is done in Africa without presents, and the success of a negotiation is to be anticipated in proportion to the importance of the present or offering sent. In the case of the Merchants this was not done. The propriety of the change was not canvassed. It emanated with Mr. Charles Grant and was carried into effect at MacCarthy's Island by himself and three or four other individuals connected with the Commerce of the Upper River, without consulting any of the influential Chiefs. It has, therefore, proved unprofitable, and the consequence is that Traders from the Interior now carry their produce to the Cazamanza and Bissao establishments where they are certain of getting a higher price for it. But I do not regard the low price which our Merchants have bound themselves to give for African produce the sole cause of the badness of the River Trade. It must also be ascribed to wars which are now ravaging many portions of the Interior. . . .

10

LORD STANLEY TO GOVERNOR NORCOTT: TERMS OF TREATIES, 13 JANUARY 1844[1]

SIR,

I have received Mr. Ingram's Despatch marked separate, of the 30th of March 1843, enclosing copies of six agreements or treaties, which he had entered into with the king and chiefs named in the margin, and I have now to inform you, and to desire that you will convey the information to the chiefs, that having laid those agreements before the Queen, Her Majesty has been graciously pleased to confirm and ratify the same.

With respect, however, to any future agreements of this nature which you may be instructed to conclude, you will bear in mind that the following words at the latter part of article 3 should be omitted.

'And may also seize every vessel or boat of other nations found carrying on the trade in slaves, in the waters belonging to the chief of——.'

In lieu thereof, the following words should be added at the end of the article: 'And if at any time hereafter it shall apear that slave trade is carried on upon the territory of——, Great Britain may put down that trade by force.'

As moreover, the principal object of the treaties entered into with African chiefs is the suppression of that traffic, it is desirable that no precise engagement upon matters of detail in commerce, such as the fixing of certain rates of duties, should be included in them.

Considering the manner in which commercial transactions are conducted on the coast of Africa, and the absence in most places of all the usual checks and restraints upon the traders, it may be apprehended that such engagements would be liable to be frequently disregarded by one party or the other, and that any chief who should wish to escape from the obligations into which he had entered with respect to the slave trade, might thereby be furnished with an excuse for annulling the treaty altogether.

If in negotiating a treaty with any one chief, you should have occasion to report that it would be desirable to enter into a specific engagement as to the rate of duties and customs to be levied on British and native goods; and if, upon reference to the Lords of the Committee of Privy Council for Trade, it should appear that such an arrangement is of importance to the interests of British commerce, it

1 *Parl. Papers*, 1865, v (412), pp. 428–9.

would then be time enough to entertain the question with regard to that particular case; but as regards all ordinary treaties of general application, you will take care that none of them contain any engagement more specific than that which forms the 5th article of the proposed treaty with the chiefs of Bimbia,[1] which is as follows:—

'The subjects of the Queen of England may always trade freely with the people of Bimbia in every article they may wish to buy and sell, in all the places and ports within the territories of the Chiefs of Bimbia, and throughout the whole of their dominions; and the Chiefs of Bimbia pledge themselves to show no favour and give no privilege to the ships and traders of other countries, which they do not show to those of England.'

For the future, therefore, no such article must be inserted as the latter part of the 5th article in the treaties now under consideration, beginning with the words 'and the chief' to the words 'free of duty', and the article above quoted from the treaty with Bimbia, should be substituted for the concluding part of the 5th article in the draft model agreement transmitted to Captain Huntley by my predecessor in his Despatch, No. 32, of 31st July 1840, namely from the words 'and the customs and dues taken', to the words 'price of the goods sold'.

II

GOVERNOR R. G. MACDONNELL TO EARL GREY: KUNNONG EXPEDITION, 10 APRIL 1849[2]

[A punitive expedition has been sent to Kunnong as a reprisal for robberies and hostile reception of the Governor.]

. . . It is not possible to conduct the Government peaceably without making an occasional example. I regret also to say that at present a very general idea of the weakness of this Government in a military point of view is prevalant amongst the Natives. To a certain degree the firmness with which, shortly after my arrival as Governor, I insisted on the King of Barra's delivering up such of Her Majesty's subjects as he illegally detained, checked the disposition to despise our force, which had manifested itself. Nevertheless frequent robberies were committed on the property of our Merchants, and since the last outrage on my own person at Keening I have every reason to suppose from authentic accounts that unless strong measures to punish that Chief be promptly taken, there will be no security for the property of our Merchants which remains at present unprotected amongst different native tribes. . . .

[1] See above, no. 20, p. 164.
[2] W.O. 1/486. *Richard MacDonnell* was Chief Justice of the Gambia, 1843–8 and Governor, 1848–52.

12

GOVERNOR L. S. O'CONNOR TO THE DUKE OF NEWCASTLE: THE BARRA WAR, 12 AUGUST 1853[1]

. . . I HAVE now the honor to report to Your Grace that I held a Palaver on the 1st. and 2nd. Instant which was attended by 'Demba Soonko', King of Barra, and 'Jalia', the rebel Chief.

2. After considerable difficulty I affected a reconciliation between the hostile parties—induced Jalia to pull the cap, bow to the knee, and acknowledge Demba Soonko as his lawful Sovereign; on the last day a treaty of amnesty and peace was duly signed, a copy herewith enclosed.[2]

Thus a Civil War, which, for nearly thirteen years has blighted the Agricultural pursuits and commercial prosperity of the fertile and widely extended Kingdom of Barra—I sincerely hope—is terminated. . . .

13

GOVERNOR L. S. O'CONNOR TO LORD JOHN RUSSELL: MARABOUT UPRISING AT KOMBO, 17 AUGUST 1855[3]

MY LORD,

I have the honour to report to your Lordship that the severe but merited chastisement inflicted upon the rebel Mahometan Chiefs of Combo, and the capture and total destruction of their strong hold of Sabagee by the combined French and British forces on the 4th Instant appears to have checked the predatory encroachments on the British Settlements in the Gambia and produced a *temporary* cessation from hostilities.

2. I entertain but little faith in their pacific intentions for I believe they want only the opportunity and season to renew their depredations and destruction of English property, and I am fully convinced that until men and means are granted me to make an expedition against Canju[4] at a favourable period of the year, and thereby cripple the Mahometan power in the Combo, Her Majesty's Settlements in the Gambia *will not be in a safe position.*

[1] C.O. 87/55. Approved in Newcastle to O'Connor, 19 September 1853.
[2] Encl. treaty, 2 August 1853: ibid.
[3] C.O. 87/60. Sabaji (Sukuku), the Marabout centre, was close to the annexed territory of British Kombo.
[4] Gunjur, about twenty-five miles south of Bathurst towards the Casamance, became the new centre for the Marabouts, but was not attacked.

3. The leader and commander of the Rebel Forces on the two late occasions—'Omar' a Moor, is an emissary from Alhadji[1] the prophet, so strongly animadverted upon in the Governor of Senegal's despatch. He is now engaged on a Missionary tour among the Mahometans and was formerly an Officer in the Army of *Abd-el-Kadir*, this at once accounts for the skilful dispositions made to resist the attack of the British. . . .

14

LORD PALMERSTON: MINUTE, MUSLIM POLICY, 17 NOVEMBER 1855[2]

It would be very unwise to set ourselves up as Enemies on Principle to the Mahommetans & whatever may be the faults & errors of the Mahommetan Religion it is at least a step in advance as compared with the devil worship of the fetish Negroes. At the same time we must be able to defend ourselves against the Mahommetans if attacked, though we ought to take great pains to let them understand that we don't wish to molest them but on the contrary wish to be Friends with them & have no intention of interfering between them and the Fetish People excepting as far as we may be bound to defend from Injury Tribes living under our Protection.

This Despatch should be sent to the War Depart. calling serious attention of Sec. of State to the necessity of some increase of Force for Defence of these places but informing him of Instructions given to Governor for his guidance. . . .

15

GOVERNOR L. S. O'CONNOR TO HENRY LABOU-CHERE: MARABOUT PEACE TREATY, 17 APRIL 1856[3]

Sir,

With reference to my despatch No 24, 15th Instant Para 34, I have now the honour to inform you that a Convention was signed this day at three o'clock by the King of Jamboor, the Almamys of Kunjur,

---

[1] Omar, the local agent of Haji Ismail (who led an anti-French *jihad* in Senegal) escaped to the Casamance where he was caught by the French. He had taken part in the resistance by Abd al-Qadir, Emir of the western sector of Algeria, who surrendered to the French in 1847.

[2] C.O. 87/60. On the basis of this minute a request was made to the War Office, 28 November 1855, for more troops from the West Indies. C.O. 87/61.

[3] C.O. 87/62. Encl. convention, 17 April 1856; and *Parl. Papers*, 1865, v (412), p. 411.

Burufut, Sabbagee, the Chiefs and representatives of Mandinarry, Katong, the King of Barra and the Alcadi of Jillifree joining in it.[1]

2. A copy of the Treaty is enclosed.

3. The Almamys and the Fodis (priests) swore upon the Koran to observe strictly the bond made between us and visit with punishment anyone 'who dug up the war' . . .

16

GOVERNOR G. A. K. D'ARCY TO THE DUKE OF NEWCASTLE: BADDIBU EXPEDITION, 26 FEBRUARY 1861[2]

. . . No sooner was the battle over when the King of Jocardo whose territory is separated from those of Baddiboo by the Creek demanded an interview with me, begging I would grant an armistice of three days whilst he brought in from Baddiboo Towns all the Head Men who were anxious for peace but afraid to come in. I consented to this arrangement but strongly advised Colonel Murray to proceed with his orders for our march to the King's Town on the morning of the 25th Instant; it was finally arranged that the Commodore should encamp at Sablea with his sailors whilst the Marines accompanied the force to Indear—all was in preparation when on the 24th I received a Message from the King of Jocardo begging to extend the Armistice one more day as the distance to the different towns was so great—this I also granted but with a message that at 8 o'clock on the 26th the Colonel and Commodore would march. For the sake of suffering humanity I was delighted to see this Potentate on board of the 'Torch' at 6 o'clock this morning when I ratified the Treaty which I have the honor to enclose and which His Excellency Governor Hill, Commodore Edmonstone, Captain Smith and Major Hill Commanding 2nd W.I. Regiment approved and attached their signatures.[3]

I trust Your Grace will be pleased to approve of all I have done—by the display of such a force as never has been seen on the Coast since the days of Governor McCarthy British supremacy is secured on the Coast for many years to come.

The Native Chiefs will think that although the Governor of Bathurst has only 300 Soldiers he can by going to Sierra Leone collect

[1] I.e. the leading Mandinka chiefs and Marabout leaders of Niumi and Kombo on both sides of the Gambia mouth.

[2] C.O. 87/71. *Colonel D'Arcy* was Governor of the Gambia, 1859–66. The expedition was occasioned by the refusal of the Mandinka chief of Baddibu to pay a fine for the pillage of traders. His capital at Saba was stormed, 21 February 1861.

[3] Encl. treaty, 26 February 1861; and *Parl. Papers*, 1865, v (412), p. 416.

3,000. Their arrogance is reduced by defeat, and a heavy fine inflicted, which I could not in reason have asked had this large exporting country of Nuts been destroyed, by our march to Indear.

Before leaving Bathurst I received the enclosed Memorial[1] from the Merchants. Your Grace will perceive I sent a guarded reply. I was anxious by a display of power and a smart action to shew the River Kings what British power could do when provoked but I had not the least intention to refuse overtures of peace conceiving it to be bad policy to annihilate the largest and richest ground nut country on the River.

I have agreed with the Chiefs to send the 'Dover' up the Creek on the 26th of March for the first instalment. I need scarce add that I will return the hostages to the hour when the indemnity is all paid.

17

THE DUKE OF NEWCASTLE TO GOVERNOR G. A. K. D'ARCY: THE BADDIBU TREATY, 5 DECEMBER 1861[2]

SIR,

I have to acknowledge the receipt of your Despatch, No 54, of the 21st August last, forwarding a treaty which you had concluded with the King and Chiefs of Baddiboo, in the River Gambia, in which it is stipulated that the King shall receive an annual payment of 600 dollars from the local Government in lieu of all customs and charges on French and British traders.

As a preliminary step of the negotiation of this treaty, you consented to deliver up the hostages who were in your hands, and to be satisfied with the payment of one-fourth of the fine originally imposed on the King and his chiefs, amounting in value to 600 *l.*, remitting the remainder of the fine, amounting to 1,800 *l.*

It appears, however, that at the date of your Despatch, and after the signing of the treaty, all the property received from the King and chiefs in payment of the fine, amounted to the value of 360 *l.*, and that you intend 'to withhold the customs' until that balance was paid; meaning, I suppose, that till then the king will not receive any portion of the 600 dollars stipulated by the treaty to be granted to him in lieu of customs.

I think it not improbable that the treaty which you have concluded may secure the good behaviour of the King and chiefs in the conduct

[1] Encl. Merchants to D'Arcy, 11 February 1861 (requesting the destruction of Mandinka and Marabout towns in Baddibu). The fine of some £1,800 was never paid in full: the Marabout of Baddibu revolted against an attempt to destrain them of goods and cattle to meet the terms of the treaty.
[2] *Parl. Papers*, 1865, v (412), p. 429.

of the trade with that country; but this advantage will be gained at an expense which must fall on the mercantile body.

The colonial expenses of the war against Baddiboo amounted to 2,379 *l.* 7 *s.* 5 *d.*, and the original fine imposed on the King and chief equivalent to 2,400 *l.*, would have paid for those expenses.

The sum to be ultimately realised is 600 *l.*, leaving a balance of 1,800 *l.* to be provided for; and you must therefore make every effort, by additional temporary taxation if necessary, to provide for that amount.

It is to be regretted that, after reducing the fine to one-fourth only, you did not take care that the whole of that portion of it was realised before the signing of the treaty, as by the terms of the treaty you are bound to pay the King the stipulated commutation, and withholding it even for a time may be misconstrued by the King and his chiefs.

You will likewise have to make provision for the annual payment of the 600 dollars to the King, which may perhaps be effected by a duty upon the certificates with which, under the treaty, the merchant must provide themselves in order to benefit by it.

Subject to these remarks, I have to signify to you Her Majesty's confirmation of that treaty.

18

GOVERNOR G. A. K. D'ARCY TO EDWARD CARD-WELL: MARABOUT UPRISING (NIUMI), 22 AUGUST 1864[1]

RIGHT HONOURABLE SIR,

Most respectfully replying to your Despatch, No. 334, of the 23d July 1864, I have to explain that I did not consider it necessary to trouble a Secretary of State with a detail of the proposed expedition to Albreda. I will now, at your order, proceed *seriatim* to detail events as they took place; and you will not fail to observe that the success which followed the expedition to M'Carthy's rendered that of Albreda unnecessary.

The noble Duke, your predecessor, was pleased, in a Despatch, No. 306, March 23d, to sanction the settlement of Fitzgerald Town; this decision gave great offence to the merchants of the town, who at the time were deeply offended with my appointed ordinance, and also with my policy towards the starving refugees from the Salum country; to such a degree did they carry their resentment, that a European merchant of some influence moved the natives of Albreda

[1] *Parl. Papers*, 1865, v (412), p. 431.

to contest my right of bestowing the soil in grant over the one inland ceded mile on the right bank of the river. The Minutes of Council will fully explain my position with regard to the disputants; and the Board, *nemine contradicente*, agreed with me, that Masamba Kokey[1] ought to be supported; during the time the troops were absent on the expedition to M'Carthy's, the chiefs were drawn up in hostile array with loaded arms on the debateable ground; the Marabouts feeling protected by some mercantile influence at Bathurst, and the Sonnin-kees[2] in this case by the Government, for although Masamba Kokey is a Joliffe by birth, yet politically is he a Sonninkee. It became necessary to act promptly to save bloodshed, and the renewal of the civil war in the kingdom of Barra. Directly after the meeting of Council, I dispatched a small boat up the river to stop the 'Dover' on her return voyage from M'Carthy's Island. Major Harley picked up my messenger off Albreda, but being short of coals was obliged to steam on to Bathurst. However he requested to be allowed to return with the troops to Albreda, after the departure of the mail on the 25th of July; this course I desired the Major should take, at the time deem-ing the occasion serious, feeling the necessity of supporting Masamba Kokey; previously, however, to the embarkation of the troops, I received a message from Masamba himself to the effect that the 'palaver was shut'.

It appears that the Marabouts were alarmed at the steps taken at M'Carthy's Island, and hearing of my determination to send the troops back to Albreda, they had yielded, and promised not to trouble the Governor any more, and they were guileless enough to confess that they would not listen again to bad advice! Consequent on this message, I countermanded the embarkation of the troops, and dispatched Dr. Sherwood as my agent, whom the natives much respect, to arrange the palaver; and his report I have the honour to enclose for your information.

I can assure you, Right Honourable Sir, that I am quite aware that the present is a time when the governors of the colonies on the West Coast of Africa are in disgrace with the public, owing to the un-popularity of the Ashantee war, yet I am sure you, Right Honourable Sir, will be as just as the Spartan mother was to her son, by allowing us to speak.

We are honoured by being appointed as Her Majesty's representa-tives over settlements occupying but a decimal part of this great continent, surrounded by a people who, since the days of the geo-graphist Shobo, have been considered the most savage and ignorant

---

[1] Chief of Kataba in Niani, Upper Gambia.

[2] The 'Soninki' strictly speaking were Serahule (Sarakole), Mande. The term was used in the Gambia region from the 1830's to mean pagan Mandinka or Wolof rulers opposed to the Marabout.

of mankind, but open to regeneration by those who comparatively may be styled the 'lords of human kind'. Alas, it is far otherwise; the merchant comes to the coast only to enrich himself, without a feeling of philanthropy in his disposition towards the aborigines, or even a thought for the honour of the flag. On the other hand, the Governor considers such aspirations as compatible with his office, and steers without flinching a different course, opposed widely to avaricious gain; he is thwarted and misrepresented in England by the merchants, the peculiarity of their business making it necessity to take the homeward trip for three months in every year. The Imperial Government, again, is not in a position to know what the people really feel, the officer administering the government of the colony being averse to sing his own praises by recording his earnest efforts in the cause of justice, truth, and humanity; they are, however, fully appreciated by the poor people. In the present instance, I feel that owing to the inhabitants of Albreda having been tampered with, it was the more necessary to demonstrate the strength of the Government; but the very moment the natives saw their error, and promised amendment, I took at once pacific steps to arrange so serious a misunderstanding, and their conduct on this occasion resembled that of rebellious children to an injured but forgiving parent . . .

[He has encouraged peaceful settlement of refugees at Fitzgerald and Berwick.]

In 1861, with a fine force military and naval, of 2,000 combatants, burning to display their prowess, I signed a peace on the field, after the successful battle of Saba,—directly the chiefs expressed contrition and gave hostages for future good behaviour.

In 1862 I did not fire a shot, but by a firm, though inexpensive demonstration, I prevented the calamity of the slaughter of 600 women and children, and the probable invasion of British territory.

In November 1862, I received from the Governor of Senegal a most tempting offer to join in a military expedition against Maba;[1] from my intimate knowledge of the country, I felt the stern expediency of this wise policy, and the more especially was this co-operation personally agreeable to me, as on the 1st of January of the following year the export tax on the produce was to commence, the measure I had framed and organised after much opposition in and out of doors, and on which the revenue almost in its totality depended; nevertheless, in obedience to His Grace's orders, I declined the proposal, and it is only now, after seeing all the distress and misery that this fanatic has caused that I minuted so strongly in Council last month on

[1] Ma Ba (Ama Ba) a Tukolor Marabout who led a *jihad* in Senegal, 1862–7, first against the Wolof and then against the French in alliance with Moors and Futa Toro Tukolor.

receiving His Excellency's second proposal of co-operation; insomuch, I did my conscientious duty, but obediently forwarded all the correspondence to you, Right Honourable Sir, taking no further action.

In 1863 I burned the stockades at Barra, and made a treaty of peace between the rival sects, literally amidst the smoke of battle.

In February 1864, with great fatigue and exposure, I prevented the civil war from spreading into British Combo, and by Commodore Wilmot's aid I made a treaty of peace between the belligerents; and in July of this same year, I originated and proposed to the Council a policy at once bold and conciliatory with regard to the perilous position our strictly neutral policy had naturally caused the settlement at M'Carthy's Island to be surrounded by earthworks and stockades, to the detriment of trade, and to the risk even of British life. This undertaking was crowned with success, and a treaty of peace signed, which has thrown 40 miles of country into beautiful cultivation; and when I reflect that none of these treaties have been broken, and that prosperity has returned to the settlment, owing to my pacific policy, the only reward I have ever received for all my exertions in the holy cause of peace, I am necessarily compelled, at the risk of being self-laudatory, to compose this hasty recapitulation of my services, and my apology for doing so may be accepted as not unreasonable; that you, Right Honourable Sir, cannot possibly be aware of all that has taken place of late years in the Senegambia, and of my devotion to His Grace's orders.

19

EDWARD CARDWELL TO GOVERNOR G. A. K. D'ARCY: MARABOUT UPRISING (KOMBO), 21 JANUARY 1865[1]

SIR,

I have received your Despatch, No. 74, of the 21st November last, reporting the steps which you had taken in consequence of your having received information that the Marabouts from Goongour, a town in Lower Combo, had burnt down a portion of the town of Bussumballa, inhabited by Sonninkees. I appreciate your desire to prevent rival tribes in the vicinity of the Gambia from engaging in open hostilities against each other; but I am compelled to remark that on the present occasion the circumstances do not appear to have called for any active interference on your part.

---

[1] *Parl. Papers*, 1856, v (412), pp. 433–4. The Mandinka town of Busumballa did not finally fall to the Marabout till 1874.

You were quite right in sending Seymour Gay, the Superintendent of Police, and a person in whom you placed confidence, to endeavour to find out the causes which led to the occurrence which had been brought to your notice, but it is from the statements made in his report that I have come to the conclusion that it was not a case for interference.

The person mainly concerned in the attack on Bussumballa appears to have been one Allse Owd, whose body was discovered, and although he seems to have been a sojourner in Goongour, he is also described as a 'stranger' there, and formerly a resident at Bathurst. His widow, whom Seymour Gay visited, and who admitted herself to be a British subject, stated that he went to war without saying anything to her about it, or giving any notice, and that he deserved his fate. It would further appear that the four men who fell with him were Joliffees and Touculors, and therefore it may be presumed, not belonging to Goongour.

I am further of opinion that the treaty made by Commodore Wilmot in February 1864,[1] does not impose such extensive obligations as you represented to the Council.

But I shall withold any formal sanction of the treaty, because however expedient and judicious it may have been under the circumstances of the case, and bearing my interpretation of it, it would be highly injurious if it were taken to compel us to intervene in such cases as the present, and to take up the quarrels of the two sects of Mahomedans and Pagans. . . .

20

GOVERNOR G. A. K. D'ARCY TO EDWARD CARDWELL: MARABOUT UPRISING (KOMBO), 21 JANUARY 1865[2]

RIGHT HONOURABLE SIR,

In consequence of a severe attack of ague, which incapacitated me from meeting the native chiefs, including the King of Combo and the deputation from the Cabba, or high priest of Goonjour, who had assembled in Bathurst by appointment, I deputed Chief Justice Mantell to preside in my absence.

2. His Honour reports to me that after a discussion and investigation which occupied four hours, no proof was adduced by the King of Combo implicating the Chief of Goonjour in the late barbarous

---

[1] In 1864 Commodore Wilmot of H.M.S. *Rattlesnake* arranged a truce between the King of Kombo and the leader of the Kombo Marabouts, Fodi Kaba, in which both parties were required to refer disputes to the Governor of the Gambia.

[2] *Parl. Papers*, 1865, v (412), pp. 434–5.

incendiary attack in the night time upon the king's town of Bussum-balla, which cruel and dastardly act was emphatically repudiated by the Chief of Goonjour.

3. It was pointed out to the chiefs present, that the existing treaty bound all the contracting parties to submit each supposed *casus belli* to the Governor of the Gambia, whose decision thereon must be guided by satisfactory proofs, and that the parties had bound themselves not to commence hostilities in the absence of the Governor's decision.

4. That upon request the Governor would probably resume the hearing of the present charge on a future day, and, in the meantime, any hostile act upon either side would violate the treaty and constitute the aggressor an enemy of the British Government.

5. Both parties expressed warmly a desire for peace, but upon a proposition that terms should be reduced to writing, and signed by them, the Goonjour people only consented, the king declaring he would not allow the outrage upon Bussumballa to pass unavenged. The chief justice, however, formed an impression that this king will hesitate ere he commits any overt act of hostility.

6. An impression has gone abroad that it is the policy of this Colonial Government to favour the fetish Negro Pagan; this is an error arising, in a great measure, I fancy, from the reports taken home by passengers who cannot possible, from their short stay, sufficiently master the subject. The Sonninkees and Marabouts are equally Mahomedans: all are circumcised, and all believe in the Mahomedan religion, and all abhor fetish, or devil worship; the breast of a Sonnin-kee is covered with gree-grees, or charms, pieces of leather in which verses from the Koran are inscribed, in like manner to the Marabout; it is difficult to know how they have been divided into different sects. I fancy accident has more to say to it than design, and in the public profession of the faith on arriving at the years of puberty a judical ceremony is recognised. I hold in my hand a latter just received from a Mandingo resident of this town, who says:—

'Allow me, Governor, to hold a tom-tom tonight (native music), in order to perform a rite on my son, which has come down in tradition from our common father, Abraham.'

Two hundred years ago, the whole country was inhabited by Mandingoes and Jolloffs, of no established religion, as the Fodeys or red caps; Mahommedan priests wandered down the coast, they preached the unity of the Deity and the inspiration of the Prophet, making proselytes in great numbers; they were feared by the simple minded Pagan oligarchy, who passed a law never to allow a writing man (a Marabout) the throne, fearful lest he would forget the common good, and work out his power to his own advantage; yet this government of headmen allowed all the rising generation to be taught to read and write the Arabic characters; a generation is passed, and all are Mahomedans; but there is a public ceremony to be performed.

'Do you renounce all drink, the conduct and policy of your ancestors.'

Will you become a clergyman, in fact?

7. It is not religion which has caused the civil war, but policy; the Marabouts want the government of the country, knowing full well that the universality of religion will surely follow the temporal power. It is to the cause of order that the Colonial Government leans; under the Marabout rule all is left to chance, every man for himself consequently it is now found difficult to deal in reason with the natives.

8. A trader is robbed! to whom has the Governor to apply for redress? formerly there was a king, with a constitutional power of life and death, and rather than lose his customs, it was to his interest to see the trader indemnified.

B. GUINEA, SIERRA LEONE

Introductory Note

UP till the end of the 1830's the Sierra Leone administration tried to arrange treaties with Bulom, Temne, Susu, and Mandinka chiefs for amity and trade, in return for promises of military assistance and arms, the return of fugitive slaves, and payments of money and goods. The type of agreement made by Governor Thompson in his 'Offensive and Defensive' alliance of 1808 with chiefs along the Rokel river was refused sanction by Lord Castlereagh; but Lord Bathurst in 1825 approved the policy of distributing stipends and presents (excluding arms) and the practice of withholding them from chiefs who fell from favour. Governor Turner carried this policy a stage further by intervening at Porto Loko to settle a title dispute on behalf of a Temne chief who would assist the colony's trade—a precedent followed by Governors Jeremie and Kennedy in 1841 and 1853. Governor Findlay and Lieut.-Governor Campbell, between 1831 and 1837, drew up the most comprehensive of early treaties to end civil war among the Susu and Temne, to lay down rules for reciprocal surrender of offenders, criminals and domestic slaves, and to provide by increased Customs a source of revenue to meet the cost of annual stipends. Both Lord Goderich and Lord Glenelg approved this method of securing widespread clientage, but the treaties were suspended until clauses on fugitives were revised. Governor Doherty reported that the chiefs evaded his proposals for revision, and his criticisms of the usefulness of past treaties reached the Colonial Office in time to lend weight to Lord Russell's plans for a new comprehensive treaty policy in 1840 and 1841.

The first agreement combining anti-slave trade clauses with traditional provisions for amity and commerce was signed with the Temne and forwarded for approval in January 1841. It immediately raised doubts about the presumption of colonial jurisdiction over British subjects in Temne territory[1] and the stipulated allowance of an *ad valorem* percentage on imports into Freetown. Lord Stanley approved this provision, provided only goods for the Temne area were affected; but the Foreign Office objected to making chiefs partners in levying duties on trade. The treaty was renewed by Governor Hill in 1857, but only stipends and not *ad valorem* duties were ever paid to the chiefs. The stipend system and new treaties based on a simplified model of 1844 were extended to the Susu of the Melakori and Nunez in 1845 and 1851 and to Bulom and Sherbro chiefs in 1852. The whole policy of stipends was questioned by Governor Kennedy who advised a change from paying goods measured in devaluated 'bars' to payments of money. The Colonial Office accepted this advice, but it was not followed by Kennedy's successor, Governor Hill. A series of expensive military expeditions by Hill in the Scarcies and the Sherbro went unchecked during Bulwer-Lytton's term as Secretary of State, until Acting Governor Smith, through the agency of the trader John McCormack, arranged a truce between the Susu and Temne in the Scarcies in 1861. New treaties were made with the chiefs of the area north of the colony and with Koya chiefs whose territory was incorporated in Sierra Leone.

By the end of the 1860's the stipend policy at Sierra Leone had survived disapproval of interference beyond the boundaries of the colony and doubt concerning the question of extra-territorial jurisdiction which the treaty system raised but did not solve. Meanwhile, the practice of sending diplomatic missions to the interior carried out by O'Beirne and Thomson in 1821 and 1841 was revived by Governor Kennedy who sent W. Winwood Reade to Falaba, Solima, and the Niger in 1869, followed by Dr. Edward Blyden to Falaba and Timbo in 1869 and 1872.

I

'TREATY OF ALLIANCE OFFENSIVE AND DEFENSIVE', 11 NOVEMBER 1808[2]

FOR the securing of Peace & the encouragement of lawful Commerce, or for mutual assistance in just & necessary war, it is agreed between the Chiefs whose names are hereunto subscribed.

1st. That if any of the Allied Chiefs shall be attacked in his own country, the others shall directly assist him by every means in their power, without waiting for further cause of war.

2nd. That if any of the Allied Chiefs shall have dispute or cause of war with any other people he shall give information of the same to the

---

[1] See below, V (B), pp. 547–8.
[2] C.O. 267/24. Between Governor T. Perronet Thompson and Temne chiefs of Mahera and Rokon on the Rokel river. The treaty was not approved: Castlereagh to Thompson, 3 April 1809, C.O. 268/18.

other Chiefs of the Alliance, who shall be bound to interfere in his behalf & if possible to bring the dispute to a fair & amicable conclusion, or otherwise to assist by all means in their power, unless the cause of war be manifestly unjust.

3rd. That in case of war or danger of any war, the Chiefs allied shall choose a Head under whose command shall be the whole forces of the said Chiefs during the war or while such danger of war shall last.

4th. That if any dispute shall arise between any of the Chiefs Allied, a General Council shall be assembled to which such dispute shall be referred and that if any Chief or Chiefs shall refuse to abide by the decision of such Council, the refusal shall be held to be a fair cause of war.

5th. That if any of the parties shall make any treaty of peace and Alliance with any other people, he shall do his utmost to cause the other parties to be included in the same.

6th. That the parties shall keep up a Friendly correspondence with each other, and shall inform each other of all events and circumstances in which the interest of the others may be concerned.

7th. That the Governor of Sierra Leone shall do his utmost to procure to the allied Chiefs every advantage of communication & correspondence with this Colony, and with Great Britain, and that those Chiefs on their part shall do every thing in their power to promote the interests of this Colony.

8th. . . . and that if those Chiefs or any of their people shall appear within this Colony & there make declaration of any wrongs or causes in question according to the forms of English law, the persons concerned therein of what nation or country soever, shall be detained on their arrival in the Colony, if the Complaint is sufficient to Justify it, until the plaintiffs can appear and proceed against them according to law, in the same manner as if the plaintiffs had been Inhabitants of this Colony: And that those Chiefs on their part shall engage to deliver up all offenders against the laws of this Colony and to procure them to be delivered up so far as in their power.

9th. That the Governor of this Colony shall engage to cause any Children or other people of the Allied Chiefs whom those Chiefs may chose to send to the Colony, to be instructed in European Arts and Knowledge, on condition that they shall be maintained without charge to the Colony of Sierra Leone and shall pay the same price to the teachers as is paid by the Inhabitants of this Colony.

10th. That if the said Chiefs shall be disposed to send any young men to learn the use of great Guns and other English fashions of War, the Governor of Sierra Leone shall cause them to be instructed therein on condition that they shall be maintained without charge to the Colony of Sierra Leone.

11th. That if any of the people of the Allied Chiefs shall with the permission of their Chiefs desire to settle within the Colony of Sierra Leone for the purpose of learning to cultivate any of the articles cultivated within the Colony, the Governor shall engage them to find a good & sufficient quantity of land for the maintenance of themselves and families free of rent for the time of their residence there.

12th. That nothing shall be done to hinder any man of the people of the Chiefs Allied from marrying any women of the Inhabitants of the Colony of Sierra Leone or any man of the Colony of Sierra Leone from marrying any woman of the people of the Allied Chiefs, but that such marriages shall rather be encouraged as tending to encourage peace and goodwill.

13th. That the Allied Chiefs when appearing with [their] proper mark and distinction shall be received by all sentries within the Colony of Sierra Leone with the same compliment as is due to all the Commissioned Officers of His Majesty's Forces; and that the Governor of Sierra Leone shall be received within the countries of the Allied Chiefs with the same or equal respect.

14th. That nothing shall prevent any other Chief from being admitted to this Treaty of Alliance and Confederacy with the consent of the greater part of the Chiefs at that time parties therein.

15th. That if any question shall arise with respect to the explanation of any part of these articles, it shall be determined by a meeting of the parties concerned with the Colony of Sierra Leone, in a manner becoming friends & Allies. . . .

2

ACTING GOVERNOR A. GRANT TO EARL BATHURST: MISSION TO FUTA JALLON, 28 FEBRUARY 1821[1]

MY LORD,

Previous to the departure of Governor Macarthy to Europe an application had been made to him by the King of the Foulahs a very powerful Prince in the interior, expressing a desire to have an Officer sent up to Teembo the Capital of his Territories, and having myself lately received a very friendly letter from that King I was induced

[1] C.O. 267/53. *Major Alexander Grant* of the Royal African Corps founded the Gambia posts in 1816 and administered them till 1822. He was Acting Governor of Sierra Leone in 1821. *Assistant Staff Surgeon O'Beirne* reached Timbo in March 1821 and returned with a delegation of Fula traders. Journal (MS. ff. 89): ibid. Both Grant and Governor MacCarthy sponsored a mission by Lieutenant F. G. Laing to the Scarcies in 1822 and to Falaba to investigate other trade routes. See Laing's *Travels in the Timannee Kooranko, and Soolima Countries*. London, 1825; reports in C.O. 267/58.

in conformity to the intentions of Governor Macarthy to dispatch on the 29th. Ulto. Mr. B. O'Beirne Assistant Surgeon to the Forces on that service. The influence of the Foulah nation extending from the Branches of the River Sierra Leone to the banks of the Niger and communicating with the principal countries of the interior renders a friendly connection with that country of much importance to our Mercantile interests, and it is with great satisfaction I have the honour to report to your Lordship that the good effect of Mr. O'Beirne's executions are already felt here in the increased supply of Ivory, Gold and Cattle brought by the Foulahs to our different Factories situated on this River; Mr. O'Beirne is merely accompanied by a few people of colour to carry his baggage and presents the expence of which will be triffling. . . .

3

ACTING GOVERNOR D. M. HAMILTON TO EARL BATHURST: RELATIONS WITH FUTA JALLON, 21 APRIL 1824[1]

MY LORD,

I have great satisfaction in informing your Lordship, that about the latter end of last January, a mission arrived in this Colony from Timbo, the capital of the Foulah Country, a place I suppose to be about three or four hundred miles North north east of Freetown. The superior of this mission was an intelligent young man, much superior to the natives of the Coast generally; he brought a letter written in the Arabic character from Almanee Abdool Kadree the King of the Foulah country, to our lamented governor, with whose name he appeared to be well acquainted; a copy of the translation of this Letter I have herein enclosed for your Lordship's information.[2] This young chief was attended by a retinue of about Sixty men, and set off from Timbo with one hundred bullocks for a present to the governor, only ten of these bullocks lived to arrive in the Colony. On his return a suitable present was sent with him from the Council to the King, and presents also made to several intermediate Chiefs between Timbo and the Colony, all of whom either by themselves or their head-men on their parts, promised there should be a free communication between this Colony and the Foulah nation. At the same time and since several hundred Foulahs have visited the Colony, in which they have expended from the best information I have been

---

[1] C.O. 267/60. *D. M. Hamilton*, King's Advocate, was Acting Governor of Sierra Leone, 1824-5.
[2] Encl. *Almamy* Abdul Kadri to MacCarthy, n.d. (requesting powder, guns, paper, &c.).

able to collect, not less than five thousand pounds worth of Gold. The absence of our late lamented Governor was much felt at the time this mission left the Colony to return to Timbo, the chief expressing a strong desire that a white man might return with him; and the Council feeling delicate in incurring the necessary expence for such a measure in the absence of His Excellency the Governor and at the same time being doubtful which of the Government officers he might approve of being sent. It is only in consequence of, and since those transactions, that I have had any hopes, during a residence of near twenty years in the Colony, of its ever becoming a place of any profit to the Mother Country, I am however now very sanguine if advantage is taken of these favourable circumstances, by sending an European to reside at Timbo with a sufficient number of the coloured inhabitants as a retinue, that in a few years a very extensive and beneficial trade will be established, and the desideratum of exploring the Interior easily attained.

I think it but an act of justice to observe to your Lordship that these prospects of advantage to this Colony have been chiefly attained by the meritorious service of Mr. Bryan O'Beirne an assistant Staff Surgeon in the Army, who conducted a mission to Timbo about two years and a half since; and who appeared to have gained the confidence and friendship of Almani Abdool Kadree the King of the Foulah country, together with that of most of the intermediate Chiefs through whose territories he passed on his way to Timbo and back.

I beg to call your Lordship's particular attention to the important Subject of residents being sent from this [Colony] to Timbo and other important places, where it may be thought their residence would prove beneficial to the commerce of the Colony, being convinced my Lord that those missions may be conducted on a very triffling expence indeed in comparison with that undertaken under the command of the late Major Peddie.

4

GOVERNOR CHARLES TURNER TO EARL
BATHURST: PORT LOKO TITLE SUCCESSION,
20 DECEMBER 1825[1]

My Lord,

I have the honour to acquaint your Lordship with the successful issue of a little Expedition on which I considered it my duty to proceed up the two rivers of Rokell and Port Locco, which, by their

[1] C.O. 267/66. *Alikali* Moriba who had driven the Susu from Port Loko in 1815 died in 1825 leaving the title in dispute among the Temne.

junction, form the river and harbour of Sierra Leone, and along the course of which lay the routes by which our intercourse with the Interior is kept up principally.

The interruption given by the Native Chiefs to this intercourse has always been severely felt by this Colony, and has been the principal Cause of the little progress which our Trade has hitherto made. Up the Rokell river lays our best country for Camwood, and the direct route to the Countries round the source of the Niger and the richest in Gold, and on from thence to Bambarra, Sego, and down the Niger to the Eastward. This route is tolerably open but at one place about 200 miles from this, where it is obstructed by a chief named Quaia, and my object in going up this River with a Military Force, was to intimidate this man, by giving countenance and assistance in powder and a few Musquets to Tickel a Mahomadou, who is employed against him and in clearing this route of all obstructions, and I have reason to hope that the arrangement which I made there will accomplish this very desirable object.

Along the Port Locco River lays the direct route to Teembo, the Capital of the Great Foulah Nation, with whom we are on the most friendly terms, and carry on considerable trade in Gold, Ivory, Wax, Cattle, Hides &c. &c. Yet at no place was more interruption offered to our Trade than at Port Locco, the Town situated at the head of the River; repeated presents had been made to the Chief with the view to his keeping the path open, but without much advantage, threats had been also used, but as it was considered that Vessels could not approach nearer than 40 or 50 miles to the Town, these threats were disregarded, and at last they blocked up the path altogether. About a month past [sic] then the old King (as he was called) Ali Karlee died, and as it was essential that a well disposed person should succeed him, I determined in order to effect this object to go up there myself, with an armed Force, in the Colonial Vessels and in boats, but as no Vessels had ever gone higher up than about half way and the Pilots would take no further charge. I had much difficulty in getting the Vessels up, but as I considered it very important for the sake of appearance, which in this Country goes further than Strength, to do so I succeeded by considerable exertions to get them all up near the Town, and one of them, within 20 yards of the houses. The presence of these Vessels with 100 White Soldiers had the best effect as they had always considered themselves secure from our Shipping. The party against whom so much complaint was made for plundering the Foulah Traders set up a Chief of their own and before my arrival got him appointed Successor to the late Ali Karlee, but in a manner at variance with the usual custom; this Chief had rendered himself very obnoxious to the Foulah King, as well as to the Government of Sierra Leone and it was important that he should not be permitted to rule the Country. I therefore acquainted the Chiefs that I could not acknowledge him, as he had already stopped our Trade with the Interior, nor keep on friendly terms with Port Locco if they persisted in keeping him in power. These considerations together with the certainty of a Civil War between the two Rivals soon satisfied them with the imprudence of the hasty step which they had taken, and they immediately caused the Chief to resign his new situation and they sent to me a Deputation with the Turban (there the Emblem of Power) to be placed by me on the head of the man I thought most proper, and as under the increased trade and population of the Country they considered themselves incompetent to maintain good order and authority, they also requested that their Country might be taken under the protection of the Government of Sierra Leone; to both these propositions I considered it my duty to accede, placing in authority, Fatima Brama[1] nephew and heir to the last Chief; and the person generally considered as the proper successor; and drawing out and signing the accompanying Convention. . . .

5

EARL BATHURST TO GOVERNOR CHARLES TURNER: PRESENTS TO CHIEFS, 23 DECEMBER 1825[2]

SIR,

I have the honor to acknowledge the receipt of your despatch of the 28th October last in which you enclose a List of Articles which you consider to be necessary as Presents to the Chiefs of those Countries with which you may think it desirable to cultivate a friendly intercourse.

I certainly am not disposed to object to the principle of distributing Presents to the Native Chiefs, as perhaps by no other means could you succeed in obtaining their good will. But I doubt very much the propriety of including arms, except of an ornamental description, among such Presents.

As I have already directed the Colonial Agent to forward a large supply of Bafts to the River Gambia, your wishes have been in some measure anticipated & I shall lose no time ordering the other articles for which you have applied to be forwarded direct to Sierra Leone.

---

[1] Fatima Brima Kamara. The convention to cede territory from Loko to the Scarcies was refused in Bathurst to Turner, 22 April 1826, C.O. 268/20, ff. 334–6.
[2] C.O. 268/20, ff. 304–5.

6

GOVERNOR A. FINDLAY TO R. W. HAY: TEMNE AND LOKO, 10 NOVEMBER 1831[1]

[He has intervened in order to end a conflict between the Temne and Loko people.]

... BEING thus invited by the Ali Karlie to use my best endeavours to rescue from bondage so great a number of human beings, and being well convinced of the hostile disposition of many of the Chiefs in the neighbourhood of the Colony, and the measures which they had adopted to ruin its commerce, I considered it a favorable opportunity while negotiating with the Chiefs for the Liberation of their prisoners to enter into into some arrangements with them for establishing a peace between the Timmanee Chiefs and that of the Loco Nation, and to open the paths through their Countries to the interior for the benefit of Commerce as well as to prevent the Chiefs of the Timmannee and Loco Nations from joining the other Chiefs who have shewn themselves so inimical to the Colony. I therefore sent Messrs. Rishton, McCormack, Campbell, McCaulay, and Savage,[2] to meet the Chiefs of the Timmanee nation, who had assembled at Marbala, and I am happy to state, that after a long and protracted discussion of one month, they succeeded in restoring the unfortunate Loco prisoners to their liberty, and in concluding a Treaty of Amity and Commerce between this Colony and the several Princes, Chieftains and Headmen of that nation.[3] By this we have secured the Friendship and aid of the Chiefs whom we had most to dread, in the event of their joining the other Chiefs, as their Territory joins the Peninsula of Sierra Leone. I herewith enclose to you a Copy of the Treaty, by which you will perceive that it will cause a little annual expence to the Colony, to meet which the Council have made an Act, for levying an additional duty on Tobacco, Brandy, and Gin, and although but small it will be more than sufficient to meet the expence incurred, besides those Merchants who have Factories, and such as may hereafter establish Factories in the Timmanee Territories will have to

[1] C.O. 267/110. The Loko towns along the Rokel on the trade route between Freetown and the Futa Jallon had failed to pay tribute to the Temne who attacked and overran them.

[2] *Henry Rishton*, Colonial Secretary. *John McCormack* and *William H. Savage* were timber traders; *H. W. Macaulay* and *B. Campbell* were employees of the Freetown firm of Macaulay and Babington.

[3] Treaty, 23 September 1831, signed by Findlay's envoys and Bai Kobolo, Temne chief of Marampa (upper Rokel), Bai Fonti; Fatima Brima, *Alikali* of Port Loko and *Almamy* Kabba (a chief of upper Rokel). Lord Goderich approved the treaty and a colonial Act for raising additional duties to pay rent to these chiefs. See below, no. 7, p. 251.

pay rent for the same to the Government of this Colony in aid of the
expence incurred by the said Treaty. . . .

7

THE TEMNE TREATY, 23 SEPTEMBER 1831[1]

[Art. I, peace and friendship between the Colony and the Temne; II,
disputes are to be referred to the Governor; III, if any signatory is attacked
the Governor will supply arms and munitions; IV, V, there are to be no
hostilities between the signatories; VI, signatories will help defend the
Colony.]

. . . VII THE contracting parties being desirous to remove every cause
of misunderstanding which may exist between them respectively,
stipulate and agree for themselves and their successors, that they, the
Princes, Chieftains, and Headmen, and their successors, will give up
to the Governor of Sierra Leone for the time being, or such persons
as he may appoint for that purpose, every liberated African who may
be brought into their respective territories, either by having been
enticed away, kidnapped, purchased, or held for any debt or
pretended claim; and that no satisfaction shall be required or made
to any person before such surrender for any purchase money which
may be alleged to have been paid, promised, or advanced on account
of such liberated African.

VIII And that if any person or persons belonging to the said
Colony, should commit any crime therein, and abscond from justice,
or being indebted within the said Colony, to avoid payment thereof
remove or take up his or their residence within any of the districts
under the Government of any of the said Princes, Chieftains or
Headmen, then, on a demand being made by the Governor of the
said Colony for the time being, for the surrender of such person or
persons, he or they shall be surrendered accordingly.

IX And that in all cases where persons, who may be considered as
domestics by the Timmanee Nation, and who may be proved to have
formed part of the family of any person living within the districts of
the said contracting Princes, Chieftains and Headmen, shall run
away, and without leave from their masters resort to Sierra Leone,
or to any factories belonging thereto, and refuse to return upon the
application of their said masters, the said persons shall be compelled,
to leave the said Colony, or the factories thereof, and be sent into the
districts which their masters may reside, being the districts aforesaid.

X And that all offences committed or done in the Timmanee
Country (not ceded to the Crown of Great Britain), and being under
the government of the Princes, Chieftains and Headmen, parties to
this Convention, by any subject of the Colony of Sierra Leone, may

[1] C.O. 267/110.

be treated and dealt with according to the laws of the said country; provided always the punishment shall never extend to death, deprivation of limb, or loss of liberty, without the consent of the Governor of the said Colony for the time being.

[XI, Temne surrendered in the recent war shall occupy villages under their headmen as free persons and with access to the Marbala market; XII, the Marbala headman, protected by the signatories, shall keep the market orderly.]

XIII And whereas the object of His Excellency the Lieutenant-Governor of Sierra Leone, is to extend the commerce and commercial influence of the said Colony, in which object the Princes, Chieftains, and Headmen, parties to the Convention, are desirous to cooperate; they do therefore stipulate and agree, that all Foulah, Sangarra, Koranko, Mahomedan, and other strangers, shall be considered under the special protection of the several contracting parties, and that they shall have free and secure passage through their several countries towards the said Colony and in returning therefrom. . . .

[XIV, there is to be no restriction on the passage of trade canoes; XVI, the property of Sierra Leone subjects is not to be seized; XVII, for keeping the paths open to trade, the Sierra Leone Government agrees to pay to the Chief of Marampa, 100 bars; the Chief of Menda, 100 bars; the *Alikali* of Port Loko, 150 bars; the *Almamy* of Rokel, 100 bars; Pa Subar Chief of Marbala, 100 bars; the Chief of Bumballa country, 50 bars.]

XVIII . . . And in order to place the several inhabitants of the Colony of Sierra Leone, and the inhabitants of the Rivers Port Logo and Rokelle, on the most amicable footing in their several trading relations, it is more particularly stipulated between His Excellency the Lieutenant Governor, Alikarlie, and Alimarmie Cabba, that in consideration of the annual custom or presents hereinafter set forth, they the said Chieftains will permit, from henceforth, any person, or persons belonging to the said Colony to form a Factory or Establishment for trade in any part of the several districts before mentioned that may be agreed upon, without any let or molestation of any kind: and that they shall not claim from such persons any rent or annual custom for any purpose whatsoever; but that the said annual custom or present to the said Chieftains, that is to say to Alikarlie, three hundred bars, and to Alimarmie, two hundred bars, which it is hereby stipulated, shall be delivered to the said Chieftains annually by the Governor of the said Colony, in the month of June in each year, shall be and remain in lieu thereof to them, and their successors forever. And that the rents now due by the owners of the present factories, being paid up for the present year, shall be considered to all intents and purposes, as being included in the above arrangement, and fully exonerated from all future rent and service; it being hereby fully understood and agreed, that His Excellency the Governor of the said Colony for the time being, shall have full right and authority to ask, demand, and receive from the several persons belonging to the said Colony, now holding Timber and other Factories within any of the territories of the said Chieftains, the amount, from year to year, which they have severally stipulated to pay for the occupation of the site thereof, or such part, or sum in composition, as he may think fit; and further to fix and require such sum in annual rent, or otherwise, in consideration of any future leave to the inhabitants of the said Colony to occupy any site within the said territories; and that any person or persons who may hereafter establish a Factory within the said districts, shall produce, to the Chieftain of such District, a certificate or letter from the Governor of the said Colony, that he or they has liberty so to do.

[XIX, difficulties arising from the treaty are to be discussed between the chiefs and a representative of the Governor.]

8

LIEUT.-GOVERNOR H. D. CAMPBELL TO LORD GLENELG: TEMNE AND LOKO, 9 NOVEMBER 1835[1]

MY LORD,

In the month of June last a representation was made to this Government by certain traders at the town of Magbellay on the neighbouring river called Rokelle, stating that their trade with this Colony had suffered interruption and themselves and their property exposure to violence and plunder in consequence of a war which has existed for some time between two native chiefs, and praying the interposition of our good offices.

My Council, to whom this application was made conjointly with myself, advised that I should communicate with the contending parties, and offer my mediation for the restoration of tranquillity and a mutual good understanding.

With a view to render such interference the more easy and efficacious I addressed myself in the first instance to Dalla Mahommadu[2] on the opposite or Bullom Shore, the most influential and intelligent chief in the neighbourhood. Having secured his co-operation I despatched an officer of the Government to the parties

---

[1] C.O. 267/129. These negotiations to end the continued Temne-Loko war were approved in Glenelg to Campbell, 26 March 1836, C.O. 268/33, ff. 119–21.

[2] *Dalla Modu*, a Mandinka Muslim chief of the Lungi area on the Bulom Shore.

themselves, for the two-fold purpose of supporting Dalla Mahommadu in a negotiation into which he had entered with them, and of pressing it to a conclusion. This mission was undertaken during the last month, and has been attended with such success that the hostile chiefs have agreed to suspend their contest, and to submit their differences to the arbitration of Dalla Mahommadu.

The war, which is I hope thus terminated, is said to date from the year 1830, since which time it has occasionally ceased and been renewed. During the last eighteen months it has been maintained without interruption. The parties are an alleged usurper of the name of Cessi Betti, on the north bank of the Rokelle; and the chief called the Alikarli of Port Logo, a person of considerable reputation and authority throughout the neighbourhood, to whom the colony pays, by treaty, an annual rent. The war is said to have arisen from a domestic quarrel: but whatever may have been its origin, it was doubtless maintained so long by the temptation of the slave trade, and the large opportunities it must have afforded for that traffic. Its termination therefore seems an object still more desirable in this view than in that of the reopening of the trade of Magbellay, which will now again be conducted with security.

9

LIEUT.-GOVERNOR H. D. CAMPBELL TO LORD GLENELG: THE MAGBELE TREATY, 2 MAY 1836[1]

... AN armistice having been established at my request I was induced on the 21st March, to proceed to the town of Mabelly, in the Rokelle River to meet the Kings and Chiefs (who had previously solicited my interference) at a general assembly, and investigate the matters in dispute, and, if possible, arrange them satisfactorily. On the 23rd March I reached Mabelly, and found on my arrival, the Kings of Marampa and Ma Simmerah Countries, and Ali Karlie of Port Locco, the head of the Army, opposed to the Chief Cessie Betty, late of Rokon.

From the Gentlemen I had sent on, some time before to Mabelly I learned that Cessie Betty, who was in a strong stockade, a few miles up the River, only wanted a summons from me, to attend the General Assembly; and that the Chiefs of all ranks, were, but waiting my presence in Mabelly, to come in, which I subsequently found to be the case.

The collecting together all the parties concerned in the disputes to

[1] C.O. 267/132. Dala Modu was appointed paramount chief on the Rokel.

be settled, the hearing of their several statements, and, the defence of their own conduct, proved to be a labour of much greater time through the exceeding deliberation with which these gentlemen proceed in everything, than I could have anticipated; and, my return to Sierra Leone was therefore delayed until the 21st Ultimo.

I have the honor to enclose herein a Copy of the Treaty of peace,[1] signed on this occasion, which, I hope will meet your Lordship's approbation; the present effect of it being, the securing of quiet and happiness to a harmless race of people, who have been rescued from the most distressed situation, and the reasonable prospect of our trade in the districts described, being restored and greatly increased.

Whilst employed at Mabelly in the arrangement of the matters above stated, I had the satisfaction of receiving a visit from Massa Packey, a powerful King of the Limba Country, situated high up on the northern bank of the Rokelle, who came down as well as on his own behalf, as the representative of two other Kings in the Limba Country, and of Bey Camah, a Timmanee King, whose territory occupies a portion of both banks of the Rokelle, and adjoins on the Western side, the country of the Limba King.

Massa Packey stated at the General Assembly, that his object in coming down to Mabelly was to learn whether I had really come up to that place, and if so, to see and enter into friendly arrangements with me, on behalf of the Kings of Limba, Bey Cemah, and himself for keeping up a constant communication with Sierra Leone. . . . As the Treaty which was conducted between Colonel Findlay and some of the above contracting parties in September 1831, was inoperative, and caused great dissatisfaction from the unequal distribution of the Custom paid, I thought it adviseable to concur with the wishes of the contracting parties on that occasion and made a new Convention which I have the honor to enclose.

Your Lordship will perceive by enclosure No. 2 there is a triffling increase of expenditure, but I have a confident hope your Lordship will not deem it worthy of notice, when the great advantages gained by this Convention in a Commercial point of view, are considered. The opening of the communications with the interior, for the introduction of British Manufactures. The authority it will give to this Government over the Native Chiefs, and consequent protection which it will afford to British Subjects, and their property, the immense increase in the shipping of Timber, for the home market, by the facility afforded in obtaining it, and lastly the security obtained for the recovery of Liberated Africans who may be entrapped. . . .

[1] Encl. treaty, 8 April 1836. Signed by Campbell and Bai Kobolo, Bai Simera (Temne chiefs), Bai Fonti, the *Alikali* of Port Loko, the chief of Rokon, Pa Suba, chief of Magbele, *Almamy* Kabba, Mahomadu Bundu, chief of Foredugu and Mahera, Tom Bendu, a chief of Rokon. The treaty was not ratified because of clauses promising to return slaves. C.O. 268/35, ff. 40–42.

10

THE MAGBELE CONFERENCE: DUTIES OF CHIEFS, 18 APRIL 1836[1]

NOTE of a Conference between the undersigned, Mabelly, 18 April 1836, at which the following arrangements were made:

It is the bounden duty

Of Bey Cobolo King of Marampa, Bey Fonti King of Mende; Ali Karlie Chief of Port Loco; Lanselley Chief of Bumbelly, and Massa Packey King of Mabelly, to keep open the road to Foutah by way of Mende, Bambelly and Woosey; also the rivers.

Of Ali Karlie Chief of Porto Loco, Ali Karlie Sa Maura, Chief of Sandu, Nardemah Mahomodoo, Chief of Tomeso, and Buggoro Suree, Chief of Tambacca, to keep open the road to Foutah by way of Bentie, Rocco, Tambacca and Tomeso. Also the rivers.

Of Alimamy Cabba to keep open his portion of the River Rokelle and also the road from Rokelle to Maharra and Masimmera.

Of Pa Suba to keep open the road from Mabelly to Mende and Port Loco.

Of Tom Bendo Chief of Rokon to keep open the road from Rokon to Masimmera and Maharra and also the river.

Of Mahomodu Bondoo to keep open the road from Fooradoogoo to Maharra and from thence to Waterloo in the Colony of Sierra Leone and also the Creeks and river in his district.

Of Bey Summerah to keep open the roads and rivers in his Country.

Of Bey Woosey to keep open the road from Woosey to Foutah.

Of Cessi Betty to keep open the roads and rivers in his neighbourhood.

Of Bey Cammah to keep open the roads and rivers in his neighbourhood.

It is understood and agreed upon that in the event of any of the beforementioned roads or any of the rivers of the Country being stopped, that it shall be the duty of every one of the undersigned Kings, Chiefs, and Headmen to use his or their exertions immediately to open the road or river again for the free pursuit of trade.

The undersigned Kings, Chiefs and Headmen have agreed with the Lieutenant Governor of Sierra Leone to send off immediately Messengers to Alimamy Bocarry the King of Foutah Jallon as well as from themselves as the said Lieutenant Governor to state to Bocarry that the undersigned have entered into a formal agreement with the

---

[1] Encl. in no. 9. These roads constituted the main trade routes from the Colony to the Futa Jallon by way of the Great Scarcies.

Lieutenant Governor of Sierra Leone that all the roads in their countries shall be kept free and open for all Traders and Travellers to pass up and down; and to call on Bocarry as an old and esteemed friend of all and in particular of Sierra Leone to use his influence in keeping the roads open from his own country down to the town of Tomeso where the authority of Ali Karlie of Port Loco and of that Chief's friends commences. . . .'

II

GOVERNOR R. DOHERTY TO LORD JOHN RUSSELL: USE OF TREATIES, 22 APRIL 1840[1]

. . . This question [of presents to chiefs] involves the general one of the advantage which the Government and Colony derive from entering into those treaties with the Chiefs of the neighbourhood: and after a good deal of consideration of the subject, and of the views and reasoning of one or two gentlemen of experience and judgement in the Colony who are unconcerned in mercantile pursuits and so far unbiassed judges, I incline to the opinion that, as those compacts have been hitherto framed and for the commercial objects which the framers of them had in view, they are not beneficial: and cannot be so under the present circumstances of the Settlement, or under any probable circumstances in which it will be placed during a long period to come. They have never been so hitherto. They have never indeed been observed. And it is a notorious fact, that even on occasion of Lieut. Colonel Campbell's second visit to Mabelly in 1837, when he was employed in confirming and gaining the accession of new parties to the Treaty & Convention of the previous year, which bound all parties to them to a strict and lasting reconciliation and amity, the Alikarlie of Port Locco, the principal subscriber on the side of the Chiefs, had his war-men as they are termed out; and was engaged then and has been at intervals ever since in active hostilities against those persons with whom he pledged himself to remain at peace, and who were themselves bound to the same conduct by the same engagement.

Nor is the Colony, though prepared for its own defence, in a condition to enforce the observance or punish the violation of such agreements, by assuming the offensive against parties who may neglect or evade, or thus treat with contempt the stipulations into which they have been enticed. The failure of any aggressive movement would much injure such moral influence in the surrounding

[1] C.O. 267/159. In reply to Russell to Doherty, 28 November 1839, ff. 262-3, C.O. 268/35 (questioning the payment of presents to Temne and other chiefs).

country as the Sierra Leone Government possesses; and even a successful invasion into the territory of a refractory ally would only have the effect of involving us in a train of disputes and hostilities, without after all ensuring an obedience which there are so many temptations to deny and facilities to escape from.

But if such be the case and those treaties are thus without utility for the attainment of their object, they must be prejudicial. The expences they occasion are not only incurred in vain, but what is of more importance cannot be so incurred without being repaid by secret disrespect for a Power which is thus supposed to allow itself to be baffled in its policy, or not to perceive that it is so.

Experience has shown them to be productive of other disadvantages. In so far as they are commercial, they disturb the natural course of trade which they are intended to improve. The merchants of Sierra Leone, for whose benefit they are devised, presuming upon the continuance and support which they promise them, neglect the ordinary arts of conciliation, and the ordinary respect for the customs and rights of the territories they trade in, which are practised and required in the case of foreign traders in other countries; and sometimes resort instead to acts of intemperance and insult—against the retaliation consequent upon which, they fatigue the Government with applications for redress, which cannot be given, and would of course be undeserved if it could.

It is the error at the same time of the merchants themselves that in their trade with the Chiefs they have found themselves so much as they have done of late years within their power. This has been occasioned by their narrow jealousies of one another. In the hope of gaining petty separate advantages they have fallen into the practice of granting to the native chiefs and headmen very large credits for their timber; and in their competition for that staple, instead of requiring the seller to bring it, as was formerly done, at least to the confines of the Colony, they consent to buy it where it grows, in many instances five, six, and seven miles from the banks of the Rivers.

It is thus rendered necessary that in their dealings with those parties they should observe greater prudence: but acting, as I state, imprudently they then feel the want of Government protection. And it is to be remarked that while demanding the fulfilment of the treaties to their own advantage, they totally omit to comply with the conditions which those same treaties impose on them of paying the rents and customs of their factories to this Government: for in this particular the 18th article of the Convention of Mabelly and of the previous Treaty of Lieut. Colonel Findlay has at all times proved a nugatory stipulation.[1]

In general cases therefore it appears to me, as in the particular

[1] See above, p. 255 and n.

instance it does to your Lordship, that the payment of presents to native chiefs, provided for by those treaties, is 'not productive of any adequate compensatory advantage'; but on the contrary is attended with loss and injury to the interests of the Government: the treaties themselves being ineffective and prejudicial. In the views upon which this opinion is formed I find myself supported by one of the ablest of my predecessors, the late Major Temple, by Lord Monteagle, and by Lord Bathurst;[1] all condemn the interference of Government in commercial relations subsisting with the jealous independent tribes of this part of Africa, as unrequired and impolitic: declaring their expenditure attending such interference to be a waste of the public resources; and recommending that the merchants should not be otherwise assisted than by being exhorted to that self-reliance in their professional undertakings which has heretofore succeeded in other parts of the world.

But concurring in these views I am nevertheless of opinion that if a short and general Treaty of amity could be negotiated with the *leading and most influential* chiefs, which should not only exclude the inadmissable clause of the last treaties relative to the surrender of fugitive slaves, but affirm that the right recognized by British law as belonging to every individual present in a British Colony, to dispose at will of his own person, it would under all existing circumstances be a measure adviseable to adopt. The question which respects these fugitives has now by the Mabelly Convention been so indiscreetly revived and agitated, that until this is done the Government will never be secure against the detention, as a measure of retaliation, of British subjects found by the Chiefs in their own territories: more especially as it is sufficiently known that the refusal of Government to send back their runaways is disapproved of by many of the Europeans of the Colony.

A Treaty of this description might further contain, in general terms, an undertaking on the part of the Chiefs to abstain from slave trade; and to treat with civility, and forbearance British Subjects trading in their territories, on the condition of their own traders meeting with a similar reception in Sierra Leone: but it would exclude all the further stipulations hitherto enacted for all alliance offensive and defensive between the contracting parties, and for authorising the intervention of the Governor in the contentions and domestic affairs of the Chiefs—stipulations which, if they were other-wise unobjectionable, are incompatible with certain instructions of Lord Glenelg . . . in which his Lordship expressly disapproves and interdicts the practice of furnishing munitions of war to the native

[1] Bathurst to Campbell, 25 November 1826, C.O. 268/26; Spring-Rice to Temple, 15 September 1834, C.O. 268/30; Temple to Spring-Rice, 14 June 1834, C.O. 267/123.

tribes, as by the 3d. article of both the last conventions is required under certain circumstances to be done.

I confess however I entertain but faint hopes of inducing the Chiefs to become parties to such an Agreement. The formal renunciation of all right to claim the surrender of their fugitive people is scarcely I fear, to be expected from them; and their knowledge of the sympathy with them, in their view of the question, which exists in the Colony is of course not likely to render them more disposed to it.

As an inducement towards gaining their concurrence it ought to be made a condition of obtaining it that all parties to the last Treaty shall receive, up to the date of the new compact, payment of those arrears of presents under the Mabelly Convention which have been withheld since June 1837; and of the annual amount of which I do myself the honor to transmit a statement herewith.[1] . . .

12

LORD JOHN RUSSELL TO GOVERNOR R. DOHERTY: CONTENT OF TREATIES, 23 JULY 1840[2]

SIR,

I have had under my consideration your despatch No. 60 of the 10th of October last with the papers therein enclosed in explanation of the obstacles which had been represented to you from various quarters as continuing to be opposed to the prosecution of lawful commerce in the different rivers which discharge themselves into the Atlantic on that part of the Coast of Africa which lies between Sierra Leone and the Gambia.

It is a subject which has engaged the serious attention of H.M.'s Government.

You are aware of the objections which the Lords Commrs. of the Admiralty entertain against the habitual employment of H.M.'s. Naval forces in those unhealthy rivers; and it is impossible, therefore, for me to hold out the expectation that the trade of H.M.'s Subjects there, can be secured against the occasional outrages of petty refractory Chiefs in every isolated quarter to which the enterprise of individual traders may carry them.

It appears highly probable indeed that excesses of that nature can only effectually be restrained by the influence and agency of the more powerful Chiefs, whose interest it should be to watch over the preservation of good order and tranquillity in those Rivers.

---

[1] Encl. 'Statement of Customs and Presents', amounting to 3,060 'bars' (£382. 10s.).
[2] C.O. 268/35 ff. 338–42.

The accompanying reports which I have received from the Board of Admiralty of Lt. H. W. Hill's proceedings in the River Nunez Septr. last, shew how much may be accomplished by judicious intervention with influential Chiefs and I very earnestly recommend to your attention that Officer's proceedings as well as his suggestions as to the advantage of entering into communication with the Alimamy of Teembo.[1]

It is in furtherance of these views that I transmit to you herewith the draft of an agreement which H.M.'s Govt. are desirous should be proposed to all Native Chiefs in the more immediate vicinity of Sierra Leone, and especially to those, who, like the Alimamy of Teembo, command the paths or communications with the interior of Africa.[2]

I should see no objection to your appending to those agreements such stipulations as may be necessary for fixing the duties, whether of Anchorage, or of Customs, to be paid by our Merchants, upon the principle of the arrangement which Lt. Hill concluded with King Saarah of Kythandy, in the River Nunez, provided that such stipulations shall have received the assent of the Merchants. But you will understand that no other stipulations are to be introduced into any of these agreements which should contain provisions contrary to the principle of the Navigation Act, and that every agreement is to be held subject to the ratification of H.M.'s. Govt.

I am averse from sanctioning stipulations for the payment of presents of fees in money or goods. If any stipulation of that nature should be considered absolutely necessary, or be insisted on as a sine qua non, in consideration of some important advantage to be conceded by a Chief, the payment to be promised must be of very limited extent and expressly reserved for H.M.'s ratification. . . .

13

TREATY WITH TEMNE AND LOKO CHIEFS, 13 JANUARY 1841[3]

. . . 13. THE Queen of England gives presents from a fund for the Chiefs. Bey Cobolo, King of Marampa 100 Bars. Bey Summerah King of Summerah 100. Bey Finti King of Mendi 100. Alikarlie

[1] Admiralty to C.O., 2 November 1839, C.O. 267/155.
[2] Encl. 'Draft of Agreement Proposed to be entered into with African Chiefs'. The terms were similar to the draft for the Niger Commissioners: see above, p. 150.
[3] C.O. 267/163. Encl. in Jeremie to Russell, 20 January 1841. The rest of the terms of the treaty were based on Russell's model agreement. All former treaties were declared void. As explained by Jeremie to Russell, 4 March 1841, in a long history of relations between the colony and Port Loko, the treaty was occasioned by the need to settle a succession dispute for the title of *Alikali* between the Temne and Susu. With some pressure from Jeremie they elected a son of *Alikali* Moriba (who had expelled the Susu from Port Loko). Jeremie did not take part in the installation ceremony, as Turner had done.

BP

Chief of P. Locco 600. Chief of Bumbelly 50. Pa Roonier, Chief of Mabelly 100. Massa Packey, King of Mabelly 50. Alimamy Cabba, Chief of Rokelle 100. Tom Bendo, Chief of Rokon 50. Mahamadu Bundoo, Chief of Faradugu and Mahara 100. Alikarlie Sa Maura, Chief of Sanda 50. Bokaree Susi, Chief of Tambacca 50. Bey Camma, King of Koolifa 50. Bey Woosee King of Simba 50. Alimamy Dalla Mahommadu, 450 Dollars. Bey Kroo, King of Mabang 100 bars. Bey Gola, King of Massimerah 50. Kino Bah Yotte Chief of Rokelle 50. Fenda Moodu, Chief of Yannie 80. Bey Foki 200. Namina Lahi 300. Brimah Cauleno 100. Mahomadu Alikarlie 100. Saulagay Byan 100. Saulagay Yemi Collo 50. Saulagay Fa Foulah 50. Ansumana Dabo 150. Ali Bundo 250. Mahomadu Sancong 100. Brimah Luke 100. Booboo Sancory 50. Saulagay Malalay 100. Nentigay Falimah Mahomadoo 100. Amarah Saule 50. Lamina Bengalie 50. A. Damma Lahay 50. All annually.

The Queen of England further agrees, that no custom or duty whatever shall be taken on the Boats or goods of the Timmanee people at Freetown or in any other port or Harbour of the Colony of Sierra Leone, but that they shall be placed on the same footing in every respect as the boats and goods of the colony. And still more fully to encourage innocent and useful Trade among the Timmanees she consents to pay to the Chief of the Timmanees for himself and the remaining Chiefs, one pound on every one hundred pounds in value of all the goods imported into the Colony of Sierra Leone, which now pays three pounds for every one hundred pounds to the use of the Colony, or such a percentage on the said goods, as would on an average of the last three years produce one thousand pounds a year which sum per Cent shall not (when ascertained by the Collector of Customs) hereafter be named; *deducting from this for the payment* the amount of the Sums stipulated to be paid to each Chief by the present article. . . .

14

LIEUT.-GOVERNOR W. FERGUSSON TO WILLIAM COOPER THOMSON: MISSION TO FUTA JALLON, 18 DECEMBER 1841[1]

You are to regard the object of your mission to Teembo as being mainly of a commercial nature.

These primary points of enquiry are suggested for your attention

[1] C.O. 267/166. *W. C. Thomson*, a member of the C.M.S. Temne Mission, was financed by a subscription of £242 from local traders. Leaving for the Futa Jallon at the end of 1841, he successfully renewed relations with the *Almamy* of Timbo. For dispatches describing the internal politics of Timbo, C.O. 267/176; and *Journal of the Royal Geographical Society*, xvi (1846).

as being matters on which it is desirable to obtain correct information.

First to ascertain which of the three Routes between this Colony and Teembo is the best and most eligible for the general course of trade; vizt. The route by the Melacourie, that by the Kambia in the River Scarcies or that by Port Loko in the Sierra Leone River; having reference not only to the mere length of route, and to the convenience of land and water carriage, but also to the liability to obstructions on the path, such as may arise from the exactions of petty chiefs &c.; connected with this is the consideration of the comparative facilities and convenience afforded on each route, by having to deal with one Chief of an extensive country, rather than the numerous petty princes and the extent of protection to trade which may be reasonably expected on each line.

Secondly, The principal causes of occasional obstructions in the path, and the means most advisable for their permanent removal.

Thirdly, To ascertain whether, and by what means the existing commercial intercourse betwixt this Colony, and the Foulah and adjacent countries is susceptible of being increased and extended. For these purposes it has been decided that you should proceed to Teembo by way of Melacourie and (unless unforseen circumstances should appear to you to render a change of purpose necessary) that you should return by way of Port Loko.

You will be furnished with boats and Canoes for the conveyance of yourself and party to the town of Melacourie, at the head of the Melacourie River, from which place your land journey will commence, and in order to conciliate the good-will, favour, and protection of Alifa Sanko, the Chief of Melacourie or in his absence of Mohamadoo Kellatugy, you will be furnished with a letter and a suitable present to be delivered to whichsoever of those persons you may find in charge at Melacourie; you will also be accompanied to that place by a brother of our neighbour and friend Amarah Mohamadoo as a special messenger charged with a letter to Alifa Sanko, commending you and the object of your mission to his protection and good offices.

From all that can be learned of the Chief of Melacourie, it appears that his influence and power are such as to enable him to afford you a safe conduct on your journey, as far as Tambacca, it will therefore be with you an object of much importance to conciliate his favor and good will.

Tambacca is represented to be the great thoroughfare through which persons necessarily pass in travelling betwixt the Coast and the Foulah Country, converging lines from various parts of the Coast meet at that town. Bokoro Soory its Chief is rich and influential, and the advantages of its position give him great power either in granting or withholding facilities to the transit of merchandize or strangers through his territories.

It may be right to apprize you that Bokoro Soory was a party to the Treaty which the late Governor Campbell entered into with the assembled Timmaney Chiefs at Mabelly in 1837, by that Treaty it was stipulated that an annual sum of fifty bars should be paid him; This Treaty was not confirmed by Her Majesty's Government and in consequence none of the stipulated payments were made.

It is doubtful whether the non-ratification of the Treaty was ever communicated to Bokoro Soory, and it is therefore probable that he labours under an impression adverse to the British Character for good faith and plain-dealing.

You are therefore fully to explain this matter to him, and further to acquaint him that another Treaty was in the early part of this year entered into at Port Loko betwixt the Governors of this Colony and the assembled Timmany Chiefs, whereby the Stipulations of the former Treaty as regards annual payments, were renewed, and in token of the scrupulous good-faith, which characterizes the Acts of the British Government a sum equal to the amount of three annual payments, was then paid to all the Chiefs, who had been parties to the Treaty of 1837, Bokoro Soory not having been represented at that meeting 150 bars were paid on his account into the hands of Alimanee Dalla Mohamadoo.

This explanation, together with the handsome present with which you are provided for him, and the assurances of the regular payment to him or his agent duly accredited of 50 bars, at Port Loko in February of each year, will, it is hoped remove any impression which he may have conceived, of a nature injurious to the character of the Government of this Colony for good faith and plain dealing.

Although it is expected that you will not make any unnecessary delay at any place during your journey, yet the importance of attaching a person of such influence as Bokoro Soory, to our interests and to our views might justify your remaining a few days at Tambacca.

It may be proper whilst at that place to ascertain whether it would be requisite for you to send on a messenger to Teembo to apprize the Alimamee of your coming, in order that he might send a party of his own people to ensure a safe conduct to yourself and your party, during the remainder of your journey, should the State of the Country in that neighbourhood appear to render such a measure necessary or expedient.

Having arrived at Teembo you will deliver to the Alimamee the letter and present intended for him, observing such formalities on the occasion as may be understood to imply dignity and importance in the giver and in the gift.

Your own discretion and good sense will be the best guides in your intercourse with the Alimamee and keeping constantly and clearly

before you the great objects of your mission, I confidently hope that
your management of the trust reposed in you, will be such as to
justify the Subscribers in their selection, and to reflect much credit
on yourself. . . .

[He is to denounce the slave trade, collect geographical information,
and record 'moral habits', religious beliefs, and systems of justice and
government.]

15

LORD STANLEY TO GOVERNOR G. MACDONALD: THE TEMNE TREATY, 10 JUNE 1842[1]

SIR,
H.M's. Govt. have had under their consideration the Treaty wh.
was concluded on the 13th of Feby 1841[2] by your predecessor the
late Govr. Sir John Jeremie with the Chiefs of the Timmanees, and
I have now to acquaint you that the Queen has been pleased to confirm & ratify the said Convention. Subject to the late Gov's. explanation of the thirteenth Article of that compact, and subject also to the
understanding that the article as now worded is not to give the
Timmanees a duty upon all goods imported into Sierra Leone from
whatever quarter coming. The attention was to raise an additional
duty of one per cent on all goods now paying the duty of three per
cent as by law established for the purpose of making up a revenue
as nearly as possible equivalent to five per cent upon such goods as
were, on the average, imported into the Timmanee Country. An
alternative was taken of paying a sum of £1000 a year, deducting the
value of the presents stipulated to be paid to the individual Chiefs.
The conditions of the Treaty obviously imply, & there ought to be a
clear understanding on that head, that no other duties be levied on
British goods imported into the Timmanee Country from Sierra
Leone. The reasons against allowing the Timmanee Chiefs to levy
five per cent on their part are very strong; and if the condition be
obtained of freeing our goods from any other duty, it is much preferable that, your Govt. & not they shd. be the Collectors; and in this
point of view whether the sum paid be an ad valorem duty or a
gross sum, it must in some way or other be reimbursed to the Colonial
funds. The mode proposed is an extra duty of one per cent upon all
imports of goods now chargeable with 3 pr. Cent & I see no very
strong objection to such an increase of duty with such an object.
Undoubtedly the arrangement is open to the objection that a burthen

---

[1] C.O. 268/38, ff. 177–82.　　　[2] See above, p. 261. *Sic* January 1841.

is laid upon the general trade of the Colony for the limited object of obtaining an exemption from duty in the Timmanee Country on such portion of the goods imported into Sierra Leone as might afterwards be sent to that Country. But it must be borne in mind that the circumstances of the case are of a very peculiar nature, and as the local authorities who have been called upon to consider the Subject, appear to be of opinion that the arrangement is advantageous to the interests of the Colony, it has not been deemed expedient to insist upon that objection to the thirteenth Article of the Treaty, the more especially as other articles allow of recourse being had to an alternative in case the arrangement to be adopted shd. be found, on experience not to be attended with the advantages anticipated from it. In the meantime it must be notified to the Timmanee Chiefs that H.M. Govt. clearly state that no other duty is to be levied on British goods in the Timmanee Country, and that in the contrary case, the payment stipulated by the Treaty will be immediately suspended.

16

GOVERNOR W. FERGUSSON TO LORD STANLEY: SHERBRO AND MELAKORI TREATIES, 18 JULY 1845[1]

MY LORD,

I have the honor herewith to enclose, for your Lordship's information, six copies of each of four Treaties which, on the part of Her Majesty's Government, I have entered into with certain Native Kings and Chiefs resident in the neighbourhood of this Colony— videlicet with 1st. Bey Sherbro King of the North Bulloms, and Tombo Booboo, his chief adviser; 2nd. Mori Lahai, Chief of Malagua; 3rd. Alimamee Ali, King of Fouricaria; 4th. Mori Moosa, Chief of Bareira.[2]

The circumstances under which I have been induced, somewhat hastily, to conclude those Treaties are detailed at length in a letter addressed to this Government by Mr Charles Heddle,[3] a merchant of this Colony, under date 7th May last.

[1] C.O. 267/187.

[2] Encl. treaties, 20 May 1845, with Be Sherbro, Mori Bokari, chief of Forekaria (Melakori), Mori Lahai, chief of Maligia (Melakori), *Almamy* Ali, chief of Forekaria, *Almamy* Mori Musa, chief of Bereire. They were promised 200 bars, 100, 300, 400, and 250 bars respectively, for the abolition of the slave trade and safeguarding British trade.

[3] Heddle to Macdonald, 7 May 1845, C.O. 267/187. *Charles Heddle*, Freetown trader, pioneered both the timber and groundnut trade in the neighbourhood of the colony. A French warship had visited the Melakori in 1845.

Mr Heddle has the merit of having originated and brought to its present flourishing and rising condition, the trade in Ground-nuts; the culture and supply of which are, as yet, almost exclusively confined to those countries with whose chiefs those treaties have been entered into.

The aggregate amount payable annually by this Government under those Treaties is, in Country language, 1,250 bars, equal to about £93–15–0.

The object contemplated in framing those Treaties is to secure to British Traders a free participation not only in the fruits of a new and promising trade, but in the commercial advantages directly and indirectly to be derived from intercourse with the Mandingo Country generally. A fair and unfettered competition for the enjoyment of those advantages was all that our merchants desired or expected. Those reasonable expectations were, however, threatened by the French, and that by a mode to which they appear, on this coast, to have resorted with singular success, on more than one occasion—as adverted to in Mr Heddle's letter. It therefore became so much the more necessary that the conduct of this Government should, to counteract this threatened evil, be at once prompt and decided. With this in view, I laid the matter before the Board of Council, by whom it was unanimously resolved that a mission should be forthwith despatched to the Chiefs of Mellicoorie and Fouricaria, to make such arrangements with them by Treaty, as might secure to British merchants the right to trade in those districts, notwithstanding any ulterior arrangements which they might enter into with the French. . . .

17

LORD STANLEY TO GOVERNOR W. FERGUSSON: SHERBRO AND MELAKORI TREATIES, 6 DECEMBER 1845[1]

[He has received the treaties made with the chiefs of Melakori.]

. . . . THE Queen is graciously pleased to ratify these General Treaties subject to the amendment of one of the Articles which is repeated in each Treaty.

The Article to which I allude is that which stipulates that the Canoes & Boats of the Several Chiefs & the produce of their Territories are to be placed on the same footing as the Boats Canoes & produce of the Colony of Sierra Leone.

With every desire to grant to the Native Chiefs the practical

[1] C.O. 268/41, ff. 27–31.

advantages which these stipulations seem calculated to secure to them, it should be impossible for Her Majesty in the present state of the Law of Navigation & with reference to our Treaties with European Powers to ratify them in the form in which they have been drawn.

The Canoes & Boats of the Natives are no doubt intended to be used for the conveyance of the produce of their respective Territories from the place of production to Sierra Leone and for traffic of this description it is quite proper to place them on an equal footing with the Canoes & Boats of the Colony, but the Causes of the Colony may also bring the produce of the Territory of one Chief from the Dominions of another, as for instance the produce of Foricaryah from Malagua which the canoes of the Natives could not do since the Navigation Act (8 & 9 Vict. C 88 S 11) prohibits the importation of Goods into any British Possession in Asia Africa or America in any Foreign Ships unless they are the Ships of the Country of which the Goods are the produce & from which the Goods are imported. A similar difficulty also arises as to intercourse with other British Possessions which by the 10th Section of the Act is confined to British Vessels.

These objections might probably be of no importance were these treaties alone to be considered, as the cases would not be likely to arise; but if a general stipulation of this kind were agreed to, other Nations with whom we have Treaties of reciprocity would be entitled to claim similar privileges for themselves & they would most assuredly use them for purposes not permitted by the Navigation Law.

A similar remark may be made on the privileges conceded to the African Produce. If all or any duties & restrictions are taken off any particular article of African Produce in the Colony, a number of Natives will be entitled to claim the same advantage for their own produce of the same kind: if they are taken off African Produce generally, these Natives will claim that all duties on their produce generally shall be taken off.

In order therefore to avoid these difficulties and at the same time to keep faith with the Chiefs by giving them the practical advantages which have been promised them, the privileges to Boats & Canoes should be granted in words placing them on the footing of Colonial Boats & Canoes only 'whilst trading between the aforesaid Colony & the Territories of the aforesaid Chief in Articles the produce of those Territories': and in lieu of the stipulations with respect to produce should be introduced a stipulation reciting the principal productions of the Country in question & providing that those productions should be admitted into the Colony duty free. I have therefore to instruct you to obtain the concurrence of the Chiefs to these alterations in the Treaties and I have to convey to you the necessary sanction to provide for the payment from the Colonial Revenues of the value of the Articles to be annually presented to the Native Chiefs with whom the several Treaties have been entered into.

18

EARL GREY TO GOVERNOR N. W MACDONALD: SUSU AND BAGA TREATIES, 28 JUNE 1851[1]

SIR,

I have received your dispatch No. 70 of the 6th April transmitting Treaties which you had concluded with Tougoh, King of the Upper Nunez & his Chiefs, and with Lamina Towle the Sovereign of the lower Nunez & his Chiefs.

I entirely approve of the terms in which these Treaties have been framed & I have much pleasure in signifying to you Her Majesty's Ratification of them, & in acquainting you that it is intended shortly to appoint a Consular Agent to reside at the River Nunez.

As you propose to conclude similar Treaties with the King of the Pongas & of the Bramiah River I shall postpone for the present the steps which will be necessary for extending British Jurisdiction over British Subjects resorting to the Countries with which Treaties have been concluded; but unless you see an early prospect of entering into Treaties with the Chiefs of the Pongas & the Bramiah, it will not be advisable to delay the measure with respect to the other Chiefs, and I have therefore to request that you will inform me by the earliest opportunity whether you are likely to be able to conclude Treaties with those Chiefs within a reasonable period of time.

[1] C.O. 267/225. These were the first treaties containing a clause ceding to the Crown jurisdiction over British subjects outside Sierra Leone. See below, pp. 539, 547. *Consul Augustus Hanson* was appointed to the Sherbro in 1853 with a commission extending north to the Nunez.

19

GOVERNOR N. W. MACDONALD TO SIR JOHN PACKINGTON: BULOM TREATY, 28 AUGUST 1852[1]

[Forwarding a treaty with Nain Sugo (Be Sherbro), King of the Kafu Buloms.]

. . . This Treaty is similar in every respect to those which I have already concluded with other Native Chiefs in the neighbourhood of this Colony, and forwarded to England for the confirmation of Her Majesty, with the following exceptions.

3. Clause 14, which promises for the surrender of criminals offending against the Laws of England within the Territory of the King of the Kaffee Bulloms, has been worded, as you will perceive, in conformity with your directions on this Head contained in your Despatch No 1 of the 28th February last.

4. Clause 18, is entirely new, and stipulates for the payment, out of the annual Stipend or Customs to be paid to the Chief, of the expenses which the Local Government, or other parties, may be put to, in consequence of any of the Stipulations of the Treaty being infringed, disregarded, or broken, either by the Chief himself, or by any of his Headmen or People.

5. I deemed it prudent and necessary to insert such a provision in this Treaty, and, if approved will do so in all future ones, in order to its acting as a check upon the lawless dispositions of the Natives, by making their Chief feel that he was held responsible, in a pecuniary point of view, for whatever expense the misdeeds of his Subjects might entail on the Local Government, or upon others subjected to their molestation; and in order also, that the Local Government should have the right, confirmed to it by Treaty, to make deduction from the Chief's Stipend, in order to meet such demands; and I have no doubt whatever of this Clause operating very beneficially, by being the means of putting a stop to the constant hinderances and annoyances to which our Traders are subjected, in consequence of the jealousy and cupidity of the Natives amongst whom they travel or reside for the purposes of legitimate Commerce.

6. Clause 19 is also new, and has reference, as will be seen, to a cession of the waterside of the Territory of the King of the Kaffee Bulloms, the opposite shore of the Sierra Leone River, made to me for Her Majesty in 1847,[2] by the then Bey Sherbro; and I have

[1] C.O. 267/229. Encl. treaty, 26 August 1852, approved, Barrow to Kennedy (draft), 29 November 1852. *Sir John Packington* was Colonial Secretary, February 1852–December 1854.
[2] *Sic*, 1846. For this cession, see below, p. 420.

inserted this clause in the accompanying Treaty in order that the Cession in question should be ratified by the present Bey Sherbro and his Chiefs and Headmen, and so prevent the possibility of any doubt or misconception respecting it in future. . . . .

20

GOVERNOR SIR ARTHUR KENNEDY TO SIR JOHN PACKINGTON: STIPENDS, 21 DECEMBER 1852[1]

SIR,

A system, with which you must be conversant, of giving presents and paying annual Stipends to Native Chiefs in Treaty with this Government and Great Britain, has existed since the foundation of this Colony.

2. Without commenting or discussing the principle involved in this system, I am of opinion that there is much to demoralize and lower the character of this Government in the present mode of paying these Stipends or presents. I will therefore shortly state the particulars for your information.

3. At a period when it was considered desirable to conciliate (or attain an object in view) by means of presents to Native Chiefs, and when money would have been of little use to them, a system of making presents in kind was established. It became, therefore, necessary to adopt some standard which the natives could understand; and instead of giving a certain sum of money, so many 'Bars' of Cotton Goods, or Rum, Tobacco &c were given in lieu thereof.

4. The 'Bar' of goods, at the time many of those Treaties were entered into, was equivalent to 2/6. A piece of Blue Baft for instance was reckoned as 10 Bars or equal to 25 shillings. This piece of Blue Baft probably cost 18 shillings in England. A piece of the like, but far inferior material, is still reckoned to these Chiefs in payment of their stipend at 10 Bars, though its first cost, or real value does not exceed 7s/9d in like manner with other goods. This fact is now as well and fully known to the native Chiefs, as to ourselves; and the results may be inferred.

5. The details of the established mode of paying these stipends or presents is as follows. The Governor orders payment of so many Bars; The Colonial Secretary invites tenders for the supply of these Bars or Goods, and then orders them from the Dealer or Trader who offers to supply them at the lowest rate, and the Recipient then

---

[1] C.O. 267/229. This policy was approved by the Treasury and by Newcastle to Kennedy, 25 February 1853, C.O. 268/45, ff. 102.

receives the goods at the hands of the Trader. The account is furnished to the Colonial Secretary, containing a certificate from two other Traders that the price charged is fair and reasonable. This account, when approved and signed by the Governor, goes forward as the Voucher for the Expenditure—"B" and "C" who certify the reasonable charge of 'A'. one day, probably have occasion to call on 'A' to perform the like office for them on the day following.

6. Under this, in my opinion, most faulty arrangement, proceed the following results. 1st When the Government intend to give a number of Bars of goods equal to £10, the recipient generally receives an amount and quality of goods, which, if re-sold (as they frequently are) would not realize £5. Thus a fraud is committed upon donor and receiver. 2nd. A most inferior quality of goods is supplied, thereby bringing our manufactured goods into disrepute, as I believe a most inferior article is imported for this sole purpose. 3d. The Governor and the Colonial Secretary know that a fraud is committed; and the native Chief goes away with the belief that the Government is dishonest, and devoid of principle as himself.

7. Those best acquainted with the African character know that a breach of faith, truth or honesty, in dealing with them, is an irretrievable step; and, I believe, to the system I am describing may partly be traced what I believe to be the serious decline, within a few years, of the moral influence exercised over native and neighbouring Chiefs by this Government. To obtain, or retain the friendship, obedience or respect of the African, he must be dealt with fairly, honestly and truthfully on the one hand, but with unflinching firmness and decision on the other.

8. Having submitted this outline of the system as it exists, the suggestion of a remedy will naturally be expected of me; and it appears to me that there is but one course to recommend namely that the system of giving goods should be discontinued, and the recipient paid in money by the Colonial Secretary in the presence of the Governor, who should be required to certify the payment.

9. By the accompanying Return it will appear that there are 59 Chiefs and Kings in receipt of annual stipend, the total amount of which is 10,280 Bars, which valued at the former Cost of 2/6 per Bar would amount to £1285 Sterling, being nearly one fourth of the present Revenue of the Colony.

10. I would not, however, pay them in money at this rate; but I would ascertain the money value of the Bar, say between 1810 and 1820, between 1820 and 1830, 1830 and 1840, 1840 and 1850, and pay them at the respective rates according to the date of the Treaty; or fix a certain sum, as an equivalent to their stipend, in goods, and allow them to make their election, which they would receive; and thus carry out the reform I propose without additional expense to the

Colony. Having made enquiry from those best informed on the subject, and well qualified to offer an opinion, I entertain no doubt that this arrangement would be received as a very great boon by all those in treaty with us.

11. It might be objected that the Colonial Money, and not goods, would be, under this arrangement, taken from the Colony, and thereby injure Trade. I would attach no weight to this objection. I believe, on the contrary, that this being the only market the recipient could go to, an increased and wholesome stimulus would be given to trade generally, instead of leaving the local Government open to the suspicion of jobbing for the aggrandizement of one or two individuals.

12. While on this subject I feel called upon to remark that individual Chiefs, comparatively without importance or influence, have been put on and taken off the List of Stipendiaries on the Colonial Funds, without any sufficient authority that I can arrive at.

13. A great majority of the Treaties guaranteeing these Stipends should not, in my opinion be renewed on the death of any Chief without the most mature consideration and distinct authority from the Right Honorable, the Secretary of State for the Colonies; the objects for which they were framed having, in some instances so altered, as to render them unnecessary.

21

GOVERNOR SIR ARTHUR KENNEDY TO THE DUKE OF NEWCASTLE: PORT LOKO TITLE SUCCESSION, 9 MAY 1853[1]

. . . Shortly after I assumed the Government of this Colony, the Alikarli or Chief of Port Lokkoh died. On the receipt of this intelligence I visited the Chiefs and people to proceed with all convenient speed to elect a Chief, as successor.

2. From their dilatory habits and the difficulty of ascertaining the public feeling over a large tract of Country and the intrigues of the numerous Aspirants to the Office, the Alikarli-ship remained unfilled on the 28th of April.

3. Finding great difficulty and embarrassment in treating with a Country without a recognised Chief, and apprehending a civil war among the many Chiefs who were candidates for vacant office, I decided upon sending up Messrs. Dillet and McCormack on a special mission to the Town of Port Lokkoh.[2] The former of these gentlemen is a Writer of some standing in the Colonial Secretary's Office, and

---

[1] C.O. 267/232. The Susu candidate was excluded in favour of a son (Mahomadu) of Fatima Brima, supported by the Temne.

[2] Encl. McCormack and Dillet to Kenndy, 4 and 7 May 1853: ibid

the latter an old merchant in the Colony and some time resident near Port Lokkoh.

4. I instructed these Gentlemen to call upon the people and various Chiefs in Treaty with us, to proceed to an election without delay, but in no way to give their support or influence to any candidate—observing a strict neutrality—and to point out to the assembled chiefs the confusion and ruin due to result from delay or want of unanimity amongst themselves.

5. The Trade and interests of this Colony render it a matter of the first importance to establish and retain an influence over the various Chiefs in the River and its neighbourhood, and I trust that Your Grace will approve the steps I have taken to this end. . . .

22

GOVERNOR S. J. HILL TO HENRY LABOUCHERE: TEMNE TREATIES, 12 MARCH 1857[1]

. . . I HAVE the honor to inform you that I returned from the Rivers Porto Lokkoh and Ro Kelle on the 6th Instant having paid an official visit to Port Lokkoh and Mabelly where I held palavers with the Timmanee Chiefs.

2. My reasons for proceeding to those native towns were, in the first place to approve agreeably to the custom of the Chief selected by the majority as Arlikarlie of Port Lokkoh, to have a new treaty[2] signed by the existing Chiefs many of those on the old treaty having died, to open the Timber Trade in the Ropet Creek and to put an end to the feuds between some of the Chiefs which threatened intestine war and injured the trade of British Merchants in those Rivers.

3. After some trouble I induced the Chiefs hostile to the Alikarlie of Port Lokkoh to shake hands with him and acknowledge his authority. The new Treaty was signed by all, and the Ropita Creek or branch of the Ro Kelle River reported to be full of good timber is now open to the Merchant Traders of this Colony.

4. I was most anxious to have a new Treaty with those Chiefs as the old one which Sir John Jeremie had signed contained a clause giving one per cent on all our Colonial Imports which could never be fulfilled in as much as it was beyond the resources of the Colony to meet the same, and the Chiefs themselves never having claimed it

[1] C.O. 267/257. As in 1853, the Temne candidate for the *Alikali* title was preferred to the Susu.

[2] Treaty, 27 February 1857, encl. in Hill to Labourchere, 18 March 1847, ibid. The Colonial Office objected to payments in 'bars' and did not confirm the treaty: Labourchere to Hill, 18 April 1857: C.O. 268/47, ff. 148–50.

seems to imply that there was some doubt respecting the matter, nevertheless to prevent any evil disposed person hereafter making it a grievance and seeking to embarrass the funds of the Government I thought it best to set the matter at rest by revoking the old Treaty altogether.

23

GOVERNOR S. J. HILL TO HENRY LABOUCHERE: STIPENDS, 14 MAY 1857[1]

. . . 2. IN reply I beg to explain that although bars are nominally introduced as more comprehensible to the Chiefs, yet since the receipt of the Secretary of State's despatch No. 19 of the 25th February 1853 all payments of stipends have been made in cash, each bar being valued at one shilling its present worth, and thereby reducing by three fifths the amount of stipends formerly paid, twelve pence paying what previously required thirty pence worth of goods to liquidate and leaving the Chiefs perfectly satisfied.

3. I also beg leave to point out that the Timmanee people are on a very different footing to any other natives trading to this Colony. They were the original owners of the soil of Sierra Leone, are our next neighbours, and all the merchandise British and Foreign sent into their country pays duties and increases the revenue of the Colony, added to which it is of the greatest consequence to set at rest the claim that might be made on this Government of one per cent on all Imports: which appears in the old Treaty made by Sir John Jeremie and approved of, a demand that could not possibly be met without the assistance of the Mother Country.

4. I assure you I was most particular in admitting on the new treaty only those Chiefs whose position warranted a belief in their influence and good will to protect British Traders and their property, and live at peace with their neighbours, and the small amount of additional salaries will not affect the resources of this colony. . . .

[1] C.O. 267/257. Hill's treaty was finally approved in Labouchere to Hill, 23 July 1857: C.O. 268/47, ff. 166.

24

GOVERNOR S. J. HILL TO SIR EDWARD BULWER-LYTTON: SUSU-TEMNE WAR, 15 MARCH 1859[1]

. . . I HAVE the honor to transmit statements received from three Liberated Africans Subjects of the Queen who were residing and trading at Port Lokkoh when that town was fired and attacked by the Soosoos.

2. I regret to remark that Dalla Moodoo a Chief of Bullom is said to have aided in this act of aggression, and although he denies all knowledge of the proceedings at Port Lockoh, I cannot acquit him of blame, as I think if not actually a participator in the burning of the town, he must have been aware of the intentions of 'Momo Sancho' and the war party, by whom it was surprised, a large amount of British property destroyed, and subjects of the Queen maltreated, and he should have warned this Government of the intended hostile movement against Port Lockoh.

3. It would appear from the enclosed statements which I believe to be perfectly correct that the Soosoo Leaders expressed their hostile intentions relative to Sierra Leone, and I have not doubt if they are not checked in time an attempt will be made by them at no distant period to plunder the frontier Towns of this Colony and carry our people to the slave mart.

4. I have expressed to Dalla Moodoo in strong terms my disapproval of his conduct imputed to him, informing him that he must not look to this Government for any countenance in this war resulting from his own bad faith towards the Timmanees, and I have no intention of placing his name as I had proposed on the List of Chiefs receiving a stipend from the Local Government until I am perfectly satisfied that he is guiltless of any partisanship with 'Momo Sancho' and the Soosoos.

5. I have to state that the Timmanees in retaliation have succeeded in destroying 'Momo Sancho's' Towns, and are now on the frontier of the Territory occupied by 'Dalla Moodoo' having already taken one of his towns, and I have no doubt they will persevere in endeavouring to drive him out of the Country as they are much exasperated at the burning of their Chief Town Port Lokkoh.

[1] C.O. 267/263. Hill had carried on a campaign against the Susu in the Scarcies, ending in a fruitless expedition against Kambia in 1858 and gradual involvement in the Susu-Temne war.

25

ACTING GOVERNOR T. H. SMITH TO THE DUKE OF NEWCASTLE: SUSU-TEMNE WAR, 23 AUGUST 1861[1]

My Lord Duke,

1. I have the honor to transmit for your approval copies of Treaties[2] between this Government and Alimamy Sattan Lahai, King of Ro Wooloh in the Cassey Country and Bey Farama, King of Ma Buntie and Kambia in the Great Scarcies River.

2. I also forward a letter received from Mr. McCormack who was sent by His Excellency Colonel Hill at the request of Sattan Lahaia to endeavour to put an end to the war between Soosoo and Timmanee Tribes in the Great Scarcies River, that Chief having promised to restore Kambia, the cause of the contest, to Bey Farama the rightful King, if the Governor of Sierra Leone would send an officer to be present on the occasion.

3. It was of great importance to this Government that Kambia should be occupied by the Timmanee people, as it is one of the principal entrepôts for the Trade passing from the interior of the Country to this Colony, and since it was taken by treachery, war has never ceased between the Soosoos and Timmanees, in consequence of which the Trade in the Great Scarcies River has been completely destroyed, and our influence seriously weakened with the Natives of the interior.

4. I am happy to inform your Grace that several Gold Strangers and Natives have already passed through Kambia from the interior of the Country, and a considerable quantity of produce has been exported from that place to this Colony, and I hope the flourishing Trade once carried on in the Great Scarcies River will be restored as soon as sufficient time has elapsed to allow of the Tribes further inland being made acquainted with the fact that the roads are now open.

[1] C.O. 267/271. *Lieut.-Colonel Smith* was Acting Governor for only a few months in 1861. McCormack persuaded Sattan Lahai, Susu chief of Rowula, Upper Scarcies, to give up his claim to the trading centre of Kambia which was restored to Temne rule in the name of Bai Farama, chief of Koya.

[2] Encl. two treaties, 10 and 11 June 1861. These were approved in Newcastle to Hill, 23 October 1861, ibid.

26

GOVERNOR SIR ARTHUR KENNEDY TO LORD GRANVILLE: MISSION TO FALABA, 15 APRIL 1869[1]

My Lord,

1. I have the honor to enclose for your Lordship's information the copy of a letter from Mr. W. Winwood Reade dated from 'Falaba' the capital of the 'Soolima' Country.

2. I encouraged Mr. Reade to undertake this journey, with some Government aid, for the purpose of opening the Road to the 'Niger' in the 'Sangara' Country.

3. Mr. Reade is also assisted by some public spirited merchants. The opening of this 'route' for traffic would add immensely to the commercial resources of this settlement, and his visit to the various Chiefs, has already been sensibly felt in the increased trade; one Merchant alone having received no less than 5,000 Hides for exportation, all of which will be paid for in English goods. 'Falaba' is about 20 days journey inland through a fine country to the North West of Sierra Leone. The climate is reported good and salubrious; and the Rokelle River, is, with one or two interruptions, navigable by Canoes for a great portion of the distance.

4. I shall keep your Lordship informed when I hear further from Mr. Reade.

27

GOVERNOR SIR ARTHUR KENNEDY TO LORD GRANVILLE: SHERBRO STIPENDS, 7 MAY 1869[2]

My Lord,

1. I have the honor to transmit the copy of an Extract from the Minutes of the Legislative Council, which explains itself.

2. I regard the Settlement at Sherbro Island and the adjoining Territory as one of the most important and promising on the West Coast of Africa. It is easy of access for Steamers of all Classes, with quick anchorage and Smooth Water at all Seasons of the year.

[1] C.O. 267/300. Reade set out in January 1869 and was the second European to visit Falaba and the Solima after Major Laing. He returned after five months with a brother of the *Mansa* Solima as emissary and made a full report on the trade routes: C.O. 267/301. A second journey took him to the Niger at Bendugu at the end of 1869: C.O. 267/302.

[2] C.O. 267/300. The Legislative Council, 6 May 1869, agreed to set aside £700 for these stipends in the Sherbro which already absorbed £8,000 a year from the colonial budget. The Treasury approved in June 1869.

3. The exports in 1867 amounted to £115,289 which increased to £116,431 in 1868.

4. A glance at the Map will show that the Sherbro Settlement forms the focus where many important Rivers meet:—the Gal Tucker, Messam, Bagroo, Bala River, Jong River, Boom Kiltum &c.

5. These Rivers with their numerous tributaries reach far into the Interior of a rich and productive Country, yielding every description of African produce. They are ruled over by numerous native Kings and Chiefs, residing at various distances from each other, but all accessible by water.

6. The extent and profit of our Trade entirely depends upon our maintaining peaceable relations with them, and holding out inducements for their keeping the peace *inter se*. To achieve this by coercive measures would be neither politic or possible. It is only to be accomplished by making it clearly the interest of all concerned to maintain Peace, and keep the navigation of the Rivers open for all legitimate Traders.

7. With this in view, I have laid the proposition now under consideration before my Legislative Council; and Your Lordship will observe that it has been unanimously and cordially concurred in.

8. The highest Stipend given to any Chief would be £100 per annum, and several Headmen &c. as little as £10—a considerable sum however to men who have never owned 10s. in money: but who are capable of doing incalculable mischief if so inclined.

9. Your Lordship is aware that a similar system has obtained for many years in the neighbourhood of Sierra Leone; and such is its entire success that there is now for the first time in the history of the Settlement, universal peace around us. So great is the influence obtained at a small outlay in Stipends, that I can send a single Policeman hundreds of miles into the Interior, under the protection of the Subsidized Chiefs; and I have this year sent a Traveller Mr. Winwood Reade as far as 'Falaba', only 60 miles short of the 'Niger' without other guard or protection than that voluntarily accorded by the Kings and Chiefs in Treaty with us.

10. The Stipends awarded to the Chiefs in the Sherbro District would of course be conditional upon their entering into a Treaty of Peace with this Government and with each other.

11. The small outlay proposed will, I feel confident, be repaid tenfold by an increase of trade, and will be further counterbalanced by the withdrawal of the Troops from that Station. . . .

28

GOVERNOR SIR ARTHUR KENNEDY TO LORD GRANVILLE: MISSION TO FALABA, 23 JUNE 1869[1]

[Forwarding a report by Winwood Reade on his return from Falaba.]

. . . 6. THE maintenance of Peace among the distant and surrounding Tribes, is all-important to the Trade and prosperity of this Settlement; and with this object in view, I propose at the beginning of the next dry Season to organize an expedition to 'Timbo' an important Town due North of 'Falaba'. The Chief and Natives of Timbo are intelligent and comparatively civilized Mahomedans carrying on an extensive Trade to the Rivers North of Sierra Leone.

7. I feel assured that by establishing peace among those tribes, through whose territory the Road passes, that a great deal if not all the Trade now directed to the Northern Rivers 'Pongas' and 'Nunez' will flow to Sierra Leone.

8. The Ali-Kali of Port Lokoh and Sankelle from whom Mr. Reade derived such Valuable Assistance, are both Allies of this Government, and the Coronation of the former 8 or 9 months ago was attended by some of the Chief Officers of this Settlement whom I sent to represent me.

9. Your Lordship will of course understand that Mr Reade uses the word 'annex' figuratively and implies only that the Chiefs to whose territory he alludes will be bound to us by ties of friendship and interest.

29

E. KNATCHBULL-HUGHESSEN: MINUTE, STIPENDS, 3 OCTOBER 1872[2]

. . . As to the general question of stipends to native chiefs, the system (in the present uncivilised & undeveloped condition of the Native Tribes) appears to work well. Its increase will of course militate against the idea (entertained a few years ago) of the gradual abandonment of these settlements on the Coast of W. Africa, but to my mind this is rather a recommendation than otherwise. England has sown

[1] C.O. 267/301. Reade recommended that the stipend system be extended to the Limba and Solima of Falaba. The Colonial Office took no action on this report.

[2] C.O. 267/316. On Hennessy to Kimberley, 1 September 1872, encl. Edward Blyden 'Report of the Expedition to Falaba', January–March 1872. *E. H. Knatchbull-Hughessen* was Parliamentary Under-Secretary in the Colonial Office, 1871–4.

the seeds of civilisation and christianity upon these coasts, and whether for furtherance of these great objects, or for the mere development of the revenues of a Country evidently teeming with undeveloped wealth, her continued presence and action is most desirable in the interests of W. Africa & of the world.

C. GOLD COAST

Introductory Note

THE two main tasks of Company and Crown administrators on the Gold Coast were to keep the peace between the coastal states and Ashanti, and, as relations with the former grew more complex, to decide how far 'protection' entailed Protectorate. From 1807 till 1821 the Governor and Council at Cape Coast were little more than ineffectual spectators of the expansion of the Ashanti Confederacy. Governor Torrane and his successors had no power to prevent invasion of Fanti territory and no jurisdiction outside the forts; treaties made with the Ashanti in 1817 and 1820 were inconclusive and not approved. The Crown inherited this weak position in 1821 and financial obligations for the rent of the forts. Refusal to admit Ashanti claims to tribute from the coastal states resulted in a clash in which Governor MacCarthy lost his life in 1824, before the Ashanti were defeated at Dodowa in 1826. It was left to George Maclean, after the return of the forts to merchant administration in 1828, to negotiate the peace of 1831 which delimited Ashanti power north of the buffer states of Denkyera and Assin, in return for a financial bond, hostages, and rules for keeping open paths for trade. The union of Fanti allies created during the war gradually dissolved, leaving only a vague allegiance to the President and Council at Cape Coast; the old practice of paying stipends and rents was not resumed.

Establishment of Crown control under the Governor of Sierra Leone brought a series of muddled attempts to define more closely the notion of 'protection' over the Fanti, while restricting sovereignty to the forts. Under the Foreign Jurisdiction Act of 1843 and declarations made by Fanti chiefs in 1844, a system of adjudication in criminal cases was continued by Maclean as Judicial Assessor. After the separation of the Gold Coast from Sierra Leone in 1850, this jurisdiction was extended when the assessor became an officer of the Supreme Court. Fanti chiefs were subjected to punishment and deposition in 1848, 1858, and 1866, when the internal security demanded by the administration as a condition of protection was challenged in various ways. Again, after 1868, the Fanti Confederation, formed initially to check an alliance between the Elminas and Ashanti, was discredited as a seditious movement when it aspired to a written constitution under leaders of its own.

Throughout this period of increasing political tension on the coast, relations with Ashanti remained on the whole peaceful. The problem of fugitive slaves, however, received no satisfactory answer, after Lord Stanley laid down in 1844 that their surrender from British territory was illegal. This topic was not covered in the treaty of 1831; and after an Ashanti raid into Assin in 1853, no new treaty reaffirming or extending its clauses could be obtained. Ten years later a refusal to return Ashanti fugitives was followed by a brief invasion of the Fanti protectorate and illustrated a weakness in defence which brought about Parliamentary inquiry into the conduct of the war. The so-called 'truce' of 1866 settled nothing and after the accession of a new *Asantehene* in 1867, Ashanti policy towards the British changed.[1]

By the end of 1873, after an invasion of the Fanti States, Sir Garnet Wolseley had forced the Ashanti to retreat. Kumasi was sacked and the treaty of Fomena in February 1874 completed the defeat of one of the strongest forest states. Meanwhile, on the coast the powers of the administration were extended by agreements with the Akwapim and Krobo in 1872 and over the Anlo in 1874. The abolition of domestic slavery and the reorganization of the Protectorate set new limits to the independence and authority of the Fanti chiefs.

I

COLONEL G. TORRANE TO THE COMMITTEE OF MERCHANTS: ASHANTI INVASION, 20 JULY 1807 [2]

... The King[3] has promised to avoid all Towns under British Forts, provided the Inhabitants of those Towns are not found in Arms against him. I on my part have sent strict orders to Tantum and Winnebah on that Subject which orders I have the honor to send with the dispatch. I had it not in my power to conclude my treaty with the King. The Fantees collected in some force to Leeward of Cormantyne. The King went out to give them Battle, I witnessed the Action which was decisive in favor of the Ashantees, who (I am confident) must conquer wherever they go, they are both numerous and brave, the Beach for Miles is strewed with the Dead in heaps of Thousands. Their object of pursuit now is Accoom the Caboceer of Assecoomah who I have already mentioned as having at the breaking out of the War betrayed his Confidence which the Ashantees reposed in him & seized nearly one Thousand he is now with the Fantee

---

[1] See above, p. 36.

[2] W.O. 1/881. *George Torrane* who had been a clerk for the African Committee and member of the Council, 1790–2, was Governor of Cape Coast, 1804–7.

[3] *Asantehene* Osei Bonsu defeated the Fanti on the coast in 1807—the first extension of Ashanti power so far south—and attacked the British fort at Anomabu. Torrane handed over two chiefs of Assin who were the occasion for the war, but the Ashanti army remained on the coast till October 1807.

Army. If the King gets him the War I conclude will cease. The King is accompany'd by 12 Kings all Men of Power, but obliged to attend in person at his call with such a force as he shall see fit to demand.

The Ashantees fight both with Musquets and bows & arrows. It doubtless was then, the intention to place a large quantity of Gunpowder to the Walls of the Fort, and they had also a plan of cutting open the Gates. The orders were given and the Day appointed when my Messenger acquainting him of my taking Cheboo changed the face of affairs. I will not pretend to offer an opinion, as to what success might attend either of those attempts. I will observe only, the King values not the lives of a few Thousands, to carry any point in which he is determined. Their Bravery I have more than once in this dispatch highly extolled, 'tis not to be surpassed; they manifest a cool intrepidity you Gentlemen would look at with surprise and admiration. In all my negociations with the King, I had cause to remark, what I have not experienced on the Sea Coast—to wit the strictest regard to his word—in fact I look on King Zey, so he is called, to be a high Character, he is of middling stature, remarkably well built, and of a handsome, and open Countenance indeed all the principal Ashantees, seem half a century advanced in civilization; to these people on the Waterside. He is attended with many Moors, and every Ashantee Man, has a Gregory, or fetesh, which is a little square cloth, enclosing some written sentences of the Koran—some have many. In fact, the Moors seem to have spread over the whole Interior of Africa.

I have received a Message from the King, importing that as soon as the War shall be over, he will return and form his camp near Annamaboe, to the end that we may arrange all points for the future Welfare of the Country; and the regulation of the Trade, and here let me observe, that an intercourse securely opened with Ashantee, offers, prospects of the highest advantage, and the more so, as the Slave trade is at an end. The Ashantees have Ivory and Gold in great abundance, and the Fantees have ever thrown impediments in the Way, so as to prevent their intercourse with us, but it appears to hold out an Object of more National importance, and one if I can be the happy Instrument of bringing about I shall deem my Service in Africa, not altogether misapplied. I mean a thorough Knowledge of the source of the Niger, and a direct and safe way of going to Tomboctu, should any more adventurers engage in that research. The conversation I have had with the Moors gives the fullest confidence of Success, in such an undertaking, and the Confidence is not a little supported by the reflection of the influence, I have with the King of Ashantee, the probable increase thereof and the vast extent of country, over which he rules, and the Aid he can further give in such an enterprise. . . .

2

TREATY WITH ASHANTI, 7 SEPTEMBER 1817[1]

TREATY made and entered into by Thomas Edward Bowdich, Esquire, in the name of the Governor and Council at Cape Coast Castle on the Gold Coast of Africa, and on behalf of the British Government, with Sai Tootoo Quamina, King of Ashantee and its Dependencies, and Boitinnee Quama, King of Dwabin and its Dependencies.

1st. There shall be perpetual peace and harmony between the British subjects in this country and the subjects of the Kings of Ashantee and Dwabin.

2nd. The same shall exist between the subjects of the Kings of Ashantee and Dwabin, and all nations of Africa residing under the protection of the Company's Forts and Settlements on the Gold Coast, and, it is hereby agreed, that there are no palavers now existing, and that neither party has any claim upon the other.

3rd. The King of Ashantee guarantees the security of the people of Cape Coast from the hostilities threatened by the people of Elmina.

4th. In order to avert the horrors of war, it is agreed that in any case of aggression on the part of the natives under British protection, the Kings shall complain thereof to the Governor-in-Chief to obtain redress, and that they will in no instance resort to hostilities, even against the other towns of the Fantee territory, without endeavouring as much as possible to effect an amicable arrangement, affording the Governor the opportunity of propitiating it, as far as he may with discretion.

5th. The King of Ashantee agrees to permit a British officer to reside constantly at his capital, for the purpose of instituting and preserving a regular communication with the Governor-in-Chief at Cape Coast Castle.

6th. The Kings of Ashantee and Dwabin pledge themselves to countenance, promote and encourage the trade of their subjects with Cape Coast Castle and its dependencies to the extent of their power.

---

[1] T. E. Bowdich, *Mission from Cape Coast Castle to Ashantee* (London, 1819), pp. 143–5. The mission was led by the Commandant of Accra, Frederick James, together with Bowdich and William Hutchison, writers for the Company, and the surgeon Henry Tedlie. A slightly different version of the treaty is given in Joseph Dupuis, *Journal of a Residence in Ashantee* (London, 1824), Appendix II, which represents the copy left with the *Asantehene*. For a discussion of these discrepancies, see W. E. F. Ward, *A History of the Gold Coast*, 2nd ed. (London, 1952), pp. 160–1 and n.

7th. The Governors of the respective Forts shall at all times afford every protection in their power to the persons and property of the people of Ashantee and Dwabin who may resort to the water-side.

8th. The Governor-in-Chief reserves to himself the right of punishing any subject of Ashantee or Dwabin guilty of secondary offences, but in case of any crime of magnitude, he will send the offender to the Kings, to be dealt with according to the laws of his country.

9th. The Kings agree to commit their children to the care of the Governor-in-Chief, for education, at Cape Coast Castle, in full confidence of the good intentions of the British Government and of the benefits to be derived therefrom.

10th. The Kings promise to direct diligent inquiries to be made respecting the officers attached to the Mission of Major John Peddie and Captain Thomas Campbell; and to influence and oblige the neighbouring kingdoms and their tributaries, to befriend them as subjects of the British Government. . . .

3

SIMON COCK TO JOSEPH DUPUIS: MISSION TO KUMASI, 31 OCTOBER 1818[1]

SIR,

The Committee of the Company of Merchants trading to Africa have received a communication from The Right Honorable The Lords Commissioners of His Majesty's Treasury, importing that Their Lordships desire that the intercourse which has been opened with the King of Ashantee should be kept up, and the advantages which may be expected to arise from it promoted to the utmost; and that, with this view, His Royal Highness The Prince Regent has been pleased to appoint you, (your long residence at Mogadore, and acquaintance with the Moorish Language peculiarly qualifying you for the station) to be His Majesty's Consul at Cormasie the Capital of Ashantee. Their Lordships further direct the Committee to make you an allowance of £500 Sterling p. annum from the period of your arrival in Africa; and to pay for your passage to Cape Coast, and journey to Cormasie, furnishing you with an escort, and with such presents for the King as may be deemed most acceptable, not

---

[1] C.O. 2/11, ff. 17–23. S. Cock was secretary to the African Committee. Dupuis' difficulties with the Gold Coast merchants and Governor Hope Smith which delayed his mission to Kumasi are recounted in a 'Narrative of the Existing Differences between the King of Ashantee and the African Company or their Servants on the Gold coast', encl. in Dupuis to Bathurst, 16 January 1820: ibid.

excluding the value of £200,[1] and with such Instructions for your Government, as may be necessary for your own safety, and useful to you in the promotion of the objects of confirming the friendly disposition of the Natives of Ashantee, and obtaining correct information of the Kingdoms further Inland.

Their Lordships have also intimated their opinion, that besides yourself, there should be stationed at Cormasie, one Officer in the Service of the African Company, qualified to establish and conduct a School at that place, if the opportunity should be afforded; and also a Surgeon with two or three subordinate Officers, as the Committee may think necessary.

Conformably to Their Lordships' said Instructions I have now by the directions of the Committee to acquaint you, that the Vessel which they have chartered to take out their annual supply of Stores to Cape Coast Castle, is the Sarah, Capt. Corser, lying in the London Docks, which is intended to leave the River on the 15th of next month at the farthest. Capt. Corser will be instructed to receive you and your Baggage on board, and to afford you every accomodation.

With respect to the Presents for the King of Ashantee, I am directed by the Committee to acquaint you that they have authorized me to purchase such articles, to the amount limited, as you may deem the best suited for the purpose. . . .

The Committee will also instruct the Governor & Council at Cape Coast, to furnish you with the necessary escort to Cormasie. . . .

[He is to stay at Cape Coast for some time to learn 'the language', obtain information on the interior, learn the business of the Company of Merchants, and to co-operate with the Governor and Council.]

It appears therefore to the Committee to be desirable to impress upon the King, that His Britannic Majesty's Government consider the Treaties [of 1817] as sacred; and the better to give effect to the amicable relations subsisting between this Country and those Sovereigns, you are hereby authorized to signify to them, that provided they will find Labourers, they may depend upon receiving, free of other expense than of carriage from the Coast, an ample supply of Hatchets, Saws, Spades, Pick-Axes, and other Tools, for opening and repairing the roads to the Coast; which the Committee deem to be an object of the greatest importance in every point of view; but especially, as it may by furnishing profitable means of employment, induce those Kings to discontinue the practice of sacrificing their prisoners and others.

As the Governor & Council have supply of these articles, sent out by the Store Ships, we recommend you taking a few of each to

[1] Subsequently raised to £500.

Cormasie, in order that you may be the better enabled to explain yourself on this point.

One object most desirable to obtain, as it would essentially assist in the realization of the views of Government, might perhaps be a Grant from the King of Ashantee, of a District, distant about 25 Miles from the Coast, subject to a certain perpetual annual rent, with full liberty to clear and cultivate the same, and to erect Houses &c. Such a spot, judiciously chosen, might open an extensive field for the employment of the Youth educated at the Company's Schools, and be the beginning of a system which might eventually extend to the cultivation and civilization of the whole Coast. You will therefore keep this object constantly in view; and seize every favorable opportunity of impressing upon the mind of the King the signal advantages that would result to the Ashantees as a people, and the immense accession of riches & strength which would be acquired by the Sovereign from the Country being brought into such an improved state. It need hardly be observed to you that this is a matter which will require to be treated with the greatest delicacy; and that no opinion upon it should be ever hazarded, by any person attached to the Mission.

Whatever may at any time pass upon this subject you will, as soon as possible, communicate to the Governor and Council, and be very careful that your Despatches are entrusted to safe hands.

It does not occur to the Committee on the present occasion to add to the foregoing any particular instructions. The enclosed paper containing Queries on the Geography Statistics; Government; Political Institutions and Relations; Wars; Laws; General Appearance of the Inhabitants; Their Dispositions; Morals; Religion; Intellectual Capacity; Arts; Sciences; Manufactures; Education &c. &c. you will find of great assistance to you in the prosecution of your enquiries; And, as opportunities may offer of gaining assistance, in this object, from others, you have several Copies herewith, which you can distribute as such opportunities offer.

It must be almost superflous to point out to you that the most important object to attain, is, to establish mutual confidence, since upon this basis alone can mutual interest be raised. And with this view, it may be good policy to defer the prosecution of any plans for immediate profit, that may have a tendency to excite the suspicion or jealousy of the Natives. For though the promotion of our commercial relations with the interior, is undoubtedly a consideration of the first importance, yet in a Country with which we have had so little intercourse, *that* should be but a secondary object. Your particular care should be to satisfy the minds of the King and his Ministers, that our professions of friendship and good will are sincere, before you allow it to be understood, that the intention is, to pursue our enquiries, and and extend the Trade beyond the boundaries of his Dominions.

For the same reasons, all enquiries relative to the geographical situation of Ashantee, or the neighbouring Countries, or the internal Government should be cautiously avoided, both by yourself and those who may accompany you, since it will be difficult to make the Ashantees credit the true motives by which the Company are influenced; and it is most probable that an unfavorable construction would be put upon the views of persons who might manifest an eager curiosity upon those Subjects. Nevertheless, you must be sensible how necessary it is to get this information; and therefore you will carefully treasure up everything you can learn, without shewing that you attach any importance to the obtaining of it.

Your acquaintaince with the characters of the Moors or Arabs, obtained during your long residence in Barbary, renders any suggestions for your government with respect to them wholly unnecessary; further, than that it will be deserving of much consideration, how far it may be politic to place confidence in any of those who are resident a[t]Cormasie, by making use of them as Interpreters, or otherwise, as they must, both from their religious principles, and self interest, be rather disposed to prejudice, than to promote our interests. You may, however, find them to be less bigoted than self interested; and by prudent measures be able to turn their influence with the Government very much to the advantage of this Country.

The Duties of a British Consul at Cormasie, must necessarily be of a peculiar nature: He must, therefore, for a time, be wholly guided by the circumstances as they arise, bearing, however, always in mind, as the general Rule of his Conduct, his duty and allegiance to his Sovereign & Country; the promotion of the Christian Religion, and the interest of British Commerce.

In every case in which you may require advice and assistance, you may always rely upon the Governor & Council at Cape Coast, to the extent prescribed by their means; by the orders of Government; and by their sense of what is proper and just in cases upon which you may apply to them. . . .

4

TREATY WITH ASHANTI, 23 MARCH 1820[1]

TREATY made and entered into by Joseph Dupuis Esquire, his Britannic Majesty's Consul for the Kingdom of Ashantee in Africa, in the name and on behalf of the British Government, with Sai Tootoo Quamina, King of Ashantee and its dependencies.

[1] Dupuis, Appendix III; W. Walton Claridge, *A History of the Gold Coast and Ashanti*. 2 vols. (London, 1915), I, 322–4. The Governor and Council refused to ratify the treaty, particularly because of the 5th clause.

1st. The King of Ashantee agrees to receive and acknowledge Joseph Dupuis, Esquire, as his Majesty's Consul at Coomassy, to the full extent and meaning of his commission, and if at any time ill health should oblige the said Joseph Dupuis to leave this country the King will receive and acknowledge any gentleman that he may appoint to succeed him.

2nd. The King of Ashantee, having taken his sacred oath of allegiance and fidelity to the Crown of Great Britain, in the person of His Royal Highness the Prince Regent, makes known to all whom these presents shall come that he will, with all his power and influence, support, aid, and protect the British interests in this country, and that he will, if necessary, on all occasions march his armies to any part of the country where the interests of Great Britain may require their aid and assistance.

3rd. The claim recently made by the King of Ashantee, on the Governor of Cape Coast Castle, amounting to one six hundred ounces of gold, or £6,400, is hereby acknowledged to be relinquished; and it is agreed that there are now no differences or palavers existing between the King of Ashantee and the Governor, or between the King and any other of His Britannic Majesty's subjects, collectively or individually.

4th. The King of Ashantee agrees and binds himself to support and encourage the commerce of this country with Cape Coast and its dependencies by all the means in his power; and pledges himself not to allow any differences that may occur to interrupt the trade with the English merchants on the Coast.

5th. The King of Ashantee claims the Fantee territory as his dominions, which the Consul, on the part of the British Government, accedes to, in consideration and on the express condition that the King agrees to acknowledge the natives, residing under British protection, entitled to the benefit of British laws, and to be amenable to them only in case of any act of aggression of their part.

6th. After the final adjustment of the present claims upon the natives of Cape Coast, the King binds himself to submit all future complaints to the Consul only, and on no account whatever to make war with the natives, at any of the English Settlements, without first allowing the Consul an opportunity of settling such differences.

7th. The Consul, on the part of the British Government, guarantees all the protection in his power to the subjects of the King of Ashantee who may have any commerce with the British Settlements on the Coast.

8th. The Consul binds himself on the part of the British Government and the Governor and Council, to keep half the path that is at present made between Cape Coast and Ashantee well cleared, and the King of Ashantee agrees to keep the other half of the path constantly in good order, so that there shall always be a free and easy communication with the Ashantee dominions.

9th. It is expressly agreed and understood that the Consul shall at all times be at liberty to visit the capital of Ashantee, and to take his departure therefrom whenever he may think fit, without being subject to any interruption or detention, and that the Consul's residence may either be at Coomassy or at Cape Coast, as he may, from time to time, deem expedient for the public good; but if at any time during the Consul's absence from Coomassy the King of Ashantee has any complaint or palaver against the natives of the British Settlements, the same is to be submitted to the Consul at Cape Coast, and if it cannot be settled without his presence at Coomassy, it is agreed that the Consul shall immediately proceed to the capital on all such occasions.

10th. The King of Ashantee, having publicly and repeatedly complained of the exorbitant prices charged on the Notes he holds from the forts for the goods he receives in payment of those Notes, and n consequence of the manifest dissatisfaction expressed by the King on this subject in particular, the Consul, in order to obviate any objections to the ratification of the present treaty, concedes this point to the King, agreeing in future to take upon himself the payment of those Notes; and the King declares he will not from henceforth receive any payment of those Notes except through the medium of the Consul.

11th. The King, on the part of his principal Captains and Counsellors, hereby acknowledges to their having also taken the oath of allegiance and fidelity to the Crown of Great Britain.

12th. In virtue of this treaty, it is mutually agreed and expressly understood that all former treaties between the King of Ashantee and the authorities of Cape Coast Castle, on the behalf of His Majesty's Government, particularly the treaty of 1817, are from henceforth to become null and void, and are hereby declared so accordingly. . . .

Supplementary Articles.

. . . 1st. The King of Ashantee having, by force of arms, subdued the Kingdom of Gaman or Buntooko, which he now governs in full and undisputed sovereignty, and whereas, from political motives, it has been deemed prudent to station troops in Amanaha, on the banks of the Assinee River, and other parts of the said kingdom, to prevent the inhabitants from trading or holding any communication with the sea coast, the King now pledges himself, in virtue of this article, to remove the before-mentioned obstacles to the commerce of the kingdom of Buntooko or Gaman; and he guarantees the same privileges of trade to the natives of that country which the Ashantees themselves enjoy, provided their intercourse with the sea coast is confined to Cape Coast Castle, or any other of the British Forts and Settlements on the Gold Coast. In promotion of this object the King has already nearly completed a road forming a direct communication to the heart of the said country of Gaman, and he hereby binds himself to support, aid and encourage the trade of the country.

2nd. The King of Ashantee, being decidedly adverse to relinquishing his claim on the natives of Cape Coast Town, and in consequence of certain private negotiations which are now pending through the medium of Mr. Smith, the Governor of Cape Coast Castle, on behalf of the parties concerned (and whereas the Consul possesses no authority to guarantee payment to the King of any sum of money on behalf of the natives of Cape Coast beyond the limit of one hundred ounces of gold, which has only tended to excite the King's anger and indignation), as well as for other reasons unnecessary to introduce in this treaty, it is hereby stipulated that the natives of Cape Coast Town, being subjects of the King of Ashantee, are excluded from participating in the benefits of either of the treaties, as the King is resolved to eradicate from his dominions the seeds of disobedience and insubordination; nevertheless in consideration of the friendship existing between him and the King of England, and as the King of Ashantee is particularly anxious to convince the world of the sincerity of his regard for the honor and dignity, as well as the interests of the British Government and people, he will endeavour, as much as possible, to avoid giving offence either to the Consul or to the authorities of Cape Coast Castle, directly or indirectly, and, therefore, whatever plans the King of Ashantee may think it advisable to adopt, in order to bring his people under due subjection, he binds himself not to destroy the town of Cape Coast, nor will he allow a gun to be fired in the town, or suffer his troops to commit any act of hostility or depredation therein on the inhabitants or on their property. . . .

5

MAJOR CHISHOLM TO GOVERNOR SIR CHARLES MACCARTHY: ASHANTI CLAIMS, 30 SEPTEMBER 1822[1]

. . . LATE events fully convince me that the King has no thoughts of giving up the Serjeant, but on the contrary is resolved to use every means in his power to injure the British Establishments. I have been informed by a number of persons, some of whom are on intimate terms, and in close correspondence with men of consideration at

[1] J. J. Crooks, *Records relating to the Gold Coast Settlements from 1750 to 1874* (Dublin, 1923), pp. 164–5. The Ashanti had seized a mulatto sergeant at Anomabu and later had him executed for insulting the *Asantehene*. This trouble brought back MacCarthy from Sierra Leone to his defeat and death at Nsamankow in 1824. The Ashanti again invaded the coastal states in 1826, attacked Accra, and were defeated in August at Akantamasu (Dodowa).

Coomassie, that he purposes attacking the town, and that on the return of a part of his Army employed on the banks of the Volta, in subduing a small State which has revolted, the necessary dispositions will be made. A Message he sent to the Cabboceers at Annmaboe on the 24th Instant, gives a countenance to these reports; he required them to declare whether they considered themselves his Subjects or were disposed to take part with the Cape Coast people against him, and signified to them that the most acceptable proof of their fidelity would be their uniting themselves to the Chiefs of Abrah. This they declined to do, and as their answer to the question respecting the people of this town was evasive, they expect nothing short of the severest vengeance at his hands.

I learn his present enmity proceeds from his not having received a Present at the change of Government similar to that given to him by Mr. Dupuis on his arrival at his Court as British Consul. The homage paid to him by the late Company and the uncontrolled authority they allowed him to exercise in their Possessions, even to the extent of levying excessive fines, in the towns protected by this and their other Forts, have given him a very unfavourable opinion of our National Character. The immense Presents he has at different times received and the readiness with which Mr. Dupuis made an addition to his annual stipend and yielded several other important points, has led him to imagine that the commerce which he controls is absolutely necessary to our existence as a Nation, and that we will ultimately concede dignity and every other consideration for the advantage of participating in it. His conduct to the Dutch who really have not either the means or inclination to make him Presents, clearly shows that he considers us profitable subjects for his rapacity. Conceiving the most effectual means would be to appear very indifferent as to his views, I have not adopted the measures which under other circumstances I would have pursued to get the Serjeant back. There is no a necessity for immediate interference in his behalf, as I am assured his life is in no danger.

6

GOVERNOR SIR NEIL CAMPBELL TO EARL BATHURST: FANTI DISUNITY, 5 NOVEMBER 1826[1]

... As soon as possible after my arrival here I assembled all the Kings and Chiefs nearest this place who were in the Campaign, and others, but it was impossible to prevail upon them to unite with the King of

[1] Crooks, op. cit., p. 239. As long as the Fanti refused to communicate these terms to Ashanti, Campbell failed to settle the peace, and relations with Kumasi remained in doubt till the arrival of George Maclean, as President of the Merchants' Council in 1830.

England to open even the most indirect communication with the Ashantees. I told them it was not to propose a Peace, but to let it be understood by the Ashantees, that if they sent Messengers here 'to ask for Peace' they might pass in safety. That it would not be for the King of England alone or separately, but for all together, and that no Peace would be granted without the strongest guarantees for the independence of every one of them. Councils were held with them in the formal manner peculiar to this country, they held several among themselves, presents brought from Sierra Leone were distributed on a very liberal scale, but they would not yield. I then told them that as none of them could unite with the King of England or accept of his mediation, they could not any longer have claims for assistance in any future war. That he was resolved to be at Peace with every Nation in Africa, who would remain peaceable, and wished them to follow the same course. As the King and people of Cape Coast were willing to find a few individuals to proceed to the Ashanti frontier I made arrangements for them, and asked a small escort through the respective territories of the Chiefs. They would not give any; circulated reports to intimidate them, and finally set off to intercept them.

The Mission could not proceed from Cape Coast. I went to Accra on the 10th of October, but none of the Chiefs came in consequence of threatening messengers sent to them and I have no doubt that the disapproval of any negotiations were proclaimed and fomented by every one at Accra. . . .

7

TREATY WITH ASHANTI, 27 APRIL 1831[1]

WE, the undersigned . . . and the other Chiefs in alliance with the King of Great Britain, whose names are hereunto appended—do consent to, and hereby ratify the following Treaty of Peace, and of free commerce between ourselves and such other Chiefs as may hereafter adhere to it:—

1. The King of Ashantee having deposited in Cape Coast Castle, in the presence of the above-mentioned parties, the sum of 600 ounces of gold, and having delivered into the hands of the Governor two young men of the royal family of Ashantee, named 'Ossor Ansah' and 'Ossoo In Quantamissah', as security that he will keep the peace with the said parties in all time coming, peace is hereby declared betwixt the said King of Ashantee and all and each of the parties

[1] Crooks, op. cit., pp. 262–4. Signed by President George Maclean, the Ashanti delegates Princess Akianva and Chief Kwagwa, King Aggery of Cape Coast, Chief Aduku, Chief Amonu of Anomabu, Chief Abuku of Akomfi, Chief Otu of Abra, Otibu, Chief of Assin, Kwadjo Otibu, king of Denkyera, Gebel, chief of Assin, Oso Oku, king of Twifu, unnamed chiefs of Apollonia, and Chief Akini of Aga. For a discussion of the terms of the treaty, see G. E. Metcalfe, *Maclean of the Gold Coast* (London, 1962), pp. 89–92.

WBP

aforesaid, to continue in all time coming. The above securities shall remain in Cape Coast Castle for the space of six years from this date.

2. In order to prevent all quarrels in future which might lead to the infraction of this Treaty of Peace, we the parties aforesaid have agreed to the following rules and regulations for the better protection of lawful commerce:—

The paths shall be perfectly open and free to all persons engaged in lawful traffic; and persons molesting them in any way whatever, or forcing them to purchase at any particular market, or influencing them by any unfair means whatever, shall be declared guilty of infringing this Treaty, and be liable to the severest punishment.

Panyarring,[1] denouncing, and swearing, on or by any person or thing whatever, are hereby strictly forbidden, and all persons infringing this rule shall be rigorously punished; and no master or chief shall be answerable for the crimes of his servants, unless done by his orders or consent, or when under his control.

As the King of Ashantee has renounced all right or title to any tribute or homage from the Kings of Dinkera, Assin, and others formerly his subjects, so, on the other hand, these parties are strictly prohibited from insulting, by improper speaking or in any other way, their former master, such conduct being calculated to produce quarrels and wars.

All 'palavers' are to be decided in the manner mentioned in the terms and conditions of peace already agreed to by the parties to this Treaty. . . .

8

GOVERNOR SIR JOHN JEREMIE: PROCLAMATION, DOMESTIC SLAVERY, 4 MARCH 1841[2]

WHEREAS undoubted information has been conveyed to us that the practice of holding persons in slavery prevails in certain parts of the British territories of Africa within the limits of this government, viz. 20th degree north to 20th degree south, as aforesaid: Now, therefore, be it known, that by the several Acts of Parliament, viz. 5 Geo. 4, c. 13, and 3 & 4 Will. 4, c. 73, commonly called the Slave Trade Abolition Act, and the Slave Emancipation Act, it is unlawful for any person to hold slaves in a British territory, or for a British subject to hold slaves in any country whatever, except India, St. Helena, and Ceylon, and that in all cases the holders are liable to severe punishment, and the persons thus unlawfully held in slavery to seizure and confiscation.

[1] The seizure of goods and persons for debt.
[2] *Parl. Papers*, 1842, xi (551), Pt. II, pp. 65–66.

And whereas undoubted information has been further conveyed to us, that it is not unusual for traders to take persons in pawn within the said limits; be it therefore also known that such holding in pawn is a holding in slavery within the meaning of these Acts; and we do hereby strictly enjoin and require all officers, civil and military, all officers of cities, towns, and others, Her Majesty's loyal subjects, to aid and assist in the execution of the laws. . . .

9

GEORGE MACLEAN TO LORD STANLEY: DOMESTIC SLAVERY, 13 AUGUST 1843[1]

My Lord,

I have the honour to acknowledge the receipt of Your Lordship's letter of the 20 of May, wherein you desire me to report to your Lordship what steps have been taken to give effect to Sir John Jeremie's Proclamation[2] in these Settlements and more particularly at British Accra.

In reply I have the honour to acquaint your Lordship that in March 1841, on the receipt of Sir John Jeremie's Proclamation, I caused it to be published and made generally known at British Accra as well as at all the other British Settlements under this Government. I also expressly made known to the European Residents that any holding, buying, or selling of Slaves by them would be considered illegal,— that any Slaves found in their possession would be confiscated, & they themselves prosecuted for any infraction of the Law. With respect to the persons denominated 'Pawns', I caused it to be made known to them, & I personally explained to many of them, that though I could not release them from the pecuniary engagements which they had contracted, yet their continuance in their Master's service must be purely voluntary on their part, and that if any attempt should be made to coerce or ill-use them, they would receive immediate protection and redress on applying to the Authorities. Since that period no infringement of the Law on the part of the European Residents has come to my knowledge.

With the system of Slavery existing among the Native population, of any Class, I have in no respect interfered, beyond, as formerly, giving every protection and redress to Slaves when ill-treated, & emancipating them on the spot where I saw reason.

Without express Instructions to that effect,—and I have never received any—I have not dared to attempt to carry out a measure which would inevitably convulse this country from one end to the other, and involve the British Settlements in continual petty, but

[1] C.O. 96/2. Approved in Stanley to Maclean, 7 December 1843; ibid.
[2] No. 8, above.

sanguinary, warfare with the neighbouring Dutch and Danish Settlements where Slavery is protected by the Local Governments. Your Lordship is aware that the physical means of this Government are of the most limited descriptions:—its moral power is indeed great, but it is based, as all moral power must be, on the implicit confidence entertained by the population generally in the inflexible uprightness, justice, & inviolable good faith of the person or persons wielding it. For the purposes, therefore, of maintaining tranquillity and order throughout a large extent of country, of ensuring protection to commerce and safety to Travellers, and for the protection, generally, and encouragement of those who are engaged in extending the blessings of education and Christianity to the Native population, I do not find my physical means, backed by my moral power, insufficient, because these are objects the reasonableness and righteousness of which are palpable to all. But I should sap the very foundations of that power, were I to attempt the execution of a measure which would bear, upon the face of it, the appearance, at least, of the grossest tyranny and injustice,—the depriving people, namely, without Compensation, of property which they have either inherited from their ancestors, from the remotest times, or acquired by their own industry. I might, indeed, hope to convince a few and, in the present state of society here, but a few—of the injustice, sinfulness, and even of the inexpediency, of holding their fellow-creatures in slavery; but I should never be able to convince them that I possessed any just right to deprive them, without compensation, by a merely arbitrary act, of a description of property in the possession and acquisition of which, however abstractly indefensible, they had been protected and encouraged by the British Government itself for two Hundred Years. Under these circumstances, and in the absence of any express Instructions on the subject, I have refrained from any general interference with the Slaves of the Natives of the Country, and have continued that system of Government with respect to them, which I practised even before the passing of the Emancipation Act of 1834, and by which it appeared to me that their gradual amelioration and eventual emancipation might be best brought about.

10

JAMES STEPHEN: MINUTE, DOMESTIC SLAVERY, 16 NOVEMBER 1843[1]

This wd. seem to be a complete defence, subject, as I think, to the following remark. Mr. Maclean, if I rightly understand him wd. distinguish between the Slaves of Europeans and the Slaves of Natives

[1] C.O. 96/2, on no. 9.

within the Queen's Dominion—holding that although the British Subject cannot, the Native African can hold such property there. If this be his meaning it is a distinction which the Law does not admit. Considering however, how very narrow the limits of the British Dominion strictly understood & accurately speaking are, it is very possible that Mr. Maclean is to be understood as referring to persons holden in Slavery outside the Forts. If this be so Sir John Jeremie's Proclamation is inapplicable to this case, nor is there any British Law that touches it.

II

GOVERNOR H. W. HILL TO LORD STANLEY: FANTI RELATIONS, 6 MARCH 1844[1]

My Lord,

An opportunity offering for England tonight I am induced thus hurriedly to acquaint your Lordship that several of the Chiefs from different parts of the Country adjacent to Cape Coast Castle, have visited me today in great state, to pay their respects on the transfer of the Government.

I have for some days been aware that an idea was believed by the natives, of its being the intention of Her Majesty's Government to pronounce freedom to all Slaves within the limits over which jurisdiction has been exercised.

I need not tell your Lordship that an attempt to carry any such measure, would cause a revolution.

The Chiefs were delighted on my informing them it was quite an idle report, and that the Export Slave Trade was all that we prohibited, they expressed satisfaction on my telling them they were not at liberty to ill-use their domestic Slaves, and if a person inherited a Slave, that person was not at liberty to sell the Slave again, but such Slave was to be considered a member of the family.

I considered it a good opportunity of establishing an agreement to their being under our Jurisdiction, and drew up the document of which the enclosed is a Copy, and which the Chiefs readily signed.

This will I hope my Lord meet with your approbation, and I think it is quite sufficient to establish the Powers of the Foreign Jurisdiction Act.[2]

I beg to mention the Chiefs expressed great satisfaction at the appointment of Captain Maclean to preside over the Trial of offenders. . . .

[1] C.O. 96/4 'Private and Confidential'.
[2] Act of 24 August 1843 (6 & 7 Vict., c. 94), see below, p. 549.

12

DECLARATION OF FANTI CHIEFS (THE 'BOND'), 6 MARCH 1844[1]

WHEREAS Power and Jurisdiction has been exercised for and on behalf of Her Majesty the Queen of Great Britain and Ireland, within divers Countries and Places, adjacent to Her Majesty's Forts, and Settlements, on the Gold Coast: We Chiefs of Countries, and Places so referred to, adjacent to the said Forts, and Settlements; do hereby acknowledge, that Power, and Jurisdiction: and declare, 'that the first objects of Law, are the protection of Individuals, and of Property.

2nd. Human sacrifices, and other barbarous Customs, such as Panyaring, are abominations, and contrary to Law.

3rd. Murders, Robberies, and other Crimes and offences, will be Tried, and Inquired of, before the Queen's Judicial Officers, and the Chiefs of the district, moulding the Customs of the Country to the general Principles of British Law.'

Done at Cape Coast Castle before His Excellency the Lieutenant Governor on this 6th. day of March in the year of our Lord 1844. . . .

13

LIEUT.-GOVERNOR W. WINNIETT TO EARL GREY: APOLLONIA, 22 MARCH 1848[2]

[Apollonia, though abandoned, is still under British jurisdiction.]

. . . JURISDICTION over the Territory of Appolonia has always been exercised by the Local Government; and the present Chieftain has at all times so far recognised that jurisdiction as to hoist the English Flag; although it seems that he has for many years been more or less in such a state of insubordination as to give considerable annoyance to the Local Government, and to prejudice the honor of the British Flag.

---

[1] C.O. 96/4. Signed by Hill (Governor of Cape Coast, 1843–5), Maclean (by whom it was probably framed), Lieutenant F. Pogson, Adjutant S. Bannerman, King Otibu of Denkyera, Chief Otu of Abra, Chiefs Otibu and Gebel of Assin, Chief Anka of Donadi, Chief Awusi of Domonsai, Chief Amonu of Anomabu, Chief Aggery of Cape Coast. Later signatories were the chiefs of Twifu, Ajumako, Gomoa, Asikuma, in March and April 1844. Hill to Stanley, 5 September 1844: ibid. Chiefs of Dixcove and Wassaw signed in July, August, and December 1844. Claridge, vol. i, p. 453.

[2] C.O. 96/13. *Commander (Sir) William Winniett* was Governor of the Gold Coast, 1846–50 and visited Kumasi in 1848.

The Expedition against him by the late Captain Maclean, during the time of his Government in one thousand, eight hundred and thirty-five, shows him to be an old offender of this description.

His spirit of insubordination came first under my personal notice from the circumstances of my wishing to pay a visit of inspection to the Fort which is situated close to the Town in which he resides, and my attempt thereupon to open a friendly communication with him.

The accompanying Documents from Mr. Swanzy, the Civil Commandant of Dixcove, from Mr. Cruickshank, the present Acting Judicial Assessor, and from His Excellency Governor Van der Eb of Elmina, which I now transmit to your Lordship will show that the insubordination, and tyranny, insolence, and intrigue of this Chieftain have now exceeded all bounds; and that to allow a day to pass without a fixed determination on my part to direct *at once* against him for the purpose of crushing rebellion and establishing good order, the energies of the Local Government here, with whatever aid I can secure from Her Majesty's Squadron, would be to temporize with a case pregnant with incalculable mischief to the well being of the British Settlements here; and to compromise British honor in the eyes of the Natives of the Country, and the French and Netherland Governments whose subjects have suffered from these outrages.

The Documents to which I have already referred, furnish against the Appolonia Chieftain the following well substantial [*sic*] charges.

I

His disregard for, and his contempt of the British Government, as shown most strongly in his contemptuous detention (if nothing worse) of Messengers sent to him on the most friendly terms; and his insolent answer to the inquiry made respecting the fate of those Messengers.

II

His profanation of the British Flag, to the great prejudice of British honor.

III

His uniformly bad treatment of Masters of British Vessels.

IV

The murder of the French Commandant of Assinie and his Boat's Crew.

V

His stopping the path and waylaying and murdering Wassaw people while on their journey to Cape Coast.

VI

His Piratical attack upon the Dutch Coast at Axim, and capture of twelve Dutch subjects.

This, My Lord, is indeed a grievous list of wrongs, to say nothing of the Seventh and last charge furnished, namely, *Intrigues with Ashante*, which while it is, from its very nature, less clearly proveable than the others, is, if true, the most important of all as it regards its bearing on the welfare of the British Settlements on this Coast.

On this last charge, fraught with so many weighty considerations, I need not enlarge to your Lordship farther than to observe that from the general tenor of this refractory Chieftain's conduct, it is quite clear that he is capable of such intrigues; and altho such a fact as the existence of this dangerous capability is not positive evidence against him, yet there can be no doubt that the charge is far more likely to be true than otherwise.

Considering then, My Lord, that in reference to a question involving so many important interests, indecision on my part would be fraught with perhaps total consequences; and finding that I have with me the unanimous voice of all classes and orders of the people of the Colony, both European and Native, my desire to avoid expense and bloodshed, has yielded to the absolute necessity of the case; and I have determined to proceed *at once* with a Force of *Four thousand, five hundred Men* against this Monster of Appolonia, Her Majesty's Brigantine 'Dolphin' accompanies me—and I have chartered the Brig 'Governor Maclean'—a Vessel belonging to Messrs. Forster and Smith of London as a Transport. . . .

14

EARL GREY: MINUTE, APOLLONIA, 17 JUNE 1848[1]

THE further information which Mr Barrow has now furnished me with confirms my opin[ion] of the unjustifiable character of Lt. Gov. Winniett's proceedings.

In the first place though the letter addressed to him by the Commodore is dated Feb. 20 & must have been received before he wrote his despatch on the 22d of March, he does not mention the fact of his having applied for a naval force in his operat[ions] against this Chief & been refused for the very sufficient reasons given by Sir C. Hotham. It was clearly his duty to have reported this circumstance. Nor wd.

[1] C.O. 96/13. And based on this, Grey to Winniett, 3 July 1848. Winniett's expedition against Apollonia was, however, carried out in March, and Chief Akka was captured, tried at Cape Coast, and sentenced to life imprisonment.

anything but a case of very great necessity have warranted his acting against the advice of an Officer of such high character without the express sanct[ion] of H.M.'s Govt.

It further appears from the evidence to which Mr Barrow has referred me that the local authorities have more than once applied for permiss[ion] to undertake hostile operations against this Chief & that such permiss[ion] has always been refused from this office—an additional reason for not acting now without instructions. Those refusals can I presume be referred to.

Nor was there anything pressing in the circumstances which had occurred requiring immediate act[ion]. The 1st ground of complaint against the Chief ought not to have been given—no messengers shd. have been sent to him—it is not our policy to extend our territory & our responsibility on the Coast of W. Africa, on the contrary it is highly desirable [not] to get into relat[ions] with these barbarous Chiefs so far from Cape Coast Castle which are likely to lead to our receiving insults which it is difficult to pass over. The complaint numbered II I do not understand, at all events redress for this injury (if it was one) cd. have been at leisure exacted by a naval force if H.M's Govt. on being referred to, considered this necessary.

The last remark applies to III. With IV, V, & VI we have nothing to do. The Lt. Govr. seems to suppose that this country is to undertake the maintenance of order amongst the barbarous inhabitants of this part of Africa. There cannot be a greater or more dangerous mistake. He will in future confine his interference to our own settlements & their immediate neighbourhood.

A despatch severely censuring the Lt. Govr. on these grounds must be prepared.

15

ACTING GOVERNOR J. C. FITZPATRICK TO KING KWAKU DUA: ASSIN, 26 FEBRUARY 1849[1]

SIR,

I have the honor to acknowledge the receipt of your communication through the Revd. Mr. Hillard respecting your desire that the Assin Chiefs should pay you an annual visit at Kumasi. When you mentioned this subject to Lieutenant Governor Winniett I believe he told you that he should consult some papers at Cape Coast Castle before he replied to you finally and as this may have encouraged you in the hope that the Assin Chiefs would be sent back, I now send you this letter which will tell you openly and honestly the truth in

[1] C.O. 96/15. *J. C. Fitzpatrick* was Judicial Assessor from 1847, Acting Governor in 1849 and 1853, and Chief Justice, 1853–7; Kwaku Dua I, *Asantehene* (1834–67).

order that as there can be no mistake, you and the English can continue good friends if you both wish it. The matter stands thus exactly. By the treaty of peace which you made with Governor Maclean in 1830,[1] the Assins were declared entirely independent of Ashantee and under British protection. You know there were three parties concerned in that Treaty, the English, yourself, and the Assins. It has been well observed towards you by the English, and towards the English by you, and I am surprized you could think for a moment that it would not be faithfully observed towards the Assins also. You make a great mistake if you think the English would cheat any people in that way. When they call a man their friend they intend that he shall be so in truth, and continue so unless it be his own fault. I have learned that you also applied to Governor Hill in his time 'to take his hands off the Assins' and he told you that they were under British protection—and you now renew the application made to Governor Winniett to me. Perhaps you think that with a new Governor you have a new chance of succeeding in your views, but be certain of this and I hope you will never allow a doubt of it to cross your mind, that no matter how her servants may be changed, the honor and good faith of the Queen of England can never be either changed or lessened. Those whom she honors with her friendship or protection, she will never desert, unless they behave bad themselves. She has lately given you a distinguished mark of her friendship in allowing Governor Winniett to visit you in Kumasie, and I can assure you, it is the wish, as well as the duty of all Her Officers here to continue on the same friendly terms with you, doing what we can to serve and oblige you and your people, recovering debts. &c. &c. and requiring from you the same civilities in return. It is better for us all to continue in this way. The riches of your Kingdom and the comforts of your People have all increased since you and Governor Maclean made peace. That Palaver was then settled and all we have to do now is to keep our words with one another and to observe honor and good faith with every man.

16

EARL GREY TO GOVERNOR SIR W. WINNIETT: ASHANTI FUGITIVES, 19 SEPTEMBER 1850[2]

. . . I HAVE considerable difficulty in giving you any definite instructions on this subject [fugitive slaves] in the absence of more complete information.

[1] *Sic*, 1831.
[2] C.O. 96/19. Based on a minute by Grey, 13 September 1850; in reply to Winniett to Grey, 4 June 1850: ibid.

3. There can be no objection, as far as I am aware, to the execution of an Agreement to surrender to the King of Ashantee persons who have fled from his Country, charged with the commission of crimes, or of offences against Ashantee law and usage, so far as their surrender does not involve any breach of the laws of humanity.

4. But with regard to runaway Slaves from Ashantee, I have to direct your attention to two Despatches of my Predecessor, Lord Stanley, of the 29th. & 30th. Decr. 1844.[1] Lord Stanley pointed out that any such surrender, where the slave had taken refuge on British Territory (as in Cape Coast Castle) would be absolutely illegal under the Statute 3d. & 4th. Geo IV c. 113: and that if the Slave was found on territory not British, but under British protection, such surrender altho' not strictly illegal as in the former case, was equally contrary to the spirit of English law, and not to be sanctioned.

5. I fully concur in these views of Lord Stanley. If, therefore, it is for the advantage of the Settlements that such an arrangement, as that you have described with the King of Ashantee, should be maintained, it is desirable that the class of persons to whom it is to apply, and the terms on which their surrender is to take place, should be defined.

17

THE DUKE OF NEWCASTLE TO GOVERNOR S. J. HILL: ASHANTI AND ASSIN, 21 JUNE 1853[2]

SIR,

I have to acknowledge the receipt of your despatches of the numbers and dates noted in the margin, relative to the invasion of the Assin territory by an armed body of Ashantees, for the purpose of taking away the chiefs of that country, Chibboo and Gabriel.

Your despatches of the 25th and 26th April, announcing the retirement of the Ashantees into their own country, and the removal of all fear for the present of our being forced into a war with them, were not received till three weeks after your first despatches had arrived, and they have relieved Her Majesty's Government from the anxiety which the earlier information could not fail to produce.

I am much gratified in expressing to you my entire approbation of your conduct in the very trying circumstances in which you were placed, and especially for the forbearing spirit which you evinced,

---

[1] C.O. 96/4.
[2] *Parl. Papers*, 1853, lxv (703), pp. 13–14. The chiefs of Assin, Otibu, and Gabiri, were tried by the Fanti for intriguing with Ashanti. They were executed in April 1853—which did not end Ashanti claims to Assin.

and the firmness you exhibited in resisting the urgency of the merchants for measures, which must have precipitated the crisis of affairs, and entailed war with the Ashantees.

My approbation is likewise due to all who were employed in carrying your orders into effect, but I must notice specially the conduct of Ensign Brownell, whose courage and self-devotion were as conspicuous as his judgement and discretion; and I have to request you will inform him that it is my intention to represent his merits to the General Commanding-in-Chief.

Your report of the creditable manner in which the natives conducted themselves is highly satisfactory, and the forbearance which they showed under provocation would do credit to more civilized nations.

I trust that your late proceedings with the Ashantees will prevent any renewed attempt on their part to disturb the peace, and I am glad to find, by your despatch of the 25th April, that in your opinion those measures will have a lasting effect.

But in order that you may be able to assume an attitude which may ensure the continuance of peace in the autumn, I have requested the Lords Commissioners of the Admiralty to order such vessels of war as can be spared for that purpose from the African squadron, to visit the Gold Coast at the close of the rainy season.

I have likewise instructed the Governor of Sierra Leone, upon your requisition, to despatch a company of the regiment stationed there to the Gold Coast, for temporary service; and the Board of Ordnance has been requested to forward to you a supply of muskets.

You will cause the muskets to be placed in store immediately on their arrival, in order that the natives may not know that they have been supplied, and be tempted to engage in hostilities, by anticipating the possession of firearms.

Your proposal to visit the King of Ashantee, at his capital, Coomassie, is a step which I must leave entirely to your discretion. But I must caution you against incurring any undue risk of your personal safety, as your detention by the king would defeat the very object for which alone your visit can be justified, and render a war inevitable.

As you have expressed an opinion in your later despatch of the 25th April, that the Ashantees are not likely to renew their attempt, it is probable that you may no longer contemplate a visit to Coomassie; but if, after mature reflection, you should decide upon doing so, the presents which you require for the king of Ashantee shall be sent out to you.

In concluding this despatch, I have to express my hope and confidence that your future proceedings with the Ashantees, will be characterized by the same spirit of moderation and forbearance, combined with watchfulness and a firm maintenance of the rights of

British territory and of our native allies, as you have evinced throughout the late crisis.

18

LIEUT.-GOVERNOR B. CRUICKSHANK TO KING KWAKU DUA: ASHANTI AND ASSIN, 5 SEPTEMBER 1853[1]

BEFORE I had any thought of being honoured with Her Majesty's
commission as Lieutenant-Governor, I wrote to you a friendly letter
by Mr. Ossoo Ansah, recommending you to renew a treaty of peace
and friendship with the Governor on behalf of the Queen and the
native tribes enjoying her protection. Ansah has returned, and brought
me your letter of the 18th August, which I only received yesterday.

2. I hasten now as Governor to carry into effect the measures
which as a private individual I had recommended. You mention that
you had received great wrong from the Assins. It is true that Chibboo and Gabil had intrigued with you, and for this they have suffered a just death; but your Majesty had no right to enter into their
intrigues, as you were well aware that they have been long under
the protection of the British Government, and no overtures should
have been received by you from them without communicating them
to the Governor. But you did more than intrigue: you sent an armed
force into the Assin country, which you knew to be under the protection of the Queen's Government; an act which by all nations is
considered tantamount to a declaration of war; and it was only the
Governor's great forbearance that prevented this fearful calamity.
Your people destroyed many villages and ravaged the country. For
this the Governor has, I understand, demanded from you compensation for those people, who look to him for protection, and upon
which he had a perfect right to insist.

3. The Queen's Government is determined to give full protection
to the Assins, but is at the same time most peaceably disposed
towards you; and to convince you of this, I am willing to forego the
demand for compensation, which the English Government will have
the generosity to make good to them in your stead. This concession
proceeds from no fear of the consequences of a just war, but solely
with the view of averting its horrors, and is made only upon the
condition of your renewing the treaty acknowledging the independence of the Assins and other tribes, who have hitherto enjoyed the
advantage of British protection. Mr. Blankson[2] will present such a

[1] *Parl. Papers*, 1855, xxxvi (456), pp. 10–11. *Brodie Cruickshank* was Chief
Justice at the Gold Coast and Acting Governor in 1853 and 1854.
[2] A native trader from Anomabu who returned to the coast after delivering the
draft treaty in January 1854.

treaty for you and your captains, which I expect you will sign in good faith. Your refusal will be a proof to me that peace is not yet restored, in which case I shall take measures to prevent any intercourse with your country from Assinee and Grand Bassam all the way to the Volta. At present there is a restriction placed upon gun-powder and other warlike stores, but I will make it general on all things, and use all the power of the Government to carry it into effect if you do not agree to my most just and moderate demands.

4. I say not this by way of threat to offend you, but to give you clearly to understand in what light I should regard your refusal to sign the treaty. If you do refuse, and war should be the consequence, upon you and your people will be the blame clearly manifest to all the world, and the issue is with God.

5. I confidently hope, however, that your sense of right and justice will convince you and all your people that I am acting with great moderation, and as one earnestly desirous to be your friend. I am anxious above all things to see our relations to each other to the tribes under British protection, restored to the same cordial footing of confidence and friendship which existed in the days of Governor Maclean.

19

KING KWAKU DUA TO LIEUT-GOVERNOR B. CRUICKSHANK: ASSIN, 28 NOVEMBER 1853[1]

YOUR EXCELLENCY,

I have the honour now to reply to your Excellency's letters on the subject of the new treaty, by Mr. George Blankson, who, according to your Excellency's request, has given the explanation and contents of them all to the hearing of myself and all my captains, since his arrival in the town; which subject we have taken into our deep consideration, and arrived at the conclusion in refusing to sign the new treaty, as I have good reasons in so doing; because I consider that I have not violated any of the rules in the old treaty since it was drawn at Cape Coast Castle, until the occurrence of the recent excitement, caused by the evil conduct of the Assins, which case I thought that I was justified in sending a body of people to escort them to Ashante country, at their own wish and request, without letting Governor Hill know of it. The reason was, that at the time the late Governor Winniett visited the capital, and about to leave, I brought under his notice the same subject, to interfere on my behalf in getting the Assins and Denkeras to return to Ashantee, and live with me, as they formerly were my subjects, after his arrival, who kindly promised in

1 Ibid., 9–10.

doing so for me; but he did not fulfil the promise, or as much as even sent to tell me anything respecting it. Since that I have had a different opinion, that I thought it unnecessary for me to bring under the notice of any Governor a subject of this nature, in consequence of which I embraced the chance in sending the body of people to escort the Assins to me, at their own free offer, will, and desire, without my asking them to come or sent to encourage them; but it was a matter that I, for several years elapsed sought, and only opportunity failed me, otherwise I would not have brought under Governor Winniett's notice. However my people met with disasters in bringing the Assins, but met with Lieutenant Brownall at Fessoowly, who was, as the representative of the Governor, stopped the people in advancing, investigated the matter, and decided in my favour; and according to the rules and custom in my country, Asamwah Quantah, the commander of the body of people, paid four ounces eight ackies gold dust, half of which was given to Lieutenant Brownall, on behalf of the British Government, and the other half on mine. Thus the case was settled, then my people returned back to Ashantee, and he to the coast; after that, notwithstanding his judgment in the matter in deciding it in my favour, but the then Governor Hill himself sent to confirm the decision by sending to tell me that the case was over, and we were at peace, and that he desired me to send a party of trade to the coast, and people to bring the remainder of my property seized by the Fantees, when the excitement took place, to show that the matter was over, and I had nothing on my part to say after. I consented at the Governor's wish, and acted upon it; but to my greatest surprise, the tradesmen returned from the coast, reported that a restriction placed on the selling of powder and warlike stores, and only a portion of my property sent to me, which conduct is not found among the whites or Europeans. In fact I was greatly annoyed at such treatment and dealings, summing up all these and put together, I consider myself blameless in the affairs throughout, from the beginning of Governor Winniett's conduct and others, and have not infringed the old treaty, which require a new to be made or renewed as you requested. In the mean time I still confirm the old treaty, and will act upon it, and in future also I shall never do anything without letting your Excellency know if it, as you have proposed, in reference to any injury that may be done to myself, or any of my subjects, the demanding of a debt or debts, or any other minor cases. Trusting you will not feel hurt of my refusing to renew the treaty, as I do not see any blame in the case on your part, but if there will be any at all is attached to the Lieutenant Brownall and Governor Hill; the former decided the case in my favour, the latter confirmed it, in sending to request me to send trade to the coast, as the matter was over; and if I was wrong in my proceedings, I ought to have been told plainly and justly, and not to be dealt with in such a way, and disappointed in many ways, independent to what I have said in writing. I send messengers to accompany Mr. George Blankson to confirm it verbally, hoping you will take my word that I will do nothing without letting you know, and wishing that you will do the same towards me. I can assure your Excellency also, that if I have violated the rules in the treaty which deserve a fine, and you asking me to lodge gold in the castle, I shall not show any reluctance in doing so, knowing that it shall be sent to me again at the expiration of the period of time fixed on delivery of the gold, as the whites of Europeans never will cheat people or depriving them of their lawful and rightful property; above all I beg your Excellency to represent the statement of the case to the British Government in England, that they might not think that I have done wrong in these matters, and refusing to sign the new treaty, as I have already given you my reasons of the same. . . .

20

SIR GEORGE BARROW: MINUTE, DOMESTIC SLAVERY, 13 NOVEMBER 1857[1]

. . . [GOVERNOR PINE] depicts Domestic Slavery & the Pawn System in the blackest colors & the latter he describes as 'the most subtle & iniquitous scheme ever devised for the purposes of Slavery, & worthy of the author of all evil'.

Major Ord who enquired into matters on the G. Coast, described Domestic Slavery as existing in its milder form & compared it to the old Patriarchal Rule:—this is the bright side of the picture, & is perhaps as far from the real state of things as Sir B. Pine's views.

But the abhorrence of the latter to the whole system has absorbed every other consideration & appears to have become a sort of monomania—whichever way he turns it meets him, & at last he has no hesitation in advising that our Protectorate of the Country should at once be withdrawn as by the recognition of Slavery, it involves the violation of English Law, & the moment that Law is fully observed by our Officers, our jurisdiction is brought to an end.

His allusion however to the maxim that every Slave who puts his foot on British Ground is free is scarcely applicable to the Gold Coast—for there is no British Ground there in the common acceptation of the term & the maxim could not be fairly extended to the case of any number of fugitive slaves who might come daily to the gates of the Forts, exclaiming 'I wish to be free'.

It is no doubt a question of extreme difficulty, because altho' we

[1] C.O. 96/41. On Pine to Labouchere, 10 October 1857: ibid.

do not recognize the system or give any direct sanction to it we are compelled to tolerate it because we have not the means of suppressing it.

But if we are to retain any jurisdiction on the Coast—his two plans are, either to put Garrisons in the Forts for the protection of Trade & of the Natives from the Ashantees & to establish a Consular Jurisdiction—or to acquire by purchase or free cession, small tracts of the country adjacent to & within reach of the Forts, to be the Asylum for fugitive Slaves & should the influx be great, to serve as a depot for Emigration to the W. Indies—these 'free Colonies' to be governed by Municipalities & made Dependencies of Sierra Leone.

These suggestions appear to me to be altogether unadvisable—& may be considered rather as the emanations of a brain so oppressed with an over-whelming notion of the horror of Slavery, that every thing must give way to it & the Protectorate be abandoned. . . .

21

ACTING GOVERNOR H. BIRD: PROCLAMATION, KROBO REBELLION, 6 SEPTEMBER 1858[1]

Whereas it has been made known to me that there is a Rebellion in Crobboe whereby much bloodshed has ensued and many lives have been sacrificed and that Odonkor Ossu, the Chief of Eastern Crobboe has been unable to reduce to order a powerful and insurgent Chief, by name, Tenoo residing in the Chiefdom of Eastern Crobboe owing to the support afforded and guaranteed to him by Ologo Pattoo the influential turbulent and refractory Chief of Western Crobboe and Noy his son and the heir presumptive to his father's stool; and that Odonkor Ossu has solicited the immediate aid and support of the Government at this juncture to enable him to maintain his just authority and to prevent his Chiefdom becoming the scene of anarchy, bloodshed and War.

And Whereas after due enquiry I am credibly informed that the said Tenoo has broken the peace of the District by engaging of his own authority in warlike operations against another Chief by name Paddie-Attah in which several lives had been lost, and, in addition, many persons severely wounded; and that Odonkor Ossu the Superior Chief of both of them was endeavouring to restore order to the District, and that Paddie-Attah submitted to his authority but that Tenoo absolutely refused to do so, owing to the support afforded

---

[1] C.O. 96/44. Ologo Patu surrendered and was imprisoned pending the payment of a fine of £10,000—only half of which was received before he escaped.

Xвр

him by Ologo Pattoo the Superior Chief of the adjoining District of Western Crobboe.

And Whereas it has been made known to me that on the above recited circumstances having been reported to the Chief Civil Commandant of the Eastern District and on his issuing Summonses for the appearance of the above named Persons before him, and on his endeavouring to arbitrate for Peace through the medium and influence of the Clerk of the District; the Officers of the Court of Justice were treated with contumely and opposed by a large armed force, and the authority of the Government was defied and set at nought by the said Tenoo, Ologoo Pattoo, Noy and their aiders and abettors.

And Whereas it is urgent and imperative for the maintenance of the peace, order and good government of the Protected Countries, and therefore for the welfare and happiness of the Inhabitants thereof that the said insurgent Chiefs and others aforesaid should be reduced to submission compelled to obey the Decrees of the Court and to acknowledge the supreme authority of the Protecting Power by submitting to its humane and equitable jurisdiction, and also, that the authority of Odonkor Ossu should be upheld in its integrity, And as it is necessary in order to accomplish these objects that the said Tenoo, Ologo Pattoo, Noy and their principal aiders and abettors should be brought to trial before the Civil Tribunal of these Settlements to answer for their grave and treasonable offences:

Now, Therefore, I do call upon all good, faithful and loyal Kings, Chiefs, Captains, Headmen and Citizens to aid and support the Protecting Power in quelling this rebellion in apprehending the ringleaders. . . .

22

GOVERNOR R. PINE TO THE DUKE OF NEWCASTLE: ASHANTI FUGITIVES, 10 DECEMBER 1862[1]

THE refuge afforded to runaway slaves and pawns under the British flag has, during my long experience, proved the source of the greatest irritation and annoyance to the native kings and chiefs, and the wound the most difficult for Her Majesty's representative to heal; and, unfortunately, I find here such questions of every-day occurrence.

While addressing these lines to your Grace, I have two claims from the powerful and much-dreaded King of Ashantee for the restoration of his subjects.

The first case is that of a slave boy, who for some weeks since

[1] *Parl. Papers,* 1864, xli (385), pp. 3-4.

escaped from his master on his way back to Ashantee, and took refuge in the kingdom of Assin, under this Protectorate.

As has been the custom, I desired the King of Assin to restore the boy to his Sovereign, and he is immediately sent down to me with special messengers.

An inquiry takes place in the hall of this castle, when the runaway boy avows himself to be a slave: that he was overloaded, and otherwise cruelly illtreated by his master: that he has taken the King's oath not to return to Ashantee; that death will be the penalty for his offence; and that by force alone will he leave the Protectorate.

The master admits the boy to be a slave, but declares that for my sake the King of Ashantee will not take his life.

The second case is that of an old man[1] (not a slave) who is claimed by the axe-bearer, sword-bearer, and followers of the King of Ashantee, who exhibit their symbols of office with much ceremony, and are considered of more than ordinary importance.

This old man is accused of having received and converted to his own use a piece of (so called) rock gold, which by the law of the country must be accounted for to the King; there is not a tittle of evidence except the remotest hearsay in support of the allegation, and the accused solemnly denies the charge. He is a man of property, and declares that the King desires only to entrap him, take his head, and afterwards possession of his property.

The King's messengers offer to swear that the accused will be fairly tried, and even if found guilty, will not lose a hair of his head.

The old man imploringly cries to me, 'Kill me if you like; that will be better than giving my head to the King.' And no one can assure me that I may rely upon the King's word; yet all would be delighted for me to restore to him his subjects.

Gladly would I try an experiment, and send back these subjects to Ashantee, for if confidence were once created between this Government and Ashantee, the greatest obstacle in the way of amicable relations between us would be removed; and if against the old man there were the slightest shadow of a *prima facie* case of criminality, my course would be clear; but as it is, I dare not deliver him up, much less the runaway boy. Their blood would be upon my head. And yet I feel that I am estranging, if not exasperating the most powerful King on this coast, and upon whom, according to his ideas, I am committing a gross injustice.

[1] Kwasi Gyani.

23

KING KWAKU DUA TO GOVERNOR R. PINE: ASHANTI FUGITIVES, 9 FEBRUARY 1863[1]

YOUR EXCELLENCY,

Yours was received safely by Ahmanquah Akkoomah on the answer of Quasie Gainie's case, because the case is between himself and his wife who was pawned to him by his family, and it happened some quarrels between them about gold, which his wife said took from the ground, and had given him, but Quasie Gainie said his wife have told lie; and the woman sworn the King's great oath that she did not tell a lie. Quasie Gainie also sworn that he likes the case should be brought forward in the presence of the King; in the meantime they were King's messengers, who were coming from different places, happened to be present there instant to bring him, and he set them eight days' time; and after the time fulfilled, he set them a time of 10 days more; again fixed them 15 days' time to come with them; and if he did not come then he is guilty according as he said the 15 days fulfilled, and refused to come the messengers condemned him to be guilty, and pronounced the woman faithfull, and claimed from her, according to the custom, oz. 4, 8 acs., to bring to the King; and the returned the gold back because the said Q. Gainie has given his own word to come to the King to settle the case for him; for this reason I return the gold back untill he comes with his wife to proof the case before me; because, he being the son of my captain, I believe him more to see his case for him. But when they returned they did not see him, but ran away to Cape Coast. I think you to be my good friend, and always believe you, that I can get back any of my slave who run away to you; but in poor George Maclean's time I made agreement with him in certificate, the one in Cape Coast Castle, and another in my hand therein, states that any Fantee person run up to me, to deliver him, and bring him to Cape Coast; and if any slave of mine also run away to Cape Coast you are to deliver him back also to me, as all the Governors that take charge of Cape Coast Castle did not move from this agreement, but always filled the rules of the said poor Geo. Maclean, except your time has destroyed the agreement; but little time before your coming, about 70 persons of Wassaw, your own subjects, ran away to my country, and the Governor of Cape Coast Castle sent a soldier to me for them, and I tried as much as possible and got them for the soldier to deliver them

[1] *Parl. Papers*, 1864, xli (385), p. 4. The Ashanti invaded the coastal area in March 1863 and retired in June, having been virtually unopposed by Major Cochrane and the Fanti forces.

to him. These persons I subsisted them oz. 4. 8 acs. gold dust to maintain themselves in the way because the Governor, being a good friend to foreshown agreement, and also to me. But when you came, any of my slave run away to Cape Coast, you and subjects take them and would bring him to me, so you have taken more of my subjects, and even my grandson, and now you are going to take Quasie Gainie also. So you must not blame me for keeping my subjects from coming down to Cape Coast, but when any disturbances arise, then all the blame is upon you because you have broken the rule of agreement. But one of my slaves Quarquah, who was witness to the said agreement, and who was the bearer of the certificate for me, is absent in the town, and I have sent messenger after him, but when he comes I will let him come with the book that you may see your guiltiness.

24

THE DUKE OF NEWCASTLE: MINUTE, ASHANTI FUGITIVES, 14 FEBRUARY 1863[1]

THE questions here discussed are some of the most painful & embarrassing which arise out of our well-intentioned but ill-advised system of 'protecting' certain Native Tribes on the West Coast of Africa. I imagine that the only advantage we claim or derive from this 'protection' is that the Tribes protected should abstain from slave-dealing and resort to legitimate commerce. But what are the *responsibilities* we incur? In the first place, the defence of the Tribes against such enemies as their obedience to our humane views entails upon them. Are we further bound to insist upon compliance by the protected Tribe with such moral laws as regulate, or ought to regulate, our own conduct? Are we bound to prevent them from giving up to the Vengeance of a Master a runaway Slave or to the punishment of death by a savage King a subject who has committed some political offence?

It is clear to me that in the two cases here mentioned—the slave boy and the old man—nothing could justify the Govr. in surrendering them after they had entered our Forts so long as the laws and practice of England remain what they are. The King of Ashantee can surely have no right to expect from us what we deny to the United States!

But the question is—ought we to *make* the King of Assin conform to our high standard of justice and humanity? It would be well if we could *induce* all these Tribes to do so, but how far are we to carry our *interference*, and does interference to this length promote in the long run the cause of freedom and civilization?

[1] C.O. 96/58. On no. 23.

I fear we must leave these protected Tribes for the present to their own course in these Matters, but though we do not forcibly prevent them we must in no way sanction them. They must not send runaways into our Forts and expect that in any case except that of clearly-proved heinous crime we will surrender them even to make 'friends' with a King of Ashantee.

I should approve of the refusal of the Govr. to surrender the man & boy & lay down some general rules in accordance with what I have written. . . .

25

GOVERNOR R. PINE TO KING KWAKU DUA: ASHANTI FUGITIVES, 21 FEBRUARY 1863[1]

. . . I HAVE carefully perused Your Majesty's last letter, and inter-rogated your messenger; but both are silent as to any evidence having been sent, and the messenger, indeed, states that you do not care for evidence.

Your Majesty speaks of an agreement with the late Governor George Maclean he should deliver you up all your runaway slaves and people, and that I am the first Governor who had broken this bargain—but I can find no such agreement; but on the contrary I find that Mr. Maclean himself says he gave up one or two persons, and those for proved crimes, upon payment of a sum of money.

I am willing to give up criminals, although there is no such agree-ment; but I do not consider Quasie Gainie a criminal until you prove him so.

Your Majesty complains that you gave up to this Government 70 of its subjects; but they had committed no crime, but were free people whom you detained, but I am sorry to say that up to this time you detain many more.

You say that I take and keep your subjects; but I never have and never will. I request them to return to you, but I cannot force them; and I trust therefore you will not prevent your subjects from coming here, because this will injure trade and show that you desire to break the friendship between us.

You also say that if disturbances arise I am to blame; but unless you cause disturbances they will not take place I hope; and, if they do, I trust you will help me to suppress them.

Your Majesty intends it appears to send a messenger named Quar Quar, who was witness to the supposed agreement with Governor

Maclean. I shall receive him well; and if he can convince me that Quasie Gainie should be delivered, I shall be happy to send him.

26

EDWARD CARDWELL TO GOVERNOR R. PINE: ASHANTI INVASION, 23 JUNE 1864[1]

... THE duty of defending the extensive territory included in the Protectorate can only be satisfactorily discharged if the chiefs to whom it belongs are united and resolute in their own defence. If they are not united, and will not take upon themselves the principal part of the exertions necessary, it will not be possible to defend them without exposing the Queen's forces to the risks of a deadly climate, and to the hazard of being virtually defeated by the disastrous consequences of that climate, before they have been able to bring the native enemy to the issue of arms.

The proper course, therefore, is to take every possible means for bringing the chiefs to an united and decided system of defence, and for this purpose to give them advice, to supply them judiciously with military stores, and in concert with the Officer in Command of the forces to furnish them with such assistance as he may be able to afford, without exposing his officers and men to any protracted residence in the interior, especially at the unhealthy season, and without weakening his force upon the coast so as to endanger the safety of the Settlements themselves. I must repeat the caution, which I conveyed to you in my Despatch of 23rd ultimo, that you should avoid, if it be in your power, the necessity of bringing to the Settlement a number of the Queen's troops too great to be properly accomodated on the coast.

Instructions to the same effect will be sent by the Secretary of State for War to Lieut.-Colonel Conran and I shall request the Lords Commissioners of the Admiralty to direct the attention of the Commodore on the station to the possibility that you may find yourself again engaged in measures of defence against an invasion of the King of Ashantee. Since, however, the experience of the past year has exhibited in so strong a light the great difficulties which attend operations on the part of Her Majesty's Forces, I rely on your using every exertion to avoid a renewal of the war. You have already received from the Duke of Newcastle the full expression of his approval of your conduct in respect of the origin of the late war,—I mean your refusal to surrender to a cruel death the two refugees demanded by the King of Ashantee; but that approval I now desire

[1] *Parl. Papers*, 1864, xli (385), pp. 16–17.

to repeat; and I take the opportunity of impressing upon you the great importance of your being clearly in the right in any case of difference which may hereafter arise. I trust that you will be careful to assure yourself that you are acquainted, as far as possible, with all the circumstances which may be alleged on either side, and that you will not permit yourself to become involved in any hostile operations until you shall have first exhausted every legitimate means of preserving peace.

27

T. F. ELLIOT: MINUTE, 18 MAY 1866[1]

[The case of John Aggery, King of Cape Coast.]

... I BELIEVE, and indeed for so long a period as 50 years as I have heard it said, The British right over the land at Cape Coast was assumed by all parties. Then doubts arose, and there was an idea of limiting the claim to lands within gun-shot of the Fort. This much around Forts is, I imagine, assumed by almost universal usage. But latterly this has been deemed too much, on account of the unpleasant dilemma about Slavery. In a despatch of the 7th of October last, Col. Conran showed that he had laudably prevented wanton blood-shed in some of the barbarous black customs close to Cape Coast, and he sent a Proclamation in which he announced that this kind of repression would be enforced for the distance of a cannon-shot from each English Fort. He was ordered to withdraw that notice.[2] Influence he might use, but he must say nothing implying extension of Territory. On the 2nd. of Nov. 1865 he reported that he had issued a Notice in order to get rid of filthiness and the roaming of pigs in Cape Coast Town under the walls of our Fort. His efforts were commendable, but the caution was repeated that he must avoid any expression which could bear the appearance of extending jurisdiction. I append these despatches for reference. The Governor's good intentions are praised, but the use or even the show of power is forbidden.

Thus it has happened that just at the moment when there could not be avoided some risk that the mind of an ignorant Chief might be unduly excited by the visit of [an] emissary to the Commons' Committee, it also was felt necessary entirely to disclaim any authority over the Town of which Aggery is called King, and which is inseperably united to our Fort, and contains the market built by us and the Government House.

Under these circumstances we received from King Aggery the

[1] C.O. 96/71, on Blackall to Cardwell, 19 April 1866; and *Parl. Papers*, 1867, xlix (198), pp. 53–54.
[2] See below, p. 439.

present letter, representing that the Governor has no right to pass laws without the previous knowledge of the King, and without *'the consent of the people'* ;—that it is a hardship that the duties of Customs go into the British Chest; that the Governor ought not to have interfered with the King's calling on the Chiefs of all neighbouring Tribes to contribute to paying for Mr. Martin's mission to England; and finally that John Aggery, the King, is about to form a Corps of Natives to be trained (as he possibly says idly) by some of H.M.'s Troops at Cape Coast, and to be maintained by the revenue of the Country.

I dismiss the minor points in Aggery's letter as being so inferior in importance to these splendid pretensions.

The moral appears to me to be that, there may be some danger in our too anxiously disclaiming any power whatever over the uncivilized people in immediate contact with our own Fort at Cape Coast, and that John Aggery, if it be only for his own sake and in order to save him from the misconceptions to which ignorant people are liable, should be effectually discouraged and repressed.

28

THE EARL OF CARNARVON TO GOVERNOR S. W. BLACKALL: JOHN AGGERY, 23 FEBRUARY 1867[1]

. . . I MUCH regret that the injudicious course taken by Aggery under bad advice has brought affairs to the present crisis. The anomalous position of the British Government on the Gold Coast affords no general principles for the decision of such questions as the present. I can only look to the history of the place, and to the nearest approach which can be discovered to a precedent, for my assistance in endeavouring to arrive at a just conclusion.

The town of Cape Coast is contiguous to, and inseparably united with, Cape Coast Castle. The Government House and the market are both situated outside the fort and within the precincts of the town. From time to time a chief was elected who, on being approved by the Governor, received the title of King, according to what may be a somewhat injudicious practice of white people on designating chiefs on the African coast. In 1856 the King of Cape Coast at that time was deposed by Colonel Ord, Her Majesty's Commissioner, in compliance with the wish of his people, who were dissatisfied with him. An interval followed of nine years, during which there was no king at all;

---

[1] *Parl. Papers*, 1867, xliv (198), p. 93. Aggery, after a short exile in Sierra Leone, was granted a pension and allowed to return in 1869.

but in February 1865 Governor Pine permitted and ratified the election of John Aggery. I find it stated in Colonel Conran's evidence before the Parliamentary Committee of 1865, that Governor Pine refused to admit his right to hold courts or appoint magistrates, and similar evidence in substance was given by Colonel Ord.

Aggery sent an agent named Martin to give evidence before the Committee of the House of Commons; and, after that agent's return, erroneous accounts are said to have been circulated of the proceedings before the Committee. There certainly has been a greater disposition than had appeared before to dispute the Governor's authority, and to set up the Native against the English Courts, which had been resorted to for many years by the natives with great benefit. After various other differences, Aggery, on the 15th of March 1866, addressed a memorial to Governor Blackall, which revealed the false ideas that he had been taught to entertain. He complained that the Governor passed British laws without making them known to Aggery beforehand, and obtaining the consent of the people; that the British Government received the revenues of Customs and all other public revenues, whilst none of them went to King Aggery; and he ended by announcing that he was about to form a corps of natives, to be trained to arms, for what he called the benefit of the country, and for purposes of self-defence. These pretensions need no comment. They are simply a claim to set aside the sovereignty and the power of the Queen at Cape Coast Castle itself, which is the chief seat of government on the Gold Coast. My predecessor replied that Aggery's pretensions must be effectually discountenanced; that he must be told that, in return for protection, we expect deference to our authority, and that he would not be permitted to make himself an exception to that rule. Aggery, however, did not alter his course. He appears to have fallen into the hands of a European, or man of colour, who had been lately dismissed from the office of churchwarden on account of his immorality; and after growing indications of disrespect for the Government, Aggery wrote his menacing letter to Colonel Conran, having previously held a meeting of his followers, at which, as reported by Colonel Conran, no fewer than 2,500 persons were assembled.

These are the circumstances under which Colonel Conran, believing, as he sets forth in his address of the 10th of December to the principal European and native inhabitants of Cape Coast, that there was grave danger, resolved upon immediately sending off Aggery by the mail steamer to Sierra Leone, with a view to the ultimate decision of the case by you or by Her Majesty's Government.

I have already said that I regret the absence of any settled law by which I could dispose of the matter. The practical question seems to be whether there are sufficient grounds for depriving Aggery of the title and position which was accorded to him by Governor Pine in the beginning of 1865. Whilst I regret that the affair should have been thus forced by him to such an issue, it is clear to me, on a review of the foregoing facts, that it would be inconsistent with the proper precautions to be observed at Cape Coast, and with that resistance which it is our duty to offer to the renewal, under the very walls of our forts, of the cruel punishments and exactions of native chieftains, to allow Aggery to resume his former position. I have, therefore, to express my approval of his deposition. I agree with you, that it will be better to avoid conferring a title so calculated to mislead as that of King, on the next person who may be elected by the people, and approved by the Governor, as the leading native authority in the town. The designation which you propose of Head man is far more appropriate.

With regard to Aggery himself, I should wish him to be treated with all reasonable consideration. I am prepared to sanction an allotment to him of a pension of 100 *l.* for his life, subject to his good behaviour, and in addition to any private means of his own. You will judge whether he should be required to reside for the present at Sierra Leone, or whether he can be permitted to return as a private person to the Gold Coast. This point I must leave to your discretion; but at first sight it seems to me that to require Aggery's residence at Sierra Leone, rather than at the Gold Coast, for one or two years, until the memory of recent transactions has passed, will be the safest course to adopt.

29

THE DUKE OF BUCKINGHAM AND CHANDOS TO GOVERNOR SIR ARTHUR KENNEDY: ELMINA FANTI, 22 SEPTEMBER 1868[1]

SIR,

I have received your despatch, No. 73 of the 13th of August, relative to the excited state of the Natives on the Gold Coast and their hostility to the Dutch.

I transmit to you copies of two letters which I have received from the Foreign Office on the same subject, and I enclose for your information and guidance a copy of the reply made to those letters by my direction.

In accordance with the contents of that letter, I have to instruct you to employ all the means in your power to restrain the Natives under British influence from every act of hostility against the Forts

[1] C.O. 96/77. For the Anglo-Dutch treaty of 5 March 1867, see below, p. 441 and n.

belonging to the Netherlands on the Gold Coast. I shall make arrangements with the Lords Commrs. of the Admiralty for sending Cruisers to the Coast, when the proper season arrives, to lend due weight and authority to the efforts of the British Authorities for the preservation of the peace. . . .

30

LORD GRANVILLE TO GOVERNOR SIR ARTHUR KENNEDY: ELMINA FANTI, 19 DECEMBER 1868[1]

SIR,

I have to acknowledge the receipt of your despatch No. 106 of the 7th Ult. reporting that you had held a lengthened conference with the Chiefs of Cape Coast and neighbourhood respecting the Fantee Nation, who submitted to you proposals for an establishment of Peace with the Elminas & for the conclusion (with the consent of the Dutch Governor at St George d'Elmina) of a Treaty Offensive & Defensive.

You likewise report the conference which you held with Colonel Boers, the Dutch Governor, at Elmina, & with the Kings & Chiefs of Elmina.

It is very much to be regretted that your attempts to induce the Elminas to accept the proposals of the Fantees [D. should have been frustrated by the Dutch Governor declining to support your recommendations] should have proved unavailing notwithstanding that the educated & intelligent inhabitants & Natives of Elmina assured you that the Elminas would accept the proposals, if the Governor of Elmina would only express a wish to that effect.

The statement made to you by the Dutch Governor that his instructions precluded him from taking or sanctioning any step which could by possibility be displeasing to & so jeopardize the Ashantee Alliance, justified you in informing him that the responsibility of the continuance of the present state of affairs must rest upon himself.

I entirely approve of your having assured Col. Boers at the same time that you would readily give him any moral support in your power, in keeping the peace but that you felt it to be your duty to abstain from any coercion against the Fantees. . . .

[1] C.O. 96/77.

31

ACTING ADMINISTRATOR W. H. SIMPSON TO KING KOFI KARIKARI: PROTECTION OF VOLTA TRIBES, 8 MARCH 1869[1]

YOUR MAJESTY,

It is with sincere regret that I am compelled to address myself to you in language of remonstrance.

2. Having visited Aquamoo for the purpose of procuring the adhesion by that people to the Treaty of Peace[2] lately made for securing the opening of the River Volta I was greatly astonished to find the Country in possession of Your Majesty's forces. Their presence was explained to me on the ground that Your Majesty had, on invitation, sent them to assist the Aquamoos in their quarrel with the Crepees.

3. Without venturing to impugn the motives which may have induced your Majesty to interfere in this quarrel, it is nevertheless my unpleasant duty to protest against the presence of Your Majesty's Troops in a Country owing and acknowledging Allegiance to the British Government and confessedly subject to its authority.

4. The settlement of the quarrel is, as Your Majesty will admit, properly within my province, and is, in fact, now the subject of my earnest endeavours, but my efforts have so far been opposed and thwarted by the Aquamoos who acting under the influence of the sense of increased power which Your Majesty's aid has given them have resolved again to attack the Crepees.

Knowing as I do the temper and feeling of all other Nations of the Protectorate I have not hesitated to expressing determination should Your Majesty's troops join in the proposed attack to lend every assistance moral and physical to the Crepees in the defence of their Country and independence.

5. Your Majesty may have been misled into the supposition that my Government had abandoned its rights and the Protectorate over the Countries situated on the east side of the Volta but the Aquamoos, Crepees, Agotims and Ahwoonlahs have never so regarded their political position; but have, on the contrary, remained faithful to their original terms of Allegiance, acknowledging the Title by purchase under which the Danish possessions and rights were

[1] C.O. 96/79.
[2] A treaty for freedom of trade on the Volta had been signed by Sir Arthur Kennedy and Awuna (Anlo) chiefs, 13 November 1868. Simpson did not succeed in detaching the Akwamu from alliance with Ashanti—part of whose army had invaded Krepi, north of Akwamu on the Volta, at the end of 1868. His policy was disapproved in Kimberley to Kennedy, 31 August 1870: C.O. 96/85.

acquired by the British and that the soil itself of their Countries is British soil.

Although not prepared to accept or adopt in their full absolute sense the views so entertained, Your Majesty will see by the Treaty which I beg to transmit herewith a copy that the British Government recognizes the Protectorate to extend over these Countries which border on the River Volta, and Your Majesty may be sure that the occupation by a Foreign power of any portion of them giving control over the river within the limits of the Protectorate will never be acquiesced in by Great Britain.

6. The material benefit to be derived from the freedom of the Volta to the Countries throughout or in proximity to which it flows will be appreciated by no one I am confident more readily than by Your Majesty. That, that benefit may be realised through the present Treaty and greatly increased Commercial intercourse spring up with Your Majesty's people is the sincere desire of my Government whose opinion it is that the more the advantages of Trade are understood and felt the greater will be the security for peace.

7. The value of this River for commercial purposes has only lately been brought into forcible notice and the interest taken and control exercised by my Government in the affairs of these Eastern Districts have in an equal measure revived and will not again be suffered to abate.

8. Whatever the reasons therefore may be by which Your Majesty has been led to accept the invitation of the Aquamoos I am yet convinced that Your Majesty's sense of justice and international obligations will readily induce you at my request at once to withdraw your forces from Aquamoo.

9. In which event I shall of course deem it my duty to guarantee the Aquamoos against attack by the Crepees and the immediate withdrawal of Domprey from Crepee and his return to his own Country.

10. Desiring to receive at Your Majesty's pleasure such friendly explanations as will remove all anxiety lest the peaceable relations which the British Government is so desirous to maintain should in any way be interrupted.

32

ADMINISTRATOR H. T. USSHER TO R. J. GHARTEY: FANTI CONFEDERATION, 8 DECEMBER 1869[1]

SIR,

I have to acknowledge the receipt of your letter of the 4th instant.

2. I am, I presume, to understand from its contents that you, assuming to represent the voice of the great Fantee chiefs in Council, are carrying on separate negotiations with Ashantee, without the knowledge and coincidence of the British Government.

3. I think you must be unaware of the folly of the course you are endeavouring to pursue. What can the King of Ashantee suppose, on receiving one statement from me and another purporting to be from the chiefs of Fantee? I am told your present Council consists of yourself, King Edoo,[2] and Mr. Bentil. I cannot for an instant admit that such an assemblage adequately represents the voice of the Fantees.

4. I wish to point out to you that you are infringing the prerogative of Her Majesty in this Protectorate, who alone, through Her representative, can deal with foreign powers. Whatever suggestions the Fantees have to make will receive every consideration, but your present attitude is one of distinct opposition to the Government.

5. You may perhaps be unaware that a considerable portion of the Ashantees detained by you have placed themselves under my protection, and are here in Cape Coast. I now distinctly request you to send down to Cape Coast the messenger from the King of Ashantee to you, and that you will co-operate with me in my efforts to relieve this country of the weight it now labours under from the misunderstanding with Ashantee. The Fantee honour in this matter will be strictly guarded by me, but it is impossible that any satisfactory settlement can be arrived at under the conditions you appear to meditate.

6. I trust that you will see the necessity of following my advice in this matter. . . .

[1] *Parl. Papers*, 1873, xlix (171), pp. 63–64. *R. J. Ghartey*, an African trader, was made first President of the Fanti Confederation in 1869 and King of Winneba in 1872.

[2] King Edu of Mankessim.

33

THE EARL OF KIMBERLEY: MINUTE, ASHANTI AND ELMINA, 10 SEPTEMBER 1871[1]

[The King of Ashanti has a claim to Elmina.]

. . . THE Dutch Govt. having repudiated the King's claim, I do not see what we can do but decide for ourselves whether we will accept the cession notwithstanding. I think we may accept it. If the Treaty is ratified, we should tell the King of Ashantee that we were willing to pay the money, but not as tribute and unless he makes war upon us because we don't admit the claim, no harm will come. He will hardly quarrel with us about the word, as of course he will continue to claim it as tribute & will represent our payment as such to those who are willing to believe him.

34

ACTING ADMINISTRATOR C. S. SALMON TO GOVERNOR SIR ARTHUR KENNEDY: FANTI CONFEDERATION, 4 DECEMBER 1871[2]

[Forwarding documents concerning the Fanti Confederation.]

. . . THE Constitution was handed to me in Government House by Mr. Davidson, the Vice-President, and Mr. Brew, Assistant Secretary; I refused to forward it officially to your Excellency on their part.

The parties have never applied for any sanction to their proceedings; I officially proclaimed them to be illegal some time since.

The taxes were to be levied throughout the whole of the Protectorate, as far as they were able to enforce their proceedings from the 1st of January next.

Mr. Grant has disavowed connection with the Confederation; I enclose copy of his letter. The people of the country, the merchants and traders, and all the kings and chiefs, except those immediately interested, are one and all utterly opposed to this new confederacy.

Kings Edoo, of Mankessim, and Otoo, of Abrah, are the only two cognisant of the actual proceedings, and even they have been partially imposed on. I have ascertained that many of the other

[1] C.O. 96/88. On Ussher to Hennessy, 6 July 1871. For the final cession of the Dutch forts by the Convention of 25 February 1871, see below, p. 446.
[2] *Parl. Papers*, 1873, xlix (171), p. 2.

chiefs mentioned, being those not immediately dependent on the two kings, know absolutely nothing of it.

Four of those mentioned as kings are very small chiefs.

The majority of the names appended to the constitution have been put down without the knowledge or consent of the parties themselves.

I have arrested all the ministry except Grant. Warrants are out against the other members of the Executive Council. I have sent for the judge. The parties will be tried in the Judicial Assessor's Court.

Two messengers have gone for the kings, one from the chiefs and another from the prisoners.

If the kings come down I shall send a magistrate to Mankessim for a day or two, to make inquiries and to obtain the seal.

This dangerous conspiracy must now be destroyed for good, or the country will become altogether unmanageable.

The people could not stand a double taxation. The Government have for a long time been attempting to do what this Confederation states to be its object, but they, the originators of it, have, more than all else, hindered us, by keeping up a state of feud and destroying unity and confidence.

They assume jurisdiction over a portion of Dutch territory.

35

THE EARL OF KIMBERLEY TO GOVERNOR SIR ARTHUR KENNEDY: FANTI CONFEDERATION, 16 JANUARY 1872[1]

SIR,

I have received your Despatch of the 16th ult. transmitting Despatches from the Administrator of the Gold Coast, reporting the proceedings of the so-called Fantee Confederation, and the steps which he had taken to check what he regarded as a dangerous conspiracy.

As the information before me does not lead me to attach so much importance to this movement, I cannot but regret that persons claiming to hold office under the Confederation should have been arrested, although they were subsequently, and apparently after a short interval, released on bail; and if on the receipt of this Despatch the proceedings which the Administrator contemplated in the Judicial Assessor's Court should not have taken place, you will instruct him to stay any proceedings and to free the parties from bail.

[1] *Parl. Papers*, 1873, xlix (171), p. 13.

But whilst I feel it necessary to give these directions, I fully recognise that the Administrator acted under a strong conviction that it was incumbent upon him to take the promptest and most effective measures for putting down a movement which, in his judgement, infringed the conditions of the British Protectorate, and was likely to prove delusive and injurious to the natives who would be affected by it.

There is hardly room for question that some of the Articles in the Constitution of the Confederation were practically inconsistent with the jurisdiction of the British Government in the protected territory. I think that the Administrator might have confined himself to issuing a proclamation warning British subjects from taking office under the Confederation, and stating that those who did so would be held responsible for their acts. He would have been quite right also in declining to recognise in any way the 'Constitution' until the Articles had been approved by Her Majesty's Government, and in publishing Mr. Grant's disavowal of participation in the proceedings of the Confederation.

Her Majesty's Government have no wish to discourage any legitimate efforts on the part of the Fantee kings and chiefs to establish for themselves an improved form of government, which indeed it is much to be desired that they should succeed in doing; but it is necessary that all parties concerned should understand that as long as they live under the protection of Great Britain, the protecting Government must be consulted as to any new institutions which may be proposed.

The manner in which the new 'Constitution' was brought into operation and certain acts were performed under it, without any previous communication with the British authorities, would be more likely to tend to discord and disorder than to further the ends which the promoters of the Constitution profess to have in view.

36

AGREEMENT: AKWAPIM AND KROBO, 21 AUGUST 1872[1]

WHEREAS unhappy differences and disputes have existed for a considerable time, whereby damage has been caused to the trade and social welfare of the Aquapem and Croboe nations, and which disputes lately threatened to disturb the peace of the nations of the Protectorate, and whose interest it is to live together in peace and friendship:

[1] *Parl. Papers*, 1873, xlix (160), pp. 143–4.

It is hereby agreed by the kings and representatives of both people that their present differences should be submitted to the Civil Commandant, whose decision, after full hearing, shall be final and binding upon both parties, and that henceforth friendship should exist between the two nations.

The following Articles being discussed and understood are agreed to:—

I. That both parties to this Agreement shall use their best efforts to discourage and prevent any molestation, interference, or depredations upon each other's plantations.

II. That the Aquapem and Croboe nations undertake and promise to arrest and deliver into the hands of the Civil Commandant of the Eastern Districts, without delay, any person or persons breaking the foregoing Article.

III. That for the better enforcement of the two foregoing Articles the king and principal chiefs of each nation do hereby bind themselves that, in the event of it being proved that any person or persons of their respective nations have broken the first Article, and the king and chiefs of that nation are unable to comply with the provision of the second Article, then a fine not exceeding two hundred and fifty pounds be imposed upon the offending nation.

IV. If any difference or dispute should in future arise between the Aquapem and Croboe nations, or between either of them and any other tribe or nation, it shall be submitted to the Civil Commandant, whose decision, after full hearing, shall be final and binding upon both parties.

> King Asah of Aquapem.
> Boafor Ansah, Chief of Akropong.
> Abbey Bio, Chief of Aducroom.
> Akautah, Chief of Lartey.
> Becknau, Chief Interpreter.
> Darcoo, Chief of Amarnacroom.
> Ashong, Chief of Apready.

Croboes.

> King Sackity of Eastern Croboe.
> King Noye of Western Croboe.
> Chief Lamee of Western Croboe.
> Agba, for Barry, Chief of Eastern Croboe.

Witnessed: G. F. Cleland, J. F. Hopkins, Lieut., 2nd W. I. Regt., William N. Fox, W. Addo, Government Interpreter, Accra.

37

ACTING ADMINISTRATOR C. S. SALMON
TO GOVERNOR J. POPE HENNESSY: SEKONDI
AND WASSAW, 7 SEPTEMBER 1872[1]

SIR,

I have to report for your Excellency's information that Dr. Horton, the Acting Commandant at Seccondee, has succeeded completely in settling the differences so long outstanding between the Seccondees and the people of that part of Ahanta and Wassaw.

2. There were great rejoicings in the town of Seccondee at the opening of the road to the interior, which has been closed for some years.

3. The effect of the good done is already apparent; at Seccondee itself palm oil is reported plentiful, and a vessel calling there, expecting to do only a slight trade, had to leave oil on the beach, not having capacity for more, and the super-cargo reported to his employer that he could have purchased 100 puncheons more.

4. Produce is reported as being ready for shipment at places on the Windward Coast, where it was never seen for a long time past.

5. I consider that any danger that may have been apprehended of disturbances on the Ahanta Coast has now passed. The great difficulty I look forward to was the opening of the roads from the Coast to the interior, the Wassaws and Ahantas having been more or less at war for five years.

6. The fact of both sides engaging in a trade conferring mutual benefit cannot fail to have the best effect.

7. The deputation I met here from Wassaw were willing to second any suggestion I made; my advice was taken respecting the opening of trade roads to the Coast and to the interior, and I gave a supply of tools to assist.

[1] *Parl Papers*, 1873, xlix (160), p. 146.

38

KING KOFI KARIKARI TO GOVERNOR R. W. HARLEY: ASHANTI CLAIMS TO ELMINA, DENKYERA, AKIM AND ASSIN, 20 MARCH 1873[1]

Sir,

His Majesty, Kalkaree, sends his best respects to your Honour, also to Messrs. Ossoo, Ansah and G. Blankson.

2. His Majesty states that, he being the grandson of Ossai Tutu, he owns the Elminas to be his relatives, and consequently the fort at Elmina and its dependencies being his, he could not understand the Administrator-in-Chief's sending Attah, *alias* Mr. H. Plange, to tell him of his having taken possession of them for Quake Fram, and notifying him also that in four months, he, the Administrator, would come to Ashantee to take away power from him.

3. He states that he has been made angry by this, and it was this which led to his sending his great captains and forces to bring him Quake Fram, of Denkerah, who dares to take his Elmina fort, &c., and also the Assins and Akims, who are his own slaves, and who have united with the Denkerahs to take power from him.

4. His Majesty further states that your Honour's restoring him these tribes, viz., Denkerahs, Akims, and Assins, back to their former position as his subjects, and also restoring the Elmina fort and people back in the same manner as they were before, will be the only thing or way to appease him, for he has no quarrel with white men; but should your Honour come in to interfere as he hears you are, that you have not to blame him, because he will then start himself.

5. That his Majesty having heard of some false information being brought to your Honour respecting your messengers and the white captives, he has requested their attesting this letter with their own signatures, of their being in health. . . .

[1] *Parl. Papers*, 1874, xlvi [C. 890], pp. 9–10.
[2] The Basel missionaries, F. Ramseyer, Mrs. Ramseyer, J. Kühne, and a French trader, J. Bonnat.

39

THE EARL OF KIMBERLEY TO CAPTAIN J. H. GLOVER: MISSION TO THE VOLTA, 18 AUGUST 1873[1]

[He is appointed Special Commissioner to the eastern districts of the Gold Coast.]

. . . THE Administrator will also be instructed to place under your orders the detachment of Houssa police now in that Settlement. And your previous relations with the Houssas, and intimate acquaintance with their character and habits, will, it is hoped, enable you to procure the recruits necessary to increase their strength to the number of 1,000, as suggested in your letter.

5. You will communicate with the Chiefs in the eastern districts, especially at Accra, and if you find them ready to take part in the projected movement in defence of the Protectorate, you will furnish them with assistance in the way of arms and ammunition, and such moderate sums of money as may be essential.

6. You will be supplied by the War Office with the requisite arms and stores, which will be transmitted direct from this country, so that you may not have to draw for anything upon the stores now on the coast; and you will be furnished with a steamer suited to the navigation of the Volta, and with three steam launches for proceeding up the river beyond the falls at Kpong.

7. A separate communication will be addressed to you on the subject of the financial arrangements of the Expedition.

8. The general object which you will keep in view is to create such a diversion on the flank and rear of the Ashantees as may force them to retreat from the Protectorate, or at all events, to so far harass and alarm them as to enable an attack to be made on them in front with better prospects of success.

9. The facilities which are afforded by a river navigable as the Volta is, to a long distance from the coast, for carrying the war into the Ashanti territory are unquestionable and it is stated that the country in the neighbourhood of that river is comparatively free from bush, and is, therefore, less unhealthy, and can more easily be penetrated than the district lying directly between the Gold Coast and the Ashantee country.

10. It would be impossible to suggest any particular line of operations. So much must depend upon the amount of support which may be afforded by the friendly tribes, the degree of opposition which

[1] *Parl. Papers*, 1874, xlvi [C. 1891], pp. 42-44.

may be encountered, the nature of the country and of the climate, the disposition of the populations of the district to be traversed, and of the neighbouring tribes, especially of the Aquamoos, that it must be left to you to judge for yourself on the spot, according to circumstances how far it may be prudent to attempt to penetrate into the Ashantee territory in the direction of Coomassie, and whether it may be practicable to march upon Coomassie itself.

11. You will, of course, bear in mind that the resources of the Ashantees are said to be very considerable, and that an advance to a great distance from the Volta must necessarily be attended with much risk, unless, indeed, you should succeed in obtaining assistance from the tribes in the eastern part of the Ashantee dominions.

12. So little is known of that part of Africa, that opinions on this point amount to little more than conjectures. If it be true, however, that the population is to a considerable extent Mahommedan, decisive successes gained against the Ashantees might cause some disruption of the ties which unite it to the Government of Coomassie.

13. But Her Majesty's Government hope that even if you should be unable to penetrate far into the Ashantee country the presence of a hostile force in the neighbourhood of the Volta will not fail seriously to alarm the Ashantees, and to make a powerful diversion in favour of the Protectorate, and they must not be understood as giving an opinion that a march upon Coomassie is an operation which it would in any case be prudent to attempt.

14. It will be advisable that you should seize any opportunity which may present itself of opening communications with the tribes on the north of Ashantee.

15. It is known that, from time to time, severe wars have been carried on between those tribes and the Ashantees, and news of an invasion of Ashantee from the East might possibly cause some movement to be made from the north.

16. Lastly, I have strongly to impress upon you the necessity of using your utmost efforts to prevent the natives who take part in the movement from putting to death captives and unarmed men, and committing the other barbarities which are too often the concomitants of native warfare.

Her Majesty's Government, when furnishing the tribes of the Protectorate with effective means to defend themselves against their enemies, have a right to require that those means shall not be used for purposes abhorrent to humanity and the usages of civilized nations. . . .

40

THE EARL OF KIMBERLEY TO GENERAL SIR GARNET WOLSELEY: THE ASHANTI WAR, 10 SEPTEMBER 1873[1]

SIR,

Her Majesty's Government wish to leave you a large discretion as to the terms which you may think it advisable to require from the King of Ashantee, but may I point out to you that the Treaty which was concluded with Ashantee in 1831, and of which I inclose a copy for your information, seems to afford a reasonable basis for any fresh Convention.

2. It would certainly be desirable to include in such a Convention an explicit renewal by the King of Ashantee of the renunciation, contained in the Treaty of 1831, of all claim to tribute or homage from the native Kings who are in alliance with Her Majesty; and further, a renunciation of all pretension on his part to supremacy over Elmina or over any of the tribes formerly connected with the Dutch, and to any tribute or homage from such tribes, as well as to any payment or acknowledgement in any shape by the British Government in respect of Elmina or any other of the British forts or possessions on the coast.

3. The King should also, for his own interest no less than with a view to the general benefit of the country, engage to keep the paths open through his dominions, to promote lawful commerce to and through the Ashantee country, and to protect all peaceful traders passing through his dominions to the coast; and it might be expedient that a stipulation should be made that a resident British Consul or Agent should be received at the Ashantee capital, if Her Majesty should think fit at any time to appoint one.

4. You will, of course, be careful to avoid as far as possible anything which may endanger the lives of the European missionaries and their families who have so long been held in captivity at Coomassie, without any fault of their own, so far as Her Majesty's Government are aware, and you will use every effort to secure their safe release.

5. You will also endeavour to procure the surrender of all the prisoners taken by the Ashantees from the tribes in alliance with Her Majesty.

6. It is a usual practice with the native tribes to demand hostages for the faithful performance of Treaties of Peace. This was done in

---

[1] *Parl. Papers*, 1874, xlvi [C. 891], p. 141. *Major-General Sir Garnet Wolseley* had served in India, Burma, and China, 1852–60, and was assistant Adjutant-General at the War Office before his appointment to the Gold Coast as Governor and Commander-in-Chief.

1831, when two hostages of high rank were delivered over to the British Government by the King of Ashantee. If you should find it advisable to make a similar demand on the present occasion, you will bear in mind that the hostages should be men of high rank and position in Ashantee.

7. It would be reasonable to exact from the King the payment of such an indemnity as may be within his means, which are said to be considerable, for the expenses of the war and the injuries inflicted on Her Majesty's Allies.

8. Lastly, the opportunity should not be lost for putting an end, if possible, to the human sacrifices and the slave hunting which, with other barbarities, prevail in the Ashantee Kingdom.

41

THE TREATY OF FOMENA, 13 FEBRUARY 1874[1]

Treaty of Peace between Major-General Sir Garnet Joseph Wolseley, C.B., K.C.M.G., acting on behalf of Her Majesty Victoria, Queen of Great Britain and Ireland, and Saibee Enquie, acting on behalf of His Majesty Koffee Kalkalli, King of Ashantee.

Article I.

There shall be hereafter perpetual peace between the Queen of England and her allies on the coast on the one part, and the King of Ashantee and all his people on the other part.

Article II.

The King of Ashantee promises to pay the sum of fifty thousand ounces of approved gold as an indemnity for the expenses he has occasioned to Her Majesty the Queen of England by the late war, and undertakes to pay one thousand ounces of gold forthwith, and the remainder by such instalments as Her Majesty's Government may from time to time demand.

Article III.

The King of Ashantee on the part of himself and his successors renounces all right or title to any tribute or homage from the Kings of Denkera, Assin, Akim, Adansi, and the other allies of Her Majesty formerly subject to the Kingdom of Ashantee.

Article IV.

The King on the part of himself and of his heirs and successors does hereby further renounce for ever all pretensions to supremacy

[1] *Parl. Papers*, 1874, xlvi [C. 922], pp. 10–11.

over Elmina, or over any of the tribes connected with the Dutch Government, and to any tribute or homage from such tribes, as well as to any payment or acknowledgment of any kind by the British Government in respect of Elmina or any other of the British forts and possessions on the coast.

Article V.

The King will at once withdraw all his troops from Appolonia and its vicinity, and from the neighbourhood of Dixcove, Secondee, and the adjoining coast line. . . .

Article VI.

There shall be freedom of trade between Ashantee and Her Majesty's forts on the coast, all persons being at liberty to carry their merchandize from the coast to Coomassie, or from that place to any of Her Majesty's possessions on the coast.

Article VII.

The King of Ashantee guarantees that the road from Coomassie to the river shall always be kept open and free from bush to a width of fifteen feet.

Article VIII.

As Her Majesty's subjects and the people of Ashantee are henceforth to be friends for ever, the King, in order to prove the sincerity of his friendship for Queen Victoria, promises to use his best endeavours to check the practice of human sacrifice, with a view to hereafter putting an end to it altogether, as the practice is repugnant to the feelings of all Christian nations.

Article IX.

One copy of this Treaty shall be signed by the King of Ashantee and sent to the Administrator of Her Majesty's Government at Cape Coast Castle, within fourteen days from this date.

Article X.

This Treaty shall be known as 'The Treaty of Fommanah'.
Dated at Fommanah, this 13th of February, 1874.

(Marked thus) X X

This Treaty was presented at Government House, Cape Coast, on the 14th March, 1874, by Quamin Enkwe, Chief-Captain, accompanied by Prince Coffee Jutin, son of the King, and signed and ratified by them and the Undersigned Representatives of the Ashantee Kingdom.

(Signed)   Coomassie—
> Coffee Jutin, his X mark, Prince.
> Quamin Enkwe, his X mark, Chief Captain.
> Kodjo Bah, his X mark, Linguist.
> Quaco Sawoo, his X mark, Fetishman.
> Edoo You, his X mark, Swordbearer.
> Kodjo Bumpabo, his X mark, Swordbearer.
> Coffee Egey, his X mark, Court Crier.
> Quacoe Nenqui, his X mark, Captain.
> Quacoe Woosoo, his X mark, Swordbearer.

Juabin—
> Kobina Ampea, his X mark, Linguist.

Beqwa—
> Quacoe Kurenkwe, his X mark, Swordbearer.

Kokofoo—
> Coffee Akenah, his X mark, Linguist.

Inkutanassie—
> Quamin Maffol, his X mark, Swordbearer.

Jusuta—
> You Essal, his X mark, Swordbearer.

Mampon—
> Quamin Essim, his X mark, Swordbearer.

Ardakanjah—
> Quamin Kaye, his X mark, Linguist.

Assarful—
> You Amponsah, his X mark, Goldkeeper.

Ackiramadie—
> Coffee Brempah, his X mark, Swordbearer.

Sawoorah—
> Acquasie Wuoosu, his X mark, Captain.

Acrofoom—
> Kodjoe Amoatin, his X mark.

Signed on behalf of Her Majesty Queen Victoria,
    (Signed) J. Maxwell, Lieutenant-Colonel, Acting Administrator.
Witnesses:
    (Signed) James Marshall, Chief Magistrate and Judicial Assessor.
        C. C. Lees, Acting Colonial Secretary.

42

TREATY WITH AWUNA, 22 JUNE 1874[1]

TREATY of Peace entered into at Jellah Coffee, this 22nd day of June, 1874, A.D., between Kings Tackie and Solomon of Accra, King Dosoo of Addah, and Charles Cameron Lees, Esq., Acting Administrator of Her Majesty's Goverment on the Gold Coast, and Commodore Sir William Natham Wrighte Hewett, V.C., K.C.B., Commanding the West African Squadron, on behalf of Her Majesty the Queen of England, on the one part, and the undermentioned representatives of the Ahwoonah nation on the other part, namely:—

Abjaba, Chief of Ahwoonah; Folu, Chief of Jellah Coffee; Cocumay (for Aholu), War Captain of Ahwoonah; Tameklo, Chief of Hoolay; Joseph Akrobolu, Chief of Teroboy; Tingee, Captain of Anyako; Tubolu, Interpreter; Afadee, Interpreter; Gelo (for Amegashy), Chief of Quittah; Posoo, Captain of Jellah Coffee; Antoquo, Chief of Anyako; Agodogo, Chief of Fiaho; Agblevo, Chief of Atiave; Nyaho, Chief of Salame; Letsha, Chief of Aveno; Saba, Chief of Afyarengba; Mogolu, Chief of Feta; Amedomy (for Antonio), Chief of Whey.

The following Articles, being fully discussed and understood, are agreed to:—

Article I.

That there shall be peace and friendship between the represented nations henceforth and for ever.

Article II.

That the River Volta shall be kept open for all lawful traders; and both parties to this Treaty shall use their best efforts to discourage any dishonest or unlawful interference with legitimate traders of whatever country or nation.

Article III.

With the view to remove any doubts which the natives might entertain as to the right of Her Majesty the Queen to occupy Jellah Coffee, Quittah, and any other places deemed necessary to be held in order to place the Ahwoonah country or any portion of it under the same jurisdiction as is exercised by Her Majesty over the other portions of the Gold Coast.

It is hereby further agreed that, should it seem fit to Her Majesty's

[1] *Parl. Papers*, 1875, lii [C. 1140], pp. 44–45. Encl. in Lees to Carnarvon, 23 June 1874.

Government they shall occupy any such places as may appear to them expedient, for and on behalf of Her Majesty the Queen of England.

In proof of our truth and sincerity, we subscribe our names to this Treaty, a copy of which is to be retained by each party. . . .

[Signatures and witnesses.]

43

PROCLAMATION: DOMESTIC SLAVERY, 17 DECEMBER 1874[1]

. . . WHEREAS the Queen's Most Excellent Majesty has resolved to abolish slave–dealing in Her Protectorate of the Gold Coast and the importation thereinto of slaves and persons intended to be dealt with as slaves and also to provide for the emancipation of persons holden as slaves within the said Protectorate:

And whereas the Governor and Legislative Council of the Gold Coast Colony have by Her Majesty's Commands enacted an Ordinance bearing date 17th December, 1874, by which all selling, buying, or dealing in slaves is declared unlawful, and is absolutely and for ever abolished, prohibited, and made penal, and another Ordinance also bearing date 17th December, 1874, providing for the emancipation of persons holden in slavery.

Now I do hereby proclaim, publish, and make known the said Ordinances to all persons whom it may concern.

And further, in order and to the intent that all the Kings, Chiefs, Headmen, and other persons throughout the aforesaid Protectorate and elsewhere may the more readily understand and obey the laws now made and enacted, I hereby require every person to take notice and observe that now and from henceforth

It is unlawful to sell or purchase or transfer or take any person as a slave.

It is unlawful to sell or purchase or transfer or take any person so as to make such a person a slave.

It is unlawful to put or take any person in pawn for or on account of any debt.

It is unlawful to bring any person, whether slave or free, into the Protected Territories from Ashantee or elsewhere in order that such person should be sold or dealt with as a slave or pawn.

It is unlawful to take or send any person out of the Protected Territories in order that such person should be sold or dealt with as a slave or pawn.

It is unlawful to make any contract or agreement for buying, selling,

[1] *Parl. Papers*, 1875, lii [C. 1139], pp. 42–43.

or pawning any person, or for bringing any person into or out of the Protected Territories to be sold or dealt with as a slave or pawn.

It is unlawful that any King, Chief, Headman, or other person should, in any palaver, or by any means whatsoever, force or constrain any person for the purpose of compelling him to remain at any place or serve any master contrary to the will of such person.

Whosoever offends against any of these laws shall be punished with imprisonment and hard labour and may also be fined.

If in any contract hereafter made it should be agreed that any person shall be put in pawn, or bought or sold or transferred, the whole contract shall be null and void.

And further, let all persons whom it may concern take notice that all children who, after the 5th day of November, 1874, have been or shall be born in the Protectorate, have been declared free. But it is not intended by any of the aforesaid laws, or otherwise, to offer inducement to any persons to leave any master in whose service they may be desirous of remaining, or to forsake the rooms where they have been accustomed to inhabit, and that it is intended to permit the family and tribal relations to continue in all respects according as used and wont except only that of slavery and such customs as arise therefrom and are thereon necessarily dependent. . . .

D. DAHOMEY, LAGOS

Introductory Note

TREATY relations with the Fon and Gun of Dahomey and with the southern Yoruba were a product of missionary contact in the 1840's and the anti-slave trade campaign. The treaties were easier to draw up than to negotiate; and Lord Stanley was not prepared to consider the reoccupation of the British fort at Whydah as a preparatory step towards winning the King of Dahomey's good will. A treaty of trade and friendship signed in 1847 was the most that could be obtained; and as the economic reasons for King Ghezo's reluctance to abolish the export of slaves were better understood after Cruickshank's visit to Abomey in 1848, Lord Palmerston fell back on the Buxton thesis of encouraging legitimate trade, and appointed a vice-consul to Whydah to expound it. The same thesis, urged on the Foreign Office by the Church Missionary Society, turned Palmerston's attention towards Lagos and Yorubaland as a centre for African 'regeneration' and for a route to the Niger. Consul Beecroft's mission to Abomey and Abeokuta in 1850 represented the last attempt to win over King Ghezo by peaceful means and confirmed the British alliance with the Egba begun by the missionaries during the previous decade. Thereafter, the Navy was ordered to proceed with a policy of blockade along the Slave Coast, and Beecroft was left free to make a show of force at Lagos. The bombardment of the port in 1851 and the installation of King Akitoye as signatory to an anti-slavery treaty produced a crop of similar agreements with chiefs in the area—including one with the King of Abomey which was never kept. At Abeokuta British influence was at its highest: Commander Forbes supplied ammunition and military advice in return for an anti-slave trade agreement at the end of 1851; and in 1852 the alliance was renewed, though Commodore Bruce would not be committed to supplying more arms and stores.

The establishment of the Lagos consulate gradually made the island a protectorate in all but name. By the end of the 1850's the need for adequate jurisdiction over British subjects and the fear of foreign competition in an expanding market led to the annexation in 1861. By the end of the decade, too, British relations with the Egba had deteriorated, after the failure of the consuls to mediate between Abeokuta and Ibadan at the beginning of the Ijaye war and because of the alarm occasioned by the establishment of a colony on the coast.

Until his departure in 1872, John Glover, as Lieut.-Governor and Administrator, was the dominant figure in the formation of British policy towards the Yoruba and their neighbours at Porto Novo. His interpretation of wars between the successor states of the Oyo empire was strictly in terms of Lagos trade, with occasional reference to southern Dahomey export of slaves. The aims of his policy were peace by diplomacy or by the threat of force and unhindered access through Yorubaland to the Niger and the Hausa states. He was immediately involved in the last stages of the Ijaye war which resulted in military action against the Egba at Ikorodu and a blockade of Egba supplies. More radical suggestions for action against Porto Novo were rejected. Mediation by Governor Blackall helped to restrain Glover in his more expansionist moods and established the rule that a policy of no interference was to be followed, unless the 'safety and well-being' of Lagos Colony were in question. A liberal interpretation of this condition brought Glover into conflict with the Egba again in 1867. Not till 1871 were representatives of the Yoruba states persuaded to meet at Lagos to settle differences; but this inconclusive diplomacy did not satisfy Glover's ambition for keeping open alternative paths to the interior in order to by-pass Egba tolls. It proved impossible to open the eastern route through Ondo. Glover, therefore, concentrated on subduing the Egba by blockade in 1872, which brought him once more to the verge of annexation at Porto Novo[1] and into conflict with Governor Pope Hennessy who arrived at Lagos in April from Sierra Leone to put an end to this initiative. Two unauthorized missions to the interior cost Glover some of the commendation he had earned for his administration of Lagos and enabled Hennessy to discredit his policy. When Glover went on leave in June 1872, he was not allowed to return. Lord Kimberley, however, did not approve of his policy being suddenly reversed. By 1874 the Glover-Hennessy dispute over relations with African states had been subsumed under wider considerations of constitutional reform and the definition of Lagos Protectorate boundaries—measures which contained the Lagos

[1] See below, V, p. 453.

administration within its own area, but did not settle the problems of economic dependency on the interior which Glover had tried to solve.

I

LORD STANLEY: MINUTE, RELATIONS WITH KING GHEZO, 14 MAY 1845[1]

Mr. Stephen,

It seems to me that there is no evidence to warrant the conclusion that the King of Dahomey is at all disposed to lend his assistance in putting down Slave Trade,—but on the contrary that there is every reason for supposing that he is not inclined to surrender the practical advantages which he derives from his present pursuits. I can scarcely, therefore, concur in the utility of making any proposition to him wh. should not be founded upon the offer of solid and tangible benefits in substitution for the profits which he might be required to renounce.

With regard to the reoccupation of Whydah, I can perceive no Colonial interest in the question. It is reasonable to suppose that the establishment and display there of British authority will have the effect of raising some additional trade, but not probably to an extent that would compensate for the expenditure to be incurred for rebuilding the fort and supporting it. I think it a great mistake to suppose that a petty trade of such a description is calculated to put down the traffick in Slaves. Why is the King of Dahomey anxious for the reoccupation of Whydah?—because he wants more trade, or more abundant supplies of bafts, rum, tobacco, musquets and gunpowder. From the slave dealers he can only obtain dollars.

All that I would venture to suggest for your own consideration on this subject is, that if Whydah is to be reoccupied, it should be done as an act of Government, not as a departmental arrangement.

2

SIR GEORGE BARROW: MINUTE, DAHOMEY TREATIES, 9 AUGUST 1847[2]

The annexed dispatch from Captain Winniett reports the result of his visit to the King of Dahomey. He has concluded two Treaties with the King—one of Amity & Commerce—the other for the Suppression

---

[1] C.O. 96/8. On Canning (Foreign Office) to Stephen, 12 May 1845.

[2] C.O. 96/11. On Winniett to Grey, 12 May 1847. The treaty for peace and trade between Great Britain and Dahomey was dated 5 April 1847; the second, renouncing the slave trade, was undated and unsigned. Both were forwarded to the Foreign Office for a decision.

of the Slave Trade. They are founded on Drafts of Treaties prepared 3 or 4 years since by Captain Foote of the Navy and were seen at the Foreign Office, to which Department all such Treaties are forwarded with a request that the Secretary of State for Foreign Affairs would state his opinion whether the Treaties should be confirmed.

The only observations that occur to me with respect to these Treaties, are,

1st. in the one for Amity and Commerce British Subjects are to be allowed to hoist a Flag of the Kingdom of Dahomey in concert with the flag of England on their respective Factories—there would be great risk, I think, in this measure, of disputes if not collision with other Powers.

2nd. in the Treaty for the suppression of the Slave Trade an engagement is made to pay the King yearly for seven years Goods to the value of 2000 dollars (about £416) of the selection of the King.

Captain Winniett states that by giving up the Slave Trade, the King will lose considerably more than 50,000 dollars (about £10,400) he proposes therefore that a considerable addition should be made to the amount stated in the Treaty, & that the person whom it is proposed to depute on a visit to the King next year, should be authorized to increase the amount.

I collect from Captain Winniett's observations that this Treaty will not be carried into immediate effect.

Captain Winniett recommends the re-occupation of Fort Whydah . . . he states that the repair of the Fort may be effected at a cost of from £500 to £750 & the expense of the Establishment, with 50 Soldiers he estimates at £1000 per annum.

He proposes also a British Resident at Abomey, the capital of the King of Dahomey, but this, I conceive, is a question for the Foreign Office.

3

LORD STANLEY TO B. HAWES: DAHOMEY TREATIES, 21 DECEMBER 1847[1]

. . . I AM to state to you in reply, for the information of Lord Grey, that Lord Palmerston thinks the Treaty of Amity and Commerce should be ratified, and he proposes therefore to signify to the King of Dahomey that Her Majesty's Government approve of the Terms agreed upon between the Lieutenant Governor and the King. Lord Palmerston also thinks that the proposed Treaty for the Suppression of the Slave Trade may be Signed whenever the King of Dahomey

[1] C.O. 96/12. *Benjamin Hawes* was Parliamentary Under-Secretary at the Colonial Office, 1846–52.

ZBP

can be induced to agree to it. As to the means of putting down the Slave Trade mentioned in the Lieutenant Governor's despatch, in regard to which Lord Grey asks Lord Palmerston's opinion; Lord Palmerston observed that they seem mainly to consist in the Treaty and in the occupation of Whydah. With respect to the Treaty I have already stated Lord Palmerston's opinion, and it must rest with Lord Grey to determine about the Fort of Whydah.

[Sir George Barrow (marginal note), December 1847.]
Lord Grey has decided that nothing shall be done with respect to Whydah, until the survey of the Lagoon [by Capt. Denham] has been effected.

4

B. CRUICKSHANK: REPORT ON A MISSION TO THE KING OF DAHOMEY, 19 NOVEMBER 1848[1]

[Summary of the minutes of two meetings with Ghezo, King of Dahomey. The economy of the kingdom cannot be abruptly changed from trade in slaves to trade in natural products.]

. . . BUT in considering the general question of the abolition of the Slave Trade, I have wandered from the territories of the King of Dahomey, to which I ought, perhaps, to have confined my report. The remarks, however, which I have made generally, will of course apply also to his particular portion of the coast. If I am required to prescribe for his case alone, I believe that a close blockade of the coast for a couple of years (by which I mean a total exclusion of all merchantmen, from Cape St. Paul's to Lagos, would compel him to give up the Slave Trade, to enable him to obtain the manufactures of Europe, which have now become indispensable to him. A blockade of this nature, however, might embroil us with the American or the French Government, and perhaps with both; and it would be attended with other evils, which render such a measure far from desirable. In the first place, it is doubtful whether the slaves now exported from his country would not, in the case of a blockade, be carried by the interior beyond Lagos, and shipped there; thus only entailing a more toilsome march upon the slaves; and in the next place it must be remembered that there is a very extensive and yearly increasing oil trade springing up along his whole coast, which bids fair at no distant day to rival the Slave Trade; and it will be seen from my report of his conversations, how much this trade had done for Porto Nuovo, Badagry, &c.

[1] *Parl. Papers*, 1850, ix (53), pp. 534-5.

It would, therefore, be altogether impolitic to give any interruption to so promising a source of prosperity for the country. I believe it is through this trade, and legitimate trade generally, that the Slave Trade is to be put down in his dominions; and this may be very much encouraged and fostered by the appointment of a Government agent at Whydah.

It does not appear to me that the appointment of a governor for the fort would be desirable, where his power would be so limited. A consul to reside in the fort, as it is acknowledged as Government ground, would perhaps be the most suitable arrangement. I forsee that a prudent intelligent man in such a situation would exercise a very beneficial influence over the King, and would eventually become his principal adviser. It would aid greatly in turning the King's mind in lawful trade, if the English Government would send out a sound practical agriculturalist accustomed to cultivation in the tropics. I have already said, that he is desirous for instruction to his people in these matters; and before anything can be expected to be done in the growth of cotton and coffee, a planter must be provided. All the expenses attending this experiment, with the exception of labour alone, must be paid by the Government, and the produce of the plantation given to the King, who will provide as many labourers as may be thought necessary. Only show him that he has a mine of wealth in the soil of his country, which he can extract by the labour of his people, and the Slave Trade in his dominions has received its death-blow. The proof, however, which must be given of the source of such a source of riches, must be the produce of the riches themselves, and therefore must the original expenses of the establishment, such as the planter's salary, and the necessary supply of plants and tools, be defrayed by the Government. No useful exertions need be expected generally among the people, until they have seen the first result; and should that result be favourable, our object is gained. The probable unsuitableness of the soil for the production of coffee or of cotton is, in my opinion, the only possible obstacle. There is certainly nothing in the appearance of the country to indicate anything of the kind, for a more fertile soil, and one more abounding in rich and healthy plantations, I have never seen. But I do not wish to pronounce too confidently before an experiment has been made, as I have seen the injury done to the coffee trees at Cape Coast by an insect which often attacks the plant when in an apparent healthy state. It might be the same in Dahomey; but I would fain hope there would be found nothing of the kind; as far as can be at present judged, everything promises well, and if the plants thrive, England may expect a large supply of cotton and coffee from this country. It must not be expected that the King and his people will set about this industrious work of themselves; as soon may we expect the confirmed gambler, sharper, or black-leg to earn his livelihood by patient and honest industry, as to see a slave-dealing king and people become suddenly painstaking agriculturists. It is not unreasonable to hope, however, that after the first harvest there will be a new spirit developed. The history of the palm-oil trade there affords a strong confirmation of this hope; in 1836, a hundred puncheons of oil were not shipped from Whydah; in the present year I am assured that 4,000 have been exported. When the King has a country with resources of this kind to fall back upon, who shall despair of fighting the battle of legal against illegal trade, upon such a far field? . . .

5

LORD PALMERSTON TO JOHN DUNCAN: APPOINTMENT AS VICE-CONSUL 29 MAY 1849[1]

SIR,
Her Majesty's Government having understood that you are about to proceed to Dahomey, on the African Coast with the laudable endeavour to introduce into that country some of the arts of civilized Life, whereby legal Commerce will be eventually promoted, and the traffic in slaves discouraged, I have to state to you that, with the view to assist and countenance your exertions in this undertaking, Her M's Govt. propose to invest you with the temporary rank and character of British Vice-Consul within the dominions of the King of Dahomey on the Western Coast of Africa; and I herewith inclose a formal Letter authorizing you to act as such.

Your previous knowledge of the King of Dahomey, and of African affairs, and of the habits of the Blacks, renders it unnecessary for me to give you any very specific Instructions for the guidance of your conduct whilst you shall act as British Vice-Consul.

It is hoped that the influence which you may obtain may enable you to prevent misunderstandings between the Chiefs and Crews of British Vessels resorting to the Ports of the Dahomey Country, for the purposes of legal trade.

With a view to such Results you will endeavour to encourage the Chiefs and People to till the soil, and to produce available exports, so that they may obtain by Barter the European commodities of which they may stand in need.

You will take every suitable opportunity to impress upon the minds of the Chiefs, and of their principle [sic] Councillors the great

[1] C.O. 267/211. *John Duncan* had sailed on the Niger Expedition and travelled through Dahomey, 1845–6. He accompanied Commander Forbes on a joint mission to the King of Dahomey in November 1849.

advantages which they will derive from the extension of legal commerce with the nations of Europe & America; and you will assure them that Her M's Govt. earnestly desire to their welfare and improvement. . . .

[Duncan is to send information on local trade and place himself under the orders of John Beecroft who is to be appointed Consul for the Bights of Benin and Biafra.]

6

LORD PALMERSTON TO CONSUL JOHN BEECROFT: MISSION TO DAHOMEY, 23 JANUARY 1850[1]

. . . THE King of Dahomey might probably object that the loss which he would sustain by the suppression of the Slave Trade would be certain and immediate, while the profit which might accrue to him from import duties on legitimate trade would be uncertain, and at all events not arising until after some lapse of time.

To obviate this objection, if made, you are authorized to say that if the King of Dahomey would immediately and entirely put an end to Slave Trade in and through his dominions, the British Government would engage to make him for a limited time, say three years, an annual present as a compensation for the loss which he would during that period sustain, it being reasonably to be expected that by the end of such a time legitimate commerce would have afforded him an income which would fully make up to him for the loss incurred by the cessation of Slave Trade. Her Majesty's Government must leave it to your discretion to make with the Chief the best arrangement which you can on this head, and you are authorized, in case of necessity, to promise an annual present, either in money or goods, at the option of the King, to be continued for three years.

If you can conclude a satisfactory arrangement, on this principle, you will draw up and sign with the King a treaty to that effect.

[1] *Parl. Papers*, 1852, liv (221), p. 4.

7

LORD PALMERSTON TO CONSUL JOHN BEECROFT: MISSION TO ABEOKUTA, 25 FEBRUARY 1850[1]

SIR,

I now proceed to give you instructions for your mission to Abbeokuta. . . .

A short time since a deputation from the Church Missionary Society waited upon me, and represented among other things that the establishment of commercial relations with the interior of Africa through the Yoruba tribe, would materially contribute to the suppression of the Slave Trade, and that of free and secure navigation on the Ogu could be obtained, most of the advantages which were proposed by the expedition of the Niger in 1842 would be attained; that traders from the banks of the Niger visit the principal markets of Abbeokuta; and that there is little doubt that the road to Egba and Rabbah, the former of which was the highest point reached by the Niger expedition, might be opened for trade through the Ogu River.

Abbeokuta, as I am informed, is the chief town of the Egba province of the Yoruba Kingdom, and contains above 50,000 inhabitants. It is situated upon the east bank of the Ogu, and that river is navigable for canoes to within a mile of Abbeokuta, and discharges itself into the sea at the Island of Lagos. Lagos is therefore said to be the natural port of Abbeokuta; but the Slave Trade being carried on at Lagos with great activity, the Yoruba people have been obliged to use the port of Badagry, between which and Abbeokuta communications are carried on by a difficult road by land.

But besides the impediments which the slave-dealers at Lagos throw in the way of legitimate commerce, the Yoruba people experience another hindrance to their prosperity, and a constant cause of alarm from the hostility of the King of Dahomey, who harasses them by an annual slave-hunt, and who is said to have threatened the destruction of the town of Abbeokuta. His enmity is said to be especially excited by the fact that the Yorubas are becoming prosperous and are gaining wealth by their commerce with the English, and by refraining from Slave Trade.

The Yorubas are represented to be a commercial people in their habits, and much trade has been carried on between Abbeokuta and Sierra Leone, by way of Badagry. It is also believed that many of the liberated Africans have emigrated from Sierra Leone to Abbeokuta,

[1] *Parl. Papers*, 1852, liv (221), pp. 29–30.

and many vessels owned entirely by liberated Africans are said to be employed in the Trade between Sierra Leone and Badagry. There is also a regular trade carried on between London and Badagry. English missionaries have been received both at Badagry and Abbeokuta with great kindness, and their valuable services in imparting religious instruction and in promoting social improvements appear to be duly appreciated by the natives. The people of Abbeokuta are said to feel a strong desire that the Slave Trade should be wholly abolished, and that legitimate traffic should be substituted for it; and the Egba chiefs manifest a favourable disposition towards the English nation.

Under these circumstances, Her Majesty's Government have deemed it advisable that you should at a suitable season visit Abbeokuta, in order to ascertain by inquiry on the spot, the actual wants, and wishes, and disposition of the Yoruba people.

I have accordingly to instruct you to proceed on this mission as soon as you conveniently can. Before you proceed, however, to Abbeokuta, it will be advisable that you should first visit the chiefs on the coast within your Consular jurisdiction, and that you should endeavour to ascertain the sentiments and intentions of such of them as have not already entered into amicable relations with Great Britain.

You will explain to those chiefs what is stated in my letters addressed to the chiefs themselves, that the principal object of your appointment is to encourage and promote legitimate and peaceful commerce, whereby those chiefs and their people may obtain in exchange for the products of their own country, those European commodities which they may want for their own use and enjoyment; so that the great natural resources of their country may be developed, their wealth and their comforts increased, and the practice of stealing, buying, and selling men, women, and children, may be put an end to; and you will impress upon their minds that it is the earnest desire of the Queen's Government to contribute in every possible way to their welfare and prosperity, if they will but listen favourably to your overtures, and will honestly follow the friendly counsel which is offered to them by the British Government.

When by personal communication with these chiefs, you shall have made yourself acquainted with their disposition, and shall have ascertained how far they may be inclined to break off their connexion with slave-dealers, and to apply themselves to legitimate trade, you will be the better prepared to undertake with advantage your mission to Abbeokuta.

With respect to any aggressive intentions of the King of Dahomey towards the Yoruba people, you will have an opportunity, during your visit to Abomey, to bring that subject under the notice of the King; you will represent to him that the people who dwell in the

Yoruba and Popo Countries are the friends of England, and that the British Government takes a great interest in their welfare, and would see with much concern and displeasure any acts of violence or oppression committed against them; that moreover, there are dwelling among those tribes many liberated Africans and British-born subjects whom Her Majesty's Government are bound to protect from injury.

It is to be hoped that such representations as these, enforced by whatever influence you and Lieutenant Forbes may have acquired over the King in the course of your negotiations upon other matters, may induce the King to make a formal promise to abstain from future aggressions against the people of Yoruba and Popo, and from molesting in any way the liberated Africans or Europeans who reside in Abbeokuta and Badagry, or who frequent the countries adjoining the territories of Dahomey.

8

H. U. ADDINGTON TO THE SECRETARY OF THE ADMIRALTY: LAGOS, 11 OCTOBER 1860[1]

SIR,

I am directed by Viscount Palmerston to transmit to you the accompanying copy of a despatch from Mr. Beecroft, Her Majesty's Consul in the Bights of Benin and Biafra, reporting the failure of his endeavours to induce the King of Dahomey to enter into a treaty for the suppression of the Slave Trade, and stating that the King of Dahomey had expressed an intention of making war on the Chiefs of Abbeokuta. I am to transmit to you also a copy of a letter addressed by the King of Dahomey to Her Majesty, stating his views with respect to the Slave Trade.

I am to request that you will lay these papers before the Lords Commissioners of the Admiralty, and that you will state to their Lordships that it appears to Lord Palmerston that it seems clear that the King of Dahomey will not be induced to enter into any agreement to abandon Slave Trade until the Chief of Lagos shall have previously been brought to enter into such an agreement, and until Slave Trade shall have been effectually stopped at Whydah.

It seems, therefore, to Lord Palmerston, that measures should forthwith be resorted to for the purpose of putting an end to Slave Trade at Lagos, and that with this view the present Chief of Lagos should be invited to enter into an agreement similar to that which was agreed to by the chiefs at Gallinas; and if he should refuse to do

[1] *Parl. Papers*, 1852, liv (221), p. 45.

so, that measures similar to those which were enforced against Gallinas, should be brought to bear upon Lagos, or that steps should be taken to replace in authority at Lagos the former chief, who is understood to be now at Badagry, and who would, it is believed, willingly subscribe to the proposed engagement.

In the meantime it would be desirable that the strictest watch which circumstances might admit of should be established, to prevent slaves from being exported from Whydah.

It is obvious that the King of Dahomey, who is the greatest originator of Slave Trade in that part of Africa in which his territory lies, will yield, in regard to that Trade, only when compelled by necessity to do so, and when he shall be quite sure that the profits which he would give up by relinquishing that pursuit, would not pass into the hands of any less conceding neighbour. . . .

9

LORD PALMERSTON: MINUTE, LAGOS, 18 FEBRUARY 1851[1]

SEPARATE & additional Instructions to Mr. Beecroft to represent to Chief of Lagos that the British Govt is resolved to put an End to the African Slave Trade and has the Means & Power to do so. That it is employing those means with increasing Success on both sides of the Atlantic. That the British Govt has made Treaties with the greater Part of the native Chiefs on the West Coast of Africa by which those Chiefs have engaged to put an end to Slave Trade within the limits of their territorial authority and to encourage lawful Commerce in the stead of Slave Trade. That Lawful Commerce is more advantageous to the nations of Africa than Slave Trade and that therefore the British Govt in putting down Slave Trade and in encouraging Lawful Commerce is conferring a Benefit upon the People & Chiefs of Africa. That Gt. B[ritain] is a Strong Power both by Sea and by Land, that her Friendship is worth having and her Displeasure it is well to avoid. That the Friendship of Gt. B[ritain] is to be obtained by the Chiefs of Africa only on the condition that they abandon Slave Trade and expel the Slave Traders, and that those Chiefs who may refuse to do these things, will surely incur the Displeasure of the British Govt. If the Chief should shew a disposition to refuse compliance Mr. Beecroft should beg him to remember that Lagos is near to the sea, and that on the Sea are the Ships and the Cannon of England; and he should also bear in mind that he does not hold his authority

---

[1] F.O. 84/858. A draft treaty was sent to Beecroft, 20 February 1851, and on the basis of Palmerston's minute instructions were forwarded, 21 February 1851: *Parl. Papers*, 1852, liv (221), pp. 83, 85–86.

without a Competitor, and that the Chiefs of the African Tribes do not always retain their authority to the End of their Lives.

10

ENGAGEMENT WITH THE KING AND CHIEFS OF LAGOS, 1 JANUARY 1852[1]

ENGAGEMENT between Her Majesty the Queen of England and the King and Chiefs of Lagos, for the abolition of the Traffic in Slaves. Signed at Lagos, on board H.M.S. 'Penelope', on the 1st day of January, 1852.

Commodore Henry William Bruce, Commander-in-Chief of Her Majesty's ships and vessels on the West Coast of Africa, and John Beecroft, Esq., Her Majesty's Consul in the Bights of Benin and Biafra, on the part of Her Majesty the Queen of England, and the King and Chiefs of Lagos and of the neighbourhood on the part of themselves and of their country, have agreed upon the following Articles and Conditions:—

Article I.

The export of slaves to foreign countries is forever abolished in the territories of the King and Chiefs of Lagos; and the King and Chiefs of Lagos engage to make and to proclaim a law prohibiting any of their subjects, or any person within their jurisdiction, from selling or assisting in the sale of any slave for transportation to a foreign country; and the King and Chiefs of Lagos promise to inflict a severe punishment on any person who shall break this law.

Article II.

No European or other person whatever shall be permitted to reside within the territory of the King and Chiefs of Lagos for the purpose of carrying on in any way the Traffic in Slaves; and no houses, or stores, or buildings of any kind whatever, shall be erected for the purpose of Slave Trade within the territory of the King and Chiefs of Lagos; and if any such houses, stores, or buildings shall at any future time be erected, and the King and Chiefs or Lagos shall fail or be unable to destroy them, they may be destroyed by any British officers employed for the suppression of the Slave Trade.

Article III.

If at any time it shall appear that Slave Trade has been carried on through or from the territory of the King and Chiefs of Lagos, the

[1] *Parl. Papers*, 1852, liv (221), pp. 191–2.

Slave Trade may be put down by Great Britain by force upon that territory, and British officers may seize the boats of Lagos found anywhere carrying on the Slave Trade; and the King and Chiefs of Lagos will be subject to a severe act of displeasure on the part of the Queen of England.

Article IV.

The slaves now held for exportation shall be delivered up to any British officer duly authorized to receive them, for the purpose of being carried to a British colony, and there liberated; and all the implements of Slave Trade, and the barracoons, or buildings exclusively used in the Slave Trade, shall be forthwith destroyed.

Article V.

Europeans or other persons now engaged in the Slave Trade, are to be expelled the country; the houses, stores, or buildings hitherto employed as slave factories, if not converted to lawful purposes within three months of the conclusion of this Engagement, are to be destroyed.

Article VI.

The subjects of the Queen of England may always trade freely with the people of Lagos in every article they may wish to buy and sell in all the places, and ports, and rivers within the territories of the King and Chiefs of Lagos, and throughout the whole of their dominions; and the King and Chiefs of Lagos pledge themselves to show no favour, and give no privilege to the ships and traders of other countries, which they do not show to those of England.

Article VII.

The King and Chiefs of Lagos declare that no human beings shall, at any time, be sacrificed within their territories, on account of religious or other ceremonies; and that they will prevent the barbarous practice of murdering prisoners captured in war.

Article VIII.

Complete protection shall be afforded to missionaries, or ministers of the Gospel, of whatever nation or country, following their vocation of spreading the knowledge and doctrines of Christianity, and extending the benefits of civilization within the territory of the King and Chiefs of Lagos. Encouragement shall be given to such missionaries or ministers in the pursuits of industry, in building houses for their residence, and schools and chapels. They shall not be hindered or molested in their endeavours to teach the doctrines of Christianity to all persons willing and desirous to be taught; nor shall any subjects of the King and Chiefs of Lagos, who may embrace the Christian faith, be, on that account, or on account of the teaching or exercise thereof, molested or troubled in any manner whatsoever. The King and Chiefs of Lagos further agree to set apart a piece of land, within a convenient distance of the principal towns, to be used as a burial-ground for Christian persons. And the funerals and sepulchres of the dead shall not be disturbed in any way or upon any account.

Article IX.

Power is hereby expressly reserved to the Government of France to become a party to this Treaty, if it shall think fit, agreeably with the provisions contained in the Vth Article of the Convention between Her Majesty and the King of the French for the suppression of the Traffic in Slaves, signed at London, May 28, 1845. . . .

11

COMMODORE BRUCE TO THE SECRETARY TO THE ADMIRALTY: SLAVE COAST TREATIES, 11 FEBRUARY 1852[1]

Penelope,
Whydah,
11 February 1852.

SIR,

It is my pleasing duty to request you will lay before the Lords of the Admiralty the accompanying engagements on the part of the Kings and Chiefs of the following places: Block-house, Elminax, Chica, Adaffie, Flohow, Porto-Segoora, Gomuluta, Little Popoe, Aghwey, Great Popoe, for the abolition of the Slave Trade, &c.; copies of letters from Commodore Forbes, of Her Majesty's Ships 'Philomel;' together with journals of his daily proceedings while employed in negotiating with the native rulers in this part of Africa, from the 1st to the 17th of January, and from the 23rd of January to the 4th of February, 1852.

Their Lordships' order of the 14th of October last required me, under certain circumstances, to blockade the port of Whydah, and the rest of the Dahomian coast. Acting upon the spirit of this order, I took upon myself to extend the blockade to all those ports and places in the Bight of Benin, from longitude 1° to 4° 30′ east of Greenwich, where I knew the Slave Trade existed. The successful result of this measure exceeds what I expected, because the end has

[1] *Parl. Papers,* 1853 (*Slave Trade* A), p. 68.

been gained in a much shorter time than I anticipated, and without the slightest temporary inconvenience to legitimate traders; in fact, it appeared that the mere declaration of blockade had the effect of bringing the Chiefs to the terms which Her Majesty's Government desired to obtain from them.

On the 16th of December I arrived off Whydah, and established the blockade, with instructions to the commanders of cruizers not to interfere to prevent vessels from completing contracts which had been entered into prior to their receiving the usual notification. On the 27th, Lagos was taken; and on the 11th of February, I had the satisfaction of declaring the places mentioned in the inclosed notice to be free, as heretofore, for the purpose of legitimate trade.

In less than two months from the commencement of our operations, three-fourths, and by far the most important, of the Chiefs, in the Bight of Benin, solemnly engaged to abolish the Slave Trade for ever within their respective territories. I must attribute the happy results which have been obtained to the zealous and faithful manner in which the several commanders have carried out my instructions to them; no one in these respects has exceeded Commander Forbes of the 'Philomel': regardless of the danger that always attends a prolonged stay on shore in this part of Africa, he has voluntarily been twenty-nine days away from his ship, travelling in the interior to Cannah, and along the coast from Whydah to Quitta; fully succeeded in his negotiations with nine Chiefs of different States, and partly with the King of Dahomey. His journals are replete with useful and entertaining matter, and they prove him to be a highly intelligent and indefatigable officer.

I shall consider what course it is necessary to adopt in respect to Dahomey, and to acquaint their Lordships with my determination as early as possible.

12

CONSUL BENJAMIN CAMPBELL TO LORD CLARENDON: KING DOCEMO, 3 SEPTEMBER 1853[1]

[Reporting the death of King Akitoye of Lagos.]

. . . IN the very unsettled state of the town, it was very impolitic that it should remain without a supreme Chief, or King. I therefore requested an interview with the Chiefs civil and military; they having assembled, and being ignorant of Ackitoye's death, I requested them to inform me, who, in the event of Ackitoye's death, was the proper person to succeed him in the Kingship of Lagos. I withheld from

[1] F.O. 84/920.

them the fact of Ackitoye's death, and told them that my reason for applying to them was, that his state of health and prostration of strength, rendering him unable to attend to business, and his life of uncertain duration, rendered it necessary in the disturbed state of the country that the matter of succession should not be in dispute. After retiring and consulting for some minutes, the Chiefs returned; and informed me that, Ackitoye's eldest son Docemo[1] would be the right-ful successor to his father. I requested them to send for him, that I might be introduced to him. On his arrival, and after his introduction, I again put the question to the Chiefs, whether Docemo would be the man to succeed in the event of his father's death; they unanimously (taking Docemo by the hand,) declared, and presented him to me, as the lawful King should his father die.

I then told them that being unanimous on that point, was very satisfactory, as Ackitoye had died during the previous night; they therefore saw their future King; upon which the Chiefs embraced Docemo, and made the usual token of submission, by prostrating themselves on the ground and snapping the left finger on the palm of the hand. On the following day, Docemo was formally acknowledged and presented as King to the people; and received a salute of 21 Guns from the boats of H.M.S. Waterwitch and Atholl; the Com-manders, and several of the Officers of these ships, being present.

13

CONSUL G. BRAND TO LORD JOHN RUSSELL: THE IJAYE WAR, 9 APRIL 1860[2]

MY LORD,

My preceding number informed Your Lordship of the retreat of the army of the King of Dahomey and that all chance of any attack upon Abbeokuta this season was over. I regret, however, to add that the Yoruba Country is in a very unsettled state, caused probably in part by the intrigues of Dahomey, who is known to have made efforts to form an alliance with the people of Ibadan. The Ibadan army is encamped around Ijaye—another large town, the 'Are' or Chief of which, has never recognized the present King of Oyo, who still claims the titular dignity of King of the Yoruba Country.

[1] *Docemo* (Dosunmu), with the advice of the consuls acted as paramount chief till annexation when he was pensioned off (see below, p. 429). He remained titular Native Authority till his death in 1885.

[2] F.O. 84/1115. The town of Ijaye between Ibadan and Oyo had become an important trade centre in the 1830's. The war arose out of the refusal of the *Are* of Ijaye to recognize a new *Alafin* at Oyo in 1859, which brought Ijaye into conflict with Ibadan. The Egba supported Ijaye. Two attempts at intervention by Consuls Brand and Foote were unsuccessful and the town was destroyed by Ibadan in 1862.

The people of Ijaye are friendly to Abbeokuta and the fear is, that the Abbeokutans may be induced to join their friends and thus a general war ensue which might last for years.

The effect of all this is an interruption of the course of trade and as we depend at Lagos, very much upon the Yoruba country for our supplies of articles of export—that interruption is severely felt here.

I enclosed the Copy of a paper which was delivered to me officially by the Revd. Messrs Crowther and Chaser and I do enclose a number of a small newspaper which for some time past has been published at Abbeokuta.[1] From these enclosures an idea of the present state of affairs in the interior may be gathered.

On the receipt of the former of these papers, I called a meeting of the merchants, which was very numerously attended and has assembled from time to time since by adjournments.

At the meeting of last Saturday, it was resolved to carry out the resolution, passed at the first meeting, of sending a deputation to the Interior, the object of which would be, in the first instance, to advise the Abbeokutans to keep out of the strife, and, in the second, to endeavour to persuade the Ibadans to give up their warlike intentions and to open the roads for the flow of peaceful commerce.

I thought, that as we had recently afforded aid to the Abbeokutans we were in a good position to be heard with deference, and I felt it right to promise to the merchants that I would send a special Messenger to support their deputation.

I have made an application to the Senior Officer for permission being given to Lieutenant Lodder, as a most competent person, to undertake this important service, an application which I believe will be granted, and the deputation will likely depart in a few days.

14

WILLIAM WYLDE TO SIR GEORGE BARROW:
RELATIONS WITH ABEOKUTA,
31 OCTOBER 1862[2]

MY DEAR SIR GEORGE,

We have done nothing here in regard to the threatened attack on Abbeokuta for the reason that we have no power to render effectual aid even if we wished to do so. We have had several letters calling our attention to the threats of the King of Dahomey but Ld. Russell has merely acknowledged their receipt. When the notification first appeared in the Papers of the Dahomian threats, I had a gentleman

[1] Encl. copies of the first Yoruba newspaper produced by the Abeokuta mission —*Iwe Irohin*, No. 9, March 1860.
[2] C.O. 147/2.

here in hot haste from the Church Missiony. Society to find out what the Missionaries should do in the event of Abbeokuta being attacked. I told him that if there really was any danger of the place being taken by the Dahomians, the Missionaries had better withdraw to Lagos, and that I thought their doing so would have a good effect, inasmuch as it would shew the Abbeokutans that they must depend upon themselves and not think that after their bad conduct to us in refusing to receive our Vice Consul[1] and continuing to persist in their war with the Ibaddans contrary to our advice, they had merely to ask for assistance and receive it as a matter of course. He did not like the advice and said he would write to Ld. Russell, but if he did so his letter has not been sent into the Office. Of course if there were really any danger of Abbeokuta being taken and sacked, as it would be by the Dahomians, we should do what we could to prevent so disastrous a result, because as our object is to civilize Africa, it would be a great blow to have all that we have hitherto done utterly destroyed by such a Ruffian as the King of Dahomey, but I think it would not be bad policy to make use of the Dahomian threats as a lever to assist our own policy—I have told you what my views are but of course if you want to know officially what answer should be returned you must write an official letter to us.

15

LIEUT.-GOVERNOR J. H. GLOVER TO LORD JOHN RUSSELL: EGBA, IJEBU AND IBADAN, 9 JUNE 1863[2]

[Glover intends to make peace between the Egba and the Ijebu.]

... SHOULD I succeed in this, I would propose that on a peace being made, (which, unless Her Majesty's Government pursue a coercive policy, will only be, when they are tired, and not before) that the Egbas shall give up Makun to its rightful master the King of Jebu, and go back to Abbeokuta. That the Ibadans give up Ipara, also belonging to the King of Jebu, and go home to Ibadan. That as an equivalent to the evacuation of Makun, we shall reconcile the Iccorodu people to their King. That ourselves and the Ibadans shall have a road from Iccordou to Ibadan subject to such [tax] on goods

[1] After the annexation of Lagos, the Egba refused to receive Vice-Consul Taylor in July 1862.
[2] C.O. 147/3. After the fall of Ijaye, the war between the Egba and Ibadan shifted south, closer to the Lagos hinterland around the lagoon markets which supplied arms to the north and foodstuffs and palm products to Lagos. *Commander J. H. Glover* had served on the West Africa Station in 1851 and on the Niger, 1857–61; he had surveyed the Lagos lagoons and commanded the gunboat at Lagos where he became Administrator of the colony, 1863–72.

as shall be decided upon by the contracting parties, (viz: Her Majesty's Government, Ibadans, and Jebus) which tax will be understood to be paid to the King of Jebu for the security of the road through his country.

This road, my Lord, is the sole object of the War. The King of Jebu by keeping this Road closed to us, throws a large revenue into the hands of the Abbeokutans who have a monopoly of the trade from Lagos via Abbeokuta to the Interior.

Your Lordship will not fail to observe that the King of Jebu, the Ibadans and ourselves, will be mutual gainers by this arrangement; the Egbas alone losing the monopoly for which they are fighting. . . .

16

LIEUT.-GOVERNOR J. H. GLOVER TO LORD JOHN RUSSELL: EGBA BLOCKADE, 14 MARCH 1865[1]

[He has blockaded the Egbas at the mouth of the Ogun and opened paths through Ijebu.]

. . . On the 17th ultimo I deemed it necessary to cut down such trees across the mouths of the River Ogun as I considered would be sufficient to obstruct the passage of Egba Troops to our farms. Your Lordship will observe that all produce or provisions had for some time past been prohibited from coming to Lagos and therefore no stoppage of trade from Abbeokuta has taken place consequent upon this measure which has been adopted to ensure the peace of the Settlement and the safety of our farms.

[Attempts by Sierra Leone settlers to breach the blockade have failed.]

5. Having at length succeeded in entirely detaching the Jebu from the Egbas I have been thereby enabled to obtain a road to the Ibadans and to enter into negotiations with those Tribes, vizt. the Jebus and the Ibadans for the purpose of permanently opening a road to the Niger through their countries—of reopening the trade of Ejerin market and of establishing the peace of the surrounding country on a permanent basis by inducing the Egbas to raise the siege of Ikorodu and return home. . . .

[1] F.O. 84/1250. At the end of March 1865, Glover defeated the Egba at Ikorodu with a mixed naval and West Indian force, assisted by Hausa police and Ikorodu Yoruba.

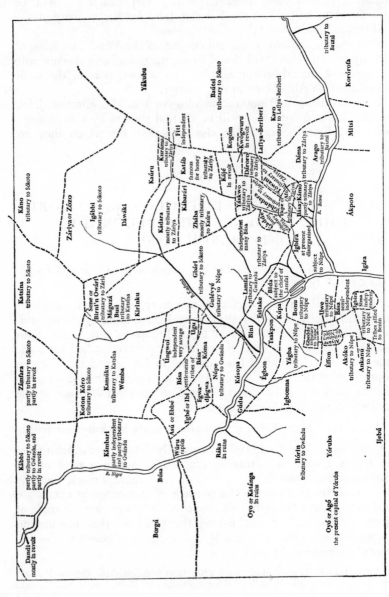

Map 3: Dr. W. B. Baikie, Political Map of the Fulani—Hausa States, 1862. No scale.

17

WILLIAM WYLDE: MINUTE, EGBA AND INTERIOR ROADS, 20 APRIL 1865[1]

LORD RUSSELL will perhaps recollect that the Egbas have for some years past entirely closed the roads leading from Lagos to the interior, and have stopped our trade with Abbeokuta whenever it suited their policy to do so.

The result of Captain Glover's present policy it to open a better and shorter road from Lagos to the Niger and to the interior, and to make the Colony entirely independent of Abbeokuta.

We shall undoubtedly have great complaints from the Missionaries at Abbeokuta, and probably also from the Church Missionary Society in London but the result of the opening of this new road cannot fail to be highly beneficial to the Colony and to the cause of Africa generally. The Egbas have been supported by our Missionaries, and until lately by this Country, because they professed to be averse to the Slave Trade, but they have deserved very little encouragement or protection either from our hands or at the hands of the Missionaries as within the last six or eight Years they have swept upward of 30 Towns & Villages from the face of the Country, one of them, the Town of Ijaye containing upwards of 60,000 Inhabitants.

I take it that the policy of the Govt. is for the Secy. of State for the Colonies to approve or disapprove, but as far as this Depart. is concerned, the result of the Policy carried out at Lagos and in the neighbouring Countries has been to put a stop entirely to the very large export trade in Slaves that used formerly to be carried on along the Shores of the Bight of Benin.

18

GOVERNOR J. H. GLOVER TO EDWARD CARDWELL: PORTO NOVO, 7 SEPTEMBER 1865[2]

SIR,

I have the honour to report for the information of H.M.G., that the state of the Town and adjacent Country of Porto Novo is such, as to require the more decided interference on the part of H.M.G.

2. On the 17th January 1852, a Treaty was executed between Commodore H. W. Bruce, Commander in Chief of Her Majesty's

[1] F.O. 84/1250. Russell approved this view: Minute n.d. [April] 1865.
[2] C.O. 147/9.

Land Forces on the West Coast of Africa, on behalf of Her Majesty the Queen of Great Britain and the King and Chiefs of Porto Novo. On the 26th April 1861, in consequence of the total violation by the King and Chiefs, of the articles of the said Treaty, it was found necessary to destroy Porto Novo by an armed Force, and to exact, from the King and Chiefs, additional articles to the said Treaty, copies of which are enclosed.

3. It is unnecessary for me to specify what particular articles of the Treaty of 1852 and the additional stipulations of 1861, have been violated since the abandonment by the French, of their Protectorate of Porto Novo. Indeed I may say that the Treaty has since been entirely ignored. I may mention that one of the final causes of the abandonment of the French Protectorate was the inability of the French Admiral to obtain from the King and Chiefs the release of a woman, a British Subject, that I had demanded.

4. The present King, Mepon, has, since his accession to the throne, during a period extending over the short space of a year, killed and sacrificed upwards of 200 people, principally women; and report goes even so far to credit him, his Chiefs and Priests with the butchery of upwards of 600 victims.

5. The case of the two women, mentioned in my Proclamation of 22nd August, Copy herewith, brought this state of things to a crisis; and you will observe, by my letter to the Senior Naval Officer in these waters, dated 18th August, copy of which I enclose, that I requested him to proceed to Porto Novo and obtain from the King the release of the woman reported to be still living. From that Officer's report, dated August 21st, you will be enabled to judge of the character of the King and his Chiefs, as well as from the insults and threatening gestures offered to the Commander of 'The Investigator' and his officers.

6. By the Senior Naval Officer's letter of 24th August, you will observe that the woman was eventually given up, and that it was the opinion of that officer that the native population would not assist this Government in placing the present King's nephew, who is a son of the late King, upon the throne—a measure which at the moment I contemplated.

7. I must observe that this opinion of the Senior Naval Officer was based on very insufficient information; and that, although the various Tribes, chiefly Yorubans, would most willingly assist in placing 'Yinrofin Dasi', the late King's son, on his father's throne, they would much rather that the direction of the affairs of the Country were at once placed in the hands of this Government.

8. The unexpected return of the Colonial Steamer, 'Eyo', from the River Nun, whither she had gone to effect some repairs, enabled me to visit Porto Novo on the 26th August. I immediately sent for

the Chiefs, who came on Board, and first of all informed them that since the British Subject had been delivered up, and the King, and Chief Agboton, had apologised to the Senior Naval Officer for the gross insult to himself and his officers, there was no danger to be contemplated for the safety of the Town of Porto Novo, on account of any hostile measures from the British Force then lying off the Town; but that, should the King of Porto Novo set fire to the Town before retreating to the interior, as I was informed he had threatened to do, there was no sum of money, which, if regained, I was not prepared to pay for his capture.

9. I informed the Chiefs that the state of things, which had existed for some months past in Porto Novo, would not be allowed to continue; that Europeans as well as Natives enjoyed no security either of life or property; that Trade was continually being disturbed by the constant and necessary interference of a Vessel of War, to compel the King to keep his engagements which he always violated immediately after her departure; that British Subjects, Natives of Lagos, were continually chained, plundered, and sold to Whydah; that all payment of debts in Porto Novo was totally ignored; that human sacrifices were of frequent occurrence and that the number of persons butchered by the Kings, Princes and Chiefs was monstrous and inhuman; that, as a security for the future, I would fine the King 20 puncheons of Oil, value £200 sterling, for the life of the British subject starved to death or poisoned by him, and 50 puncheons, value of £500, as compensation to the Merchants for the removal of their goods, the injury done to their trade, and the expenses to the three Steamers sent for their protection; that they would have seven days allowed them to pay the fine, in order that I might be enabled to report the circumstances to H.M.G. by this Mail; that, as it was impossible that a Vessel of War could be entirely devoted to the protection of British life and interests at Porto Novo, and to enforce the maintenance of the Treaty, a British Agent would henceforward reside in Porto Novo, agreeably with Article 4 of the said Treaty.

10. After two prolonged interviews with the Chiefs, on board Her Majesty's Ship 'Handy', I succeeded in obtaining a promise of payment of the fine; but they distinctly refused to recognise the Treaty, or to receive the Agent.

11. I informed them that I should refer the matter to the decision of H.M.G., having first, however, communicated with the European Merchants in Porto Novo, and received their reply, my rejoinder to which is also enclosed.

12. Having officially notified to the King my definite intentions, and requested the Senior Naval Officer to render the assistance required, I left Porto Novo in Her Majesty's Ship 'Investigator' on the 30th August.

13. I may report that, up to the present date, not a gallon of the fine has been paid—from the total inability of the King and Chiefs to procure it, the people all steadily refusing to bring the Oil in from the Country, to have it seized by the King and Chiefs, without payment, stating that, as the misconduct of the King and Chiefs has brought upon them the displeasure of H.M.G. (although not upon the People of the Country) the King and Chiefs might pay the fine themselves. The King and Chiefs have endeavoured to obtain the Oil from the Merchants on trust. This request has been steadily refused.

14. I would venture with all respect, to advance the opinion that three courses are open to the British Government, viz.

1st. To depose the present King, and to place the son of the late King 'Yinrofin Dasi', on the throne. This is an experiment which we before tried at Lagos in 1851, and which failed, resulting in the ultimate occupation of this Settlement by the British Crown:

2nd. To compel the King to adhere to his Treaty, by receiving the British Agent ashore. These two measures will entail the necessity of the constant presence of a Man of War, and, often, the interference of a Military Force, carrying with it a vast expense in maintaining 'de facto' though not 'de jure', the Government of Porto Novo;

3rd, and lastly, the annexation of the Town of Porto Novo, and its immediate district, which should be confined within the narrowest limits consistent with the safety and protection of the peace. I must observe that any one of these measures can be adopted with ease; but the one, easiest of all, and which would best meet the wishes, not only of the European Merchants, but of the majority of the Native Community, would be the third and last step I have proposed. These people are so thoroughly tired of the brutality and exactions imposed on them by the King and the small 'clique' of Chiefs and Princes who surround him, that they would gladly hail the advent of any other power, which would give them security for their lives and property, and ensure them equal justice, which British Law alone can ensure.

15. Should H.M.G. see fit to adopting my last proposition, I would respectfully observe that the increase to the Revenue of this Colony would suffice for more than treble the increased Expenditure, which the occupation of Porto Novo might entail. No additional Forces, either Naval or Military would be required, and we should at once shut up the only opening left to the Egbas, and thereby secure firmly and permanently the peace of the whole Country. And, although it would finally close the Slave traffic at Whydah, it would be a measure which would cause satisfaction to all the surrounding Tribes, who, together with ourselves, are equally desirous of curbing the Egbas and restoring the trade and prosperity of the Country.

19

EDWARD CARDWELL TO GOVERNOR J. H. GLOVER: PORTO NOVO, 23 OCTOBER 1865[1]

. . . I REGRET that such a serious state of affairs should have arisen [at Porto Novo] and I am now in communication with the Foreign Office on the subject: but I lose no time in informing you that the annexation to Lagos of the Town of Porto Novo and the immediate district which is one of the measures which you propose, is not likely to receive the sanction of H.M's. Governt. [D. and would moreover be opposed to the opinion expressed by the Select Committee on the West Coast of Africa against any further extension of territory on that Coast].

20

EDWARD CARDWELL TO GOVERNOR S. W. BLACKALL: DOMESTIC SLAVERY, 3 FEBRUARY 1866[2]

[Domestic slavery at Lagos is to be abolished.]

. . . I NEED scarcely remark that this state of things is inconsistent with the provisions of the Imperial Act 3 and 4 William IV, cap. 73, which has made all the Queen's dominions free soil, and by which, therefore, every person in Lagos has been free since it became a British Colony. I am fully aware of the extreme difficulty which a Governor must encounter in having to assume the control of a territory under British Jurisdiction, in which domestic slavery, as in every part of Africa, is a constituent element in the fabric of society, and appreciate the endeavours of the late Governor Freeman and the present Lieutenant-Governor, to facilitate the transition from slavery to freedom.

But, unfortunately, as could hardly have been helped, the Ordinances which have been passed for that object are at variance with British law.

The Ordinances to which I allude are, first, the one passed in 1863 for registering all 'slaves' in the settlement of Lagos, and in which provision is made that in the case of a slave being apprenticed the period of apprenticeship shall be guided by the original cost of the slave, the present market value of slave labour, &c.

The second Ordinance relates to the Slave Commission Court in which provision is made for settling the amount of compensation

---

[1] C.O. 147/9.   [2] *Parl. Papers*, 1874, xlvi [C. 1007], pp. 1-2.

to be given to the late owners of slaves being inhabitants of Lagos, &c.

When Colonel Ord was appointed Commissioner to inquire into matters on the West Coast of Africa, the question of slavery at Lagos was one of the questions which he was to consider, and on his arrival in that Colony he communicated with the Lieutenant-Governor on the subject.

In reporting the result of their communications, the Lieutenant-Governor remarked, in his despatch to me, that the Slave Commission Court, which was to supersede the Slave Registry Court, was 'a safety-valve for the disaffection of the serf, while, on the other hand, it afforded the master a certain amount of protection against the total or immediate loss of what he had been accustomed to consider his property'.

The Lieutenant-Governor, however, felt that both in its language and working, there was in the Ordinance constituting the Court, an actual though indirect recognition of slavery in British territory, and he announced his intention of limiting its operations as much as possible in the first instance, and eventually altogether, to territory not British, but he left the Ordinance in the shape in which it was originally framed.

I need scarcely inform you that a Colonial Ordinance made in violation of an Act of the Imperial Parliament, is *ab initio* illegal and void, and I have now advised Her Majesty to disallow the two Ordinances above mentioned, and they are disallowed accordingly.

In what terms, and with what precautions, you are to announce their invalidity or their abrogation to the Colony is a matter requiring your serious consideration. You will be careful to take such steps as may avoid disturbances in Lagos or conflict with neighbouring Chiefs whose slaves might take refuge in Lagos; and you will consider whether it would be advisable on the same occasion to recommend labourers and servants to continue with their employers while well treated by them.

I should hope that after the repeal of the Ordinances the ordinary Courts of the Colony might take cognizance of all complaints of violence or compulsory detention, but if you should think it necessary to have prescribed punishment for such offences, or to have an Ordinance regulating the relations of master and servant, I should wish you to frame such Ordinance, and send it to me for consideration, taking care that it contains no recognition of slavery in any shape.

With regard to fugitive slaves from the neighbouring territories, I need only remark that a Fugitive Slave Law in Africa is out of the question, and that it will be for the Chiefs, therefore, to take precautions against their slaves entering British territory, and for the

Colonial Government to take care that no official inducements are held out to fugitives, and to warn them that if after entering British territory they again quit it, they must do so at their own risk.

But the readiest and most effectual way of escaping from all these embarrassments, is to confine British territory within the smallest compass which may be practicable, and if it should be found that British law cannot be fully established in the Island of Lagos, and in the towns occupied by us, we must confine the area of British territory, as at the Gold Coast, to the land occupied by the Government buildings, constituting the rest of the territory acquired from Docemo, a Protectorate where our influence could be used to soften and gradually destroy slavery, without our authority being called on to abolish it.

Supposing, however, that you do not find this course necessary, I should wish you to define the boundary of the settlement, so that the British territory be restricted to the Island of Lagos, and the towns of Badagry, Palma, and Leckie; but I should be glad to receive your opinion whether it is absolutely necessary to retain the three towns abovementioned, and whether, without holding them, the principal stream of trade would not find its way through the mouth of the Lagoon to the town of Lagos.

In any case it will be requisite, in order to secure the Customs Revenue, to keep sovereignty over the sea-board and the waters of the Lagoon.

The question still remains of the permanent retention at Lagos of a detachment of regular troops, which I requested you in my despatch of the 20th ultimo to report upon.

21

THE EARL OF CARNARVON TO GOVERNOR S. W. BLACKALL: MISSION TO IBADAN, 21 MARCH 1867[1]

SIR,

I have to acknowledge the receipt of your desp: No 6 of the 15th Ult. enclosing a copy of one from the Adm[inistrator] of Lagos with a report from Lt. Gerard, whom he had sent on a mission to the King of Yoruba and the Bashorun of Ibadan on the occasion of a war between those chiefs and the Ijeshas.

I entirely approve of the views you express with regard to the policy of non-interference with the wars of the natives, unless requested by both parties to act as mediator, [A. and even in the event of such a joint request being received I am of the opinion that a

[1] C.O. 147/13.

policy of non-interference should still be adhered to unless the settlement of the dispute in question shall appear to be of essential importance to the safety & well being of the Colony]. I have to request that you will instruct Captain Glover to act on those views.

I am glad that in the present instance Lt. Gerard's mission was apparently successful.

22

THE DUKE OF BUCKINGHAM AND CHANDOS TO GOVERNOR S. W. BLACKALL: RELATIONS WITH THE EGBA, 23 NOVEMBER 1867[1]

SIR,

I have received Colonel Yonge's Despatch No 48 of the 28th October, accompanied by one from Commander Glover, Administrator of Lagos, reporting a riot at Abbeokuta, the destruction of Churches, plundering of the Christians and partial demolition of their houses; but happily with no loss of life.

I have received this intelligence with great concern. Abbeokuta is in no sense within British jurisdiction, but the account of violence towards Christian converts at any place must be a subject of much regret.

The enclosures of Commander Glover's despatch consist of a correspondence between himself and the Egba Government. It would appear that Commander Glover had placed Constables on a road which is in the course of construction between Ebute-Metta and Otta, and that the Egbas remonstrated against this assumption of jurisdiction. There can be no doubt that Otta lies beyond any boundary line which has ever been contemplated for what is called the 'Protectorate' of Lagos, and therefore that Commander Glover was in fact encroaching if he stationed British Constables at or near Otta. His design of extending the Protectorate, without previous report to or sanction from Her Majesty's Government, is further apparent from his proposal to the Egba Government to make Otta and the Country Northward of it, neutral.

I disapprove of Commander Glover's having attempted to enlarge the Lagos territory and jurisdiction, entirely on his own motion, without leave, and contrary to what he must well know to be the policy of H.M.G.

He ascribes the outbreak at Abbeokuta to a plot of the King of Jebu, formed three months previously. No evidence, however, of this is adduced, and the event followed rapidly on his own measures to which I have referred.

[1] C.O. 147/13. Drafted by T. F. Elliot and approved by the Parliamentary Under-Secretary C. B. Adderley.

The tone in which Commander Glover, in his letter to Abbeokuta of the 2nd of October, denounced Mr. Johnstone[1] the Secretary of the Government as liable to the penalties of a felon and to the forfeiture of his life was equally unbecoming and illjudged.

I regret to say that I am compelled to view the whole of Commander Glover's proceedings with great dissatisfaction. You will of course communicate to him Copies of this and of my other Despatches on his policy.

23

ADMINISTRATOR J. H. GLOVER TO CAPTAIN
P. SHEPPARD: INTERIOR ROADS,
7 SEPTEMBER 1871[2]

[Representatives from the Egba, Oyo, and Ibadan Yoruba have met at Lagos with envoys from Benin, Ijaw, Ketu, and Ilaro.]

. . . 3. I WILL now refer your Excellency to my Despatch, No 79 of the 19th August 1869,[3] wherein I reported my visit to Odé for the purpose of ascertaining the practicability of establishing a Trading Station on the Beach at that place (within our Territory) in order to enable us to obtain supplies from Ijesha (a Country in the Interior) in the event of the Egbas repeating their invasion of Ijebu Country, which caused such depression to the Trade of Lagos during the years 1863, 1864 and 1865. At the time of my visit to Odé (viz August 1869) the principal Town of Ijesha was invested by the Ibadans or Yorubas; and being aware that Ijesha must ultimately fall (and that the Ibadans, having secured their rear by the reduction of Ijésha would re-open the question of the Road to Lagos, via Iperu and Ikorodu, which had been closed against them by the united action of the Egbas and Ijebus) my efforts to open friendly communication with the Ijoh Chiefs, and thereby effect an entrance to the Interior of the Effon and Ijesha Country, and again to the Westward by Igbessa, Illaro and Ketu, have been increasing, in order that when the current events, which I am now reporting, (and which justify the anticipation I entertained in 1869) should take place, this Settlement might (to a certain extent) be independent of Abbeokuta for one or more inlets to the interior for its Imports.

4. I am not yet in a position to report to your Excellency that I

---

[1] Sic, G. W. Johnson, a returned Yoruba from Sierra Leone and secretary to the Egba United Board of Management which had attempted to levy Customs on trade with Lagos. The missionaries were allowed to return in 1872.

[2] C.O. 147/21. Captain Sheppard was Officer Commanding at Sierra Leone and Acting Governor in 1871.

[3] Not received by the Colonial Office. See map p. 368.

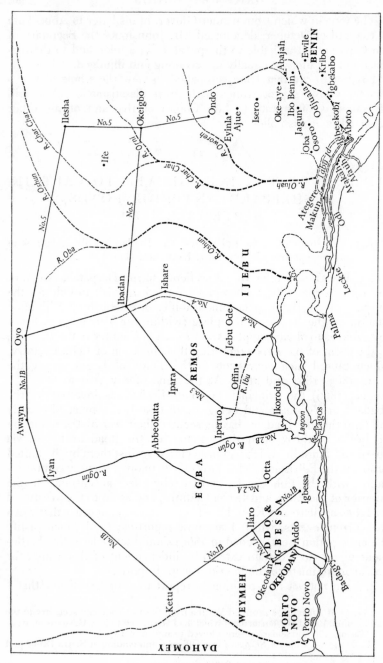

Map 4: J. H. Glover, Yoruba Interior and Trade Routes, 1871.

have entirely accomplished the opening of the Road to Ibadan, via Ijesha, Doko and Abotoh on the Lagoon, but Messengers have been despatched both ways (viz via Abbeokuta, Ibadan, Ijesha, Doko and Abotoh, and from Abotoh upwards), and I do not anticipate more than the usual delay attendant upon all progress and development in Africa.

5. Your Excellency will observe seven different Routes, on the Chart, for Trade and Intercourse with the Interior, only two of which are partially open to us and the Yorubas (Viz No 2A and No 2 B), but continually obstructed by the Egbas; and until within the last two months, closed to all Government messengers, and still shut to all White men, and at present closed against the Yorubas and Ijeshas.

6. Hitherto the Ijebus have been entirely guided by the Egbas, who to retain for themselves the Monopoly of the Roads, (Viz No 2A and No 2 B), close the Illaro Road, and induce the Ijebus to allow to Europeans, Lagos Traders, Yorubas or Ijeshas, to pass up or down. That this may be clear, I will observe that the Roads coloured blue, are those only partially open from Lagos to the Interior.

7. The opening of Road (No 5) from Abotoh on the Lagoon via Doko, Ijesha, and Ibadan to Oyo, will destroy for the Egbas their hitherto Monopoly; and it will then be their interest to remove all obnoxious impediments (viz plundering and kidnapping) to our use of their Roads (marked Blue); and the Ijebus will, for the same reason, open Roads Nos 3 and 4, in order that they may obtain Traffic which would otherwise be diverted from them to Road No 5.

8. The intention of the Yorubas was, and is, to fight for Road No 3, as your Excellency will observe by enclosure No 2; and unless I succeed in opening Road No 3 by the establishment of Road No 5, I shall be unable to prevent the breaking out of hostilities between the Yorubas, Egbas, and Ijebus; hence my endeavours, since 1869, to establish communications with the interior via Road No 5.

9. I have impressed upon the Yorubas that the opening of Road No 5 will obtain for them, peacefully, all that they desire to achieve by fighting; and that until it can be shown that the Road No 5 fails to give them what both themselves and this Government desire (viz open intercourse with the Interior) they will be wrong in going to War. So far as I can form an opinion, the Yorubas will be guided by the advice this Government has given them, unless Abbeokuta, by some hostile act, should bring on a war which, I believe, both Parties consider unavoidable, but for the pressure which the geographical position and moral influence of this Government enables it to exercise on the Interior Tribes. This influence was exemplified only the other day, when on its becoming known that I remonstrated with some Egbas sent to kidnap on the Otta Road, they were immediately

withdrawn. The kidnapping Party was sent by the Township of Igbein (in Abbeokuta) whose Chief, Solanke is one of the persons alluded to in Enclosure No 3, paragraph 2 of Despatch dated 3rd June 1871 (see Enclosure).

Up to this point matters have arrived; and I trust that this Government may be enabled, both by its Council [sic] and endeavours, to open Road No 5, to preserve peace between the Egbas, Yorubas, and Ijebus, and at the same time, effect for the Yorubas open intercourse with Lagos (via Road Nos 3 and 4) without which intercourse, no Peace of long duration can now be looked for.

10. In conclusion I have to report that I this morning received information that the Messengers of this Government which were despatched to Ibadan via Abotoh and the Ijesha Country have reached that place.

24

THE EARL OF KIMBERLEY: MINUTE, INTERIOR ROADS, 15 NOVEMBER 1871[1]

IT is evident that the opening of road No 5 will effectually turn the flank of the Egbas. The Administrator seems to be pursuing a wise policy—approve him and say I shall learn with much satisfaction that he has succeeded in establishing a secure communication with the interior free from the interference of the Egbas.

25

THE EARL OF KIMBERLEY: MINUTE, RELATIONS WITH THE YORUBA, 6 AUGUST 1872[2]

I AGREE much with Mr. Herbert. There are as far as I understand the matter two questions. 1. The fugitive slave difficulty. On this we can make no concessions. 2. The trade with the interior.

The tribes near the coast have a monopoly from their geographical position of the trade with the country beyond them. They therefore object to open roads through their country. The King of Ijebu puts the question plainly—'The Lagos people sell to the Jebus, and Jebus to their neighbour & the neighbour to the interior & vica versa to the

[1] C.O. 147/21. Approved in Kimberley to Glover, 18 November 1871.
[2] C.O. 147/23. On Hennessy to Kimberley, 25 June 1872. *J. O. Payne*, trader and sheriff of Lagos, had been sent by Glover to report on trade routes through Ijebu Ode. Governor Pope Hennessy wrote unfavourably of Glover's policy: see below, p. 452.

Coast. This is the custom of the whole countries in the interior and the Governor must not interfere.'[1]

Capt. Glover's policy has been too ambitious. We should be satisfied as a rule with cultivating friendly relations with all the surrounding tribes, and when we endeavour to feel our way to direct intercourse with tribes further in the interior should do so with much caution, and not attempt to force on such intercourse by coercive measures.

26

ADMINISTRATOR J. H. GLOVER TO THE EARL OF KIMBERLEY: RELATIONS WITH THE YORUBA, 7 NOVEMBER 1872[2]

. . . In the beginning of 1871, a promise was obtained from the Yorubas, that they would abstain from attempting by war, to obtain a direct Road to Lagos, until they had given the new Road a trial for a period of Thirteen Moons, after such a new Road should be opened; it being the opinion of the Lagos Government, that the opening of the new Road would necessitate concessions on the part of the Egbas and Ijebus, in order that the commerce of the Interior should not be diverted from them.

On the other hand the new road would place the trade of Lagos, in a position less dependent than at present, on the goodwill or caprice, of the Egbas and Ijebus.

This policy, after having been patiently and laboriously followed up since 1867, was brought to a successful issue by the Mission, so ably conducted by Mr. Goldsworthy during the months of April, May, June and July of the present year.

In June Mr Goldsworthy was recalled, and the entire policy of the Lagos Government disavowed by Mr Pope Hennessey, altho' your Lordship had been most fully informed, and had approved of the course pursued. . . .

The result of the policy which Mr Pope Hennessey was persuaded to introduce by those whom he considered, 'the well disposed and intelligent portion of the inhabitants', may be summed up as follows, —namely, Restriction of Territory to the Island of Lagos, and the Towns of Badagry, Palma, and Leckie. The rendition of Slaves, by the ex-King (henceforth to be styled the King of Lagos) and connived at by the Local Government, and every principle of good government, sacrificed to the demands of the Egbas and Ijebus,

---

[1] Encl. King of Ijebu to Payne, n.d. [1872].

[2] C.O. 147/23. Glover had sent the Collector of Customs, *R. T. Goldsworthy*, to survey the route to Ibadan and Oyo through Ijebu Ode. The Ijebu refused to keep this eastern route open; and Goldsworthy's report showed (as Hennessy pointed out) the extent of Yoruba mistrust of Glover's policy.

in the hope to obtain thereby, a renewal of Trade which had ceased thro' the intrigues of a Mr Mills, and the Sierra Leone Egbas in Lagos, and would have been speedily reopened, but for, the insidious councils of this Clique, having succeeded in working upon the vanity and culpable weakness of Mr Pope Hennessey . . .

[Trade is still at a standstill, as Glover has warned.]

It is History repeating itself. The Goths in the 5th Century came down to taste the sweets and luxuries, which the trade of the East, had brought to the shores of the Mediterranean; in the same way, the ragged, hungry hordes from the Interior are pushing each other down to the Coast.

The same desire influences the Ashantees. Our Trade on the Coast, whether at Lagos, or the Gold Coast, is the tempting bait. . . .

27

THE EARL OF KIMBERLEY: MINUTE, RELATIONS WITH THE YORUBA, 24 NOVEMBER 1872[1]

. . . I WOULD thank Capt. G[lover] for his full and able statement of his views. Capt. G[lover's] was a bold policy, but it is open to the serious objection that it distinctly allied the British Govt. with one set of tribes with a view to coerce another set into opening communications to the interior. That Capt. G[lover] was hostile to the Egbas & Jebus and wished to crush them, I don't believe. He wanted to play one party off against the other in order to promote the interests of Lagos. I fear we shall have serious troubles. We cannot however as far as I can see do anything more than we have done to avert them. . . .

28

THE EARL OF KIMBERLEY TO GOVERNOR J. POPE HENNESSY: INTERIOR ROADS, 28 NOVEMBER 1872[2]

SIR,

I referred your desp: No 81 of the 15th Septr., forwarding Mr. Goldsworthy's account of his mission to the Yoruba Country with a Report upon it by the Acting Admr. of Lagos, to Captain Glover for his observations and I transmit to you herewith a copy of the reply which I have received from that officer, together with the copy of a letter addressed to him by Mr. Goldsworthy.

[1] C.O. 147/25.
[2] C.O. 147/26. The interior roads were not opened till July 1874.

These papers deserve your careful consideration.

Although Capt. Glover may have been over sanguine in his expectations of opening peacefully a new road to the interior and thus establishing a communication independent of the Egbas and Jebus, I entertain grave doubts whether you have acted prudently in suddenly reversing Capt. Glover's policy, and whether you have not been misled by persons at Lagos, acting exclusively in the interests of the Egbas & Jebus.

These doubts have been confirmed by your despatch of the 28th October reporting that the Egbas and Jebus have refused to open the roads on the ground, it appears, that certain concessions have not been made to them as to the delivery of slaves & restriction of British territory to which, as you are well aware, H.M's. Govt. are not prepared to consent.

29

ADMINISTRATOR G. C. STRAHAN TO GOVERNOR G. BERKELEY: INTERIOR ROADS, 4 NOVEMBER 1873[1]

Sir,

I did not consider it necessary to trouble your Excellency with the various rumours which were current here on my arrival as to the probability of the Egba roads being again closed, as I was not then in a position to judge of the reliability of the information upon which these rumours were founded.

Although I am not prepared to state that there is a perfect confidence among the mercantile community that the present state of things will last, I am happy to inform your Excellency that nothing has occurred since my arrival to lead me to anticipate any stoppage of trade with the interior from that cause. Several markets have been held during the last three weeks to which large quantities of produce have been sent from Abbeokuta.

I regret to state that the Jebu roads still remain closed. I took advantage of the intended departure of King Docemo's Apena the other day for Jebu, to send to the King a short message informing him of my arrival at Lagos, sending him my compliments and expressing the hope that we may be 'good friends', and I am not without hopes that the Apena, to whom I have fully explained the policy of Her Majesty's Government as regards the neighbouring tribes, may succeed in showing to the King of Jebu and his people that it is their interest to establish commercial relations with this Colony upon a settled and permanent footing.

[1] C.O. 147/26.

E. NIGER DELTA

Introductory Note

By contrast with the settlements and forts, relations with the Ijo, Ibibio, and Efik chiefs of the Delta states, like those on the Slave Coast before 1861, were conducted almost exclusively through the Admiralty and the Foreign Office. The object of policy was to regulate the palm oil trade on European terms and secure an end to the export of slaves. Between 1836 and 1838, three trade treaties were made with the House of Pepple at Bonny, with the net effect of weakening the authority of King Dappa Pepple and increasing his dependence on the British Navy to uphold his position against factions hostile to his rule. An abortive slave trade treaty made in 1839 went unratified and unobserved, when promised compensation was never paid. Palmerston, however, insisted on the principle of compensating Delta chiefs, and treaties and payments were arranged with Kalabari and Bimbia chiefs in the early 1840's. A second anti-slave trade agreement with Bonny in 1841 was not ratified, after Commander Tucker exceeded his instructions by promising King Pepple $10,000 annually. Serious hostility towards British traders led the Foreign Office to order closer naval supervision which resulted in the seizure and deportation of the High Priest Awanta in 1847. Naval officers such as Commander Hotham, however, were not convinced that all blame lay with African traders and were reluctant to execute a Foreign Office request to enforce payment of debts contracted under the 'trust' system which was the basis of Oil Rivers commerce. Two new treaties to end the slave trade and to secure equal trading rights were obtained in 1848, in return for annual presents to the value of $2,000.

The appointment of consuls to the Delta, beginning with John Beecroft, coincided with commercial changes in the early 1850's resulting from the establishment of steam communication and from political instability in the Delta states. Increasingly, the consuls were drawn into economic and political disputes, while making payments to chiefs under the treaty system and concluding new agreements for the protection of British subjects at Bonny, Old Calabar, New Calabar and the Cameroons. Beecroft upheld the Egbo Society rulers of Duke Town against insurgent slaves, by phrasing an agreement with King Archibong to include references to customary law, in return for a clause on the abolition of human sacrifices. At Aqua Town and Bell Town in the Cameroons more agreements for dollars were made and the election of a chief was supervised and approved in 1852. The following year, the Foreign Office acknowledged Beecroft's practice of settling disputes arising from commercial treaties by imposing fines on traders. By 1854, this informal empire controlled from the consulate at Fernando Po was extended again to Bonny, where Beecroft assisted an alliance of traders and disaffected partisans of the former Regent to depose and exile King Dappa Pepple. This position, achieved by Beecroft, was confirmed in 1855 by his successor, who ordered the destruction of a town at Old Calabar and intervened to prevent reprisals when a supercargo murdered a relative of the King of Aqua Town.

During the last years of the 1850's, however, it was made clear that consuls had no jurisdiction over British subjects in the Delta: codes of laws to regulate trade were not approved by the Foreign Office, because British traders could not be bound to observe them; consuls were permitted to help form Courts of Equity on the model of one at Bonny, but they were forbidden to interfere in their hearings or to act as a court of appeal until 1862;[1] the practice of installing and deposing chiefs was called in question in 1861 and disapproved. Throughout the rest of the 1860's, the consuls' power remained formally limited by these instructions as the problems which encouraged their illegal acts grew more acute.

War in the late 1860's between Okrika, Bonny, Brass and Calabar, and the foundation of a new Delta state by Ja Ja who contested Bonny sources of palm oil behind the coastal ports, threatened a complete stoppage of trade. Consul Livingstone's intervention achieved little more than a clarification of the issues at stake and the knowledge that British traders were divided in their support. As the conflict intensified, 1869–71, the use of force was authorized by Lord Granville, and a peace was arranged for the Kalabari dispute. By the beginning of 1873, the chiefs of Bonny and British traders were ready to acknowledge Ja Ja as King of Opobo and his right to control customs, oil markets, and the entry of shipping for trade. At the same time consuls were given new powers of jurisdiction under the West African Order in Council of 1872 and moved their court and consulate from its outpost in the Bight of Biafra closer to the troubled frontier at Old Calabar.

I

BONNY TRADE REGULATIONS, 25 JANUARY 1836[2]

King Pepple's House, Grand Bonny,
25 January 1836.

Article 1.

IT is hereby agreed, between the undersigned H. B. Majesty's Subjects and the King of Bonny, that no English Subject shall from this time be detained on shore or maltreated in any way whatever by the King or natives of Bonny under any pretence; by so doing, they will bring themselves under the displeasure of the King of

---

[1] For the growth of extra-territorial jurisdiction, see below, V (B), pp. 539–41.

[2] F.O. 2/1, ff. 77–79 and v. Signed Lieutenant R. Tryon, Anna Pepple, Manilla Pepple, H. L. Corran, Christopher Jackson, Joseph Rennie, Henry Trodsham, L. Grant. Lieutenant Tryon who had seized four Spanish slave ships at Bonny was imprisoned by the head of the house of Anna Pepple and released only after a display of force by a vessel of the West Africa Squadron. See K. Onwuka Dike, *Trade and Politics in the Niger Delta 1830–1885* (Oxford, 1956), pp. 70–72; and cf. G. I. Jones, *The Trading States of the Oil Rivers* (London, 1963), pp. 111–12; and Appendix, pp. 221–2.

England, and be declared enemies of Great Britain, and that the Men of War, on any complaint will immediately come up the Bonny to protect the English Vessels.

2.

In case of any misunderstanding between the Captains of the English Vessels and the King or Gentlemen of Bonny, that all and every English Captain will go on shore, free of molestation and will, with the King and Gentlemen of Bonny, peaceably settle all disputes between the parties.

3.

English Captains having any complaint against any of the natives of Bonny, will come on shore, and lay his or their complaint before the King, and they hereby promise to give the complainant redress, by punishing the offender, and if any English seaman shall ill treat a Bonny man he shall be punished by the Captain of the Vessel to which he may belong.

4.

That for the future, all books made between the Traders and English Captains, shall bear the signature of such responsible officer, belonging to the Ship with the date and name; by his not doing so, the case shall be decided by the Captains of the Merchant Ships, lying in the River, who will see, that the Trader's or Native's loss be made good.

5.

That after the Captain or Supercargo has paid the regular Custom, the trade shall be opened, and upon no account, shall the trade of any Vessel be stopped; excepting the Captain or Supercargo act in opposition, to any of the annexed agreements, and refuses to pay the fine, imposed by the other Captains, for the infringing of these rules.

6.

That every vessel's property shall be properly protected, and that no King, Gentleman, or Native of Bonny, shall roll away the casks of any Vessel from the Cask house on any pretence whatever.

7.

That the King will be responsible for all monies, Oil, or goods, that may be owing to the English Captains, so that the Vessel may not be detained before sailing; and that the Captains of the English Ships, will see all just debts incurred by any vessel, are paid by her to Bonny men with Bars, or Oil, before leaving the River.

2

REAR-ADMIRAL SIR PATRICK CAMPBELL TO COMMANDER CRAIGIE: TRADE RELATIONS WITH KING PEPPLE, 11 MARCH 1837[1]

SIR, *The Thalia.*

I enclose herewith, for your information, a copy of some articles to regulate the Trade, in the River Bonny which were drawn up, under the direction of Acting Commander Puget, of H.M. Sloop Trinculo, in January 1836, and Signed by Lieut. Tryon of that Sloop, King Anna Pepple, and another Chief named Manilla Pepple, and by four Masters and a Mate of different English Merchant Vessels, then lying in the Port.

The Trade of the Bonny being of considerable importance and extent, I have to desire that you cause all proper countenance and protection to be given to His Majesty's Subjects engaged therein; sending one of the small cruizers into the River occasionally for that purpose.

And you will take an opportunity of proceeding thither yourself, to congratulate the new King on his accession to the Sovereignty of the Bonny, and to express a hope that the Trade will continue to be carried on, in the same amicable and friendly manner, that it has hitherto been.

It would be proper to obtain the ratification of the New King to these regulations respecting the Trade in the Bonny, and to make the same generally known amongst the British Shipping in the River.

3

BONNY CONVENTION, 9 APRIL 1837[2]

H.M. Brig *Lynx.*

THE undermentioned Masters of British Merchant Vessels lying in the River Bonny having met Lieutenant Henry V. Huntly in conformity to the wishes of Robert Craigie Esqr. Senior Officer and Commander of H.M. Sloop Scout to confer upon the subject of rules

---

[1] F.O. 2/1, ff. 77–79.

[2] F.O. 2/1, ff. 91–92. Articles 4–7 of the 1836 treaty were changed in accordance with this convention on the advice of British traders at Bonny; and King William Dappa Pepple (head of the Manilla Pepple house) with the support of British naval officers had the regent, Anna Pepple, deposed. Dike, op. cit., pp. 75–77. These treaties were approved by the Board of Trade, 7 December 1837, and in Lord Palmerston to Admiralty, 28 December 1837.

for the benefit of the British trade in that river it was unanimously resolved.

1st. That it should be clearly impressed upon the King and Chiefs of the Bonny territory that a Vessel of War can always be called by the Masters of British Vessels in the river and will always come in whenever protection is required by the said British Ships, that while the British are most desirous of having their trade with the Bonny territory carried on upon the most friendly terms yet every case of insult to the Flag or oppression to a British Subject will be severely resented whenever it is made known.

2ndly. That Article Six suggested by Commodore Robert Craigie and read by me was unanimously desired to be added to the Treaty of Jany. 1836.

3dly. That the following articles should also be added to that Treaty.

Should any Master of a British Merchant vessel give his goods or any part thereof out upon trust for Oil or any produce whatever to any Chief, trader or other person belonging to the Bonny Country, the King will not hold himself responsible for such goods or for the payments of them; but the person so trusting his goods must do so at his own risk and the King further agrees that should any Master of a British Vessel seize or take away to his Vessel or elsewhere any Canoe having in her any oil or other produce the same being embarked for another Vessel that he the King upon the seizure being complained of and proved by any Master of a British Vessel, or by the trader sending off the said Oil or produce will stop the trade of such Ships until the seized Oil or produce shall have been returned to the proper owner, and such return proved before the King to have been made and acknowledged by the proper owner.

This article is not to be considered as preventing any private arrangement respecting oil or produce between any two or more Masters or traders.

4th. When a British Ship comes into the Bonny river to trade she shall offer to pay or pay customs if demanded in goods and according to the practice of former times, this custom shall be paid within seven days or upon the seventh day to the King or only to the King, unless he shall appoint another person to receive it but the whole custom shall be paid to one person and the King agrees to divide it on shore according to the laws there existing.

The King further agrees that upon no pretence shall the payment of the custom be refused if offered within seven days, or upon the seventh day provided it is offered to be paid to the King or person appointed by the King to receive it, but that should the custom so offered be refused the Ship shall open trade as if it had been paid nevertheless the Ship shall pay the custom whenever it may be demanded afterwards. . . .

4

J. BLACKHOUSE TO THE SECRETARY TO THE ADMIRALTY: CONDITIONS FOR A TREATY WITH BONNY, 8 APRIL 1841[1]

SIR,

With reference to previous correspondence respecting Agreements [D. Treaties] with African Chiefs for the suppression of the Slave Trade; I am directed by Viscount Palmerston to transmit to you, to be laid before the Lords Commissioners of the Admiralty copies of correspondence which has recently passed between this office and Her Majesty's Treasury upon that subject of Agreements with the Chiefs of Bonny & of the Cameroons and I am to request you will state to the Lords of the Admiralty, the opinion of Lord Palmerston that, in the agreement proposed to be concluded with the King & Chiefs of Bonny it will be better to specify the conditions to be entered into by both parties: and that those conditions should be, That the Slave Trade shall be totally put an end to within the dominions of the King of Bonny. That Great Britain will make for five years an annual Gift to the King & Chiefs of Bonny, of Goods to the value of Two Thousand Dollars; That the first Gift shall be made on the ratification of the Agreement, on condition that from that time & for ever Slave Trade shall be totally put a stop to in the said Dominions and that no slave shall be passed through or exported from these Dominions; and that at each future time of making the gift there shall be furnished to Great Britain a Document from the Merchants frequenting the Bonny certifying the fact that no Slave Trade has to their knowledge existed there during the preceeding year: and if at any time whatever, either from the want of that Document or from any other circumstance it shall appear that Slave Trade has been carried on through or from the Bonny the Presents will be discontinued, the Slave Trade will be put down by Great Britain by Force, & the Chiefs of the Bonny will subject themselves to a severe act of Displeasure on the part of Great Britain.

[1] F.O. 84/383.

5

COMMANDER WILLIAM TUCKER TO THE SECRETARY TO THE ADMIRALTY: TREATY WITH BONNY, 22 AUGUST 1841[1]

H.M.S. *Iris*,
Off the River Bonny.

SIR,

With reference to your letters of the 12th and 23rd April 1841 Nos. 34 and 43 and their enclosures from the Foreign Office and Treasury.

I beg to report that on the 18th. Inst. I anchored Her Majesty's Ship under my command on the outside of the Bar off the mouth of the River Bonny, and proceeded into the River in Her Majesty's Steam Vessel 'Pluto', to arrange, if possible, a Convention for the total abolition of the Slave Trade for ever in the dominions subject to the jurisdiction of King Pepple and the Chiefs of the Bonny, as per Instructions contained in those letters and their enclosures, which, after a great deal of trouble, I arranged and procured the signature of the King and of the greater part of the Chiefs. A copy of which I beg to transmit for the information of their Lordships, and to report, that the King and Chiefs proposed and for a long time insisted upon several articles being inserted which I considered totally inadmissable, as they would have been used as so many loop holes for evading the Convention, strongly confirming in my opinion, so often expressed in my letters, that the King and Chiefs of the Bonny will never abolish the Slave Trade, so long as slave vessels have opportunities of taking off slaves from New Calabar, or at any of the mouths of the Delta, even to the Benin.

And if I needed stronger confirmation in my opinion, the Kings and Chiefs insisted that the Convention was not to interfere in any way with their Laws and customs respecting Domestic Slavery in their Dominions, their general method of getting rid of their bad subjects and Slaves, and their principal means of purchasing Canoes and Yams &c. from the Eboe country being with Slaves they possess, And as the Instructions I received did not direct me to interfere with their national Laws and Customs respecting their Domestic Slavery and it would have frustrated the wishes of the British Government for the abolition of the Export or Foreign Slave Trade, I did not insist upon it, though I feel convinced it may and will be used for the sale of Slaves to the natives of other parts of the Delta, to be resold

[1] F.O. 84/385.

or transferred by them to European Slave dealers whenever an opportunity offers.

I beg to call their Lordships' attention to the alteration of the Instructions in the 3rd Article, which states 'the Man of War bringing the annual gift shall furnish the document', instead of 'King Pepple shall furnish the document', because the King stated, and it appeared very clear to me, that he had no power to force the Captains of the Merchant Vessels to sign the document, and some of them from ill-feeling to him might report falsely that the Slave Trade had been carried on during the preceeding year and he not have the power of making the said Captains prove the correctness of their Reports, whilst others from the fear of having their Trade stopped by the King and Chiefs, a common place with them when they are offended, and of being detained in the River, would not give the information if they saw it carried on openly, whereas the Commander of the Man of War bringing the annual money can obtain the signatures and investigate the truth of any reports which may be made of the Slave Trade having been carried on in the Bonny since the ratification of the Treaty.

I have also to call the attention of their Lordships to the 6th Article, which makes the gift payable in dollars instead of goods, because the King made a particular point of it, as he will have to divide among his Chiefs, and also because the sending out the goods would injure the Trade of the British Merchants here, who would not then be able to dispose of their goods of the same kind.

Also to the 8th Article, which the King insisted upon being inserted and which I agreed to as of no moment.[1]

I beg also to inform their Lordships that the King considered the Treaty ratified, and expects the first payment will be sent to him immediately on the receipt of this. . . .

6

COMMODORE C. H. HOTHAM TO THE SECRETARY TO THE ADMIRALTY: SEIZURE OF AWANTA, 3 MAY 1847[2]

SIR,   *Penelope.*

I request you will inform my Lords &c that I have received a despatch from Comm[ander] Birch informing me of the murder of two English Seamen belonging to the bark 'Rienze' on or about the 6th of Nov. last and that he had in consequence seized the person

---

[1] According to this article King Pepple might resume the slave trade, if British policy regarding abolition changed. The treaty was not approved: F.O. to Admiralty, 31 December 1841; but other engagements to end the slave trade made at this date with Calabar and Cameroons chiefs were allowed.

[2] F.O. 2/3, ff. 105–8.

of the principal Instigator and carried him on board the Waterwitch from whence he was subsequently forwarded to the Tortoise.

The fact of the murder is distinctly proved in the despatch, but the provocation is nowhere to be found, and considering the peaceable character of the Natives, and the many years uninterrupted commercial intercourse, I cannot bring myself to believe that the Blacks are entirely wrong and the English perfectly right.

However under any circumstances the murder required redress, and the means which Comm[ander] Birch adopted were to seize the person of Awanta[1] the High Priest, or Ju Ju Man, and remove him from his Country.

From the very first it appears that the King and Chiefs had promised redress, and before the arrival of the 'Waterwich' the actual murderers were all executed and that the culpability of Awanta—the instigator, and Master of the Slaves who committed the crime was by all parties distinctly admitted. The papers before me prove that the Chiefs called upon Comm[ander] Birch to execute Awanta, acknowledging that justice required it, and even regretted that the sacred character of his person removed him from the pale of human laws, and enabled him to commit crimes of great atrocity with impunity. Their only stipulation was that his body should be interred in the Country, otherwise their good fortune would assuredly forsake them.

Reviewing all the circumstances, I am disposed to believe that Comm[ander] Birch has acted properly, but it is difficult to form a judgment in a matter where superstition enters so largely into the scheme. It will be my duty to cause one of H.M.'s Ships, commanded by an officer of discretion to visit the Bonny more frequently, and watch the effect which this summary measure may have on the Natives.

Up to the period of redressing the murder, I consider Comm[ander] Birch to have acted prudently but I perceive that afterwards, the shrewdness of the Masters of the English Vessels got the better of his judgment, and regret that he allowed himself and his vessel to be made an instrument in the hands of the Traders. The policy of my Predecessors has always been never to interfere in commercial matters, the trade of Africa is formed on credit, the ignorant black adheres to all the stipulations, and performs his part creditably and well: there may be exceptions but, on the whole, their behaviour will stand a favorable comparison with that of more civilized Nations; and, therefore it would be unwise to attempt coercion for the recovery of debt, or to lead the Merchants to believe that their speculations would be backed by Military power.

[1] Awanta was high priest of Bonny. He was possibly set ashore at some other part of the coast.

However the situation of Comm[ander] Birch was difficult and great allowance should be made for an oversight.

As the traders now in the river Bonny addressed the letter, marked A.[1] I availed myself of the opportunity to return the answer marked B which I hope will meet with their Lordship's approbation.

In the meantime, this Awanta is a Prisoner in the Tortoise, where I shall keep him until I receive their Lordships' commands, and in the event of his death, his body shall be sent back to the Bonny.

7

H. U. ADDINGTON TO THE SECRETARY TO THE ADMIRALTY: PAYMENT OF DEBTS, 6 JANUARY 1848[2]

. . . WITH respect to the alleged insecurity of the Persons of British Subjects legally trading in the River Bonny; and to the Dishonesty of the Native Traders in that River, I am to state to you that Lord Palmerston is of opinion that Commodore Hotham ought to be instructed to compel King Pepple and the Chiefs of the Bonny, by force if necessary, to respect the Lives and Property of H.M.'s Subjects; and that the Commodore will be justified in enforcing the Payments of the Debts due to British Subjects in cases where the [D. Payment of] Period in which such Debts ought to have been liquidated has exceeded the period usually allowed by the Custom of the Trade or agreed upon in the particular case, and where the Payment of such Debts is withheld from Motives of Fraud or Hostility.

8

COMMODORE C. H. HOTHAM TO THE SECRETARY TO THE ADMIRALTY: PAYMENT OF DEBTS, 27 MARCH 1848[3]

SIR,

Your Despatch No 14 dated 14th Jany. 1848 conveying a letter from Mr Addington authorizes the Officer commanding this Squadron to enforce the payment of debts due to British Subjects in cases where the period within which such debts ought to have been liquidated has exceeded the period usually allowed by the custom of the Trade.

2. Proper and reasonable as it certainly is that the Commander in Chief of this Station should be furnished with discretionary powers enabling him to meet the various cases which may arise, still I feel it

[1] Encl. British traders to Hotham, 19 March 1847 (requesting protection).
[2] F.O. 2/3, ff. 205 and v.   [3] F.O. 2/3, ff. 223–6.

my duty to state, that if publicity is given to the discretionary authority vested in him the mercantile Agents trading in the Bonny, will eagerly enter into the field of competition, and, for the prospect of early cargoes, offer trust to any amount and any extent.

3. The object of our general endeavour is to extend the range of British manufactures, and open new fields of trade, but if a system of credit is sanctioned or tolerated, endless disturbances will arise and the presence of men of war will be demanded, not to collect sums of money due to our Merchants, but to avenge murders and assassinations, the fruit of the misconduct of our own Captains.

4. There can be no clearer proof of the propriety of the course I advocate than the present state of the Bonny; trust has been abolished by general consent; the Trade is conducted with propriety and order, and the Masters of Merchant Vessels are loud in the praise of the results.

5. Our object is, I presume to retain the larger share of African trade; we gained it through good faith and strict probity we maintain it through good feeling our conduct is contrasted most favourably with that of the French but the moment we adopt their system and place ourselves on a level with them, there is an end to our superiority, and a proportionate advantage gained to our rivals. . . .

9

LORD PALMERSTON TO CONSUL JOHN BEECROFT: APPOINTMENT AND INSTRUCTIONS, 30 JUNE 1849[1]

SIR,

Representations having been made to Her Majesty's Government from time to time by Persons engaged in Legal Trade in the Bights of Benin and Biafra, stating that it would be desirable that a Person should be appointed to reside in that part of Africa, as Agent on the part of H.M.'s Government, for the purpose of regulating the legal Trade between British Merchants and the Ports of Benin, Brass, New and Old Calabar, Bonny, Bimbia, the Cameroons, and the Ports in the Territories of the King of Dahomey, H.M.'s Govt. have determined to make such an Appointment; and being informed by the Commodore commanding on the West Coast of Africa that it will be agreeable to you to hold it, I have to inform you that the Queen has been graciously pleased to confer that appointment upon you, and that a Commission under the Sign Manual will be prepared accordingly and will be transmitted to you at the same time with this Despatch.

[1] C.O. 267/211 for final draft; F.O. 84/775 for draft and deleted section.

It is not intended, nor desired, that this Appointment should interfere with that which you hold from Spain as Governor of Fernando Po, the Duties of which, I am assured, may be found compatible with those of your Appointment of Consular Agent on the part of H.M.'s Govt. for the purpose above specified.

You have been selected for this Appointment in consideration of your general knowledge of African Affairs, and of the Habits of the Blacks, and because of the influence which you appear to have acquired over the Native Chiefs of the places to which your Consular Jurisdiction will extend:—That influence, it is hoped, may enable you to prevent Quarrels and Misunderstandings between those Chiefs, and the Crews of British Ships resorting to those Parts for the purposes of Trade, and thereby on the one Hand legal Commerce will be promoted, while on the other hand the Slave Trade, which can scarcely coexist with legal Commerce will be much discouraged.

With a view to these Results, you will endeavour to encourage the Chiefs and People to till the Soil and to produce available Exports, so that they may obtain by Barter the European Commodities which they may stand in need of.

You will take every suitable opportunity to impose upon the minds of the Chiefs, and their Principal Councillors, the great advantages which they will derive from the extension of legal commerce with the Nations of Europe and America; and you will assure them that H.M.'s Govt earnestly desire to contribute to their Welfare and Improvement. [D. H.M.'s Governmt. in establishing this Consulate in the Bights of Benin and Biafra, have no intention to seek to gain Possession, either by purchase or otherwise of any portion of the African Continent in those parts, nor of any neighbouring Island. H.M.'s Governmt. merely wish to avail themselves of such means as natural resources of the Country, the wants of the Natives, and the favourable disposition of the Chiefs and Rulers, aided by the protection and influence of the British Governmt. may afford, to encourage and extend British Commerce, and thereby to displace the Slave Trade.]

You will transmit to me from time to time the best Information which you can procure as to the means by which Commercial Intercourse with the Chiefs on the Coast and in the Interior can be extended, and as to the points of the Coast which may appear to afford the greatest Facilities for Commerce;—And you will also state what kinds of European Commodities are most sought after by the Natives.

You are at liberty to continue to make Fernando Po the Chief Place of your Residence, but you will from time to time visit, either in a Ship of War, or otherwise, according to Circumstances, the Rivers and Places within your Consular Jurisdiction.

It will be your Duty at all times to keep up a cordial intercourse and good understanding with H.M.'s Naval Officers on the West African Station, and to communicate to them any Information which may come to your knowledge from time to time respecting the Slave Trade; and H.M.'s Naval Commanders will be instructed to afford you every facility and assistance in their power to aid you in the performance of your duties.

You will receive in other Despatches General Instructions for your Guidance in your Consular Functions, and also in matters relating to the Slave Trade.

It may be right here to inform you, that when H.M.'s Government first contemplated making this Appointment, so long ago as the Month of August 1844, a communication was made to the Government of Madrid with a view to ascertain their Sentiments upon the Subject. This step was considered due to the Spanish Government in consequence of the Appointment which you hold as Governor of Fernando Po. But no answer has been received to that Communication; and as the Spanish Government has been several times reminded upon the subject, H.M.'s Government assume the continued silence of the Spanish Government as implying that they have no objection to your being appointed to the Office which H.M.'s Govt. have now conferred upon you.

10

LORD PALMERSTON TO CONSUL JOHN BEECROFT: PAYMENTS TO KING PEPPLE, 16 AUGUST 1850[1]

SIR,

I herewith transmit to you a copy of the Treaty[2] for the Supression of the Slave Trade, which was concluded in your presence on the 21st Novr. 1848 by Captain Eden on behalf of Her Majesty with King Pepple and the Chiefs of the River Bonny, by which it is stipulated that an annual present of Goods of British Manufacture to the value of $2000 shall be granted to King Pepple. On the conclusion of this Treaty King Pepple made a statement to Captain Eden, a copy of which I enclose, of the articles with which he would wish to be supplied for the first annual Present; and on the visit of H.M.S. 'Rattler' to the River Bonny at the close of last year, he stated to

---

[1] F.O. 84/816. Beecroft also concluded a new trade treaty with Bonny, 3 October 1850: Jones, op. cit., Appendix, pp. 222–5.

[2] *Parl. Papers*, 1850, ix (53), p. 427. Presents for similar slave trade treaties were also forwarded to King Eyo and King Archibong of Old Calabar and to King William of Bimbia.

Commd. Cumming that he wished to be supplied with 1000 dollars worth of muskets, long Danes, flint locks, and 1000 dollars worth of Powder, Tobin's H.B.

The Articles named by King Pepple to Captain Eden for his first Present not having yet been forwarded to him, I have requested the Lords Comm[issioners] of H.M.'s Treasury to cause those Articles, as well as those which he requested from Commd. Cumming for his 2nd Present, to be forthwith prepared and to be sent to the Admty. in order to be forwarded to you; and I have now to instruct you to repair, as soon as you shall have received them as may be compatible with your health &c with your other arrangements, to the River Bonny, and to deliver them to King Pepple, provided that you shall be satisfied that the Treaty has been duly observed.

You will state to King Pepple on delivering the Presents that H.M.'s Govt. regret that owing to accidental circumstances the delivery of his first annual Present has been so long delayed; and you will enquire what Articles he desires to be furnished with for his 3d Present. . . .

II

CONSUL JOHN BEECROFT TO LORD PALMERSTON, 27 OCTOBER 1851[1]

[An explanation of the terms of the Agreement, 15 February 1851, with King Archibong of Duke Town, Old Calabar.]

. . . WITH regard to the 1st Article of that Treaty, your Lordship has instructed me to inform you what the 'Egbo' law is, and, with regard to the 3d. article, your Lordship has requested me to transmit an explanation of the meaning of the expression 'Chop Blood'.

Your Lordship also instructs me to furnish the reasons which induced me to agree to the stipulations contained in Articles 2, 4 & 5, which articles appear to your Lordship to be open to more or less objection; and with regard to Article 6, your Lordship desires to be informed what Crimes are punished by Death in the district under King Archibong's jurisdiction.

I beg leave to state, for the information of your Lordship, that the 'Egbo' is at once the Legislature, and Police Establishment of Old Calabar. Formerly, its whole purpose seemed to be that of keeping the slaves in awe and subjection by working on their superstitious fears and ceremonies. So rapid, however, within the last few years, has been the advance of civilization in Old Calabar, that, at present though retaining many of the old *forms* they have lost their old

---

[1] F.O. 84/858. For the terms of the Agreement, see Dike, op. cit., p. 158. This explanation was approved in Granville to Beecroft, 27 January 1852, F.O. 84/886.

influence, and no act of oppression can be committed through its agency without notice being taken thereof. The influence of the Christian missionary fast supersedes that of Egbo, so far as the superstitious ideas connected with it are concerned, and it now simply forms the Legislative and Executive Government of Old Calabar. As Civilization advances, so may we hope for corresponding advances in good government. At present, however, no government, or order, can exist in Old Calabar, without Egbo in its present form.

The Criminal law of the Country, or, in other words, Egbo Law, visits Homicide alone with the punishment of death. Punishments for assaults on the person are inflicted on the principle of 'just retaliation'; the offender suffers the same mutilation of his person as he has inflicted on his victim; and, unless satisfaction is given the injured person in the shape of heavy fines, the breaker of another's limb, is punished by having his own broken. Theft is sometimes punished by lopping off a portion of the thief's ear.

'Chop Blood' is the act, or form of oath whereby persons vow friendship, to each other, or, in other words, swear to stand by, and assist each other under all circumstances aggressive or defensive. It is done by making a slight incision in the arm, each one sucking a drop of the other's blood.

In furnishing your Lordship with the reasons which induced me to agree to the stipulations contained in Articles 2, 4 & 5, I beg leave to remark, that I had no desire to aid the slave powers to subdue an attempt at self-liberation. There are many grades of what they call slaves in Old Calabar. I know how well the deserving ones are generally cared for, and to what a position in the country they attain by good conduct and industry. It is not that one class is a slave class in a degraded position—could your Lordship go near a Grand Egbo Assembly with one of the principal gentlemen at right hand, your Lordship would then see how few could be shown whose origin could not be traced to an obscure slave family. With the exception of the late duke Ephraim, and Mr. Young's family, there are scarcely one without the blot, (if blot it may be called) of slavery on their Escutcheon. The very lowest class is composed of those recently arrived from some interior country, or living continually in the 'bush' without opportunities of raising themselves; cut off from European Intercourse and Trade.

Recalling these points to your mind, your Lordship will consider the *cause* of the insurrection. The decapitations and sacrifices at a great man's death, were, a few years ago, much worse, and carried to a greater extent than ever we had cognizance of, and, until now, it has been carried on, perhaps with milder features, and less openly, but still to a deplorable length. It was not at the death of a great man of pure family alone, that these sacrifices were made; but amongst those who had risen from the slave ranks even, if their means were commensurate. The victims were in either case, people belonging to the family, and not the lowest slave was always the first chosen. The consequence was, that upon the death, or serious illness of any sufficiently great man, there was a desertion of all, or most of those who did not consider themselves secure, and away to the 'bush' and plantations they ran until the manes were appeased and sufficient blood had been spilled. They often had to wait so long, that other ties and connexions were formed, and they remained away altogether, and became outcasts from the Calabar community: others remained out from their dislike to, or fear of, the succeeding 'head of family' and many, because they were aware, in the event of their return, they would be the first in the next *counting of heads.*

This lamentable waste of human life, it has ever been the endeavour of the English frequenting the river to put a stop to, but they were always reminded that it was no part of their business to interfere with national customs, pursued from time immemorial; and many captains and supercargoes have excited much of the displeasure of the Chiefs by their pertinacity: even the missionaries were unable to produce any effect on the opinion of the natives on this subject.

I need not say, my Lord, how desirable to any civilized and Christian community, the abolition of this odious practice must seem. The Suttee of India was a trivial matter compared with this: for here as many as five, or six wives were often buried with a King, and two hundred decapitated as well. After Eyamba, duke Ephraim, (Eyo Duke) and young John Duke's deaths, the number of those slaves, or, more properly outcast retainers, were greatly increased; and consequently their means of subsistence shortened, for they cultivated not, and having always had their necessities provided for, when working at home, not only the means, but the method of procuring means, was lost or unknown to them.

Your Lordship may be aware that the profits of their trade with the English supports the Town part of the community; and that the confidence of the English in the natives, after so many years of intercourse, is so great, that the amount of property intrusted to them for carrying on trade with the interior is startlingly enormous to those unacquainted with the system. At this time there must have been at least *Seventy thousand* Pounds in their actual possession, besides One hundred and thirty thousand Pounds more in their power, if these lawless savages got the ascendency. At this juncture the outcasts united, and, according to the mode before explained, swore fidelity to each other, and 'tasted blood' upon the matter,—not an union for the assertion of their rights,—a return to their position in social scale, and a repeal of the laws of sacrifice: but an union to obtain for themselves by their powers and law of might, as much as they could obtain of the property in the Town, making the custom of human sacrifice their plea and excuse. There was great alarm excited from their numerical strength and deportment, and also from the fear that they might be joined by the very lowest scale of the population; a scene of anarchy, confusion, and plunder would have been the result and all the British property on shore could have been lost, and that afloat in the river much endangered. I was sent for, and arrived before anything had been carried to extremes, with a force sufficient to protect British property. I did not proceed to coercion, and make war palaver on the disturbers, taking part with the powers that be, but called them to appear before me, and state their grievances. They met, and their principal, indeed only real one, was that arising from the inhuman law involving their safety.

I showed them that I was prepared to oppose and punish their threatened proceedings endangering British Interests; and at the same time seized upon opportunity of endeavouring to obtain an abolition of the murderous customs at the death of a chief, or man raised to station in their society, and I happily accomplished it by promising my support to the traders (Brokers to the English ships, and holding such an amount of British Property) upon the condition that the law was annulled: and entered into an agreement, which gave me power, upon satisfactory evidence of any of these insurgents themselves, to seize, remove, or punish by fine or otherwise, any Chief or headman who should in future take the life of man upon the death of another. This principal grievance removed, the slaves gave up hostilities, and disbanded.

Thus I treated them, my Lord, not as slaves, nor the higher powers as slave masters: but the whole as a community, a part complaining truly of a barbarous and inhuman custom held by the more powerful division. I took advantage to do away with a law which has been a disgrace to a partially civilized place, and all Europeans connected with the Trade. It saved the loss of an immense sum (£200,000) to English merchants, and allayed the storm in a manner which could have been done only by myself, for no one else knows so well how to deal with African character. I trust, my Lord, after what I have stated, it will not be viewed as aiding to suppress an attempt at self liberation, for your Lordship must view the retainers of these people in a different light to mere *slaves*: and to have done otherwise than I did, would have laid me open to severe animadversions at home, had the British Property suffered. Domestic Slavery I had no right to interfere with, had I met it, much less a state of things constituted as the 'River Town associated emigrants' have framed their government, and kept their society (not a kingdom) together.

I have always been fully aware, that no agreement made by me could be of force, until approved and ratified, and the other parties to the agreement in question are also aware that no clause can be carried into effect until sanctioned by Her Majesty's Government. . . .

12

CONSUL JOHN BEECROFT TO LORD CLARENDON: CAMEROONS DISTURBANCES, 16 AUGUST 1853[1]

My Lord,

I beg leave to state for your Lordship's information that I left this place for Cameroons on the 8th of June last, in the English merchant schooner 'Cosmopolitan' in consequence of some outrages committed on the person of a British Subject, the supercargo of a vessel trading in that River, by one of the Natives; and other petty disturbances that occurred there about the same time.

The party referred to was a Mr. Ellis, trading the Brig 'Timbuctoo' of Bristol; the statement of Ellis, backed by some of the other agents and masters of vessels in the River, I beg to enclose herewith.

I inflicted the penalty of Five Puncheons of Palm oil on Jacko, the aggressor, for this breach of the 2nd. Article of the Commercial Treaty with Cameroons.

I beg also to state for your Lordship's information that I found it necessary to inflict a fine of 1 Puncheon of Palm oil on a white trader, Captn. Pounsbury, of the Brig 'Mohawk' of Bristol, for the unlawful detention of a native Chief named Joss of Joss' town.

After arranging some other petty matters, I left the River on the 18th. and arrived at this place on the 20th of the same month.

13

CONSUL JOHN BEECROFT: JOURNAL [JANUARY 1854][2]

On January 19th H.M. Consul, John Beecroft Esqr. arrived in Bonny to investigate King Pepple's conduct & at the request of the masters conveyed two letters of December 17th & December 31st.

January 20th at 10 A.M. went on shore and convened a meeting of King Pepple & Chiefs—the first point entered upon was Pepple's reason for trying to commence a war with New Calabar—which he

---

[1] F.O. 2/9.

[2] F.O. 84/950. Encl. in Beecroft to Clarendon, 20 February 1854. For a discussion of the position of the Bonny chiefs during Pepple's deposition, see Dike, op. cit., pp. 142–4. Pepple was taken to Fernando Po and Ascension from where he made his way to London, eventually winning his claim to be restored with £7,523 compensation for his seven years of exile.

denied & said such was never his intention; the Chiefs said it was
his intention, & that they accompanied him as far as in sight of
Young Town, without knowing his intention was otherwise than to
visit his mother's country Billa—& upon arriving there, he requested
them to lay in wait at a certain point, which the Calabar men must
pass on their way to the Ships—which they refused, telling him they
did not come to war.

The next question was relative to whether if the Consul reinstated
him—prohibiting him from all Trade and allowing him two thirds
of the Coomey for his support, he would remain as King and conduct
the Business of the Country as formerly; upon consideration, he
answered he would do so.

The Chiefs were then asked if they would keep him as King upon
these terms. They answered they were tired of his rule & did not
wish him to remain King any longer, bringing a series of charges
against him—such as oppression & tyranny.

The Consul then enquired who they had appointed for his suc-
cessor if he was removed from being King, as he could not allow the
Country to remain, without a head-man; they answered Prince
Dappo the son of elder Brother than Pepple & rightful heir. The
Consul informed them he should draw up certain laws, restricting
him from all Trade &c. allowing him two thirds of the Coomey
for his support & that his whole time must be given to governing the
Country; to all of which they were agreeable.

Upon Prince Dappo being proposed, Pepple claimed the protection
of the Consul & begged to be removed to Fernando Po—to which the
Consul consented.

Shortly afterwards the whole of the Chiefs said that sooner than
Pepple should be taken away they would let him be King again—
they also said they thought if he was taken away the Eboe men would
not pay either his debts or theirs—it was elicited from them that the
chief reason they did not wish him to go was that they might be called
upon to pay his debts & that it was contrary to their Jew Jew; the
Consul explained, he was not taking him away, but allowed him to
go, at his own request. The Chiefs then retired to discuss & afterwards said they did not care where Pepple went—if he paid his debts
first.

The whole of this day & the 21st were devoted to hearing palavers
& going through the book.

On the 23rd Pepple was pronounced deposed & Prince Dappa
formerly elected King under the title of King Dappa—the boats
of H.M.S. Antelope firing a salute of 21 Guns. . . .

14

LORD CLARENDON TO CONSUL JOHN BEECROFT: RELATIONS WITH KING AMAKIRI, NEW CALABAR, 29 JUNE 1854[1]

SIR,

I have received your Despatch S[lave] T[rade] No 1 of the 20th of February last, enclosing a Journal of your Proceedings from the 18th of January to the 10th of Feby, whilst visiting various rivers in the Bight of Biafra, and reporting the circumstances under which you had thought it necessary to withhold the first of the three Annual Presents promised to King Ammacree of New Calabar by the Treaty of August 8th 1851.

I have read your Journal with much Interest, and I have to inform you that I approve your Proceedings as reported therein.

I have also to express my approval of your having, in consequence of King Ammacree's Violation of the Treaty of 1851 in the matter of the Slave Vessel 'Restaurada' withheld the present due to that Chief.

You will retain in your possession the Articles composing that Present, until you shall be satisfied that Ammacree is fairly entitled to receive it, and when that Time comes, you will report to me what Articles should be sent for his second and third Presents.

15

LORD CLARENDON TO CONSUL J. W. B. LYNSLAGER: DESTRUCTION OF OLD TOWN, NEW CALABAR, 8 MAY 1855[2]

SIR,

I have received your Despatch S[lave] T[rade] no 1 of the 27th of January last, enclosing a Journal of your Proceedings on a visit in H.M.S. 'Antelope' to the Rivers Bonny, & New, and Old Calabar; and I have to express to you my Approval of your Proceedings as reported therein.

With reference especially to the destruction of Old Town in the Old Calabar River, by H.M.S. 'Antelope' at your requisition in consequence of the Chiefs of that Place having violated the 6th article of the Treaty of Feby, 15th. 1851, relating to the Abolition

---

[1] F.O. 84/950.
[2] F.O. 84/975. *J. W. B. Lynslager* was Consul at Fernando Po, 1854–5, and alternated with *Consul T. J. Hutchison* till 1858.

of human sacrifices, I have to inform you that under the circumstances of the Case, H.M's Govt. approve of your Conduct in having called upon Lieut. Young to destroy the Town in question.

16

LORD CLARENDON TO CONSUL J. W. B. LYNSLAGER: RELATIONS WITH KING AQUA, CAMEROONS, 9 MAY 1855[1]

SIR,

I have received your Despatches marked Slave Trade Nos 4 and 5 of the 3d of March enclosing a Journal of your Proceedings at Aqua Town, in the Cameroons River, and at Bimbia.

With regard to the Enquiry set on foot by you as to the affair in which Ned Aqua the brother of King Aqua was killed by Mr William Walker Supercargo of the British Hulk 'Alexander Great'; I have to instruct you to transmit to King Aqua a full and clear statement in writing of all the Facts of this Case, shewing that the British Consul and the Commander of H.M.S. 'Antelope' had done all that depended on them to secure the Ends of Justice, and that those Ends were defeated by the Refusal of the King to take the Steps which were indispensably necessary in order to bring Mr Walker to Trial. And King Aqua should therefore be warned not to allow any British Subjects to be molested on account of this Homicide, and he should be told that you hold in Deposit the sum of £50 as compensation for the nearest Relations of Ned Aqua.

I have at the same Time to observe that the System pursued by British Supercargoes in these Rivers of giving Credit to the Natives and of endeavouring to recover such Debts by forcibly detaining their Persons, is calculated to give rise to occurrences similar to that now under consideration: and if the Supercargoes cannot devise a better mode of trading, it will become impossible for British Authorities to attempt to maintain Peace in the Rivers of the Bight of Benin.

17

ACTING CONSUL JOHN LAUGHLAND TO LORD JOHN RUSSELL: REMOVAL OF KING AQUA, CAMEROONS, 21 JANUARY 1861[2]

[Reporting measures taken against theft in the Cameroons.]

. . . THESE robberies have lately become so numerous that no property on the Beach is now safe and the Chiefs have been unable to put a stop to them. I therefore requested that every case should in future be brought before the Equity Court (which is composed of the Supercargoes and Native Chiefs) and to have the guilty parties punished.

I have also to report that King Aqua has again sacrificed one of the Abo people without any reason whatever but boasting that he did not care for any of the treaties he had entered into with our Government, and in order to show this, he personally put the head of the poor victim on a pole, went into the River in his Canoe ringing bells and beating drums and exhibited it to the horror and disgust of every European in the River. This as well as his general conduct caused the Supercargoes and all his own Chiefs to present a request to me to dethrone him, which I at once assented to and declared him no longer King well knowing that he had frequently broken every Treaty entered into, and was the cause of almost every quarrel in the River amongst Europeans and natives, as well as being continually drunk and seldom ever paid a penny of the trust he received from the ships.

I have in the meantime appointed Dido Aqua Chief of the Aqua Country and to receive half Comey[1] for the next twelve months and should his conduct be satisfactory to all parties during that time I agreed to make him King and order payment of the full Comey. . . .

18

LORD JOHN RUSSELL TO ACTING CONSUL JOHN LAUGHLAND: KING AQUA, CAMEROONS, 2 MARCH 1861[2]

SIR,

I have received your despatch S[lave] T[rade] no 1 of the 21st of Jan. last reporting your proceedings on the occasion of your late visit to the Cameroons River; and I have to convey to you my approval of the steps taken by you to procure compensation to British Supercargoes for the goods stolen from their stores & also to procure the punishment of the offenders; with respect however to the deposition of King Acqua I am to state to you that although no doubt it was a proper measure in the circumstances stated by you, it should not have proceeded from you but from the Chiefs as you possess no authority as British Consul either to depose one Chief or to set up another.

You should have confined yourself to advising & confirming the act of the Chiefs.

---

[1] I.e. half the export duty on palm products.   [2] F.O. 84/1147.

19

EQUITY COURT REGULATIONS, OLD CALABAR, 5 MAY 1862[1]

AGREEMENT between the British and other Supercargoes, and the Native Traders of Old Calabar.

At a meeting of the British & other Supercargoes and native traders, resident at Old Calabar, held on Board Her Britannic Majesty's Steam Vessel 'Griffon' Commander Perry the following code of bye laws and agreements subject to such modifications or additions as may be sanctioned by H.B.M. Consul for the better regulation of trading matters between the parties hereunto subscribing was unanimously agreed to, & sanctioned by Richard Francis Burton Esquire, Her Britannic Majesty's Consul for the Bight of Biafra & the Island of Fernando Po.

Article I. That an equity Court be established in the Old Calabar Country to keep in their integrity the following bye-laws and regulations, and that the Court shall consist of all the Supercargoes, a corresponding number of the Chief traders of the locality being admitted at each meeting to hear the decisions of the Court but the Kings alone shall have a vote in the proceedings.

Art. II. That a majority of votes at each meeting have the deciding power, on any subject brought before the Court, the Chairman's vote being equal to two.

Art. III. That this body have a monthly sitting, unless in special cases, when it may be summoned at any time; that a Supercargo each in his turn according to seniority, be elected Chairman for a month; and that a report of each meeting be forwarded to Her Britannic Majesty's Consul at Fernando Po.

Art. IV. That a Court House be erected at the joint expense of the Supercargoes now trading in the river, on the ground where Whitehall once stood, to be under the protection of Her Britannic Majesty's Consul, the aforesaid ground having been granted to Her Britannic Majesty's Consul for that purpose by the late King Duke Ephraim.

Art. V. That any one member of this Court have the power of appeal against its decisions to the Consul, and until his next visit

---

[1] F.O. 84/1176. The regulations were signed by Richard Burton, Commander Perry, W. Donaldson, R. McGowan, W. Roy, Irvine and Inglis (supercargoes), Duke Ephraim, Tom Eyo Honesty, John Eyo, Egbo Young Ofo, Doctor Eyo, Brassy, Antica Ambo, Black Davies, Egbo Young, Yellow Duke, Brassy Henshaw, George Duke, Henshaw Duke. A similar agreement was made for the Cameroons, 19 May 1862, omitting Article 16.

or communication all action of judgement be suspended, and if on examining this appeal it be found frivolous or invalid, the appellants are to be fined at the discretion of the Court.

Art. VI. That this Court shall apply the fines levied by it, to the expense of the erection of the Court house & keeping it in order, or otherwise, as the Court may think expedient; that the fines of Palm Oil be sold by Public Auction.

Art. VII. That any supercargo or native after receiving a formal notice to appear at the Court & failing to attend at the time fixed for meeting, shall have half an hour's grace allowed and if not present at the expiration of that time, shall be considered as refusing to attend, and shall be fined at the direction of the Court unless he can produce satisfactory reasons for such non-appearance in defiance of the rules of the Court.

Art. VIII. That any native refusing to pay any fine that may be inflicted by this Court shall be stopped from going on board any Ship in the river, either for trade or any other purposes; and any super-cargo refusing to pay a fine shall be denied the privileges of the Equity Court.

Art. IX. That all Comeys be paid to the Kings or other recognised authorities at the time, of Duke and Creek Towns, one half to each town as arranged on board H.M.S. 'Alecto' by Commander Raby; the Comey to be paid at the rate of 20 Coppers per registered ton; and no further claim is allowed to any person whatever beyond this.

Art. X. That all Comey be tendered on the arrival of a Vessel in the river, without any breakfast or ceremony of any kind, and if not accepted, the Supercargo may commence trade immediately. The said Comey to be paid, in Cargo, by said Ship when subsequently demanded.

Art. XI. That Comey having been paid or tendered, no hinderance shall be offered to the obtaining of Wood and Water for any Ship's use.

Art. XII. That the ground given as a site for a Cask house to any Supercargo shall be paid for in the case of Hulks at the rate of one H[ogshead] of Rum and three hundred Kroos of salt per annum, and in the case of sea going Ships, consigned to a supercargo who has no permanent Hulk then the same goods shall be paid for each Ship loading with Country produce in this river.

Art. XIII. After the Comey has been paid or tendered to the Kings or recognised authorities, every person desirous of disposing of any country produce in any quantities whatever to the Shipping shall be at liberty to do so in his own name without hinderance or molesta-tion from any one.

Art. XIV. That in the event of any trader making an agreement to take goods from any Ship at a certain rate, all such agreements shall be perfectly binding: and in the case of the goods not being paid for by the specified time, such goods may be sold for what they will bring, and any loss sustained thereon shall be made good, at the instance of the Court, by the defaulting trader to the Supercargo with whom the agreement has been made.

Art. XV. That no trust whatever be given to any native trader after date hereof and it is hereby distinctly understood and agreed to, that no claims whatever for any trust given to any native after date of this, shall be allowed to be brought before this Court as claims, but if any Supercargo shall hereafter give trust he does so on his own responsibility.

Art. XVI. That in the case of already existing debts, it is hereby agreed, that in order to obtain all such outstanding trust prior to this date, any supercargo can summon before this Court any debtor or his guarantee, and upon such debt being proven, a time for payment shall be fixed by the Court, and if within that time the debt has not been paid up, then a notice shall be given to the Kings or any other recognized authority, demanding such debtor to be delivered up to the Court until his debt be paid; and should a debtor not be delivered up according to notice, the Court shall consider the expediency of stopping trade, or adopting such measures as may ensure compliance with their demand. And further, in order as far as possible to do away with trust it is agreed that no trade casks shall from this time be given out as heretofore, except for the obtaining of a debt already existing, and subject to the same rule as a debt.

Art. XVII. That for the protection of the Shipping, and in order to facilitate the adjustment of disputes or quarrels arising from between Supercargoes and Natives, it is agreed that all such matters be in the first instance referred to the Court and if upon investigation it be found impossible to adjust such matter peaceably, then the Court shall refer it to the Consul, and while awaiting his decision, the contending parties shall be bound to keep the peace in such sums as the Court may think fit to decree, according to the circumstances of the parties implicated; and further all disputes between white men and natives, shall be without prejudice to the Shipping, all parties agreeing to abide by the decision of the Consul.

Art. XVIII. That if at any time after the usual Comey has been paid or tendered, any Supercargo can prove that the trade of his Ship has been stopped, by blowing Egbo[1] or by any other means direct or indirect upon any pretence whatever, then the Kings or recognised authorities for the time are to be held responsible for such stoppage, and shall pay one puncheon of good Palm Oil per day for every one hundred Tons registered tonnage to said Ship as

[2] I.e. placing under an embargo.

compensation for loss incurred. The said Oil to be paid at such time and in such manner as may be directed by the Consul.

Art. XIX. That property on shore in Cask houses, shall be strictly inviolate, and the Kings or recognised authorities shall prohibit their subjects from entering any Cask house, unless by written authority from the White trader to whom the Cask belongs.

Art. XX. That a legally qualified Pilot shall be paid at the rate of one Copper per registered Ton, for bringing up any vessels and the same for taking her out to sea but unless a legal certificate be presented by a Pilot, signed by H.B.M. Consul, it shall not be allowed that the native authorities can claim any pilotage whatever. But it shall be lawful for a certified Pilot to claim one half the foregoing pilotage when he shall not have been sent for, or his serviçes demanded.

Art. XXI. That a Ship being ready to proceed to sea, or having sent for a Pilot to bring her up the River, the Pilot shall proceed on board without delay under pain or forfeiture of his pilotage and any further penalty which may be adjudged by H.B.M. Consul.

Art. XXII. That it shall be unlawful to blow Egbo under any pretence on persons, premises, or property of any British subjects resident on shore.

Art. XXIII. That the Kings and Chiefs of Old Calabar, pledge themselves, that no British subject, shall from this time, be defamed on shore or maltreated in any way, or under any pretence; and if the Kings or Chiefs do so they will incur the displeasure of Her Majesty the Queen of England, and be declared enemies of Great Britain; and the Men of War will, upon such complaint being made to them, immediately come to Calabar River, to protect British Subjects.

Art. XXIV. That these laws be considered the existing laws between British supercargoes and the Native traders at Old Calabar, and all former Codes shall be by these abolished relating to trade. . . .

20

LORD CLARENDON TO CONSUL C. LIVINGSTONE: THE BONNY-OPOBO WAR, 23 MAY 1870[1]

Sir,

Since my Despatch of the 13th Instant was written I have received through the Admiralty a copy of a Despatch from Commodore Dowell, dated the 3rd. Ultimo, reporting the failure of his attempt to mediate between the contending Chiefs of Bonny, and I have also

[1] F.O. 84/1326. *Charles Livingstone*, brother of the explorer, was consul at Fernando Po, 1864–72.

received a letter, of which copy is inclosed, from King George Pepple deprecating any attempt at interference as useless until Ja Ja[1] has been driven away from the Andouly.

I presume that the failure of the Commodore will have prevented you from acting upon the Instructions contained in my Despatches Nos 16 & 20 of the 8th. ult. & 13th. inst. and under the present circumstances I wish you to refrain from interfering in this matter unless a more favourable opportunity present itself, and you think your intervention would be successful.

I regret to learn that British Subjects have been taking part in this quarrel, by furnishing Ja Ja with Arms and Ammunition, and I wish you to make it publickly known that H.M's. Govt. entirely discountenance and disapprove of the interference of British Subjects between rival factions.

I approve the Circular which you addressed to the Traders of Biafra and Benin, warning them not to enter the Andouly and Opobo Rivers while the war lasts, but you will endeavour to prevent the Bonny Chiefs from injuring British property in those Rivers.

21

CONSUL C. LIVINGSTONE TO LORD GRANVILLE: THE BONNY-OPOBO WAR, 23 AUGUST 1870[2]

My Lord,

With reference to Instructions in Despatch No 23 of June 3, 'To endeavour to prevent the Bonny Chiefs from molesting the property of British subjects established the Opobo', 'to protect them from personal injury or violence; and, if necessary, to ask for the assistance and support of a man of war for this purpose', I have the honour to state that I called at Bonny and Opobo on my return from the other Oil Rivers.

The Traders could not account for the movements of the Bonny fleet of war canoes; the impression was, that directly the rains were over in September, there would be a continued attack, by Bonny and Okrika, to drive Jaja from the Opobo; and that the war would never end until the oil markets were opened.

---

[1] With the decline of the House of Pepple in the 1860's, the way was open for ex-slaves such as Oko Jumbo and Ja Ja to rise to power in the Delta markets. Ja Ja succeeded as head of the Anna Pepple House in 1863, and when civil war broke out at Bonny in 1869, he established himself in the Andony area behind Bonny, effectively controlling the avenues of trade along the Bonny and Opobo rivers.

[2] F.O. 84/1326. Livingstone called in a warship to blockade Ja Ja's river trade and forced an agreement from him for a temporary truce.

As this was likely to become a war of extermination, ruinous to both rivers, another effort for peace seemed desirable. Jaja was ill when we entered the Opobo, but came on board next day 'to shew his respect'.

I said he would be recognized as Chief of Opobo, if he let Bonny Traders into the Oil markets; he had now to keep half his men in war canoes, which greatly crippled his trade. H.M. Govt. would prevent Bonny from attacking him in future; and it was better to yield than prolong the war, as he might be beaten some day when off his guard, and obliged to flee into the bush.

After consulting his Chiefs, he agreed to open the markets, if his people were returned. He did not ask for those who had been killed in the war, nor for such as preferred to remain in Bonny.

As the Bonny Chiefs had always denied killing anyone in cold blood after the fight, it seemed that Jaja's people could easily be produced, and the war ended.

I asked Jaja to send two of his Chiefs with us to see his people in Bonny, and conduct them through the creeks to Opobo; but he wished the Bonny Chiefs to come to him as he was lame. On our return, the Bonny Parliament, after a debate of 3 days and 2 nights, and trying to have Fernando Po as the place of meeting appointed 4 Chiefs to accompany us to Opobo and settle all the details of a Treaty with Jaja. Nothing was accomplished by their stiff interview, and for the first time, the Bonny Chiefs admitted that the war had broken out in all the small towns, and there had been a general massacre in which they had lost as heavily as Jaja.

I told Jaja that all his people who survived would be returned, but as the Bonny Chiefs could not raise the dead, it was idle to talk about them. I then laid the Treaty before them as the basis of a fair settlement. The Bonny Chiefs agreed to sign it, but Jaja refused. I reminded him that he had stopped the Trade of 10 English Firms in the Bonny for a Year, and this could no longer be tolerated. He replied that he would never open the oil markets; he would keep the Bonny Traders out of them for a thousand years.

Having reason to believe that the surrounding tribes had allowed Jaja to settle in the Opobo, because he promised to bring Trade there, I was satisfied that a stoppage of Trade would immediately cause these Tribes to bring pressure on Jaja and compel him to open the markets. I informed Jaja that as he declined any reasonable settlement, I should now stop his Trade, and place the matter in the hands of the Captain of this man of war. . . .

22

LORD GRANVILLE TO ACTING CONSUL
D. HOPKINS, 5 SEPTEMBER 1871[1]

[Acknowledging dispatches of July and August 1871 reporting the war between Bonny, Okrika, New Calabar, and Brass.]

... You further report that you have negotiated a truce of 3 months, dating from the 15th of July, and that you have forbidden British Subjects to sell Arms or Ammunition of War to the Natives, or to interfere in any way in the quarrel.

I entirely approve your proceedings and I trust that your warning to the Traders will not be disregarded, as I attribute the existence of so serious a state of affairs in districts hitherto peaceable, to reckless commercial rivalries and to the unwarrantable interference of British Subjects in Native disputes, notwithstanding the advice and remonstrances of H.M.'s Consul.

I have spoken strongly in this House to a deputation of the principal African Merchants who lately called upon me: they did not deny the charge, and promised, after holding a general meeting, to give me a satisfactory assurance that such instructions should be sent to their agents as will prevent a repetition of the proceedings of which I complained.

I agree with you that the time has arrived for H.M.'s Govt. to interfere for the preservation of peace, and you are accordingly authorized to state to the Chiefs that H.M.'s Govt. desire to prevent the outbreak of a general War which would be ruinous to Trade and to the prosperity of a rising and thriving Country, and that if they will submit their quarrel to you for arbitration you have full power & authority to settle it.

[D. I gather from your Despatches that the Chiefs would gladly agree to this proposal, and if so, it is possible, although I hope improbable, that you may find it necessary to insist upon their complying with the terms you dictate to them.

H.M.'s Govt. are most anxious to avoid any resort to force except as a last recourse, but they authorize you, if absolutely necessary, to call upon the Naval Authorities for such support as you may require to enforce your decision if it should be contested.][2]

As regards the merits of the quarrel, so far as I understand it, it appears to me that the natives of New Calabar were clearly in the wrong when they seized in the Waters of a Power with whom they

[1] F.O. 84/1343. *David Hopkins* was Acting Consul in 1871 and Consul at Old Calabar, 1873–9.
[2] Omitted by Lord Granville's instructions.

were at peace a canoe belonging to that Power simply because it was conveying some natives of a Tribe with whom they were at War. This was an unjustifiable act of aggression calculated to provoke War, which deserves punishment, and for which I think the Chiefs of New Calabar should be fined. With respect to the proposed interference of Bonny, I need hardly remind you that by the 3rd Article of the Treaty of Jany 23 1854[1], the Chiefs pledged themselves except in case of being attacked, not to enter into a Foreign War without first satisfactorily explaining their reasons and the necessity for doing so, and paying their debts to the Traders, and H.M.'s Govt. will in any case insist upon their complying with the provisions of this Article.

I cannot undertake to prescribe the terms of Peace that you should dictate to the Rival Chiefs. This can best be done on the spot, and I prefer to leave matters in your hands [D. with a warning that you must not resort to force except as a last resource, and that you should not dictate any terms that you would not feel justified in assuming the responsibility of enforcing.]

But in any agreement that you may conclude with the Chiefs for the establishment of a general Peace you should insert a stipulation for the future reference of all disputes to H.M.'s Consul. . . .

23

ACTING CONSUL D. HOPKINS TO LORD GRANVILLE: THE NEW CALABAR, BONNY AND OKRIKA TRUCE, 27 OCTOBER 1871[2]

H.M.S. *Dido*,
Bonny.

MY LORD,

I have the honour to report that since my Despatch No 25 was mailed I proceeded with Mr Simpson the Special Commissioner of the Niger, in the trading steamer 'King Masaba' to the River Nun, and on arrival there he was informed that H.M.S. 'Pioneer' was waiting for him in the Brass River, and we proceeded in my Consular boat through the Akassa Creeks to join that ship.

At the request of Mr. Simpson I called a meeting of the Kings and Chiefs of Brass. . . .

After Mr Simpson had finished his business I requested the people

[1] For this treaty see Jones, op. cit., Appendix, pp. 225–7.
[2] F.O. 84/1343. Encl. treaties between New Calabar and Bonny chiefs, 27 October 1871, and between Okrika and New Calabar Chiefs, 28 October 1871. For texts, see Jones, op. cit., Appendix, pp. 233–7. These were approved in Granville to Hopkins, 9 December 1871: F.O. 84/1343.

of Brass to attend me, and I informed them I had instructions to inquire into their grievances and arbitrate between them and New Calabar with whom they had intended going to war. After a protracted sitting I ascertained that they had really very little cause to quarrel with the neighbouring tribe, but that they being friends with Okrika men with whom Calabar had long been at enmity, their one cause of complaint was that Calabar had prevented Abassa from passing through the creeks to Okrika and Bonny. The Abassa men are dwellers on the banks of the Niger, and makers of Canoes, it was from them principally that the Bonny and Okrika men purchased their canoes. I noted all the Brass men had to say and gave permission to one Brass Chief to go down to Bonny, to be present at my meeting with the Kings and Chiefs of Bonny and New Calabar. . . .

[H.M.S. *Dido* was placed at the Consul's disposal by Captain Chapman.]

It is my pleasing duty to inform your Lordship that I have successfully made peace between the Natives of Bonny and New Calabar, and between Okrika and the latter people. The war that has so long disturbed this Country, preventing the people from going about their peaceful occupations in security, is happily at an end for ever. I have much pleasure in bringing to your Lordship's notice the aid and assistance I have received from King George Pepple, Oko Jumbo, and all the Chiefs of Bonny; without their valuable assistance it would have been impossible for me to have made this perpetual truce between New Calabar and Okrika.

The Calabar men have of their own free will promised to use their best endeavours with Ja-ja to bring about a settlement of the difficulties between that Chief and Oko Jumbo. The Eboe markets that Ja-ja now holds do not belong to him exclusively or to Oko Jumbo, but to *all* the people of Bonny, and his monopoly of them is ruining hundreds of natives. . . .

[He will go to Brass to inform the chiefs of his success.]

The Obiartuboo had been spoken of by Bonny and Okrika as one market, and the Okrikas claimed an equal right with the New Calabar in it, but when I discovered that Obiartuboo was a large tract of country embracing all the New Calabar Oil markets on the River's banks, and that the Calabar men had held undisturbed possession of the same for a great number of years I decided to recognize it as theirs exclusively. To the Okrikas I have secured the Deobo markets, and the right of fishing in all the creeks and rivers they have so long been kept out of by the people of New Calabar. . . .

24

CONSUL C. LIVINGSTONE TO LORD GRANVILLE: THE BONNY AND OPOBO TRUCE, 7 JANUARY 1873[1]

H.M.S. *Pioneer*.

MY LORD,

While visiting the oil rivers last month, Commodore Commerell V.C.; C.B. arrived with the news that H.M. Governmt. had determined to settle the Bonny—Opobo difficulty. At the request of that able officer I placed myself at his disposal to render him all the assistance which some years of experience in African palavers might suggest.

We first enquired whether the rival Chiefs would submit the settlement of their long standing differences to the friendly arbitration of the Kings of New Calabar and Okrika, with the Commodore and Consul as referees: and next obtained the consent of these two Kings to become arbitrators. After the usual African delays, two Kings, twenty six Chiefs and thirty one servants with all their luggage were embarked on H.M. Ships Rattlesnake and Torch. Directly the King and Chiefs of Bonny heard that they were to meet Jaja inside Opobo bar, they refused to proceed, although they had agreed to leave the choice of the place to the Commodore. The Consul went on board the Torch and told the King and Chiefs of Bonny that Jaja had sworn juju never to cross the Opobo bar, and surely enlightened men like them would not refuse to go inside that bar in an Eng. man of war. They had all along claimed the Opobo as theirs, and it could be no humiliation to visit a part of their own country. 'No' said they, 'we will go to Fernando Po and you must bring Jaja there'. The reply was, it is solely for the benefit of Bonny that we are working: England can derive no advantage from the settlement of this quarrel, as she is now getting all the oil of the country through other channels; and Jaja would of course prefer to be let alone.[2]

The Commodore will now insist on your keeping your word. 'We don't know', said George 'that this will be for our benefit, however we agree to go, but all wish the Consul to understand that we feel slighted in not being taken on board the Commodore's ship.' I told them that the Commodore would gladly have taken them all on board the Rattlesnake but he had already twenty New Calabar men

[1] F.O. 84/1377.
[2] William Wylde (marginal note): This is not the case; the roads from the interior are barred by the Opobo chiefs to the natives who want to trade with Bonny and the produce of their country is therefore lost altogether to Brit. trade.

on board, all he could accomodate; besides Jaja might object to the Bonny chiefs being in the same ship with the Calabar arbitrators: and that the Consul has assured the Commodore that under these circumstances, and especially as they were now in one of the finest ships of the squadron, the Bonny Chiefs were too sensible men to feel hurt at not being taken on board the Rattlesnake.

On meeting Jaja the rival chiefs signed an agreement to abide by the decision of the arbitrators. All met again next day on board the Pioneer in sight of the other four ships of the Squadron. King Amacree of New Calabar, presided with great dignity and sat at the head of the table; his Chiefs were on his right with Jaja and the Opobo Chiefs behind them. The Okrika Chiefs sat on his left with the Kings & Chiefs of Bonny seated behind. A difficulty arose at the beginning as to which side should speak first. The arbitrators decided that Bonny must. After indulging in mutual recriminations, both sides proceeded to serious business and seemed desirous of a settlement. The discussions lasted till the afternoon of the third day. The Arbitrators then retired for Consultation, and after their return Prince George Amacree, brother of the King, in a speech of remarkable power, announced the unanimous decision of the Arbitrators. A treaty[1] based on the decision of the arbitration was drawn up at once and signed by the Kings & Chiefs of Bonny & Opobo; and by the Commodore & Consul.

[1] Encl. treaty between the chiefs of Bonny and Opobo, 3 January 1873: Jones, op. cit., Appendix, pp. 237–9. A trade agreement on behalf of British traders was signed, 4 January 1873: Dike, op. cit., p. 223.

V

COMPANY AND CROWN
ADMINISTRATION

A. THE WEST AFRICAN SETTLEMENTS

1. *Definition and Expansion*

Introductory Note

UP till the early 1870's, the pattern of limited expansion in British West Africa falls roughly into three periods: after 1807 there was a certain amount of consolidation and a number of annexations in the Gambia and near Sierra Leone, terminated by Lord Bathurst in 1826; from then till the 1840's the interests of the British Government on the coast were reduced to a minimum; and lastly, a series of acquisitions were made between 1850 and 1863, followed by a policy of restraint which was gradually modified by new factors and a changing appreciation of the needs of the settlements in the Colonial Office.

Desire for trading posts and need for land to settle discharged soldiers and liberated Africans were the motives behind the annexation of Mac-Carthy Island, the cession of a strip of the Barra shore in the Gambia, and the series of treaties concluded by the administrators of Sierra Leone with the chiefs of Bulama Island, the Isles de Los, the Banana Islands, and the south and north banks of the Sierra Leone river. The colony which had been recognized by the Charter of 1799 to be co-extensive with the peninsula, spread westwards to the sea and to Waterloo and Kent villages in the south. Requests for further expansion in the Sherbro, North Bulom, and Port Loko areas and the annexation of the island of Matacong in 1826 were refused. With the exception of two small (and useless) purchases in the Gambia on the Deer Islands in 1834 and at Kombo in 1839, Bathurst's policy of no extension of sovereignty was maintained throughout the 1830's. The abortive plan to shift the Court of Mixed Commission from Freetown to Fernando Po and the return of the forts to the Merchants in 1828 completed a decade of indecision and withdrawal.

Investigation into charges of assisting the slave trade on the Gold Coast and the acceptance of recommendations of the Select Committee of the House of Commons in 1842 ended the period of administrative attrition, though Bathurst's policy was not immediately changed. With Earl Grey at the Colonial Office, Governor Macdonald was firmly restrained from expanding to the Bulom Shore and from altering the southern boundary of the colony, fixed at Calmont Creek in 1848. In the same year, Grey opposed a suggestion of the Foreign Office to purchase the Danish forts and a plan prepared by Palmerston to obtain territory in the Gambia to prevent French expansion from their post at Albreda. Two years later, however, Grey agreed that shortage of Gold Coast revenue was sufficient reason for acquiring the Danish forts and that the need for more land to support the liberated Africans at Bathurst justified the settlement of part of Kombo. A second annexation at Kombo was allowed in 1852 and the French post at Albreda was acquired in 1857. When the Portuguese flag was removed from Bulama Island—claimed by Sierra Leone, but not occupied, since 1840—Governor Kennedy was ordered by the Duke of Newcastle to send a resident agent there. In the Bight of Benin, as a result of Russell's treaty policy and the policy of the Lagos consuls in the 1850's, the Foreign Office persuaded a reluctant Colonial Office that it was necessary to annex Lagos for humanitarian and commercial reasons. The Lagos annexation of 1861 was preceded by the cession of part of Koya territory in Sierra Leone and was closely followed by the annexation of Bendu and Sherbro Island. Bulama was formally annexed and a garrison was sent there in 1863. On the Gold Coast the administration of the eastern district was extended as far as Keta near the Volta mouth. By then, too, Lagos had been expanded to Badagri, Palma, and Lekki to ensure control of markets and Customs on the lagoon.

For the moment, these represented the limits of Colonial Office patience with new responsibilities in the name of trade, revenue, and the anti-slavery campaign. An ambitious attempt by Lieut.-Governor Glover to extend Lagos Protectorate to towns in southern Yorubaland was disallowed along with his designs on Porto Novo and his partition of the area west of Badagri with the French. The boundaries of the colony and its outposts were fixed provisionally by Colonel Ord in 1864, and British sovereignty on the Gold Coast was firmly kept to the forts in 1865. Similarly, a proposal to annex territory along the Melakori rivers north of Sierra Leone in the same year and offers to found a British colony at Victoria in the Cameroons were rejected out of hand. The Select Committee of 1865, in slightly ambiguous resolutions, confirmed Colonial Office caution and demanded immediate withdrawal from the Upper Gambia and possibly from other parts of the coast.

Troops left MacCarthy Island in 1866; but a token administration still remained. The Gambia example was a fair illustration of policy elsewhere —retrenchment, rather than abandonment. In these circumstances, Consul McLeod's plan for a Niger colony at Lokoja in 1867 was not supported by the Foreign Office which also dismissed as groundless British traders' claims to interfere with French posts in the Melakori on the basis of treaties concluded there in 1826. For financial reasons part of Koya territory west of Freetown was given up by Governor Kennedy in 1869 and a garrison of troops was removed from the Sherbro in 1870. On the other hand, British claims to Bulama were obstinately maintained and were only terminated by international arbitration in favour of the Portuguese. Other cases were considered on their merits. Two efforts were made to define European possessions according to spheres of influence and trade after 1865, when negotiations were begun to exchange Gold Coast forts with the Dutch and to cede the Gambia to France. Both examples indicated a desire on the part of the Colonial Office to improve Gold Coast revenues and to get rid of a financial burden. From 1866 till early 1870 there was a rare unanimity between politicians and officials on the desirability of ceding the Gambia. Repeatedly, the step was postponed because of indecision over what compensation to ask for, unwillingness to take the proposal before Parliament, and, finally, by the outbreak of the Franco-Prussian War and a change of attitude on the part of Lord Kimberley in July and August 1870 towards the question of safeguarding the commercial and civil rights of British subjects at Bathurst. A year later the negotiations were broken off. On the Gold Coast the exchange of Dutch and British forts which provoked much more violent local opposition was completed at the beginning of 1868. By August 1870, Kimberley, following the advice of the Gold Coast administration, was ready to go further and purchase the Dutch forts—though not at the Dutch price of £80,000. Five months later the forts were sold by the Anglo-Dutch Convention of 1871 at the cost of only £24,000 for stores and fixtures. To complete the extension of British jurisdiction along the coast, Administrator Ussher called for the occupation of the Volta mouth east of Keta—a move delayed till after the Ashanti War.

A third important test for the limits of colonial control was at Lagos and Porto Novo where Administrator Glover posted constables outside the Protectorate and blockaded the Dahomey port in defiance of orders from his Governor-in-Chief. The clash between Glover and Pope Hennessy over this policy which led to Glover's removal contributed to the debate in the Colonial Office on the question of British policy on the coast as a whole. The decision not to take Porto Novo followed the line laid down by Cardwell in 1864; but neither at Lagos nor on the Gold Coast by 1873, was there a serious possibility of withdrawal from territory already acquired. The relationship between Customs revenue and expansion, well understood on the coast since 1850, was now acknowledged as a sufficient reason for altering colonial boundaries. By 1874, other sectors adjacent to British settlements, particularly north of Sierra Leone, began to be considered from this point of view.

I

PURCHASE OF TERRITORY ON THE SIERRA LEONE RIVER, 11 JUNE 1787[1]

KNOW all Men by these Presents, That I King Tom, Chief of Sierra Leone, on the Grain Coast of Africa, by and with the Consent of the other Kings, Princes, Chiefs, and Potentates, subscribing hereto,

[1] *Parl. Papers*, 1789, xxxiv (626), p. 12. *King Tom* was subordinate to the paramount chief of the Koya Temne, Naimbanna, with whom it was necessary to make a new treaty, 22 August 1788, which repeated the description of the ceded territory. See J. J. Crooks, *A History of the Colony of Sierra Leone Western Africa*, p. 361.

in Consideration of the Presents, as by a List annexed, now made me by Captain Thomas Boulden Thompson, of His Britannic Majesty's Ship Nautilus, Joseph Irwin, Esquire, and the Reverend Patrick Fraser, in Behalf of, and for the sole Benefit of, the Free Community of Settlers, their Heirs and Successors, lately arrived from England, and under the Protection of the British Government, have granted, and by these Presents do grant, and for ever quit Claim to, a certain District of Land, for the settling of the said Free Community, to be theirs, their Heirs and Successors, for ever; that is to say, All the Land, Wood, Water, &c, which is contained from the Bay, commonly called Frenchman's Bay, but by these Presents changed to that of St. George's Bay, Coastways, up the River Sierra Leone, to Gambia Island, and Southerly or Inland, from the River Side Twenty Miles. And further be it known unto all Men, That I King Tom do faithfully promise and swear, for my Chiefs, Gentlemen, and People, likewise my Heirs and Successors, that I will bear true Allegiance to His Most Gracious Majesty George the Third . . . and protect the said Free Settlers, His Subjects, to the utmost of my Power, against the Insurrections and Attacks of all Nations or People whatever. And I do hereby bind myself, my Heirs and Successors, to grant the said Free Settlers a Continuance of a quiet and peaceable Possession of the Land granted, their Heirs and Successors, for ever. In witness whereof I and my Chiefs have set our Hands and Seals this Eleventh Day of June 1787.

(L.S.) × The Mark of King Tom,
(L.S.) × Chief Pabongee,
(L.S.) × Queen Yammalouba.

Witness to the executing the above,
  and of the Presents[1] made,
    T. B. Thompson,
    Joseph Irwin,
    Patrick Fraser, A.M.

2

HENRY DUNDAS TO LIEUT.-COLONEL FRASER: GOREE, 11 NOVEMBER 1800[2]

SECRET.

. . . As it is certainly a matter of some importance both with a view to the Security of Goree and to the Trade carried on with that part

[1] The presents amounted to about £59 worth of trade goods.
[2] C.O. 268/18. After capture, the fort at Gorée was commanded by Fraser till 1803, when he was replaced by Colonel Charles Stevenson. The post surrendered to the French in 1804 and was recaptured the same year.

of Africa to dispossess the Enemy of that position, it is His Majesty's pleasure that on your arrival at Goree, you should, in concert with the Commanding Naval Officer, lose no time in making an attempt for this purpose, should it appear to you and the said Officer practicable and likely to succeed with the Force under your respective Commands. In the event of your obtaining Possession of the Place, of which I entertain little doubt, should the Enemy receive no Reinforcements before your arrival, you will consider of the best means of rendering it most conducive to the encouragement of the Commercial Intercourse established with that part of the Coast (particularly the Gum Trade) with the least possible expence to this Country in maintaining the Position and at the least risk to the Lives and Health of the Troops under your Command. . . .

3

COMMITTEE OF THE COMPANY OF MERCHANTS TO THE TREASURY: GOLD COAST FORTS, 9 APRIL 1812[1]

. . . OF the particular Forts recommended by the Commissioners to be abandoned;[2]

Succondee—has a good landing-place, and considerable gold-trade; it is situated in a fertile country; the natives are remarkably quiet and tractable, and more favourable to cultivation and improvement than any on the Gold Coast. As we have here only a Settlement, and the Dutch a respectable Fort, on the capture thereof a mere mark of possession might be left at our own.

Commenda—has some gold and ivory trade; furnishes corn and yams; is useful as a stopping place on proceeding to windward; and is of importance, as the only place in our possession which furnishes canoes.

Tantum—valuable as a point of communication; is a place where the trade in slaves has been extensively carried on; it yields some gold and ivory, and abundance of provisions.

Winnebah—is useful in many respects; it is most fertile, and good corn country; has plenty of fish, and stock, a good landing place, and should on no account be abandoned; as it is, in certain seasons, the only place on the Gold Coast which can supply fresh water to the shipping; it is also necessary to keep up the communication between

---

[1] *Parl. Papers*, 1816, vii (506), pp. 104–8. The members of the Committee at this date were: Miles Wynne, Thomas Morton, N. B. French, Thomas Reed, John Vaughan, John Noble, James Barnes, George Barnes, Robert Rolleston, James Swanzy.

[2] By the West African Commissioners Columbine, Ludlam, and Dawes. The latter two had visited the forts in 1810. *Parl. Papers*, 1812, x (101), pp. 11–13, 89.

Accra and Annamaboe, as must be evident to every person informed of the mode of travelling in that country.

Pram Pram—a dependence on James Fort, Accra, has weaker claims to notice, but in our opinion it should not be abandoned until a general peace shall have determined the footing that we are permanently enabled to retain in Africa.

Whydah—on the subject of this Fort, we are so far in the situation of the Commissioners, that we can only form an opinion from the report of others; but we are well assured, that the people in that neighbourhood, in many respects, exhibit strong evidence of an advance in civilization beyond what is apparent on other parts of the Coast; it is one of the most populous and fertile districts, and produces cotton and indigo in abundance; and there is a French Fort, and also a Portuguese Fort, within musket-shot of ours, so that the relinquishment of the British Fort (its destruction is out of the question, being too far inland to be effected from the sea, and it being certain that the King of Dahomy will not allow it) would give to either of the others the additional advantage to be derived from its abandonment by the British. Regarding this Fort, the Committee have only to add that, although no advantage is at present derived by the British traders from its occupation, it occasions an annual expense to the public of no more than 600 *l.*; how far the saving of this sum may be deemed an object, under the circumstances stated, the Committee wholly submit to the consideration of your Lordships.

On this part of the subject we feel it incumbent to add, that in the event of relinquishing any of the British Settlements, or taking, and afterwards abandoning, any of those now in the occupation of other European nations, the presents or allowances usually made to the chiefs of the country, must, for the preservation of peace, and of the means of intercourse, be continued to them, until they shall be otherwise provided for; scarcely any saving therefore would be immediately made by the abandonment of any of the Forts. Our duty requires also, that we should not conceal from your Lordships, that the capture of the Dutch Settlements will not be affected without difficulty or loss, in a climate so unfavourable to the European constitution; and that the animosity which it will create among the inhabitants of the Dutch towns, when it is known that our object in this measure is to deprive them of their accustomed trade, will require for some time the presence of a considerable force.

Of the propriety of selling or letting any of them, as proposed by the Commissioners, it is only necessary to say, that it is utterly impracticable.

These gentlemen state the average charge of maintaining each of the Out Forts is about 1,400 *l.* or 1,500 *l.* per annum, and that the profit made by the officers in the command of them respectively, is from 800 *l.* to 1,200 *l.*; can it then be imagined, that any man will be found willing to settle in Africa, to subject himself to this positive loss?

Upon the assumption of the Commissioners, that if the Forts were in the possession of individual merchants, the spirit of enterprize and command of capital might increase the trade, which the Commissioners say, may probably not have been pushed to the full extent of which it is capable, owing to the want of sufficient means; we cannot but observe that in this instance, as in other parts of their Report, particularly where they remark that the commerce of the Gold Coast has never been found sufficient to defray the expenses of the Companies engaged in it, the Commissioners seem to have been unacquainted with the nature and constitution of this Company; they appear to have imagined that this Committee have hitherto been the traders, and that the trade has languished and proved unprofitable in our hands for want of capital and energy. Your Lordships, however, know that, restricted as we are from trading in our corporate capacity, we have no benefits or advantages whatever arising from the trade; nor any funds, beyond the annual grant from Parliament, for the maintenance of the Forts; and that the importance or value of the trade is not to be estimated by the little profits made by some of the officers in charge of the Forts, which profits have never before been deemed of sufficient consequence to become the subject of calculation or remark.

The trade to Africa is now, and has been during the last 60 years, perfectly free and open to the capital and enterprize of all British merchants without exception, who have constantly enjoyed, without charge, the full protection and advantage of the Forts.

In adverting to the observations of the Commissioners on the dilapidated state of the Forts, we cannot forbear to avail ourselves of the opportunity of urging the necessity for affording them additional protection. That some of them are in bad repair, and in an imperfect state of defence, we are ready to admit; but your Lordships will allow us to observe, that we cannot suffer this fact to be stated against us as a matter of reproach. . . .

4

EARL BATHURST TO GOVERNOR SIR CHARLES MACCARTHY: GAMBIA POSTS, 20 JULY 1816[1]

[Acknowledging the report of Colonel Brereton on the occupation of James and St Mary's Islands in the Gambia.]

. . . As the only objects which His Majesty's Government had in view in reoccupying an Island in the Gambia, were the extinction of the Slave Trade which has lately been carried on in that Quarter to a great extent, and the revival of the Gum Trade formerly carried on from thence, His Majesty's Government will be ready to approve the occupation of either Island which you may consider best calculated for the purpose in view; but you are not to consider yourself authorized to incur any expence which may have for its Object a permanent Establishment, or to erect any Buildings beyond what may be absolutely necessary for the protection of the small Detachments of Troops employed in that River under Colonel Brereton. The mere fact of its occupation by a British Force will be sufficient to deter the Dealers in Slaves from a continuance in this illegal Traffic, and if the Merchants consider that there is a prospect of carrying on from thence the same Trade with the Natives which has heretofore been carried on at Senegal, they will take the necessary measures for making on the Island which you may finally determine to occupy, an adequate Depot for their Goods. You will not fail to transmit to me, without delay, an Estimate of what additional Expence the occupation of this Island will lead to, in order that His Majesty's Government may decide how far its permanent retention may under existing Circumstances be a means of expediency.

5

GOVERNOR SIR CHARLES MACCARTHY TO EARL BATHURST: ISLES DE LOS, 2 JANUARY 1818[2]

My Lord,

Understanding that it is in the contemplation of the Government of the United States of America to form an Establishment of their People of Colour on some part of Africa near this place and being

[1] C.O. 268/19.
[2] C.O. 267/47. The occupation was approved by the Committee for Trade, 25 April 1818: C.O. 267/48; and a treaty of cession was concluded by MacCarthy and the chief of the Isles de Los, 6 July 1818.

thoroughly convinced that such a measure would not only prove highly prejudicial to the Interest of this Colony, but ultimately prevent all Commercial intercourse with Great Britain I beg leave to solicit of your Lordship to adopt such measures as you may deem most advisable to prevent an Establishment of that nature being formed either to the North of Sierra Leone or nearer to the South than Cape Palmas.

The loss which the British fair dealer daily suffers in consequence of the smuggling carried on by the petty Traders of this Colony with the Isles de Los renders it highly desirable that those Islands, at present inhabited by two British Subjects (Messrs Samo and Leigh) should be occupied with a small Military Force. As the case now stands, the Trade of the important Rivers of Scarcies, Ryo Pongas, Ryo Nunez, Ryo Grande, and Sherbro', is nearly engrossed by Americans through the agency of those *two* British Subjects, who purchase the whole of their Merchandizes from Foreigners in exchange for African produce. A Military Establishment would of course prevent such intercourse and secure to His Majesty's subjects that branch of Commerce which they have so honorably and dearly purchased.

6

GOVERNOR SIR CHARLES MACCARTHY TO EARL BATHURST: ANNEXATIONS, SIERRA LEONE, 19 JULY 1819[1]

[Reporting a Convention made with the Temne for the cession of land on the left bank of the Sierra Leone river.]

. . . YOUR Lordship will perceive that such an acquisition was not only desirable for the purpose of establishing the soldiers lately discharged from the West India Corps, and such captured Negroes as we may hereafter receive, but that it will also secure the rest of the Colony—that by extending it towards the Sherbro and Caramancas Rivers, it will give in a great measure to this Peninsula the same advantages as an Island. I have not yet obtained any correct survey of these Rivers (Sherbro and Camarancas) but I have strong motives to think that the distance to the latter from Waterloo, does not exceed eight or ten miles, at most, and is probably less.

[1] C.O. 267/49. The convention of 25 May 1819, ceding Temne lands at Ma Porto (Waterloo) and Robump (Hastings), was approved in Bathurst to MacCarthy, 30 November 1818: C.O. 268/19.

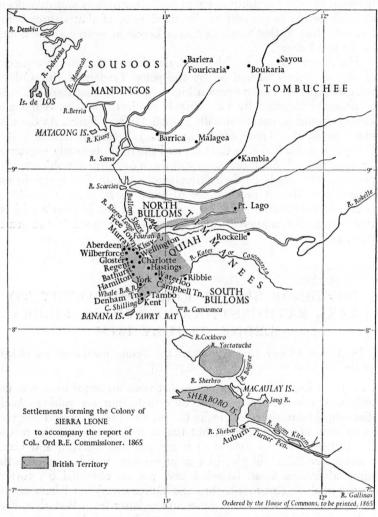

Map 5: Sierra Leone Settlements, 1865.

7

ACTING GOVERNOR D. M. HAMILTON TO EARL BATHURST: ANNEXATIONS, SIERRA LEONE, 11 NOVEMBER 1824[1]

[Forwarding a Convention with chiefs for the cession of territory along the north bank of the Sierra Leone river.]

. . . I was induced to do so, not only from the representation of several of the timber Merchants of the advantage that would result to the Timber Trade by this Act, but also from a persuasion of the sound policy of the measure as a means of extending our influence and Trade in the immediate neighbourhood of the Colony.

8

GOVERNOR CHARLES TURNER TO EARL BATHURST: ANNEXATIONS, SIERRA LEONE, 18 OCTOBER 1825[2]

[Reporting a successful expedition to the Sherbro and the cession of the Plantain Islands and Sherbro coast.]

. . . By this Treaty which I hope will meet with your Lordship's approbation, it will be seen that upwards of 100 Miles of Sea Coast is added to this Colony, a circumstance which in this particular case will tend greatly to increase its trade and general prosperity by throwing open, and securing the exclusive trade of five large Rivers, navigable a great way into the interior, and known long to have been the most fertile in rice, Camwood and various products of this Country. As regards the Slave Trade the district now ceded to us has, for many years back been the theatre of its most active operations in this, or perhaps any other part of Africa. . . .

[1] C.O. 267/60. Encl. convention, 2 August 1824, with Bai Mauro, ceding one mile of the north shore and the islands of Bance, Tasso, and Tombo; approved in Bathurst to Turner, 30 January 1825: C.O. 268/20.
[2] C.O. 267/66. Encl. convention, 24 September 1825, with King Banka: disallowed in Bathurst to Turner, 19 December 1825: C.O. 268/20,

9

EARL BATHURST TO GOVERNOR CHARLES TURNER: REFUSAL OF ANNEXATIONS, 22 APRIL 1826[1]

SIR,

I have the honor to acknowledge the receipt of your dispatch No. 91 of the 20th of Decr.[2] last, in which you enclose a copy of a Convention which you had concluded on the 12th of that month with several Chiefs the lawful proprietors of the Bacca Loco Territories, for ceding the Sovereignty there to His Majesty.

Having already conveyed to you the sentiments of His Majesty's Government upon the subject of a Convention of the same nature which you had concluded with several Chiefs in the Sherbro River, I can only refer you generally to my instruction of the 19th of Decr. last, although I must at the same time express my regret that you did not await H.M's commands respecting your proceedings in the Sherbro before you entered into similar agreements with the Chiefs of other Tribes in the immediate vicinity of the Colony itself; nor can I omit expressing my disapprobation of the publication in the Gazette of the Colony of the Convention of Bacco Loco, before it was known whether it would receive the sanction of His Majesty; and I persuade myself that you will take care for the future to prevent similar unauthorized publications of the measures of your Government.

I entirely concur with you in opinion as to the propriety of cultivating the closest relations of amity with the Native Chiefs; & of using every effectual means for prevailing on them to abandon the detestable traffic in which they have hitherto been engaged. That such has been the sole object which you have sought to accomplish, by the arrangements which you have recently adopted, I entertain no doubt; but I cannot too strongly impress on you the necessity of avoiding entering into any treaty with a view to the acquisition of Territory or Rights of Sovereignty. . . .

[1] C.O. 268/20, ff. 334-6.
[2] In C.O. 267/66. On this basis the annexation of Matakong was also refused: Goderich to Campbell, 9 June 1827: C.O. 268/26, ff. 290-2.

10

LORD STANLEY TO ACTING GOVERNOR J. CARR; ANNEXATION OF NUNEZ TERRITORY, 8 NOVEMBER 1841[1]

SIR,

I have to acknowledge the receipt of your desps. Nos. 32 & 33 of the 16th & 18th of Augt. in which you announce your intention to send a Mission to Teimbo & to conclude treaties for the suppression of the Slave Trade with Thomas Caulker & all the Chiefs who command the line of Coast from Sierra Leone to Cape Mensurado.

As H.M. Govt are unable to concur in the propriety of the suggestions which you have thrown out as to the expediency of obtaining the Sovereignty of the River Nunez & of the Waters of the Chiefs in question I lose no time in acquainting you that you are to consider yourself prohibited from concluding any Treaty or agreement which should have the effect of binding H.M. to give military aid to African Chiefs, or to assume any right of Sovereignty, or protection over any portion of the soil or waters of Africa. Cases may occur (I hardly think it possible they should) in which [D. such an engagement may be justifiable; but I repeat that in none is that engagement to be entered into] it may be deemed advisable ultimately that H.M. shd. enter into such an engagement, but I repeat that in no case are you to take any step which may fetter the discretion of the Queen's Govt. If at any time application should be made to you to place an African Chief or his territory under the Sovereignty, or protection of the Queen, the utmost to be done, & that most sparingly, & in instances of extreme urgency shd. be to forward such application to H.M.'s Govt, but independently & irrespectively of the other terms of the Treaty.

11

G. W. HOPE TO VISCOUNT CANNING: APOLLONIA, 4 MAY 1844[2]

MY LORD,

With reference to my Letter of the 11th Oct. last enclosing the copy of a letter from Mr. Maclean, President administering the Government of the Forts on the Gold Coast relative to the establishment of a French Settlement in that Quarter, I am directed by Lord Stanley to transmit to your Lordship for the information of the Earl

[1] C.O. 268/38, ff. 113–15.   [2] C.O. 96/4.

of Aberdeen, the copy of a further letter from Mr. Maclean explanatory of the grounds on which he considers that portion of the Coast which he designates as the Appollonian Coast, to be British Territory.

Mr. Maclean suggests that the line of Coast which he includes under that name should be re-occupied by H.M.'s Government or that it should be formally & finally abandoned. Lord Stanley, however, does not see the necessity of adopting either of those alternatives.

His Lordship conceives that we have no claim in fact to more than the Fort situated on that part of the Coast & known as 'Appollonia Fort', & that in practice we have confined ourselves to the limits of that Fort; & his Lordship would therefore propose with Lord Aberdeen's concurrence to instruct the Lieut.-Governor of the British Forts on the Gold Coast that he must not insist on any claim to territorial possession on the Appollonian Coast beyond the limits of the Fort.

12

EARL GREY TO GOVERNOR N. W. MACDONALD, 7 NOVEMBER 1846[1]

[Acknowledging dispatches reporting resistance on the Bulom Shore, Sierra Leone, to the settlement at Clarkson.]

. . . In my desp[atch] of 4 Augt. last, I expressed to you my strong disapprobation of the steps you had taken for occupying the Territory, called Clarkson, on the Bullom Shore, an error, which has caused most serious apprehensions to be entertained for the peace and security of the Colony of Sierra Leone.

It is unnecessary therefore on the present occasion that I should enter into any further consid[eration] of the general policy of the measures you have adopted but there are some points mentioned in your Desps. which require to be noticed.

1. The practice of bribing the neighbouring Chiefs with presents of Rum, Tobacco, and Cloth to induce good conduct and peaceable behaviour towards the Local Govt. is highly objectionable—but your statements on this subject are so vague and imperfect that it is impossible for me without further inform[ation] to give you any definite instructions respecting it. I must request therefore, that you will report to me how long this practice has existed. . . .

---

[1] C.O. 268/41, ff. 174–80. Macdonald had consolidated the occupation of the Bulom Shore 'Square Mile' at Clarkson, begun by Lieut.-Governor Fergusson for liberated Africans, but not reported to the Colonial Office. Both Stephen and Hawes in minutes of July 1846 opposed this expansion: C.O. 267/191.

13

EARL GREY TO ACTING GOVERNOR B. PINE: SIERRA LEONE BOUNDARY, 2 DECEMBER 1848[1]

SIR,

I have the honour to acquaint you that since Governor Macdonald has been in this country, I have had under my consideration the Despatches enumerated in the margin respecting the Southern Boundary of Sierra Leone, and especially no. 70 of the 7th June 1847 containing the report made by yourself on the legal bearings of the Question, and accompanied by a Chart which much facilitates the examination of the subject.

2. The conclusion which I have arrived at is that although the name of the River Caramanca is introduced both in the Act of Parliament and in the original Charter, yet the intention undeniably was to make the Colony consist of the 'Peninsula' of Sierra Leone, and that inasmuch as Calmont Creek is the only boundary to the Southward which is consistent with that condition, while the course of the Caramanca is now known to be altogether different from what was apparently assumed when the Charter was drawn up; inasmuch also, as it does appear in the general course of practice to have been recognized, accordingly, the Creek must be deemed to be, as a matter of fact the existing Southern Boundary of the Colony. I do not think that it would be possible more strictly to define it without applying for an amendment of the Act of Parliament; nor on the other hand would it be expedient to extend it beyond the present practical boundary without endeavouring by some previous cession of the Country lying beyond it, to provide against collision with the Natives by whom the ground is already occupied.

3. But I do not perceive that such evils exist, either from smuggling or from want of Jurisdiction as call for measures of this serious character; and certainly I do not think that any positive gain is to be expected which would justify H.M.'s Govt. in seeking an extensive enlargement of Territory in Sierra Leone.

4. I have to instruct you therefore that Calmont Creek is to be deemed the existing limit of the Colony to the Southward, and that I see no reason at present for endeavouring to exchange it for another Boundary.

[1] C.O. 268/43, ff. 13–16.

14

H. MERIVALE TO THE TREASURY: DANISH FORTS, 1 DECEMBER 1849[1]

. . . LORD Grey has been most anxious to discover some mode of raising in the British Possessions in Africa a Revenue applicable to those measures of improvement, the extension of which he has regarded as of so much importance, and to provide the means of increasing the number and efficiency of the Schools, of opening new lines of communication and improving those, which already exist, and undertaking other Public Works without adding to the Amount of the Vote annually submitted to Parliament.

With this view the L[ords] C[ommissioners] of the Treasury have concurred with Lord Grey in approving of the suggestion offered by the Lt. Govr. of the Gold Coast for the imposition of very moderate Duties upon Spirits and a few other Articles extensively consumed in this part of Africa. From the communications Lord Grey has had with Sir Wm. Winniett during his stay in this country, and also with several of the principal merchants trading to the Coast, he sees no reason to doubt, that the produce of these Duties, if they are successfully levied, will be amply sufficient not only for the objects I have mentioned, but also to defray the whole expense of the Establishments, at the different Forts, (including a Local Corps, which it is proposed to substitute for the present Military Force) for which Parliament is now called upon to provide. But there is this difficulty in levying the duties, that the Danish Forts and the territory over which Denmark claims Jurisdiction, being so intermixed with the British Possessions, unless the authorities, under which these Forts were placed were to concur in imposing the same duties, those imposed in the British Territory would to a considerable extent be evaded. Their L[ordships] will perceive, from the extract already referred to from the Despatch of the Acting Lt. Govr. of the Gold Coast, that this concurrence on the part of the Danish authorities has not been obtained. The transfer to H.M. of the Danish Settlements would at once remove this obstacle to the collection of the proposed Duties and Lord Grey is assured by those he considers to be best able to form a judgment on the subject that no other difficulty is to be anticipated, & that a very considerable Revenue arising from these duties may confidently be reckoned upon.

7. On the other hand the additional expenditure, which would be

[1] C.O. 96/17. Based on a minute by Grey, 7 August 1849, on F.O. to C.O., 12 July 1849 (urging purchase of the Danish forts for £10,000). The Treasury agreed to apply to Parliament, 19 December 1849.

necessary would be exceedingly moderate [A. would cost in additional establishment to Brit. Possessions £1340 and for Danish Forts £1150] & Sir Wm. Winniett has no doubt of its being in his power to meet both these charges without making any addition to the Parliamentary Vote even for the present year; he is equally confident, that if the measures now in contemplation should be adopted, in the course of two or three years even the present vote may be dispensed with.

9. [*Sic.* The present troops of the West India Regiment are to be replaced by a local militia paid for from colonial revenues.]

10. While the advantages of the cession of territory will be thus considerable it is proper to add, that [Lord Grey apprehends that there can be no room for doubting that the actual value of the property which in consequence of that cession it will be necessary to purchase far exceeds the price, which the Danish Govt. has expressed its willingness to accept for it. The Lt. Govr. of the Gold Coast and Mr. Forster, one of the principal merchants trading to that part of Africa, whose opinion is entitled to very great weight, have both reported, that they consider the sum, which is asked, to be much below that, which the Buildings and their contents are worth without allowing anything for the Rights of Sovereignty, which would be transferred along with them];[1] and I am in conclusion to express Lord Grey's opinion, that the present is an opportunity of establishing on a firm foundation & extending British influence in this part of Africa which cannot be neglected without great risk to the permanency of the improvements, which has already been effected. Even while held by Denmark it will be observed, that the possession of these Forts by another Power is stated by the Acting Lt. Governor of the Gold Coast to have led to embarrassing questions as to the extent of the respective Rights of jurisdiction which belong to the two nations. While these Forts are in the hands of the Danes there is no danger of their being made use of in any way to countenance a revival of the Slave Trade in a region where it is now happily extinguished & thus as the influence of the two countries is directed towards the same objects, there is comparatively little probability of any serious difference arising. The case would be very different if the Forts were in other hands, & the Danish Govt. is so anxious to be relieved from these possessions, that if the offer now made to H.M.'s Govt. should not be accepted there can be little doubt that they will be transferred to some other Power; & if, unfortunately, this should be one less sincerely anxious than Denmark to assist to the utmost in the suppression of the Slave Trade, there is but too much danger that the private gain to be easily made by persons entrusted with authority on the

[1] Section transposed from ff. 3-4 to f. 23 of the draft.

Coast of Africa by conniving at the Slave Trade might prove too powerful a temptation to be resisted, & that these Forts might be used to countenance, instead of to put down, that detestable traffic, The result would not be merely the revival of that traffic, but most probably also, to involve this Country in differences of a very serious character with the Power which might have acquired these Forts & might have allowed them to be thus abandoned.

But on the other hand, should the offer now made be accepted, this Country would obtain almost exclusive jurisdiction over a great extent of Country of the highest natural capabilities & inhabited by a numerous population already manifesting a strong disposition to improve the advantages they possess, & requiring nothing, as it is believed, but the superintendence & direction of an enlightened European Govt. to become industrious & thriving communities. The soil & climate are fitted for the cultivation of most kinds of tropical produce, & above all, it has been ascertained that the cotton plant grows with singular facility, & is even now almost without cultivation to be found in considerable abundance. If judicious means are adopted to direct the attention of the natives to the cultivation of this article (on which subject Lord Grey proposes to address another communication to their Lordships) there seems to be no reason why in the course of a few years, cotton should not be added to the list of Exports from this part of Africa & a new and valuable source be opened for the supply of the raw material of our most important manufacture.

15

CONVENTION FOR THE CESSION OF THE DANISH POSSESSIONS ON THE COAST OF AFRICA TO GREAT BRITAIN, 17 AUGUST 1850[1]

... ARTICLE I.

In consideration of the sum of ten thousand pounds sterling to be paid by Her Majesty the Queen of the United Kingdom of Great Britain and Ireland to His Majesty the King of Denmark, on the exchange of the ratifications of the present Convention, His Danish Majesty cedes to Her Britannic Majesty, her heirs and successors, in full property and sovereignty, all the forts belonging to the Crown of Denmark, which are situated on that part of the Coast of Africa called the Gold Coast or the Coast of Guinea, and which comprise Fort Christiansborg, Fort Kogensteen, and Fort Prindsensteen, with

1 *Parl. Papers*, 1851 (213), p. 2.

their appurtenances and all the guns and stores contained therein; together with all other possessions, property, and territorial rights whatever belonging to His Danish Majesty on the said coast. . . .

16

EARL GREY TO GOVERNOR R. G. MACDONNELL: KOMBO, GAMBIA, 25 FEBRUARY 1851[1]

SIR,

I have received your dispatch No. 67 of the 31 Decr. last transmitting a copy of a Treaty (with the documents) which you have concluded with the King & Chiefs of Combo for the cession of a small tract of ground near Cape St Mary & about 8 miles distant from the Town of Bathurst in the Gambia.

Altho' I am generally reluctant to sanction any new acquisition of Territory on the Coast of Africa, I concur with you in regarding the possession of this small tract of Country so contiguous to the Settlement as highly desirable on account of the comparative salubrity & fertility of the soil.

I have therefore laid the Treaty before the Queen & Her Majesty has been graciously pleased to approve of it. . . .

17

PROCLAMATION: CESSION OF ALBREDA. FREETOWN, 21 APRIL 1857[2]

. . . WHEREAS a Convention between Great Britain and France was concluded in London on the seventh day of March in the year of our Lord one thousand eight hundred and fifty-seven, in which it is, amongst other things, agreed:

1st. That Her Majesty the Queen of the United Kingdom of Great Britain and Ireland relinquishes the right hitherto enjoyed under Treaty by the subjects of Her Britannic Majesty of trading from the mouth of the River St. John to the Bay and Fort of Portendic inclusively.

2nd. His Majesty the Emperor of the French cedes to Her

---

[1] C.O. 87/48. Encl. convention, 26 December 1850 (by which the chief of Kombo renounced tribute and rents for an annual stipend). A portion of Kombo had also been annexed in 1840 and approved by Russell: C.O. 87/23, Huntley to Russell, 28 July 1840. A further cession at Kombo was made by treaty, 24 May 1853, and included the town of Sabaji.

[2] *Ordinances of the Settlements on the Gambia, 1818–79* (London, 1882), p. 545.

Britannic Majesty the French factory or *comptoir* at Albreda on the north bank of the River Gambia, on the Western Coast of Africa, together with all possessory or other rights whatever appertaining to the said factory.

Now, therefore, I do hereby publish, proclaim, and make known for the information of all concerned that British trade with Portendic has been relinquished as aforesaid. . . .

I. F. Smyth, Colonial Secretary.

18

LORD JOHN RUSSELL TO THE DUKE OF NEWCASTLE: ANNEXATION OF LAGOS, 7 FEBRUARY 1861[1]

[Measures which may be taken to assist Abeokuta.]

. . . But there is another measure which would in my opinion be attended with the most beneficial results, both as regards the suppression of the Slave Trade, and the encouragement of lawful Commerce in the Bight of Benin, namely that the Town and Island of Lagos should be taken possession of by the British Government.

Since the establishment at Lagos of its present Chief, King Docemo, that Island has virtually been under British protection, the King's authority being only maintained by the continued presence in the Lagos Lagoon of one of Her Majesty's Gun Boats. If that protection were withdrawn, the place would, in all probability, shortly fall into the hands of its former Chief King Kosoko, under whose rule it would speedily become again the head quarters of Slave Dealers, as it was until Kosoko was expelled by a British force.

King Docemo is moreover unable to govern the people under him, and to keep order among the traders assembled at Lagos without the constant support and interference of Her Majesty's Consul, who is in reality the Chief Authority in the place. Her Majesty's Government are thus in fact burdened with the responsibility of governing and defending Lagos, whilst they do not enjoy any of the advantages of Sovereignty.

If instead of this anomalous quasi Protectorate, Lagos were placed under British authority, the state of uncertainty and periodical alarm that prevails there would be put an end to, and the feeling of security which could not fail to spring up, would have a most beneficial influence in extending the valuable trade already carried on from

[1] C.O. 96/58. Much of this was derived from Consul Brand to Russell, 9 April and 14 April 1860: *Parl. Papers*, 1862, lxi (339), pp. 4–5; and Wylde, Minute, 14 August 1860: F.O. 84/1115. Russell pressed the matter again on 21 March and 10 June: C.O. 96/58.

Lagos and its neighbourhood, the existence of which is due to the expulsion of the Slave Dealers from Lagos by a British force in 1845, [sic] and their exclusion ever since, by the measures taken to prevent the return of Kosoko.

To shew Your Grace the extent and value of this Trade, and how rapidly it has sprung up, I have the honor to enclose for your information the accompanying Extracts from Reports which have been received from Her Majesty's late Consuls at Lagos. It will be seen from these Papers that the value of the Palm Oil & Cotton exported from the Bight of Benin in the Year 1857 amounted to the sum of £1,062,700 and the value of these exports since that date would have been made more considerable if it had not been for the Slave hunting Expeditions of the King of Dahomey.

I do not doubt that Your Grace will concur with me that it would be impossible for Her Majesty's Government to allow Lagos again to fall into the hands of the Slave Dealers, nor could they view with indifference the establishment there by French Agents of a Depôt for Negroes to be exported as Labourers to the French Colonies, a measure which might still be carried into effect if the French should fail in procuring a supply of labor for their Colonies from other than African sources.

But the defence of Lagos would be far more easy if the place was actually under British Government, and there would then be no difficulty in preventing the interference of foreign nations with Lawful Trade by Schemes of black Emigration.

Moreover, the occupation of so important a point as Lagos, could not fail to produce a great moral effect upon the minds of the Inhabitants of the surrounding Country, and would go far to secure the tranquillity of the neighbouring District. From this District we have, within the last few years, derived a supply of Cotton which tho' hitherto small, is rapidly increasing, and which, according to the information received by Her Majesty's Government, is capable of an almost unlimited extension.

For these reasons I do not hesitate to recommend to Your Grace's favorable consideration, that Lagos should be taken possession of and occupied. It might afterwards be considered whether it should be constituted a British Colony.

It would, it is believed, not be difficult to obtain from the present Chief the cession of his Rights, in return for which it would probably be necessary to assign him an allowance out of the Revenues of the Port, and there is no cause to doubt that the inhabitants would gladly become British Subjects.

The expense of maintaining such a Colony would not be considerable, and would, in my opinion, be amply repaid by the advantages which I have pointed out.

If your Grace should agree in these views, I would propose to intrust Her Majesty's Consul at Lagos to enter into a negotiation with King Docemo for the cession of his rights.

19

LORD PALMERSTON: MINUTE, ANNEXATION OF LAGOS, 3 MARCH 1861[1]

As it is supposed that the French want to form a military establishment at Lagos might it not be useful that we should get this Lagos Chief to enter into Treaty with us to place himself & his territory under British Protection with Engagmt. not to alienate any Part of his Territory without our Consent.

20

SIR FREDERIC ROGERS TO LORD WODEHOUSE: ANNEXATION OF LAGOS, 19 JUNE 1861[2]

MY LORD,

I am directed by the Duke of Newcastle to acknowledge the receipt of the letters addressed to this Department by the Foreign Office on the 7 Feby., the 21st. March & the 10th Inst. recommending that the Island of Lagos on the West Coast of Africa, should be taken possession of by the British Government & I am to request that your Lordship will state to Lord John Russell that His Grace is very much averse to any extension of our Dependencies on that Coast, & can only concur with his Lordship in the present case on the ground of the importance which he attaches to it as the means of preventing a renewal of the Slave Trade in the Island & its neighbourhood, & of promoting legitimate commerce, especially the trade in cotton.

The Duke of Newcastle desires me to remark that some Troops will be necessary for the occupation of Lagos & some expense must be incurred for its Civil Government and that as no Troops can be spared from the West Coast of Africa for that purpose, nor any aid given from the small Parliamentary Grant for the Gold Coast,

---

[1] F.O. 84/1141; and cf. Consul Foote to Russell, 9 January 1861 : ibid. (reporting the visit of a French warship to Lagos and relations between the French firm of Victor Régis and Kosoko).
[2] C.O. 96/58. *Sir Frederic Rogers* (Lord Blachford) was Land and Emigration Commissioner, 1846–60, and Permanent Under-Secretary at the Colonial Office, 1859–71. Draft based on Newcastle's minutes, 25 February and 17 June 1861. T. F. Elliot confined himself to repeating the F.O. arguments (minute, 11 June 1861); C. S. Fortescue agreed with the F.O. requests, but raised the question of the cost of a garrison for Lagos and the need for a new vote on the Colonial estimates (minute, 16 June 1861).

application must be made to the War Office to find some Black Troops & a Vote of Parliament will be necessary to pay such expenses as the taking possession may entail.

If these matters are arranged, His Grace would suggest that Lord John Russell should direct the Consul at Lagos to take such steps as may be requisite for taking temporary possession of the Island.

21

LAGOS TREATY OF CESSION, 6 AUGUST 1861[1]

TREATY between Norman B. Bedingfeld, Commander of Her Majesty's Ship 'Prometheus', and Senior Officer of the Bights Division, and William McCoskry, Esq., Her Britannic Majesty's Acting Consul, on the part of Her Majesty the Queen of Great Britain; and Docemo, King of Lagos, on the part of himself and Chiefs.

Article 1.

In order that the Queen of England may be the better enabled to assist, defend, and protect the inhabitants of Lagos, and put to an end to the slave trade in this and the neighbouring countries, and to prevent the destructive wars so frequently undertaken by Dahomey and others for the capture of slaves, I, Docemo, do, with the consent and advice of my Council, give, transfer, and by these presents grants and confirm unto the Queen of Great Britain, her heirs and successors for ever, the port and Island of Lagos, with all rights, profits, territories, and appurtenances whatsoever thereunto belonging, and as well the profits and revenue as the direct, full, and absolute dominion and sovereignty of the said port, island, and premises, with all the royalties thereof, freely, fully, entirely, and absolutely. I do also covenant and grant that the quiet and peaceable possession thereof shall, with all possible speed, be freely and effectually delivered to the Queen of Great Britain, or such person as Her Majesty shall thereunto appoint, for her use in the performance of this grant; the inhabitants of the said island and territories, as the Queen's subjects, and under her sovereignty, Crown, jurisdiction, and Government, being still suffered to live there.

Article 2.

Docemo will be allowed the use of the title of King in its usual African signification, and will be permitted to decide disputes between natives of Lagos with their consent, subject to appeal to British laws.

[1] *Parl. Papers*, 1865, v (412), p. 421. The orders for annexation had been sent in Russell to Foote, 22 June 1861, *Parl. Papers*, 1862, lxi (339), p. 5. The C.O. approved these orders, 22 June 1861: C.O. 96/58.

Article 3.

In the transfer of lands, the stamp of Docemo affixed to the document will be proofs that there are no other native claims upon it, and for this purpose he will be permitted to use it as hitherto.

In consideration of the cession as before-mentioned of the port and island and territories of Lagos, the representatives of the Queen of Great Britain do promise, subject to the approval of Her Majesty, that Docemo shall receive an annual pension from the Queen of Great Britain, equal to the net revenue hitherto annually received by him; such pension to be paid at such periods and in such mode as may hereafter be determined.

Additional Article to the Lagos Treaty of Concession, 18 February 1862

King Docemo having understood the foregoing Treaty, perfectly agrees to all the conditions thereof; and with regard to the 3d Article consents to receive as a pension, to be continued during his lifetime, the sum of 1,200 (twelve hundred) bags of cowries per annum, as equal to his net revenue; and I, the undersigned representative of Her Majesty, agree on the part of Her Majesty to guarantee to the said King Docemo an annual pension of (1,200) twelve hundred bags of cowries for his lifetime, unless he, Docemo, should break any of the Articles of the above Treaty, in which case his pension will be forfeited. The pension shall commence from the 1st of July of the present year, 1862, from which day he, the King, resigns all claim upon all former farmers of the revenue.

22

SIR GEORGE BARROW: MINUTE, ANNEXATION OF BULAMA, 18 OCTOBER 1861[1]

THE Order in Council of 18 May 1860, annexing the Island of Bulama to the Colony of Sierra Leone ought I think, to be now forwarded to the Governor.[2]

It was detained in the first instance because the War Office insisted on a whole Company with 2 Officers & an Assist. Surgeon being sent there, the Barracks &c. having to be provided by the Colony.

[1] C.O. 267/269. *Sir George Barrow* was Clerk in the Colonial Office, 1825–72. Bulama Island about 300 miles north of Sierra Leone had been claimed but not annexed by MacCarthy in 1818: the claim was considered valid by Russell in 1841, but no formal colony was established: C.O. 268/38, ff. 77–78.
[2] By Newcastle to Hill, 2 November 1861: C.O. 267/269.

Governor Hill, who was in this country at this time, promised to report, on an early occasion, whether the Col. Legislature would provide for this unexpected outlay—but he failed to do so—until in Jany. 1861 when he reported that he hoped the Barracks for a Company would be completed in about 9 Months from that time—the War Office subsequently deciding that half a Company should be sent there—a further delay however, took place in the construction of the Barracks, owing to the loss of the Vessel carrying the materials for the work—& no later progress has been reported.

But shortly before the Governor had given notice of the preparation of the Barracks, he reported (in Decr. 1860) that he had taken possession not only of the Island of Bulama, but of other Territories, & a correspondence was carried on between this Department & the Foreign Office on the subject—the Governor being apprized (in April 1861) that a correspondence was going on between H.M.'s Govt. and the Governt. of Portugal & desiring him to confine his operations to the Island of Bulama.

As the Portuguese Govt. do not appear to have made any rejoinder to the representations made to them by the Foreign Office in April last, I think the correspondence may be considered as concluded & at any rate there is no reason why the Order in Council annexing the *Island* of Bulama to the Colony of Sierra Leone should not be sent out—apprizing the Governor in a short despatch of the general purport of that correspondence.

23

GOVERNOR S. J. HILL TO THE DUKE OF NEWCASTLE: ANNEXATION OF BENDU, 14 NOVEMBER 1861[1]

1. I have the honor to inform your Grace that I proceeded on the 6th instant in Her Majesty's Steam Ship 'Torch' to the Sherbro for the purpose of procuring the deed of cession from the Chiefs giving Bendoo to the Crown of Great Britain. I arrived there on the 7th and on the 9th the Chiefs assembled, and without the slightest hesitation signed the Treaty.

2. After completing the Bendoo Treaty, the Chiefs of the Bagroo came forward and begged their Country might also be added to British Territory, as it would prove the only means by which the peace and prosperity of the Native Inhabitants of the Bagroo could be secured.

3. Taking into consideration the fact that if the Bagroo fell under

[1] C.O. 267/271. Encl. conventions, 9 November 1861, with Sherbro chiefs.

the power of any other European Nation, its vicinity to this Colony would probably induce to misunderstandings with the Government of Sierra Leone and possibly lead to more serious results, I ventured to accept the offer of the Chiefs, and prepared a Treaty which they signed ceding their Country to the Queen.

4. The Bagroo is the finest navigable River in the Sherbro, it has been lately surveyed at the request of the Lords of the Admiralty by a Mr. Mann, Botanist, it yields the finest timber required by the Admiralty, its general soil is most productive, and there is but one opinion throughout the Colony that the acquisition of this Territory is of vital importance to the Merchants engaged in the timber trade, as well as in securing a supply of this much desired article for the Royal Dockyard.

5. The Bagroo being a Dependency of this Colony secures it from any interference on the part of Foreign powers, tends to protect the inhabitants from aggression on the part of their neighbours, induces to peace among themselves, destroys in so much of Africa that great evil the slave trade, advances civilization, and any expenditure its acquisition may entail on this Colony will be a small item compared to the advantages pecuniary and otherwise derived from its occupation.

24

SIR GEORGE BARROW: MINUTE, ANNEXATION OF BENDU, SIERRA LEONE, 12 DECEMBER 1861[1]

. . . As these several cessions are to stop the slave trade and to establish legitimate trade and will cost this Country nothing I suppose they may be approved with the concurrence of the Foreign Office?

25

DUKE OF NEWCASTLE: MINUTE, ANNEXATIONS, 14 DECEMBER 1861[2]

I see no help for it & this must be done, but the 'suppression of the Slave Trade' is leading us into serious Territorial complications, on the whole W. Coast of Africa.

[1] C.O. 267/271.
[2] Ibid. The cession was approved in Newcastle to Hill, 15 December 1861: C.O. 267/271.

26

GOVERNOR H. S. FREEMAN TO THE DUKE OF NEWCASTLE: LAGOS TERRITORY, 9 JULY 1862[1]

My Lord Duke,

I have the honor to enclose herewith copy of an Ordinance passed by the Provisional Legislative Council of [Lagos] for the collection of Export and Import Duties of two per cent at all the Ports within the Territory of Lagos—including from Leckie and Palma on the East to Badagry on the West.

It being the unanimous opinion of the Council that the duties should be imposed simultaneously at Lagos, Palma and Badagry, I proceeded to that place in Her Majesty's Gunboat 'Handy' on the 27th Ultimo to make the necessary arrangements to that effect.

The Chiefs, eight in number, who already considered themselves under the British law and protection gladly consented to receive a pension in lieu of the duties they had hitherto claimed on the Trade, for they never could collect them without much trouble and delay; and they have therefore agreed to receive each the sum of Thirty six bags of Cowries per annum amounting altogether to Two hundred and eighty eight bags a year which, at the present value of cowries will equal about two hundred and sixty pounds. Besides this they are each to be presented with one white hat a year.

Some expense will be incurred to keep up the Civil Establishments at Badagry and the other Ports, but the balance of revenue to the Treasury of this Settlement will be such as I trust will enable us next year to convert the two per cent Import and Export duties into an Import duty of three per cent doing away with the Export duty altogether. . . .

27

GOVERNOR S. W. BLACKALL TO THE DUKE OF NEWCASTLE, 6 FEBRUARY 1863[2]

[Forwarding a report on his visit to the Sherbro, recently ceded to Sierra Leone.]

13. The whole District which I visited, with the exception of the upper part of the Bagroo river, was a succession of small Islands covered with Mangrove, and at low water surrounded by mud. The channels between these Islands are very narrow and shallow. There

[1] C.O. 147/1.   [2] C.O. 267/277.

is little or no cultivation, and with the exception of a few miserable villages, the only habitations to be seen are the Factories established by the Merchants, around which the persons employed are located in the usual huts of the country. These Factories are the Depositories for the rice, Palm oil, Ground nuts, and other produce, brought by canoes down the Boom, Kittam, Jongh, Bagroo, and some other smaller rivers from the interior; and for the various articles sent up the River to barter for the produce; the Sherbro river being the outlet. This produce is reembarked in coasting vessels for Freetown, and, and, in some few instances, shipped direct for France or England, as vessels of 300 or 400 Tons can, though with great difficulty, ascend the Sherbro river.

14. Until the Proclamation of June 1862, all Goods for the Sherbro were received duty free, and the owners were entitled to export them from this Colony out of Bonded warehouses. But, by the Proclamation referred to, all Laws of the Colony were declared to be in force, and though nothing had been done, up to my arrival here, to carry them out, I directed the attention of the Collector of Customs, to this matter, and the Duties are now levied.

15. This has caused some dissatisfaction amongst the Traders; but as I forsee very considerable expenses in the Establishment of both a Military and a Civil Force in that part of the Colony, it would be impossible to forgo the levying of these duties; for there is no prospect of revenue accruing from any other sources.

16. Except for the purpose of protecting Trade, and suppressing the Slave Trade, both Imperial Questions, I see no advantage likely to accrue to this Colony from the annexation of the Sherbro. The country does not afford, so far as I could see, any capability of being turned to account by Agricultural improvements, and the climate is decidedly unhealthy. . . .

[A small steamer is needed for communications with the Sherbro, Isles de Los, and Bulama.]

28

T. F. ELLIOT: MINUTE,
AFRICAN ANNEXATIONS, 16 MARCH 1863[1]

. . . [This despatch] affords a picture of what are the new acquisitions which we are making on the Coast of Africa; low Islands covered with mangrove, surrounded by mud, the channels between them narrow and shallow, little or no cultivation, and only a few miserable villages. To rule over this happy land, the Governor calls upon us (and justly)

[1] Ibid, on no. 27.

for Managers with strong moral and physical constitutions and no mean legal acquirements; Barracks; Troops; Police; Customs Officers Surveyors and the means of constant Steam communication with the Capital. If we supply these things, they must be costly,—if we refuse them, what have we gained by the enlargement of Territory? Unless to exercise power and do good, must not such extensions be rather a mockery and discredit?

For my part the useful information supplied by Governor Blackall in this despatch appears to me very suggestive of what would be our true policy in these African Regions. We should have two or three civilized and well ordered Stations at which Merchants could place their goods in security and ship them in larger vessels for export to Europe, but the Traders should be left to themselves and do the pedling work in such waters as those of the Sherbro, as they seem already to have been doing very contentedly, costing us no money and involving us in no responsibility. We should supply the centres of civilization, but commerce should be left to insinuate itself with the suppleness and sagacity which are the best instruments of commerce, and without our undertaking to provide a whole apparatus of Custom Houses and Troops and Lawyers at the mouth of every African River. . . .

29

THE DUKE OF NEWCASTLE: MINUTE AFRICAN ANNEXATIONS, 17 MARCH 1863[1]

THIS is all that can be done for the present, but I fear we must soon consider the alternative of a very considerable increase of Establishment in these unhealthy territories or abandoning those which have been recently annexed.

30

LIEUT.-GOVERNOR J. H. GLOVER TO THE DUKE OF NEWCASTLE: ANNEXATION OF BADAGRI, 10 JULY 1863[2]

MY LORD DUKE,

I have the honour to report that I succeeded in bringing to a peaceful settlement the disturbed state of the Town of Badagry without proceeding to any coercive or hostile measures. The Chiefs and People have since ceded it to the British Crown fearing as they themselves described that they might become 'Niggers for the

[1] Ibid, on no. 27.   [2] C.O. 147/3.

Frenchmen' that [is] Slaves. I have increased the Pension of the Chiefs in fair proportion to our increase of the Duties raised and I am happy to be able to report to your Grace that the Chiefs and People are perfectly happy and contented under the arrangements as set forth in the Treaty of Cession.[1]

I have full confidence that by taking the Protection of Okeodan, Pocrah and Addo with its River into our hands, Badagry will in a short time compete with Lagos in its amount of Exports, indeed the entire trade of that part of the Interior will come down the River Addo to Badagry instead of as heretofore going to Porto Novo.

31

LIEUT.-GOVERNOR J. H. GLOVER TO THE DUKE OF NEWCASTLE: LAGOS PROTECTORATES, 6 NOVEMBER 1863[2]

[Defending his extension of a protectorate to Addo, Okeodan, Ipokia, to forestall the French; the Yoruba wars have disrupted Lagos trade.]

. . . To the North and East, nothing was to be done by friendly mediation to bring the war to an end, or indeed to place our relations with the Egbas and Ijebus upon a more friendly footing; but to the North-west and West, the horizon looked brighter. The people of Okeodan and Addo had long sought our Protection and assistance, a fine River with a depth of $4\frac{1}{2}$ fathoms washed the bank of Okeodan, the great Slave market of the Egbas. The King of Pocrah added his request to those of Addo and Okeodan, and I visited those places to ascertain personally the feelings of the People; intending to report the same to Her Majesty's Government; but I found that the French authorities would give me no time, and that if anything was to be done to check (at least for the moment, until the approval of Her Majesty's Government be made known) the grasping Policy of the French Authorities at Porto Novo, who were seeking to absorb all the surrounding Country to their Flag, and thus reduce Lagos to a mere Town upon a sandy Island insignificant in itself, and contemptible for all time (as it was then) in the eyes of the surrounding Tribes, to destroy its legitimate revenue and cause it to be a constant Burden upon the Mother Country.

After I had restored order at Badagry and the People had returned peaceably, the French flag was introduced into the Town, and large

[1] Encl. treaty, 7 July 1863. Addo, Ipokia, and Okeodan were taken under British protection by treaties, 27 and 29 June, 4 July 1863. These were refused sanction.

[2] C.O. 147/4. Glover arranged a treaty, 1 August 1863, with the French at Porto Novo to demarcate British and French spheres either side of the Addo river. It was never ratified by either government, and the French withdrew from Porto Novo in January 1865.

Presents made to induce them to hoist the Flag and declare for its Protection; at the same time I received Monsieur Daumas' Despatch claiming not only Appa, but Eastward of Badagry; and at a later date, I was assured by Monsieur Baron Brossard [de Corbigny] that their claims extended to Beshi, nine miles from Lagos.

My Lord Duke, at this time it was being discussed in Abbeokuta to bring up the French from Porto Novo; and I hesitated no longer in accepting the Protectorates, which shut off alike, the French from Abbeokuta, and the Egbas from the Coast. . . .

[These measures have impressed the Egba that the British can enforce a blockade; he has avoided hostilities between Okeodan and Porto Novo; action had to be taken before the Colonial Office could be consulted.]

32

T. F. ELLIOT: MINUTE, EUROPEAN RIVALS, 12 DECEMBER 1863[1]

THERE certainly appears some force in Capt. Glover's representations. The main source of our difficulties seems to have been the jealous and annoying spirit of our French neighbours.

I do not think that it is at all a good policy to multiply our stations on the Coast of Africa. But if we do choose to create a new Station, it seems to me necessary to take sufficient Territory to make it self-supporting by admitting of the successful collection of a Customs revenue, and sufficient to give us elbow room relatively to other European Powers. The Gold Coast experience proves enough of the evil of having close European neighbours; and it would be a misfortune to have the same immediate proximity to the French at Lagos.

33

EDWARD CARDWELL TO ACTING GOVERNOR W. J. CHAMBERLAYNE: MELAKORI ANNEXATION, 22 SEPTEMBER 1865[2]

SIR,

I have the honor to acknowledge the receipt of your despatch No. 90 of the 19th ultimo, transmitting Mr Huggins's report on the civil war in the Moriah country.

---

[1] C.O. 147/4, on no. 31.
[2] C.O. 267/284. *Colonel Chamberlayne* was Officer Commanding at Sierra Leone and Acting Governor, 1865–6.

In that report Mr. Huggins[1] suggests, and you recommend, that the sea board of that part of the Country should be annexed to the Colony of Sierra Leone, in accordance with treaties concluded with the Natives in the years 1826[2] and 1827. I cannot sanction this proceeding: to revive a treaty which has been inoperative for 38 years appears hardly fair to the present possessors of the territory; and moreover it is not the policy of H.M.'s Govt. to extend the dominions of this country on the West Coast of Africa.

You will do well to impress upon the minds of traders or others that if they settle for purposes of their own again beyond the limits of the Colony of Sierra Leone, they do so entirely at their own risk, and that H.M. Govt. cannot be responsible in any way whatever for the damage which may be done to their property by the Natives.

34

NOTICE: CAPE COAST CASTLE, GOLD COAST TERRITORY, 16 SEPTEMBER 1865[3]

IT is hereby notified for the general information and guidance of the public in the Protectorate—

That according to custom and usage, the territory belonging exclusively to Great Britain on the Gold Coast, extends to the distance of a cannon shot (or five miles) from each of the undermentioned castles and forts; having ordnance mounted thereon for the defence of the Protectorate in general; viz:—

The Castle	
Fort William	
Fort Victoria	} Cape Coast, Seat of Government.
Fort George	
Fort Dixcove	
Fort Anamaboe.	
Fort James	} Accra, Dutch territory
The Castle Christianburgh	excepted.

within which distances, none but British laws can be recognised, or enforced upon any account whatever (respecting, however, as far as practicable, native laws and usages).

Annual customs will not be permitted to take place within these distances, without the permission of the Lieutenant Governor, who

[1] Encl. Huggins to Chamberlayne, 31 July 1865. *H. J. Huggins*, Queen's Advocate and Chief Justice of Sierra Leone, 1863–6, had been sent to investigate traders' complaints in the Melakori. A proposal for cession of the right to levy Customs was also refused.

[2] The articles of the treaty of 18 April 1826 with Susu chiefs ceding territory near the Melakori had not been approved by Lord Bathurst.

[3] *Parl. Papers*, 1867, xliv (198), p. 19.

will (upon being assured by the chiefs and head men, that peace and order shall be maintained, by their respective flags and companies) grant leave to hold such customs in such places as may seem best for the public peace and their own amusement.

And it is further notified, that any person or persons who may on these occasions take the life of a fellow-creature will at once be arrested by the civil power and brought to trial.

Last year several lives were lost at Secondee, and only a few days ago, at Mumford, several men were shot dead, by one company having fired on another, which would have been much worse were it not for the timely interference of Mr. Bentil, who, at the risk of his own life, put a stop to the disgraceful proceedings, for which Colonel Conran, the Lieutenant Governor, takes this opportunity of thanking him publicly.

35

EDWARD CARDWELL TO LIEUT.-GOVERNOR CONRAN: GOLD COAST TERRITORY, 23 NOVEMBER 1865[1]

Sir,

I have to acknowledge your Despatch, No. 114 of 7th October, enclosing the copy of a notice which you have issued, in which you define the limits of Her Majesty's possessions on the Gold Coast. I am unable to approve the step which you have taken, in declaring the territory within five miles of eight separate British forts to be British territory, and I have to instruct you to recall the notice in which this is done. Whatever influence you may be able to exert in discouraging or repressing barbarous customs, leading to the loss of life, will be very proper, and I shall be happy to approve your exercise of it; but the extension of British territory is a different matter, and cannot receive my sanction.

36

EDWARD CARDWELL TO GOVERNOR S. W. BLACKALL: WITHDRAWAL FROM UPPER GAMBIA, 23 MAY 1866[2]

[Acknowledging a petition from Gambia merchants for protection.]

. . . His Majesty's Government cannot regard the Upper Waters of the Gambia as being under British protection, and when Traders

[1] Ibid., p. 90.
[2] C.O. 87/84. The Gambia merchants had petitioned against the abandonment of MacCarthy Island: memorials, 21, and 23 August 1865, encl. in D'Arcy to Cardwell, 20 January 1866.

establish Factories on the Shores of Countries beyond the limits of British jurisdiction, they must be prepared for the risks which they incur in doing so.

With respect to McCarthy's Island, the Merchants are aware that in pursuance of the recommendations of the Select Committee of the House of Commons Her Majesty's Government have decided that the Island should no longer be occupied by any Detachment of Her Majesty's Troops. [D. and that time has been allowed them to remove from thence if they thought fit to do so, but it is understood that they prefer remaining with such protection as the Local Government may be able to afford them.

I approve of your intention to endeavour with Colonel d'Arcy's assistance, at once to organize a Volunteer or Pensioner's Force which, with the able bodied men already located at McCarthy's Island and armed for defence, would probably obviate the danger of any attack from a Native Force; and in conformity with your suggestion, I have the honour to authorize you to present to the Merchants the Steamer 'Dover' if they can take upon themselves the management and maintenance of the vessel, as they have urged the necessity of the frequent appearances of a steamer in the Upper River, especially with reference to the protection of their Factories above McCarthy's Island.]

[A. I shall avail myself of the return of Captain Bridie to obtain the information which you say he will be able to give me respecting the state of affairs at McCarthy's Island, & in the Upper Waters of the Gambia. For while on the one hand, it is desirable to encourage legitimate commerce as much as possible it is very necessary not to hold out to traders the same appearance of continued military protection as before, after that we shall, in deference to the opinion of the Committee have withdrawn our force. The arrangements to be made in consequence of that withdrawal will require careful consideration & I shall address you further upon the subject by an early opportunity. . . .][1]

[No help is to be asked from the French Governor of Senegal for military operations against the King of Bundu.]

[1] In Cardwell's hand. Capt. Bridie died on his passage to England.

37

SIR FREDERIC ROGERS TO E. HAMMOND: DUTCH FORTS, 17 JANUARY 1867[1]

SIR,

I am directed by the Earl of Carnarvon to acknowledge your letter of the 12th. Inst. stating that the Netherlands Minister at this Court has mentioned that the Netherlands Government were disposed to meet the wishes of H.M.'s Government in regard to an interchange of Territory on the West Coast of Africa and requesting to be apprized of Lord Carnarvon's views on the subject.

I am desired to state in answer, for the information of Lord Stanley, that Lord Carnarvon, on a careful consideration of the rights, interests and relative position of the two Countries, believes that it would be conducive to their mutual advantage to conclude an agreement on the following basis:

1st. That the meridian of the Sweet River should henceforward be the boundary between the Possessions of the two Countries on the Gold Coast, Great Britain ceding to the Netherlands all her Possessions to the Westward of that Meridian, and the Netherlands ceding to Great Britain all her Possessions to the Eastward of the same—2ndly. that both Governments should for a considerable period enforce the same tariff of Customs duties within their respective Territories. . . .

38

LORD CARNARVON TO THE WAR OFFICE: OCCUPATION OF ADDA, GOLD COAST, 22 FEBRUARY 1867[2]

SIR,

I have laid before the Earl of Carnarvon your letter of the 7th Inst. transmitting a copy of a letter from Col. Conran Command[ing] the Troops at the Gold Coast in which he reports the occupation by a detachment of Addah a Trading Station on the Bank of the River Volta, and requesting that Secretary Lt. Genl. Peel may be informed whether his Lordship approved of the occupation by the Troops of that new post on the G. Coast.

---

[1] C.O. 96/75. These terms served as the basis of the Anglo-Dutch treaty of 5 March 1867. The British exchanged Dixcove, Sekondi, Beyin, Komenda and the Denkyera, Wassaw, and Apollonia protectorates for Mori, Kormantin, Apam, and Dutch Accra; a 3 per cent. *ad valorem* tariff was to be levied at all ports.

[2] C.O. 96/75. Draft by T. F. Elliot.

Lord Carvarvon requests that you will lay before Genl. Peel the enclosed copy of a despatch which he is about to send to the Governor in Chief of the W. Africa Settlements on the subject of the disturbances which have so long existed at the Volta, and that you will state to him that he gathers from the correspondence sent home that the occupation of the trading Station at Addah is only a temporary measure to give confidence to the Traders in that quarter, & not for any measures of offence.

'Addah Fort', which was ceded by Denmark in 1850 has never been occupied by Troops—and the Trading Station at Addah where the 30 men have been stationed has been hired for the occasion by the Local Governt.

39

WILLIAM WYLDE: MINUTE, NIGER SETTLEMENT, 8 MAY 1867[1]

WE have not heard anything lately of French designs in the Niger, but I have heard from several sources that the French Govt have of late years been considerably pressed to make settlements in that River and it is undoubtedly true that an expedition organized by the French about two years since for the ascent of the Niger & probably with the view to establish a settlement there was wrecked on its way out.

I take it that all our interests require it that there shall be free access to the Niger and that we should not be justified in taking exclusive possession of the mouths of that River ourselves any more than we should submit to their being occupied & closed by the French.

The greater the traffic on the Niger the more probability there will be of the People becoming civilized and of the resources of the Country being developed, and I think we may safely leave our Traders to obtain their share of the Trade.

I think it would be very inadvisable to adopt Mr. McLeod's suggestions in regard to taking possession of the Islands in the Delta of the Niger.

LORD STANLEY: MINUTE, NIGER SETTLEMENT, [MAY 1867]

CERTAINLY. We want no more W. African settlements.

[1] F.O. 84/1278. On Consul McLeod to Stanley, 19 March 1867 (urging annexation of Niger territory).

40

GOVERNOR S. W. BLACKALL TO THE DUKE OF BUCKINGHAM AND CHANDOS: FRENCH ON THE GOLD COAST, 27 MARCH 1868[1]

MY LORD DUKE,

I have the honor to enclose to Your Grace the Duplicate of a Despatch from the Administrator of the Gold Coast, reporting that he had received information to the effect that some officers of the French Sloop 'Renadin' landed at, and claimed a small place 20 miles North-East from Cape Coast, called 'Apopoo'[2] which I presume to be 'Akimfoo' as shewn on the Admiralty Chart....

41

T. F. ELLIOT: MINUTE, FRENCH ON THE GOLD COAST, 18 APRIL 1868[3]

THE whole coast for upwards of 100 miles to the eastward of Cape Coast (with the single exception of a few Dutch Forts which have now been ceded to us) has belonged to us for years without contest and beyond dispute. Any attempt of the French to establish themselves on any point there would be unendurable. It is plain that they have now in Western Africa some officers of indiscreet zeal, or else that they wish to try by experiment the length of our forbearance.

I am persuaded that the proper course is prompt and firm remonstrance.

I submit that a copy of this despatch should be sent to the Foreign Office. For the present I should say that the supposed intentions of the French Officers rest upon rumour, and that we cannot but assume that they must be mistaken. I should beg however that it may be forthwith represented to the French Government, that with the exception of the Dutch Forts recently ceded to Great Britain, the whole Coast for upwards of 100 miles to the Eastward of Cape Coast Castle has long been under the well known and undisputed Protectorate of this Country, and that any Establishment there by another European power could only be made by the concession &

---

[1] C.O. 96/76.
[2] Amotu, the site of a French fort in 1786. It had been visited by Lieutenant Crespin of the *Renaudin*.
[3] C.O. 96/76, on no. 40.

agreement of Gt. Britain. Unless therefore, the report which has reached the ears of the British Authorities is wholly unfounded, we must hope that the French Government will at once give orders to repress any attempt on the part of their Officers through an indiscreet zeal to encroach on places well known to be within the jurisdiction of Great Britain.

42

SIR GEORGE BARROW: MINUTE, GAMBIA EXCHANGES, 21 MAY 1869[1]

THIS would be a good opportunity of ceding the Gambia to the French (but not Bulama—which is under arbitration)—on condition of their relinquishing any rights of Sovereignty over Moriah & Samo Countries—but there is one obstacle viz that it has been suggested to the Foreign Office that certain Factories on the Coast offered by the French in exchange for the Gambia might possibly be made available as an offer to the Dutch in exchange for Elmina. . . .

43

GOVERNOR SIR ARTHUR KENNEDY TO LORD GRANVILLE: WITHDRAWAL FROM KOYA, SIERRA LEONE, 23 JULY 1869[2]

[Part of Koya, annexed to the colony, is to be given up.]

. . . 7. IT is, I think, needless to discuss the necessity for the original annexation of this Territory. It is clear to me that it is now unnecessary, impolitic, and expensive to maintain it.

8. I have no doubt of the necessity which existed for the punishment of an aggressive and turbulent neighbour. But the advance of Civilization and intelligence has rendered a recurrence of such proceedings highly improbable if not impossible.

9. Should your Lordship concur in the general views I have expressed, I would draw up a temporary Treaty or Special agreement between this Government and the King Bey Cantah and Headmen of Quiah for your Lordship's approval, and have it executed here and in Quiah with due formality.

10. Some of the accompanying papers will illustrate the state of the Quiah territory, and the manner in which British Laws were administered therein, when I assumed the Government. It is a task beyond

---

[1] C.O. 267/300, on Kennedy to Granville, 29 April 1869.　　[2] C.O. 267/301.

our grasp, unless at great increase of expense, and extension of our Executive Machinery.

44

THE EARL OF KIMBERLEY: MINUTE, GAMBIA EXCHANGE, 2 AUGUST 1870[1]

State to F.O. that to prevent misunderstanding I think it would be advisable to inform the French Govt. confidentially that whilst France is at war, it will be impossible to renew the negotiations, and that H.M.'s Govt. must reserve to themselves the liberty before negotiations are resumed to consider the objections which have been raised in the settlement and elsewhere to the cession [of the Gambia to France].

45

THE EARL OF KIMBERLEY: MINUTE, DUTCH FORTS, 4 AUGUST 1870[2]

I THINK we should decline to engage ourselves to pay £80,000 [for the Dutch forts] or any other particular sum, but we might agree to take the Dutch 'fixtures' at a valuation *provided* we see our way to paying the money. It would be out of the question to ask Parliament to provide the money. It must therefore be found by the Settlement, but we ought not to bind the Settlement to pay it without consulting Sir A. Kennedy, and ascertaining distinctly that the money will be forthcoming. I should be disposed to write to the F.O. that we think the Dutch Govt. should be informed that we cannot bind ourselves to pay £80,000 or any particular sum: but that if the Dutch Govt. will agree that the amount shall be left to valuation, we will write to our authorities to report whether the necessary sum can be provided out of the revenues of the Gold Coast and if they report in the affirmative, we will conclude the necessary arrangements.

[1] C.O. 87/98A, on F.O. to C.O., 27 July 1870. The Colonial Office had just received memorials from the Manchester and Bristol Chambers of Commerce, 4 and 30 July, protesting against the intended cession of the Gambia to France, without a promise of compensation for any loss of trade or property on the part of British merchants.

[2] C.O. 96/86, on F.O. to C.O. 5 July 1870. For the history of the cession of the Dutch forts see Douglas Coombs, *The Gold Coast, Britain and the Netherlands 1850–1874*. London, 1963.

46

CONVENTION BETWEEN THE NETHERLANDS AND GREAT BRITAIN, 25 FEBRUARY 1871[1]

HER MAJESTY THE QUEEN of the United Kingdom of Great Britain and Ireland, and His Majesty the King of the Netherlands, being desirous to proceed with the regulation of the respective interests in their Colonies in the friendly spirit which has constantly marked the relations between both Kingdoms, and taking into consideration that the mixed dominion exercised on the Coast of Guinea by Great Britain and the Netherlands has occasioned to the native populations much harm, which did not cease after the interchange of territory stipulated by the Treaty of March 5, 1867, and the remedy for which is not to be expected until the two Powers shall carry out, with regard to their respective possessions, the principle of abstaining from or giving up mixed dominion or mixed possession, have with a view of concluding arrangements for that purpose, named as their Plenipotentiaries. . . .

[The signatories to the convention are listed.]

Article I.

His Majesty the King of the Netherlands transfers to Her Majesty the Queen of the United Kingdom of Great Britain and Ireland all the rights of sovereignty, jurisdiction, and property which he possesses on the Coast of Guinea.

Article II.

Her Majesty the Queen of the United Kingdom of Great Britain and Ireland accepts those rights, and the obligations resulting from them towards the populations hitherto placed under the authority of the King of the Netherlands.

The British authorities will take care, as far as possible, that no person belonging to these populations, who may during the dominion of the Netherlands, have participated in quarrels or hostilities with independent tribes or tribes dependent on Great Britain, shall be annoyed or troubled on that account.

Any persons who, within a period of six years after the actual transfer of the aforesaid possessions, may wish to remove to other Netherlands possessions or to foreign places, shall be at liberty to do so by the British Authorities . . .

[1] J. J. Crooks, *Records relating to the Gold Coast Settlements from 1750 to 1874* (Dublin, 1923), pp. 393–6; and Coombs, pp. 152–55.

[Art. III. All buildings and grounds are included in the transfer; for stores and other articles compensation up to £24,000 will be paid to the Netherlands.]

Article IV.

The Africans freed from military service in the Netherland Transatlantic possessions, and who have not made use of the liberty mentioned in Article II, to remove from the coast, shall, provided they conform themselves to the laws and regulations introduced or established by the British Authorities, be allowed to continue to dwell by themselves, in the manner adopted by a large number of them, in any part of the present Netherland Guinea.

Article V.

Netherland subjects, provided they conform themselves to the laws and regulations of the British Government, shall be treated on the Coast of Guinea on the same footing as British subjects, in regard to their right to proceed thereto or to travel therein, or to establish themselves within the same; or to hold temporarily therein any houses, manufactories, warehouses, shops and premises, which may be necessary for the purpose of their residence or trade, by wholesale or retail, carried on either in person or by agents whom they may think fit to employ.

Netherland subjects, Netherland vessels and goods imported or exported in Nertherland vessels, shall be treated on the Coast of Guinea on the same footing as British subjects, vessels, and goods, in all that regards commerce, navigation, duties of import or export, local dues, trade duties, prohibitions, impositions, warehousing, bounties and drawbacks, without any distinction as to the respective flags under which articles of lawful commerce may be imported or exported, or as to place of origin, departure or destination. . . .

[Art. VI. The Convention shall be ratified as soon as possible.]

47

ADMINISTRATOR H. T. USSHER TO GOVERNOR SIR ARTHUR KENNEDY: EASTERN GOLD COAST, 6 MARCH 1871[1]

[Jella Koffi on the eastern Gold Coast is under British jurisdiction.]

. . . 4. WITH regard to the definition of purely British Territory, and of territory supposed to come under British jurisdiction, I should not recommend that any territory should be declared purely British

[1] C.O. 96/87. Approved in Kimberley to Kennedy, 19 April 1871: ibid.

beyond the actual limits of the Forts. The acquisition of any additional land as territory, even short of the absolute annexation of the entire protectorate, would necessitate the immediate abolition of domestic slavery within that acquired territory, and might induce grave complications with the natives; while the action of the law as it at present stands would be crippled by the anomaly of the Chief Magistrate exercising the functions of a Judicial Assessor to Native Chiefs and dealing with Native questions according to an undefined mixture of British and native law, within the limits of territory absolutely declared to be British, and where native law would be null and void. The present assumption that every act done by Her Majesty's Government on the Gold Coast is in the name of, and by and with the consent of the Natives, is, in my opinion at least, sufficient for all practical purposes.

5. As regards the definition of British jurisdiction there can be little doubt that if the River Volta is to be utilized and the distracted border or debatable land to be converted into a prosperous trading Country, the sea coast to the Eastward of the Volta, to three miles beyond the old Fort of Quittah, should be re-occupied. The River Volta itself will be of comparatively little use to the Revenues of the Settlement unless both sides of the mouth are occupied. The numerous creeks and lagoons communicating with Jellah Coffee and the Volta would enable the traders and others to land all their goods duty free at Jellah Coffee, and pour them into the present protected districts to the detriment of those merchants who are honestly collecting and paying Customs dues to the Government. In return for this, a large portion of our legitimate produce would find its way to Jellah Coffee, aided by the steam traffic which I shortly expect to see on the river.

6. These disadvantages to the present protected Territories have hitherto been neutralized by a long series of wars. Now that peace may be said to be established they will soon make themselves sorely felt.

7. Our jurisdiction in the interior districts must, I apprehend, remain as it is and it will diminish or increase according to the firmness or otherwise with which the local Government is enabled to deal with the Native Chiefs. In 1866 and 1867, in fact up to 1869, our orders were not respected in the interior, and great lawlessness prevailed; but from the gradual cessation of active hostilities, and from the increased power of the local government (derived from its improved revenues) that lawlessness is rapidly diminishing. Of late I have brought down and punished Chiefs from the interior, who have for many years set the Government at defiance.

8. The actual assumed jurisdiction of the protected districts (after the cession of the Dutch Settlements) should I apprehend to be from

Fort Appolonia in the Windward or Western District to Quittah on the Ahunah Coast—a coast line of about 250 miles. The interior jurisdiction in a northerly direction would be generally accepted, with more or less effect to the borders of Ashantee; with the exception of the territory between the river Volta and Quittah where I should only recommend that a strip or tongue of land bounded on the North by the Ahunah 'Lonjo' or lagoon should be declared within British jurisdiction. The more northerly Trans-Volta districts of Cupee and Aquamoe, the latter not well disposed to the British Government, will be effectually neutral, or rather friendly, as soon as a steamer makes her appearance on the river. . . .

48

ADMINISTRATOR J. H. GLOVER TO GOVERNOR SIR ARTHUR KENNEDY: PORTO NOVO, 1 NOVEMBER 1871[1]

[Proposing to annex Porto Novo.]

. . . 3. ON the decision of this question by Her Majesty's Government will depend the peace of the Yoruba Country for many years to come. Porto Novo is the last market left to the Egbas for their Slaves, and from which they can obtain supplies of Powder, added to which, the Revenue of this Settlement is adversely affected by Porto Novo to the amount of some Ten thousand pounds per annum.

4. I have on previous occasions pointed out to Her Majesty's Government the state of Porto Novo (see Despatches dated Lagos No 6 of 4th February and No 15 of 20th March 1868), that I hesitate on this occasion to say all that I see and feel upon this subject; it is a question of vital importance to Lagos and the Inhabitants of the surrounding Countries; I will therefore only add that whatever determination may be arrived at by Her Majesty's Government, no assistance either Naval or Military will be needed or asked for by me, in carrying out the instructions which, I cannot but hope, I may receive upon this subject.

49

E. H. KNATCHBULL-HUGHESSEN: MINUTE, PORT NOVO AND ANNEXATION, 9 DECEMBER 1871[2]

I HAVE not maps before me sufficiently accurate to judge how the question is affected by the geographical position of Porto Novo. I

[1] C.O. 147/21.   [2] Ibid., on no. 48.

think the question suggested by Sir G. Barrow shd. certainly be asked of Capt. Glover. Upon the whole question I should say that in all probability Capt. Glover is right as to the immediate—possibly permanent—good effect upon Lagos to be obtained by the annexation. But there are some local as well as general considerations to be taken into acc[ount]. Locally speaking, what would the effect be upon the minds of the other neighbouring states, if we, acting upon petitions & letters from the subjects of a neighbouring King (who, assuring themselves to speak the sentiments of their whole country, are not able themselves to strike the blow which would free them from an oppressive & odious tyranny) should annex a Kingdom with the Chief of which we are not at war, upon grounds, so far as it appears, of general philanthropy. Would not the general confidence in us be diminished & might not the consequence be an implication in native wars & embarrassments from which our whole policy has been to keep ourselves clear if possible? In this point of view, I shd. rest the refusal to annex upon the opinion of Sir A. Kennedy, clearly expressed, & wld. observe that the increased financial prosperity of Lagos would be dearly purchased by the loss of native confidence in British honesty & that stronger ground for interference must be shown. Then would come the question as to Capt. G[lover's] reasons as to the peace of the Yoruba country—there, generally speaking, we must look to our policy elsewhere. No the more strongly that I advocated the annexation of the Diamond fields, but then the circumstances were exceptional, the person whom we believed to be the legitimate owner of the country, & his people, earnestly desired annexation, and British subjects formed a large portion of the population [A. the establishment of a settled form of Govt. was also essentially necessary]. These features were *added* to the great importance of the acquisition and the well-being of a large British Colony & the probable development of the whole country consequent upon annexation. But, on the other hand, we refused Fiji, which to my mind was a stronger case for annexation than Porto Novo (according to my present information). Time will show whether Public opinion in England will approve or condemn that refusal, but I see a difficulty—if there [is] no other—in annexing the country of an unwilling King after refusing to annex a country when everyone wished for annexation. These, however, are all remarks subject to *revision*—the ground to take is, I think, the *inexpediency* of exceeding [or the] *undesirability* of running counter to the opinion expressed by Sir. A. Kennedy, who is well able to judge the matter & is not a timid adviser.

50

THE EARL OF KIMBERLEY: MINUTE, ANNEXATIONS, 11 DECEMBER 1871[1]

I AM altogether against Captain Glover's proposal. On similar grounds of philanthropy we might be called upon to annex Dahomey, Ashanti, Abbeokuta, & for anything I see (except the difficulty of the enterprise) the greater part of Africa. Inform Capt. G[lover] that H.M.'s. Govt. cannot entertain the proposal.

51

HENRY HOLLAND: MINUTE, FRENCH EXPANSION, 30 SEPTEMBER 1872[2]

... IT remains to be considered whether any steps should be taken to prevent the French occupation of the Scarcies Rivers. As I have pointed out ... we appear to have recognized their occupation except in countries which are practically dependencies of S. Leone. It cannot be contended that the Great & Little Scarcies are dependencies of Sierra Leone, but they are even nearer to that Settlement than the Mellecourie River; & Sir A. Kennedy in his Despatch of the 3d July 1868 says that the occupation of these rivers by any European power would take a large portion of Sierra Leone trade at the source.

The Treaties with the native chiefs in respect of the Scarcies are substantially identical with those in respect of the Mellecourie & Fouricaria districts, and it would be difficult therefore, if the French press on, to raise any objections, provided that British merchants have the same freedom of trade the French merchants have. But as these Scarcies rivers are so near to S. Leone, it might be desirable to learn what are the intentions of the French Govt., & if possible to make some arrangements with them, by which the interests of British merchants & free trade up these rivers may be served. ...

[1] Ibid., on no. 48.
[2] C.O. 267/316. *Henry Holland* was Assistant Under-Secretary in the Colonial Office, 1870–4; and as Lord Knutsford he was Secretary of State for Colonies, 1888–92.

52

THE EARL OF KIMBERLEY: MINUTE, FRENCH EXPANSION, 8 OCTOBER 1872[1]

WE ought not to have a 'dog in the manger' policy. Either we should take steps to open the trade of these rivers ourselves, or we should let the French do so. I do not understand that anything is proposed in the nature of active measures on our part: and it is quite possible that it may be objectionable to take any such measures. But I should like to have Mr. Hennessy's opinion on this point. I would therefore write to him pointing out that we cannot reasonably object to the extension of the influence of another European nation in these rivers provided there is no exclusion of our trade, unless we occupy the ground ourselves. . . .

53

GOVERNOR J. POPE HENNESSY TO THE EARL OF KIMBERLEY: LAGOS EXPANSION, 30 DECEMBER 1872[2]

[Reporting on the question of Lagos boundaries, domestic slavery, and Administrator Glover's policy.]

. . . 34. I ARRIVED at Sierra Leone at the end of [February 1872] and soon found that Captain Glover was taking active steps to accomplish the project which my predecessors and each succeeding Secretary of State had condemned.

35. The spreading of 'distrust among the neighbouring nations', which Your Lordship connected with Captain Glover's Porto Novo policy, was in full operation before I could reach the Coast.

36. The annoyance he caused was not confined to the Native States. He entered into an argumentative correspondence with the French Consul and printed it in large posters. The French Merchants and others complained that the tone of his letters to the Consul was not courteous. Your Lordship censured this proceeding. . . .

37. I wrote to him twice from Sierra Leone conveying to him the instructions of the Government that he should withdraw the Steamer 'Eyo' from Porto Novo. In compliance with Your Lordship's wishes I warned him that if he now failed to carry out the instructions he received on this subject his conduct 'would be viewed with serious displeasure by Her Majesty's Government' . . .

[1] C.O. 267/316.   [2] C.O. 147/24.

38. Before I reached Lagos, I reported to your Lordship (writing from Elmina on the 10th of April 1872) that Captain Glover had received the despatches conveying Your Lordship's instructions but that he had not carried them out. On the 6th of April I transmitted Captain Glover's reasons for refusing to carry out his instructions I added that I was not satisfied with his reasons.

39. Meanwhile, though he spent large sums of Public money in pushing his own policy in opposition to the clear instructions of the Government, he reported to me that the state of affairs at Lagos was very gloomy—that all trade was stopped—and he begged me to come to Lagos as quickly as possible. I arrived at Lagos on the 24th of April. I found the Settlement in as gloomy and lamentable a state as Captain Glover had reported. His policy had not only spread distrust among the neighbouring nations but it seemed to have isolated him from every honest and intelligent man in the community. Mr Gerard the magistrate whom he had stationed in the 'Eyo' at Porto Novo informed me that Captain Glover had spent in January 1872 £84 of public money in bribing Porto Novians to rebel against their King.

40. I was not many minutes in Lagos before he began to speak of his Porto Novo policy. He said it was absolutely essential to extend the boundaries of Lagos in that direction. He hoped I was not going to prevent him from doing it. He undertook if I would read a mass of papers he had collected on the subject to convince me that the Settlement should be extended beyond Porto Novo both for fiscal and political objects.

41. I said there was no use in our discussing the matter for it was not a question of my opinion or my policy; that I was merely the medium of conveying the instructions of the Secretary of State; that I must beg him to retire without further delay from the position he had taken up at Porto Novo, and that any attempt to extend the boundaries of Lagos in that or any other direction should cease.

42. Without noticing a hasty remark he then made respecting a former Secretary of State, I cannot well avoid quoting what he repeated more than once, to this effect, in speaking of the boundary question:—'what does the Government mean by interfering with my policy?'

43. When I ventured to point out that the European Merchants and the Native Traders disapproved of his encroaching policy also, he said 'They are Egba sympathisers. They are as bad as Egbas'.

44. When I gave the positive orders that your Lordship's instructions about the withdrawal of the 'Eyo' from Porto Novo should be no longer disobeyed, he said 'It will be necessary to give the British Subjects there some days notice that my Protectorate of Porto Novo is to be removed or they will all be murdered'. I declined to sanction another day's disobedience of instructions from home. He again

dwelt on his own long experience of the place, and the very slight knowledge of Lagos and Porto Novo affairs that certain great people had,—adding that he would not share in the responsibility of the bloodshed and murder which would instantly take place at Porto Novo when it was 'out of his grasp'.

45. The result however of compelling him to carry out your Lordship's wishes was just the reverse of what Captain Glover anticipated. The withdrawal of all pretension to extend the jurisdiction of Lagos beyond Badagry produced a most satisfactory change at Porto Novo. Friendly messages were exchanged with Lagos, a brisk trade sprung up, and the good feeling thus established with the Natives on that part of our frontier seems to be permanent.

46. The Lagos trade with Porto Novo since the renewal of Captain Glover's encroaching policy is far greater than it has been in any corresponding period. . . .

[Glover has assumed unlawful jurisdiction over the Yoruba town of Otta.]

67. Your Lordship will therefore see that the Protectorate of Lagos had been unlawfully extended to Porto Novo on the [West] and to Otta and Isheri towards the North. A line drawn from Porto Novo to Otta and then to Isheri on the River Ogun covers an immense extent of Territory usurped by Captain Glover without authority, Territory which it would be in the last degree injudicious for the British Government to hold. . . .

54

E. H. KNATCHBULL-HUGHESSEN: MINUTE, WEST AFRICA POLICY, 23 FEBRUARY 1873[1]

. . . But the real truth is that the difficulties and troubles of the West African Settlements do not arise so much from mistakes on the part of this or that Administrator as from the inherent viciousness of the whole system under which we find ourselves administering the governments on that coast. I am dealing only with Lagos today and would say this—that it was perfectly possible—had we chosen to do so—to have refused Docemo's cession and never to have occupied the place. Having accepted the cession and possessed ourselves of Lagos, it was perfectly possible to have seized from the weak hands of native Kings such territory as we deemed necessary for the security of our settlement, or, better still, to have accepted other cessions or bought the places desirable to hold. But to do neither one

[1] C.O. 147/24.

thing nor the other—to leave boundaries undefined, jurisdictions uncertain & administrators uninstructed as to either one or the other, was a course which required no great faults on the part of the officer administering the Government in order to produce a state of difficulty and confusion which, in fact, the greatest prudence and circumspection could hardly have avoided. Natives are to be governed either by fear of the dominant race, or by a conviction that it is to their own interests that the desired form of government should exist. Either alternative was—and possibly still is—open to us in the case of the West African Tribes. But *neither* has been fully and fairly tried. They have been left—(both by the action of Capt. Glover & that of Mr. Hennessy—and I am bound to say, of the British Govt. itself) uncertain of our intentions towards them— even doubtful whether we desire or intend to keep Lagos—and have come to regard the community of merchants there as people whom it is desirable to starve out and get rid of, instead of looking to them as in truth they should, as the channel through which their country should & would reap the greatest commercial advantages. They look upon the attempts to open roads as something conceived in the interests of the Foreign occupiers of Lagos rather than as that which cannot fail to be of the greatest benefit to their own country, and their whole position as regards British occupation is uncertain & unsatisfactory. To this state of things the report of 'Sir Charles Adderley's Committee' contributed not a little, & I am at a loss to conceive how the half-and-half policy of Great Britain—occupying territory as if she was ashamed of it & felt she had no business to be there—coaxing one day & threatening the next—can have been expected to produce anything but confusion & disaster. Whatever may be the Policy of this or any other Government, *Public Opinion* will not permit the withdrawal of British Authority from the W. Coast of Africa. Then what is to be done? Why did we ever occupy Lagos? To put down slavery and to extend Christian Civilization. Are these still considered objects worthy of our attention? If not— the sooner we withdraw the better, & if English opinion will endure the withdrawal, no doubt a certain amount of expenditure will be saved & we shall be spared some trouble. But if these are still objects to be aimed at, & if, as I think, a great country which has undertaken certain responsibilities of that kind cannot evade or abandon them without loss of honour & character, then surely some definite course of action should be adopted, and a more certain policy be established. If this be conceded, it seems to me that there are only two courses before us. The best thing that could happen for Lagos—and indeed for the whole of West Africa—whether as regards the safe & certain extension of commerce or the general & gradual improvement of the natives—would be that the whole of the sea-board should be under British control, and that the Egbas, Ijebus and others should thus have brought to bear upon them a power & influence which would oblige them for their own sakes, to open up roads into the interior, and would gradually teach them the value of a well regulated trade, & imperceptibly lead them into an improvement & civilization. For this purpose & from this point of view I am bound to say that I think the annexation of Porto Novo, and the holding of all the sea-coast from thence to Leckie, would be most desirable & most generally beneficial. But I take it to be the policy of Her Majesty's Government that this is not to be attempted—even if the people of Porto Novo should desire it—at all events as long as the King lives & objects. If this be the case we must (for the moment & until the force of circumstances oblige this annexation, which I think may not improbably be the case) put aside the question of holding the coast from Badagry to Porto Novo, and leave this latter still to remain an Egba outlet, damaging Lagos and paralysing to a certain extent our efforts to improve the condition of the Country. But apart from the Porto Novo question, two alternatives present themselves to us: One, to maintain our present position—to avoid offending native tribes by asserting our right to boundaries which may be disputed—to let it be clearly understood that we desire nothing more than we have—and to try by persuasion and conciliation, to induce the natives to look upon our merchants and us as friends and benefactors, and to aid us in extending trade & commerce & opening up the resources of the country. The other, and as it appears to me the wiser alternative is this—I should appoint Commissions—or empower the Administrator as may seem best—to define the boundaries of British Territory. I should then proclaim it as such, let it be clearly understood that upon British Territory no runaway slave law can exist. With regard to the *Protected* Territory I should not interfere with slavery as it exists, but I should govern that territory through the Native Kings, securing their adhesion & fidelity by a moderate stipend, and establishing district courts for the trial of criminal offences. I should then go a step further, and offer stipends to the Government of Abbeokuta & the Jebus, contingent upon their opening and securing the safety of traffic upon the roads to & through their respective countries. My belief is that if this course were adopted, the trade of Lagos & the coast would be so largely developed and the revenues of the Settlement so greatly increased that no expense would eventually fall upon this country, whilst the advent of Christianity and of civilization would be secured, & the best hope afforded of the ultimate improvement of the native Tribes in the interior.

55

THE EARL OF KIMBERLEY: MINUTE, LAGOS EXPANSION, 25 FEBRUARY 1873[1]

MR HENNESSY's despatch is able, and he brings a formidable indictment against Capt. Glover. Both in my opinion are in the wrong. Capt. G[lover] evidently thought that 'a man who had been 9 years on the coast' was entitled to pursue his own policy regardless of his instructions, & Mr H[ennessy] forgot that a man who has been a few weeks on the coast should act with great caution in reversing a policy long pursued by the local authorities, or rather in checking and moderating it, for that rather than reversal was what was needed. However the mischief is done & the question now is how to repair it. Capt. Glover has ceased to be administrator, & must on no account return. Mr Fowler the representative of Mr H[ennessy's] hasty policy has ceased to act. Mr Berkeley & Capt. Lees are free from bias, & ought to be able to bridge over the transition period till Capt. Strahan takes up the Government. I should think it would be better not to take any decided measures as to the boundary question till Capt. S[trahan] holds the reins. But in the meantime Mr Keate might be instructed to inquire and report. I put out of the question retirement from Lagos. The place must be held, by force if necessary. I would not attempt to extend our sovereignty to Porto Novo. I would keep generally within the lines laid down by Mr. Cardwell in 1864, that is, I would only hold under British *sovereignty* Lagos, Badagry, Palma & Leckie, not allowing any trade by sea within the limits of the Coast (coloured yellow in the map) except on payment of duties to us. This I apprehend is our present position. The rest of the territory should be only '*protected*'. The slave question apart from all reasons of other kinds, makes this essential. The most important point remains namely to define the boundaries of the Protectorate. On this I would ask for a report from Mr Keate, adding I think that as far as possible the status quo should be maintained pending further instructions, but care should be taken not to weaken our position or encourage the natives to suppose that we contemplate withdrawing from Lagos & the protectorate connected with it.

[1] C.O. 147/24, on no. 53.

56

A. W. L. HEMMING: MINUTE, SIERRA LEONE EXPANSION, 8 OCTOBER 1874[1]

MR GRANT advocates the acquisition of territory adjacent to Sierra Leone, with the view of increasing the revenue by enabling the Govt. to prevent the importation of goods without payment of Customs Duties. The difficulty sought to be provided against is the same as that felt at the G. Coast, which has led to the occupation & establishment of Customs Houses at Quittah & other places, and which at Lagos is the cause of the desire for the annexation of Porto Novo.

[Includes a small sketch map of the Sierra Leone river area.]

. . . In 1867 or 1868 the French Govt. took possession of the country adjacent to the Mellicourie River & built a blockhouse at the mouth of the River. They also claimed to exercise a Protectorate over the neighbouring tribes. The Govr. of S. Leone (Sir A. Kennedy) pointed out that it was most undesirable to have any other European Power settled so near to S. Leone and he stated that in his opinion & that of the leading commercial men such an occupation would materially injure the trade & prospects of the Settlement. H.M.'s Govt. however did not think they could oppose a French Protectorate if it did not extend to countries which were practically dependencies of S. Leone, & if English merchants had in that territory the same freedom of trade as French merchants had. A good deal of correspondence took place with the F.O. & the Govr. on the subject, but although we have never distinctly recognized the right of the French to occupy these rivers & the adjacent territories (with the Chiefs of which we already had treaties) yet we never distinctly denied it. Subsequently negotiations were set on foot to put an end to all difficulties & discussion by an exchange of territory between France & England on the W. Coast. The proposals made (& accepted) were that England should cede the Settlement of the Gambia, & all sovereignty or political influence over tribes to the north of the River Dembia, & that France should cede all sovereignty or political influence in respect to natives dwelling between the R. Dembia & the R. Shebar.

The negotiations however fell through owing to the breaking out of the Franco-Prussian War in 1870.

[1] C.O. 267/327. On William Grant to Colonial Office, 6 October 1874. Grant was a Sierra Leone trader with posts in the Melakori. Lord Carnarvon agreed to this proposal for extended Customs in the Scarcies and ordered the Administrator of Lagos to report on the possibility of a similar solution to difficulties with Porto Novo: C.O. 147/30, Carnarvon to Strahan, 4 September 1874.

In 1872, Govr. Hennessy sent home a report by Professor Blyden of an expedition to Falaba in which he expressed his fears that the French would occupy the Great Scarcies River as they had done the Mellecourie & other rivers north of S. Leone . . .

[Further information requested by Kimberley has never been furnished.]

I believe that the negotiations dropped in 1870 are now likely to be resumed, and in such event we may probably assume that the F.O. would propose to the French Govt. the same terms & boundaries as were previously agreed upon.

If the negotiations were successful we should be at liberty to extend our sovereignty & levy Customs Duties along the whole coast between the Dembia & Shebar Rivers, & it cannot be doubted that the result would be a great increase of revenue to S. Leone: an increase which would be most welcome & desirable. At present the finances of the Settlement are at a very low ebb, whilst there are various important works, such as drainage, water supply, establishment of a sanitorium &c., which are delayed for want of funds.

As Govr. Berkeley is in this country it might be worthwhile to send him a copy of Mr. Grant's letter & ask for his observations.

2. Constitution and Government

Introductory Note

JUST as the location and size of the forts and settlements owed much to the Merchants and the Sierra Leone Company, so, too, their government before 1843 contained a legacy of the Sierra Leone Instructions and Charter of 1791 and 1799 and the long tradition of trading-house management on the Gold Coast. The nineteenth-century constitution of West African possessions was a progressive adaptation of earlier institutions to the forms of Crown colony administration copied from colonies elsewhere and an effort to achieve a semblance of co-ordination and unity.

Experiments in settler representation at Sierra Leone did not survive for more than a decade and the number of original councillors was soon reduced from eight to two with increased legislative and judicial powers under the Court of Directors in London. By the Charter of 1799 the Governor and advisory council formed a court of record and were assisted in municipal administration by a Mayor and three Aldermen, elected by the Council, with civil and criminal jurisdiction. These were continued when the colony was taken over by the Crown in 1808; and in 1811 a Chief Justice was appointed and acted in conjunction with the Mayor's Court as Recorder of Freetown. For the rest, the Governor's instructions in 1811 added a few clauses similar to those issued to West India governors concerning the powers and duties of the Council; and the Company system —without the directors—survived intact.

On the Gold Coast the forts were run by officials in the service of the Committee of Merchants, in return for salaries and profits from private trade. Some reforms were made to increase the powers of the Governor and Council at Cape Coast in 1804; but the West African Commissioners of 1810 and the House of Commons Committee of 1817 were highly critical of the state of the forts, their number, and the lack of supervision over the spending of Parliamentary grants. Appointment of officers by the Crown was recommended and supported by Governor MacCarthy's observations in 1818 and by charges of extravagance in 1820—which influenced the Treasury's decision to ask for the abolition of the African Company and the transfer of its possessions to the Crown in 1821. Similarly, in the Gambia where the Committee of Merchants took no interest in exercising control under an Act of 1783, it was left to the Governor of Sierra Leone to make provision for administration in 1818, when a Police Court and a Settlement Court were introduced and Bathurst traders were encouraged to advise a military commandant on the enactment of local regulations.

By the Charter of 1821 the Gambia and the Gold Coast were made dependencies of Sierra Leone. The Governor was given a council of nine; two assistant judges were appointed to the Chief Justice's Court of Record; and the Mayor's Court was abolished. Commissioners of Requests were nominated along with Justices of the Peace. In the Gambia a lieut.-governor was appointed in 1829 to correspond with the Colonial Office but his legislation was passed by the Council of Sierra Leone. On the Gold Coast four of the eight forts were abandoned and Justices of the Peace were commissioned at the others whose administration came directly under the Governor of Sierra Leone, till the Merchants regained control in 1828. Charges of owning slaves and assisting Portuguese slavers resulted in an inconclusive investigation of the forts by Captain Tucker and by Dr. R. Madden, 1839-40; and a Select Committee of the House of Commons was summoned to hear evidence on the government of the settlements as a whole.

The recommendations of the 1842 Committee for the separation of the Gambia and the return of the forts to Crown control were accepted at the Colonial Office by Lord Stanley. From the beginning of 1843 the settlements were considered as conquered colonies and a general Act was framed by G. W. Hope, giving the Crown power to regulate them by Order-in-Council. Under this Act the Gambia acquired a governor and council with executive and legislative powers, a colonial secretary, collector of customs, a chief justice and a military commandant. In 1850 the Gold Coast forts which had been administered by a miscellany of naval officers and traders were given a similar constitution; and Lagos and its dependencies and, finally, Sierra Leone, were constituted as crown colonies in 1862 and 1863. With the exception of the Gambia, a small number of unofficial members were nominated to the legislative councils of the settlements, though in the case of Lagos this concession lapsed after 1865.

The Charter of 1866 which united the settlements again under Sierra Leone preserved the administration of each possession intact and provided for joint consultation by correspondence and tours of inspection by the Governor-in-Chief. In 1874 events on the Gold Coast and the feeling the

the houses of the rich and great, nay of the first officers of the state, are not exempted from the nocturnal intrusion of house-breakers, insomuch that even the Lord Chancellor and Honourable Speaker of the House of Commons have lately experienced the common danger, and the deplorable want of the ancient '*Maxima securitas*'. That fundamental system of *English polity* is so little known among us at present, that many well-meaning persons are induced, by their fears, to wish for *security*, on a much less eligible plan, formed on the model of the arbitrary system of government in France, commonly called *police*, the introduction of which would be an utter perversion of the first principles of *legal* government in England. The inhabitants even of the most distant settlements under the crown of Great-Britain must not adopt any *polity* that is essentially *inconsistent* with the *Maxima securitas*, ordained and required by the common law of England.

The community of free African settlers, however, have already adopted (as I am informed) a small variation from the old English model of numerical divisions, by forming themselves into divisions of *dozens*, instead of *tithings* or *tens*; but as this little change is by no means *inconsistent* with the true principles and intention of our legal English *frankpledge*, I am at liberty to acknowledge a most hearty approbation of it, as being an arrangement far more convenient and effectual for securing perfect subordination, peace, and good government, even that the antient legal divisions into *tens* or *decinaries*, because each *dozen* will have one *chief* or *headborough*, and one *assistant headborough*, to govern and lead a complete complement of ten *deciners*; so that the division may still with propriety retain the old *legal* name of a *tithing* or *decinary*; and the *hundred division* may be rendered literally and strictly an *hundred* families, by appointing one *hundreder*, two *chiefs* of *fifties*, and one town clerk (or clerks of the hundred) over every *eight dozens*;. . . .

2

EXTRACT FROM THE SIERRA LEONE COMPANY ACT, 6 JUNE 1791 (31 GEO. III, c. 55)[1]

. . . xliv. AND, for the better and more effectually establishing and carrying on of the Trade and Business of the said Company, be it further enacted, That it shall be lawful for His Majesty, His Heirs

---

[1] B.T. 6/70. The St. George's Bay Company first met in February 1790 and the bill for incorporation was sponsored by its first chairman, *Henry Thornton*, banker, philanthropist, and M.P. for Southwark. The title of the company was changed in the course of enactment.

and Successors, to make unto the said Company a Grant, by Letters Patent under the Great Seal of Great Britain, of so much and such Part of all Tract or District of Land, situate and being at Sierra Leone, on the Coast of Africa, and commonly called or known by the Name or Description of the Peninsula of Sierra Leone, as already may have, or shall hereafter, by any Grant, Purchase, or Cession from any of the Kings, Princes, or Chiefs having Right therein, become vested in His Majesty, His Heirs and Successors, with full Power, Liberty, and Privilege to and for the said Company to purchase of and from all Kings, Princes, and Chiefs, or other Power having right to make Sale thereof, so much Land as shall include the whole Tract or District so commonly called or known by the Name of the Peninsula of Sierra Leone as aforesaid, as the same is bounded on the North by the River Sierra Leone, on the South by the River Camaranca,[1] on the East by the River Bunce, and on the West by the Sea, to hold the same, and the whole Use, Property, and Possession of the said Peninsula (as well as such Part thereof as may have so been vested in His Majesty as aforesaid, as also such additional Part so to be purchased by them under the Authority of this Act, and His Majesty's said Grant) unto the said Company and their Assigns, upon such Terms, Conditions, and Reservations to be inserted in the said Grant, as His Majesty, His Heirs and Successors respectively, shall judge expedient.

xlv. Provided always, and be it enacted, That nothing in this Act contained shall extend or be construed to extend to affect the rights of any other British Subjects trading to Africa, so as to prevent or in any manner obstruct the Ships or Vessels belonging to British Subjects from anchoring in Sierra Leone or Caramanca Rivers, or in any of the Creeks, Bays, or Harbours within the Limits specified in this Act, for the purpose of refitting and repairing. . . .

3

INSTRUCTIONS TO THE SUPERINTENDENT AND COUNCIL OF THE SIERRA LEONE COMPANY SETTLEMENT, 1791[2]

. . . Constitution of the Government of Sierra Leone.

16. In the appointments given to you as well as the address of this letter, you will understand what we now more formally notify, that

---

[1] The southern boundary of the ceded territory was mistakenly thought to extend to the Karamanka river.

[2] L. E. C. Evans (ed.), 'An Early Constitution of Sierra Leone', *Sierra Leone Studies*, XVIII (1932), pp. 26–77 (from the Melville Collection of State Papers); and for sections 6–12, 53, 86, see Harlow and Madden, op. cit., pp. 459–61.

the Government of the Peninsula of Sierra Leone is to be vested in a Superintendent and Council. We proceed now to describe the nature and exercise of your powers; but shall first particularize the Order in which you are respectively to rank.

1. John Clarkson, Esq. (*Superintendent*)[1]
2. Mr. Alexander Falconbridge
3. Mr. James Cocks
4. Dr. John Bell
5. Mr. John Wakerell
6. Mr. Richard Pepys
7. Mr. James Watt
8. Mr. Charles Taylor

General Powers of the Superintendent and Council.

17. As our Superintendent and Council you are hereby invested with the Government of the Peninsula of Sierra Leone in all matters, civil, military, political and commercial, to hold the same under the authority which we ourselves possess, until a new Constitution shall be fixed, and to conduct them agreeably to our Orders. And when you have not specific orders from us, you are, looking to the general principles already explained to you and the scope of our general instructions, to act with the same power as we ourselves might do in such case, being responsible to us for the exercise of this discretion. All Acts and Orders of your Board are to run in the name of the *Superintendent and Council of Sierra Leone*, even though the Superintendent may not have been present or may have been out-voted.

18. Our servants at Sierra Leone are to be under obedience to your authority. They are to receive from you their Orders and Instructions as well as those which we ourselves may think proper to give as those originating in your Council. They are also to report their proceedings to you (all which reports are to be recorded on your Consultations) to receive their salaries from you, and to be liable to your suspension. In conformity to this arrangement, the specific instructions which we think should be given to each of them respectively at the commencement of their several employments, will be transmitted to you that they may be issued through the channel of your Board: and we hereby require that each and all of them, whether Members of the Council or otherwise pay a prompt and implicit obedience to your Resolutions when signified in due form; for on the subordination of all our servants to the supreme power at Sierra

---

[1] *Lieut. John Clarkson*, brother of the Rev. T. Clarkson (one of the directors of the Company), who had recruited African settlers in Nova Scotia in 1792 and was subsequently appointed Governor in August with increased powers and a reduced Council of two. He left at the end of 1792, leaving the colony in the charge of William Dawes and Zachary Macaulay.

Leone the peace and well-being of the Colony essentially depend.

19. Mr. Falconbridge having been dispatched before the formation of the Council was completed, we were obliged to give him some separate instructions of which we now furnish a copy for your information.

Duties of the Superintendent and Council.

20. The principal duties of the Superintendent and Council will be the forming of General Regulations for the good order and prosperity of the Colony, the providing of general means of defence, the chief administration of justice, the prevention and correction of abuses of every kind, and also the general charge of all pecuniary interests of the Company, and the chief care and control of trade, cultivation, building and all other concerns, etc., conformably to the Orders which by this and any further Letters they receive from the Court of Directors.

Powers and Duties of Superintendent.

21. The Superintendent is in every respect to have the precedence in the Colony; he is to be our Representative with the native chiefs; he is to head the Military, to command the Fort, and is to take the chair in the Council, where he is to have a casting vote, that is to say where the numbers including himself are on each side equal, he is to have another vote to decide the question. He is to introduce such questions for discussion as he thinks proper, which shall be disposed of before any questions introduced by any other member of Council shall be discussed, so that he do not put off the proposed motion of any member longer than two meetings. He may correspond with the Court of Directors, if he pleases, without communicating his letters to the Council, which no other member of Council is officially to do. He is always to be concluded by the resolutions of the majority, and to see that the determinations of the Council are executed. It will be his business also to summon the Council who are to meet twice a week at least, which if he should fail in doing, you are to meet of your own accord at the Council House giving him notice of it. But you are to observe, that neither the Superintendent nor any of the Council is to issue money, make appointments, or act in any other matters of his own authority without the sanction of the Government on the spot.

22. In the case of the death or resignation of the Superintendent, the senior Councillor on the spot is in all respects to stand in his place, until a Superintendent is appointed by the Court of Directors; and in case of his absence from the Council on service or on account of sickness, the next member of the Council in rank is to preside there . . .

[23–24 The Council are to keep records of meetings and duplicates of despatches.]

Appointment of Servants.

25. In case any places should become vacant, except the seats in Council, you are to make temporary appointments to them, we give you as already mentioned the power of suspending any of our servants, but you are to understand that this power is to be exercised only after a servant is charged and found guilty by the Government of an offence meriting this punishment. If however there should be strong appearance of guilt, the party may be immediately and during the time of his trial (which should be carried on without delay) suspended from the exercise of any office he may hold in our service; if he is fully acquitted he is to be restored to the exercise of his office; but if ground of suspicion remains, he may be removed from such office until the Court of Directors finally determines his conduct. Your proceedings in all such cases are to be fully stated to us.

26. In case the creation of any new office should appear to you necessary, we give you liberty to make a temporary appointment stating at large in your consultations the circumstances which constituted such necessity, in order that we may have full materials for forming a correct judgement. . . .

[27.–28. Servants appointed were John Beckett, Mr. Peppard, Mr. Jefferson, Mr. Jones, and Mr. Strand, Secretary to the Council.]

Committee.

29. We submit to your consideration that in consequence of the variety of business to be transacted by the Council, it may be convenient to form yourselves into distinct committees who may report their opinions on particular points to the Council for their ultimate decision.

30. Every member of the Council and every servant of the Company unless especially excepted by us is to be restricted from trading, from purchasing or holding land either in the Company's district or from the native Princes and from taking presents.

Principle of Internal Legislation.

31. The Directors consider it as a fundamental principle on which the Company ought at all times to proceed, and as a point in the highest degree essential to the welfare and comfort of the resident members of the Settlement, to ensure to them a due share in its internal Legislation; and they trust that they shall e'er long be able to institute a plan for that purpose adapted to the infant state of the Colony, and capable of being extended by degrees in proportion to its growing population and prosperity. At present however they deem

it advisable to abstain from doing more than thus recognizing and recording the principle itself, and they avail themselves of this occasion to observe that they have thought it most conducive to the effectual accomplishment of their views in establishing the Colony to take experience for their guide, and to proceed gradually and circumspectly both with respect to the gradual application of general principles and especially with regard to sending out Settlers from this country, a measure in which peculiar caution has in every view been thought absolutely necessary.

Administration of Justice.

32. In order to provide for the present administration of Justice in the Colony, each member of the Council is to possess the powers and exercise the functions of a Justice of the Peace, and if any member of the community shall violate any Law of England (such law being of a class not inapplicable to the state of the Colony) he shall be apprehended and detained on the Warrant of a Justice. If his case is one of that inferior sort which is subject by the Law of England to the decision of one or more Justices of the Peace, it shall be so decided without delay. If it is one not subject to such decision he shall be committed *for trial* by the Justice by whose Warrant he was apprehended and tried if it be practicable, within fourteen days, by a jury that shall be summoned for that purpose, and the trial shall proceed according to the Law of England. In case the prisoner be a black man or person of colour, at least one-half of the persons empanelled for the jury shall be blacks or people of colour, and if a white man, at least one-half shall be white men, with the usual right of challenge. The Council shall summon the jury and shall sit as judges. You are in no case however to proceed to Capital punishment, but shall substitute for Capital offences some punishment short of death, and of a kind that is recognized by the laws of England substituting *fines* for corporal punishment as much as possible; and a majority of the Council shall in all cases have a power to be exercised impartially and on weighty grounds according to the equity of the case to mitigate the punishment, or grant a free pardon, recording their proceedings in every such instance, and the reasons on which they act. In cases of conviction as above for murder the Council are at liberty either to punish the criminal on the spot or to send him to England for trial, provided such witnesses as will be sufficient to substantiate the charge, are willing also to come over being indemnified for their expense and loss of time by the Company.

33. Civil suits shall be tried also by a jury according to the Laws of England and full costs of suit may be imposed on the parties who are cast according to a tariff to be published by the Council.

Debts.

34. We cannot at present lay down any permanent system respecting debts; but in the meantime you will act agreeably to the following Regulations:

Cases of debt under £2 shall be determinable by a Justice of the Peace who if satisfactory proof is brought of the debt, shall issue a Warrant of Distress on the personal property of the debtor.

If the debt be above £2, a Warrant of Distress shall in like manner be issued, but the goods shall not be sold until the debt is proved by a jury, before one or more of the members of the Council nor shall the property be sold for three months, provided security sufficient in the opinion of the Council is offered by the debtor. In case the personal property is insufficient the whole or part of the Debtor's real property may be sold in like manner.

If from the sale of the real and personal property a sum sufficient to discharge the debts should not be produced, the Creditor shall be at liberty at any future time to apply to the Council for a fresh Warrant of Distress, pointing out to them the former determination in his favour and an entry on the judicial record that the sum before raised was insufficient, and then a fresh Warrant of Distress or sale as above shall be granted him; and so *toties quoties*.

In all cases where the debt shall amount to more than £10 and there shall be no property of the debtor found within the Colony to answer the debt, the Creditor shall be at liberty to take the person of the debtor in execution, and he shall be detained in prison thereon for three years, or until satisfaction of the debt; but a discretionary power shall be vested in the Council on his delivering up all his real and personal estate upon oath for the equal benefit of all his Creditors to liberate his person, but not to discharge his future effects, nor shall such future effects be discharged, even after three years imprisonment, until full payment of the debts.

The members of the Council shall not in any case be imprisoned for debt, but their effects and salaries shall be liable to attachment and distress in the same manner as those of other debtors.

Election of Peace Officers.

35. The settlers may select from among themselves Twenty Housekeepers out of every hundred, and out of every twenty so chosen the Council may choose ten for Constables. . . .

4

GRANT OF LAND AND CHARTER OF JUSTICE TO THE SIERRA LEONE COMPANY, 5 JULY 1799[1]

WHEREAS by an Act of Parliament passed in the Thirty-first George Third, entitled 'An Act for establishing a Company', &c. the Sierra Leone Company was incorporated, and the Crown enabled to grant the peninsula of Sierra Leone to the Company; and whereas the Company, in pursuance of this act, raised a large capital or stock, entered upon the business for which they were incorporated, and purchased from the natives of Sierra Leone a part of the said peninsula, and formed a considerable establishment, and built a town called Freetown, and laid out plantations, and have also carried on trade with this country in the natural productions of Africa: and whereas the Company, in the year 1792, received as settlers upwards of eleven hundred blacks, who had been taken under the royal protection in America, and they are about to receive in like manner under their protection near 600 Maroons from the island of Jamaica; and whereas there is great want in the Colony of a competent authority for its government, and for the administering of justice in civil causes, and for the trying and punishing of capital and other criminal offences, and of misdemeanors committed there, and in the Company's other factories and settlements: and whereas the Company have lately applied to His Majesty by petition to that effect, His Majesty being desirous to afford all fitting encouragement to the Sierra Leone Company, and to the Colony of Sierra Leone, grants to the Company so much of the peninsula as is vested in him, with full power to purchase from all having right to make sale thereof, so much land in addition thereto as shall include the whole tract commonly known by the name of the Peninsula of Sierra Leone, all which lands so granted are hereby created one independent Colony, by the name of the 'Colony of Sierra Leone': and His Majesty grants that the Court of Directors may make laws, statutes and ordinances for the government of the Colony, so as the same be not repugnant to the laws of England, and impose reasonable fines, penalties or forfeitures for any breach thereof: and have full power to nominate and appoint a Governor and three Council, for the government of the Colony and the factories or settlements dependent thereon, and at their pleasure to recall them and appoint others; and that the Governor

---

[1] *Substance of the Report of the Court of Directors . . . 26 March 1801* (London, 1801), pp. 41–48. The Charter allowing the directors to increase the governor's authority over the rebellious Nova Scotians did not arrive in Sierra Leone till November 1800—a month after some 500 Maroons had landed and helped to put down the uprising; and B.T. 6/70.

and Council so appointed may make laws, statutes and ordinances for the government of the Colony, not repugnant to the laws of England, to be in full force within the Colony, until the Court of Directors shall think fit to disapprove of the same.

And His Majesty further grants and appoints, that there shall be within the town of Freetown, a body politic and corporate, by the name of 'The Mayor and Aldermen of Freetown', to consist of a mayor and three aldermen, and that Thomas Cox shall be the first mayor of Freetown, and George Ross, Alexander Smith, and Peregrine Francis Thorne, the first aldermen thereof, who shall take the oaths of office and allegiance before entering on their offices, the mayor to continue in office until another person shall be duly elected and sworn, as hereinafter is directed, and the aldermen to continue in their offices for the term of their natural lives, unless their places shall be avoided, or themselves removed in the manner hereinafter mentioned.

And His Majesty further grants and directs, that the Governor and Council shall yearly, on the first Monday in the month of September, elect one of the aldermen of Freetown to be mayor for one year, from the 19th September in every year, and until another shall be duly elected and sworn into the office.

And that the person so chosen shall, on or before the 29th day of September next after he shall be chosen, take the usual oaths of office and allegiance, and continue in office for one year, and until another shall be elected and sworn into the office.

And in case the mayor shall happen to die in office, the Governor and Council shall elect one of the aldermen to be mayor for the remainder of the year.

And the mayor shall, after the determination of his office, continue to be one of the aldermen of the town, until his place be avoided or himself removed; it being provided, that the mayor for the time being shall be capable of being re-elected from time to time, so often as the electors shall think fit. . . .

. . . And his Majesty further grants and ordains, that the Mayor and Aldermen of Freetown shall be a Court of Record, by the name of 'The Mayor's Court of Freetown', to try and determine all civil suits between party and party, that may arise, or may have arisen, within the Colony of Sierra Leone, or any of the Factories subordinate thereunto, except such suits be between natives of Africa only, not become settlers, and except where the cause of suit shall not exceed the value of forty shillings, provided that no person interested in the suit shall sit as judge, and that if the voices are equal, the Mayor or senior Alderman shall have two. And His Majesty further directs, that James Wilson shall be the first Sheriff under this Charter; the Sheriff to be sworn to continue in office, to be elected, removed, or disqualified, as in the case of the Mayor and Aldermen; and the Sheriff so elected and sworn, shall have full power to summon Juries, execute and make return of all process of the Mayor's Court, and of any other courts erected by this Charter: and in case of his absence the Deputy or Under-Sheriff shall do all acts in his name.

And his Majesty also specifies what shall be the form of proceeding of the Mayor's Court in civil actions, and how to proceed if an action be brought against the Mayor or Sheriff, or against the Company, or in case a defendant withdraw himself out of the jurisdiction of the Court, it being provided in all cases where the action to be tried would, if the parties were resident in England, be tried by a jury in some of the courts of law, every such action shall be tried in the Mayor's Court, before a jury, according to the practice of the English courts, or as near thereto as circumstances will admit.

And his Majesty further ordains, that the money and effects of suitors, which shall be ordered by the Mayor's Court to be deposited for safe custody, shall be deposited with the Governor and Council, subject to the orders of the Court; and that the Court of Directors may appoint an Accountant General of the Mayor's Court, who shall do all things necessary to carry into execution the orders of that Court, relating to the payment of the suitor's money and effects, and to the keeping of the accounts, under such rules as shall be made by the Court of Directors, according to such rules as are observed by the Accountant General of the Court of Chancery of Great-Britain, or as near thereto as circumstances will admit.

And his Majesty authorizes the Mayor's Court to administer oaths, to frame rules of practice, nominate clerks, and do all other things necessary for the administration of justice, and the due execution of the powers given them (subject to the approbation, controul and alteration, of the Court of Directors, who shall likewise have full power to make rules for the better administration of justice) and also to settle a table of fees, to be approved by the Governor and Council, and written out fair, and constantly fixed up in some open part of the room where the Court shall be held, and also to vary and alter such table of fees as they shall think fit.

And his Majesty further ordains, that there shall be an appeal from the sentence of the Mayor's Court, within fourteen days after such sentence, to the Governor and Council, who are appointed a Court of Record, to receive such appeals, and to hear and determine the same: it being provided that no person interested shall sit on any appeal, and that the Governor or Senior Council, where the voices are equal, shall have two voices, and that their determinations shall be final, where the matter does not exceed 400 *l.* but that where it does, or where there shall not be a sufficient number of the Governor and Council disinterested, appeal may be made to the King in twenty-one days, on giving security to pay interests and costs in case the decree shall be affirmed; the sentence upon such appeals to be put in execution by the Mayor's Court, and if they neglect it, by the Governor and Council.

And as a more easy method of recovering small debts, would promote industry and support credit, his Majesty appoints, that there shall be within the town of Freetown, a court which shall be called 'The Court of Requests, for the Town of Freetown, and the Factories and Settlements thereof', and that the Governor and Council shall nominate not more than twenty-four, nor fewer than eight, of the principal inhabitants of Freetown, to be commissioners to hear and determine suits in a summary way, under such rules as shall from time to time be sent to them under the hands of the Court of Directors any three or more of which commissioners shall have full power to hear and determine all such suits as shall be brought before them where the debt or matter in dispute shall not exceed the value of forty shillings; all the commissioners so appointed to continue in office until the first Monday in the month of September next after the arrival of this charter, and three or more of them in rotation as they shall agree, shall sit one day in every week, from the hour of nine to eleven in the forenoon, or longer, if the business shall require, to hear and determine all such causes. And on the first Monday in the month of September next after the arrival of this charter, one-third of them shall be removed by ballot, and an equal number nominated by the Governor and Council, and on the first Monday in the month of September in the succeeding year, half of the two-thirds of the said commissioners who shall have the longest served in such office, shall in like manner be removed, and others nominated, and so from year to year.

And his Majesty further grants and ordains, that the Governor and Council shall be the justices of the peace in and for the town of Freetown, and throughout the Colony of Sierra Leone, and all the Factories and Settlements subordinate thereto, in the same manner and with the same powers, as justices of the peace constituted by commission under the great seal of Great-Britain, for any country, city, or town-corporate in England; and having first taken the oaths of office and allegiance, shall and may hold quarter-sessions of the peace four times in the year, and shall be a Court of Record, in the nature of a Court of Oyer and Terminer and Gaol Delivery, and shall be commissioners of Oyer and Terminer and Gaol Delivery, for the trying and punishing of all offenders and offences (high-treason only excepted) committed or to be committed within the town of Freetown, or elsewhere within the Colony of Sierra Leone, and any of the Factories or Settlements subordinate thereto; and that they may proceed by indictment, or by such other ways, and in like manner, as is used in England, as near as the circumstances of the place and inhabitants will admit, and that they may for that purpose, command the sheriff to summons grand and petit juries, and administer the usual oaths taken by grand and petit juries, and by witnesses; and that they may proceed to the arraignment, trial, conviction, and punishment of persons accused of any crimes or offences (high-treason only excepted) in the same manner, as near as the circumstances of the place and inhabitants will admit, as any of the justices of the peace or commissioners of Oyer and Terminer and Gaol Delivery usually do.

And his Majesty grants unto the company all fines imposed by the different courts, with full power to sue for the same, and commands the different courts and officers to cause all such fines to be paid to the company.

And his Majesty further empowers the mayor's court to grant probates of wills, and letters of administration, in a manner specified.

It is further provided, that if the Company remove the seat of their presidency, the like jurisdiction, &c. shall be continued at the new seat of presidency; and that if the Company should for a time lose the possession of their settlements, the same shall not be construed to be a dissolution of the above Corporation or Courts, but that the Court of Directors may, after the settlement is restored, reappoint the same.

And it is also provided, that if at any time the Court of Directors shall judge it expedient, they may augment the number of council to eight, and the number of aldermen to six.

And it is further provided, that his Majesty reserve unto himself full power to revoke, alter, and annul this grant, and to grant new powers to the Company.

And it is finally declared, that these letters patent, or the enrolment thereof, so long as the same shall remain in force, shall be in all things valid and effectual in law according to the true intent of the same, and shall be construed in the most favourable sense for the Company in Courts of Record, or elsewhere notwithstanding any nonrecital, misrecital, defect, or uncertainty. . . .

5

SELECT COMMITTEE REPORT ON THE PETITION OF THE COURT OF DIRECTORS OF THE SIERRA LEONE COMPANY, 1804[1]

... Having laid before the House the recent Progress of the Colony, and its present Situation, it becomes the Duty of your Committee to state the Objections to which, under such Circumstances, a Determination to support the Colony on the one Hand, or to evacuate it on the other, would be liable.

The principal Objection which must attend the Maintenance of the Settlement, arises from the total Inadequacy of the Company's Funds to discharge, or even contribute to that Expenditure which is necessary for its Preservation. It is sufficiently manifest from the Inconveniences already experienced in the Colony, that during its Continuance, it will be essentially necessary to support a local Government capable of maintaining Order amongst its Inhabitants, and affording them Protection. The Expences of the Civil Establishment for some Years to come cannot be estimated at less than £10,000 per Annum; that of completing the proposed Works has been estimated at £8,000. It also appears, that the Defence of the Colony will require the present Volunteer Force to be permanently kept up, the Expence of which has been estimated at about £4,000 per Annum; or, if that Establishment should be discontinued, a regular Garrison must be maintained at the constant Establishment of One hundred effective Men, exclusive of the proportion of Artillery Men before mentioned, which, considering the numerous Casualties in that Climate, and great Expence of supporting them, would exceed the Sum above stated.

It not only appears that these future Charges, which must be considered as indispensable, cannot be defrayed by the Sierra Leone Company in the present State of their Funds; but that some of the Measures recently adopted, and Expences consequently incurred, have been proceeded on in the confident Expectation that the Parliamentary Grant of £10,000 in the Year 1802, would be Annually renewed.

Your Committee cannot, however, state the Charges to which the Support of the Colony may in future subject this Country, as Objections to the Grant now proposed, without at the same Time

[1] *Par. Papers*, 1804, v (24), pp. 7–9. Apart from the increasing insolvency of the Company which the Treasury was reluctant to remedy, the settlement had been unfavourably reported on by Captain Benjamin Hallowell in January 1803. In July 1804 a further Parliamentary grant of £28,000 was made to cover expenses, 1803–4.

adverting to the Obligations of the Government towards the Maroons and Nova Scotians, established there under its Authority. That the British Government is bound by every Consideration of Justice and good Faith, to continue its Protection and Support to this numerous Description of Colonists, does not admit of Doubt; and it appears difficult to calculate the Inconvenience and Expence which would attend their Removal; to which must be added that of affording them such a Compensation as might be deemed equitable for the Houses and Lands they would be compelled to abandon; nor has any Situation been suggested to Your Committee where they could be maintained with greater Facility, and in a Manner equally consistent with their former Habits and Occupations. It may be considered therefore as doubtful, in the peculiar Circumstances under which the Colony is placed, whether its Evacuation may not lead to Expence as great as that with which its Support will be attended; and where there appears a Necessity in either Case of incurring considerable Expence, it may be thought reasonable to prefer the System, the Foundation of which is already laid, and connected with the Pursuit of a distinct and important Object.

It remains for Your Committee to state, as far as they are enabled from the Evidence before them, the future Prospects of the Colony, and the Degree to which it may be expected that the Objects of its Institution will be attained, should it receive the necessary Support.

There appears little room to doubt that the Colony, when placed in a respectable State of Defence, may, by setting an Example of Industry, and displaying the Advantages of Law and Justice, as well as the Ascendancy which its Government may obtain over the Minds of the neighbouring Chiefs, exert a considerable and beneficial Influence over the Manners and Habits of many of the surrounding Nations. From the disposition to Industry already evinced by the Colonists, it may reasonably be hoped, that when Security is established, Cultivation will be gradually extended throughout the greatest Part of the Territory of Sierra Leone. The Facility with which free Native Labourers have been induced to seek employment in the Colony, and the Satisfaction they appear generally to have given to their Employers, forms a leading and interesting Feature in the History of the Colony; and there is Reason to believe, that to whatever Extent Cultivation may be carried, this Demand will always be supplied. The Amount of Labourers of this Description admitted into the Colony has already, at One Period, exceeded Three Hundred, and a greater Number than that required have generally been found to offer themselves for Service.

It appears notwithstanding, that while the Traffic in Slaves is continued on the Coast of Africa, however beneficial the Effects produced by the Colony of Sierra Leone on its own immediate

Neighbourhood, its Influence cannot be expected to extend far beyond the Limits of its own Territory; at the same Time a Foundation will be laid, from which, should Events lead to any material Change in the System of African Commerce, that Influence may be more widely and successfully diffused.

Upon the whole, Your Committee, from a full Consideration of the State of the Company's Funds—of the Necessity of supplying their Deficiency—of the Uncertainty attending the constant Renewal of the Parliamentary Grants which may hereafter be found necessary —and of the Interest of the British Government in the Colony, as connected with the Maintenance of the Maroons and Nova Scotians, who are its Inhabitants, have been led to conclude, that the Objects for which the Colony was instituted, may be more easily and effectually attained by transferring the Civil and Military Authority to the Crown; for which Purpose it may be reasonably expected that a partial Surrender of the Rights of the Company may be obtained from the Proprietors, provided Security is given for the Prosecution of the Objects originally proposed.

Unless such a Transfer should be effected, and until it takes place, there does not appear to Your Committee any better Means of discharging the Obligations of Government towards the Nova Scotians and Maroons, or of obtaining the other beneficial Purposes proposed by the Institution of the Colony, than by supporting the Company's Government as now established.

6

THE SIERRA LEONE COMPANY TRANSFER ACT, 8 AUGUST 1807 (47 Geo. III, c. 44)[1]

... AND whereas the said Company, convinced of the Expediency of relinquishing the Government and Management of the said Colony, have expressed a Desire to make, and have humbly entreated His Majesty to accept a Surrender to His Majesty of all the Tract or District of Land granted to them by the said Letters Patent, or of which the said Company are possessed, or which they do now enjoy by Purchase or otherwise, in Addition to the said Lands so granted

---

[1] B.T. 6/70. Overtures for transfer had been made by Thornton in 1805 and a preliminary agreement was sent to the Company by the Committee for Trade and Plantations in September 1806. The Directors, as late as November 1806, still endeavoured to surrender no more than the Charter of 1799—retaining the Act of Incorporation, land, and buildings: Thornton to Fawkener, 20 November 1806: ibid. But two days later, when it was clear the Committee for Trade would not alter the terms of transfer, the Company agreed to surrender all; and in response to a decision of the Crown Law Officers, Zachary Macaulay sent a formal petition to Parliament through the Committee for Trade, 15 December 1806.

to the said Company; and they are further desirous that their Existence as a Body Politick and Corporate should cease and determine within such Period of Time, shorter than that limited and declared in and by the said Statute, as is deemed by the said Company sufficient for them to settle their Affairs; for confirming and giving Effect to such intended Surrender, and for limiting the Duration of the said Company: May it therefore please Your Majesty that it may be enacted; and be it enacted by the King's most Excellent Majesty, by and with the Advice and Consent of the Lords Spiritual and Temporal, and Commons, in this present Parliament assembled, and by the Authority of the same, That the said Letters Patent and Grant, and every Matter, Clause, and Thing, therein contained, shall, and the same are hereby declared to be henceforth null and void; and the said Company shall be, and they are hereby divested of and from all that Tract or District of Land commonly called and known by the Name or Description of *The Peninsula of Sierra Leone*, and all Forts, Castles, Buildings, or Estate, which have been since purchased or otherwise acquired by the said Company in addition thereto, or which now are possessed or claimed by the said Company in or about the said Peninsula; and the said Tract or District of Land, and all Forts, Castles, Buildings, or Estate so purchased or otherwise acquired, possessed, enjoyed, or claimed by the said Company, shall henceforth be, and the same and every of them are and is hereby declared and enacted to be fully and absolutely vested in His Majesty, His Heirs and Successors, for ever.

II. And be it further enacted, That, at the Expiration of Seven Years from and after the passing of this Act, the said *Sierra Leone* Company shall cease to be a Body Politick and Corporate, to all Intents, Constructions, and Purposes whatsoever; any Thing in the said Act to the contrary thereof in anywise notwithstanding.

III. And be it further enacted, That in case any Difference shall arise respecting any Building or Buildings as aforesaid, whether the same is or are such as within the Meaning of this Act are to be surrendered by the said Company, and vested in His Majesty, His Heirs and Successors, it shall and may be lawful for the Governor that shall be appointed by His Majesty for the Government of the said Colony, or in his Absence for the Lieutenant Governor, and he is hereby authorized and required, after due Examination of the Matter, to determine whether any such Building or Buildings is or are to be surrendered and vested in His Majesty, His Heirs and Successors, or to remain in the possession of the said Company; and such Determination shall be final.

IV. Provided always, and be it further enacted, That it shall not be lawful for any Person or Persons whatsoever, inhabiting, or being, or who shall at any Time hereafter inhabit or be within the said

Peninsula or Colony of *Sierra Leone*, either directly or indirectly, to deal or traffick in, buy or sell, or to be aiding or assisting in the dealing or trafficking in the buying or selling of Slaves, either within the said Peninsula or elsewhere.

7

ZACHARY MACAULAY TO EDWARD COOKE: MEMORANDA, GOVERNMENT OF SIERRA LEONE, 11 APRIL 1808[1]

1. MR. THOMPSON to be directed to proceed to Sierra Leone in the Ship of War which is about to sail thither, and to succeed Mr. Ludlam in the Government of the Colony on the 1st October 1808 or sooner should Mr. Ludlam before that time vacate his Situation. Mr. Thompson in the interim to fill the Situation of first in Council. If this arrangement be adopted, Mr. Ludlam to enjoy the Salary of Governor till the period of his resignation and Mr. Thompson an inferior Salary, perhaps that which Mr. Ludlam will enjoy as Commissioner.

2. The Governor and Council to enjoy & exercise until further orders, the same legislative & judicial functions with which the Sierra Leone Company's Governors and Council were invested by His Majesty's Charter of Justice, their proceedings being of course subject to the approbation of His Majesty instead of that of the Court of Directors.

3. The Governor to be further invested with the various civil and military powers usually conferred on the Governors of the British Colonies.

4. To direct that all the Ordinances and Regulations which may be adopted by the Government of the Colony, whether they respect its internal administration its defence from foreign attack, or its relations with the Native Powers; in short all their proceedings of a public nature, with the reasons on which such proceedings are founded and the correspondence which may be entered into, be regularly recorded and that copies of the same be transmitted from time to time to His Majesty's principal Secretary of State.

5. To direct that all the Engagements made to the present Colonists, on the subject of Grants of Land, by the Sierra Leone Company; and all the Stipulations entered into between the Company

[1] C.O. 267/24. *Zachary Macaulay* who continued to direct much of Sierra Leone administration from London had been a plantation manager in Jamaica. A member of the Clapham Sect, he governed Sierra Leone under the Company, 1794-5 and 1796-9, and was Secretary of the Company till dissolution. He was Honorary Secretary of the African Institution, 1807-12, helped to found the Anti-Slavery Society in 1823, edited the *Reporter*, and invested heavily in Sierra Leone trade.

and Native Chiefs, be considered as binding on the present Government.

6. To direct that, agreeably to the provisions of the Act of Parliament transferring the Colony to the Crown the Governor shall immediately proceed to decide what part of the Buildings erected in the Colony, by the Sierra Leone Company, shall be surrendered, along with the fortifications, to the Crown; and what part shall be continued in the possession of the Company.

N.B. In the discussions which took place, preparatory to the Transfer, between the Lords Committee of the Privy Council for Trade and Plantations and the Court of Directors; it was agreed that the Company should only retain such Buildings as had been erected by them for commercial or agricultural purposes.

7. To make it understood that his Majesty's Government are anxious to carry into full effect those views of policy which have led to the Abolition of the Slave Trade; and that it is their wish that the Colony of Sierra Leone should afford to the surrounding Natives an example of a mild but firm and well ordered Government, and of secure and productive Industry; and that the influence which its growing strength and its growing commercial importance may give it over the neighbouring Chiefs should be exerted in composing their differences, and inducing them to pursue plans of peaceful Industry.

8. In conformity with these general principles to instruct the Government of Sierra Leone, to encourage and patronize every rational Scheme for improving the condition of Africa; to favour the introduction of persons into that Country who may be disposed to instruct the Inhabitants in useful arts or to set them an example of profitable Cultivation; to direct the attention of the British Slave Traders who now reside on the Coast, to the pursuit of Agriculture and of a Trade in the natural productions of Africa; to take every proper opportunity of pointing out to the African Chiefs the various Channels into which the Industry of their people may be advantageously directed; to extend and improve as much as possible the British influence in Africa, by making Treaties with the Native Powers which, where it shall prove practicable, may comprize a recognition of the Abolition of the Slave Trade by Great Britain and an engagement mutually to discourage and prevent the revival of that Trade by any other Nation, and which may secure privileges and immunities in favour of British planters or Traders who may settle among the Natives; to adopt every practicable expedient for opening fresh Channels of Trade between Africa and Great Britain; to promote all eligible plans for exploring the Interior, and particularly to endeavour to open a direct communication between the highest navigable point of the Sierra Leone River and the Foulah Country and also with the

Niger; to encourage the acquisition of the native languages by the Servants of Governments and others in the Colony, and to consider a proficiency in these as forming a ground of preference in designating persons to particular Situations; & to use their best endeavours to excite Industry, to repress immoral practices, and to maintain and encourage Religion and Virtue, both within the Colony and as far as their influence may extend, among the Natives.

9. To require from the Governor and Council a full statement of their views respecting the System of Policy which appears to them best suited to the circumstances of the Colony, in regard to the different branches of its internal administration, civil, judicial, and military, in regard to its political relations with the Native Chiefs, and in regard also to the promotion of Agriculture, Commerce and Civilization, both within the Settlement and by means of the Settlement among the surrounding Natives.

10. More particularly to require from them an opinion on the following points viz.

1. The nature and extent of the Establishment requisite for the Colony, with a Statement of the Salaries which it would be proper to annex to the different offices.

2. The conditions on which Grants of Land ought to be made by the Government to Individuals.

3. The best mode of increasing the population of the Colony and of insuring a regular supply of Labourers.

4. The additions which it would be proper to make for the fortifications with an Estimate of the Expence. This ought to be accompanied by an account of the present State of the Fortifications.

11. To require full information on all subjects connected with the State and progress of the Colony, as well as with the State and conditions of Africa in general.

12. To direct that regular Accounts and Vouchers of money expended, be furnished.

13. To direct that a copy of all the local regulations which are now in force in the Colony be transmitted to England.

8

ROYAL INSTRUCTIONS TO GOVERNOR C. W. MAXWELL, 15 JUNE 1811[1]

[The Governor will also receive a Royal Commission.]

. . . 2nd. AND We do hereby direct that the Person whom We have appointed or shall hereafter appoint to be Our Chief Justice of Our

[1] C.O. 268/18, ff. 228–56. *Lieut.-Colonel Maxwell* was Commandant of Gorée and governed Sierra Leone, 1811–14. No formal instructions had been sent to his predecessor, T. P. Thompson.

said Colony & the Secretary of Our said Colony together with One other Person to be chosen by you from amongst the most considerable of Our Protestant Inhabitants residing in Our said Colony (Two of whom We do hereby appoint to be a Quorum) be Our Council for Our said Colony and have & enjoy all such Powers, Privileges, and Authorities as are contained in Our said Commission under the Great Seal of Our United Kingdom of Great Britain & Ireland and in these Our Instructions to you and they shall meet together at such time or times place or places as you in your discretion shall think necessary and expedient. Nevertheless in Case of Death or absence of You Our Governor & of Our Lieutenant-Governor or Commander in Chief for the time being it is Our Will and Pleasure that the said Chief Justice shall not be capable of taking on himself the Administration of Government. But that in such case, execution of all Powers & Authorities vested in you by Our Commission Under Our Great Seal of Our United Kingdom of Great Britain and Ireland and by these Our Instructions shall devolve upon the Member of Our said Council next in Seniority to the Chief Justice for the time being who shall be present in the Colony.

[The Council is to be called together, the Governor's Commission is to be read and oaths administered to the members.]

4th. And if it should at any time happen that by the death departure out of the said Colony suspension of any of our said Councillors or otherwise there should be a Vacancy in Our said Council Our Will and Pleasure is that you signify the same to us through One of Our Principal Secretaries of State by the first opportunity that We may under Our Sign Manual constitute and appoint another in his stead to which end you are whenever such Vacancy happens to transmit unto Us by One of Our Principal Secretaries of State the names of three or more Persons Inhabitants of Our said Colony whom you shall esteem best qualified for such trust.

5th. But that Our affairs may not suffer for want of a due number of Councillors if ever it shall happen that there shall be less than three residing in Our said Colony We do hereby give and grant unto You the said Charles Maxwell full Power & Authority to choose as many persons out of the Principal Inhabitants of Our said Colony as will make up the full number of the Council to be three and no more which Persons so chosen and appointed by you shall be to all intents and purposes Councillors in Our said Colony till either they shall be confirmed by Us or Our said Council by the nomination of others by Us under Our Sign Manual and Signet shall have three or more Persons in it.

6th. And it is Our Will & Pleasure that you do & you are hereby authorized and empowered to suspend and remove any of the members of Our said Council from sitting Voting and assisting therein if you shall find just cause for so doing and also in like manner to suspend Our Chief Justice or Secretary of Our said Colony from the execution of their Offices and to appoint others in their stead Until Our Pleasure shall be known. It is nevertheless Our Will and Pleasure that you do not suspend or remove the said Chief Justice or Secretary of Our said Colony or any of the members of Our Council when they shall have been confirmed by us as aforesaid without good and sufficient cause and in case of suspension of any of them you are to cause your reasons for so doing together with the charges and proofs against such Person and his Answers thereunto to be duly entered upon the Council Books and forthwith to transmit Copies thereof to Us through one of Our Principal Secretaries of State.

Nevertheless if it should happen that you should have reasons for suspending any of the said persons not fit to be communicated to the Council you may in that case suspend such Person without such Communication but you are thereupon immediately to send to us by One of Our Principal Secretaries of State an account of your proceedings therein together with your reasons at large for such suspension as also your reasons at large for not communicating the same to the Council and Duplicates thereof by the next opportunity.

[Absence without leave from the colony shall cause a member to forfeit his place in the Council.]

8th. You are forthwith to communicate such and so many of these Our Instructions to Our said Council wherein their advice and consent are mentioned to be requisite as likewise all such others from time to time as you shall find convenient for Our service to be imparted to them.

9th. You are to permit the members of Our said Council to have and enjoy freedom of debate and vote in all affairs of Public concern that may be debated in Council.

10th. And whereas by Our Commission under Our Great Seal of Our United Kingdom of Great Britain and Ireland you are empowered with the advice and consent of a Majority of the Council to make, inact and ordain, such Laws & Statutes and Ordinances as shall be thought reasonable and necessary for the welfare and good Government of Our said Colony You are therefore to give all possible attention to the Exercise of this Power and Authority using it with such moderation and discretion as that at the same time nothing be omitted to be provided for that may promote the objects for which the Power is given the number of the Regulations may not create perplexity or the severity of them complaint and dissatisfaction and above all things you are to take especial care that the said Laws

Statutes and Ordinances are not repugnant but as near as may be agreeable to the Laws and Statutes of this Our Kingdom of Great Britain regard being had to the situation & Circumstances of the place & the condition of the People & that all Laws Statutes and Ordinances whatever be transmitted within six months or sooner after the making thereof to Us through one of Our Principal Secretaries of State for Our approbation or disallowance and Duplicates thereof to the Committee of Our Privy Council for Trade & Plantations for their Information.

[Rules for the framing and style of laws, statutes and ordinances.]

12th. It being of the greatest importance that Justice be everywhere speedily and duly administered and that all disorders delays and other undue practices in the administration thereof be effectually prevented We do particularly require you to take especial care that in all Courts established within the said Colony of Sierra Leone Justice be impartially administered and that all Judges and other persons therein concerned do likewise perform their several duties without delay or partiality.

13th. You shall not by Colour of any Power or authority hereby or otherwise granted unto you or mentioned to be granted unto you take upon you to give grant or dispose of any place or office within Our said Colony which now is or shall be granted under the Great Seal of Our United Kingdom of Great Britain and Ireland or to which any Person is or shall be appointed by Warrant under Our Signet and Sign Manual any further than that you may upon the Vacancy of any such Office or place or upon the suspension of any such Office by you put in any fit Person to officiate in the interval till you shall have represented the matter unto Us through one of Our Principal Secretaries of State which you are to do by the first opportunity and till the said Office or place is disposed of by Us Our Heirs or Successors under the Great Seal of Our United Kingdom of Great Britain and Ireland or until some Person shall be appointed thereunto under Our signet and sign manual or until Our further directions be given therein.

[Ministers and teachers are to be appointed and the Protestant religion protected.]

15th. In whatever relates either to the Troops to the repairs and supply of Fortifications already erected or to the erecting New ones where it may be necessary you are to form your measures and opinions upon Plans and estimates of the greatest frugality availing yourself of every advantage and material which the nature of the Country can afford or which may be supplied from any parts of the neighbouring Coast and to this end you are to use the Naval Craft which you may

find there which you shall take out with you or which shall be hereafter sent you to the greatest advantage.

[Commerce is to be furthered and trade monopolies avoided.]

17th. It is no less essential for preserving to Our subjects free and
open commerce and for preventing that undue preference which is
meant to be particularly guarded against that all Officers whatsoever
Civil or Military should be restrained from carrying on any private
Trade or Traffic whatsoever on their own account further than may
be absolutely necessary for the supply of mere personal Wants it will
therefore be necessary that Our Will and Pleasure in this respect
should be fully & expressly signified and made Public in all parts of
the Colony under Your Government. . . .

[The abolition of the slave trade is to be enforced and piracy put down;
commissions of marque are not to be granted; the governor is not to come
to Europe without permission; in case of his death, the next senior member
of council will succeed; freedom of action is reserved by the Crown to
change instructions.]

9

SELECT COMMITTEE REPORT ON THE AFRICAN FORTS, 25 JUNE 1817[1]

[The annual Parliamentary grant to the African Company should be
continued; trade at the forts has declined since 1807, though it might be
encouraged to increase.]

. . . 4. THE conditions of the forts and settlements belonging to the
Company, appears to Your Committee, from all the information
they have received, to be by no means good, either as to repairs or
means of defence. Of their eight[2] forts and settlements, the greater
part appear to want the means of defence, against even an attack of
the natives, the security derived from them consisting, rather in
opinion and in the interest which the natives have in trading with
them, than in their intrinsic strength. It is evident, however, that
such a security among tribes, whose character is described by the
servants of the Company, as selfish, unjust and perfidious, must be
extremely precarious. A melancholy proof was afforded of this, by
the murder of one of their governors in 1812. . . .

The bad repair of the generality of their forts is admitted by the
Company, who ascribe it to an insufficiency of the annual parliamentary grant. This grant has varied in different years; on an average

[1] *Parl. Papers*, 1817, vi (431), pp. 3–9.
[2] Apollonia, Anomabu, Accra, Cape Coast, Dixcove, Komenda, Tantumkweri,
Winneba.

Ii BP

of fifty-eight years, from 1750, when the present Company was established, to 1807 inclusive, it has been 13,431 *l.* per annum; since 1807, it has been 23,000 *l.* per annum. It follows, therefore, according to the statement of the Company, that without a considerable increase of the parliamentary grant, they will not be able to maintain their present establishments on a secure and respectable footing, much less to take any effectual steps towards maintaining and extending a communication with the interior, and introducing education and civilization among the natives.

5. Your Committee now proceed to the last and most important subject for consideration; viz. the policy which it may be most expedient to adopt in future with regard to these settlements. This subject involves two questions;—1st, Whether those settlements should be abandoned altogether; and 2dly, Whether, if continued, they should be maintained under the present system; viz. the exclusive government and direction of the African committee with the aid of Parliament, or whether with a view to economy, to the interests of general trade, and to the ulterior objects of African civilization, a more advantageous system may not be adopted.

With regard to the first question; as the entire abandonment of the forts is understood to imply that of the trade also, and as this would not only be a present loss, though to an inconsiderable amount, to the country, but entirely cut up by the roots all chance of extending the existing trade, of opening new sources, and of improving the state of the country, and its inhabitants, by education and civilization, Your Committee can by no means recommend this policy to Parliament.

With regard to the Second Question, Your Committee feel more difficulty in deciding upon it.

The advantage of carrying on the trade by the medium of the Company, is represented to be, 1st, A saving to the Public in the pay of their officers and servants in Africa, who receive their salaries, &c. in goods, which are purchased by the African Committee of Management here, and sent out in a store-ship, freighted for that purpose; by which means, it may be alleged, that those officers receive them at a cheaper rate there, than they could otherwise obtain them, and the public has the advantage of securing the payment of the salaries, &c. in British exports, at a mercantile profit, instead of bills of exchange, which might perhaps be employed in the purchase of foreign articles. As, however, it has not been suggested to Your Committee, that free traders labour under any disadvantage from the want of this accomodation; and as Mr. Banks,[1] the witness before referred to, distinctly states, that traders on that coast would find no difficulty in obtaining whatever goods they might order by private ships; added to which,

[1] Ibid, pp. 6 and 8.

Mr. Hutton states, that he has himself received goods at as low a freight as the Company charge, Your Committee are disposed to think it probable, that the connections and skill of individual merchants might enable them to receive goods as cheap, or nearly as cheap, as the Company's servants do under the present arrangement.

The second advantage arising from the management of the Company, is represented to be in the local experience of their governors, who rise to the chief commands through subordinate stations in their service; which gives them an opportunity of becoming acquainted with the language, habits, and manners of the natives, and thereby enabling themselves the better to discharge the duties of their business.

From the best consideration which they have been enabled to give the subject, under the means of information which they possess, they are inclined to recommend that the governor in chief should be appointed by Government, with supreme authority extending over the whole of the British settlements on the Gold Coast; that the number of those forts and settlements should be diminished by the disposal or abandonment of such as may, upon strict inquiry, appear not to be of service in a sufficient degree fully to compensate for their expense. That the inferior officers universally, including the chief officers of such out-forts as may be retained, should be appointed by the same authority, and according to the same routine of promotion as at present; subject to the control of the governor in chief, with power of suspension by him in cases of misconduct, and of removal by the Government of this country; and that the number of the African committee be reduced from the present number of nine to six, giving the chairman the casting vote. It is the opinion of Your Committee, that by the reduction of some of the settlements and forts a saving may be made, so that not only the remainder may be kept up, but the ulterior objects which Your Committee have in view, for promoting the improvement of the country, may be pursued with a very small addition to the present expense to the Country. Your Committee cannot conclude their Report without distinctly stating to the House, that a principal motive which induces them to recommend the continuance of an establishment on the Gold Coast, and the aid of Parliament for its maintenance, is the instruction and improvement of the natives of that country, in which but little, if any thing, has been hitherto accomplished. As one method conducive to this purpose, they would recommend the establishment of schools at all the settlements which may be retained; and that in the selection of schoolmasters, a preference may be given to the writers and factors, who will become supernumerary by the discontinuance of some of the factories and forts, so far as they may be properly qualified.

10

GOVERNOR SIR CHARLES MACCARTHY TO EARL BATHURST: GOLD COAST FORTS, 9 OCTOBER 1818[1]

[Reporting the death of General Daendels, Governor of Dutch Elmina; all administrators on the Gold Coast are merchants and traders.]

... CONCEIVING it the duty of an officer abroad to communicate such information as he may suppose to lead to the advantage of his Country, I shall upon that principle beg leave to state to your Lordship that from the knowledge I have acquired, & I believe not on light grounds, I fear that unless a radical change takes place with respect to the Administration & the management of the whole of the Forts—and the same is placed under the immediate rule & charge of His Majesty's Government there is no likelihood of any advantage being obtained for the Commerce of Great Britain, commensurate in the smallest degree to the expense incurred yearly for the maintainance of those Establishments. They are all open to Foreigners without any duty being raised on imports or exports in aid of the public expence and therefore Foreigners, and them only derive a clear gain from our charges. The Governors of Forts are the sole Individuals (except at Cape Coast) receiving Salaries permitted to Trade, they actually being placed in that situation where their interest lies in opposition with their duty use all their influence and authority to preserve for themselves an advantageous monopoly—but prejudicial to all commercial enterprises. The Governor and Officers at Cape Coast and the Governor in the smaller Forts employ the whole of their time as traders in their stores—and their putting on a Scarlet Military dress after their morning avocation does not raise the dignity or importance of our Country—the assumption of the Character of private Merchants or traders—civil officers and Military men cannot be supported by the same individual—if the trade is clearly advantageous, a considerable saving could be obtained, as there can be no necessity of granting large Salaries to carry on trade, and if otherwise the officers ought to be satisfied with the allowance they receive from the public, and in lieu of preventing other individuals from trading, they ought to encourage all enterprises for the benefit of commerce and abstain from them.

[1] C.O. 267/47. Referred to the Treasury.

II

WILLIAM HUTTON TO EARL BATHURST, 16 MAY 1820[1]

[Some of the Gold Coast forts should be abandoned and the African Committee be required to keep accurate accounts of expenditure.]

... BUT although my suggestions in these particulars as well as others of less moment, have been implicitly followed, I lament to find that the annual Parliamentary Grant to the African Committee, *instead of being decreased*, has been lately *increased* from £23,000 to £28,000.

I conceive it therefore my duty distinctly and unequivocally to state, that this Grant might be reduced with the greatest propriety, and without injury to the Nation, to £13,000; and hence will result a saving of £15,000 annually. Indeed when your Lordship considers that the original Grant for the support of the Forts on this Coast did not exceed £13,000, at a time we had seven more Settlements to support, namely, Appolonia, Succundee, Commenda, Tantum, Winnebah, Whydah, & Pram Pram, it will doubtless be matter of surprise, how the African Committee can account for ths enormous increase of the public Expenditure, while it must be glaringly manifest that the reduction of seven of our Establishments ought at least to produce a proportionable reduction of the Parliamentary Grant; instead of which, the African Committee are constantly calling on His Majesty's Government for a further increase: in short it was only very lately that they succeeded in an application for an Increase of £5000 annually. ...

[The Dutch Government have reduced salaries and expenditure on their forts to £4,100 per annum.]

12

GOVERNOR SIR CHARLES MACCARTHY: MEMORANDUM RELATING TO THE CONSTITUTION OF SIERRA LEONE, [1820][2]

AT the time the Charter was granted by His Majesty to the Sierra Leone Company in the year 1800 the Colony of Sierra Leone had only one Town (Free Town) then not the half of its present size, and its whole population then residing in that town consisted of the

[1] C.O. 2/11, ff. 144–51. *William Hutton* had accompanied Dupuis on his mission to Kumasi and was appointed Acting Consul—a post not recognized by the African Committee or the Governor and Council at the forts. See above, p. 285.
[2] C.O. 267/42. Encl. in MacCarthy to Hill, 16 November 1820.

Nova Scotia & Maroon Settlers with the few Europeans then in the Company's Service. In 1808 the Colony was transferred to the Crown, and continued to be governed by virtue of the same Charter till the middle of the year 1811 when a Chief Justice and a new Charter was sent out from the Country; this new Charter appears to have been modelled from the old one, with the addition of some of the Clauses usually inserted in the Commissions given to the Governors of the West India Islands; and was at that time when the population of the Colony did not amount to Two Thousand persons, all residing in one Town, perhaps the best Constitution for such a place, but there being now Twenty Towns or Villages on the Peninsula with a Population of about 12300 captured negroes, free Africans from neighbouring countries & other persons, who are rapidly advancing towards English Manners and Ideas, and are accumulating considerable permanent property, and it being advisable to extend the Colonial Laws for the Government and protection of the persons established at the Gambia, Isles de Loss, and other Dependencies not forming part of the Peninsula; the present Charter therefore is inadequate for the present State of the Colony, and, I conceive, of no use whatever to the Dependencies thereof—the most eligible plan to remedy which I should apprehend would be to revoke the present Charter and to grant the Governor such Commissions as are usually granted to the Governors in the West India Islands and by which and the Royal instructions together with their own Bye Laws those Islands, I believe, most of them are governed, omitting in such Commissions those Clauses relating to a House of Assembly.

Another peculiar inconvenience is the want of a Supreme Court to include a Court of King's Bench, Common Bench and Exchequer, the latter to take Cognizance of Cases within the Jurisdiction not amenable to the Court of Vice Admiralty. The Chief Justice might be assisted in this Court by Two of the Members of Council—the present Court of the Recorder of Freetown, the Judges of which are the Chief Justice, in his Office of Recorder, the Mayor and three Alderman; and which is a Court of Law and Equity; and which has also the power of granting Probates of Wills and Letters of Administration.

A Power lodged somewhere to take cognizance of matrimonial Causes similar to that of the Ecclesiastical Courts in this Country I have observed many times to be much wanted.

On a reference to the Constitution of Sierra Leone it will appear that there is no adequate provision made for the Administration of Justice out of the Peninsula of Sierra Leone, and therefore that such instructions as I have deemed it my duty to establish for the guidance of the Officers who have held the subordinate Command of the Isle de Loss and of our Settlements on the River Gambia as well as the appointment of *Magistrates* were only granted upon the *necessity* of the case and not upon positive Law, and therefore subject to Cavils at some future period.

To prevent those serious evils should it not be considered necessary to alter or revoke the Charter of Sierra Leone? it would be expedient after the preamble relating [to] the transfer of the Forts to the Crown to express that in order to provide for the future Government of the Forts & territories on the Gold Coast the Captain General & Governor in Chief of the Colony of Sierra Leone or in his absence the Lnt. Governor or Commander in Chief with the Council of the Colony or the Major part thereof should have power and authority to make, enact and ordain Laws Statutes ordinances for the peace welfare &c &c for those Forts & territories as also the Isle de Loss, Settlements in the River Gambia &c.

That the Governor should have power & authority whenever he might deem expedient to get out Commissions of oyer & terminer of Gaol delivery for such parts of the Colony & Dependencies.

The Number of Members of Council I should propose to be increased to Seven.

13

TREASURY MINUTE: GOLD COAST FORTS, 15 DECEMBER 1820[1]

MY LORDS read a letter from the African Company, dated 22 September last, relative to the proposed transfer of the settlements upon the Gold Coast to His Majesty, and enclosing particulars relative to those Forts; and a list of the officers and servants now in the employ of the Company.

My Lords also read a letter from Governor McCarthy, of the 16th November 1820, transmitting a copy of the Charter for the Governor of Sierra Leone, and a Memorandum relative thereto.

In pursuance of the several Acts of Parliament before recited, the whole of the British forts and settlements upon the Gold Coast of Africa, have become vested in the Company created by the said Act of the 23 Geo. 2, c. 31, and have been entirely governed and managed by officers and servants appointed by them; but the whole expense of such management has, for many years past, been entirely defrayed by sums granted by Parliament for the support of these forts; the said Company having in their corporate capacity no funds whatever, out of which any part of such expenses could be defrayed, and having no beneficial interest in the said forts.

[1] *Parl. Papers*, 1821, xxi (724), p. 4. The Treasury had already resolved, 21 July 1820 (ibid., p. 3) to transfer the forts to the Crown. The African Company was abolished by Statute 1 & 2 Geo. IV, c. 28 (7 May 1821).

My Lords also read the Reports of the Committees of the House of Commons of the 13th June 1816, and 25th June 1817, appointed to inquire into the concerns of this Company.

Upon a full consideration of this subject, it appears to my Lords, that it will be expedient to submit a Bill to Parliament, for abolishing the Company created by the Act of the 23 Geo. 2, c. 31, and for vesting all the forts, and the property and effects of the said Company, in His Majesty; and for enabling His Majesty to grant such reasonable allowances as he may see fit, to such of the officers and servants of the said Company, who may not be retained in the government or management of the said Forts, or otherwise employed in His Majesty's service; and for charging the allowances so granted, upon the Consolidated Fund.

14

COMMITTEE OF AFRICAN MERCHANTS TO EARL BATHURST, TRANSFER OF THE FORTS, 29 JUNE 1821[1]

[Requesting the African Committee be paid the Parliamentary grant for 1821 in order to settle debts already contracted.]

. . . THE Committee are desirous of submitting to your Lordship, some remarks upon the change of the character of these Settlements which will be produced by their annexation to, 'and making them Dependencies on the Colony of Sierra Leone, and subject to all such Laws, Statutes and Ordinances, as shall be in force in the said Colony, or as shall at any time thereafter be made, enacted, or ordained by the Governor and Council of the said Colony, and shall not be disallowed by His Majesty, in the same manner as if the said Forts, Possessions, Territories or Islands, had originally formed part of the said Colony of Sierra Leone'.

Upon these provisions of the Act, (which formed no part of the Bill as laid before the Committee) they felt it proper to observe, that the Gold Coast Settlements consist simply of Forts, without any Territory; and therefore, as the Act describes Sierra Leone as a 'Colony', the operation of it will be to prevent their having any commercial intercourse whatever (even with the Natives) but what may be carried on direct with the Mother Country, (with the exception of the article of Wine by the Navigation Laws) except in those cases of urgent necessity, in which the Governors of Colonies are permitted to open their Ports; and then only, subject to the orders of the Governor & Council of the Colony of Sierra Leone, 900 miles distant.

[1] C.O. 267/54.

In the judgement of the Committee, the Forts on the Gold Coast cannot be retained as *'Colonies'* without the annihilation of their Trade, unless the System of the Laws by which the Trade of the British Colonies is governed, be relaxed in almost every essential point; and if that were to be done, the consequence could not fail to lead to much hardship, oppression and injustice, for want of a rule for the regulation of commercial intercourse with them. . . .

[The chiefs should continue to be paid monthly rents and stipends.]

15

CONSTITUTION OF THE COLONY OF SIERRA LEONE AND ITS DEPENDENCIES, 17 OCTOBER 1821[1]

[Terms of the Sierra Leone Company Act, 1791, the Act transferring the Colony to the Crown, 1807, and the Act for abolishing the African Company, 1821.]

. . . Now know ye, that we, having considered the premises, and being willing and desirous to provide for the future good government, as well of the said forts and possessions so heretofore acquired, pur-chased, enjoyed, claimed, or held by the said African Company, as of all and every other the territories, islands, or possessions on the West Coast of Africa, between the 20th degree of north latitude and the 20th degree of south latitude, which now do, or at any time here-after shall or may belong to us, our heirs and successors, do by these presents, by virtue and in pursuance of the said recited Act, and of our special grace, certain knowledge, and mere motion, order, direct, and appoint, that all and every of the said forts and possessions so heretofore acquired, purchased, enjoyed, claimed, or held by the said African Company, and also all territories, islands, and possessions which now do, or at any time hereafter shall or may belong to us, our heirs and successors on the West Coast of Africa, between the 20th degree of north latitude and the 20th degree of south latitude, shall be annexed to and made dependencies on, and the same are hereby annexed to and made dependencies on the said colony of Sierra Leone. And that from the publication of these presents in the said colony of Sierra Leone, as hereinafter directed, the same shall be and they are hereby made subject to all such laws, statutes, and ordi-nances as shall be in force in our said colony, or as shall at any time hereafter be made, enacted, or ordained by the Governor and Council of the said colony, and shall not be disallowed by us, our heirs and successors, in the same manner as if the said forts, possessions,

---

[1] *Parl. Papers*, 1855, xxxvii (383), p. 10. Proclaimed at Sierra Leone, 28 February 1822, and at Cape Coast, 29 March 1822.

territories, or islands had originally formed part of the said Colony of
Sierra Leone. . . . And we do further by these presents, for us, our
heirs and successors, will establish, and ordain, that from and after
the publication of these presents, there shall be nine or more councillors advising and assisting our Governor of our said colony of
Sierra Leone for the time being. And we do by these presents
nominate, make, ordain, and constitute our trusty and well-beloved
Edward Fitzgerald, our Chief Justice, or our Chief Justice of our
said Colony for the time being; our trusty and well-beloved Daniel
Molloy Hamilton, our advocate, or our advocate of our said colony
for the time being; our trusty and well-beloved Dudley Feneday, our
secretary, or our secretary of our said colony for the time being; our
trusty and well-beloved Thomas Stuart Buckle, our surveyor of
lands, or our surveyor of lands of our said colony for the time being;
our trusty and well-beloved Kenneth Macaulay, esquire, our trusty
and well-beloved Alexander Grant, esquire, our trusty and well-
beloved Joseph Reffell, esquire, our trusty and well-beloved John
O'Neil Walsh, esquire, our trusty and well-beloved, Andrew Nicoll,
doctor of medicine, our trusty and well-beloved John Hope Smith,
esquire, and our trusty and well-beloved William Dawson, esquire,
thenceforth councillors of our said colony, to continue in their said
office of councillors during their natural lives, unless suspended from
their said office, or absent from the said colony for the space of one
year without leave given them under our Royal signature, or until
other councillors shall be chosen and appointed by us, under our
signet and sign manual in their stead. And we do further hereby
give and grant to our said Governor full power and authority to
suspend any of the members of our said Council from sitting, voting,
or assisting therein, if he shall find just cause for so doing, and if it
shall at any time happen that by the death, departure out of our said
colony, or suspension of our said councillors or otherwise, there shall
be a vacancy in our said Council (any five whereof we do hereby
appoint to be a quorum), our will and pleasure is, that our said
Governor do signify the same unto us by the first opportunity, that
we may, under our signet and sign manual, constitute and appoint
others in their stead. But that our affairs at that distance may not
suffer from want of a due number of councillors, if it ever shall
happen that there be less than nine of them residing in our said
colony, we do hereby give and grant unto our said Governor full
power and authority to choose as many persons out of the principal
inhabitants thereof as shall make up the full number of our said
Council to be nine, and no more, which persons so chosen and
appointed by him shall be, to all intents and purposes, councillors
in our said colony, until either they shall be confirmed by us, or that
by the nomination of other by us under our sign manual and signet,

our said colony shall have nine or more councillors in it, resident in our said colony. And we further by these presents ordain, will, and appoint, that our Governor of our said colony, or in his absence our Lieutenant-Governor or Commander-in-Chief for the time being of our said colony, together with our Council of the same, or the major part thereof, shall have full power and authority to make, constitute, and ordain laws, statutes and ordinances for the public welfare and good government of our said colony, under the like conditions, and subject to the same limitations and restrictions, as those imposed on that behalf on the Governor and Council of our said colony in the Letters Patent of his said late Majesty hereinbefore recited. But to the end that nothing may be done or passed to the prejudice of us, our heirs and successors, by our said Council, we further ordain by these presents, that our Governor of our said Colony, or in his absence our Lieutenant-Governor or Commander-in-chief for the time being, may and shall have a negative voice in the making and passing of all laws, statutes and ordinances as aforesaid. And we do further by these presents will, ordain and appoint, that from and after the publication of these presents in our said colony of Sierra Leone as hereinafter directed, our court of record in our said colony, called and known by the name of "The Court of the Recorder of Freetown,' shall consist of our Chief Justice of the said colony for the time being, and two such members of the Council as shall be appointed by the Governor of our said colony for the time being, assistant judges thereof, in lieu of the mayor and aldermen of Freetown for the time being, as ordained and appointed in and by the Letters Patent of his said late Majesty hereinbefore recited. And we hereby will and ordain, that they, or any two of them (whereof our said Chief Justice for the time being, resident in Freetown, to be one), shall, and the same are hereby authorised to hear and determine all civil suits, actions, and pleas between party and party that shall or may arise or happen, or that have already arisen or happened, within our said colony of Sierra Leone, or of any of the forts, settlements, islands, or territories subject or subordinate thereto, except when the cause of action or suit shall not exceed the value of 40 s. Provided always, and it is hereby further ordained and directed, that if such Chief Justice and Recorder, or any of the said assistant judges should be anyway interested in the event of any action or suit, no such Chief Justice and Recorder, or Assistant Judge, shall sit or act as a judge in such suit or action, but the same shall be heard and determined by such of them as shall be no ways interested therein; and in all cases where the number of voices shall be equal in the determination of any action of suit, the Chief Justice, or in his absence the senior assistant judge present, shall have two voices. And we do further direct, that the said Court of the Recorder of Freetown, hereby constituted, shall proceed in the same manner and form, and subject to the same rules, as to trial by jury and otherwise, and to the same remedy and right of appeal, as were, in and by the said Letters Patent hereinbefore recited, directed and provided, in respect of the Court of the Recorder of Freetown constituted by such Letters Patent; and that all rules of practice made by the one court, and now, or at the time of publication of these presents, remaining in force, shall be observed and followed in and by the other, until, by the authority of that other, the same be varied or repealed. And we do further will and direct, that no action, cause, suit, or proceeding, depending in the said Court of the Recorder of Freetown at the publication of these presents, shall be voided, abated, discontinued, or annulled for or by reason of any change in the constitution of the said court, effected by these presents, but that the same shall be respectively transferred in their then present condition to, and subsist and depend respectively, and be prosecuted, tried, and determined respectively in the said Court of the Recorder of Freetown hereby constituted and established, to all intents and purposes, as if they had been respectively first commenced, brought, and prosecuted in the last-mentioned court. And we do further will and direct, that each person so nominated or appointed one of the assistant judges of the said Court of the Recorder of Freetown as aforesaid, shall, prior to the entering upon the execution of his said office, take an oath before the Governor, Lieutenant-Governor, or other Commander-in-chief for the time being, for the due discharge of the same; which oath the said Governor, Lieutenant-Governor, or Commander-in-chief for the time being, is hereby empowered to administer. And we do further, by these presents, will and establish, that our said Governor, Lieutenant-Governor, or other Commander-in-chief, and Council of our said colony for the time being, shall be, and they are hereby constituted a Court of Record to receive, hear, and determine appeals from as well the said Court of the Recorder of Freetown as from any other superior court of common law now established, or to be in future established, in our said colony, pursuant to these presents, in the like cases, and subject to the like limitations, rules, and directions as to their proceedings therein, and subject also to the like right of appeal from their judgment, sentence, or decree, to us in our Privy Council, when the debt, damages, or things, or matter in dispute, shall exceed the value of 400 *l.*, and upon the like conditions as to security to be thereupon given by the appellant, as were in and by the said Letters Patent hereinbefore recited, directed, and provided in respect of appeals to the Governor and Council of the said colony, and from them to his said late Majesty in his Privy Council, respectively: provided, always, and it is hereby ordained, that no such member or members of our said Council as shall be at time judge or judges of the court from which such appeal shall be so made, shall be entitled or permitted to vote upon such appeal: provided also, that no appeal be allowed from any sentence, order, or decree of our Courts of Chancery of our said colony, to us or our Privy Council, unless the debt, damage, or thing, or matter in dispute, shall exceed the like sum or value of 400 *l.* sterling, and that such appellant do also give good security that he will effectually prosecute such appeal, and answer the condemnation money, and pay also such costs and damages as shall be by us awarded, in case such sentence, order, or decree so appealed from be affirmed: provided nevertheless, and our further will and pleasure is, that when the matter in question related to the taking or demanding of any duty payable to us, or to any fee of office, or annual rent, or other such like matter or thing where the right in future may be bound, in all such cases an appeal may be had from the judgment of our said Governor and Council as aforesaid, or from the sentence, order, or decree of our Court of Chancery of our said colony, to us in our Privy Council, though the immediate sum or value appealed for be of a less amount than 400 *l.* sterling. . . .

[Use of the Great Seal; custody of idiots and lunatics.]

And we do further by these presents ordain, direct, and establish, that from and after the expiration of three months from the publication of these presents hereinafter directed, the authority of the Court of Requests for the Colony of Sierra Leone, for the recovery of small debts within the said colony, as constituted by the Letters Patent of his said late Majesty hereinbefore recited, shall cease and be abolished. And we do by these presents authorise and require our said Governor, by and with the advice and concurrence of our said Council, prior to the expiration thereof, to nominate and appoint certain justices, or other commissioners, in and for particular districts, upon whom the authority of the said court, henceforward to cease and be abolished in and throughout the said colony as aforesaid, may regularly devolve, and that the said justices or other commissioners may and shall proceed to the hearing and determining of all matters of debt or damage, under forty shillings value, in the same or the like manner and form, as near as circumstances will admit of, as any Commissioners of Requests usually and lawfully do within that part of our United Kingdom called England, and that such Commissioners shall assemble at such times and places as our said Governor, with the advice and concurrence of our Council as aforesaid, shall from time to time appoint. . . .

[Governor and Council are empowered to constitute civil and criminal courts and appoint commissioners of oyer and terminer.]

16

[R. W. HAY]: MEMORANDUM, POSSESSIONS ON THE WEST COAST OF AFRICA, 9 MAY 1826[1]

IT no doubt would be premature whilst Commissioners[2] both Civil & Military are engaged in preparing Reports on the African Coast, to enter into any discussion on the propriety of retaining all our present Settlements in that quarter. Their extreme unhealthiness is a fact unfortunately too well established, but without entering into this very material part of the question, it is presumed that Government would not consider it advisable to embark in any very great expense in replacing our Forts on the Gold Coast in a state of Military defence, should it be pronounced by the Engineer Officers who have been recently employed in inspecting them, that a considerable sum of money would be required for that purpose.

The recent death however of the Governor of Sierra Leone, & the appointment of a Successor[3] who must shortly proceed thither, render it extremely desirable that no time should be lost in bringing this matter again under the consideration of His Majesty's Government & that before a new Governor goes out, it should be finally determined how far the present system should be adhered to, & whether one might not be advantageously substituted, which would not entail such waste of human life, & so great an expenditure of the public money.

There can be no doubt that the climate of that part of Africa is most destructive to the European constitution, for although some portion of the mortality, which is found to prevail in that quarter, may be attributed to the irregular habits of the Troops which are sent out there, still the gradual falling off within a very short time of all the public Servants of the Colony, whatever their habits of life or occupations may have been, too clearly demonstrates that at certain Seasons of the year no common precautions are of any avail against the decided unhealthiness of the atmosphere.

A great improvement may probably be effected by taking care that those who are sent to this quarter on the public Service, shall arrive in the most favorable Season of the year, & shall be removed when their health requires it to a different Settlement, but still the enclosed List will sufficiently prove that our possessions on the West Coast of Africa cannot be retained without a great sacrifice of a

[1] C.O. 325/37.
[2] Commissioners Major J. Rowan and H. Wellington were already on tour. See above p. 187.
[3] Sir Neil Campbell who arrived in August 1826 to replace Major Charles Turner.

number of valuable lives. The Estimates laid before Parliament will shew the expense of our three Establishments at Sierra Leone, the Gambia, & Gold Coast, and although it is proposed to make reduction on the whole, by a different distribution of the Public Servants employed, yet the saving will not exceed £1,500 or £2000 per annum & the whole of the Revenue raised within the Colony is required for the completion of various public works which are now carrying on there.

In considering the advantages which belong to the three British Settlements on the Coast, it will be sufficient for our purpose at present to take into consideration the policy of maintaining possession of some of the Forts which belong to us on the Gold Coast, & the reasons which have been urged for not withdrawing altogether from so unhealthy a Region.

The chief arguments which have been employed for keeping at least two of the Forts which we at present possess, are the loss which our Merchants would sustain by the want of some secure place of deposit for their goods, or for their own protection in case of necessity, & the check which by our influence we are enabled to impose on the prosecution of the Slave Trade in that part of Africa.

The island of Fernando Po[1] has often been pointed out as a far more eligible spot, both in point of climate, & in local advantages, for the formation of a Settlement, than any which can be found upon the mainland adjoining, & there can be no doubt that as far as the safety of our Merchants & the prosperity of their Trade is concerned, they would benefit considerably by removing their Establishments from the Gold Coast to this Island. In regard to the other object to which we have adverted, the prevention of the Slave Trade, there is no place so advantageously situated for enabling us to block up the mouths of the Rivers, on which this odious traffic is most actively carried on or for affording us the means of introducing into the Interior of Africa the taste for Trade of a better description.

It is understood that a claim to Fernando Po (though the claim is of so doubtful a character as scarcely to be recognizable) might be brought forward by either Spain or Portugal, in the event of the British Government proceeding to form a Settlement on that Island —but as both these Powers are bound to give us their best assistance in putting down the Slave Trade, the rightful claimant could not reasonably object to our forming there what might in the outset

[1] Two British traders had claimed ownership of the island in 1819 and both the Committee for Trade and the Admiralty urged that a settlement be formed there. In 1825 the Foreign Office recognized that it was a Spanish possession. The plan to transfer the Mixed Commission Court there from Sierra Leone—approved by a Select Committee of the House of Commons in 1830—was abandoned in 1832, after use of the island as a naval station and a location for liberated Africans: C.O. 82/3, 5 and 6.

be only considered as a Naval Depot, from whence our Cruizers might most effectually watch the movements of those engaged in this Traffic.

As the Island, where it is cleared on the North Eastern Extremity is said to be free from all unwholesome qualities which belong to the opposite shore, our Ships of War, which are now compelled to resort to Ascension for refreshment & for the recovery of their sick, will be able to repair here for that purpose, & it may be a matter for after consideration [*sic*] whether it may not be advisable to locate here some of the Liberated Africans to whom the task of gradually clearing the Island of Timber may in the mean time be assigned.

17

EARL BATHURST TO GOVERNOR SIR NEIL CAMPBELL: GAMBIA BOARDS OF COMMERCE, 24 NOVEMBER 1826[1]

SIR,

I have to acknowledge the receipt of your dispatch No. 16 of the 23rd. of Septr. last respecting the Establishment of two Boards of Commerce at the Gambia.

As I can see no necessity for there being two Boards of this description in an infant Colony, where no proper system of Government has yet been established, I recommend to you to take an early opportunity of abolishing them, explaining to the Merchants that one of your first objects on revisiting the Gambia will be to consider the propriety of organizing a Board of this description under proper regulations & restrictions, & that in the meantime you will be ready to pay attention to the representations on commercial matters which they may consider necessary to bring before you.

18

EARL BATHURST TO GOVERNOR SIR NEIL CAMPBELL: GOLD COAST FORTS, 21 MARCH 1827[2]

[Forwarding the Sierra Leone Estimates for 1827.]

. . . [D. You will perceive that the alterations which have been made in the Civil Establishment of Sierra Leone are few and inconsiderable; that it is intended to make a larger provision for the support

---

[1] C.O. 268/26. The Boards do not figure again in correspondence, though the Gambia merchants met frequently to consider petitions.

[2] C.O. 268/26, f. 212. The garrisons at Dixcove and Anomabu were already withdrawn in 1826.

of the Settlement in the Gambia;] it is not proposed to apply to Parliament for more than a very limited & temporary grant on account of the Forts on the Gold Coast, as it has appeared to H.M's Government that the interests of this Country do not require that any Civil Government should be kept up there for the future, or that any Garrison should be maintained there after the expiration of the present year.

It will be incumbent upon you therefore, immediately upon the receipt of this despatch to take measures for withdrawing such Officers of Government as may be stationed at any of the Forts; & I trust that you may not find it incompatible with your convenience to proceed in person to Cape Coast Castle for the purpose of concluding the other arrangements which must be adopted for giving effect to the views of H.M's Government.

Upon your arrival at Cape Coast Castle you will assemble such British Merchants as may be residing there, & with whom you appear already to have communicated on this subject, & you will announce to them that it is proposed to evacuate the forts altogether, at the expiration of the year, as soon after that period as a due attention to the security of the lives and properties of those who may be inclined to remain for mercantile purposes, will permit. You will inform them also that if in consequence of this measure, they should feel desirous of removing themselves & their Establishments, you will be ready to afford them every assistance which they could reasonably expect for that purpose; and if they should propose to you to remove at once, you will then withdraw the Troops and Public Stores, & cause the Forts to be demolished, or at least rendered unfit for Military occupation.

But if the Merchants should on the contrary express their wish to remain on the Coast, you are authorized to assure them that you will maintain Military occupation of Cape Coast Castle during the present year, at the conclusion of which you will place them in possession of Cape Coast Castle, & of the Fort of Accra, if they should desire it, & assign to them a limited number of guns, together with two or three hundred stand of Arms, a proportion of accoutrements, and a moderate quality of ammunition.

You will also acquaint them that if in the event of their asking to remain on the Coast, they should think it expedient to embody themselves and their labourers into an armed Militia, you could hold out to them the expectation, that for the first year, a sum not exceeding Two Thousand Pounds by way of outfit & pay, £1500 for the second year & £1000 afterwards, would be assigned to them under proper Regulations, for the support of such Militia, which would be liable to be inspected from time to time by an officer whom you would dispatch for that purpose. But you must distinctly apprize the Merchants that in the event of their preferring to remain in possession of the Forts, it must be entirely at their own risk, & that they would under no circumstances have to expect any assistance from you for the purpose of carrying on hostile operations against the Native Tribes, nor any aid whatever beyond that which has been defined, for the purpose of protecting the forts against aggression; for although there might be an occasional appearance of a Ship of War on the Coast, in order to demonstrate to the native powers that the interests of the British Residents in this quarter are not lost sight of by the Government at home, yet the Captains of H.M's Ships would receive strict orders to abstain from all interference in any contest which the Merchants might be engaged in ashore.

It must also be explained to them that as the Forts, when they shall have been evacuated cannot be considered in any other light than as Factories, & in no degree dependencies of Sierra Leone, His Majesty's Government will not be considered responsible after the expiration of the present year, for the payment of what is usually called the ground rent of the Castles, or for presents of any description to the native authorities; nor will they be answerable for any further disbursement for repairs or improvements in these buildings beyond what it has been settled to contribute for that object in the present year.

I have pointed out in the annexed Estimate the arrangements which you are to make for disposing of the Civil Officers of Government who are now on the Establishment of Cape Coast Castle, & with respect to the Pensioners of the late African Company I recommend that you discharge their Claims forthwith by granting them a moderate compensation out of the monies lodged in the Civil Chest at Cape Coast Castle.

Of the native Labourers you will probably think it expedient to retain a select number for the new Establishment at Fernando Po.

With regard to the Public Stores, you will appropriate a sufficient number of heavy brass Guns for mounting a Battery at Bathurst in the Gambia, & you will send the remainder of the Guns to England.

Whatever articles in Store may be found useful in forming the proposed Establishment at Fernando Po, should be retained and allotted for that purpose.

I am inclined to think that the Merchants whether they decide upon remaining at Cape Coast Castle or not, are fairly entitled to be relieved from all further payment of duties on their trade; & you will, therefore, give directions for that purpose without delay; but you will resist any application which may be made to you for a return or drawback on the amount of duties actually paid.

You will convey under your own charge to Sierra Leone all the monies and effects which are lodged in the Civil Chest of Cape

Coast Castle, & carry the amount thereof to the general Account of your Government.

19

RULES FOR CONDUCTING THE AFFAIRS OF CAPE COAST CASTLE AND ACCRA, 31 DECEMBER 1828[1]

[With the approval of His Majesty's Government the management of the forts is entrusted to an elected President and Council of merchants, subordinate to the Committee of Merchants in London; the President and Council of five are to meet once a month; they are to submit names of persons to be appointed as magistrates.]

. . . 14. THE number of acting magistrates to be limited to five, and vacancies in that number to be filled up by the President and Council from those gentlemen who, agreeably to Rule No. 4, have received their commissions.

15. The President and Council to transmit to the committee every six months the names of any additional merchants who may have completed a residence of 12 months, and who are in their opinion fit persons to be appointed magistrates and members of Council, in order that if the Committee should concur in the same opinion, the names of such merchants may be submitted for the approbation of His Majesty's Government, that they may receive their commissions as magistrates.

16. A report of the state of the country, the forts, trade, &c. signed in the same manner, to be transmitted half-yearly.

17. The establishments at Cape Coast Castle and Accra, and the pay and allowances to the persons composing the same, to be stated in the annexed list.

18. The general principle of the establishment being voluntary service, the members of the Council and other British residents are to act without pecuniary reward in their several offices for the defence of the forts and preservation of order and good government, on which depend their own personal safety and commercial prosperity.

19. The secretary is restricted from trading, in order that his time be devoted entirely to the public service.

20. The captain of the guard is to perform the duties of captain

---

[1] *Parl. Papers*, 1842, xi (551), pp. 147–9. Sir George Murray had, however, insisted on retaining Cape Coast and Accra as dependencies of Sierra Leone, and was prepared to recommend up to £4,000 as an annual grant for their maintenance —a figure subsequently reduced by Lord Goderich to £3,500. See Harlow and Madden, op. cit., pp. 499–501.

and adjutant, attending personally to all the minutiae of the troops in which the lieutenants receiving no pay, and having their own concerns to attend to, can afford him little assistance beyond that which may result from the portion of attendance necessary to qualify themselves for their offices. He is also to perform the duty of engineer or surveyor of the repairs of the Castle, and deliver to the President and Council, for the purpose of being transmitted to the Committee, regular monthly returns, in duplicate, of the state and pay of the troops . . .

[The surgeon is to send returns of casualties; accounts of expenditure and inventories are to be forwarded to the Committee.]

26. Fifty men, in addition to the regular troops, are to be provided by the resident merchants and traders, in such manner and in such proportion as the President and Council may direct, to be trained, and exercised as a militia, so as to qualify them to assist in the defence of the forts when required.

27. All appointments at Cape Coast Castle to be made by the President and Council except when it may be required to send from this country a captain of the guard, surgeon, or secretary to the Council; in which case the appointments to those stations are to be made by the committee.

28. The President and Council to be empowered to suspend or dismiss any officer in their service for misconduct, incompetency or neglect of duty.

29. All judicial proceedings, both at Cape Coast Castle and Accra, to be conducted publicly, and in the presence of not less than two magistrates.

30. Apartments to be provided in the Castle for the Captain of the guard, surgeon secretary, and the persons in subordinate commands of the troops.

31. The President and Council may also allot apartments to other British residents, upon their engaging to keep them in repair.

32. The fort of Accra to be a dependency on Cape Coast Castle, under the management of the resident merchants; the officer to command the fort to be appointed by the President and Council, to whom he shall be accountable for the due application of the moneys issued to him, with a right of appeal to the committee, in all cases of dispute with the President and Council.

33. The salaries of the President, captain of the guard, surgeon, and secretary, to be paid by bills drawn by them respectively upon the committee, each bill to be marked with the signature of the secretary, as having been entered in the public accounts, and those drawn by the three last to be countersigned by the President.

34. The remainder of the grant to be applied by the Committee

to the purchase, shipment, and insurance of goods, for the pay of the troops and other necessary objects.

35. The passage-money of the officers sent from home to be paid by the committee.

36. The existing regulations established by the instrument by which the forts were transferred to the merchants by Major Ricketts, dated the 25th June last, or so many of them as the President and Council may deem necessary for the security of the persons and property of the inhabitants, and the preservation of order and good government in the place, to be continued under the direction of the magistrates.

37. The committee to be responsible to Government for the due application by them of the moneys voted by Parliament for the support of the forts.

(signed) George Barnes
Rob. Brown
M. Forster

J. G. Nicholls, Sec. London, 31 December 1828.
(Approved) George Murray, Downing-street, January 1829.

20

C. E. TREVELYAN TO JAMES STEPHEN: GOLD COAST FORTS, 10 JUNE 1840[1]

SIR,

The Lords Commissioners of Her Majesty's Treasury having had under their consideration your letter, dated 6th ultimo, transmitting copies of communications from the Secretary of the Admiralty, and Rear-Admiral the Hon. George Elliot, with a report from Captain Tucker on the state of the forts of Cape Coast Castle and Accra, I am commanded to acquaint you, for the information of Lord John Russell, that my Lords concur in the opinion, that the system at present prevailing of supplying slave-trading vessels from these forts should be put a stop to by Her Majesty's Government.

With respect to the course proposed to be adopted, their Lordships would suggest how far it would be practicable to stop this evil effectually, without taking the government of the forts into the hands of the Crown, and reverting to a system which, when it existed, was the subject of so much animadversion in the House of Commons.

---

[1] *Parl. Papers*, 1842, xi (551), p. 131. After the capture and condemnation of the Spanish slave vessel, *Dous Amigos*, which had traded for provisions at Cape Coast, Russell ordered an inquiry and pressed the Treasury for the resumption of Crown control over the forts to enforce the Act of 1824 (5 Geo. IV, c. 13) prohibiting British subjects from traffic with slavers. Reports by Commander William Tucker in 1840 and 1841 are in C.O. 267/167.

At present an allowance of 3,500 *l.* per annum (to which 500 *l.* per annum has been added for the last and present years) is made to the merchants for the keeping up of these forts. My Lords apprehend that this grant would never be made, if the country were aware that the protection of these forts is given to the slave trade; my Lords therefore consider, that the parties should be informed that no grant will be recommended to Parliament in a future year, if the system continues, and that some agent or officer should be appointed to reside at Cape Coast Castle, or in some other proper situation, to report to Her Majesty's Government the proceedings of the merchants and others in reference to this subject.

21

JAMES STEPHEN: MINUTE, GOLD COAST, 18 NOVEMBER 1841[1]

EVERY thing which comes from Cape Coast Castle strengthens my conviction that neither the Merchants here nor their Agents there are to be trusted. Here you observe a distinct acknowledgement that Mr. Hanson died possessed of some hundred domestic Slaves, and that this was well known to the home authorities, who employed them and paid for their services. That is Slavery went on in fact long after it was abolished in Law, and this was known both to Mr. McLean and to his employers. Mr. MacLean writes about Slavery and of the rashness of overturning the foundations of Society in the very terms and spirit of the West India Legislatures 10 years ago. We are surely not now to learn that the sooner such foundations are overturned the better, and that the Negro race are amongst the most inoffensive of the race of man in the enjoyment of freedom.

I take Mr. Barnes[2] to be an Attorney, or at least a Commercial man accustomed to Legal business. But he is no great Lawyer. I fear the same must be said of the Authors of the Rules which he quotes. By what lawful authority or precedent or principle a scheme of Colonial Govt. could be formed and set in action by such a document I cannot imagine. It is the single example I ever saw or heard of in which something like a compact between the Secretary of State and four gentlemen in London was drawn out as a substitute for an Act of Parliament or a Royal Commission. If it was designed to have the effect which Mr. Barnes ascribes to it, of detaching the Gold Coast Settlements from Sierra Leone, the framers of the Paper

---

[1] C.O. 267/165, on Maclean to Russell, 13 April 1841. J. W. Hanson had died leaving a large number of domestic slaves who were apprenticed out by Maclean.

[2] *George Barnes*, Gold Coast merchant and member of the Merchants' Committee in London. For the Rules, see above, p. 503.

must have forgotten—1st. That by an Act of Parliament of, I think, 1820,[1] those Settlements were placed under the authority of the Legislature of Sierra Leone, and secondly that the Commission of the Gov[ernor] of Sierra Leone gave him executive authority over them. Sir John Jeremie held such a Commission and had an undeniable right to exercise the power he assumed.

Besides this is a mere rudum pactum. These Gentlemen were nothing but Contractors to administer this Govt. cheaply. Mr. Attorney might as well complain of my taking my business into my own hands or of my substituting another Attorney for him. My right to do either is incontestable and not less clear is the right of the Govt. to control these Merchants or to supersede their authority altogether.

I ought perhaps to say that I never even heard of the arrangements of the Gold Coast Committee, till many months, perhaps some years, after they had been made, I, therefore, never had an opportunity of objecting to the Lawfulness of them. . . .

22

EXTRACT FROM THE SELECT COMMITTEE REPORT, 1842[2]

Gold Coast

IN the first place, then, we recommend that the Government of the British Forts upon the Gold Coast be resumed by the Crown, and that all dependance on the Government of Sierra Leone should cease.

We fully admit the merits of that Administration, whether we look to the Officer employed, Captain Maclean, or to the Committee under whom he has acted, which, with the miserable pittance of between 3,500 *l.* and 4,000 *l.* a year, has exercised, from the four ill-provided Forts of Dixcove, Cape Coast, Annamboe, and British Accra, manned by a few ill-paid black soldiers, a very wholesome influence over a Coast not much less than 150 miles in extent, and to a considerable distance inland; preventing within that range external Slave Trade, maintaining Peace and Security, and exercising a useful though irregular Jurisdiction, among the neighbouring Tribes, and much mitigating and in some cases extinguishing some of the most atrocious practices which had prevailed among them unchecked before. We would give full weight to the doubts which Captain Maclean entertained as to his authority, until specifically

---

[1] *Sic*, Statute 1 & 2 Geo. IV, c. 28 (7 May 1821).
[2] *Parl. Papers*, 1842, xi (551), pp. iv–v. The Committee met from 12 April and reported on 5 August 1842.

so instructed, to prevent vessels, suspected of being intended for the Slave Trade, but not having Slaves on board, from trafficking in lawful goods within his jurisdiction; and we do not infer from that circumstance, that the Government of these Forts had any partiality for an abominable Traffic, which, on the contrary, they have done much to check; but we think it desirable, for the sake of enlarging the sphere of usefulness of these Settlements, and of giving greater confidence in the character and impartiality of their Government, that it should be rendered completely independent of all connexion with Commerce, by a direct emanation of authority from the Crown, and that it should be placed, with increased resources, in direct and immediate communication with the general Government of the Empire.

We recommend, further, the reoccupation of several of the Forts, such as Apollonia, Winnebah and Whydah, abandoned in 1828, when the Government was handed over to the Committee of Merchants, and the reconstruction of others, on however small a scale, on other similar points. In some cases the climate will be found to be not worse, in others better, than on other parts of the coast of Africa; but this evil may be very much mitigated, if not entirely removed, by the employment of such Europeans only as are already inured to a tropical climate, and of British Subjects of African descent, who, we believe, may now be found, either within our African Settlements or our West India Colonies, fitted for almost every branch and grade of service; and we look upon such Establishments as of high importance, not for the extension of Territory, but of that control over the Slave Trade, and wholesome moral influence over the Neighbouring Chiefs, which we have described as having been exercised by the existing Forts, and which is much needed at those places to which we have particularly alluded, as well as others.

23

JAMES STEPHEN: MINUTE, RIGHTS OF BRITONS IN THE SETTLEMENTS, 20 JUNE 1842[1]

I CANNOT undertake to express an opinion (for I have no clear opinion) how far it wd. be prudent to state in answer to this Despatch, that which I believe to be the real answer to the greater part of it. It is this—

If some 50 or 60 of the Queen's subjects will settle themselves as a distinct Community in a settlement some hundreds of miles distant

[1] C.O. 87/28. On a memorial by the 'Merchants and Inhabitants of Bathurst' 2 April 1842, requesting a charter of government, courts, and a legislative assembly.

from any other British Colony, they have no fair right to expect the advantages of the Institutions, Legislative, Judicial and Financial of the other parts of the British Dominions. They cannot afford to pay for them: and the British Treasury ought not to afford it. In the very nature of such an enterprise it is implied that all parties will submit to the inconveniences of living under a very rude system of law & of Judicial Administration. They have not the materials from which Legislative and Judicial Bodies could safely and properly be composed. If we paid a Judge to live there he must pass $\frac{4}{5}$ of his time in idleness. A Queen's Advocate was sent there, and it was soon found out that there was nothing for him to do. If a Legislature were to be established there would hardly be a white man in the place, who wd. not either be one of the Legislators or a Partner or a near kinsman or an inveterate enemy of one of them. I should answer the complaint if it might be answered frankly by admitting that it was at once quite true, and incurable.

The moment men become Colonists, no matter where, they set up pretentions, which at home in a parallel situation no one dreams of making. There are many parts of the British Islands where Inhabitants might complain with equal truth and much greater reason, of grievances like those of the Gambia Merchants: but no such complaints are made because every one at home feels that if he settles himself in places extremely remote from the Metropolis, he must abandon the Metropolitan advantages of being well looked after by the Legislature, the Magistracy, the Police, and so on.

The mischiefs of a local Legislature, of local Courts, and of a local management of Finances in these petty Settlements where they do exist, afford topics of complaint quite as strong as any which the Merchants of the Gambia have to allege . . .

[The example of the West Indies is cited as a warning against peculation and legislative inactivity.]

Assemblies in such places have for centuries preferred to have a noxious marsh to windward of the Capital Town to the expense of draining it. In fact I believe that a bad Govt. or extremely defective Govt. is the essential condition of all such Societies, and that it is a mere illusion to pretend to rescue Colonists in that situation from that inconvenience. Of course it should be done as much as possible, but this is not the aim and object of the Gambia Merchants. Their complaint really is that a mere handful of men cannot have advantages which belong to the Members of a large Society.

24

G. W. HOPE: MEMORANDUM, WEST COAST OF AFRICA, 3 DECEMBER 1842[1]

MR STEPHEN,

I send you with this a copy of the Report of the Committee upon the West Coast of Africa.

Of the recommendations contained in that Report, Lord Stanley proposes as soon as it can be done, to carry into effect some, abandoning or postponing others.

I   As to the Gold Coast.

1st. Lord Stanley proposes to resume the Government into the hands of the Crown as recommended; but does not adopt the further proposal of making it independent of Sierra Leone, considering the Settlements as forts or factories, rather than Colonies.

2nd. He is prepared to appoint a Judicial Officer as well as a Governor—such Judicial Officer to have the jurisdiction, or rather the duty proposed by the Committee, of trying cases beyond the actual British Dominions, by consent of the Natives. The range of British dominion he proposes to confine, as at present in strictness it is, to the walls of the Fort.

3rd. He considers the appointment of a Chaplain or some one to take charge of the Intestate Estates, advisable. Possibly this latter duty might be combined with the Judicial Officer.

4th. He proposes to make the pay of the Troops really in amount what it is now only nominally—being paid in Merchandise; but otherwise he does not wish materially to increase the establishments at first.

On the further alterations suggested by the Committee, he is, I think, inclined to suspend his judgment until he shall have a report from whoever is sent out as Governor.

II   As to the Gambia.

1st. He is not adverse to the employment of a Steamer for the river, as suggested; but on this, he wishes the Admiralty to be consulted, in order to judge of the expense.

2d. He adopts the separation of the Govt. from that of Sierra Leone, with the appointment of a judicial Officer & a Legislature to consist of a Governor and Council—the Governor having power to act on his own responsibility; but he postpones acting on the other suggestions.

[1] C.O. 96/2.

III   As to Sierra Leone.

The principal suggestions, as far as this office is concerned, having reference to Emigration, and that subject being now under separate consideration with the West India Body,[1] I need not here advert to them.

On the advisability of the changes proposed, however, and on the question how they can be legally effected, Lord Stanley wishes, before proceeding further, to have your views, tho' I think the alterations would not be attended with any great legal difficulty, except as regards the very anomalous position of the Judicial Officer on the Gold Coast.

The maintenance of the Troops on their existing footing,—they being not in fact (or rather not de jure though de facto) under martial law would also, I apprehend, be attended in point of form, with some awkwardness: and as Lord Stanley does not wish, at present at all events, to have them converted into a part of the regular army, Mr. Smith's suggestion of directing the Governor of Sierra Leone to pass an Ordinance embodying them as a Militia, wd. seem the simplest mode of acquiring some legal power of maintaining discipline. . . .

25

JAMES STEPHEN: MINUTE, WEST AFRICAN SETTLEMENTS, 26 DECEMBER 1842[2]

. . . 1. FOR the resumption of the Government of the Gold Coast no formality whatever is necessary. The functions of the Committee of Merchants rest entirely on a Despatch from this Office, and by a similar Despatch they may be abrogated.

2. The Judicial Officer who is to execute beyond the precincts of the Queen's Dominions Justice rather than Law, would be encumbered rather than aided by any form of legal appointment. There is no apparent good reason why a Judicature, which in its exercise is to be quite independent of all positive Law, should in its institution seek a legal basis. All the manuscript and Seals which legal subtlety could bring together would of course be unavailing to legalise the appointment of an English Judge beyond the Queen's Dominions except indeed as an Act of Parlt. might be said to render it legal within the local range of the Authority of Parlt. But how to frame such an Act is I suppose an insoluble problem.[3] We are about to make an usurpation which the goodness of our motives, and the

---

[1] *Parl. Papers*, 1842, xiii (479).   [2] C.O. 96/2.
[3] For the Foreign Jurisdiction Act, 24 August 1843, see below, p. 549.

necessity of the case are to justify, and I suppose that such a justification would not be improved by an abortive attempt to give a semblance of Law to that which, ex hypothesi, is to be lawless. If the Arbiter Judge is fit for the employment, he will not be critical about his Commission.

3. The appointment of a Chaplain is of course to be effected by a Letter to the Treasury, followed by a Despatch to the Head of the local Govt.

4. As it is decided that the Government is to charge itself with the Care of 'Intestate Estates' (you mean of course the Estates of unrepresented deceased persons, whether Testate or Intestate) a Law will be necessary for that purpose, and such a Law ought I apprehend to be of local origin.

5. As to the pay of the Troops, this of course is the subject of a Letter to the Treasury, and requires no other formality.

6. With regard to the employment of a Steamer for the Gambia, it will of course be necessary to write to the Admiralty for an Estimate of the Expense and to the Treasury for an authority for it.

7. As the Settlements at the Gambia are to form a distinct Colony with distinct legislative and Judicial Establishments, an Act of Parliament will for two reasons be necessary for that purpose,— first, because an existing Act of Parlt. has provided otherwise[1]— secondly, because the projected institutions are not such as it is competent to the Crown in the unaided exercise of the Royal prerogative to create.

8. If the Government of the Troops at the Gold Coast and at the Gambia cannot be placed under the British Mutiny Act, it must of course be provided for by local Enactments—altho perhaps the word 'Militia Law' is not the most accurate term by which such an Enactment could be described. . . .

[He has abandoned the attempt to express an opinion on the 'advisability' of these changes.]

It could answer no good purpose to trouble Lord Stanley, or you, with an argument to prove, that the recommendations of the Committee are wrong, not in details, but in their essence. Yet such is the only opinion which I could express on the 'advisability' of these changes, if I wrote what I really thought. I would not be deterred from doing so by the dread of appearing arrogant if there could be the slightest prospect of any advantage from the attempt. But to what end trouble you with a discussion to prove, that the value of these African Settlements, to our Commerce, or that their utility as preventives of the Slave Trade is enormously exaggerated—that in

---

[1] Statute 1 & 2 Geo. IV, c. 28 (1821) and letters patent placing the forts and settlements under the government of Sierra Leone.

fact they are nothing else than Factories kept up at the expense of the Nation at large for the profit of half a dozen inconsiderable Merchants, who avail themselves of our national sensibility on every subject on which the Commercial wealth or the National importance of Great Britain are concerned—that the Trade of them all put together is of less value to us, present or prospective, than the Trade with the Isle of Skye—that we are recklessly increasing & dispersing our Colonial Empire in all directions and creating a demand for Naval and Military Force which there are no means of meeting, except by weakening that Force where its presence is most needed—that in short neither the Gambia nor the Gold Coast are worth retaining—or that, if retained, they should be placed exclusively in the hands of the Mulattoes or Negroes from the West Indies, and left to maintain themselves like the American Settlements of Liberia. . . .

P.S. The Act of Parliament for creating a Legislature at the Gambia would merely authorize the Queen to create a Legislative Council either by nominating the Members of it, or by a delegation whether partial or total of that power to the Gov[ernor] and would declare that the Gov[ernor] with the advice of the Legislative Council when so nominated shd. have power to make Laws for the peace, order and good government of the Settlement, such Laws not being repugnant to the Law of England, but being subject to be confirmed or disallowed by the Queen in such manner and on such conditions as the Queen should appoint.

26

G. W. HOPE: MINUTE, WEST AFRICAN SETTLEMENTS, 30 JANUARY 1843[1]

Ld. Stanley,

Pray see my minute to Mr Stephen of decr. 3d. & his reply.

I think that from the nature of our settlements on the W. Coast of Africa it would be much better if the power of legislating for them were vested as in the case of conquered Colonies in the Crown. The term Colonies in fact seems one which the effects of the climate on Europeans will probably never permit to be properly applicable to them and to extend to places where Englishmen can't live the doctrine that they carry when they go there, their rights with them, seems absurd.

I would propose therefore to bring in an Act giving such power to the Crown as regards the whole Sett[lements] on the West Coast of Africa. We also propose as you will remember to include in the same Bill Port Essington[2] & the Falkland Islands. . . .

[1] C.O. 96/2. On no. 25.
[2] A settlement in the northern territory of Australia.

27

THE WEST AFRICAN SETTLEMENTS AND FALKLAND ISLANDS ACT, 11 APRIL 1843 (6 & 7 VICT., c. 13)[1]

WHEREAS divers of Her Majesty's subjects have resorted to and taken up their abode in divers places on or adjacent to the coast of the continent of Africa and on the Falkland Islands: And whereas it is necessary that Her Majesty should be enabled to make further and better provision for the civil government of the said settlements: Be it therefore enacted by the Queen's most Excellent Majesty, by and with the advice and consent of the Lords Spiritual and Temporal, and Commons, in this present Parliament assembled, and by the authority of the same, That it shall be lawful for Her Majesty, by any order or orders to be by Her made, with the advice of Her Privy Council, to establish all such laws, institutions, and ordinances, and to constitute such courts and officers, and to make such provisions and regulations for the proceedings in such courts, and for the administration of justice, as may be necessary for the peace, order, and good government of Her Majesty's subjects and others within the said present or future settlements respectively, or any of them; any law, statute, or usage to the contrary in anywise notwithstanding.

2. And be it enacted, That it shall be lawful for Her Majesty, by any commission or commissions under the Great Seal of the United Kingdom, or by any instructions under Her Majesty's signet and sign manual, accompanying and referred to in any such commission or commissions, to delegate to any three or more persons within any of the settlements aforesaid respectively the powers and authorities so vested in Her Majesty in Council as aforesaid, either in whole or in part, and upon, under, and subject to all such conditions, provisoes, and limitations as by any such commission or commissions or instructions as aforesaid Her Majesty shall see fit to prescribe: Provided always, that notwithstanding any such delegation of authority as aforesaid, it shall still be competent to Her Majesty in Council, in manner aforesaid, to exercise all the powers and authorities so vested as aforesaid in Her Majesty in Council: Provided also, that all such Orders in Council, commissions, and instructions as aforesaid, and all laws and ordinances so to be made as aforesaid, shall be laid before both Houses of Parliament as soon as conveniently may be after the making and enactment there of respectively.

3. And be it enacted, That this Act may be amended or repealed by any Act to be passed in this Session of Parliament.

[1] *Parl. Papers*, 1855 xxxvii (383), pp. 3–4.

28

LETTERS PATENT: CONSTITUTION OF THE GAMBIA SETTLEMENTS, 24 JUNE 1843[1]

[The Letters Patent of 20 December 1841 are revoked]

... AND we do hereby order, direct and appoint that all and every— our said territories, islands, and possessions in the River Gambia and its dependencies, do forthwith cease to be annexed to and be dependencies on the said colony of Sierra Leone: And further know you, that, in pursuance and exercise of the powers so vested in us aforesaid by the said receited Act of Parliament passed in the sixth year of our reign, we, of our especial grace, certain knowledge, and mere motion, by this commission under the Great Seal of the United Kingdom aforesaid, delegate to the persons hereinafter named, within the said settlements in the River Gambia and their dependencies, the powers and authorities so vested in us in our Privy Council as aforesaid; but upon, under, and subject to all such conditions, provisoes, and limitations as by this our commission, or by the instructions under our signet and sign manual accompanying the same, are prescribed: And we do declare our pleasure to be, and do hereby declare and grant, that the Governor for the time being of the said settlements in the River Gambia and of their dependencies, and such other persons, not being less than two, as are hereinafter designated, shall constitute and be a Legislative Council for the said territories, islands, and possessions: And we do hereby direct and appoint, that the persons other than the said Governor constituting the said Legislative Council be such public officers within the said settlements and their dependencies as shall be designated, or such others persons within the same as shall from time to time be named for that purpose by us, by any instruction or instructions, or warrant or warrants, to be by us for that purpose issued under our signet and sign manual, and with the advice of our Privy Council, all of which Councillors shall hold their places in the said council at our pleasure.

And we do hereby authorise, empower, and enjoin such Legislative Council to make and establish all such laws, institutions, and ordinances as may from time to time be necessary for the peace, order, and good government of our subjects and others within the said present or future settlements in the River Gambia and in its dependencies; and our pleasure is, that in the making and establishing all

[1] *Parl. Papers*, 1855, xxxvii (383), pp. 44–45. Similar charters were issued for the Gold Coast, 24 January 1850, Lagos, 5 March 1862, and Sierra Leone, 27 May 1863.

such laws, institutions, and ordinances, the said Legislative Council shall conform to and observe all such rules and regulations as shall be given and prescribed in and by such instructions as we, with the advice of our Privy Council, shall from time to time make for their guidance therein: Provided nevertheless, and we do hereby reserve to ourselves, our heirs and successors, our and their right and authority to disallow any such ordinances in the whole or in part, and to make and establish from time to time, with the advice and consent of Parliament, or with the advice of our or their Privy Council, all such laws as may to us or them appear necessary for the order, peace, and good government of our said settlements and their dependencies, as fully as if these presents had not been made.

And whereas it is expedient that an Executive Council should be appointed to advise and assist the Governor of our said settlements in the Gambia, and of their dependencies for the time being, in the administration of the government thereof, we do by these our Letters Patent authorise the Governor of our said settlements and of their dependencies to summon as an Executive Council such persons as may from time to time be named or designated by us in any instructions under our signet and sign manual, addressed to him in that behalf . . .

[The Governor is authorized to keep a public seal.]

. . . And we do hereby give and grant to the Governor of our said settlements and of their dependencies, for the time being, full power and authority, in our name and on our behalf, but subject, nevertheless, to such provisions as may be in that respect contained in any instructions which may from time to time be addressed to him by us for that purpose, to make and execute in our name and on our behalf, under the public seal of our said settlements, grants of land to us belonging within the same to private persons for their own use and benefit, or to any persons, bodies politic or corporate, in trust for the public uses of our subjects there resident, or of any of them.

And we do hereby authorise and empower the Governor of our said settlements in the Gambia and of their dependencies, for the time being, to constitute and appoint judges, and, in cases requisite, commissioners of oyer and terminer, justices of the peace, and other necessary officers and ministers in our said settlements, for the due and impartial administration of justice, and for putting the laws into execution, and to administer, or cause to be administered, unto them such oath or oaths as are usually given, for the due execution and performance of offices and places, and for the clearing of truth in judicial matters.

And we do hereby give and grant unto the Governor of our said Settlements in the Gambia and of their dependencies, for the time being, full power and authority, as he shall see occasion, in our name and on our behalf, to remit any fines, penalties, or forfeitures which may accrue or become payable to us, provided the same do not exceed the sum of 50 *l.* sterling in any one case; and to respite and suspend the payment of any such fine, penalty or forfeiture exceeding the sum of 50 *l.* until our pleasure thereon shall be made known and signified to such Governor.

And we do hereby give and grant unto the Governor of our said settlements in the Gambia and of their dependencies, for the time being, full power and authority, as he shall see occasion, in our name and on our behalf, to grant to any offender convicted of any crime in any court, or before any judge, justice, or magistrate within our said settlements, a free and unconditional pardon subject to such condition as by any law or ordinance hereafter to be in force in our said settlements may be thereunto annexed, or any respite of the execution of the sentence of any such offender, for such period as to such Governnor may seem fit.

And we do hereby give and grant unto the Governor of our said settlements in the Gambia and of their dependencies, for the time being, full power and authority, upon sufficient cause to him appearing, to suspend from the exercise of his office within our said settlements any person exercising any office or place under or by virtue of any commission or warrant granted, or which may be granted, by us. . . .

[In the case of death or absence of the Governor, the Lieutenant-Governor or the Colonial Secretary is to administer the settlements.]

29

GOVERNOR N. W. MACDONALD TO EARL GREY: SIERRA LEONE LEGISLATIVE COUNCIL, 11 FEBRUARY 1847[1]

. . . WITH reference to the Return of the form of the Government of this Colony, I have prepared it in accordance with the terms of the Charter, which in my opinion confers a Legislative but no executive Council on the Colony; at all events my Lord ever since I have had the honor to serve here it has always been held by the whole of my Predecessors in the Government, as well as by the Council itself, that there is no Executive Council properly so called, but that the Executive Authority is vested in the Governor alone.

Should they however, as well as myself have been in error on this point, may I respectfully request Your Lordship will be pleased to

[1] C.O. 267/197.

declare how the executive Council is, or ought to be composed; for it would appear desirable, should such a Council be deemed necessary here that, like other Crown Colonies, where an Executive Council exists, it should not be constituted of the whole of the present members of the Legislative Council.

It is perhaps right that I should here remark my Lord, that the Governor has often occasion to submit matters of an executive nature for the consideration of the Council as at present constituted; and has on most occasions received their opinion thereupon (instances are however not wanting wherein the Council considering themselves strictly a Legislative body, have respectfully declined to entertain or give any opinion on an Executive question submitted to them). But the mere fact of the Council entertaining under their consideration an Executive measure, in their desire to assist the Governor, would scarcely, I opine my Lord, be sufficient to cloth them with the character, as well as the responsibility of an 'Executive Council'. For in the present opinion, as regards the character of the Council, an opinion I have never heard questioned, viz. that it is not Executive, it is *optional* with the Governors to submit, or not as he thinks proper any Executive question for their consideration; whereas were there an acknowledged Executive Council it would, I presume my Lord, *be imperative* on the Governor to submit all executive matters to them beforehand for their decision; a course which, in my humble opinion my Lord, would tend rather to impede, than to advance the public service, for I cannot conscientiously aver my Lord, that here, there is either wisdom or safety, at all times, in the multitude of Councillors. . . .

30

JAMES STEPHEN: MINUTE, SIERRA LEONE LEGISLATIVE COUNCIL, 12 APRIL 1847[1]

THE explanation (which I ought to have given before) is as follows:—
It is debated whether, under the existing Charter, the Council are, or are not, a Body bound to advise the Gov. in his Executive capacity; & of course the obvious way of answering that enquiry is by saying what the charter means. But that is (to myself at least) an insuperable difficulty. Of all the legal Instrumts. which I ever examined it is the most hopelessly obscure. I understand it to have been prepared by a Gentleman who was formerly a Clerk in this Office & probably it is the only document of the kind he ever read. What he meant by the

[1] C.O. 267/197. Stephen had already recorded his opinion that the 1821 Charter gave legislative power to the Sierra Leone Governor and Council 'in the most indistinct and circuitous terms', but the Crown had never given executive power outside the boundaries of the colony. Minute, 18 April 1841: C.O. 267/163.

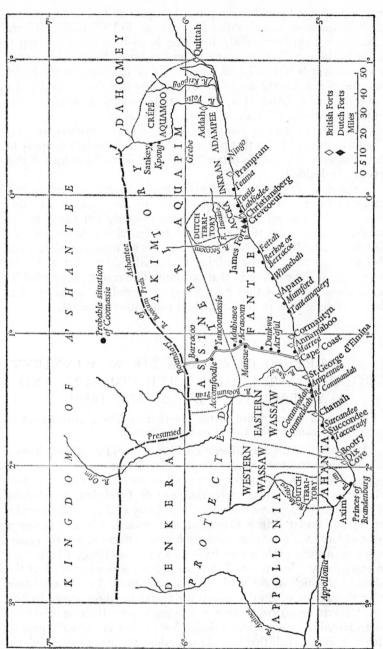

Map 6: The Gold Coast Forts and Interior, 1865.

greater part of it I could never guess. I suspect he had no meaning at all. The question whether the [Legislature D.] Council of Sierra Leone is a Legislative Body has long been involved in as much doubt as the question whether it is an Executive Body. Many years ago some words were slipped into an Act of Parliamt. in the belief that they wd. settle the doubt by ascertaining that the Council had a power to make Laws. The power at this moment rests on that foundation which, after all, is but an equivocal one.

You may ask then why not long since set all these matters straight. The answer is, that, for that purpose, it wd. be necessary to apply to Parliamt. & to tell a story better kept out of sight. So at least it was repeatedly decided.

In the case of S. Leone it seems to me wise or necessary to look rather to the practice than to the Law—to the sense put on this Instrumt. by custom than to the sense properly belonging to the words. Besides, I shd. think that it wd. be desirable to know not only how far this Body has de facto been acting as a Council of advice; but also to know what is the opinion of the Members of it as to the advantage of their acting in that capacity. The result will, probably, be to show, first that they have always so acted, &, secondly, that their own judgmt is in favour of their continuing so to act.

31

EARL GREY TO GOVERNOR SIR W. WINNIETT, GOLD COAST LEGISLATIVE COUNCIL AND ASSEMBLY, 19 DECEMBER 1850[1]

[There is to be no return to the pre-1842 system of government as suggested by some of the Gold Coast merchants.]

. . . BUT, on the fullest consideration I can give to the subject, it does not appear to me that any advantage which might result from such a measure would compensate for the evil of an alteration in a system which has been as yet, scarcely tried; nor do I feel that the relations of the local Government with that great body of Native Tribes who are already under British Protection and towards whom it is now a great object to render that protection more effective, are yet established on a sufficiently secure basis to warrant a change which must so extensively effect them. But I am not the less persuaded of the advantages which would result in some cases to the Local Legislature from the advice of the European residents, to whom every facility ought therefore to be given for making known their opinions on measures which are in contemplation before they are actually passed. Hence it is my wish that you should adopt the practice (already in

[1] C.O. 96/19.

force in Ceylon, where, as in your Government, there is a considerable commercial Body unrepresented in the Legislature) of publishing drafts of intended Ordinances in some easily accessible shape, with a view to invite comments and representations respecting them. Such comments would be entitled to increased weight if they came from any body authorized to declare the opinions of the Commercial community. I should accordingly be glad if a Chamber of Commerce, or some similar Institution could be established.

[No more members are to be admitted to the Legislative Council;[1] he agrees with the suggestion to use the Fanti chiefs as local government agents.]

. . . 8. With this view I fully approve of the proposal (which was, in fact, anticipated by my Despatch of 14th August) for constituting a yearly meeting of Chiefs, to make, under proper superintendence, and subject to the confirmation of the Governor, general Laws and Regulations for the management of the Native Tribes. And I hope that the difficulties attending such a project will not prove so considerable as they may at first sight appear; since the practice of meeting together and making Laws or Treaties by common consent seems to be in accordance with the ordinary habits of many African races.

9. I approve also of the proposal of making an annual payment to such Chiefs as should form part of the Assembly. What ought to be the amount of that payment is a question of some difficulty. I understand Messrs. Bannerman and Cruickshank to propose a small one merely with the view of making up for the loss of those Presents which were formerly made to the Chiefs by the British Government. I am of the opinion that the measure should go further, and I should approve of their receiving salaries on a more liberal footing so as to compensate them for the loss of the advantages which they formerly derived from their power of compelling their followers to submit to their exactions. If I am correctly informed as to the state of society which existed in this part of Africa before it was modified by the influence of British power, the Chiefs were enabled to maintain their station and to live in the manner considered suitable to their rank, by means of exactions of a very arbitrary character, and by the forced and gratuitous services of their people. These sources of income could not but fail with the establishment of a more regular system of Government, and it would be good policy to prevent the discontent which this is calculated to excite in the Chiefs, and give them a substantial interest in the maintenance of the protectorate, by allowing them as a substitute for what they have lost, salaries or emoluments sufficient for their support in a style of living fully equal to

[1] The Gold Coast Legislative Council consisted of the Governor, the Judicial Assessor (later Chief Justice), the Collector of Customs, and two merchants.

that to which they have been accustomed, the duty being imposed upon them in return of acting as the Executive Officers of the Government in maintaining order and carrying the law into effect. Great care should be taken to make the performance of these duties the condition on which the proposed payments should be made, lest they should reduce those who might receive them to the character of idle dependents on the Government.

10. I have said that the condition on which the Chiefs should receive these salaries ought to be that of maintaining the general regulations which may be established, and enforcing order in their several districts. For this purpose they should have the assistance of a certain number of the inhabitants of each district, who (if this slight distinction were likely to afford any encouragement to their exertions) might be enrolled as Constables, receiving some small annual fee for this trouble. The Chiefs should not have the power of inflicting punishments for offences by their own authority: but should be required to bring the offenders to be dealt with by the nearest Magistrate.

11. To provide the funds necessary for making these payments and meeting some other expenses for which provision will I think be required, it appears to me most advisable to have recourse to taxes on lands and houses, or perhaps to a poll-tax. . . .

[The revenues from taxation are to be used for roads, medical care, education, accommodation for officials and hospitals, as in New Zealand].

32

GOVERNOR S. W. BLACKALL TO THE DUKE OF NEWCASTLE: LEGISLATIVE COUNCIL REPRESENTATION, 16 DECEMBER 1863[1]

MY LORD DUKE,

I have the honor to acknowledge the receipt of Your Grace's Confidential Despatch of [18th] October 1863. And in conformity with the instructions therein contained, I communicated to the Merchants Your Grace's permission that they should recommend one of their Body for a Seat in the Legislative Council of this Colony.

2. In order to detain the opinion of the Merchants in the most legitimate manner, I called for a return from the Collector of Customs of the names of the thirty largest Importers during the current year. From this list I selected six Gentlemen whom I know to have taken most interest in the late Chamber of Commerce and Mercantile

1 C.O. 267/268.

Association,[1] both of which may be said to have become extinct, and I requested them to form themselves into a Committee, to put the Mercantile Body together, if possible revive their Association, and to obtain in the manner most agreeable to themselves the recommendation of the Merchants generally.

3. I enclose to Your Grace a Copy of the proceedings which were held and a Letter from five of the Committee announcing that Mr. Ezzidio[2] was recommended for a seat in the Council to represent the Mercantile Body for three years.

4. At the same time Your Grace will perceive that the recommendation was not unanimous, and the Merchants request further weight at the Board.

5. I have thought it right however to accept Mr. Ezzidio's appointment and I have nominated him to a seat in the Legislative Council subject to Your Grace's approval and also subject to any limitation of time Your Grace may determine, as to the right of the member so chosen to a seat in the Council.

6. It appears to me that on the whole, considering this to be the first time that the Mercantile Body were called on to act together, the result is not unsatisfactory, though no doubt a more educated representative than Mr. Ezzidio could have readily been selected, but he has been I believe ere now the organ of a powerful Body here and I consider there will be no longer any excuse for outdoor Petitions from these Parties, as their grievances can be brought under the immediate notice of the Council and Executive.

7. In such a Colony as this, and in a first attempt such as this, I need hardly say that *Color* as to choice was made a material element. The anticipations of this caused me to make the suggestion to Your Grace in my original Despatch that one Merchants should be selected by that Body and that I should have the power of naming another. Your Grace will perceive that there is a strong desire that Mr. Levi,[3] who had a considerable number of Votes should be placed in the Council, as well as Mr. Ezzidio. I have undertaken to place this request before Your Grace, but if Your Grace considers that the official Predominance would be too seriously lessened by such an addition it might be intimated to Mr. Levi that his claims would be considered on the first vacancy.

8. At the same time I have to submit to Your Grace that it will be most imperative to make the 'Treasurer' a Member of the Legislative

---

[1] The Mercantile Association, revived in 1863, was constituted as a Chamber of Commerce in 1864.

[2] *John Ezzidio*, a Nupe liberated slave, had been clerk, trader, preacher, and Mayor of Freetown. Kennedy later appointed a second unofficial member, the African trader, *William Grant*.

[3] John Levi's appointment to Council had been allowed to lapse.

Council next year which would add another official, as against one more non official Member.

33

GOVERNOR S. W. BLACKALL TO EDWARD CARDWELL: REORGANIZATION OF THE SETTLEMENTS, 21 SEPTEMBER 1864[1]

[The West African posts have been instrumental in checking the slave trade as much as the Squadron.]

... 11. I DO not think, then, that the expenditure of £18,355 for the Settlements on the West Coast of Africa can be considered extravagant or without valuable return to British interests; and I will proceed to consider how far the Governors of these Colonies are outside the control of the Colonial Secretary.

12. A regular monthly steam communication is now established between these settlements and Liverpool. A Despatch from Lagos, the most distant of these Settlements, would leave on the 8th (say of August,) and arrive at Liverpool on the 10th of September. A reply leaving Liverpool on the 24th September reaches Lagos on the 23rd. October, being a course of Post of 76 days. But from Sierra Leone or the Gambia the course of Post is little more than half that period; and I shall allude to this hereafter, as one reason for the scheme which I should propose regarding the future Government of these Settlements.

13. Taking 76 days, however, as the course of Post, it cannot be fairly said that the Governors of the West Coast of Africa are far removed from the control of the Secretary of State. Excepting the North American, and some of the West Indian Colonies, none are so much within it; and though it may be necessary to act without authority on an emergency, such as an absolute attack on our own Settlement, I am satisfied no Governor of the present day would engage in hostilities without the sanction of the Secretary of State; and late proceedings in the Gold Coast amply prove this...

[14-15, events at Lagos were known to the House of Commons; 16, West African posts helped to end the slave trade; 17, governors should be paid, as in Sierra Leone from the Imperial Chest, not through the local legislature; 18-20, the use of Parliamentary votes can be justified by the need for communications, defence and the extension of trade.]

21.... I should propose one General Government in place of the present four Governments in the Settlements on this Coast. I conceive that one Policy carried out by whoever may be appointed to the General Government, would be more likely to be in accordance with

[1] C.O. 267/281. Occasioned by a report of a Commons Debate on West African Estimates, *The Times*, 19 July 1864.

the Home policy than the present of what I must call four Policies.

22. I call these 'Four Policies' because there is given to each settlement a Colonial Staff, with high sounding titles, executive and legislative functions, all independent one of another. The consequence has been, so far as I understand, that the Merchants at the Gambia are in the ascendant; certainly at Sierra Leone the Governor, aided by his Executive Council, which is well selected, and composed of valuable and tried public servants, is the ruling Power; at Cape Coast Castle, judging from an extract which I give from a Despatch written by Commodore Wilmot, during the late occurrences there, the Governor appears to be without any valuable advice, and more likely to be bewildered than assisted by his Councillors, who are a democracy in themselves. . . .

24. At Lagos, on the contrary, the complaint appears to be that the Governor is an 'Autocrat', and neither possesses nor desires any councillors.

25. At each of these stations we have, as I have observed, a civil staff with high sounding names, in addition to Governors in Chief and Commanders of the Forces; Vice Admirals and Chancellors of the same. We have Colonial Secretaries, Chief Justices, Collectors of Customs; but in addition we have officers commanding the Troops, and Commissariat and Medical Staff. With regard to the Civil branch, they are generally paid, (and, consequently, underpaid,) from Colonial funds; thereby pretty well insuring an inferior class of men, particularly where professional education is required; whilst the military expenditure is an many cases unnecessary and wasteful.

26. It is then to remedy these evils and to reduce expenditure, that I propose a 'point d'appui' nearer than England by establishing a Government at Sierra Leone which should control other settlements. . . .

[27-28, centralisation would end anomalies in the military command of the Settlements; governors should be employed who have had experience outside Africa; 30-31, three colonial steamers should be attached to Sierra Leone; 32-35, the squadron could be reduced, blockades enforced.]

36. A great deal has been said and written against our extension of territory in Africa, and the dangers and expense consequent thereon, with remarks that we should not be led away by a desire for extending our Rule. This is true to a certain extent; but like many other general rules, is subject to exceptions. Judicious extension of Territory may lead to increased powers of self support on the part of the Colony. I believe that by judiciously entering into arrangements for the acquisition of Territory by Treaty, from the Native Chiefs on the Sea board, we should do more to relieve England from the expense of the Squadron for suppression of the Slave Trade, than by any other

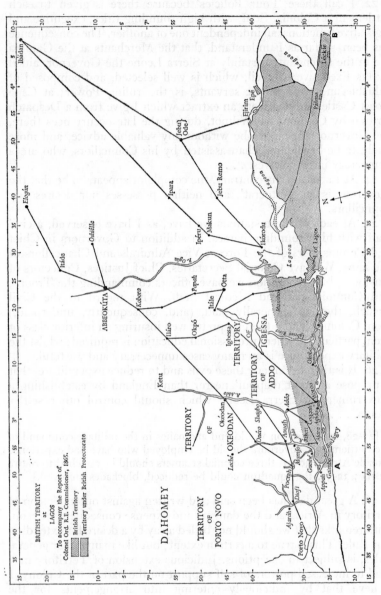

Map 7: British Territory at Lagos, 1865.

means; more particularly if we can obtain establishments at the outlets of the large Rivers. We should also have great control in preventing disturbances in the interior by regulating commerce, and whilst we prevented the export of Slaves, we might, when necessary, prohibit the importation of arms and ammunition.

37. If Parliament will really take into its consideration the whole of the Imperial expenditure on the West Coast:—not the Civil expenditure only, I think considerable reduction may be effected; but it will be utterly useless to enter on this enquiry, with any hope of real reduction of expenditure, or improvement, as to the settlements on the Coast, if it is to be confined to the small amount of about £19,600, and if the only question raised be—whether this sum should be withdrawn, and the Settlements left entirely to their own resources, I cannot help saying that I think much higher and more important results should be sought for, and expected from such an enquiry.

38. Our relations with Foreign Powers should be better regulated. It is well known that the English and French policies of Colonization are materially different; but there is no reason why they should be made, as they apparently are at present, antagonistic. We had our Settlement at the Gambia River, I believe, before the French looked to Trade therein; but, at present, the complaint at the Gambia is that the French, having obtained access to the Gambia River, have much injured British commerce. At Sierra Leone a different policy has been successfully pursued. But again—at Lagos—no sooner had we commenced levying customs dues in order to raise a revenue than the French Government took possession of Porto Novo, and declared it a Free Port, interfering seriously with the Port of Lagos. I believe it indubitable that every one 'on the spot' advised, at the time of the Establishment of Lagos, that Porto Novo, and Whydah, if possible should also be occupied; but that fear of increase of Territory causing increased expense weighed, I presume, with the British Government; though no doubt this is one of the instances (and I would give others,) where a judicious extension of Territory would ensure larger means of support.

39. It appears to me that it would be advantageous both to France and England if the Governments would come to some definite arrangement regarding their Settlements on this Coast, by which this mutual jealousy and interference might be avoided; and I would advise this even at the cost of an exchange which might, in the first instance, appear disadvantageous. . . .

[40, the French emigration scheme is as justifiable as recruitment of coolies from India and China; 41, 'protectorates' should be avoided because of the problem of domestic slavery; 42, but slaves once on British territory should not be returned.]

34

COLONEL H. ST. GEORGE ORD TO THE RIGHT HON. C. S. FORTESCUE: REORGANIZATION OF THE SETTLEMENTS, 12 JUNE 1865[1]

... The first step that suggests itself is the appointment of a Governor in Chief for the whole of the settlements, who should also be Governor of Sierra Leone, the administrators of the Gambia, Gold Coast, and Lagos, being termed Lieutenant Governors, and holding the same position in respect to the Governor in Chief as do the Lieutenant Governors of the Windward and Leeward Islands, in the West Indies, to the Governors in Chief of Antigua and Barbados.

The Lieutenant Governors would have the assistance within their own settlements of an Executive Council, and the object of these Councils being not so much to support the policy of the Executive as to give advice in questions of emergency, it would be well that they should be composed chiefly of gentlemen of ability and local experience in colonial affairs, and not exclusively of officials.

The Governor in Chief should also have the aid of a similar Council, which should be entirely distinct from the Executive Council of Sierra Leone, and be termed the Council of General Government; and of this General Council the Lieutenant Governors and the members of the minor councils would also form a part, and thus in any question affecting the interests of a Colony, its Lieutenant-Governor and some of its Council could be summoned to Sierra Leone, to give the Governor in Chief the benefit of their local experience, or the Governor in Chief could hold his Council in the Colony, with the aid of members of the General Council brought from Sierra Leone.

It is not considered necessary to propose any modification in the legislature of Sierra Leone; there has recently been a slight alteration in its constitution, giving it a more liberal character, and as circumstances justify its further enlargement, it will no doubt be accorded by the Government. The legislature of the minor settlements should be carried on by a council nominated by the Crown, consisting partly of merchants and planters, acting under a uniform system of

[1] *Parl. Papers*, 1865, v (412), p. 385; and 1865, xxxvii (170). *Colonel H. St. George Ord* had served as Commissioner to the Gold Coast, 1855–6, and was sent to examine the state of the West African settlements in 1864. His recommendations were considered by the Select Committee of 1865 and partly incorporated in their report.

regulations laid down by the Governor in Chief, by whom all local ordinances would have to be approved before they became law.

The administration of justice might be left to the officers of every settlement whose circumstances allowed of its maintaining the necessary independent establishment for the purpose. This should consist of a judge, and one or more police magistrates, according to the requirements of the place. If the judge were dispensed with, it would be requisite to make arrangements for securing the visits of a judge from one of the neighbouring Colonies, who would hold periodical gaol deliveries. If necessary the Gambia might thus be aided from Sierra Leone, and the Gold Coast from Lagos. . .

[Financial measures and the use of steamers for communications; a saving of £73,584 by decreasing military expenditure is proposed.]

35

REPORT OF THE SELECT COMMITTEE OF THE HOUSE OF COMMONS ON BRITISH ESTABLISHMENTS IN WEST AFRICA, 26 JUNE 1865[1]

Resolved,—
That it is the opinion of this Committee:

1. That it is not possible to withdraw the British Government, wholly or immediately, from any settlements or engagements on the West African Coast.

2. That the settlement on the Gambia may be reduced, by M'Carthy's Island, which is 150 miles up the river, being no longer occupied; and that the settlement should be confined as much as possible to the mouth of the river.

3. That all further extension of territory or assumption of Government, or new treaties offering any protection to native tribes, would be inexpedient; and that the object of our policy should be to encourage in the natives the exercise of those qualities which may render it possible for us more and more to transfer to them the administration of all the Governments, with a view to our ultimate withdrawal from all, except, probably, Sierra Leone.

4. That this policy of non-extension admits of no exception, as regards new settlements, but cannot amount to an absolute prohibition of measures which, in peculiar cases, may be necessary for the more efficient and economical administration of the settlements we already possess.

5. That the reasons for the separation of West African Governments in 1842 having ceased to exist, it is desirable that a Central

[1] *Parl. Papers*, 1865, v (412), p. iii.

Government over all the four settlements should be re-established at Sierra Leone, with steam communication with each Lieutenant Government.

6. That the evidence leads to the hope that such a central control may be established with considerable retrenchment of expenditure, and at the same time with a general increase of efficiency.

7. That in the newly acquired territory of Lagos the native practice of domestic slavery still, to a certain degree, exists, although it is at variance with British law; and that it appears to your Committee that this state of things, surrounded as it is by many local difficulties, demands the serious attention of the Government, with a view to its termination as soon as possible.

36

CHARTER OF GOVERNMENT FOR THE WEST AFRICAN SETTLEMENTS, 19 FEBRUARY 1866[1]

. . . WE do hereby constitute on the said west coast of Africa one Government-in-Chief, which shall be called the Government of Our West Africa Settlements, and shall, until otherwise provided by Us, comprise Our four Colonies or Governments aforesaid under the respective designations and with the limits hereinafter expressed, that is to say, Our Settlement of Sierra Leone, comprising all places, settlements, and territories which may at any time belong to Us in Western Africa between the fifth and twelfth degrees of north latitude, and lying to the westward of the tenth degree of west longitude; Our Settlement on the Gambia, comprising all places, settlements, and territories which may at any time belong to Us in Western Africa between the twelfth and fifteenth degrees of north latitude, and lying to the westward of the tenth degree of west longitude; Our Settlement on the Gold Coast, comprising all places, settlements, and territories which may at any time belong to Us in Western Africa between the fifth degree of west longitude and the second degree of east longitude; Our Settlement of Lagos, comprising all places, settlements, and territories which may at any time belong to Us in Western Africa between the second and fifth degrees of east longitude.

7. And whereas by an Act made and passed in the sixth year of Our reign,[2] intituled 'An Act to enable Her Majesty to provide for the Government of Her Settlements upon the Coast of Africa and in the Falkland Islands,' it was enacted, that it should be lawful for Us, by any Commission under the Great Seal of Our United Kingdom, or by

[1] *Laws and Ordinances of the Gambia*, p. 244.   [2] See above, no. 27.

any instruction under Our Sign Manual and Signet accompanying and referred to in any such Commission, to delegate to any three or more persons within any of the Settlements aforesaid, either in whole or in part, and subject to all such conditions, provisions. and limitations as might be prescribed by any such Commission or instruction, the power and authority to make and establish all such laws, institutions, and Ordinances, and to constitute such courts and officers, and to make such provisions and regulations for the proceedings in such courts, and for the administration of justice, as might be necessary for the peace, order, and good government of Our subjects and others within Our then present or future Settlements on the said coast.

8. We do further declare Our pleasure to be that there shall be within each of Our said four Settlements a Legislative Council, which shall consist of you Our said Governor and of such other persons or officers not being less than two in number within each of Our respective Settlements, as shall be named or designated by or by virtue of any instruction or instructions, cr by any warrant or warrants to be by Us for that purpose issued under Our Sign Manual and Signet, and with the advice of Our Privy Council; all of which persons and officers shall hold their places in the said Council during Our pleasure.

9. And We do further by this Our Commission under the Great Seal of Our United Kingdom aforesaid delegate to the persons who within each of Our said Settlements shall compose the Legislative Council thereof full power and authority, subject always to such conditions, provisions, and limitations as aforesaid, to establish such Ordinances not being repugnant to the law of England or to any order made or to be made by Us with the advice of Our Privy Council, and to constitute such courts and officers, and to make such provisions and regulations for the proceedings in such courts and for the administration of justice as may be necessary for the peace, order, and good government of such Settlements.

10. And We do further declare Our pleasure to be that you shall have a negative voice in the passing of all such Ordinances as aforesaid; and We do also hereby reserve to ourselves, Our heirs and successors, Our and Their right and authority to disallow any such Ordinances as aforesaid, in the whole or in part, such disallowance being from time to time signified to you through one of Our principal Secretaries of State; and also to make and establish from time to time, with the advice and consent of Parliament, or with the advice of Our or their Privy Council, all such laws or Ordinances as may to Us or them appear necessary for the order, peace and good government of Our said Settlements, or any of them, as fully as if these presents had not been made; and We do further declare Our pleasure to be that in the making and establishing of all such Ordinances

every such Legislative Council shall conform to and observe all such rules as may from time to time be directed or appointed by any instruction or instructions issued by Us with the advice of Our Privy Council.

11. And we do further declare Our pleasure to be that, for the purpose of advising you, there shall be within Our Settlement of Sierra Leone an Executive Council, which shall be composed of such persons or officers as may from time to time be named or designated, and shall observe such rules in the conduct of business as may from time to time be directed or appointed by or in virtue of any instruction addressed to you or them under Our Sign Manual and Signet.

[Authorization to use the Public Seal, make land grants, appoint judges, remit fines, grant pardons, suspend officials.]

18. Our will and pleasure is, and We do hereby direct, that in the execution of this Our Commission, and in the exercise of the command hereby vested in you, you be resident in Our Settlement of Sierra Leone, except when the interests of Our service may render your presence desirable in any other of Our said Settlements.

[In the case of the Governor's death or absence, power is to be vested in a Lieutenant-Governor or the Senior Military Officer.]

20. And We do further declare that so long as you or (as the case may be) the said Administrator of the government of the West Africa Settlements shall be absent from any such Settlement all and every the powers and authorities aforesaid, so far as the same shall be exerciseable within such Settlement, shall be vested in such person within the same as may have been appointed by Us by warrant under Our Sign Manual and Signet to administer the government thereof; and in case there shall not be within such Settlement any such Administrator, then We declare that the said powers and authorities shall, in the Settlement of Sierra Leone, be vested in the Senior Military Officer aforesaid, and shall in the Settlement of Lagos, and in the Settlements on the Gambia and Gold Coast respectively, be vested in the Collector of Customs, or officer lawfully acting as such Collector. . . .

37

A. W. L. HEMMING: MEMORANDUM, GOLD COAST, MARCH 1874[1]

[A review of the findings of the House of Commons Committee of 1865.]

. . . ALTHOUGH a great preponderance of opinion in favour of the concentration of the Settlements under a central Government was

[1] C.O. 806/12 (*Confidential Print*).

presented to the Committee, yet subsequent experience has shown that, at all events as regards the Gold Coast, it may be questioned whether the system has succeeded. Colonel Ord, who strongly advocated its adoption, considered the fact that it had for a length of time been in successful operation in the West Indies was a sufficient ground for proposing its trial in the Settlements, but the circumstances in the two cases are so very different as materially to lessen the force of the argument.

In the West Indies there is no vague and undefined jurisdiction like the Protectorate on the Gold Coast, neither are there powerful savage neighbours like the Kings of Ashantee and Dahomey, with whom an error of judgement or lack of discretion on the part of an Administrator may involve Great Britain in difficulties and war. Besides it may be observed that the West India Islands, which are subordinate to Barbados and Antigua, are none of them at more than the distance of a day's steaming from the seat of Government, and the majority are much nearer. It does not seem as if, in weighing the evidence in favour of a central government, and the placing of it at Sierra Leone, sufficient account had been taken of the position of constant hazard and danger in which we have always stood on the Gold Coast. So far as regards the consequences which might result from maladministration, the Gold Coast is incomparably the most important of all the Settlements, and requires the constant presence of an officer of experience and position, who is able and willing to act on his sole responsibility.

[There have been difficulties in the relations between the Governor-in-chief and his subordinate Administrators.]

. . . If it is not thought advisable to place each of the Settlements under a separate Government, the natural arrangement would seem to be that Sierra Leone and the Gambia should form one Government and that the Gold Coast and Lagos should be united to form another. These two Settlements are only 300 miles apart, and similar questions of native policy are likely to occur in each, so that it would seem desirable that they should be governed by an officer well acquainted with native matters, who could adopt a uniform system of dealing with such subjects.

38

CHARTER OF GOVERNMENT FOR THE GOLD COAST COLONY, 24 JULY 1874[1]

I. WHEREAS, by certain Letters Patent, under the Great Seal of Our United Kingdom of Great Britain and Ireland, bearing date at Westminster the nineteenth day of February, 1866, in the twenty-ninth year of Our reign, provision was made for the Government of Our Settlements on the West Coast of Africa, as therein is more particularly described: And whereas, by a Supplementary Commission under the Great Seal aforesaid, bearing date at Westminster, the eighth day of November, 1872, in the thirty-sixth year of Our reign, We did empower Our Governor and Commander-in-Chief of our West Africa Settlements to grant pardons to offenders in the manner and upon the terms therein mentioned: And whereas by Our Commission under the Great Seal aforesaid, bearing date the twenty-fifth day of July, 1873, in the thirty-seventh year of Our reign, We did constitute and appoint Our trusty and well-beloved George Berkeley, Esquire (now Companion of Our Most Distinguished Order of Saint Michael and Saint George) to be, during Our will and pleasure, Our Governor and Commander-in-Chief in and over Our said West Africa Settlements: And whereas it is expedient that provision should be made for the Government of Our Settlements on the Gold Coast and of Lagos, apart and separate from the Government of Our other Settlements on the West Coast of Africa; And whereas by an Act made and passed in the sixth year of Our reign, intituled, 'An Act to enable Her Majesty to provide for the Government of Her Settlements upon the Coast of Africa and in the Falkland Islands,' it was enacted that it should be lawful for us, by any Commission under the Great Seal of Our United Kingdom, or by any Instructions under Our Sign-Manual and Signet accompanying and referred to in any such Commission, to delegate to any three or more persons within any of the settlements aforesaid, either in whole or in part, and subject to all such conditions, provisions, and limitations as might be prescribed by any such Commission or Instructions, the power and authority to make and establish all such Laws, Institutions, and Ordinances and to constitute such Courts and Officers, and to make such provisions and regulations for the proceedings in such Courts and for the administration of justice as might be necessary for the peace, order, and good government of Our subjects and others within Our then present or future Settlements on the said Coast: Now know ye that We do by these Our Letters Patent, under the Great Seal

[1] *Parl. Papers*, 1875, lii [C. 1140], pp. 97–99.

aforesaid, declare Our pleasure to be that Our said Letters Patent of the nineteenth day of February, 1866, Our said Supplementary Commission of the eighth day of November, 1872, and Our said Commission of the twenty-fifth day of July, 1873, shall be, and they are hereby revoked so far as regards Our said Settlements on the Gold Coast and of Lagos, or any part or parts thereof; and We do further declare Our pleasure to be that those Settlements shall constitute, and they are hereby erected into a separate Colony under the title of the Gold Coast Colony.

II. And We do further declare Our pleasure to be that Our Settlement on the Gold Coast shall, as heretofore, and until otherwise provided by Us, comprise all places, settlements, and territories which may at any time belong to Us in Western Africa between the fifth degree of west longitude and the second degree of east longitude. And Our Settlements of Lagos shall, as heretofore, and until otherwise provided by Us, comprise all places, settlements, and territories which may at any time belong to Us in Western Africa between the second and fifth degrees of east longitude.

III. And We do further declare and appoint that the Government of Our said Colony shall be administered by a Governor duly commissioned by Us on that behalf.

IV. And We do further declare Our pleasure to be that there shall be within Our said Colony a Legislative Council, which shall consist of Our said Governor for the time being, and of such other persons or officers, not being less than two in number, from each of Our said Settlements, as shall be named or designated by or by virtue of any Instruction or Instructions, or by any Warrant or Warrants to be by us for that purpose issued under Our Sign Manual and Signet, and with the advice of Our Privy Council; all of which persons or officers shall hold their places in the said Council during Our pleasure.

V. And We do further by this Our Commission under the Great Seal of Our United Kingdom aforesaid delegate to the persons, who within Our said Colony shall compose the Legislative Council thereof, full power and authority, subject always to such conditions, provisions, and limitations as may be prescribed by any Commission or Instructions, to establish such Ordinances not being repugnant to the Law of England or to any Order made or to be made by Us with the advice of Our Privy Council, and to constitute such Courts and officers, and to make such provisions and regulations for the proceedings in such Courts and for the administration of Justice as may be necessary for the peace, order, and good government of such Colony.

VI. And We do further declare Our pleasure to be that Our said Governor shall have a negative voice in the passing of all such Ordinances aforesaid: and We do also hereby reserve to Ourselves, Our heirs and successors, Our and their right and authority to disallow any such Ordinances as aforesaid, in the whole or in part, such disallowance being from time to time signified to him through one of Our Principal Secretaries of State, and also to make and establish from time to time, with the advice and consent of Parliament, or with the advice of Our or their Privy Council, all such law or Ordinances as may to Us or them appear necessary for the order, peace, and good government of Our said Colony as fully as if these Presents had not been made. And We do further declare Our pleasure to be that in the making and establishing of all such Ordinances the said Legislative Council shall conform to and observe all such rules as may from time to time be directed or appointed by any Instruction or Instructions issued by Us with the advice of Our Privy Council.

VII. And We do further declare and establish that the Laws now in force in Our said Colony shall continue in force as long and as far only as they are not repugnant to or repealed by any Ordinance passed by the Legislature of Our said Colony.

VIII. And We do further declare Our pleasure to be that, for the purpose of advising Our said Governor, there shall be for Our said Colony an Executive Council, which shall be composed of such persons and constituted in such manner as may be directed by any Instructions which may from time to time be addressed to Our said Governor by Us under Our Sign-Manual and Signet, and all such persons shall hold their places in the said Council at Our pleasure. . . .

39

THE EARL OF CARNARVON TO GOVERNOR G. C. STRAHAN: GOLD COAST COLONY, 28 AUGUST 1874[1]

SIR,

In my despatch of the 3rd instant I had the honour to transmit to you a Charter passed under the Great Seal on the 24th July, erecting the Settlements of the Gold Coast and Lagos into one Colony under the style of the 'Gold Coast Colony'; and in that despatch I also transmitted to you Her Majesty's Commission appointing you to be Governor of the new Colony, together with Her Majesty's Instructions under the Sign-Manual and Signet.

2. In other despatches, from time to time, I have explained to you my general views of the policy to be observed on the Gold Coast on various matters, and it is my present purpose to address a few observations to you on some of the steps to be taken, under the powers conferred by the Charter and Instructions, in order to bring the new institutions into practical operation.

[1] *Parl. Papers*, 1875, lii [C. 1140], pp. 70–71.

3. You will now find yourself at the head of a Colony consisting of two divisions, which, though they have been brought into connection for reasons of proximity, community of interests within certain limits, and general facility of administration, yet differ considerably also in some of their political and social characteristics, and have been governed hitherto under dissimilar laws administered by independent Courts.

4. In both divisions of the Colony the law of England has been the basis of the system of justice administered by the Courts, but the local enactments passed by the Legislatures of the two Settlements have naturally been diverse.

5. Those laws of course until altered remain in force, but you will make it an object of policy, whilst retaining the principles of the law of England as the general rule under which justice is to be administered, to provide for the supercession of the present heterogeneous and defective legislation of the two extinct Legislatures by laws which shall be, as far as possible, uniform, simple, and complete. And it will further be an object of policy to amalgamate the judicial systems of the two Settlements in subordination to a single Supreme Court, with provisions for administering justice as far as possible at convenient places in each district.

6. It may probably also be found desirable to confer on this Court the jurisdiction of the Judicial Assessor's Court at the Gold Coast, so as to avoid the confusion which may arise from a multiplication of jurisdictions.

7. The instructions accompanying your Commission designate as members of your Executive Council eleven, besides yourself, the Administrator of Lagos, the Senior Military Officer, the Colonial Secretary, and the Queen's Advocate. In view of the frequent absence from various causes of public officers on the Gold Coast, the probable removal of the regular troops, and the necessity of having two members present besides yourself to form a quorum, I should be glad to receive any suggestion you may desire to offer as to the addition by Royal warrant at a future time of some other public officer to the Executive Council.

8. The instructions do not give you power in the first instance to add to the number of persons designated therein as Members of the Legislative Council; but I have not lost sight of the fact that, as the Sessions of the Council will be held sometimes at one Settlement and sometimes at the other, and as its work will relate to the affairs of communities differing in many of their characteristics, it may be necessary to nominate to the Legislature, a larger number of persons than would otherwise be desirable, so as to secure the attendance of a due number of persons having special knowledge of the subjects of legislation; and I shall be prepared to receive your suggestions as to

the nomination of, say one or two, additional Members beyond those designated in the Commission. But you will in no case lead any person to understand that he has any prospect of being appointed to the Legislative Council until the sanction of the Secretary of State has been given.

9. You will of course for the present regard the revenues of the two Settlements as distinct funds to be separately estimated and accounted for, and you will not allow the funds of the one to be applied to the disbursement of the other, except on the understanding that the sum disbursed is to be regarded as an advance.

10. The Customs systems of the two must also at present be regarded as distinct until amalgamated under the direction of a Controller or Treasurer presiding over the financial affairs of the United Settlement. Even then the Consolidated Department will be obliged to administer two systems of taxation, the assimilation of the tariff of the two Settlements being at this moment unfortunately impossible.

11. I presume you will see no objection to the amalgamation of the defensive forces of the two Settlements, the bulk of the force as heretofore remaining at the Gold Coast and Lagos being charged annually a sum in proportion to the average strength of the force there quartered.

12. I need hardly point out to you the advantages of at once consolidating as far as possible this and other services of the United Colony.

13. At first it will, in my judgment, be the most prudent course to charge to Gold Coast funds (which have this year been subsidized by a grant from the Imperial Exchequer) the whole of the salaries of those high officers—such as yourself, the Colonial Secretary, the Queen's Advocate, and the Inspector-General of Police—who, though nominally on the establishment of the Gold Coast, render service in relation to the affairs of both Settlements; but, in future, Lagos should bear its fair share of the charge for the salaries of these officers, and if later it should appear that its finances are in a prosperous condition, I think it would not be unfair that the Settlement should repay a sum representing either wholly or in part the arrears of its share of the amount now exclusively borne by the Gold Coast. . . .

B. COURTS AND EXTRA-TERRITORIAL JURISDICTION

Introductory Note

THE two problems fundamental to the reception and application of English and colonial laws on the coast were the organization of the courts under a professional judiciary and the jurisdiction of these courts in the immediate neighbourhood of the settlements. On the example of Sierra Leone, there was a tendency for each colonial capital to found its own judicial establishment for Africans as well as Europeans and to extend the powers of the colonial court to ensure redress for and against British subjects beyond the narrow confines of the colonial frontier. The growth of such courts and jurisdiction was far from uniform. Before 1821, the Committee of Merchants and its agents had no powers of jurisdiction on the Gold Coast; Sir Charles MacCarthy while administering Senegal had no commission to settle civil cases and no more than a warrant to hold courts martial for a criminal offence; and in the Gambia it was left to the Governor of Sierra Leone to provide the first rudimentary justice.

After transfer to the Crown, Sierra Leone by a Charter of 9 August 1809 possessed a court of record, under a chief magistrate, a vice-admiralty court, a court of quarter sessions, a mayor's court, a police court and, from 1819 till 1870, a court of mixed commission. The Governor's council was both a court of appeal and a source of law by local enactment. The Charter of 1821 retained the old judiciary (with the exception of the Mayor's court) and provided for justices of the peace and commissioners of requests. Subsidiary courts were established in the Gambia, 1822-5, under the Chief Justice of Freetown on tour; and in 1829 the Governor of Sierra Leone framed a local Act for jurisdiction over British subjects at Fernando Po, though it did not affect the administration of the temporary settlement in the Bight of Benin. In 1829, too, seven Justices of the Peace were commissioned at Cape Coast and Accra. The Gambia was given a court of common pleas and a court of appeal in 1832.

The Charter of 1821 had established the powers of the Freetown Recorder's Court over all Africans born in the colony, as well as the original settlers and their descendants. By the end of the 1820's it was recognized that liberated Africans had the same legal rights as other inhabitants and could serve on juries for both civil and criminal cases. The danger of allowing crimes to be committed with impunity beyond the frontier was emphasized by Governor Doherty in 1839, but a colonial Act framed in 1841 to give local courts powers to hear such cases was disallowed for want of the authority of a parliamentary statute. On the Gold Coast, however, an irregular jurisdiction was exercised in criminal cases by Maclean as president of the Cape Coast Council, 1830-43. Such jurisdiction was not disapproved, provided it was defined by agreements with African chiefs; and the Colonial Office under Lord Stanley (with considerable reservations by James Stephen) appointed a judicial assessor to try cases 'by consent of the Natives' outside the forts. The Foreign Jurisdiction Act of 1843 was used to justify the procedure. On the advice of the Law Officers, an Order-in-Council of 3 September 1844 made Cape Coast a place of trial; the consent of the Fanti chiefs to joint jurisdiction was obtained in a number of declarations in the same year. Gradually, the scope of this extra-territorial jurisdiction was enlarged to include civil as well as criminal cases under a Supreme Court Ordinance of 1853 and an Order-in-Council of 1856.

In Sierra Leone the question of jurisdiction over British subjects in neighbouring territories was raised again in 1849 and was made to depend on treaties with African chiefs and the determination of the status of liberated Africans by statute in 1853. The surrender of offenders to colonial justice, however, required an additional Act for Sierra Leone in 1861.

It was not till 1858 that Sierra Leone followed its former dependencies by establishing a Supreme Court under the Chief Justice. At Lagos no such elaborate system was introduced: a police court, criminal court, slave court, and commercial tribunal were set up on doubtful authority in 1862; and a chief magistrate and two assessors were appointed to hear all cases in a chief magistrate's court by an Ordinance of 1863. A petty debt court was retained, after criticism, and incorporated with the chief magistrate's court in 1866. In 1870 a court of requests was established to deal with debts under £50.

Unification of the settlements in 1866 brought attempted reform of some of the differences that had grown up in judicial practice between the four colonial capitals. Governor Blackall laid down general principles which served as the basis for Ordinances of 1866 and 1867 setting up a Court of Summary Jurisdiction and a single Supreme Court with appellate jurisdiction. At the same time juries for civil cases were abolished, together with appeals to the Governor and Council in civil cases of less than £400. In all other cases, both civil and criminal, there was appeal to Privy Council. In 1871, further reforms to ensure an inexpensive system of appeals by sending the Chief Justice on tour and reducing the responsibilities of chief magistrates outside Sierra Leone, were examined by the Colonial Office, but were postponed by the Ashanti War. Immediately after the war, however, a few changes were made. In 1874 a vice-admiralty court, a court of summary jurisdiction, and police courts were retained under the Supreme Court at Sierra Leone, with a chief justice, Queen's advocate, and police magistrate. In each of the other three settlements there were chief magistrates, as heads of the local judiciary, with commissioners of requests at Bathurst, a judicial assessor on the Gold Coast, and civil commandants both at the forts and at Lagos, with powers of summary jurisdiction. In August 1874 a new Order-in-Council under the Foreign Jurisdiction Act of 1843 was prepared for the extension of British courts and laws into the protected territory of the Gold Coast colony. The usefulness of the Chief Justice's appeal court at Sierra Leone was again questioned and a more simple system of procedure in civil cases was planned. Slowly, the Colonial Office moved towards the Supreme Court Ordinance of 1875.

Meanwhile, the lack of legal redress which had been felt in the Delta and near Sierra Leone was remedied by the Foreign Jurisdiction Act of 1871, by which the subjects of 'uncivilized Powers' became liable for crimes and offences committed within twenty miles of the colony, and by the West African Order-in-Council of 1872, under which consular courts were established.

I

REPORT OF THE COMMISSIONERS OF INQUIRY: JUDICIAL ESTABLISHMENT, 11 APRIL 1827[1]

... THE Governor and Council constitute a Court of Record, to hear and determine appeals from the Court of the Recorder, or other superior courts of the colony; and, when the matter in dispute exceeds the value of 400 pounds, a further appeal may also be had to the King in Council.

The Colonial Courts are as follows:

The Court of Royal Commission.

The Court of Vice Admiralty.

The Court of the Recorder of Freetown.

The Courts of Quarter Sessions, and of Oyer and Terminer.

The Court of Requests, and the Police Court. . . .

[No other courts have been established.]

The commissioners of the Royal Court, constituted under the great seal, are the governor, chief justice, commissary judge of the Mixed Courts, King's advocate, colonial secretary, and others specified in the commission; three of whom may form a court, one of the four first named always presiding.

This court was established for the trial of offences committed on the high seas, and for offences relating to the slave trade, when committed on those parts of the shores of Africa, where no local British jurisdiction exists. But hitherto, few occasions have occurred for bringing its powers into operation.

The chief justice is the judge of the Vice Admiralty court, which has power and jurisdiction similar to that of the corresponding courts in the West India islands; but since the establishment of the courts of Mixed Commission in the colony, the business in this court is much reduced. The chief justice, as recorder, presides likewise in the court of the Recorder of Freetown, aided by two assistant judges, appointed by the governor, from amongst the members of council. This court is stated by the chief justice, to resemble most closely the Court of

[1] *Parl. Papers*, 1827, vii (312), pp. 92–95. By Major J. Rowan and Henry Wellington. For courts introduced under the Sierra Leone Charter of 1799, see above, p. 470.

Common Pleas in England, and to be also a Court of Equity; it sits every month, and the term or session seldom exceeds one day. Although two assistant judges are appointed, one of these, in addition to the chief justice, or in cases where the chief justice is party to the action of suit, the two assistants only may constitute a court; and in all cases where the number of voices shall be equal, the chief justice, or in his absence, the senior assistant judge present, has two voices.

It is empowered by the charter to hear and determine all civil suits, actions or pleas, which may happen within the colony of Sierra Leone, or any of the forts, settlements, islands or territories, subject or subordinate thereto. In all cases where the action to be tried, would, if the parties were resident in England, be tried by a jury in some of the courts of law, it is directed that such action shall be tried before a jury in the court of the Recorder, according to the practice of the courts of law in England, or as near thereto as circumstances will permit. Formerly, the jurisdiction of the court did not extend to cases wherein the litigants were natives of Africa, not become settlers in the colony, unless both parties should by consent submit their case to the determination of the court. This clause is omitted in the charter as last revised.

The chief justice and other members of the council usually preside at the sessions of the peace and of oyer and terminer; where, as in the court of the recorder, the chief justice is assisted by two members of council. These sessions are held in March, June, September, and December, and generally complete their business in from three to five days. . . .

[Judges regulate their practice in the same way as circuit judges in England; by the Charter of 1821 the Court of Requests was abolished, to be replaced by district justices or commissioners.]

By an Act of the Governor and Council, dated in October 1825, the jurisdiction of the commissioners was extended so as to embrace all suits and actions where 'the debt, duty, or matter in dispute did not exceed the value of ten pounds;' provision being made that, where the sum exceeded forty shillings, appeal might be had, if in the Gambia or on the Gold Coast, to their respective courts of common pleas; and in any other part of the colony, to the court of the recorder of Freetown, the judgements of which court to be final. The act empowers the justices or commissioners, where the debt or duty or damage adjudged does not exceed forty shillings, to commit the defendant to gaol for not less than three or more than six weeks; if the sum exceed forty shillings, but not five pounds, then for any time not less than six weeks or more than three months; and in the event of the sum exceeding five pounds, for any time not less than three or more than six months. These commitments to be in full satisfaction of the judgments respectively. Commissioners of requests sit once a week in Freetown, and form what is there called a court for the Recovery of Small Debts.

The Police Court of Freetown is supposed to be attended twice a week by two magistrates (a member of council) and one of the other magistrates) so that by the presence of two, a kind of petit session should be formed; the member of council always presiding. The proceedings are to be recorded by a clerk of police, who is maintained on the civil establishment for the purpose.

The judicial establishment available for the duties of the foregoing courts (independently of the governor and council) consisted, in 1825 and the beginning of 1826, of the following individuals:

The chief justice.

The King's advocate.

The sheriff.

The clerk of the crown and of the recorder's court.

The coroner of Freetown, and two practising attornies.

Seven justices in the commission of the peace.

The mayor of Freetown, and three aldermen.

Eight commissioners of requests, besides eight district magistrates, three of whom are also coroners for three country districts.

The courts in which the chief justice presides, have already been specified. The King's advocate is understood to be the governor's legal adviser, and the public prosecutor; his duty in these capacities admits of his practising as an advocate or attorney in the courts.

The sheriff, who is annually appointed by the governor and council, is at present the agent of a mercantile house. His duties correspond to those of sheriffs in England.

The present clerk of the crown and of the court of the recorder, is also one of the writers in the office of the colonial secretary.

The coroner of Freetown, is stated, by the chief justice, to have been sometimes appointed by the governor, and sometimes elected by the freeholders. The individual at present holding the situation is a Maroon.

Neither of the two individuals practising as solicitors and attornies, has been professionally educated. One is a European, who also acts as King's advocate and registrar of the Vice Admiralty Court: the other, a person of colour, born and educated in England, and actually engaged in mercantile pursuits.

Of the seven justices in the commission of the peace for the colony, one is a military officer, and the other six hold civil situations under the government.

The mayor and aldermen of Freetown are appointed by the governor and council. The present mayor is one of the early Nova

Scotian settlers. The senior alderman, one of early Maroon settlers; the second, a person of colour, born in the West Indies; and the third, a young European, clerk in a mercantile house.

Of the commissioners of requests, three are magistrates, and five are engaged in trade; and of these, two are persons of colour.

The district magistrates, three of whom are also coroners, are either the local superintendents, or hold situations in their respective districts, as clergymen or teachers under the church missionary society.

2

SIR GEORGE MURRAY TO ACTING GOVERNOR H. J. RICKETTS: JUSTICES OF THE PEACE AT THE FORTS, 20 NOVEMBER 1828[1]

[The Forts have been handed over to the merchants at Cape Coast and Accra.]

... I HAVE had much communication with several of those [merchants] belonging to London who are engaged in Trade with the Gold Coast, respecting the terms upon which it may be proper that His Majesty's Government should lend their assistance in enabling the Merchants to maintain possession of the Forts in question. And I now transmit to you, for your information and guidance, copies of two communications which I have caused to be made to Messrs. Barnes, Cock and Brown and Forster,[2] for the purpose of laying down and explaining the arrangements and conditions under which the Forts of Cape Coast Castle and Accra are still to be considered as Dependencies of your Government, and maintained at the Public charge, altho' governed in all respects by the Merchants resident upon the spot, in the character of Justices of the Peace.

With the view, therefore, of providing for the municipal regulation of the Forts, it will be necessary that you should constitute the following persons, viz: Mr. John Jackson Mr. Wm. Hutchinson Mr J. Thursfield Pierce Mr Robert Roberts Mr James Swanzy to be Justices of the Peace for Cape Coast Castle, and the following Persons, viz: Mr. James Bannerman Mr. Richd. Fred. Fry, to be Justices of the Peace for Accra.

And you will also, if necessary, take measures for passing an Act for enabling the said Justices to exercise to the fullest extent, all such powers as may legally be used by Justices of the Peace, with a view to the suppression and punishment of offences against the laws, leaving it of course to the Courts of Sierra Leone to take cognizance of crimes and misdemeanours over which the Jurisdiction of the Justices of the Peace may not extend.

[1] C.O. 268/28, ff. 179–82.   [2] See above, p. 505.

3

R. W. HAY TO LIEUT.-GOVERNOR A. FINDLAY: JURISDICTION UNDER THE SIERRA LEONE CHARTER, 27 FEBRUARY 1830[1]

SIR,

The Charter of Government of Sierra Leone authorises the Governor, with the advice and consent of the Council, to erect Courts of Record, and other Courts for determining all causes, civil and criminal, arising within the Colony, and to issue special Commissions of Oyer and Terminer and Gaol Delivery, limited to the District, and Crimes or Misdemeanours specified in such Commissions.

The Court of the Recorder of Free Town which is established by that Charter, can, perhaps be not legally holden at any place except Free Town itself. But under the general power to which I have referred, there seems no reason to doubt that it would be competent to you, with the advice of the Council, to establish the necessary Tribunals for the decision of Civil and Criminal causes in any Districts, too remote from Free Town to be properly subjected to the Jurisdiction of the Recorder's Court.

As it will be necessary that justice should be administered to the Settlers at the River Gambia, without subjecting them to the inconvenience of resorting to Free Town, you will propose to the Council the enactment of such laws and the issuing of such Commissions, as may be necessary for that purpose. In framing Acts of this nature, you will especially avail yourself of the assistance of the Chief Justice. The only particular Instruction which it seems to me necessary to give you on the subject, is, that the Court to be erected at the Settlement on the Gambia should be held by the Chief Justice at those seasons of the year when he can most conveniently absent himself from Sierra Leone; and that the Court at the Gambia should be constituted as closely as possible, upon the model of the Recorder's Court at Free Town.

It will probably be most convenient that all Capital cases, if any should occur, should be tried at Free Town, but of this the Chief Justice will be the most competent Judge.

[1] C.O. 268/28, ff. 333-5.

4

GOVERNOR R. DOHERTY TO LORD JOHN RUSSELL: EXTRA-TERRITORIAL JURISDICTION, SIERRA LEONE, 29 NOVEMBER 1839[1]

[Following the murder of a Freetown Maroon in Koya country, Doherty has arranged for the surrender of British subjects by Chief Momodu Bundu of Foredugu.]

. . . At the same time it is to be observed, that the gravest offences committed in the countries adjacent to the Colony by the Subjects of the Queen, have been hitherto liable to remain altogether unpunished, from the neglect of the native chief, on the one hand, and the refusal, on the other, of the tribunals of the Colony, or of Her Majesty's Government in England, to interfere in such cases. Nor is impunity from those causes without example. An instance occurred in the year 1837, in which two colonists being arraigned before the Court of Royal Commission in Freetown for the murder of a person who was likewise a subject of Her Majesty, at the town of Mabelly, the Court declared itself to be without jurisdiction: while no punishment was inflicted by the Ali Karlie of Port Locco, the chief in whose dominions Mabelly is situated. In like manner it had previously happened in the year 1834 that a man named William Cole, charged in Freetown with high treason & murder, was ordered to be released by Lord Stanley, because the crimes imputed to him were alleged to have been committed at Cobolo, beyond the limits of the Colony: nor was any attempt made, before or subsequently, to bring him to trial at that place. But it is obvious to remark that were such impunity to become general or even probable, the knowledge and anticipation of it might be attended, among a population like that of Sierra Leone, with the most disastrous and melancholy consequences; and I have therefore to request that your Lordship will be pleased to inform me, whether the tribunals of the Colony can be invested with any general authority to try offences committed by British subjects beyond the limits of the Peninsula; and if that should be the case whether, in the event of my being still enabled to conclude an amended treaty with the parties of the Convention of Mabelly,[2] Her Majesty's Government would approve of the introduction into the new compact, in room of the 10th article of the former one, of a stipulation for the surrender of the Sierra Leone Government by the contracting Chiefs, of British subjects who may commit crimes within their territories.

[1] C.O. 267/154.   [2] See above, p. 254.

5

JAMES STEPHEN: MINUTE: EXTRA-TERRITORIAL JURISDICTION, SIERRA LEONE, 22 SEPTEMBER 1841[1]

[Acting Governor Carr has tried to secure the release of Sierra Leone liberated Africans from Temne chiefs in Koya country, and has threatened war, annexation and the suspension of stipends; he has offered to try cases against British subjects for offences in Koya, in Sierra Leone courts.]

. . . ON these facts I would observe.

First, that the Timmanee people must be considerably perplexed to understand our dealings with them. The former Governor Colonel Doherty proclaimed to the Emigrants from the Colony that if they would migrate into Countries beyond the Queen's Dominions, the Queen's Government could afford them no protection there. This Proclamation was made known to the Timmanee Chiefs. They will now learn that such is not the policy or the Law of the Sierra Leone Govt.

Secondly, I have no doubt that Mr. Carr is right in thinking himself bound to reclaim British Subjects held in slavery. But I should qualify this obligation by saying that it does not arise in a case where British Subjects are captives of War in a Foreign Country, where they have been fighting and where such captivity induces Slavery as an established and legal consequence.

Thirdly, the menace of war, if acted upon, will involve a great expenditure—inevitable perhaps, but certainly much to be regretted, and if avoidable to be most anxiously avoided.

Fourthly, I know not under what Authority Mr. Carr proposes to treat for the Sovereignty of the Quiah Country. It may be a wise measure, but it is certainly a questionable one. The motives in favor of it have I think been explained by Sir J. Jeremie and by Dr. Madden. But I apprehend that it has never yet been sanctioned.

Fifth. It appears to me that Mr. Carr is in error in stating that the Courts of Sierra Leone can punish British Subjects for offences committed in the Timmanee Country. There are I know certain local Acts of recent date which authorize this. But I take such Enactments to be mere nullities. The local Legislature has none but local powers. If any one British Colony can make a Law which is valid beyond its own precincts any other Colony may do the same, and a British Subject in a Foreign Land might in respect of the same action be amenable to the Courts of from 30 to 40 Colonies in as many different ways. Parlt. alone can make Laws binding on British

[1] C.O. 267/164, on Carr to Russell, 20 July 1841.

Subjects beyond the Realm. For this reason Parlt. interfered to give jurisdiction to the Courts of Canada, of Honduras, of N.S. Wales and of the Cape Good Hope, over the Offences of British Subjects committed in Foreign and Barbarous Countries immediately adjacent to these Settlements.

I should propose to frame for Lord Stanley's consideration a Draft of an answer to this Despatch in accordance with these views. But I believe that it would be right to request his Lordship's instructions for such a Draft, in the first instance, and before it is actually prepared.

6

EXTRACT FROM THE SELECT COMMITTEE REPORT: GOLD COAST JURISDICTION, 1842[1]

The Judicial Authority at present existing in the Forts is not altogether in a satisfactory condition; it resides in the Governor and Council, who act as Magistrates, and whose instructions limit them to the administration of British Law, and that, as far as the Natives are concerned, strictly and exclusively within the Forts themselves; but practically, and necessarily, and usefully, these directions have been disregarded, a kind of irregular jurisdiction has grown up, extending itself far beyond the limits of the Forts by the voluntary submission of the Natives themselves, whether Chiefs or Traders, to British Equity; and its decisions, owing to the moral influence, partly of our acknowledged power, and partly of the respect which has been inspired by the fairness with which it has been exercised by Captain Maclean and the Magistrates at the other Forts, have generally, we might almost say, uniformly, been carried into effect without the interposition of force. The value of this interposition of an enlightened, though irregular, authority, (which has extended, in some cases, and with advantage to humanity, even to an interference in capital cases,) is borne witness to, not only by parties connected with the Government of the Settlements, who might be suspected of a bias in its favour, but also by the Wesleyan Missionaries, and even by Dr. Madden, who, objecting to its undefined extent, and to the manner in which, in some respects, it has been carried out, yet still bears high testimony to its practical value, to its acknowledged equity, and to its superiority over the barbarous customs which it tends to supersede. Even the duration of imprisonment, of which he complains, has been usually adjudged to offences which would have incurred a severer penalty in most civilised countries, and would certainly, if left to the arbitrary decision of native chiefs, or to the

[1] *Parl. Papers*, 1842, xi (551), pp. v–vi.

'wild justice' of private revenge, have been punished by death, and that frequently of the most cruel kind. Still, however, it is desirable that this jurisdiction should be better defined and understood, and that a Judicial Officer should be placed at the disposal of the Governor, to assist, or supersede, partially or entirely, his judicial functions, and those now exercised by the Council and the several Commandants in their magisterial capacity; but we would recommend, that while he follows in his decisions the general principles, he be not restricted to the technicalities of British Law, and that altogether he should be allowed a large discretion.

It is to be remembered that our compulsory authority is strictly limited, both by our title and by the instructions of the Colonial Office to the British Forts, within which no one but the Governor, his Suite, and the Garrison reside; and that the Magistrates are strictly prohibited from exercising jurisdiction even over the Natives and Districts immediately under the influence and protection of the Forts. All jurisdiction over the Natives beyond that point must, therefore, be considered as optional, and should be made the subject of distinct agreement, as to its nature and limits, with the Native Chiefs, and it should be accommodated to the condition of the several Tribes, and to the completeness of the control over them, which by vicinage or otherwise we are enabled to exercise. Their relation to the English Crown should be, not the allegiance of subjects, to which we have no right to pretend, and which it would entail an inconvenient responsibility to possess, but the deference of weaker powers to a stronger and more enlightened neighbour, whose protection and counsel they seek, and to whom they are bound by certain definite obligations.

These obligations should be varied and extended from time to time, and should always at least include (as many of the Treaties now in existence on that Coast already do) the abolition of the external Slave Trade, the prohibition of human sacrifices, and other barbarous customs, such as kidnapping, under the name of 'pan-yarring', and should keep in view the gradual introduction of further improvements, as the people become more fitted to admit them.

7

THE FOREIGN JURISDICTION ACT, 24 AUGUST 1843 (6 & 7 VICT., c. 94)[1]

Whereas by treaty, capitulation, grant, usage, sufferance, and other lawful means, Her Majesty hath power and jurisdiction within divers countries and places out of Her Majesty's dominions: and whereas

[1] *Parl. Papers*, 1855, xxxvii (383), pp. 4–7.

doubts have arisen how far the exercise of such power and jurisdiction is controlled by and dependent on the laws and customs of this realm, and it is expedient that such doubts should be removed: Be it therefore enacted by the Queen's most Excellent Majesty, by and with the advice and consent of the Lords Spiritual and Temporal, and Commons, in this present Parliament assembled, and by the authority of the same, that it is and shall be lawful for Her Majesty to hold, exercise and enjoy any power or jurisdiction which Her Majesty now hath or may at any time hereafter have within any country or place out of Her Majesty's dominions, in the same and as ample a manner as if Her Majesty had acquired such power or jurisdiction by the cession or conquest of territory.

2. And be it enacted, that every act, matter, and thing which may at any time be done, in pursuance of any such power or jurisdiction of Her Majesty, in any country or place out of Her Majesty's dominions, shall, in all courts ecclesiastical and temporal and elsewhere within Her Majesty's dominions, be and be deemed and adjudged to be, in all cases and to all intents and purposes whatsoever, as valid and effectual as though the same had been done according to the local law then in force within such territory or place.

3. And be it enacted, that if in any suit or other proceedings, whether civil or criminal, in any court ecclesiastical or temporal within Her Majesty's dominions, any issue or question of law or of fact shall arise for the due determination whereof it shall, in the opinion of the judge or judges of such court, be necessary to produce evidence of the existence of any such power or jurisdiction as aforesaid, or of the extent thereof, it shall be lawful for the judge or judges of any such court, and he or they are hereby authorized, to transmit, under his or their hand and seal or hands and seals, to one of Her Majesty's Principal Secretaries of State, questions by him or them properly framed respecting such of the matters aforesaid as it may be necessary to ascertain in order to the due determination of any such issue or question as aforesaid; and such Secretary of State is hereby empowered and required, within a reasonable time in that behalf, to cause proper and sufficient answers to be returned to all such questions, and to be directed to the said judge or judges, or their successors; and such answers shall, upon production thereof, be final and conclusive evidence, in such suit or other proceedings, of the several matters therein contained, and required to be ascertained thereby.

4. And whereas it may in certain cases be expedient that crimes and offences committed within such countries or places as aforesaid be inquired of, tried, determined, and punished within Her Majesty's dominions; Be it enacted, that it shall and may be lawful for any person having authority derived from Her Majesty in that behalf, by warrant under his hand and seal, to cause any person charged with

the commission of any crime or offence the cognizance whereof may at any time appertain to any judge, magistrate, or other officer of Her Majesty within any such country or place as aforesaid, to be sent for trial to any British colony which Her Majesty may by any Order or Orders in Council from time to time appoint in that behalf; and upon the arrival of such person within such colony it shall and may be lawful for the Supreme Court exercising criminal jurisdiction within the same to cause such a person to be kept in safe and proper custody, and, so soon as conveniently may be, to inquire of, try, and determine such crime or offence, and upon conviction of the person so charged as aforesaid to correct and punish him according to the laws in force in that behalf within such colony, in the same manner as if the said crime or offence had been committed within the jurisdiction of such Supreme Court; provided always, that before any such person shall be sent for trial to any such colony as aforesaid it shall be lawful for him to tender for examination to the judge, magistrate, or other officer of Her Majesty to whom the cognizance of the crime or offence with which he is charged may appertain, within the country or place where the same may be alleged to have been committed, any competent witness or witnesses, the evidence of whom he may deem material for his defence, and whom he may allege himself to be unable to produce at his trial in the said colony; and the said judge, magistrate, or other officer shall thereupon proceed in the examination and cross-examination of such witness or witnesses in the same manner as though the same had been tendered to a trial before such judge, magistrate or other officer, and shall cause the evidence so taken to be reduced into writing, and shall transmit a copy of such evidence to the Supreme Court before which the trial of such a person is to take place, together with a certificate under his hand and seal of the correctness of such copy; and thereupon it shall be lawful for the said Supreme Court, and it is hereby required, to allow so much of the evidence so taken as aforesaid as would have been admissable according to the law and practice of the said Supreme Court, had the said witness or witnesses been produced and examined at the trial before the said court, to be read and received as legal evidence at such trial: Provided also, that if it shall be made to appear at such trial that the laws by which the person charged with any criminal act would have been tried had his trial taken place before a judge, magistrate, or other officer of Her Majesty in the country or place in which such act may be alleged to have been committed, vary from or are inconsistent with the laws in force within such colony, in respect either of the criminality of the act charged, or of the nature or degree of the alleged crime or offence, or of the punishment to be awarded for the same, such Supreme Court is hereby empowered and required to admit and give effect to the laws by which such person would have been tried as aforesaid, so far as but not further or otherwise than the same relate to the criminality of such act, or to the nature or degree of such crime or offence, or to the punishment thereof: Provided also, that nothing herein contained shall be construed to alter or repeal any law, statute, or usage by virtue of which any crime or offence committed out of Her Majesty's dominions might, at the time of the passing of this Act, be inquired of, tried, determined, and punished within Her Majesty's dominions, or any part thereof, but the same shall remain in full force and effect, anything herein contained to the contrary not withstanding. . . .

[5, 6 Law officers are empowered to send convicts for execution or conviction to British colonies and carry out a sentence of transportation.]

7. And be it enacted, that if any suit or action shall be brought in any court within Her Majesty's dominions against any person or persons for anything done in pursuance of any such power or jurisdiction of Her Majesty as aforesaid or of this Act, then and in every such case such action or suit shall be commenced or prosecuted within six months after the fact committed, and not afterwards, except where the cause of action shall have arisen out of Her Majesty's dominions, and then within six months after the plaintiff or plaintiffs and defendant or defendants shall have been within the jurisdiction of the court in which the same may be brought; and the same and every such action or suit shall be brought in the county or place where the cause of action shall have arisen, and not elsewhere, except where the cause of action shall have arisen out of Her Majesty's dominions; and the defendant or defendants shall be entitled to the like notice, and shall have the like privilege of tendering amends to the plaintiff or plaintiffs, or their agent or attorney, as is provided in actions brought against any justice of the peace for acts done in the execution of his office by an Act passed in the 24th year of the reign of King George the Second, intituled 'An Act for the rendering Justices of the Peace more safe in the execution of their Office, and for indemnifying Constables and others acting in obedience to their Warrants;' and the defendant or defendants in every such action or suit may plead the general issue, and give the special matter in evidence; and if the matter or thing complained of shall appear to have been done under the authority and in execution of any such power or jurisdiction of Her Majesty as aforesaid or of this Act, or if any such action or suit shall be brought after the time limited for bringing the same, or be brought and laid in any other country or place than the same ought to have been brought or laid in as aforesaid, then the jury shall find for the defendant or defendants; and if the plaintiff or plaintiffs shall become nonsuit, or discontinue any action after the defendant or defendants shall have appeared, or if a verdict shall pass against the

plaintiff or plaintiffs, or if upon demurrer judgment shall be taken against the plaintiff or plaintiffs, the defendant or defendants shall and may recover treble costs, and have the like remedy for recovery thereof as any defendant or defendants hath or have in any cases of law. . . .

[7. Repealing sections of Acts of 6 Geo. IV, c. 33 and 6 & 7 Will. IV, c. 78, concerning the jurisdiction of consuls in the Levant and the Ottoman empire.]

8

LORD STANLEY TO LIEUT.-GOVERNOR H. W. HILL: GOLD COAST JURISDICTION, 16 DECEMBER 1843[1]

[The resumption of Crown control of the forts has been delayed while Hill was in England where he has conferred with the Colonial Office and the African Committee.]

. . . As the Forts & Settlements on the Gold Coast are Dependencies on the Government of Sierra Leone, you will be guided, so far as they may be applicable to the circumstances of your Government by the Royal Commission & Instructions which are furnished to the Governor of that Colony, & I therefore transmit to you a copy of those Instructions by which you will be apprised of the general powers & functions with which that officer is invested.

On your arrival at Cape Coast Castle you will cause H.M.'s Commission appointing you Lieut. Governor of the Forts & Settlements to be publicly read & promulgated & you will take the oaths prescribed for the occasion, administering them afterwards to such persons employed in the public service as you may think proper.

You are aware that Mr. Maclean the Officer at present in charge of the Forts has expressed his readiness to accept the Office of Judicial Assessor & Magistrate.

The power of this Officer within British Territory (so long as no Court is established with Civil & Criminal Jurisdiction) must be derived from his Commission as a Justice of the Peace, which he already holds from a renewed Commission to the same effect from yourself. When the Forts were placed under the charge of the African Committee in 1828, it was arranged that all the members of the Council should be appointed Justices of the Peace & empowered to form among themselves a Court for the trial of offences [D. (not amounting to felonies & misdemeanours)] [A. cognizable by Justices of the Peace] & that the said Justices should likewise be authorized to exercise all such powers as might be legally conferred upon them with

[1] C.O. 96/2.

a view to the preservation of the peace of the Dependencies & to the protection thereof against assault or rebellion & for the repression of the Slave Trade within the limits of the Forts, it being understood that all crimes and misdemeanours [A. beyond the jurisdn. of Justices of the Peace] committed within the limits of those Forts shall be cognizable & punished by the Courts of Sierra Leone.

In the event of a Council being constituted by Her Majesty it would be right to consider whether the members should not be vested with the powers above stated and authorized to form a Court over which Mr. Maclean would preside as [D. Judicial Assessor] [A. Chairman]. For the present Mr. Maclean will receive such general assistance as he may require in the exercise of his magisterial functions, as well as from those who already hold Commissions of the Peace from the Governor of Sierra Leone, as from others to whom you may think proper to issue such Commissions.

As regards any powers to be exercised by Mr. Maclean among Tribes not within British Territory, as proposed by the Select Committee of the House of Commons on the state of the British Possessions on the West Coast of Africa, I need scarcely observe that it must rest with the sovereign power in each Territory to authorize or permit the exercise of any jurisdiction within that Territory whether according to British Laws or the Laws there prevalent.

I do not however at the present moment propose to enter fully into the consideration of this branch of the subject.

The provisions of the Foreign Jurisdiction Act of last Session (6 & 7 Vic. c. 94) will I have no doubt assist H.M.'s Government in executing the plan proposed by the Select Committee more fully than can be done by the mere appointment of the assessors which however has been made with reference to its provisions.

To this Act, as affecting the two cases of murder at Winnebah, Mr. Maclean's attention has already been called in a despatch dated the 29th Septr. last.[1] The reply to that despatch may possibly afford sufficient information to enable me to advise Her Majesty as to the propriety of conferring general powers on the Assessors under it.

In any case I have to request that you will call upon Mr. Maclean for a report with that view specially adverting to the circumstances which under the first section of the Act are required to enable H.M.'s Government to apply its provisions [A. and in transmitting the report you will accompany it by an expression of your own opinion upon the subject. In the meantime however I wd. not be understood as desiring

---

[1] James Stephen and Lord Stanley considered that non-British subjects at Winneba might be tried under the Foreign Jurisdiction Act, if Maclean had exercised such jurisdiction in the past so that its exercise became an established right. Stanley to Maclean, 29 September 1843, C.O. 96/2. Maclean did claim such jurisdiction—but only within the powers of a justice of the peace. Maclean to Stanley, 2 February 1844, C.O. 96/4.

that the exercise of the jurisdiction which has been established by Mr. Maclean in the case of crimes and misdemeanours committed among the neighbouring tribes shd. be abandoned or interrupted. On the contrary it is my wish that it should be maintained. To take an opposite course wd. according to the concurrent testimony of all persons conversant with the habits of the natives not only be most detrimental to the maintenance of order & civilization at the moment, but render its restoration at a future period very difficult.]

[Maclean's appointment will relieve Hill of his judicial functions; there will be a Parliamentary grant of £4000 for 1844 free from military charges, and an establishment of seven officers costing £2,620; the forts are to be limited to Cape Coast and Accra.]

9

GOLD COAST JURISDICTION ORDER IN COUNCIL, 3 SEPTEMBER 1844[1]

[Recital of the West Africa and Falkland Islands Act and the Foreign Jurisdiction Act of 1843.]

. . . AND Whereas Her Majesty hath power and jurisdiction within divers countries and places adjacent to Her Majesty's Forts and Settlements on the Gold Coast in Africa Her Majesty is pleased by and with the advice of Her Privy Council to order, and it is hereby ordered that all Judges, Magistrates, Assessors and other Officers duly appointed to exercise the said power and jurisdiction in the name and on behalf of Her Majesty within the Countries and Places afores[aid] shall in the exercise thereof observe until further Order such of the local customs of the said Countries and places as may be compatible with the principles of the Law of England and in default of such customs shall proceed in all things as nearly as may be according to the said Law of England, and in further pursuance of the powers by the said Acts of Parliament vested in Her Majesty, Her Majesty is pleased by and with the advice of Her Privy Council to appoint the Settlement of Cape Coast Castle and the Colony of Sierra Leone as British Colonies to which it shall be lawful for any person having authority derived from Her Majesty in that behalf by warrant under her hand and seal to cause any person charged with the Commission of any Crime or offense the cognizance whereof may at any time appertain to any Judge, Magistrate, or other Officer of Her Majesty within the Countries and Places aforesaid to be sent for Trial, or in order that Sentences passed within such Countries and places as aforesaid may be carried into effect within such Colonies. . . .

[1] *Parl. Papers*, 1855, xxxvii (383), p. 81. Forwarded to Governor G. Macdonald with additional instructions, 20 November 1844; C.O. 267/218.

10

LIEUT.-GOVERNOR H. W. HILL TO LORD STANLEY: TRIALS AT CAPE COAST, 27 JANUARY 1845[1]

MY LORD,

I have the honor to inclose to your Lordship the Acting Judicial Assessor's Notes on the trial of 'Quashie Andoful' of the Village of Ampamah in Goomnah, for the murder of his Father's Wife named 'Eduah' about the commencement of September last.

The trial took place on the 10th Ultimo when the Court found the Prisoner guilty and sentenced him to death.

This sentence was carried into effect on the 20th. Instant by the Criminal being hung at the Village where the murder took place, which is about 50 miles distant from this in a North-east direction.

In reporting this case, and also with reference to my dispatch No. 2 of the 7th. Instant reporting another capital sentence being executed, I have the honor to inform your Lordship that the Judicial Assessor presided at both trials as the Assessor to the Native Chiefs assisted by the Magistrates according to the Agreement or Treaty made with the Native Chiefs, copies of which I forwarded to your Lordship in my despatch No. 40 of the 5th, August last; twelve of the Native Chiefs or Pynins were also assembled as a Jury, and the Court was held in public in the Town of Cape Coast, not in Her Majesty's Fort.

The order and regularity observed throughout the proceedings has been most satisfactory towards establishing a proper and fair system of Trial.

Both executions taking place at so great a distance from this Castle is a convincing proof of the general desire of the Natives to be under the jurisdiction of the British Authorities.

[1] C.O. 96/6. Stanley had already approved other cases heard by Maclean with a caution that he was not to restore fugitive slaves: C.O. 96/4, Stanley to Hill, 30 December 1844.

II

ACTING GOVERNOR B. PINE TO EARL GREY, EXTRA-TERRITORIAL JURISDICTION, SIERRA LEONE, 23 OCTOBER 1849[1]

[Notices prohibiting the involvement of British subjects in native wars are ineffectual.]

... 8. Soon after my arrival in the Colony in 1842, a very flagrant outrage was committed by a person born in the Colony, upon the persons and property of some of the native people in the Bolom Country. The Chiefs sent to the then Governor Colonel George Macdonald, to request that the offender might be taken up, and punished by this Government, or that permission might be given to them to punish him according to native law. I was consulted by His Excellency upon the case, and Sir John Jeremie's Ordinance was placed before me; but I was compelled to advise that under the circumstances the Law would not reach the offender and that the Local Ordinance was inoperative, inasmuch as the Colonial Legislature, in passing it, had largely exceeded its powers; and considering the cruel and barbarous modes of punishment adopted by the Natives I also advised the Governor that he had better give the Chiefs no reply whatever, to their request to be allowed to punish the man lest His Excellency should, in some degree, become a party to the infliction of punishment which neither humanity nor our own laws would permit.

[Lord Stanley has disallowed Sir John Jeremie's Ordinance and he has pointed this out to Governors Fergusson and Macdonald.]

... 13. The intercourse which, during my administration of the Government, I have upon various occasions, had, with the peoples of the countries in our vicinity has confirmed my opinion of the importance of extending our jurisdiction over British Subjects residing in those countries, and of, as far as practicable providing a legal means of preventing their involving themselves in native wars.

14. The measure which I would respectfully suggest for effecting these objects is, that an Act of Parliament should be passed enacting 1st. That British Subjects committing in any place within 300 miles of the Colony, an offence which, if committed within its limits would be cognizable by its Courts, shall be tried and punished in the same manner as if the offence had been committed in the Colony 2nd.

---

[1] C.O. 267/208. The question was referred to the Board of Trade which produced a draft report in January 1850 and recommended an Order-in-Council, under the Foreign Jurisdiction Act of 1843.

That British Subjects, who, within certain limits, shall involve themselves in native wars, either by becoming actual combattants, or by supplying the belligerents with arms or munitions of war, shall be deemed guilty of a high misdemeanour and punished with a certain fine and imprisonment. . . .

12

EARL GREY TO GOVERNOR N. W. MACDONALD: EXTRA-TERRITORIAL JURISDICTION, SIERRA LEONE, 24 JULY 1850[1]

SIR,

I received in Decr. last a desp. from Mr. Pine, dated the 23d. October in which he points out the importance of extending British Jurisdiction over British Subjects residing in Countries adjacent to Sierra Leone under the dominion of Native Princes; and recommending that an Act of Parliament should be passed for effecting this.

The object is clearly of such importance that I could not hesitate to promote it so far as this could be done without prejudice to any of those principles which it is desirable to preserve as regulating the relations between Great Britain and the uncivilized Powers with which Her Colonial Possessions bring Her into contact. But since I felt that some important questions of jurisprudence were involved in any proceeding tending to the exercise by H.M. of jurisdiction out of Her own Possessions, I deemed it expedient to request that the Queen in Council might be advised to refer this matter to the Lords of the Committee of Council for Trade and Plantations and that they might be requested to report their opinion, whether the powers given to H.M. by the Act 6 & 7 Vic. Cap. 94 could be made available for the whole or part of the purposes contemplated by Mr. Pine's desp. and, if not, what course they would recommend in order to effect those objects. Their Lordships accordingly submitted to H.M. the Report of their opinion which is contained in and approved by the Order in Council[2] which I now have the honor to transmit.

You will find it stated in this Order that it is not competent for H.M. under the Act 6 & 7 Vic. Cap. 94, of her own authority to exercise any jurisdiction within any of the Territories adjacent to Sierra Leone, but that such powers may be ceded to H.M. by means of Treaties entered into with the Native authorities, and that it will be then competent for H.M. in Council, by any Order to be made for that purpose to authorize the trial at Sierra Leone of any person charged with the Commission of any offence 'the cognizance of which

[1] C.O. 268/43, ff. 172–8.
[2] Order-in-Council, 13 July 1850, *Parl. Papers*, 1855, xxxvii (383), p. 34.

may, in pursuance of any such Treaty, appertain to any judge, magistrate, or other of H.M.'s Officers, within any such Territories'.

You are probably aware that under the powers given by the same Act, a jurisdiction has been acquired by H.M. in the Territories adjacent to the Forts on the Gold Coast, and that by this means the neighbouring Chiefs and Tribes have been induced to have recourse to a great extent to British Tribunals for the repression of crime, and to relinquish their own barbarous usages.

The immediate object which Mr. Pine had in view was different, his object, (like that of Sir J. Jeremie in framing the Ordinance which was necessarily disallowed) was rather to create a jurisdiction under which British Subjects, guilty of crimes within the Territories adjacent to Sierra Leone, might be lawfully tried and punished within the Colony, instead of being left to the alternative either of a dangerous impunity, or of being subjected to the unrestrained vindictiveness of the Natives.

The Act in question is deemed (as you will learn from the subjoined Report) large enough to serve this purpose likewise. It is however essential that you should keep one point in view. Although it be very desirable to prevent British Subjects from intermeddling in the wars and dissensions of the Native Tribes, this object must not be pursued to the extent of making Treaties for the surrender of such British Subjects, to be dealt with as offenders, unless they are actually charged with some crime known to the law of England and the Colony. The reasons for this limitation are fully stated in the report of the Committee of the Council for Trade and Plantations.[1]

I have now to direct that should any opportunity offer for carrying into effect the recommendation contained in that report, you will take advantage of it by making Treaties with the neighbouring chiefs for the surrender of criminals, and to state that as soon as any progress has been made in obtaining such Treaties, on your reporting it to me the necessary Order in Council will be issued appointing Sierra Leone to be the Colony to which any person charged with the Commission of an Offence within the Territories comprized in the Treaty may be brought to Trial.

[1] An Act of Parliament would be necessary for such new crimes, offences, or penalties.

13

H. E. COCKBURN AND W. P. WOOD (LAW OFFICERS) TO EARL GREY: STATUS OF LIBERATED AFRICANS, 21 OCTOBER 1851[1]

My Lord,

We are honoured with your Lordship's Commands signified in Mr. Elliot's Letter of the 13th Instant stating that he was directed to transmit to us the accompanying Extract of a Despatch from the Governor of Sierra Leone, and to request that we would take the same into consideration, and report to your Lordship our joint opinion.

1st. Whether an African liberated from Slavery by legal process in Her Majesty's Mixed Commission Courts becomes ipso facto a British Subject in the full acceptation of that term &

2ndly. Whether a liberated African in the event of his committing any offence out of the Jurisdiction of a Colony would be amenable to the same Jurisdiction by which a bona fide British Subject could be tried within the Territories of Native Chiefs with whom Treaties may have been concluded.

In obedience to Your Lordship's Commands we have taken into consideration the Extract of the Despatch above referred to, & have the honor to report that in our opinion both Questions should be answered in the negative.

14

SIR JOHN S. PACKINGTON TO GOVERNOR N. W. MACDONALD: DEFINITION OF BRITISH SUBJECTS, 28 FEBRUARY 1852[2]

Sir,

I have to acknowledge your despatch No 183, of the 25th Nov last, in which you represented the difficulties which must in your opinion arise from the views entertained by some authorities in Sierra Leone, and confirmed by the Law Advisers of the Crown, that Liberated Africans, resident in Sierra Leone, are not British Subjects, and, consequently, not included in any Treaty entered, or to be entered, into by independent Chiefs in the vicinity of Sierra Leone, for the delivery of 'British Subjects' guilty of offences cognizable by the Laws of England for the purpose of trial within the Colony.

2. I fully appreciate the importance of the question there raised, but believe the difficulty in question to be removable without resort being

[1] C.O. 267/225.   [2] C.O. 267/230.

had to legislative measures.[1] The act of 6th & 7th [Vict.] C. 94 which confirms to the Crown jurisdiction acquired by usage or treaty, over parties guilty of offences out of Her own Dominions, does not apply either in language or in intention to British Subjects only. On the contrary, at the Gold Goast, where some of its provisions have been put in practice, the jurisdiction which it gives is exercised over persons not British Subjects, but Natives of neighbouring territories whose Chiefs are under British protection. And you will observe that in neither of the Orders in Council of 3rd. Sept. 1844 or 13th July 1850, are, 'British Subjects' mentioned as such.

3. When, however, you were directed by my Predecessor's Despatch of 24th. July 1850 to make Treaties with neighbouring Chiefs for the delivery of Offenders, your attention was naturally drawn to the case of British Subjects only, because the particular object in view was the trial and punishment of British Subjects or those regarded as such: the circumstances that Liberated Africans were not really British Subjects not having been at all adverted to.

4. But the Treaties would have been equally valid, and the jurisdiction given by the Act would have equally attached, if they had been more generally worded and had extended to others besides British Subjects.

5. I annex a letter which has been received from the Law Advisers of the Crown to whom my Predecessor had referred the question, which makes this point clear.

6. All that is necessary therefore is, that you should so word the Treaties as to comprehend Liberated Africans: The words might be either 'criminals being British Subjects or Liberated Africans' or, 'British Subjects or others, residents in Sierra Leone' as you may deem advisable.

7. I regret the inconvenience which this may occasion, being aware of the difficulties which may possibly occur as to the renewal of negociations with Native Chiefs; but it appears necessary for the accomplishment of your purpose: and I have therefore delayed advising Her Majesty to confirm your Treaties with Bey Ingar, Sattan Lahai, and Bey Farima,[2] transmitted with your Despatch No 7 of the 4th. Ult., until you are able to reconsider them with a view to this alteration, if you find it practicable. The Treaty with Fourecaria would likewise require revision.

8. I am aware that other difficulties, besides that supposed to have arisen under the 6 and 7 [Vict.] C. 94 may possibly occur from the circumstance that Liberated Africans are not British Subjects. For these it may become, at some future time, expedient to provide in some general way: you will, however, remember in the meantime that

---

[1] The opinion, too, of T. F. Elliot: minute, 25 October 1851: C.O. 267/225.
[2] Treaties made in August and December 1851.

the Legislature of Sierra Leone has power to naturalize these persons, and thereby to entitle them to all the privileges & protection due to born subjects of The Crown in Sierra Leone: and that I see no objection to encouraging individuals or proper character to avail themselves of this opportunity to the fullest extent.

15

J. D. HARDING (LAW OFFICER) TO SIR JOHN S. PACKINGTON: NATURALIZATION, 25 AUGUST 1852[1]

... WE have the honor *to report that* we are of opinion that under the provisions of the Stat. 10th & 11th Vict. C. 83 Colonial Acts Statutes or Ordinances imparting to any person the privileges of Naturalization, can only effect the status of such persons, or confer such privileges on them within the limits of the Colonies & Possessions & that consequently the Ordinance in question will not effect the intended object, by rendering liberated Africans British Subjects to all intents & purposes so as to bring them within the scope of the existing Treaties with the Native Chiefs. . . .

[An Imperial Statute will be necessary to determine the status of liberated Africans.]

16

THE EARL OF MALMESBURY TO CONSUL JOHN BEECROFT: CONSULAR JURISDICTION, 13 OCTOBER 1852[2]

[An African British Subject, Jonathan Scott, has been tried for manslaughter by Beecroft at Fernando Po.]

... UNDER all these circumstances, I do not see the necessity for Scott's having been put in Irons, and kept in such severe confinement, as he alleges, nor for his wife having been denied access to him.

With reference to the remark which you make in your Despatch, that you would be fully justified, as [Spanish] Governor of Fernando Po, in allowing Scott to be tried by a Jury of his Countrymen, and in abiding by their decision, I have to observe that there does not appear to be any legal ground for trying him in that Spanish possession.

If Her Majesty the Queen has even by usage, or sufferance, any jurisdiction over the place where the shot was fired, or, if the shot was in Law fired 'on the High Seas,' I am of the opinion that the

[1] C.O. 267/230.   [2] F.O. 2/7.

nearest British Colony either appointed by Her Majesty by Order in Council, or having an Admiralty or other Court exercising Jurisdiction for offences committed by Her Majesty's Subjects on the High Seas, would be the proper Tribunal according to the circumstances. A prosecution before such a court, however, would probably fail in the case of Jonathan Scott for want of the necessary Evidence.

Upon the whole therefore, I deem it expedient to instruct you immediately on the receipt of this Despatch to release Jonathan Scott.

For your future guidance I have to inform you, that you have no jurisdiction to imprison at Fernando Po, or to try in that Island, either before a Jury or otherwise, British Subjects charged with offences committed either in Africa, although within the limits of your Consular Commission, or on board of British Vessels on the High Seas beyond the limits of your Spanish Jurisdiction.

I have further to inform you, that British Subjects before conviction by a competent Court are not to be kept in Irons by H.M. Consuls, nor to be subjected to severe treatment as to diet & sleeping accomodation, but only to be confined for the purposes of safe custody, and not as a punishment. . . .

17

SIR GEORGE BARROW: MINUTE, STATUS OF LIBERATED AFRICANS, 20 JANUARY 1853[1]

Mr Merivale,

Certain Treaties were concluded by the late Governor of Sierra Leone with Chiefs in the vicinity of the Colony,[2] which were not ratified, as other Treaties had formerly been, owing to a question having arisen whether 'British Subjects' (who were to become amenable under those Treaties) included 'Liberated Africans'. The Law Officers decided that Liberated Africans as such, were not British Subjects. It was then to be considered whether the Treaties could not be so altered as to included Liberated Africans: the late Governor thought that the Chiefs having once concluded the Treaties would not agree to alter them. To remedy this state of things he passed an Ordinance constituting the Liberated Africans within the Colony British Subjects. The Law Officers however reported that this Ordinance would not constitute the Liberated Africans British Subjects *without* the Colony—& that an Imperial Act would be required for that purpose. Before proposing such an Act, the new Governor was directed to report whether he concurred with his Predecessor in the danger of attempting an alteration of the Treaties.

[1] C.O. 267/229.   [2] With the Chiefs of the Nunez area. See above, p. 561.

Governor Kennedy now reports that neither he nor his Council see any difficulty in the case, & that it is only a question of time & expense (the latter of which he says will be considerable). He recommends however that the Treaties, as they now stand, should be ratified & alterations made in them from time to time, as opportunities may occur. He points out at the same time that the *status* of the Liberated Africans *within* the Colony has become an important question.

The Ordinance which was passed in the Colony would have settled that, but unfortunately it was disallowed, because it did not accomplish all that was intended at the time.

It appears to me that there are two courses open—1st. To ratify the Treaties as proposed by the Governor—& to direct him to bring forward another Ordinance for naturalizing the Liberated Africans *within* the Colony—or 2ly. to propose to Parliament a Bill for constituting Liberated Africans bona fide British Subjects.[1]

18

AN ACT TO REMOVE DOUBTS AS TO THE RIGHTS OF THE LIBERATED AFRICANS IN SIERRA LEONE, 20 AUGUST 1853 (16 & 17 VICT., c. 86)[2]

WHEREAS doubts have been entertained whether Africans who have been liberated, or taken and received under the protection of the Crown, under the provisions of the Acts for the Abolition and Suppression of the Slave Trade, and are domiciled in the colony of Sierra Leone and its dependencies, are British subjects, and doubts have been also entertained as to the authority of the local legislature of that colony in legislating in relation to the rights and obligations of such Africans: Be it enacted by the Queen's most Excellent Majesty, by and with the advice and consent of the Lords Spiritual and Temporal, and Commons, in this present Parliament assembled, and by the authority of the same as follows:

1. All liberated Africans domiciled or resident, or who hereafter may be domiciled or resident, in the colony of Sierra Leone or its dependencies, shall be deemed to be and to have been for all purposes as, from the date of their being brought into or of their arrival in the said colony, natural-born subjects of Her Majesty, and to be and to have been capable of taking, holding, conveying, devising, and

---

[1] H. Merivale thought both courses of action necessary: minute, 21 January 1853; C.O. 267/229.
[2] *Parl. Papers*, 1855, xxxvii (383), pp. 36–37.

transmitting any estate, real or personal, within the said colony of Sierra Leone and its dependencies: Provided always, that it shall be lawful for the legislature of Sierra Leone, by any Ordinance to be passed in the manner and subject to the conditions which are or may be by law required in respect of such Ordinances, to alter or repeal any of the provisions of this Act, so far as they relate to rights to real property within the colony of Sierra Leone and its dependencies, and generally to make such provisions in relation to such rights as to such legislature may seem expedient.

2. And whereas treaties have been from time to time entered into, by or on the behalf and with the sanction of Her Majesty, with the kings and chiefs of certain African territories and tribes in the neighbourhood of the said colony of Sierra Leone, for the purpose (amongst others) of providing for the security of the persons and property of British subjects, and for the surrender of criminals, being British subjects, guilty of any offence cognizable by the laws of England, for trial in such colony as Her Majesty may appoint: In all such treaties as aforesaid made or which may be made between the officer administering the government of Sierra Leone for the time being and such kings or chiefs as aforesaid, and sanctioned by Her Majesty, her heirs and successors, the terms 'British subjects' and 'subjects of the Queen of England' shall be held, for the purposes of such treaty, to comprehend all liberated Africans domiciled or residing in Sierra Leone and its dependencies.

3. Any magistrate or other officer whom the officer administering the government of Sierra Leone shall appoint to demand or to take charge of any British subject who shall be surrendered according to the provisions of any such treaty for trial in Sierra Leone shall be deemed and taken to be an officer of Her Majesty, to whom the cognizance of the crime or offence with which such British subject may be charged appertains, within the meaning of the Act of the sixth and seventh year of the reign of Her present Majesty, c. 94, intituled, 'An Act to remove doubts as to the exercise of power and jurisdiction by Her Majesty within divers Countries and Places out of Her Majesty's Dominions, and to render the same more effectual.'

4. For the purposes of this Act, the words 'liberated Africans' shall mean and include all persons dealt with or detained as slaves who heretofore have been or hereafter may be seized or taken, under any of the Acts for the abolition or suppression of the Slave Trade, by Her Majesty's ships of war or otherwise, and liberated or delivered to the officers appointed to protect, receive, or provide for such persons, and all other persons who, as having been dealt with, carried, kept, or detained as slaves, may have been taken and liberated, or received, protected, or provided for, under any of the said Acts.

5. Provided always, that nothing in this Act shall in anywise

prejudice or interfere with any of the provisions in relation to such liberated Africans as aforesaid of the laws in force for the abolition or suppression of the Slave Trade.

19

J. D. HARDING (LAW OFFICER) TO THE EARL OF CLARENDON, 25 SEPTEMBER 1856[1]

[Concerning the legal status of Liberated Africans residing at Old Calabar.]

. . . IN obedience to Yr. L[ordship's] commands I have taken this question into consideration & have the honour to report:—

That the question of the right of liberated Africans to be considered as British subjects has on more than one occasion received the attention of the Colonial Dept. & I would beg to refer to the Reports of the Law Officers to Earl Grey 21st Oct. 1851 & 23rd Feby. 1852, & to the Duke of Newcastle 3rd Aug. 1853; as also to the Statute 16 & 17 Vic cap. 86 upon this subject, from which it will appear that in the absence of any special legislation, they cannot be so considered even in the Queen's Dominions. This being so, I am of the opinion that they cannot legally be so considered when voluntarily returning to & resident in the territory of the Native Chief whose subjects they were by birth.

I have of course answered this question upon the principles of British & International Law; whether by usage any right to British protection (such as exists to some extent in the Levant) independently of birth or naturalization, is known at Old Calabar, I cannot say. If there be any such usage, they are entitled to benefit of it.

I am ignorant whether any Treaty exists in the present case with the Chief of Old Calabar.

I need scarcely however point out to Yr. L[ordship] the difficulty of acting in such a case with a Native Chief according to the strict rules of international or of British Law, of which he is probably ignorant, & the application of which, even in his own fashion he cannot appreciate, & which will practically result only in the abandonment to barbarism & ill usage of these liberated Africans, who are all partially civilized, & some of whom are Christians; who returned to his territory from the Queen's Dominions by his express permission, & are living within the bounds & under the care of an English Christian Missionary Station.

I would respectfully submit whether (if none exists) some distinct Treaty or Agreement should not forthwith be negotiated with the

[1] C.O. 147/10. Encl. in F.O. to C.O., 7 December 1865. The Colonial Office was not informed of this opinion till this late date.

Chief of Old Calabar on this subject; & whether in the meantime he might not be warned in general terms that H.M. Govt. took the most peculiar interest in the well being of these persons, & would not fail to resent as an insult to itself any ill usage to which they might be imposed. If H.M. Consul or the Captain of H.M.'s Ships were to pay him a special and formal visit for the purpose, it might have a good effect, & any measure taken on the spot which might have the effect of raising these individuals in the estimation of the people & merchants of Old Calabar, & impressing upon them the determination of H.M.'s Govt. to protect & encourage them, would be desirable.

[In a particular case reported by Consul Hutchinson, no decision can be given for want of evidence.]

. . . There is too much reason . . . to suppose that these liberated Africans have excited the jealousy of British traders merely by engaging in the Palm oil trade, & that this has (in effect) led to their being exposed to the ill will of the natives; thus when they are attempting to do the very thing which H.M.'s Govt. would be most desirous that they should do, viz, after receiving some education & embracing Christianity, returning to their native country & there embarking in that particular trade which of all others best promotes cultivation & commerce, & most effectually checks S[lave] T[rade] they are met with the jealous hostility of British Traders, & I fear thereby exposed to degradation & ill usage by the natives.

The whole policy of H.M.G. in this matter (for which it has made & still makes great sacrifices) is thus effectually thwarted & defeated, & Africans, tho' liberated from actual slavery, are prevented from returning to their native country with any security, or from there engaging in the staple trade of West Africa, a state of things which H.M.'s Govt. cannot be expected to tolerate, especially formally brought under its notice, & going on as it were under the shadow of its Flag, a British Man of War, a British Consul, Missionaries, & Merchants being on the spot.

These however are matters entirely beyond my province, & I ought to apologize for entering upon them; which I only do in consideration of the extreme importance of the principles & policy involved in the case.

20

TREATY WITH SHERBRO AND LOKO CHIEFS: SURRENDER OF CRIMINALS, 7 APRIL 1860[1]

. . . 14. THE Queen of England shall have the right to demand the surrender of criminals, or other persons being British Subjects, or Liberated Africans, or others resident in Sierra Leone, accused of any crime or offence committed within the Colony of Sierra Leone or its Dependencies cognizable by the Laws of England, for the purpose of being tried for such offences in Sierra Leone, or such other place as the Queen of England has already appointed or may hereafter appoint for that purpose; and the said Chiefs, parties to this Treaty, hereby bind themselves to secure and surrender all British subjects or Liberated Africans, or others resident in Sierra Leone who may be charged with any crime or offence as aforesaid upon demand being made for them by His Excellency the Governor of Sierra Leone, or any other competent authority.

Article 15. The Queen of England shall have the right to demand the surrender of all criminals, who, being convicted of any crime or offence in any part of Her Dominions, may be found in the territories of the said Chiefs, and also the surrender of all British subjects or Liberated Africans accused or charged with any crime or offence cognizable by the Laws of England, committed within the territories of the said Chiefs, or elsewhere, and found within the territories of the said Chiefs, for the purpose of being punished or being tried for such crime or offence in Sierra Leone, or such other place as the Queen of England has already appointed or may hereafter appoint for that purpose, and the Chiefs, parties hereto, bind themselves and their Successors to secure and surrender all such criminals, British subjects and Liberated Africans so convicted, accused or charged as afore-said, upon demand made for them by the Governor of Sierra Leone, or any other competent authority. . . .

21

ACT FOR THE PREVENTION OF OFFENCES IN TERRITORIES NEAR SIERRA LEONE, 11 JULY 1861 (24 & 25 VICT., c. 31)[2]

WHEREAS the inhabitants of the territories adjacent to the Colony of Sierra Leone, extending to the Rio Grande or Bulola to the north of

[1] C.O. 267/268. Encl. in Hill to Newcastle, 26 September 1860.
[2] *Ordinances of the Colony of Sierra Leone* (London, 1909), vol. ix, pp. 1687–8.

the Colony, to the river Gallinas to the south of the Colony, and for five hundred miles to the east of the Colony, being in an uncivilised state, offences against the persons and property of such inhabitants and others are frequently committed by Her Majesty's subjects within such territories with impunity: For remedy thereof, be it enacted by the Queen's most excellent Majesty, by and with the advice and consent of the Lords Spiritual and Temporal, and Commons, in this present Parliament assembled, and by the authority of the same, as follows:—

1. The laws which are now or which shall hereafter be in force in the Colony of Sierra Leone for the punishment of crimes therein committed shall be and the same are hereby extended and declared applicable to all Her Majesty's subjects within any territory adjacent to the said Colony, and being within the limits as aforesaid; and every crime or offence committed by any of Her Majesty's subjects within any such territory in contravention of any such laws shall be cognizable in any such Courts, and shall be inquired of, tried and prosecuted and, on conviction, punished in such and the same manner as if the same had been committed within the said Colony.

2. And whereas it is necessary to prevent as far as may be the commission of crimes by Her Majesty's subjects within such territories as aforesaid, and to provide for the arrest, commitment and bringing to punishment of any of Her Majesty's subjects by whom any such crimes may be perpetrated: Be it therefore enacted that it shall be lawful for the Governors of the said Colony to address to any one or more of Her Majesty's subjects being within or about to resort to any such territories as aforesaid, one or more commission or commissions authorizing him or them to exercise within such territories the office of a magistrate for the purpose of preventing the perpetration therein by any of Her Majesty's subjects of any crimes or offences, and for the purpose of arresting, committing to custody and bringing to trial before such Courts as aforesaid, any of Her Majesty's subjects charged on sufficient evidence before him or them with the commission of any such crimes or offences within any such territories; and it shall be lawful to the Governor of the said Colony, by any such commission or commissions as aforesaid to define with all practicable and convenient precision the local limits within which the jurisdiction of any such magistrate or magistrates shall be so exercised, and to which it shall so extend. . . .

[Commissions may be withdrawn at any time; copies are to be sent to the Secretary of State for Colonies for approval.]

4. Nothing herein or in any such commission or commissions contained shall extend or be construed to extend to invest Her Majesty, Her heirs or successors, with any claim or title whatsoever to dominion

or sovereignty over any such territories as aforesaid, or to derogate from the rights of the tribes or people inhabiting such territories, or of chiefs or rulers to such sovereignty or dominion.

22

GOVERNOR S. W. BLACKALL TO EDWARD CARDWELL, 20 APRIL 1866[1]

[The draft Ordinance prepared by the Chief Magistrate and Queen's Advocate of Sierra Leone for the reorganisation of the judicial establishment of the Settlements will be forwarded later.][2]

. . . 3. The General Principles which I propose to embody are:

1st. A general Supreme Court for West Africa Settlements to consist of One Chief and two Puisne Judges, the Chief Justice and one Puisne Judge to be resident at Sierra Leone and one Puisne Judge at Lagos.

2nd. To establish at each Dependency a Magistrate, defining the cases which are to be tried and determined by him.

3rd. Establishing Circuits to be presided over by a Judge of the Supreme Court, having jurisdiction over all cases not triable by the Magistrate, and being a Court of Appeal in such cases as appeals may be given from the Magistrate's decision.

4th. Constituting the Supreme Court of three a general Court of Appeal from the decision of any one Judge.

5th. Establishing new Courts of Request, Escheat Etc. for Sierra Leone.

6th. Appeals direct to Privy Council.

4. I have now to bring under your special consideration the appointment of a Judicial Assessor at the Gold Coast. If such a Court is to be continued it appears to me that it would be advisable to make it only a Court of Appeal as against any decision of the Chiefs, and should be presided over by the Administrator, and that he should have full power to refuse any case on his own responsibility. No lawyers should be permitted to practice in this Court, and it should only be held once in each month.

5. The other Courts at the Gold Coast should not be allowed in any way to interfere with the Native Courts as between Natives.

6. The Native Courts should be compelled to refuse to interfere, and to refer to the British Courts, all disputes in which a British Subject may be concerned.

7. I feel satisfied that the judgement given directly by the Queen's representative, without any expensive machinery, would be more

[1] C.O. 267/287.
[2] Ordinance, 16 November 1866, set up a Supreme Court and a Court of Summary Jurisdiction.

readily recognised than any other; and the pride of a Chief would be less hurt at his decision being appealed from to such a Court; whilst making it imperative that one of the parties must be a British Subject to enable a case to be brought into the other Law Courts would be a security against their being called on to act in Slave Cases.

23

GOVERNOR S. W. BLACKALL TO LORD CARNARVON, 14 JANUARY 1867[1]

[Re petitions against Ordinance No. 4, 1867 abolishing the use of juries in civil cases.]

. . . A WANT of respect for the value of an oath is the great blot on the jurors of this Colony. In the year 1853 it was found necessary to abolish grand juries because they would never find a true bill for slave dealing; but these same men now come in as petit jurors, and if they were ready to forget their oaths on one occasion, there is no reason to suppose they would not do so on another; but the most fatal injury done to a mercantile community like this, by the want of confidence in juries, is, that the public are always at the mercy of unscrupulous lawyers, who trade upon the passions of the jurors to alarm honest men into paying costs rather than face a trial. It was stated to Colonel Ord by the leading merchant here, that he would sooner submit to a heavy loss than risk a trial before a Sierra Leone jury in civil action.

6. The same complaint has been made very lately from the Gold Coast; and so, it appears to me, must it be where the community is so limited, education so backward, and prejudice so rife. Sir Benjamin Pine says, that no man would have a chance against an Akoo with an Akoo jury; but he might have gone further, for though there are at present but few original Akoos left, the influence of the chief of the tribe, Macauley, is continued, and any person electing to go to his tribunal previous to going to law courts will be secure of a verdict. . . .

24

SIERRA LEONE SUPREME COURT ORDER IN COUNCIL, 26 FEBRUARY 1867[2]

[Recital of 4 Vict. cap. 13.]

. . . AND whereas courts of civil and criminal justice have been established by Ordinances in Her Majesty's Settlements on the

[1] *Parl. Papers*, 1867, xlix (197), p. 20.
[2] *Laws and Ordinances of the Gambia*, p. 308.

Gambia, the Gold Coast, and of Lagos in Western Africa, and it is expedient to provide a court of appellate jurisdiction to hear and determine appeals from the said courts respectively, it is therefore ordered by the Queen's most Excellent Majesty, by and with the advice of the Privy Council, as follows:

1. That the judges for the time being of Her Majesty's Supreme Court of the Settlement of Sierra Leone shall be and they are hereby constituted a court of record to receive, hear, and determine appeals from the court of civil and criminal justice of the Settlement on the Gambia, the court of civil and criminal justice of the Settlement on the Gold Coast, and the court of civil and criminal justice of the Settlement of Lagos in Western Africa, and such court of appeal shall be styled and called 'The West Africa Court of Appeal.'

2. That it shall be lawful for the plaintiff or plaintiffs, defendant or defendants, against whom any sentence, judgment, or decree or order of any of the said courts of civil and criminal justice shall be given for or in respect of any sum or matter at issue above or exceeding the value of 50 *l.* sterling, to appeal therefrom to the said court of appeal; and together with such further costs as shall be awarded thereon.

[The judges are authorized to make rules and regulations for the court.

4. That it shall be lawful for any person who shall think himself aggrieved by any final judgment, sentence, or order of the said West Africa Court of Appeal, to appeal to Her Majesty, Her heirs and successors, in Her or their Privy Council. . . .

25

GOVERNOR SIR ARTHUR KENNEDY TO EARL GRANVILLE: PROTECTION OF BRITISH SUBJECTS, 7 JUNE 1870[1]

[Whobay, a native of Imperi, has been acquitted after trial for the murder of a British subject outside the Sierra Leone Boundary.]

. . . THE broad fact which appears to me to result from these proceedings, if the Law and ruling of the presiding Judge be correct, is, that any British Subject may be seized without form of Law or pretext, within British territory, carried over a Boundary Line (which neither Native or European could accurately define) and there murdered with impunity.

This state of things cannot fail to be highly discouraging to British Traders within, or without our Boundary, and the decision when

[1] C.O. 267/306. Referred to the Crown Law Officers, 15 July 1870. See below, no. 26.

fully known, and understood will doubtless suggest to the Native Mind a very easy mode of either recovering or discharging debts or any other obligation.

I think it is unnecessary for me to trouble Your Lordship with my opinion or comments upon this matter affecting as it does, the most important interests of Society as well as the lives and property of all residing under Her Majesty's Rule on the West Coast of Africa.

I have not thought it necessary to call for any formal report from the Crown Prosecutor who has informed me verbally that he concurs in the *Law* as laid down by the Chief Justice.

There are obvious steps to be taken to amend omissions or mistakes, but I deem it more prudent to let the matter rest till the question is dealt with as a whole.

26

R. P. COLLIER, J. D. COLERIDGE, TRAVERS TWISS (LAW OFFICERS) TO EARL GRANVILLE: COURTS OF EQUITY, 12 JULY 1870[1]

MY LORD,

We are honoured with Yr. L[ordship's] Commands signified in Mr. Otway's letter of the 2nd inst., stating that he was directed to request that we would furnish Your L'p. with our opinion upon an important question, that has been raised as to the constitution of certain Courts of Equity established at various trading places on the W.C. of Africa, beyond H.M.'s jurisdiction.

That these Courts have been formed either by Treaty or Agreement with the Native Chiefs to settle disputes between the Natives & Traders, & that they may have exercised the power of inflicting punishments & levying fines. That they have provided a simple & efficient means of administering justice, & settling disputes, & that their decisions have always been acknowledged by the natives & Traders on the West Coast.

A Statement was enclosed showing by what authority & in what manner these Courts were constituted.

That a case was recently brought before Mr. Chalmers, the Chief Magistrate of the British Colonial Court at Cape Coast, the particulars of which we should learn from the enclosed correspondence the defendant pleaded in his favour a decision previously given by one of the Courts of Equity, but that the Judge set aside the plea on the ground that there was no evidence of the legal competency of the Court in question.

[1] C.O. 96/86.

That this decision has given rise to a serious question as to the competence of all these Courts of Equity, & Mr. Otway was therefore to request that we would furnish Yr. Lp. with our advice upon the following points:

1st. Whether the Court of Equity at Brass (the one in question) & those at other places on the West Coast established under similar circ[umstances] in the territories of independent chiefs & acknowledged by them, are legally constituted, & whether their decisions can be considered as having legal force, if not, what measures, if any, can be taken to place them upon a proper footing;

2ly. Whether the decision of Mr. Chalmers was right & proper in the case in point under the circ[umstances].

In obedience to Yr. Lp's. commands, we have the honor to *Report*

That the Courts in question appear to us to be useful institutions, to the working of which it is undesirable to oppose obstacles. It may perhaps be worth the consideration of H.M.'s Govt. whether means might not be taken to encourage and improve such tribunals, & possibly even to place them by legislation on some more recognized footing. At present, however, we are unable to advise Yr. Lp. that the judgments of these Courts are entitled to the same respect in law, as the judgments of the regularly constituted tribunals of recognized & civilized communities.

It does not appear further that the protection of the so called Court was set up & claimed by the defendant in a proper manner, & on both these grounds we are of opinion that the judgment of the Chief Justice was correct.

27

B. COHEN, J. D. COLERIDGE, TRAVERS TWISS (LAW OFFICERS) TO THE EARL OF KIMBERLEY: EXTRA-TERRITORIAL JURISDICTION, 6 SEPTEMBER 1870[1]

... THERE is no objection, in our opinion, to give jurisdiction to the Colonial Court in respect of offences committed at places out of British Territory against persons who by residence within a British Colony under circumstances, which constitute a domicile by the Law of Nations, have acquired a British National character. The same principles of jurisprudence, which warrant the extension of the jurisdiction of the Colonial Courts in respect of offences committed

[1] C.O. 267/308. In a case similar to that of Whobay's, a Kru labourer could not be committed for trial in Sierra Leone (though he claimed he was a British subject) for a murder done outside the colony. Kennedy had him deported to Cape Palmas. Kennedy to Kimberley, 3 August 1870: C.O. 267/306.

against persons entitled to British protection under our municipal law, will in our opinion sanction the extension of that jurisdiction to the cases of persons, upon whom the British national character is impressed by the Law of Nations.

28

AN ACT FOR EXTENDING THE JURISDICTION OF THE COURTS OF THE WEST AFRICAN SETTLEMENTS TO CERTAIN OFFENCES COMMITTED OUT OF HER MAJESTY'S DOMINIONS, 31 MARCH 1871 (34 VICT., c. 8)[1]

WHEREAS the inhabitants of certain territories in Africa adjoining Her Majesty's Settlements of Sierra Leone, Gambia, Gold Coast, and Lagos, and the adjacent protectorates, not being within the jurisdiction of any civilised Government, and crimes and outrages having been and being likely, unless restrained by law, to be committed within such territories against British subjects and persons resident within any of the said Settlements, it is requisite to provide for the trial and punishment of such crimes and outrages:

Be it therefore enacted by the Queen's most Excellent Majesty, by and with the advice and consent of the Lords Spiritual and Temporal, and Commons, in this present Parliament assembled, and by the authority of the same, as follows; that it is to say,

1. Crimes or offences committed within twenty miles of the boundary of any of the said Settlements or of any adjacent protectorate by any of Her Majesty's subjects, or by persons not subjects of any civilised Power, against the persons of British subjects or of persons resident within any of the said Settlements, shall be cognisable in the superior courts exercising criminal jurisdiction within any of the said Settlements, and shall be inquired of, tried, prosecuted, and, upon conviction, punished in such and the same manner as if the crime or offence had been committed within such Settlements.

2. Any person known or suspected to have committed a crime or offence within the first section of this Act may be apprehended in any of the said Settlements, and kept in custody therein, in the like manner as if the said crime or offence had been committed within such Settlement.

[1] *Ordinances of the Gambia*, iii, p. 160.

29

SIR HENRY HOLLAND: MEMORANDUM, ADMINISTRATION OF JUSTICE ON THE WEST COAST OF AFRICA, 18 JULY 1871[1]

I HAVE seen Sir A. Kennedy upon these papers relating to the Administration of Justice. Practically the questions for consideration are 1. Whether the Summary Court should be abolished. 2. Whether there should not be a Court of Appeal. 3. Whether Juries should not be again allowed in civil cases.

As to the *first* Sir A. Kennedy was called upon to repeat the number of cases brought before the Court, and how long it took to try them, as the delay in hearing cases has been complained of.

He stated to me that he had a great mass of papers upon this matter, which he has not yet had time to consider & which he considers—and in this I am disposed to agree with him—should only be properly dealt with by a lawyer. There is no substantial wrong or mischief being done, though he considers that the Court may be improved, and he proposes to delay reporting until the new Queen's Advocate has got out to the Colony & examined into the procedure of the Court.

I wd. suggest that this proposal be assented to.

2. As to the *second* question. I think it very desirable that there should be a good Court of Appeal for the W. African Settlements in civil cases, and in criminal cases upon points of law as in England. The Appeal Court is at present composed of Mr. Huggins & the Chief Justice, W. Phillipps in his report has fully stated the jurisdiction of the Court. He suggests the appointment of another Judge of the Supreme Court. Sir A. Kennedy concurs in this view, not merely on the general ground that a satisfactory Court of Appeal will thus be provided, but because it will enable him to provide for circuit courts being held by a judge of the Supreme Court at the other Settlements. I think this would be a very great improvement. It seems hardly possible, judging from experience, for the Chief Magistrates at these Settlements to avoid being mixed up with petty local squabbles, & accusations of partiality and incompetency, are consequently freely bandied about to the great discredit of justice. A judge of high position coming from Sierra Leone would be clear of all this, & I should be glad to see all really important criminal & civil cases tried at each settlement by a judge of the Supreme Court.

Upon this question Sir A. Kennedy promises a report when he has

[1] C.O. 267/311.

had the opportunity of discussing the matter with the new Queen's Advocate & estimating the probable expense of such a change. It appears to me that the other Settlements may be properly called upon to contribute.

As to the 3d question—No reason has been brought forward for altering the decision which after careful consideration of the question was arrived at by Lord Carnarvon in 1867, & it has been conformed by subsequent Secretaries of State. Juries are still summoned for criminal cases.

30

E. HAMMOND TO SIR HENRY HOLLAND: CONSULAR JURISDICTION, 11 OCTOBER 1871[1]

SIR,

I am directed by Earl Granville to transmit to you a Draft Order of Her Majesty in Council, for the regulation of Consular Jurisdiction in the Territories of independent Chiefs situate upon the Old Calabar, Bonny, Cameroons, New Calabar, Brass, Opobo, Nun and Benin Rivers on the West Coast of Africa.

The Order is (as you are aware) required in consequence of a decision of the Colonial Judge at Cape Coast, that the sentences of the Courts of Equity in West Africa, which had hitherto settled Trading disputes between British subjects and natives, could not be recognized as legal, and it is therefore necessary to establish a Tribunal for the hearing of such cases, as well as for the trial of crimes and offences committed by British Subjects in the Independent states on the West Coast of Africa.

The Consul is, in Lord Granville's opinion, the only person who can properly be invested with such powers and authority, although the Draft Order gives the Courts of Equity, which have hitherto worked well, powers of arbitration and of settling minor Trading disputes subject to the sanction of the Consul.

The Memorandum attached to the Order explains the reasons why provisions and alterations have been inserted in the Order, in accordance with the advice of competent persons, and before referring it to the Law Officers of the Crown, Lord Granville would be glad to be favoured with any observations or suggestions that the Earl of Kimberley may have to offer thereupon.

C.O. 96/90.

31

SIR HENRY HOLLAND: MINUTE, CONSULAR JURISDICTION, 16 OCTOBER 1871[1]

THIS draft Order adopts in the main the provisions of the Fiji Order in Council, which is now ready for H.M.'s sanction.[2]

It will be seen from Mr. Vivian's Memorandum that in deference to the Consul's suggestion the punishment of imprisonment is omitted, but this does not appear to me to be an improvement. As the Order now stands the Consul could inflict a flogging in any case, and moreover an arbitrary power is given to fix the equivalent punishment to a fine without any limitation. I would suggest that the penalty of imprisonment should again be resorted to. If however it should be decided otherwise, a special power should be given to the Consul to fix the equivalent punishment, as at present the Order is deficient in this respect.

I have suggested one or two minor alterations in the wording.

Send the draft back to the F.O. stating that in Ld. Kimberley's opinion it appears well adapted to carry out the desired object, but pointing out the object above referred to, and adding that a few minor alterations are suggested for consideration.

32

C. VIVIAN TO CONSUL C. LIVINGSTONE, 9 NOVEMBER 1871[3]

[Most of his alterations to the Draft Order on consular jurisdiction will be included; the Colonial Office has approved and has suggested Lagos as a place for imprisonment.]

. . . I FEAR your suggestion that the Courts of Equity should act as Juries instead of Assessors only, cannot be adopted. Our first object is to get a thoroughly impartial Court, which would not be the case if people so much interested as the members of the Courts of Equity must necessarily be, are allowed a voice in deciding the guilt or innocence of the accused. The Consul is the only person who can be *thoroughly* impartial—and *in all* our Orders in Council, he alone is given the right of this decision.

[1] C.O. 96/90.
[2] This Order-in-Council was not in fact applied, because of the establishment of a government of Fijian chiefs and settlers in June 1871 over whom a consul had no jurisdiction in a 'constituted' state.
[3] F.O. 84/1343.

I fear a legal difficulty will be raised as to the composition of the Courts of Equity, which (I believe?) are composed of *Foreign* as well as British Agents as well as some of the Native Chiefs and it will be difficult for the Queen to confer any Powers on Foreigners. . . .

33

CONSUL C. LIVINGSTONE TO EARL GRANVILLE: CONSULAR COURT REGULATIONS, 29 APRIL 1872[1]

MY LORD,

I have the honour to transmit herewith 'Rules and Regulations framed under Her Majesty's Order in Council of the 21st day of February 1872, by Her Majesty's Consul at Old Calabar'. If approved by Your Lordship, they are to be printed, as directed by Article 2 of the above Order in Council. This same Article 2 makes it impossible for the Consul to act under the Order in Council until he has received printed Copies of the Rules and Regulations, and affixed and exhibited them in the Consulate and Courts of Equity.

The two rules on page 1 are framed under Article 1 of the Order in Council. It is intended to secure the 'peace, order and good Government of Her Majesty's subjects' in the oil rivers. Perhaps most of the outrages in the oil rivers have been caused by the Traders taking law into their own hands. The recent Bimbia outrage on C. Townsend was caused by that youth putting a Cameroons native in irons. On arriving out, I met a Cameroons Trader who boasted of having put the Chief Charley Dido in irons on board his ship, because that Chief owed him some 'trust'. The Chief sent order to his people to arm themselves, and seize two white Traders, who happened to be up the river on a pleasure trip, and put them in irons. The other Agents took arms, and brought the two Traders back before Charley Dido's people were ready, otherwise there would have been loss of life on both sides. The Trust System betrays the Traders into these lawless acts. Rule I removes the main prop of the Trust System by prohibiting the seizure of persons and property of the natives by the Traders.

Rule II provides for the observance of the stipulations of Treaties in regard to Comey. In this river the Comey, half a crown a ton on the oil shipped by steamer, is paid directly after each steamer leaves. The Chief in this, and other rivers, generally takes the Traders word for the amount he has shipped, but in some rivers the Chiefs have complained that the Traders cheat them by false statements.

[1] F.O. 84/1346. For the West African Order-in-Council, 21 February 1872, see A. C. Burns, *History of Nigeria* (London, 1929), pp. 318–29.

As each Trader receives from the Captain of the steamer duplicate bills of lading, these will be accepted as vouchers in cases of dispute, and there will be no difficulty, under this rule, in deciding on the exact amount of the Comey due.

The last part of the Rule is to prevent unjust accusations.

The Rules for Civil and Criminal justice are chiefly taken from the rules of the Zanzibar Consular Court, with such alterations as the different circumstances seem to require.

34

RULES AND REGULATIONS FRAMED BY HER MAJESTY'S CONSUL AT OLD CALABAR, 29 APRIL 1872[1]

WHEREAS Her Majesty hath, by sufferance, power and jurisdiction over her own subjects in Old Calabar, Bonny, Cameroons, New Calabar, Brass, Opobo, Nun, and Benin Rivers; and whereas Her Majesty, by Her Order in Council of the 21st day of February, 1872, hath made provision for the due and effectual exercise of such power and jurisdiction, and hath given Her Majesty's Consul at Old Calabar full power and authority to make and to enforce, by fine, banishment or imprisonment rules and regulations for the peace, order, and good government of Her Majesty's subjects being within the said territories; and for the observance of the stipulations of any Treaty, Convention, or Agreement now existing, or which may hereafter be made between Her Majesty, her heirs and successors, and the chief or chiefs of any of the said territories.

And whereas the following rules and regulations for the purpose aforesaid having been made by the Consul at Old Calabar, all persons concerned are to take notice that—

I. No British trader in any of the territories situate upon the Old Calabar, Bonny, Cameroons, New Calabar, Brass, Opobo, Nun, and Benin Rivers, or any part of the said territories, is permitted to take the law into his own hands; or to seize and put under restraint the person or property of any native or native chief under any pretext whatever.

II. Should a difference or contention arise between the chief of any of the aforesaid territories and a British trader as to the amount of comey due to the former by the latter, the Consul may examine on oath, and cause the trader to bring into Court all the duplicate bills of lading for the amount in dispute; and the trader, if found guilty of a breach of Treaty, Convention, or Agreement, shall be fined or

[1] F.O. 84/1346; and C.O. 147/31.

banished, as ordered in Article III of Her Majesty's Order in Council of the 21st day of February, 1872; but in order to prevent unjust charges being brought against British traders the chief must, on complaint, deposit 2 *l.* in the Consul's hands, which sum will be forfeited if the charge is found to be unjust. . . .

[Rules of procedure; in civil cases the court hears all claims; there is appeal for claims above 40/-.]

Criminal Justice.

13. British subjects in the territories aforesaid are amenable to punishment, (a) for any breach of Treaty Convention or Agreement between Her Majesty and the chief or chiefs in the aforesaid territories; (b) or for any violation of any rules and regulations; or (c) for the violation of any rule and regulation for the peace, order and good government of Her Majesty's Subjects within the aforesaid territories; or (d) for offences against Her Majesty's Order in Council of the 21st day of February, 1872; or (e) for any act which a court of justice, having criminal jurisdiction in Her Majesty's dominions, would deem to be a crime, misdemeanour, or offence. . . .

[Form of charges, warrants, fines; court procedure.]

REORGANIZATION OF THE COURTS OF EQUITY.

[Traders enrolled as members of the Courts are to hold monthly meetings.]

. . . 4. All suits, disputes, differences, and causes of litigation of a civil nature arising between British subjects at —, shall be heard and determined, in the absence of the Consul, and with the consent of the parties to the suit, by the Court of Equity whose decision must, however, in all cases be submitted to the Consul for his final sanction before it can be carried into effect; and the decision of the Court of Equity, after being submitted to by the Consul, shall be deemed and taken to be the decisions of Her Majesty's Consul in such dispute or cause of litigation, and shall have the like effect and operation, and shall be entered and recorded as such, and shall be final and conclusive, and shall not be open to appeal.

5. It shall be lawful for the Court of Equity, but subject to the sanction of the Consul, in like manner to hear and determine any suit of a civil nature within — between a British subject and a subject of the native chief or chiefs; or a subject or citizen of any other foreign State or Government in amity with Her Majesty: Provided always, that the native or other foreigner who may be party to such suit, either as complainant or defendant, shall have consented to submit to the jurisdiction of the Court of Equity, and will give such

security that he will abide by its decision, and will pay such expenses as the Consul and Court shall adjudge.

6. It shall be lawful for Her Majesty's Consul to enforce his decision, or that of the Court of Equity, when sanctioned by him in favour of or against a British subject in a civil suit, dispute, difference, or cause of litigation, by distress and sale. . . .

[The consul may settle a dispute by amicable agreement; the Court may determine compensation for assault; minutes of proceedings are to be kept.]

10. And it is further ordered that it shall be the duty of the Court of Equity to appoint, at the Consul's request, not less than two and not more than four disinterested British subjects of good repute, being members of the Court of Equity, to sit with him as assessors in the trial of the more important cases.

35

DRAFT PROCLAMATION DEFINING THE NATURE AND EXTENT OF THE QUEEN'S JURISDICTION ON THE GOLD COAST, [AUGUST 1874][1]

. . . WHEREAS by an Act of Parliament made and passed in the Session of Parliament holden in the sixth and seventh years of our reign, intituled 'An Act to remove doubts as to the exercise of Power and Jurisdiction by Her Majesty within divers Countries and Places out of Her Majesty's Dominions, and to render the same more effectual,' it is, amongst other things, enacted that it is and shall be lawful for Us to hold, exercise, and enjoy any power or jurisdiction which We now have or may at any time hereafter have, within any country or place out of Our Dominions, in the same and as ample a manner as if We had acquired such power or jurisdiction by the cession or conquest of territory:

And whereas We have by grant, treaty usage, sufferance, and other lawful means acquired, and do hold, exercise, and enjoy power and jurisdiction in divers countries on the west coast of Africa, near or adjacent to Our Gold Coast Colony:

And whereas by an Order made by Us in Council, bearing date at Osborne House, on the sixth day of August, in the year of our Lord one thousand eight hundred and seventy-four, it was amongst other things ordered that it should be lawful for the Legislative Council of Our said Gold Coast Colony for the time being by Ordinance or Ordinances to exercise and provide for giving effect to all such power and jurisdiction as We might at any time, either before or after the

[1] *Parl. Papers*, 1875 [C. 1139], pp. 3–6.

passing of the said Order in Council, have acquired in the said territories adjacent to the Gold Coast Colony:

And whereas the extent and nature of Our power and jurisdiction, as now actually holden, exercised, and enjoyed by Us in the said territories have not been anywhere by Us fully declared:

And whereas it is expedient, for the guidance and information, as well as of the Legislature of Our said Gold Coast Colony, as for that of the native Chiefs and Rulers living under Our protection in the said territories, that the nature of Our power and jurisdiction, as well as their local limits, be declared by Us.

Therefore We do declare as follows:—

Our power and jurisdiction which We have acquired as aforesaid extends amongst other things to—

I. The preservation of the public peace and the protection of individuals and property.

II. The administration of civil and criminal justice, including—

(1) The constitution and regulation of a Superior Court of Justice such as that which has been hitherto known as the Judicial Assessor's Court, of District Magistrates' Courts, native Courts, and such other Courts as may from time to time be deemed expedient to create.

(2) The enactment of laws relating to crimes, wrongs, personal rights, contracts, property rights, and fiduciary relations similar to those prevailing in Our Gold Coast Colony, but framed with due regard to native law and customs where they are not repugnant to justice, equity and good conscience.

(3) The determination of appeals from native Tribunals to magistrates, or to some superior Court.

(4) The apprehension and trial of criminals and offenders of all kinds in any part of the said territories.

(5) The supervision and regulation of native prisons.

III. The extinction of human sacrifices, pannyaring, judicial torture, and other immoral, barbarous, and cruel customs.

IV. The abolition of slave trading.

V. Measures with regard to domestic slavery and pawning.

VI. The protection and encouragement of trade and traders, including the construction, maintenance, and improvement of roads, paths, bridges, harbour works, water ways, telegraphs, and other public works, which benefit trade and promote civilization.

VII. The maintenance of an armed police force for the preservation of internal order and the prevention of foreign aggression, and the organization of the military forces of the native Rulers in alliance with Her Majesty.

VIII. The settling by the authority of the Governor of Our Gold Coast Colony of disputes arising between different Chiefs and Rulers in the said territories.

IX. The promotion of the public health, including the imposition, with the assent of the native Chiefs, of sanitary rates in towns and villages.

X. The establishment of municipalities.

XI. Public education, including industrial and religious training.

XII. The raising of a revenue by licenses and customs, and by such direct imposts as the native Chiefs and Rulers, or a major part of them, may agree to.

And further, We declare that the under-mentioned territories are those within which at the present time We have power and jurisdiction as aforesaid.

[List of territories to be inserted by the local authorities in the first instance.]

C. DEFENCE

Introductory Note

APART from the West Africa squadron which was primarily for use against the slave trade, West African forces were drawn from British African and West India units and from locally raised volunteers. The West African Corps which had been disbanded in 1783 and revived again in 1800 was merged with the West India Regiments; and these, like the Corps, were partly recruited from liberated Africans from 1811 till the 1830's. By 1834 the African Corps and the Sierra Leone Militia had fallen in numbers to a mere 530—half the number of men available when the Corps was at full strength at the end of the Napoleonic Wars. The first units of the West India Regiments were sent to the Gold Coast forts in the 1840's; and in 1850 recruiting began for a Gold Coast Corps which the Colonial Office insisted on placing under Army regulations. The new corps, never more than a hundred strong, was disbanded in 1863. The Gambia and Sierra Leone command was divided in 1855; the Freetown Militia was abolished; and Bathurst had to rely heavily on naval parties, local volunteers, and assistance from the French at Gorée to bring up the West India garrison to sufficient strength to defend the colony in local wars. This strength was depleted by the departure of troops for Lagos in 1861. Not till the ineffectual campaign against the Ashanti, 1863-4, were two complete West India Regiments brought to West Africa.

Immediately after the crisis it was planned to withdraw most of this force; but Hausas could not be persuaded to enlist for service outside Lagos, and a memorandum by Captain Clarke questioned the policy of using coloured troops at all on the coast. The Governor-in-Chief, however, was prepared to make reductions, provided an Armed Police Force was raised and naval gunboats were available for emergencies. In 1869 the Colonial

Office, the Admiralty, and the Foreign Office arranged for nine vessels to be stationed permanently along the coast, and the West India troops were reduced to only four companies. Difficulties arising from restrictions placed on the use of naval vessels by the Commodore of the squadron and the deterioration of relations with Ashanti made complete withdrawal of British colonial troops impossible. But at the beginning of 1873 there were no more than 375 men of the West India Regiment on the coast, supplemented by 1,250 police and volunteers. The Colonial Office still clung to the view that somehow the Fanti could be armed and prepared to form the backbone of Gold Coast defence. This view was rudely shaken by invasion of the protectorate and by the appointment of Major-General Wolseley who swept away the piecemeal policy of the previous half-century with the decision to use European troops.

I

LIEUT.-COLONEL TORRENS TO BREVET MAJOR WINGFIELD: AFRICAN RECRUITMENT, 1 NOVEMBER 1811[1]

Sir,

I am directed by The Commander in Chief to acquaint you, that with a view to the completion of the West India Regiments, by recruiting on the Coast of Africa, His Royal Highness the Prince Regent has, in the name and on behalf of His Majesty, been pleased to approve of a Recruiting Depôt being formed either at Sierra Leone or Goree, and placed under your command. . . . You will therefore proceed, with the least possible delay, to Africa, and report yourself to Lieut. Col. Maxwell at Sierra Leone; who, from his local information, will be enabled to state to you what situation upon the Coast will be the most eligible for having the Depôt.

I am further to inform you, that it has been judged expedient, that such eligible Negroes as may be found amongst the cargoes captured under the Slave Abolition Act, should be appropriated to this Service. But as it will be highly necessary to bring the military service into repute by the encouragement of voluntary enlistment, The Prince Regent has approved of a bounty of eight guineas being given for each recruit, under such regulations as may leave at least three guineas for his equipment in necessaries. The usual bounty of fifteen guineas is not proposed, in the hope that the sum of eight guineas will answer the purpose; under the idea, that such trifling articles of inducement, more acceptable to the Negroes than money, may be furnished by a portion of the latter sum. . . .

[1] *Parl. Papers*, 1812, x (370), p. 1. A recruiting station was set up by Governor Maxwell at Bance Island, and the Africans enlisted (mostly liberated slaves) were sent to the West Indies to be formed into units of the Royal African Corps.

2

EARL BATHURST TO GOVERNOR CHARLES TURNER: AFRICAN RECRUITMENT, 21 JANUARY 1826[1]

SIR,

Having taken into my consideration the casualties which have occurred during the preceding year among the troops stationed on the Western Coast of Africa, it has appeared to me that it would be most expedient that the Royal African Corps should in future be recruited with Blacks provided that you should find it practicable to enlist them in the Settlements under your Govt., either from the Natives, or from those Africans who may have been more recently introduced into the Colony, & I rely upon your zeal for carrying this measure into effect. . . .

3

SIR GEORGE MURRAY TO LIEUT-GOVERNOR H. J. RICKETTS: SIERRA LEONE MILITIA, 18 FEBRUARY 1829[2]

SIR,

I have received your despatch No 7 of the 11th of Decr. and am glad to learn from you, that you anticipate no difficulty in the formation of a Militia Force, for the preservation of the internal tranquillity of the Colony, and for its defence if necessary.

I am of opinion, however, that before any steps are taken for appointing the officers, it will be desirable to frame a law, which you will transmit to me for regulating the application of the principles upon which this Militia is established, keeping in view what I have already stated in my despatch of the 21st of January last, I would recommend that you should not, in the outset, aim at bringing large numbers of men under arms—four Companies of 75 Rank and File, or Three Companies of 100 Rank and File, will answer every immediate purpose.

First, it should be established by Law that each District of the Colony should be liable to furnish its quota of Men according to the extent and population of the District but that it would rest with the

[1] C.O. 268/20, f. 137.
[2] C.O. 268/28, ff. 221–4. There had been a Corps of Volunteers organized in 1804 and an abortive attempt to form a militia in 1811. The new militia force was raised in 1831, but saw little action.

Officer Administering the Government in Council to fix the number of Men who should be called out and the period of their services.

Secondly, the appointment of the Officers should be vested in the Officer administering the Government.

Thirdly, It must be decided by the Council whether the service in the Militia shall be performed gratuitously under any circumstances and whether the Men should be provided with clothing or any appropriate Dress, but it must be enacted that remuneration for the service and expence of Dress, can only be provided by the Colony, His Majesty's Government undertaking once for all to furnish the arms and accoutrements.

I may further state that I see no necessity for appointing from home an Inspecting Field Officer unless it should be thought particularly desirable to select an Officer of the Line for that purpose, in which case his pay would be provided by the Colony.

4

LIEUT.-GENERAL LORD FITZROY SOMERSET TO HERMAN MERIVALE: GOLD COAST CORPS, 19 JANUARY 1850[1]

SIR,

I have the honour to acknowledge the receipt of your letter of the 7th Instant, transmitting for the consideration of the Commander in Chief, the copy of a Letter which has been addressed to Earl Grey by the Secretary at War, enclosing an Estimate of the Expense of maintaining a local Force to consist of 3 Companies of 100 men each to be substituted for the present Military Force on the Gold Coast, the future annual expenditure of which would be £6,750 10. 0. The duties required from this Force would partake more of the character of those ordinarily performed by the Police, than by the Troops, and therefore it is very desirable to employ men acquainted with the Country, and Inhabitants, and the opinion of the Commander in Chief is requested on the proposed organization of this Force. . . .

If a Corps of Police is required for the Gold Coast, the preferable arrangement would seem to be, that it should be raised and officered, and the Expense thereof defrayed out of Colonial Funds, without reference to the Military Department. . . .

---

[1] W.O. 1/498. *Lieut.-General Lord Fitzroy Somerset* was Secretary at the Horse Guards, 1827–52, and Commander-in-Chief, 1852–4. By the end of 1851 the Gold Coast Corps consisted of two sergeants and ninety-five rank-and-file who did not replace the 1st West India Regiment which had garrisoned the forts since 1843. The Corps mutinied in 1862 and was disbanded.

5

HERMAN MERIVALE TO LIEUT.-GENERAL LORD FITZROY SOMERSET: GOLD COAST CORPS, 29 JANUARY 1850[1]

. . . I AM to request you will observe to His Grace that though the duties of the proposed Corps will be in part those of a police, it is absolutely necessary that it wd. also be an efficient military force capable of repelling the attacks to which H.M.'s possessions on the Gold Coast must always be liable from the surrounding barbarous tribes, & also that these possessions consist of mere ports on the Coast, and do not at present afford a revenue sufficient for the purpose of defraying the expense of the Corps. His Lordship is also of opinion that the Corps would be more useful and command more respect if considered to form part of His Majesty's Army like the Cape Mounted Rifles and the Ceylon Rifle Regiment, than if it were placed on a different footing, and that it is also on many accounts desirable that it should be brought under the provisions of the Military Act, which would not be the case, if it were to be considered as a mere body of Police. . . .

6

T. F. ELLIOT: MINUTE, WEST AFRICA GARRISONS, 18 OCTOBER 1862[2]

THIS [dispatch] is a demand from Governor D'Arcy for a restoration of the Gambia Garrison to its usual strength, on the ground that its reduction entails heavy expense and inconvenience in keeping the Colonial Militia on foot. This involved, as Sir G. Barrow truly points out, the general question of the amount and distribution of Black Forces. The state of the case may probably be present to the Duke of Newcastle's mind, but I subjoin, in case it should be of any use, a short sketch of the correspondence.

On a Foreign Office letter of 1 Nov. 1861, respecting Vera Cruz, the question was raised of withdrawing some of the Colored Garrisons from the West Indies but the subject was not at that time considered fit for action on account of threatening aspect of our relations with the United States.

But a subsequent War Office letter of the 11th of Feby. 1862

[1] W.O. 1/498.
[2] C.O. 87/74, on D'Arcy to Newcastle, 11 August 1862 (reporting the transfer of one-third of his garrison to Lagos).

suggested an increase of the Black Regiments from three to four. The Duke of Newcastle concurred and suggested that two might suffice for the West Indies and two be permanently allotted to Africa.

On the 18th of August the War Office forwarded a letter from the Horse Guards explaining various military difficulties in the way of this arrangement.

On the 9th of Sept. last the Duke of Newcastle replied that His Grace's proposal had been based on the idea of a reduction in the West Indies and that he was confident that one Regiment could not do the work required on the Coast of Africa. Without questioning the military considerations pointed out in the letter from the Horse Guards, His Grace feared that the present arrangements were inconsistent with the Resolutions of the Committee of the House of Commons, and said that he could propose no other scheme for placing them more in harmony.

Thus the matter at present rests. The observations offered by the Horse Guards on the difficulty of placing the existing officers and men permanently on the unhealthy and irksome Coast of Africa, and on the special advantages which have been found necessary to induce those of the Gold Coast Corps, to accept those terms on the Gold Coast, certainly appear very weighty. On the other hand we have become involved in such large territorial acquisitions on the Coast, and our Native neighbours there are so restless, that our present force seems very inadequate. That restlessness may possibly itself be an evidence of the absence of a sufficient show of Troops to inspire respect.

7

EDWARD LUGARD TO FREDERIC ROGERS: WEST INDIA REGIMENTS, 29 MAY 1863[1]

SIR,

Referring to my letter of the 23d February and your reply of the 28th March relative to the arrangements to be made on the disbandment of the Gold Coast Corps I am directed to acquaint you for the information of the Duke of Newcastle, that Earl de Grey having consulted the Field Marshal Commanding in Chief, on the Subject, finds that it will be impracticable to maintain an additional West India Regiment on the West Coast of Africa, without raising a 5th West India Regiment.

In order however to keep the annual expense hence arising within the sum now provided for the four West India Regiments, the Gold Coast Corps and the St. Helena Regiment, it has been determined,

[1] C.O. 96/63.

among other measures, that the Establishment of the existing and proposed new West India Regiments shall in future consist of 750, instead of 800, rank & file. . . .

8

THE MILITARY SECRETARY TO THE WAR OFFICE: WEST INDIA REGIMENTS, 14 JANUARY 1864[1]

SIR,

With reference to your letter of the 1st instant, I am directed by the Field Marshal Commanding in Chief to inform you that, as it appears the Duke of Newcastle is desirous that only one and not two companies should be withdrawn from British Honduras, his Royal Highness has caused instructions to be issued for the distribution of the West India regiments as follows, viz:

1st West India Regiment	4 Companies—Head Quarters, Bahamas.
	3 Companies—Cape Coast Castle.
	1 Company—Belize, Honduras.
2d „ „ „	2 Companies—Head Quarters, Barbados.
	1 Company—Demerara.
	1 Company-Corosal, Honduras.
	2 Companies—Jamaica.
	2 Companies—Cape Coast Castle.
3d „ „ „	3 Companies—Head Quarters, Sierra Leone.
	3 Companies—Gambia.
	2 Companies—Lagos.
4th „ „ „	8 Companies—Head Quarters, Cape Coast Castle.
5th „ „ „	8 Companies—Head Quarters, Raising at Jamaica.

W. F. Forster.

[1] *Parl. Papers*, 1865, xxxvii (71), p. 27.

9

CAPTAIN A. CLARKE: CONFIDENTIAL MEMORANDUM, JUNE 1864[1]

[A permanent military establishment is needed for the West African Settlements; this will require an immediate expenditure of at least £42,000 for barracks, forts, and hospitals.]

. . . 58 Composition of Force.

THE military force occupying the several settlements on the African Coast consisted of detachments of the 1st and 2nd, and the whole of the 3rd and 4th West India Regiments.

The detachments are about to be withdrawn, and the garrison confined to the 3rd and 4th Regiments only; proposed to be distributed as follows: On the Gambia—Three companies of the 3rd West India Regiment at Bathurst, furnishing detachments to Cape St, Mary, McCarthy's Island, and Fort Bullen.

In Sierra Leone, the head quarters and five companies of the 3rd West India Regiment at Free Town, giving detachments to Bulama, Sher[b]ro, Waterloo and British Quiah. On the Gold Coast, the head quarters and six companies of the 4th West India at Cape Coast Castle, detaching garrisons to Accra, Dix Cove, Anamaboe, Winnebah, and Quittah. The remaining two companies of the 4th are quartered in the Island of Lagos.

With each of these detachments, are one or more of the medical staff; and at Bathurst, Free Town, Cape Coast Castle, and Lagos, officers of the Commissariat are attached, with an officer of the Store Department at the three former places.

The military staff is confined to a fort adjutant at the same stations, and the senior officer of each reports direct to the departments in England.

The military works are in charge of regimental officers detached from the corps as Acting Engineers, who are at present at the head quarters of each Command.

Formerly a Clerk of Works having the temporary appointment of an Acting Engineer, had charge of the entire Coast; this officer has, however, recently died.

When the entire force of the Coast did not exceed 500 men, the services of this officer were sufficient; should the present strength be kept up, another arrangement will become necessary, such as I have detailed elsewhere.

[1] W.O. 33/13: *Confidential Print*, No. 0228, pp. 58–65, 66–67. See R. H. Vetch, *Life of Lieut.-General Sir Andrew Clarke* (London, 1905), p. 83; and for his views on the settlements, *Parl. Papers*, 1865, v (412), Qq. 4259–490.

The West Indian troops quartered on the Coast both officers and men, at the time of my visit, were very healthy and in admirable order.

The detachment of the 2nd, quartered at Cape Coast, composed principally of liberated Africans, were chiefly old soldiers and inured to service, as they had been several times engaged with the natives on various parts of the Coast; a fine body of men, clean and soldier-like on parade and steady in quarters, their officers had every confidence in them, as they had, on more than one occasion, given proof that they could be relied upon in action.

The men of the 3rd West India are not in appearance inferior to those of the 2nd; but they are recruited more from the West Indies, where the negroes do not form so good a material for soldiers as the native Africans.

The 4th West India, chiefly creoles, were only very recently raised, but, from their appearance on parade or in quarters, they might have been taken for much older soldiers. This regiment suffered much from climate, and has lost a larger number of men than usual from dysentery. They were not reconciled to the country, and pined for their homes more even than would Europeans.

To these circumstances, it is conceived, the difficulty that is felt in obtaining recruits in the West Indies is due, as the accounts of the country those serving in Western Africa send back to their families deter others from enlisting. . . .

65. *Substitution of European Troops.*

I have elsewhere spoken of the high state of discipline and admir-able order of the West India Regiments I saw on the West Coast, which, bearing in mind the trying and peculiar circumstances under which this had been accomplished, reflected the highest honour and credit on their officers. I trust, therefore, that I shall not be mistaken in the following proposal.

These troops at present, strength for strength, cost the same as English soldiers. Recruited now chiefly from the West Indies, they suffer almost as much, if not more, when taken to Western Africa, than would white men who were ordinarily sober and steady.

66. Their powers of endurance, or of extra exertion, altogether fail when continuous exercise is called for.

They each require the same, and in some cases more transport and aid than English soldiers, and they have not those moral qualities which the latter possess to sustain them in times of pressure, difficulty, and disaster. They cannot move with the same rapidity, and if broken or separated from their officers, they are said to be wholly unable to act for themselves.

The very nature of African war requires great mobility and a freedom from encumbrances; this latter increases, while the former diminishes, with numbers.

The coloured troops, more especially the liberated Africans, now so scarce among them, have often given examples of courage and great devotion to their officers; but still they fall short of the European soldiers in these respects.

Disciplined they are formidable in African war, but they are not so feared by their own race as are the white men. To come into collision with the latter is the negro's dread, nor has he become free from a certain awe which deters him from even threatening his life.

For these and other reasons, I believe that if the costly and profitless experiment of British settlement and colonization is to be continued in tropical Africa, it is worthy of consideration, both on the grounds of great economy and increased efficiency, whether it would not be desirable to substitute for the black troops one eighth their number of white soldiers.

The present strength of the force on the West Coast consists of two regiments, or about 1,600 men, involving an expenditure of not far short of 60,000 *l.* a year, and an immediate outlay for their barracks of not less than 100,000 *l.*

Two hundred white soldiers would be more than equal to the work that could be expected from the present number of West Indian men, bearing in mind that the performance of the police duties, now carried out by the troops and which ought not to devolve upon them, would not be continued by the Europeans.

Major Blackall, the Present governor of Sierra Leone, is now organizing an armed native police, which will relieve the military in that colony from work that could be better and more economically done by a civil force. . . .

[The native police consists of 21 officers and 212 men, costing £30,172 10*s.*]

10

GOVERNOR SIR ARTHUR KENNEDY TO EARL GRANVILLE: REDUCTION OF GARRISONS, 29 APRIL 1869[1]

MY LORD,

I have the honor to acknowledge the receipt of Your Lordship's Despatch No 26 of the 26th March 1869, on the subject of the concentration of Troops and the employment of Gun Boats on this Coast, in lieu thereof.

[1] C.O. 267/300.

2. The present Stations of Troops on this Coast are as follows:

	Officers	Men
Gambia	15	151
Sierra Leone	23	352
Sherbro	2	31
Cape Coast Castle	10	253
Accra	3	38
Lagos	3	76
Total	56	901

3. I have already recommended the withdrawal of the Detachment from Lagos, and arrangements are in progress for an increase in the Armed Police Force of Houssas to replace them, and chargeable to Colonial Funds.[1]

4. If the proposed arrangement for stationing two Gun Boats between Gambia and Lagos be carried out, I should immediately take steps for the withdrawal of the Detachments at Sherbro and Accra; and if circumstances permit, decrease the Force at Cape Coast, where the improved Revenue will, I trust, soon admit of an increased outlay for the organization of an efficient Police.

5. The Force and expensive Staff at the Gambia might be decreased on the condition of its being periodically visited by a Gun Boat during the healthy Season. African disturbances seldom occur, and are never carried on, in the Rainy Season.

6. Your Lordship requires my opinion to what extent, and in what manner the employment of Her Majesty's Cruizers would enable me to dispense with the presence of Soldiers at some of these Stations; and whether in any case, Troops could not be withdrawn from some of the Smaller Stations.

7. I have already answered a portion of these questions.

8. I would propose that all these stations should be visited periodically by a Gun Boat, to enable the Administrators to visit their outlying Stations in a manner calculated to support their authority.

9. It is difficult to convey to Your Lordship a full comprehension of the moral effect which a visit from a Gun Boat has upon the African mind. Such visits properly timed, and carrying a competent civil officer to adjust incipient differences, would save the ultimate outlay and loss of thousands of pounds.

10. British interests are becoming daily more important on this Coast, and Traders and their property cannot, I think, be justly or safely to the sole protection of a Police drawn from a People only emerging from barbarism.

11. The present cessation of the Slave Trade, affords a golden

[1] Kennedy to Granville, 26 April 1869: ibid. Referred to the War Office.

opportunity for educating the people in the Arts and profits of Peace, which if once understood and felt by them, would be a sure guarantee for permanent industry and tranquillity.

12. The regular communication which now exists between Sierra Leone and all other of our West African Settlements, would enable the Governor in Chief at any time to despatch a Gunboat with a few soldiers in aid of the Civil power, and thus nip any disturbances in the bud.

13. Common foresight with reasonable and timely preventive measures, will at all times ensure Peace. These measures must depend upon the presence of a Gun Boat.

14. The present position of our Trade and its daily increasing importance are, I think, little understood by the general Public. Fifty thousand Tons of 'Palm Oil' alone (worth Two Million Sterling) has left this Coast in British Bottoms during the last year; and I have already in another Despatch informed your Lordship that the Exports of the hitherto Valueless and insignificant Settlement of Lagos have increased from £153,341 in 1863 to £517,253 in 1868. Such growing interests should not be jeopardized by the withdrawal of both Troops and Ships of War.

15. In conclusion I would take the liberty of stating that I am not a believer in the habitual use of physical force; and your Lordship may be assured that I shall never desire to keep a Ship or a Soldier beyond the time I think they can be prudently dispensed with.

II

COMMODORE W. M. DOWELL TO THE ADMIRALTY: WEST AFRICA SQUADRON, 8 FEBRUARY 1869[1]

H.M.S. Rattlesnake

... In the event of the Lords Commissioners of the Admiralty deciding to abolish the Slave Blockade on this Coast, in consequence of the total cessation of the Slave Trade, as reported in my letter of the 7th. Inst., No 22, I think it my duty to state, for their information, my opinion that the Squadron under my command might be considerably reduced.

2. It consists of the 'Rattlesnake' and seven Cruisers a steam store ship, the Investigator and Pioneer, and the stationary store Ships 'Flora' & 'Vindictive', at Ascension and Jellah Coffee. I consider that *four* cruisers in addition to the Flag Ships, would be sufficient, if the

[1] C.O. 267/303. *Commodore W. M. Dowell* was Senior Officer of the West Africa Squadron, 1868–70, before it was merged with the squadron at the Cape of Good Hope.

blockade is raised, to meet all the requirements of the Station, vizt. the protection of our settlements from the Gambia to Lagos and the guarding of our Commerce and the interests of the British merchants and Traders in the Bights, the oil Rivers, and on the South Coast. . . .

[These vessels are to be distributed: one to the Gold Coast, one to the Niger Delta, one for the annual Niger expedition, and one for the mouth of the Congo.]

12

SIR GEORGE BARROW: MINUTE, WEST AFRICA SQUADRON, 20 APRIL 1869[1]

I was deputed by Lord Granville to attend at the Admiralty on this subject—and I did so yesterday, when Sir Sydney Dacres, Admiral Hornby & Mr. Layard of the Foreign Office were present.

The conclusion come to was that the reduction of the Squadron to the extent proposed by Commodore Dowell, with reference only to the protection of trade, is greater than would be advisable, for the present at least.

That trade extends along a sweeping line of Coast from the Gambia, northwards, to the River Congo, southwards, in the latter part of which pirates have been encountered.

It was arranged that there should be maintained on the Coast at present, besides the Commodore's Vessel 4 Cruizers 2 Flat-bottomed Vessels for the Rivers 2 Reliefs—4 Cruizers always being on service . . . making 9 in all, which is a reduction of the force proposed when the Admty. asked the Secretary of State's sanction for the force to be employed at the several coastal stations.

The Admiralty had already sent Commodore Dowell's letter to the Foreign Office, & it is now sent here, in order that both Offices may express concurrence at the result of yesterday's conference on the subject.

13

ARTHUR OTWAY TO THE SECRETARY TO THE ADMIRALTY: WEST AFRICA SQUADRON, 30 APRIL 1869[2]

Sir,

I have laid before the Earl of Clarendon your letter of the 23d. inst. inclosg. a copy of a desp. frm. Comre. Dowell, expressing an opinion that the Slave trade on the W. Coast of Africa may be considered to have totally ceased, & suggesting that the blockade

[1] C.O. 267/303, on Admiralty to C.O., 19 April 1869.
[2] C.O. 267/303. The Admiralty decided to maintain five warships and one steamer. Admiralty to C.O., 15 November 1869: ibid.

should be abolished and the squadron reduced; & in reply to the inquiry of the Lds. of the Admiralty as to whether Lord Clarendon concurs in the views of Comre. Dowell, I am to state that His Ldp. has much pleasure in signifying his entire concurrence in the opinion of the Commre. that the export of slaves from the W. Coasts of Africa may be considered as having come to an end, and Lord Clarendon is of opinion therefore that the force & distribution of the Squadron may be regulated apart from Slave trade considerations.

His Ldp. further desires me to state that he considers this a fitting opportunity to bear testimony to the zeal, singleness of purpose & unwearied perseverance with wh. the officers & crews of H.M.'s Ships employed in the arduous duty of the suppression of the Slave Trade on the W. Coast of Africa & elsewhere have invariably performed their duties, thro' whose exertions the success that has been achieved in the suppression of the Slave Traffic on the W. Coast is mainly attributed.

Lord Clarendon has learnt from the reports that have been rec[eived] fm. the Comrs. of H.M.'s Cruisers on the African Coast, & from other sources, that consequent upon the suppression of the slave trade legitimate traffic has largely & rapidly increased, and this satisfactory state of things His Ldp. attributes chiefly to the protection afforded by Brit. Cruisers whose constant presence it is or the knowledge on the part of the native chiefs that a ship of war is within reach, that prevents them from engaging in petty wars among themselves, or in disputes with European traders, the effects of wh. are to put a stop for a time to peaceful & profitable trade.

Under these circums. Lord Clarendon, is inclined to the opinion, subject to the judgement of the Lds. of the Admty. that the reductions proposed by Comre. Dowell, if carried out to the full extent suggested, would scarcely leave the ships enough for the encouragement & protection of the valuable & increasing Brit. trade wh. is being developed on the African Coast.

His Ldp. observes that it is proposed to assign one vessel only for the protection of the British settlements fr. the Gambia to Lagos, and for the guarding of our commerce & interests & he would submit for their Ldps. consideration whether taking into consideration the long line of coast, upwards of 1200 miles, that is included within the above-mentioned places, an additional cruiser might not be allotted for this portion of the coast.

On the South coast also Ld. Clarendon thinks that an additional small vessel might be advantageously employed; but before any decision is come to as to the amount of naval force to be employed for the future on the African Coast, His Ldp. would submit whether the Secretary of State for the Colonies might not with advantage be consulted upon the subject.

Lord Clarendon would consider a Squadron composed of 7 cruisers including a Post-ship, together with 2 smaller vessels fitted for navigating the African rivers, making a total of nine vessels, not more than sufficient to meet the requirements of the service. If experience should prove that a smaller force would suffice, the squadron could be easily reduced, but his Ldp. does not think it would be prudent to have a smaller force on the coast than that above suggested, at any rate for the present.

14

EARL GRANVILLE TO GOVERNOR SIR SIR ARTHUR KENNEDY: NAVAL EXPEDITIONS, 28 JUNE 1870[1]

SIR,

I have the honor to ack. the receipt of your despatch No 83 of the 23rd ult enclosing a copy of a correspondence between Capt. Walshe, Civil Commandant at Sherbro, and the Commander of H.M.S. 'Rocket' and calling attention to the obstacle which the General Instructions of the Admiralty to their officer on the Sierra Leone Division offer to the obtaining of redress for outrages committed by natives within the limits of your Government, as in the recent case at Gundama.

It appears to me that Commander Wright judged correctly in refusing to proceed on an expedition to a place five or six miles from the point which his vessel could reach, and when this object was not the protection of life and property, but the punishment of crime and the recovery of captives.

In order to prevent or punish such outrages as the one above alluded to, it is the duty of the Governor to organise at the expense of the Settlement an efficient armed Police to take the place of the Troops who are in the course of being withdrawn, and unless this is done it cannot be doubted that great distress may ensue.

15

COMMODORE W. M. DOWELL: INSTRUCTIONS FOR THE SENIOR OFFICER ON THE WEST COAST OF AFRICA, 18 MAY 1870[2]

. . . THE General duties to be performed by the Squadron on the West Coast are to protect legitimate Trade and to assist the Governor in Chief of the West Coast Settlements and his Administrators.

[1] C.O. 267/305.   [2] C.O. 267/308. Encl. in Admiralty to C.O. 14 July 1870.

It will be specially the duty of the Cruiser stationed on the Sierra Leone Sub Division to assist and cooperate with the Governor-in-Chief whenever he makes a requisition for his services; and the same support and assistance is to be rendered to the Administrator of Cape Coast Castle, on his requisition by any vessel detached to the Gold Coast. Officers in Command are not however to consider the foregoing as a reason for remaining permanently either at Sierra Leone or Cape Coast Castle, and, when not actually required by the Governor-in-Chief, or by the Administrator, they are to cruise and visit any part of the Coast within the limits of their station which may appear necessary, always keeping the Governor-in-Chief (or the Administrator as the case may be) informed of their intended movements in order that they may be communicated with in case of emergency.

Should any case arise in which requisition may be made by the Governor or Administrator for the service of either of the Cruisers upon diplomatic missions, the the officer administering the government will send a civil officer on the mission, with clear instructions for his guidance and action, and copy of these instructions will be furnished to the officer in command. Should the civil officer fail in his mission he will then place the matter in the hand of the naval officer in command, who will use measures of coercion or not as upon his instructions he may feel justified, remembering that the responsibility of any action he may take in the matter will rest entirely upon himself, and that in no case would he be justified in employing force without special authority from his senior officer, or on the representation of the Governor or Administrator that coercive measures are necessary for the protection of life or property, or that they have been authorized by the Home Government. Under no circumstances are officers and men to be landed from H.M.'s Ships for service on shore *except for the actual protection of life.*

Should it be considered necessary to send Troops from one part of the Coast to another the services of the Cruiser on that part of the station would be available, but as the accommodation in the Gun Vessels is very limited, not more than 50 Troops are to be embarked at any one time, or for conveyance to a greater distance than can be reached in twelve hours steaming by day.

[Colonial authorities are to pay for coal consumed when vessels are employed for their service.]

... The cruiser stationed on the North of Sierra Leone Sub Division for the six healthy months of the year is to be directed to visit the River Gambia once during that period, and, having communicated with the Administrator at Bathurst, she may, if considered desirable, proceed up the River as far as MacCarthy's Island to shew the Flag; but she should not remain in the River longer than ten days, and whilst in it the same sanitary precautions should be observed as are directed for Vessels employed in Niger Expeditions.

Unless under special circumstances, H.M. Ships are not to be employed in the Rivers, and whenever the Senior Officer may consider it necessary to send a Vessel up any of the Rivers, he is to make a special Report to me, detailing the reasons which induced him to do so, and he is to send duplicate of the same to the Secretary of the Admiralty by the first opportunity.

16

SIR GEORGE BARROW: MINUTE, WEST AFRICA SQUADRON, 20 JULY 1870[1]

I DID not perceive that the Cruiser to be stationed on the S. Leone Subdivision is only for 6 healthy months of the year. . . . My attention was called to it in a private letter from Sir A. Kennedy. When the conference was held last year between this Office—the Admty.—the Foreign Office & the War Office as to the Naval Force to be maintained on the Coast no such limitation of service was hinted at, & the removal of the Troops from the Settlements would probably not have been considered practicable—if it had not been forseen that no naval force would be available *for half the year*.

17

EDWARD LUGARD TO THE COLONIAL OFFICE: STRENGTH OF WEST INDIA REGIMENTS, 3 MAY 1871[2]

. . . REFERRING to the correspondence that has taken place upon the subject of the reduction of the force on the West Coast of Africa, I am directed by Mr. Secretary Cardwell to acquaint you that the Major General Commanding in the West Indies has reported that he he is in a position to send 87 men from Demerara to complete the establishment of the four Companies of the 2d. West India Regiment stationed on the West Coast of Africa; but before incurring the expenditure incidental to this service Mr Cardwell requests me to be informed whether, referring to the hope expressed by Governor Kennedy when in this country, to the effect that the four Companies then in West Africa might after so long time be reduced to two, Lord Kimberley considers that it will be necessary to send the proposed relief.

[1] C.O. 267/308, on no. 15.   [2] C.O. 267/313.

18

E. H. KNATCHBULL-HUGHESSEN: MINUTE, REDUCTION OF TROOPS, WEST AFRICA, 8 MAY 1871[1]

I THINK the matter should be referred to Sir A. Kennedy. As the cession of the Gambia is not likely to take place the matters relating to the cession of the Dutch forts are complicated, and the attitude of the Ashantees by no means reassuring, I do not feel at all certain of the propriety of reducing the number of troops especially before the Police forces have been duly organised in the several settlements. If the Report of the Parliamentary Committee of 1865 had resulted in our gradual withdrawal from these settlements, it would have been a different matter, but as it seems to me we are to keep them, I confess I do not look with much satisfaction at the 'saving' effected by the withdrawal of troops. I am afraid we run the risk of having some day or another, the overpowering and massacre of a settlement by Natives Tribes. Then follows indignation in England, and a Military Expedition which vindicates England's honor, and at the same time sweeps away (and a good deal more) the 'annual saving'— However, the point at issue just now is one on which the opinion of Sir A. Kennedy may be taken.

19

GOVERNOR SIR ARTHUR KENNEDY TO THE EARL OF KIMBERLEY: WEST AFRICAN DEFENCES, 9 JUNE 1871[2]

. . . 4. THE complications at the Gold Coast and Dutch Elmina as your Lordship is aware continue to exist as they did in 1869, though the peace has not yet been broken.

5. These complications will continue to exist till the proposed transfer of Elmina is effected, and probably for some time after. Any reduction of force at this time would but court disaster, and probably necessitate an enormous after-Expenditure.

6. The force at the Gold Coast is now lower than it ought to be, and when the transfer is about to take place, I shall be obliged to reinforce it for some time, from the two weak companies at Sierra Leone.

7. A Police Force at the Gold Coast is now in process of being

[1] C.O. 267/313, on no. 17.   [2] C.O. 267/313.

increased and trained, to replace the Military when it is safe to remove them; but I should be in no wise responsible for the reduction of the force at present.

8. The same remarks apply to some extent to Sierra Leone.

9. When I addressed the letter dated 29th. September 1869 to Your Lordship's predecessor, I assumed that the Cession of the Gambia to France would be effected.

10. That project having been abandoned, it will I fear always be necessary to have a small force in hand at Sierra Leone; in case of emergency.

11. From a group of despatches from the Administrator of that Settlement, by the present mail, Your Lordship will observe that the most influential Merchants there are determined to keep up a chronic agitation and invasion panic for the purpose of obtaining a greater or less number of Troops.

12. If the statement of these Gentlemen can be relied upon, and if their anticipations are at all likely to be realized, I think the circumstances would justify my application for a larger force than I now have at my disposal.

13. I may frankly state that if I had been aware of the conditions under which the services of the Gunboats are obtainable, I should have greatly modified my proposals respecting the maintenance of peace and protection of trade upon the Coast.

14. I have no fault to find with the Commodore, Senior Officer, or Officers individually, but I cannot repress the opinion that the present mode of carrying out the Service is unnecessarily expensive, ineffective, and prejudicial to the health of the Officers and Crew.

15. It would be probably considered presumptuous in me to offer an opinion upon a professional subject, but I am quite ready to submit my reasons for holding this opinion for Your Lordship's judgement if you require it.

16. I will yield to no one in an honest desire to economise public funds, and my proceedings and recommendations on this Coast, and elsewhere, have I humbly think, given earnest of it; but I cannot acquiesce in the withdrawal of the small body of Troops at present on this Coast under existing circumstances.

17. On the contrary I would earnestly recommend that the Companies should be kept up to their full strength.

20

EDWARD LUGARD TO THE COLONIAL OFFICE: WEST AFRICAN DEFENCES, 13 JULY 1871[1]

. . . I AM directed by Mr. Secretary Cardwell to acknowledge the receipt of your letter of the 7th Instant, with its enclosed copy of a despatch from the Governor in Chief of the West African Settlements, upon the subject of the Military Force required for the protection of those Settlements.

In reply I am to request that you will acquaint the Earl of Kimberley that, under the circumstances stated by Sir Arthur Kennedy, there appears to Mr. Cardwell to be no alternative at present but to increase the force in these Settlements and that instructions will accordingly be sent out to the General officer Commanding the Troops in the West Indies to complete the establishment of the four Companies of the 2d. West India Regiment now stationed on the West Coast of Africa.

Mr. Cardwell observes that the Governor in his despatch of the 9th June last, attributes his inability to reduce the military force, in some measure, to the unsatisfactory working of the Gun boats on that station, and that had he been aware of the conditions under which the services of these Gun boats were available he would have greatly modified his proposals for the maintenance of peace and protection upon the Coast. Mr. Cardwell considers it desirable that Sir A. Kennedy should give the reasons which have led him to this conclusion, and would be glad if Lord Kimberley would call for them with a view to a communication, if it be found expedient, being made to the Lords Commissioners of the Admiralty, upon the subject.

21

LORD LANSDOWNE TO THE COLONIAL OFFICE: HAUSA POLICE, 10 JULY 1872[2]

. . . I HAVE laid before Mr Secretary Cardwell your letter of the 3d. Instant with its enclosed draft of a despatch which the Earl of Kimberley proposes to address to the Governor in Chief of the West African Settlements in reply to one in which the Governor

[1] C.O. 267/313. Kennedy provided a minute to this dispatch which he was shown while in London repeating his resentment at the Admiralty's refusal to place gunboats under the orders of the Governor-in-Chief.
[2] C.O. 267/318. *Lord Lansdowne* was Under-Secretary for War, 1872–4.

recommends that a body of armed Houssa Police should be substituted for the detachment of West India troops now stationed there.

In reply I am to request that you will state to Lord Kimberley that Mr. Cardwell entirely concurs in the proposal to withdraw the West India troops from the Coast of Africa so far as in his Lordship's judgment it can be done with safety.

22

RETURN OF TROOPS AND ARMED POLICE AT THE WEST AFRICA SETTLEMENTS, FEBRUARY 1873[1]

S. Leone	2nd. West India Reg.	210
,,	Armed Police	200
Gambia	Militia	67
,,	Armed Police	76
,,	Volunteers	37
(McCarthy Island) Militia		43
Gold Coast	2nd. West India Regt.	165
,,	Armed Police (Houssas & Fantees)	300
,,	Volunteers	250
Lagos	Houssa Armed Police	250
		1,598
or, deducting G. Coast Volunteers who are apparently not yet armed		250
		1,348

23

THE EARL OF KIMBERLEY TO COLONEL R. W. HARLEY: DEFENCE OF THE FORTS, 12 MAY 1873[2]

[The Fanti have suffered defeat; the British forces have withdrawn to Cape Coast.]

... TURNING now to that which presses for most immediate consideration—the provision to be made for the defence of the British forts

---

[1] C.O. 147/27.
[2] *Parl. Papers*, 1874, xlvi [C. 890], pp. 27–29. *Colonel Harley* was Administrator and Governor-in-Chief at the Gold Coast, 1872–3.

and as far as possible of the towns adjacent to them, in the event of the continued advance of the Ashantees, and their prolonged occupation of the adjacent territory—I am satisfied by the general tenor of your despatches that you correctly appreciate the extent of your responsibility, and are making the best disposal of the forces at your command. It is of course of the first importance that the forts carrying the British flag shall be firmly held. With regard to Cape Coast Castle and Elmina I am glad to be assured that there is no question of the practicability of holding them with a moderate or even a small force. With regard to the minor forts, although their defence may not be in an equal degree vital to the maintenance of our position on the coast, every effort must be made to protect them, and I have no doubt that after providing for the two principal forts, you will have made such arrangements as you could for the defence of the other places which are most liable to attack.

6. The commencement of the rainy season will, I conclude, greatly impede active operations on the part of the Ashantees, but it appeared, nevertheless, to Her Majesty's Government, that in order to provide against the contingency of prolonged attack upon Elmina or the other forts it was advisable that you should receive an immediate addition to your defensive force.

7. It has been determined, therefore, to send immediately an additional ship of war with a detachment of Marine Artillery and Infantry, and arrangements have been made for the immediate despatch of a suitable ship with fifty marines of each of these branches of the service, commanded by an experienced officer. You may expect this vessel to arrive very shortly after you receive this despatch. The same opportunity will be taken of sending you a large additional supply of ammunition of various kinds, and of rockets, together with a portable field gun, which may be of service either at one of the outlying forts, or elsewhere beyond Cape Coast Castle. It has been thought advisable to send these supplies, in consequence of the accounts which you have transmitted, showing the enormous expenditure of ammunition, resulting from the peculiar mode in which the Fantees conduct their operations. As, however, you have not intimated that the large supplies already in the settlements had commenced to run short, it is possible that it may not be necessary to make use of what is now sent. I am very reluctant to give you any instruction which might be construed as enjoining an improper economy in the supply of arms and ammunition to the Fantees; and I approve of your having furnished them in large quantities. I rely, however, on your bearing in mind that a prodigal expenditure of ammunition can only be justified by the possibility of some success being obtained through it, and that the cost of the settlement will be very heavy. Every opportunity should be taken of impressing upon

the Fantees that their great hope of repelling the invader lies in the judicious use of the munitions of war with which they have been so freely provided, and that much may depend upon their not wasting the stores placed in their hands.

8. I have further arranged with the Secretary of State for War for the transfer to the Gold Coast with as little delay as possible, of a reinforcement of the West India Infantry, which will probably consist of four companies of rank and file, with a full staff of officers.

9. Although it has been determined thus largely to increase the strength of the West India regiment on the West Coast of Africa, it is not proposed to maintain such a force permanently in the settlements. For reasons into which I have not now time to enter at length, Her Majesty's Government have come to the conclusion that an armed police force possesses many advantages for the special service to be performed in West Africa over a regular military force. I desire, therefore, that you will at once take such measures as you may be able, for raising a force of Houssa police for service on the Gold Coast, and increasing the number of Fantee police, and that you will report to me what number of police you are of opinion that it will be desirable to maintain for the ordinary requirements of those settlements, on the assumption that detachments of the West India troops will no longer be kept there, and bearing in mind the expediency of not being entirely dependent on a force composed exclusively of Houssas or Fantees. . . .

24

MAJOR-GENERAL SIR G. WOLSELEY TO EDWARD CARDWELL: GOLD COAST FORCES, 13 OCTOBER 1873[1]

Sir,

I have the honour to request that the troops (strength as per margin)[2] which, before my departure from England, I requested might be held in readiness for service in the Ashantee Expedition, may be dispatched to this station at the earliest possible date after the receipt of this letter.

In making this request, I bear fully in mind the instructions which I had the honour to receive from you before leaving England, and I do not make this demand hastily, or without having freely communicated with those who have experience on the coast, and

[1] *Parl. Papers*, 1874, xlvi [C. 892], pp. 233–7.
[2] Two battalions of infantry (1,300 men), detachments of the Royal Artillery and Royal Engineers, and a section of the Administrative Service. The War Office approved, 18 November 1873.

knowledge of the immediate circumstances. On the other hand I remember your desire that my decision as to the employment of European troops should be arrived at 'as soon after my arrival on the coast as I might be enabled to form it with sufficient knowledge of the circumstances and satisfaction to myself'. I have, therefore, consulted all those whose experience and knowledge was at my disposal, and I have studied the question in its various bearings.

From these consultations and this study, results my firm conviction of the necessity for the employment of European troops, and of the perfect feasibility of employing them without undue risk, for the purposes which your instructions specify, namely 'to free these settlements from the continued menace of the attacks of the Ashantees and to accomplish the further objects of my mission.'

There is, Sir, but one method of freeing these settlements from the continued menace of Ashantee invasion; and this is to defeat the Ashantee army in the field, to drive it from the protected territories, and, if necessary, to pursue it into its own land, and to march victorious on the Ashantee capital, and show not only to the King, but to those chiefs who urge him on to constant war, that the arm of Her Majesty is powerful to punish, and can reach even to the very heart of their kingdom.

By no means short of this can lasting peace be insured; one truce after another may be made, but they will again and again be broken, for the Ashantees have learnt to believe that they may with impunity invade and lay waste the protected territory, and dwell there unmolested by the white man, till they arrive under the very walls of our forts. . . .

[The history of former invasions 1807-31 and the present stalemate call for a 'signal chastisement' by British troops.]

It cannot, I think, be doubted that under the influence of civilization and European protection the Fanti tribes have grown less warlike and more peaceful than formerly. Yet even in their best times they were no match for the Ashantees. When left alone they were conquered and overrun, and when, later, English officers cast in their lot with them they could not be induced to turn out their whole strength, for I am able to state that the numbers reported as having taken the field are enormously exaggerated, and that there were never 10,000 men present under arms. Sir Charles Macarthy was outnumbered by the cowardly defection of his native allies and the success of the earlier actions of this present year, and the presence of English officers failed to induce the natives to stand firm. On one excuse or another they retreated from before the enemy, whom they now believe to be too strong for them, and against whom they are evidently very reluctant to fight.

I have held interviews with the kings. I have seen the greedy mercantile spirit in which the war is viewed by them and the excuses made to delay their departure for the field. They tell me they have little influence in raising their men, that their men prefer trading to fighting, and have gone to far countries to hide. The Cape Coast people actually claim the privilege of being the last to turn out to fight the invaders of their country.

In the face of these facts, ignorant as I am as yet of the force which may be raised by the officers employed in recruiting along the Coast, whether it is to be counted by thousands or by tens only—ignorant as I must also for some time be as to what force the surrounding kings will produce—and the hour having arrived when on account of the advancing season my decision as to the need for European troops must be made, it is impossible for me to say that my prospects are such that I dare undertake to carry out my mission with native forces, only, nor would the Government or the country hold me excused were the valuable lives of the British officers who have volunteered for this expedition sacrificed, and the prestige of our country lowered by the desertion of these native forces, a result which I forsee is too likely were I to rely solely upon them, and give them no nucleus of first-rate material to set them an example, and afford them a point on which to rally.

Under no circumstances, it appears to me, could I rely on such native troops alone to pursue the war into the enemy's territory. Nor would their presence serve to show the power of Her Majesty as would that of a body of English soldiers. . . .

[Cites the opinions of Dupuis, Governor Hill, and Governor Pine on the need for disciplined troops.]

With these forcible opinions in support of the necessity of trained and disciplined troops, and with your instructions before me, I consider it my duty to state that, in my opinion, the desired effect cannot be obtained by the employment of West Indian regiments alone. In the first place, the moral effect of their presence upon the Ashantees is not to be compared with that which a similar number of Europeans would exert; and, in the next place, they are not physically by any means as capable of withstanding the climate, still less exertion and fatigue.

It is a well-known fact here that Europeans suffer from the climate less than black men from other localities.

The Medical Reports of the Expedition of 1864 say that 'Black troops have none of the hardihood and spirited endurance of the white man. They suffer more from the effects of the climate on their arrival than white men do. They are not accustomed to very onerous duties which they had to perform on this occasion.'

And you will find that Captain (now Sir A.) Clarke, in his Report of 1864,[1] strongly advocates the substitution of an European force for a West Indian regiment, owing to their suffering less from the climate, having more power of endurance, and being able to do the same work with fewer men. I might also refer you to the opinion of Colonel de Ruvignès, that 'the West Indian troops are worse than useless, and are constantly embroiled with the natives.'

I have no wish to depreciate the West Indian regiments, but I could not enter upon my task with that confidence which is so necessary for success were I not supported by some of Her Majesty's English troops.

I consider, therefore, Sir, that (1) the service required cannot be performed solely by any force indigenous to the country; and (2) that the service for which I require these troops is of paramount importance to the main object of my mission—viz., the establishment of a lasting peace with the Ashantee nation. . . .

D. LAND, FINANCE AND CUSTOMS

Introductory Note

THE implementation of company and crown policies in West Africa was paid for by subsidies voted in the United Kingdom Parliament—including estimates for the Navy and the resettlement of captured slaves—and by taxation in the settlements. From 1793 till 1811 the Sierra Leone Company received a total of £141,000 in Parliamentary grants and £70,000 in bills of exchange. Grants to the Committee of Merchants between 1807 and 1821 varied between £20,000 and £30,000 a year. When this largesse terminated, military expenditure which had been covered by some of the grants continued to be borne partly on War Office estimates and partly by the colonies themselves. Colonial accounts for West Africa were first audited by the Audit Department in London in 1830. Civil expenditure in the 1830's fell to its lowest point in the nineteenth century—no more than £13,500 in 1835; and when the Merchants were invited to run the forts again they received only £3,000 to £4,000 a year from 1828 till 1843.

The position changed slowly in the 1840's, when the settlements were forced to rely on Customs to pay for local administration and the cost of their own defence. Either they had little to tax in the way of imports or exports or, as at the Gold Coast, there were objections to *ad valorem* duties because of competition from foreign posts. The failure of the poll tax introduced in 1852 and the extra cost of running the Danish forts, however, led to the re-establishment of taxes on trade in 1856 and to negotiations with the Dutch for parity of duties. The purchase of the Dutch forts in

[1] See above, no. 9.

1871 resulted in the immediate abolition of *ad valorem* duties and the retention of only specific duties on arms, tobacco, gunpowder, and spirits.

Other methods of raising revenue had been tried by the Sierra Leone Company. In return for land grants, the Nova Scotians and Maroons were required to pay a quit rent. The threat of escheat in 1800 and the report of the African Commissioners of 1827 are evidence of the failure of this policy, when Africans refused to take up grants or to have them registered. The only other local sources of revenue available to the Company were a small commission and freight charges for transporting produce and *ad valorem* duties limited to 2½ per cent. A recommendation for a system of rents on town and rural lots passed unheeded by the Colonial Office in 1811. In the Gambia land grants were made irregularly, before a local Act of 1839 required registration by a magistrate. A beginning of registration was made in Freetown about the same time, but high fees discouraged further grants of Crown land. It was not till 1851 that indirect taxes on trade were supplemented by an ordinance to raise revenue on houses and land. Further legislation setting up a commission to register titles in 1857 did little to reduce the number of squatters, and cost more in salaries than it recouped in fees, before it was rescinded in 1867. Governor Kennedy set up a land court and employed a surveyor from 1869; but records were defective and occupants could not be compelled to establish their claims as a basis for taxation. In the Gambia, the registration of Crown land at Kombo was carried out more efficiently in 1854 and paved the way for a land and produce tax in 1864, which was disapproved, though not abolished. In the same year it was discovered that the administration on the Gold Coast had for some time issued titles for lands outside the fort at Cape Coast, which did not belong to the Crown. At Lagos, Governor Freeman in 1862 demanded registration of all titles, and by Ordinance No. 95/1863 Commissions were appointed till 1866 to verify claims. Grants in fee simple were adopted and all earlier grants were declared null and void. Glover dealt with tenure out of court and proposed a registration ordinance in 1869 which was never confirmed. A practice of selling 'Crown' lands was noted at Lagos after Glover's departure in 1872, though all Crown grants were registered by the Surveyor's office and all private conveyances by the Collector of Customs.

The retrenchments of 1865 and the unification of 1866 did little to stop an increase in annual expenditure at the settlements which tripled during the decade to £170,000. Administrators were instructed in stricter methods of accounting and presenting their estimates, while the Richmond report on Customs collection in 1869 brought about a reform of the most important revenue department on the coast. But only Sierra Leone and Lagos retained both *ad valorem* and specific duties; and the settlements at the beginning of the 1870's were forced to rely on the Imperial Government to an extent unforeseen a decade before. The Colonial Office disliked, but tolerated, Pope Hennessy's abolition of the Sierra Leone house and land tax, road tax, market dues and *ad valorem* duties—which left only specific duties as the mainstay of the local budget. The Office fought successfully to retain a subsidy from the Treasury for steamers carrying African mail; and in 1873 Lord Kimberley secured for Lagos a loan of

£20,000. In 1874 the Ashanti expedition was estimated to have cost £815,000; and to this burden was added an advance of £35,000 to pay for additional salaries and public works in the Gold Coast Colony.

I

TERMS OF THE SIERRA LEONE COMPANY TO THE SETTLERS, 3 NOVEMBER 1791[1]

EVERY such Settler from Great Britain producing a certificate under the Company's seal, which will be granted by the Directors in London, shall have a garden lot of one acre, within a convenient distance from a town, of which the situation shall be determined by the Council, on their arrival, and shall have in a neighbouring district *twenty acres of land* for himself, *ten* for his wife, *and five* for each child that he shall carry out. The usual reservations respecting mines and minerals will be made in favour of the Company.

Each such Settler shall be exempted from all quit-rent until midsummer 1792. An annual quit-rent of not more than one shilling sterling per acre shall from that time be chargeable on the land that shall have been granted to the Settlers, in half-yearly payments, the first of which shall be paid at Christmas 1792. No addition shall be made to this quit-rent for three years ending at midsummer 1794, from which time the Company shall be at liberty to charge an additional rent that shall be settled for the next three years (the first half year's rent being payable at Christmas 1794,) on such terms as not to exceed a two per cent tax on the gross produce of the lands. At the end of the said three years, viz. at midsummer 1797, the Company shall have liberty again to raise their rents, and to fix them permanently at a rate that shall not exceed four per cent of the produce.

Any such Settler may have, besides his lot before mentioned, a number of additional acres, not exceeding forty, on his depositing with the Company in London fifty pounds for each additional ten acres that he pleases to take, and he shall receive back from the Company's warehouses at Sierra Leone, implements of husbandry for his own cultivation, and stores for consumption, to the amount of his whole deposit. The Council at Sierra Leone shall supply him with the said stores only in proportion to the progress of his cultivation.

Every such Settler shall be carried out at the Company's expence, shall have three months provisions granted for himself, his wife, and family, from the time of his arrival, according to the usual allowance

---

[1] C.O. 267/34. Encl. in Macaulay to Peel, 15 January 1812. In 1800 the Maroons were offered three acres per man, two for a wife and one for each child; and a quit rent of 20 cents (1s.) per acre was to be levied in cash or labour at the rate of one half-day for each 20 cents. *Substance of the Report of the Court of Directors, 26 March 1801* (London, 1801), pp. 55–57.

in the Army, and half the said allowance for the three succeeding months. He shall have such baggage and furniture carried free of freight for the use of himself and family, not exceeding one ton, as he chuses to take.

There will be no room in the Company's first ship for any goods to be carried out in freight, except articles wanted by the Settlers for their own use and consumption.

All lots of land, except those granted for women and children, shall be forfeited to the Company, if one-third of the said lots shall not be cleared and cultivated within two years, from the time of being granted; and every Settler shall, after the said term of three years, be obliged to proceed to the cultivation of the lots which he holds in right of his wife and children, making the same degree of progress: and no acre shall be considered as cleared, if more than ten trees are left standing.

The Settlers who go out shall give a joint bond from themselves, and some other sufficient person to be approved by the Company, for fifty pounds, as a security for their passage out and home; and for goods, which, at the discretion of the Council, they shall thereupon be allowed to have on credit from the Company's stores at Sierra Leone, for their own use, and for the purpose of cultivation, to an amount not exceeding thirty pounds. The Company will never insist on enforcing payment of the bond, so far as to take the passage money out, provided the settler shall stay twelve months; and they will not insist on the passage money, either out or home, provided the Settler or his wife is obliged to return on account of ill health, and provided he shall bring with him a certificate, to be given by the Council at Sierra Leone for that purpose, stating that they are satisfied with the Surgeon's report, as to this point. If any person shall chuse rather to deposit fifty pounds into the Company's hands in London, a bond will not be required; and he shall have the whole fifty pounds returned him at the end of one year in stores from the Company's warehouses. The Directors however will not always require the said deposit or joint bond for fifty pounds, in the case of artificers and husbandmen, who are well recommended, nor will they require it in other particular cases in which they shall judge the bond unnecessary.

There shall be Settlers houses built by the Company of three different sizes and descriptions, according to the plans to be sent out from home; and every Settler shall either rent a house of such description as he prefers, paying ten per cent. per ann. by way of rent to the Company, on the value of it; or shall be at liberty to purchase the house he occupies at prime cost, at any time within three years from his arrival; the ground on which it stands being given him by the Company.

All the Settlers on their landing, shall unite in assisting to clear the ground intended for the town: or, if they do not work themselves, they shall pay a commutation in money for the share of labour due from them.

The Company will give instructions to their commercial agent to sell to the Settlers the merchandize and provisions by their first ships, at a profit to themselves of about ten per cent.

The produce of the Settlers will either be bought by the Company at a fair price, or carried by the Company's ships on the Settlers' own account; they paying two and one-half per cent commission, and the customary freight and charges; and in the latter case the Company's agent will be instructed to give them credit for a proportion of the value of the produce not exceeding two thirds.

In case the Company should think proper to lay a duty on any articles imported into or exported from their settlement, they engage never to carry any such duty to an higher amount than two and one half per cent. on the imports and two and one half per cent. on the exports.

2

COUNCIL MINUTE, SIERRA LEONE: LAND GRANTS, 27 DECEMBER 1800[1]

Present: J. Gray Acting Governor. R[ichard] Bright Member of Council.

THE Governor and Council having taken the Subject matter of the Company's Estate into their consideration as far as relates to Grants and Transfers of Land, the registering of transfers of Town Lots Resolved:

1st. That all persons who have been, or may be convicted of having been concerned in the late Rebellion against the Company's Government have and be considered to have forfeited their Lands and other property in the Colony.

2nd. That all persons who refuse to take their Grants, and who now have no Grants for their Lots of Land be considered to have forfeited the same.

3rd. That all Lots of Land for which no Grants can be produced, be either sold or otherwise disposed of according as the Governor and Council may see fit.

4th. That all persons being possessed of Grants for their Lots be desired to bring them to the Secretary's Office, on Thornton Hill, on or before the 10th. of January, and that new Grants be drawn out ready to be delivered in lieu of the old ones by the 15th. of the same month.

[1] C.O. 267/92: Appendix B, MS. Report of Commissioners Rowan and Wellington, 1827.

RI BP

5th. That from this day no transfer of Land shall be of any Validity in law, or pleaded in any of the Courts of Justice, unless such Transfer has been regularly entered in the Register at the Secretary's Office, and that no such Transfer be registered, except where the new purchaser binds himself to the observance of this Condition: Vizt That a quit rent of One Shilling Currency or twenty Cents per Acre per annum, shall be regularly paid to the Sierra Leone Company for the said Land.

6th. That no Transfer of Town Lots be from this day Valid in Law unless they be regularly registered at the Secretary's Office.

3

THE EARL OF LIVERPOOL TO GOVERNOR E. H. COLUMBINE: SIERRA LEONE EXPENDITURE, 19 DECEMBER 1809[1]

... A LIBERAL sum has been provided with the sanction of Parliament for the Salaries of the Establishment, and I find that over and above this allowance Bills to the amount of nearly £59,000 have been presented to the Treasury since the Settlement was resumed by the Crown in the month of July 1807. Many of the Services for which the Bills in question have been drawn were under taken without previous authority from home, and will consequently remain charged against the Drawers until the necessary Explanations are produced.

In order to put a stop to this irregularity and to prevent the recurrence of it under your authority, I am to signify to you, His Majesty's Commands that you do not on any occasion, other than of the most urgent necessity (which you will immediately communicate to me) authorize the commencement of any Work or Sanction any Appointment without first apprizing me thereof. . . .

4

REPORT OF THE COMMISSIONERS OF INQUIRY: LAND GRANTS, 11 APRIL 1827[2]

... IF we may venture to propose any particular mode of remedy, it would be to suggest the expediency of reverting to what may be considered the origin of the evil, the grants to the Nova Scotian settlers. These may be divided into two parts; the first being that proportion of land (one-fifth of the whole) which was allotted to them shortly after their arrival in the settlement; and the other the

[1] C.O. 268/18, ff. 12–13.   [2] *Parl. Papers*, 1827, vii (312), pp. 72–73.

remaining portion, which they have, we believe, in no instance received. Under their present circumstances, it is thought that the second portion of land would be of little value to them in the distant situations, where only it would now be practicable to allot it; and from every thing which could be learned from several of their number with whom we conversed, there is reason to believe that they would feel satisfied by having the present possession of the first portion secured to *themselves*, free of quit-rent, and the inheritance in like manner to their children. The improvement of the land must, from the first, have been a condition understood, if not expressed, and therefore no injustice would be done by the insertion of a clause of resumption, in the event of a specific improvement not being made within a reasonable and defined period; and this clause, if acted upon, would, in all probability, induce the Nova Scotians either to cultivate themselves, or dispose of their lots to persons to whom their situation would render them valuable; should this not be the case, it would be open to the government to resume the land, and appropriate it to the disbanded soldiers, liberated Africans, or others.

The terms upon which lands were promised to the Maroons, (App[x] A. No 25,)[1] are so clearly defined, that little difficulty would have been experienced in enforcing the conditions, had not a precedent of non-compliance been established by the Nova Scotians; and it was possibily a consideration of this kind which partly influenced the governor and council, in the resolution recorded in the minute of the 18th April 1803, a copy of which will be found in the Appendix (B. No 21.)[2]

No subsequent act of council which we have been able to find, repeals the minute there quoted, although acts during the administration of Governors Columbine and Maxwell annul all grants which had been made by Governor Thompson. It is true that a proclamation was issued by the governor and council, on the 1st of June 1812, acquainting the Nova Scotians and other holders of lands from the Sierra Leone Company, that the governor and council were ready to confirm their title to such lots; but that the conditions before stipulated as to the oath of allegiance, quit-rent, and cultivation, must be complied with. On the same day an act passed the council by which the quit-rent upon grants of all descriptions of land was considerably increased above that which had been proposed by the Sierra Leone Company, or specified in the terms offered by that company to the Maroons.

It may readily be supposed that the minute of council before cited was more likely to increase than diminish the objections of the Nova Scotians to submit to the condition of a quit-rent; and the provisions of the militia act of 1811, appear greatly to have excited the feelings of

[1] See above, p. 611, n.   [2] C.O. 267/92.

the Maroons; while the increased rate of quit-rent created, with respect to both classes, a new obstacle in the way of compliance; so that few, if any, of either class availed themselves of the proffered confirmation, as will be seen by the Return (Appendix A No 26.)—where 22 grants only are stated to have been registered during the administration of Governors Columbine and Maxwell.

It appears to depend upon the weight attached to the minute of council of the 18th of April 1803, and the construction put upon the acts of subsequent governors in council on the same subject, (which, as far as it has been able to trace them, will be found in the Appendix (B. No 21,) whether the Maroons should not also be exempt from the payment of quit-rent, for any lands possessed by them up to that period. The quantity did not probably in any case exceed three or four acres; but were it greater, the question would, it is presumed, be decided upon its own merits independently of this consideration.

Whether the Maroons be made liable to quit-rent or not, the third clause of their agreement with the Sierra Leone Company, if observed, sufficiently provides for the improvement of their land, or for its reversion to the colonial government in case of default. If therefore this clause were inserted and enforced, the Maroons would, like the Nova Scotians, be compelled either to cultivate their lands, to dispose of them to others, or forfeit them to the government, by which they might be advantageously appropriated, as being perhaps the most valuable of any hitherto granted.

The obstacles which the claims of the Nova Scotians and Maroons have hitherto presented, being once cleared away, little difficulty would exist with respect to the others; as in almost all the grants made to subsequent settlers, the condition of a quit-rent and generally of cultivation or other improvement, has been inserted. . . .

5

GOLD COAST POLL TAX ORDINANCE, 19 APRIL 1852[1]

AT a general meeting of the chiefs and headmen of the towns and districts upon the Gold Coast under British protection, held at Cape Coast Castle on the 19th day of April 1852, in the presence of his Excellency Major Hill, Governor and Commander-in-Chief, and the civil and military officers of his government, it was unanimously resolved and agreed upon,—

1. That this meeting, composed of his Excellency the Governor, his Council, and the chiefs and headmen of the countries upon the Gold Coast under British protection, constitutes itself into a

[1] *Parl. Papers*, 1855, xxxvii (383), p. 83.

Legislative Assembly, with full powers to enact such laws as it shall seem fit for the better government of those countries.

2. That this Assembly be recognized by Her Majesty's Government as legally constituted; that it be called the Legislative Assembly of native chiefs upon the Gold Coast; that it be presided over by his Excellency the Governor, who shall have the power to assembly, prorogue, and adjourn it at pleasure, and that its enactment, sanctioned and approved of by the Governor, shall immediately become the law of the country, subject to the approval of Her Majesty the Queen, and be held binding upon the whole of the population being under the protection of the British Government.

3. That this Legislative Assembly, being thus duly constituted, having taken into consideration the advantages which the chiefs and natives derive from the protection afforded them by Her Majesty's Government, consider it reasonable and necessary that the natives generally should contribute to the support of the Government by submitting from time to time to pay such taxes as may be determined upon by the majority of the chiefs assembled in council with his Excellency the Governor.

4. That it appears to the chiefs at present assembled in Council that the most productive, the least burdensome, and the most equitable tax which, in the present state of the country can be levied, would be a poll tax upon the gross amount of the population enjoying the protection of the British Government.

5. That, entertaining the views here expressed, the chiefs and headmen do for themselves and their people voluntarily agree to pay annually to the Government the sum of 1 s. sterling per head for every man, woman, and child residing in the districts under British protection.

6. That the collection of this tax be confided to officers appointed by his Excellency the Governor, assisted by the chiefs, who, in consideration of annual stipends to be paid to them by the Government, agree to give in their several districts their cordial assistance and the full weight of their authority in support of this measure, and to aid the tax-gatherers in taking a census of the population and in collecting the tax.

7. That pay-notes, specifying the services to be rendered, and the amount of pay to be given to each chief or headman, be immediately granted under the hand and seal of the Governor, payable annually after the collection of the tax, upon certificates given by the tax-gatherer of the district that the services specified have been duly performed.

8. That it shall be competent for the tax-gatherer to sue any person refusing to pay the tax before the native chief of the district, or an English magistrate, as for common debt, and that the master

of a house or head of a family be considered responsible for the whole of the inmates of the house.

9. That any obstruction offered to the gatherer, or assault made upon him in the execution of his duty, shall be punished by a fine or imprisonment, one-half of all such fines to be paid to the chief of the district or town.

10. That it shall be competent for the tax-gatherer, and chief of a district, subject to the approval of the Governor, to make such local arrangements for facilitating the collection of the tax as may be found expedient.

11. That the revenue derived from this tax, after payment of the stipends of the chiefs, and other expenses attending its collection, be devoted to the public good, in the education of the people, in the general improvement and extension of the judicial system, in affording greater facilities of internal communication, increased medical aid, and in such other measures of improvement and utility as the state of the social progress may render necessary, and that the chiefs to be informed of the mode of its application, and entitled to offer such suggestions on this point as they may consider necessary.

12. That a proclamation based upon these resolutions be issued by His Excellency the Governor to carry them into full effect during this current year; and that such proclamation, issued with the full concurrence of the legislative assembly of the native chiefs upon the Gold Coast, shall have in every respect the force of a law, and be held binding upon the whole of the native population being under the protection of the British Government. . . .

(signed)

George Fynn Aggery, Chief of Cape Coast; Caboceers of Cape Coast, Attah Coffee, Coffee Amoah, Coffee Coomah, Coffee Chinguran, Quabino Menyah; Amnoney, Chief of Annamaboe; Appeah, Caboceer of Annamaboe; Quakee Ephram, Chief of Denkera; Ampontin, Captain to Chief of Denkera; Effien, Captain to Chief of Denkera; Chibboo Arbarbeo, Chief of Dixcove; Caboceers of Dixcove, Essein Mensah Coomah, Addabee, Thomas Coffee, Ahmanckie Brokenta, Addabee; Quamin Deawool, Caboceer of Secondee; Quamino Ammoah, Chief of Abrah; Quashie Ankah, Caboceer of Donassie; Thomas Solomon, Caboceer of Donassie; Chibboo Coomah, Chief of Yancoomassie; Gabil, Chief of Mansu; Yuo Fansee, Caboceer; Bondequay, Chief of Winnebah; Quoro Cootooacoo, Chief of Mumford; Quamino Menyah, Chief of Mumford; Quashie Eccoom, Chief of Aggonah; Yuow Doodoo, Chief of Aggonah; Edoom Ashantee, Chief of Assam; Endow Ampah, Captain of Mumford; Quamino Ahwil, Chief of Agah; Cudjoe Bahyinnie, Chief of Appolonia; Caboceers of Appolonia, Amakay and

Quacoe Yarkoo; Captains of Appolonia, Tandoe Ayoun Coffee, Arleah Coffee Essergoe, Ahwooshie Quamino, Amatay Cudjoe, Bocary; Quacoe Arfoal, Chief of Queen Ann's Point; Akinny, Caboceer of Eccoonfee; Coffee Appray, Caboceer or Quarmin; Coffee Andoe, Chief of Emyenebrim; Ackaafoo, Chief of Commendah; Quabino Pankeran, Captain of Commenda; Quamino Ashum; Horkoo, Caboceer of Commenda; Coffee Mensah, Captain of Commenda; Quashie Essanpon, Captain of Commenda; Addoo, King of Fantee; Enimilly, King of Warsaw; Quacoe Andoe, Interpreter to the King of Warsaw; Captains, Quoro Bocoroe, Quabino Geetoh, Coffee Artobrah; Coffee Enimil, Chief of Boosoomchie; Cudjoe Barcoon, Chief of Sekkay; Quamino Bassanin, Chief of Takquah; Quabino Ebboo, Chief of Eppinto; Coffee Kaye, Chief of Eppinto; Quacoe Mensah Mamfee; Coffee Beddoo Bansoo; (Enimilly on behalf of:) Tandoe Quabino, Chief of Peppasal, Quashie Kessie, Chief of Mansu, Coffee Boroah, Chief of Empohor, Coffee Ammonoo, Chief of Daddeasa; Quamino Ahrohomah, Chief of Adjumacoon; Quamino Ebbeasah; Quamino Ahquah Ennoo; Quamino of Abbarsen and Eyen; Quabino Ahmorquah, Chief of Essicoomah; Jepay Abbansah, Chief; and Stephen J. Hill, Governor.

6

GOVERNOR A. KENNEDY: INSTRUCTIONS FOR THE GUIDANCE OF DISTRICT MANAGERS, 9 JANUARY 1854[1]

I. THE Clerk of Police in each District will be required to keep a Register of all Fines and Fees imposed by the Magistrate. This Register is not to supersede the Magisterial Record of cases decided, which in addition to its other uses will be required as a check upon the fines and fees entered in the Book especially kept for that purpose by the Police Clerk.

II. It will therefore be necessary, that all decisions involving any Fine or Fee should be entered either in the Hand-writing of the Manager or be authenticated by the presence of his signature.

[Statements of revenue are to be transmitted to the Colonial Secretary and a monthly abstract laid before the Governor.]

VII. It must be regarded as a first principle, that no expense of any nature or kind whatsoever, not previously mentioned in these instructions can be incurred without the previous knowledge and sanction of His Excellency the Governor, for which a Requisition shall be made. . . ; should circumstances of an unforseen nature

[1] C.O. 267/235. Encl. in Kennedy to Newcastle, 10 January 1854.

however arise, which render it necessary that immediate action involving expense should be taken, the District Manager may do so upon the understanding, that he is immediately to report the circumstances to His Excellency, in order that His Excellency may be prepared to sanction in due form a liquidation from the Colonial Treasury of the expense so incurred: His Excellency's sanction for Disbursements of this nature will be according to Form D., to be prepared by the Manager.

VIII. The Manager of each District will report to the Colonial Surveyor the state of any Bridge or Building within his District that may require to be repaired, and the Manager of Districts will from henceforth be relieved from the task of making Estimates or preparing Requisitions to be forwarded to the Governor through the Colonial Secretary. That duty will in future devolve upon the Colonial Surveyor.

IX. His Excellency, the Governor will not entertain any applications for the service of any Work or Building from the Manager of any District, unless it can be shewn that an unsuccessful attempt has been made to obtain the attention of the Colonial Surveyor thereto.

X. The Manager of each District is required at once, to furnish His Excellency the Governor through the Colonial Secretary with an account of all the tithes of every description of Timber in his possession; and also a nominal return of all persons who are engaged in cutting, sawing or splitting Timber in his District.

XI. The Manager of each District will henceforth be required to keep a Book, in which he is to insert a detailed Account according to form E. of every description or Timber received by him as tithe, shewing the quantity received, the name of the party from whom he received; and the quantity cut, sawed or split on account of which, payment has been made; in order that His Excellency the Governor may have the means of ascertaining any arrears of the tithe that may be due to the Government.

XII. No person is to be allowed to cut or saw Government Timber, without a Licence first had and obtained from the Executive, on the recommendation of the District Manager; and it is to be distinctly understood, that His Excellency the Governor reserves to himself the right of dictating on behalf of the Crown, the terms on which the licences are to be granted, whether on the payment of tithe or some other equivalent.

XIII. A Return of Persons Licensed to cut or saw Government Timber must be forwarded every half year, to the Office of the Colonial Secretary, for the purpose of being registered therein.

XIV. The Manager of each District will receive directions from His Excellency the Governor, as to the manner in which he is to dispose of Timber received by him as tithe; and he will carefully preserve all approved Requisitions or other documents authorizing the delivery of Timber, in order to verify the credits which he may take in his Account Book for the issues.

XV. The Managers of Districts are not at liberty to dispose or make use of Timber received as tithe in any way whatever on their individual authority.

XVI. In collecting the House and Land Tax for each year, the Managers of Districts will be guided by the provisions of the Ordinance of the 14th April 1851.

XVII. His Excellency the Governor expects, that due diligence will be used by the Managers to send in to the Commissioners the Assessement Rolls for each District, within the period specified in the warrants addressed to them by the Commissioners, agreeably to the 5th Clause of the House and Land Tax Ordinance.

XVIII. The Assessement Rolls will as heretofore be returned to the Managers of Districts for the purpose of enabling them to collect the Tax assessed.

XIX. His Excellency the Governor desires to call the attention of the Managers to the necessity of their having the List of Defaulters (which is a Return of persons failing to pay the amount for which they are charged on the assessment Roll;) in the hands of the Colonial Accountant by the 10th day of May in each year.

XX. The Colonial Accountant will then issue his Warrant, authorizing the Managers of Districts, to enforce if necessary by levy and Sale of the goods and chattels of the Defaulters, the payment of the amounts for which they are in default.

XXI. The Managers of Districts are hereby warned of the necessity of making a return to the Warrant of the Colonial Accountant within sixty days after they have received it, attached to a further statement with respect to the Defaulters, according to the form hereunto annexed F.

XXII. Managers of Districts are expected to be very careful with regard to the manner in which their Books of Counterparts of Certificates of payment are kept. Each person paying the Tax, is to be required to attach his signature or mark to the counterpart in presence of a witness or witnesses.

[Counterparts are to be dated and sent in to the Colonial Secretary.]

. . . XXV. The Managers of Districts will be expected to make a Return to His Excellency the Governor, through the Colonial Secretary, of the persons who make payment in labour instead of money.

XXVI. This Return will embrace the number of days work performed by each person, as well as designate the Road or other locality on which the work was done.

XXVII. The Manager will recommend some useful Public Work (*other than Road Work*) on which House and Land tax defaulters may be employed. Especial care must be taken that these defaulters are not called out during the usual period for Road repairs.

XXVIII. All Requisitions for articles, except those relating to Works and Buildings, are to be forwarded to His Excellency the Governor through the Colonial Secretary.

7

GOVERNOR A. KENNEDY TO SIR GEORGE GREY: SIERRA LEONE HOUSE AND LAND TAX, 24 AUGUST 1854[1]

Sir,

Herewith I have the honor to transmit for your approval, and Her Majesty's Confirmation 'An Ordinance to Amend the Law for raising a Tax on Lands and Houses within the Colony of Sierra Leone'.

2. This Ordinance does not differ in principle from that in present operation,[2] it however corrects many faulty details and omissions which the working of the existing law has brought to light.

3. I will notice such alterations only as appear to require explanation; The 4th. Clause enacts a Tax upon empty, or unoccupied Lots. These in some situations in Towns or Villages, are found to be a great nuisance; the property of some absentee or Bankrupt, are most unsightly, and being generally a receptacle of filth; it is desirable that they should be sold into solvent hands, who can improve and make use of them.

4. The 5th. Clause enacts that all Rural Lots be assessed as containing *three* acres, this I have ascertained to be about the average quantity; heretofore such Lots were assessed but for one acre which was manifestly under the fact.

5. In the former Ordinance there is no penalty upon persons refusing to afford the necessary information to the Assessor; the 12th Clause of present Ordinance remedeys this evil which caused endless trouble, mistakes and loss of time.

6. The 17th Clause empowers the Governor to appoint a Clerk to the House and Land Tax Commissioners. I would beg to refer you to my despatch No 69 dated 5th May 1854 on this subject; such an Office is absolutely necessary; it also empowers the Governor to appoint sub accountants in the absence of 'Managers' in a district.

[1] C.O. 267/241.
[2] An Ordinance of 1851 imposed 1s. in the pound on houses whose rental value was over £5, 5s. on all houses under £5, and a tax of 6d. an acre on land. Just over £3,000 was collected in 1852.

7. The 23rd Clause empowers the sale of Lots for two years arrears of Taxes. It must be remarked that these Lots are of little value; that they were originally free grants from the Government, or granted on a nominal payment; That the lots proposed to be so dealt with are generally public nuisances and receptacles of filth or that they are virtually abandoned.

This Ordinance has undergone mature consideration and discussion and has passed the Council unanimously.

8

FREDERIC ROGERS (LAND BOARD) TO HERMAN MERIVALE: GAMBIA LAND REGISTRATION, 30 SEPTEMBER 1854[1]

[Concerning the respective rights of the Crown and British settlers over land in the annexed territory of Kombo in the Gambia; according to the New Zealand precedent, land titles made before annexation are not valid until confirmed by a Crown grant.]

. . . 8. THE cession of this territory by the King of Combo seems in no respect distinguishable from that of the Northern Island of New Zealand by the Native Chiefs; and we presume that the grants to British Subjects made previously to such cession will in both cases be considered equally invalid in point of law.

9. The question however still remains what are the equitable claims of those persons who may have acquired Lands from the Natives. But on this we find it impossible to express an opinion without much fuller information. . . .

10. It may however facilitate the treatment of this question if, even in the absence of the requisite information and subject to such corrections as that information may render necessary, we suggest the outline of a course which it may perhaps be found practicable to pursue.

11. In the first place we assume that the legal principles laid down in the case of New Zealand may be considered as practically settled— and if so applicable to the present case.

12. Next we collect from Governor Macdonnell's report, above quoted, that the land is wanted partly for the residences of merchants, and other Europeans, partly for the cultivation of the Natives who, he anticipates would be glad to take them at moderate rents; whence it would seem to follow that the usual practice of dividing the Land into Town and Country allotments may conveniently be followed, and that the Governor should have authority to leave to the Natives

---

[1] C.O. 87/58. This opinion was accepted by the Colonial Office: Grey to O'Connor, 13 October 1854.

unsold land, certainly of the latter, and probably of the former class. We collect that it also forms part of Government policy to make free grants of land to Natives likely to cultivate them . . . and particularly to African pensioners.

13. Thirdly the imposition of a land tax on all private lands is recommended not only as a mode of obtaining revenue but as it tends to control the evils which may arise from the recognition of native grants, to diminish the value of such grants, and therefore to facilitate negotiations with their claimants. . . .

[The Gambia Government is to divide the area into lots and hear claims for Crown grants.]

9

GOVERNOR H. CONNOR TO SYDNEY HERBERT: GOLD COAST POLL TAX, 4 MAY 1855[1]

[Forwarding the poll tax accounts for 1854, consisting of £3,624 in receipts and £3,872 expenditure.]

. . . Observations.

THE disturbances in the Leeward Districts at the beginning, and in the middle of the Year 1854, caused a considerable diminution in the Receipts of Poll Tax in that Year, and a large expenditure of the Reserve Fund; and the attention of the Governor was so much taken up with the military preparations rendered necessary by the disturbances, that probably fewer works of benefit to the Country were attempted, than even the small receipts from the Poll Tax, not otherwise used, would have allowed.

The principal Expenditure has been, in the pay notes of the Chiefs, the Salaries and Expences of the Poll Tax Collectors, the Salaries of Magistrates, appointed at the different Forts, to administer justice to the people, the Salary of Dr. Sawkins, appointed Physician for the Africans and parts of Salaries of the Governor, and other Officers of the Government at Cape Coast Castle: His Excellency Governor Hill made large reduction in the Salaries in the year 1854. The Salary of the Collector General of the Poll Tax was reduced, from £600 a year to £150, with a Clerk at £75 a year; that of each Magistrate was reduced from £200 to £100, except in the case of Anamaboe to £150, which is now also reduced to £100; that of Collector of Customs from £150 to £100, and the addition to the Salary of the Colonial Secretary was reduced, from £200 to £150.

If it were known what additional trouble the Poll Tax gives to the Governor and Colonial Secretary, it would not be thought, that the

[1] C.O. 96/33.

addition to their Salaries was a compensation for it: the Acting Governor is entitled to an increase to his Salary from the Poll Tax at the rate of £75 a year; of this he had in fact received £3. 18. 2, and he can state, that, the main part of his trouble and anxiety, as Acting Governor, has been with respect to the Poll Tax: as Chief Justice, or Judicial Assessor, no part of his salary is derived from the Poll Tax.

With respect to what is to be done for the benefit of the People and Country, His Excellency avoids making promises, his own authority will probably last so short a time, that he can attempt but little, and of course, he ought not to make promises for a new Governor; he, however, will tell what he has done himself, he has appointed two Schoolmasters in the Wassaw Country in addition to the School-masters at Cape Coast Castle, Donassie, Commenda and Appolonia; he has Magistrates at Quittah, Christiansborg, James Fort, Winnebah, Cape Coast and Dixcove; and Anamaboe is visited by the Acting Assistant Judicial Assessor; he has sent Dr. Sawkins to Dixcove to be both a Magistrate there, and also a Physician for the Africans, and he has recommended to Her Majesty's Secretary of State, that, each Military Surgeon, at the different Forts, shall be appointed also to be a Physician for the Africans, and he has also recommended to the Secretary of State, that the sum of £200 shall be laid out in the purchase of tools to be sent out here, for being given away:—he is also anxious to do as much as he can, in the repair of the Market place at Cape Coast. . . .

10

J. E. TENNENT TO HERMAN MERIVALE: GOLD COAST DUTIES, 18 MARCH 1856[1]

SIR,

I am directed by the Lords of the Committee of Privy Council for Trade, to request that you will bring to the attention of Mr. Labouchere the accompanying letter enclosing a copy of a Memorial the original of which has been addressed to the Secretary of State for the Colonies on the subject of the Ordinance by which the import of duties have been recently increased to 3 per cent in the British Settlements on the Gold Coast of Africa.

The facts mentioned by the Memorialists serve to sustain the apprehension expressed by their Lordships in Mr. Booth's letter of the 16th November 1855 that the operation of this measure if enforced as then contemplated might be attended with possible injury to British trade in the competition to which from our close

[1] C.O. 96/39. The Colonial Office decided to continue the new duties: Barrow, minute, 15 December 1860, ibid.

contiguity to the Dutch Settlements it is necessarily exposed on that portion of the African Coast.

The Memorialists state that the trade is already showing symptoms of being attracted towards the Dutch Stations at Elmina and Moree Fort and My Lords feel it right to renew the expression of their former opinion that the Governor should be instructed vigilantly to observe the practical effect of the Ordinance and if found prejudicial that the question of retaining the duty on its increased scale should again be brought under the consideration of the Secretary of State.

II

LIEUT.-GOVERNOR W. HACKETT TO THE DUKE OF NEWCASTLE: CROWN LANDS AT CAPE COAST, 12 MAY 1864[1]

[Various Governors have considered lands at Cape Coast to be property of the Crown.]

... 2. BEFORE entering on the matter of the proposed cession I beg to draw Your Grace's attention to some documents which have fallen under my notice since I had occasion to report to Governor Pine on this subject, and which seem to me to be important as shewing the manner in which the lands in and about this town have been dealt with for more than forty years. I think on a review of these documents it will be apparent that the Governors of these Settlements have for a series of years considered the lands of Cape Coast to be the property of the Crown; and this at least is certain that most of the houses in Cape Coast are erected on lands held under titles derived from that source. ...

12

T. W. C. MURDOCH (LAND BOARD) TO T. F. ELLIOT: SIERRA LEONE CROWN LANDS, 15 JULY 1864[2]

[Reporting on the Sierra Leone Rules and Regulations for the Sale of Crown Lands.]

... THE Regulations divide the Land into Town, Suburban and Rural and prescribe the form and size of the Lots—they provide for the Sale of all Land by auction, at an upset price for Town Lands of 20s.

[1] C.O. 96/64.
[2] C.O. 267/282. This opinion was referred to Blackall, 23 July 1864, without recommendation.

per Lot (of from 3000 to 6000 square feet) for suburban Lands of 10s. per Lot of the same size—and for Country Lands of 4s. 2d. per acre—the last to be exclusive of cost of Survey—they allow the sale by private contract of Land offered at Auction but not bought—and they require payment of the purchase money in 4 instalments ¼th. within three months of the sale and the remaining ¾ths at 6, 9, and 12, months respectively from the day of sale. Failure to make the requisite payments at the specified dates will involve forfeiture of the Land and of the instalments already paid. The grants are to contain the reservation of a right of resumption by the Crown for public purposes, and the mode of assessing the compensation for such resumption is defined. The boundaries of Blocks are to run as nearly as circumstances will admit in straight lines in the direction of the Cardinal Points of the Compass—the shortest side being about ⅔ths of the longest. Surrendered or escheated Lands are to be sold by auction, but under special circumstances may be granted to the actual holder on such terms as the Governor may prescribe. The Governor is also authorized, with the concurrence of his Executive Council, to make arrangements for the sale of blocks of Country Land of a size, and at a price, to be determined by him, without putting them up to Auction.

3. With the exception of this last provision, and of the recital in the Preamble to which I have before alluded, I see nothing in these regulations to object to. The upset price of Town Lands will vary according to the size of the Lot, from about £7 5. to £14. 10 pr. acre—and the upset price of Suburban Lands will be of course half that amount. The mode of payment is made more favorable to the purchaser than we have been in the habit of considering desirable, but the point is one on which the Colonial Government may be considered capable of forming a better opinion than we can in this Country. The Clause that gives the Governor power to sell Country Lands in Blocks, at a price to be fixed by him with the concurrence of his Executive Council, is, at appears to me, the most questionable provision in the regulations. It is possible that this power might be abused for the advantage of influential members of the community, and its exercise, whether rightly or wrongly, would probably give rise to suspicions of abuse. I would suggest, therefore, that if the regulations are approved by the Secretary of State the Governor should be informed that his power must not be exercised by him except under very special circumstances, and that in every instance of its proposed exercise he should report the case to the Secretary of State, with a full explanation of his reasons, and should not conclude the arrangement without the Secretary of State's approval.

13

T. W. C. MURDOCH (LAND BOARD) TO
T. F. ELLIOT: GAMBIA LAND TAX, 19 JULY 1864[1]

SIR,

I have to acknowledge your letter of 14th inst., with a Despatch from the Governor of the Gambia enclosing an Ordinance passed by the Legislature of that Colony entitled 'An Ordinance to facilitate the collection of a Land Revenue in British Combo'.

2. Governor d'Arcy reports that with a view to raise a Revenue in this Territory, he had organized the collection of a small Tax on the Crops brought to Market, but that payment having been resisted by some person he found he had no legal power to enforce it. He therefore, proposed to his Council the enactment of an Ordinance imposing a Tax at 8d. an Acre. The Governor expresses a doubt whether that amount is not too high, but says that having received so much assistance from the Council he was unwilling to decide against them on this point. He therefore recommended that the Ordinance should be confirmed.

3. There can I think be no doubt that a Tax of 8d an Acre is altogether excessive. It is double the price of the fee simple of land in the North American Colonies and Natal, and if regarded as rent would represent a price far higher than the price in the most prosperous and richest of the British Colonies. Such a Tax can hardly fail to discourage the increase of Settlers and the occupation of Land. In this respect, therefore, the Ordinance requires, I think, Alteration.

4. But again the Ordinance provides that the only tenure of land in British Combo shall be by yearly leases, subject to be cancelled for non payment of rent or non compliance with the other conditions of the Ordinance. So uncertain a tenure must evidently discourage anything but the most superficial cultivation, and must fail to attach the Settler to the Soil. Whatever facility it affords for the collection of rent is more than counter-balanced by its discouragement of careful and laborious cultivation.

5. The Ordinance further provides that the cultivator shall not be allowed to take his crops off the ground or sell them till he has paid his rent—a condition which would probably make it impossible for him in many cases to do either. And in that event the Manager is authorized to take possession of the farm produce and summon the defaulter before the Magistrates, who may thereupon order the sale of the produce for payment of the rent—or, if there be no produce available, may order a distress on the defaulter's goods. Where the

[1] C.O. 87/81. Despite this view, the Ordinance, 15 June 1864, was not rescinded.

farm produce or goods of the defaulter are insufficient to pay the rent and cost of proceedings, the Magistrates are authorized to direct his summary ejection from his land.

6. This Ordinance appears to me to be framed altogether in too rigorous a spirit towards the occupants of land in Combo. I am not aware whether there are any political reasons which dissuade the absolute alienation of the Soil in that District—but if not it would I think be a wise policy to sell the Land to the Settlers outright. . .

[The principles of the Sierra Leone Land Ordinance are recommended.]

14

LIEUT.-GOVERNOR J. H. GLOVER TO EDWARD CARDWELL: LAGOS DUTIES, 2 MAY 1865[1]

[Forwarding the Blue Book for 1864.]

. . . WITH regard to the taxes, duties, and other sources of revenue of this Settlement, the remarks made by His Excellency Governor Freeman in his report of last year are still applicable to the subject. A system of direct taxation, at all events to any extent, would be injudicious in the present undeveloped state of this Settlement. I had most certainly desired to institute a system of licences, similar to that carried on at Sierra Leone and elsewhere, on the sale of wines and spirts &c. Circumstances have prevented me from carrying out my views in this respect; but I am still of opinion that such a tax would be a just and fair one, and would be beneficial in its effects. As matters stand, however, our principal and almost entire revenue is derived from our customs duties. It is upon these alone that we must rely; and had our tariff been raised to that of other Colonies a very sufficient revenue would have accrued to the Settlement, even under the unfavourable circumstances which have influenced the trade of the past year. I trust, however, that the brighter prospects of the present year, caused by the opening of the roads to the Yoruba country, will do away with any necessity for increasing our duties. A very great and unfavourable influence is exercised upon the general duties of this port by the facilities afforded to merchants (principally foreign ones) of landing their goods on the beach near Porto Novo, and after paying a comparatively trifling duty to the King of Dahomey, who claims the sea beach as his territory, conveying the said goods through Cotenoo Creek to Porto Novo, and passing them thence into the interior, thus placing the Lagos merchants at a manifest disadvantage

[1] *Colonial Reports*, Part II (London, 1865), pp. 26–27.

by under-selling them. The only draw-back to this mode of proceeding was the inconvenience and oppression to which they might at any time be exposed, on account of occasional arbitrary measures on the part of the King of Dahomey, and these measures were more than once exercised. Perceiving this an attempt was made by this Government, by granting peculiarly favourable terms to importers landing goods 'in transit' for Porto Novo, to turn the Cotenoo trade into its natural channel through Lagos; and it was anticipated that after the passing of Ordinance No. 8 of the 6th April 1864, granting half duties, or a drawback of 50 per cent. on goods intended for Porto Novo, the additional sense of security afforded by this mode of importation would have counter-balanced the advantages which even under these very favourable circumstances were still presented by the discharge of goods at Cotenoo. Unfortunately the system has not worked well, and instead of resulting in a gain, has been the cause of considerable loss to this Government. I may here remark that a very extensive traffic in slaves is carried on from Abbeokuta and the countries beyond, through the said creek of Cotenoo and others leading from Porto Novo towards Whydah; and could these passages be permanently blocked up, a severe blow would be inflicted upon the Porto Novo slave dealers, while our revenue would, as above demonstrated, receive great benefits from the measure. . . .

15

SIR GEORGE BARROW: MINUTE, GOLD COAST DEBT, 13 MAY 1865[1]

UNDER the Head of *Revenue* in the Estimates [for the Gold Coast] is a sum of £1395 'by balance actually due by the Colonial Governt. on account of expenses consequent upon the Ashantee invasion & of which it is presumed H.M.'s Govt. will decide to re-imburse the Colonl. Chest.'

I remarked on a former occasion that this item, as worded, is not one of *revenue* at all—but a debt due by the Colonl. Govt. & even if paid by H.M.'s Govt. would leave nothing in the shape of revenue.

But Col. Ord has explained that it is a piece of gaucherie—& that the Col. Govt. have in fact expended that sum.

The Treasury, however, now refuse to make it good—so that expenditure will exceed the revenue by £1395—on the other hand one of the items of expenditure is £2000 set apart for the Crown Agents—which past experience shews will never be remitted—the expenditure therefore *at the Gold Coast* will be within bounds £600.

The Colony is owing the Crown Agents £2051—but the Treasury

[1] C.O. 96/69.

have just paid them the £1000 inserted in the Parliamty. Grant for arrears of 'expenditure'—which reduces the debt to £1051 & which will go on increasing during the current year.

I suppose there can be no doubt that the £1900 on account of Native Levies must be paid from Army Funds.

16

EDWARD CARDWELL TO GOVERNOR G. A. K. D'ARCY: GAMBIA DUTIES, 23 NOVEMBER 1865[1]

Sir,

I have received your despatches Nos. 2 & 7 of the 4th Septr. & 2d. Octr. reporting that the Revenue of the Gambia, which is principally derivable from Exports had for the present ceased, & that after borrowing £695 of the Imperial money collected by the Postmaster, there remained in the Colonial Chest on the 1st. Ult. a balance of only £124. 7. 6., altho' the Heads of Departments & others had agreed to allow their Salaries to stand over for some time.

I need scarcely remark that this is a most serious state of affairs & shews how unsafe it is to rely to too great an extent on Export duties only.

I have, therefore, to instruct you to procure the enactment of an Ordinance for imposing additional taxes to meet this . . . I think it would be desirable to impose a small ad valorem duty of 2 pr. Ct. on all goods imported into the Colony which are now free of duty, to raise the present duty of 1d. a lb. on tobacco to 1d. & to place a specific duty on Gunpowder & arms.

You will at the same time understand that the Export duty on Ground-Nuts and Hides is not to be disturbed.

17

W. E. FORSTER TO HUGH CHILDERS: WEST AFRICAN FINANCES, 27 JANUARY 1866[2]

Sir,

With reference to the recommendations of the Committee of the House of Commons which inquired last Session into the Colonies on the West Coast of Africa, I am directed by Mr. Secretary Cardwell to transmit to you, for the information of the Lords Commissioners of the Treasury, the enclosed Memorandum prepared at his desire by

[1] C.O. 87/83.
[2] C.O. 267/288. *William Forster*, M.P., was Parliamentary Under-Secretary at the Colonial Office for a few months in 1865 and 1866. *Hugh Childers* was Financial Secretary to the Treasury, 1865–6.

Mr. Elliot, Assistant Under Secretary in this Department, and by Major Blackall, Governor of Sierra Leone, on the re-modelling of the West African Governments, and on the pecuniary aid necessary to restore their finances and provide for their future annual requirements.

On a review of all the circumstances of the case, Mr. Cardwell is prepared to recommend the following proposals to their Lordships favourable consideration.

1st. To apply to Parliament in such form as their Lordships may deem most suitable, for the means of discharging the accumulated debts of these Settlements to the amount of £21,880.

2ndly. To ask for a Grant of £17,000 for the purchase of the two Steamers both for the intended concentration of Civil Authority in the hands of one Governor in Chief, and also for admitting with safety of the Military reductions now in course of completion.

3rdly. To submit to Parliament for the approaching Financial Year a Vote of £22,500 which will cover the cost of the new Government in Chief, defray the estimated annual expense of the two steamers, and make provision against the constantly accumulating deficiency which has heretofore embarrassed these Colonies, and has produced so heavy a demand this year on account of past liabilities.

It will be observed that the effect of these arrangements is to remove a Wing of a Regiment which costs £22,500 in Africa, and will cost £9,500 less in the West Indies, even though there should be no ultimate reduction in the number of Troops maintained.

Although it is necessary to ask at the present moment so large a Civil Grant, Mr. Cardwell trusts that the proposed changes in the Constitution and general management of the different Settlements will so alter their character, as to lead eventually to a large reduction in the annual demand upon Parliament.

18

HUGH CHILDERS TO FREDERIC ROGERS: WEST AFRICAN FINANCES, 10 MAY 1866[1]

. . . MY LORDS are of opinion that in order to prevent the recurrence of such heavy liabilities to the Crown Agents, as have lately pressed upon the Finances of the West African Settlements, the safest and simplest course will be to make the expenditure by the Agents in this Country for the Stores, Salaries, &c., the first charge upon the Parliamentary Vote, and the scale by which the Drafts of the Governors upon this Board are to be regulated. For this purpose the Governors of the Settlements should be directed to send, previous

[1] C.O. 267/288.

to the commencement of each colonial financial year, an estimate in detail of stores and services, for which payment will have to be made in England during that year. When this has been approved by the Home Government, and the amount of the Parliamentary Vote for the year has been determined, the amount of the Vote required to meet the payments to be made in this country should be deducted from the total of the Vote, and the Governors informed of the specific sums which remain as the amount within which they are authorized to draw upon this Board for the general service of the Colonies, and they should be informed that all supplementary requisitions must be preceded by the payment into the Treasury Chests in the respective Colonies of the amount required to meet all charges in respect of such requisitions, or they must be in each instance accompanied by sufficient remittances.

Instructions should also be, at the same time, given that all the stores of European manufacture or produce should be demanded from this Country, otherwise the debts of the Colonies will simply become local instead of foreign, with a heavy percentage, in addition, for the local profit. . . .

19

GOVERNOR SIR ARTHUR KENNEDY TO THE DUKE OF BUCKINGHAM AND CHANDOS: SIERRA LEONE LAND GRANTS, 14 SEPTEMBER 1868[1]

. . . 5. PRIOR to the 19th February 1857, all Land Claims or applications for Crown Lands, were examined and filled up by the Colonial Surveyor in Executive Council, by whom the Grant was completed and issued if found correct.

6. This system was carried on till 1857, in which year the Ordinance No 93 of 19th February 1857 was passed to relieve the Council of labour, and vesting the jurisdiction in Commissioners at a fixed Salary which was from time to time increased.

7. This Ordinance remained in force till 1867 when an Ordinance (No 5 of 19th June 1867) was passed, abolishing the Office of Commissioners and vesting the jurisdiction in the Judge of the Court of Summary Jurisdiction, which Law is still in force. . . .

[Fees have been paid, but few grants have been issued since then.]

. . . 10. From the passing of the Ordinance No 5 of 1867, it has remained a dead letter: no case, new or old, has been heard under it: applications have naturally ceased.

[1] C.O. 267/295.

[Salaries to commissioners and clerks, 1857-67 totalled £2,663. 5s. 2d.; the total of fees paid in was £777. 7s. 6d.]

. . . 12. Your Grace is aware that there are numerous villages in this Settlement; and by a reference to the Office of the Registrar, I find that not five per cent of those occupying Crown Lands and Allotments, have *any* Grants or title at all, and many have obtained and held their allotments by fraud.

13. There are no complete or reliable maps of Grants or allotments, either Town or Country.

14. I am informed, and believe, that in many cases *Second* Grants have been issued for lands, where first Grants were still in existence: thus the amount paid in salaries (£2,663) between 1857 and 1867, has mainly been productive of mischief and, in many cases, of great injustice.

15. I need not point out to Your Grace the dangerous complications which must inevitably arise in a Settlement where real property is daily increasing in value, if this unaccountable and discreditable state of things is permitted to continue, the more especially, when I inform Your Grace that the people of this Settlement value their allotments, and cling to them, with as much tenacity as an Irish Peasant to his 'Spot of Land'.

18. I am of opinion that it would occupy an energetic and industrious Judge and two Clerks for 18 months at least, to bring up these formidable arrears. I do not believe that the Assistant Judge has either health, time or energy to accomplish the task in *any period* of *time* in *connection with his other duties*. The people are naturally very anxious to obtain their legal titles to their holdings, and the demand for Grants would greatly increase if the Court were in working order, and a fee of £1 1s. od. in addition to those received, would be payable to the Treasurer on the issue of each Grant.

19. It would be obviously necessary for some Officer to watch cases where the Crown is interested, as many allotments now valuable would undoubtedly be escheated to the Crown.

20. A reliable Surveyor (one above taking bribes) must also be attached to the Court, to measure and record every Grant *as soon as approved:* this is the life of the whole matter. If measurement were dishonest or defective, it would open a field to endless litigation, and bring the Executive into still greater disrepute. . . .

20

J. HALES: MINUTE, WEST AFRICAN CUSTOMS, 16 SEPTEMBER 1869[1]

MR. RICHMOND'S Report discloses many abuses in the working of the Customs Departments at S. Leone, Gambia, & Gold Coast—Lagos comes out best. The Gambia Report has already been received & the removal of Mr. Kneller was the consequence.

At S. Leone Mr. R[ichmond] discovered great neglect in carrying out the provisions of the Customs Ordinances—the wrong men were doing work which did not belong to their sphere, and there was field for the perpetration of much fraud. On visiting one Warehouse belonging to the Crown on 9 Feb./69 he found that the last entry in the Locker's Stock Book (which should contain an accurate record of all goods received into & delivered from the Warehouse) was made on the 17th April 1868.

Bulama.

Mr. R[ichmond] states that owing to the Coast on one side only belonging to the British Govt. it is almost impossible to keep a strict supervision over the craft trading in the neighbourhood. Duties are levied on Imports & Exports. 38 craft with articles liable to duty had discharged their cargoes between 1st April & 31st Dec. 1868—the cargoes appeared to have been satisfactorily accounted for. Upwards of £270 was received f[ro]m Ground Nuts alone between the above dates. Assistance of Police very valuable for the protection of the Revenue.

Sherbro.

All vessels intending to visit the Sherbro are obliged to call at S. Leone before proceeding to their destination a practice which involved unnecessary delay & which should in Mr. R[ichmond's] opinion be discontinued.

Gambia.

Mr. R[ichmond] was prepared to find a great laxity of practice at this Settlement, from what he had seen cursorily on his way to S. Leone, but the result of his enquiries satisfied him that there was *no system at all*. Many provisions of the Ordinance of 1866 were

[1] C.O. 267/302. On Kennedy to Granville, 9 August 1869. *Arthur Richmond* had surveyed the Customs posts in West Africa, February–April 1869. These findings were referred to West African Administrators with instructions to remedy the numerous defects brought to light. Granville to Kendall, 23 September 1869: ibid.

altogether ignored. No steps are taken by Customs Officers to satisfy themselves that the goods landed correspond with those for which entries have been passed. No examination of goods not liable to specific duties is made & the Merchants are allowed to land the same when & where they chose (this will account for Mr. Brown's regret at losing Mr. Kneller). On the 1st day of Mr. R[ichmond's] visit, March 6, not a single entry was found in the Cash Book since the 27th Feb. although several entries had been received between these dates, & the Feb. accounts had not been balanced. Mr. R[ichmond] took a few vessels at hazard and found that 20 barrels of meal appeared on the manifest of the 'Amazon' from Demerara, but that duty had only been paid on 14—duty involved 1s/10d. 'Elizabeth' from London— four kegs, 3 cases, 50 bags of rice & 20 casks assigned to Quin (another supporter of Mr. Kneller) not accounted for—duty involved £1-10-10. The deficiencies were paid by the Merchants on representation, from Mr. R[ichmond] but doubtless many other vessels escaped. The Revenue is defrauded to a great extent as regards the accounts of the Mail Steamers.

Though the Revenue collected exceeds £1,000 a month, not a single Officer from the Collector downwards is under security to the Crown —& in the event of any defalcation the Settlement would sustain a considerable loss. The Customs duties are collected under an Ordinance of 19 March 1866 which has recently expired and Mr. R[ichmond] suggests that an opportunity might be taken of assimilating the duties in S. Leone & the Gambia.

Gold Coast.

Manner of collecting the Revenue unsatisfactory; Collectors inexperienced men, and the Ordinances regulating its collection unsatisfactory. Mr. R[ichmond] could not discover that Dr. Jones Acting Collector, took any share of the duties of the port (Dr. Jones holds so many appointments that this is not to be wondered at). Under s. 17 of Ordinance VI of 1867 articles imported actually for the personal use & consumption of Governt. Officers are exempted from duty, and Mr. R[ichmond] found it impossible to ascertain the quantities, as no record of any kind is kept of the articles landed under these conditions.

The 3d. Clerk in the Customs Dept. is said to be very incompetent & almost useless & Mr. R[ichmond] thinks he might be altogether dispensed with.

None of the officers are under Bond for the fruitful discharge of their duties. At Cape Coast, the 2d. Clerk who is cashier retains sums for a fortnight before handing them over to the Acting Collector, who is Treasurer for all the receipts of the Settlement & has no Bank to deposit them in.

There is only one Warehouse, belonging to one of the merchants; he keeps one key and the Landing Waiter the other, but no record whatever is kept at the Custom House of the goods therein deposited. The Acting Collr. (Dr. Jones) actually admitted that he did not even know where the Warehouse was situated, or what it contained. Mr. R[ichmond] suggests that the Revenue could benefit considerably by the introduction of the Warehousing System, which is desired by the leading Merchants, who had several grievances on other subjects connected with the Customs arrangements.

Accra.

The Civil Commandant is Sub-Collector here, and cannot possibly do his duty in the latter capacity. Mr. R[ichmond] began making a list of all articles landed according to the permits on which the duty had not been paid, but it became so long that he had to give it up in despair. The omissions (so far as he had gone) were pointed out to the Clerk & £20 was recovered.

Lagos.

The Imports of 1868 show an increase of 98 per cent over those of 1863 and the Exports an increase of 237 per cent for the same dates.

The Jerquer's Report Book is well kept though not posted up quite as close as Mr. R[ichmond] could have wished. He selected several ships which had arrived in 1868 with cargoes & satisfied himself that the duties had been paid on all the goods appearing in the manifest, but the practice which also prevails at S. Leone & Gambia, of delivering packages without ascertaining the real contents, renders it impossible to say whether the proper amount of duty has been collected & Mr. [Richmond] recommends that one package in five should be opened.

The Warehousing system is in its infancy at Lagos & is hardly ever employed except in case of goods for exportation. At the time of Mr. R[ichmond's] visit there were only 2 goods deposited in 2 Warehouses, of each of which the Customs retained one key and the Merchants the other. Lagos is the only Post where the Collector & all his officers find security, the Collector £2,000; but the objection is that the security is offered by the Merchants. . . .

21

GOVERNOR J. POPE HENNESSY TO THE EARL OF KIMBERLEY: SIERRA LEONE TAXES, 12 MARCH 1872[1]

[The Road Tax Ordinance of 1872 has been repealed because of hardship.]

. . . 2. MY attention was drawn to the operation of the Road Tax by the enclosed letter from the Reverend Benjamin Tregaskis dated 6th of March 1872.

3. Mr. Tregaskis states that a Widow named Sarah Cooper, a member of the Wesleyan Church, had been summoned on the 4th of March 1872 to appear at the police Court on the 6th instant, for having failed to pay the Road Tax of 15/6d. due for 1869 or in default thereof having failed to perform six days labour on the public Roads: that she stated in Court her widowed condition and inability to pay, but, after a brief procedure, was sent to gaol.

4. It was further stated that on the same day, 4th. of March 1872, her late husband Thomas Cooper was also summoned to appear on the 6th. for a tax of 1s/6d due in 1869, and having since failed in default of payment to work on the roads; whereas he died last November.

5. I ascertained that Thomas Cooper was the same person whose case had been represented to the Government on the 22nd of September 1870. At that time his blanket had been seized for the House and Land Tax. It was alleged he was sick. It was proved he was occasionally an inmate of the pauper Hospital. In this man's statement he said 'my wife is a sickly woman. Almost all her clothes she pawned and sold to support me'.

6. The fact that this man, who died the year after the state of his health had been brought to the notice of the Government, was nevertheless summoned on the 4th. instant to the Police Court as a Road Defaulter, convinced me that little attention was given to the question of the ability or inability of those called on to work.

7. Knowing Your Lordship's wishes that I should patiently consider any complaints of the operation of a law which affects the interests of as large a class of Her Majesty's Subjects in this Settlement, I lost no time in testing the accuracy of Mr. Tregaskis' allegations.

8. I began with the cases of Thomas and of Sarah Cooper and found that Mr. Tregaskis' statements were correct.

[1] C.O. 267/316. Hennessy also abolished all other forms of direct taxation, including the much-hated House and Land Tax, timber licences and market dues.

9. The enclosed copy of a Minute I sent to the police Magistrate with his reply, and the Queen's Advocate's opinion thereon,[1] will enable Your Lordship to see the steps I took before exercising the clemency of the Crown and remitting the five days imprisonment and hard labor Sarah Cooper was undergoing.

10. I found that batches of thirty or forty people, men and women. were being brought up every day before the Police Magistrate, and, in default of paying the Tax with costs of the Summons, were sent to prison for five days with hard labor.

11. The system was so faulty, and the prisoners so numerous that there appeared to be no time for any investigation or notes on each case; and although this is March 1872 the cases being dealt with were all arrears of 1869.

12. From a return the Queen's Advocate was good enough to procure for me it appears that the number of Defaulters of Road Tax for 1869 sent to the Police Magistrate to be disposed of within a recent period was 1909. The day I proposed the repeal of the Tax the number of 1869 defaulters still remaining on the Police Magistrate's Books to be dealt with was 548.

13. I also called for a Return shewing the financial value of the Tax. I enclose for Your Lordship's information a copy of this Return, from which it appears that deducting the receipts from the cost of collection the Nett Cash result for last year was £163. 18. To this must be added the estimated value of one year's compulsory labor, £80 shewing the total value of the Tax to be only £243. 18. 0.

14. I am however informed by Mr. Jenkins the Surveyor General that the actual value is really less than this, for he says he finds the compulsory labor of defaulters often useless; and that sometimes they deliberately spoil the Roads so that the item of £80 is probably too great.

15. Speaking of the system as far as it concerns his department he said it was an obstacle to really putting the Roads in good order.

16. As I have already made a few trifling reductions of permanent expenditure which will more than counterbalance the loss of the Road Tax, I had no hesitation in submitting the Repealing Ordinance to the Legislative Council by whom it was passed unanimously and with a strong expression of general satisfaction.

17. I take this opportunity of saying that Your Lordship's despatch No. 239 of the 6th of January 1872 on the subject of a somewhat similar enactment (the House and Land Tax Ordinance) is engaging my earnest attention.

[1] Encl. E. G. Alston, Queen's Advocate, and H. Bravo, Police Magistrate, to Hennessy, 16 and 8 March 1872.

22

ACTING ADMINISTRATOR H. FOWLER TO GOVERNOR J. POPE HENNESSY: LAGOS LAND GRANTS, 14 OCTOBER 1872[1]

[The price of Crown Land has been raised to £3 per acre, with 30s. fee.]

... 5. I AM informed the idea for charging so high a price was that protection was guaranteed and a Grant in fee simple given for the land.

6. I have hesitated during my administration to give such Grants for land outside the Island of Lagos as I hardly feel myself justified in giving Grants in fee simple for land over which I believe it was intended to exercise a Protectorate only without authentic instructions from Your Excellency on the subject.

7. The land herein referred to is that marked in Colonel Ord's Map as 'Territory under British Protectorate' which accompanied his report in 1865.

8. The Treaty for the Cession of the Island of Lagos Grants 'the port and Island of Lagos with all rights profits territories and appurtenances whatsoever thereunto belonging' with 'the direct full and absolute dominion of the said port, Island and premises', and Your Excellency is aware of the questions raised as to the Territory belonging to the Island of Lagos.

9. I find 104 acres of the territory outside the Island of Lagos have been granted in 66 Grants in fee simple and have realized in actual payments £385 13. 9. but there are balances still due on some of the Grants.

10. I would most respectfully submit to Your Excellency's consideration whether it is not advisable to encourage Natives especially of Semi Civilized class such as the Brazilian Emancipados to settle on the land in the neighbourhood of Lagos as they are good farmers, but it is ridiculous to suppose that they can afford to pay £3 per acre and 30/- for the Grant.

[1] C.O. 147/27. The Colonial Office delayed ordering the lowering of the land price till boundaries with the Egba had been fixed.

23

J. HALES: MINUTE, AFRICAN MAIL SUBSIDY, 7 NOVEMBER 1872[1]

. . . THE anticipated facility of communication between the 4 Settlements undoubtedly led the Select Committee of 1865 to recommend the Central Govt. System. The expenses of the Imperial Govt. in connection with the Gambia were formerly large, and a great saving was effected by the withdrawal of the Troops, and the Parliamentary Grant (which between 1861 and March 1871 varied from £9,000 off to £1000).

The withdrawal of the subsidy for mail service therefore seems inexcusable, but I suppose we must wait for an answer from the Treasury. . . .

24

WILLIAM LAW TO SIR ROBERT HERBERT: LAGOS LOAN, 13 JANUARY 1873[2]

SIR,

The Lords Commissioners of Her Majesty's Treasury have had before them your Letter of the 6th Inst., representing the financial embarrassment in which the Settlement of Lagos has been involved through the temporary cessation of Trade in consequence of the roads being closed by the neighbouring tribes, and urging upon my Lords the necessity of immediately advancing from the Imperial Treasury not less than £20,000 for the use of the Settlement, to be repaid from the proceeds of Debentures which the Colonial Government has been instructed to issue to the Extent of £25,000.

My Lords desire me to acquaint you, in reply, that in deference to the strong recommendation of the Earl of Kimberley, they are prepared to direct the advance of £20,000, upon the terms of repayment above mentioned, in such manner as His Lordship may consider best calculated to assist the Government of Lagos in its present difficulties.

[1] C.O. 87/103. On Thomas Brown (Gambia Merchant) to Kimberley, 6 November 1872 (protesting against the termination of a Government subsidy to the African Mail service).
[2] C.O. 147/29.

25

SIR ROBERT HERBERT TO WILLIAM LAW: WEST AFRICAN FINANCES, 13 JANUARY 1874[1]

SIR,

I am directed by the Earl of Kimberley to request that you will draw the attention of the Lords Commissioners of the Treasury to the correspondence noted in the margin respecting the discontinuance of the sum formerly voted from Imperial Funds in aid of the local Revenues of Sierra Leone on account of the 'Sherbro'.

In the draft Estimates of this Department for 1873-4 a vote appeared for £5000 on this account. Those estimates were forwarded to the Treasury in the Colonial Office letter of the 4th of December 1872. In a despatch received from the Acting-Governor in Chief on the 27th of January 1873 he expressed a hope that no aid would be needed from Imperial Funds on this account, as he contemplated apportioning the expenditure amongst the West African Settlements —the chief share of the expenditure for 1873 falling on the Gold Coast which had an estimated surplus of £11500.

The views of Mr. Hennessy are communicated to the Treasury in the Col. office letter of the 1st of February 1873 and their Lordships in the Treasury letter of the 8th of that month expressed the satisfaction with which they had learned that the votes were to be relieved from this charge—adding at the same time that they fully understood that such reduction of the Estimate was a measure the continuance of which could only be decided by experience.

As their Lordships are aware the Ashantee Invasion has subsequently rendered the Gold Coast for the moment insolvent. Lagos is but slowly recovering from the very serious difficulties caused by [D. the stoppage of the roads] the prolonged stoppage of the trade with the interior. Gambia with a decreasing Revenue which depends [D. on one article] almost entirely on the export of Ground nuts the source of which has been lately unfavourable, is quite unable to render any assistance. Nor is Sierra Leone itself equal to the charge. The hopes of a buoyant Revenue at one time entertained as a consequence of Mr. Pope Hennessy's Financial Policy have not as yet been fulfilled. The Governor writing on the 17th of November reports the probability of a large deficit at the close of the year 1873. And in making his estimates he apparently took into account a vote of £4000 from Imperial Funds on account of the 'Sherbro'—as through inadvertence he had not been formally apprised of the decision arrived at by the Imperial Govt. upon the representations of Mr. Pope

[1] C.O. 267/322.

Hennessy. In the Estimates for the current year though the utmost economy has been used, the Expenditure has only just been brought within the Revenue and in his calculation the Governor has for the reason above stated included a vote of £5000 from Imperial Funds on account of the 'Sherbro'.

The cash balances of the Colony which appear to have been steadily decreasing during 1873 do not now probably amount to more than a nominal sum, and in the Estimates for 1874 no items have been inserted for the expenditure on sanitary works, which are absolutely necessary & must therefore be undertaken without any considerable delay.

In this state of the Finances of the West African Settlements generally, Lord Kimberley feels that there is no other course open to him but to move their Lordships to present to Parliament a Supplementary Estimate for £4000. . . .

26

WILLIAM LAW TO THE COLONIAL OFFICE: AFRICAN MAIL SUBSIDY, 18 MARCH 1874[1]

. . . With reference to Sir H. Holland's letter of the 3rd. Instant and previous correspondence respecting the payment of the Gambia Mail Subsidy, I am commanded by the Lords Commissioners of Her Majesty's Treasury to request that you will state to the Earl of Carnarvon that under the circumstances therein represented and in compliance with His Lordship's recommendation My Lords will not insist upon a contribution on account of the Mail Service Subsidy being exacted this year from the Settlement. I am, however, to request that you will express to the Earl of Carnarvon Their regret that the Settlement is unable to make any contribution to relieve Imperial Funds from this charge, and that you will move His Lordship to give the necessary instructions that the Governor of the Gambia may be called upon for a contribution on the part of the Settlement towards the Service in question before the preparation of the Estimates for the Settlement for 1875.

[1] 87/107.

27

WAR OFFICE: PRÉCIS, COST OF THE ASHANTI EXPEDITION, 13 APRIL 1874[1]

. . . 18. A TREASURY MINUTE of the 24th February 1874 estimated the cost of the Ashanti Expedition under the three heads below given: 1. War Office; 2. Colonial Office; 3. Admiralty. The details were estimated as follows:—

1. War Office. Warlike Stores 145,000 *l.* Deduct 60,000 *l.* to be replaced by the Colonial Office, and 55,000 *l.*, value of obsolete stores not

required to be replaced leaves	30,000
Provisions and forage	100,000
Clothing 45,000 *l.* Deduct 4,000 *l.* to be replaced by Colonial Office, and 2,250 *l.* to be repaid by Admiralty, leaves	38,750
Medicines and Surgical Instruments	4,000
Field Allowances	9,000
Carriers and Labourers	40,000
Daily Pay and Allowances for the Troops from 1st December 1873 to 31st March 1874	31,267
Total for the War Office	257,093
Estimate	260,000

2. Colonial Office. Expenditure up to the 31st of January, 180,000 *l.* It was estimated that the expenditure for February and March would raise this sum to 220,000 *l.*: but 70,000 *l.* were to be charged in the Estimates of 1874-75. Thus the amount chargeable by the Colonial Office in the Estimates of 1873-74, for Expenditure up to 31st March, was   150,000

3. Admiralty   280,000

Thus the whole estimated cost of the War was 760,000 *l.*, of which 690,000 *l.* were to be charged in the estimates for 1873-74, leaving 70,000 *l.* to be charged to the expenditure of 1874-75. But, besides these amounts, 55,000 pounds worth of old arms and stores have been served out to the natives, and were not required to be replaced. Including this sum, the Ashanti expedition would have cost 815,000 *l.* . . .

[1] W.O. 33/26. Confidential Print, 1874 [W.O. 0563].

SIR ROBERT HERBERT TO WILLIAM LAW: GOLD COAST SUPPLEMENTARY GRANT, 22 MAY 1874[1]

SIR,

I am directed by the Earl of Carnarvon to request that you will inform the Lords Commissioners of the Treasury that his Lordship has had under consideration the special expenditure which is likely to become necessary at the Gold Coast and Lagos when the fresh administrative arrangements, of which he recently gave an outline in the House of Lords, are brought into effect.

It is impossible to estimate with any approach to accuracy the probable revenue of these Settlements during the ensuing year, as the interruption of trade through the Ashantee war and other causes has rendered the receipts of the year 1873 altogether useless as a criterion of what may be expected when commercial operations have been freely resumed.

It is not impossible that the anticipations of a largely increased revenue at the Gold Coast may yet be verified; but, as the financial future of this Settlement is now uncertain, Lord Carnarvon is of opinion that no time should be lost in requesting Parliament to make provision for the more immediate requirements of the Settlements.

I am accordingly to request that their Lordships will cause to be prepared and presented to Parliament, at the earliest possible time, a Supplementary Estimate providing for a 'contribution in aid of the revenue of the Gold Coast' of 35,000 *l*.

This sum Lord Carnarvon would propose to expend as follows, it being understood that the proportions to be assigned to each head may be varied as may be found convenient:—

	£
Additional salaries	6,000
Telegraphs	10,000
Buildings and roads, and repairs of same	15,000
Miscellaneous	4,000

As his Lordship thinks it very desirable that he should have entire freedom to alter or vary the objects on which the grant is to be expended, I am to request that only the aggregate sum may be proposed in the vote, without the particulars now given for their

[1] *Parl. Papers*, 1875, lii [C. 1140], p. 11.

Lordship's information. The necessary explanations will, of course be given in moving the vote.

The strictest economy will be enjoined in every case, and if the local revenue permits of any portion of the above services being performed from that source, the Imperial grant will be to that extent left undrawn.

As in previous cases, it is, of course, understood that this grant of 35,000 *l.* is in the nature of an advance, and that any surplus Colonial funds which may become available for the purpose shall be devoted to the repayment of it.

INDEX